MW00333021

THREE YEARS A SOLDIER

THREE YEARS A SOLDIER

The Diary and Newspaper Correspondence of Private George Perkins, Sixth New York Independent Battery, 1861–1864

Edited by Richard N. Griffin

Voices of the Civil War
Peter S. Carmichael, Series Editor

The University of Tennessee Press / Knoxville

Copyright © 2006 by The University of Tennessee Press / Knoxville.
All Rights Reserved. Manufactured in the United States of America.
First Edition.

The Voices of the Civil War series makes available a variety of primary source materials that illuminate issues on the battlefield, the home front, and the western front, as well as other aspects of this historic era. The series contextualizes the personal accounts within the framework of the latest scholarship and expands established knowledge by offering new perspectives, new materials, and new voices.

Frontispiece: George and Almira Perkins. The following inscriptions appeared on their gravestones: "Geo. Perkins. Died Oct. 15, 1890. Aged 49 yrs. 7 mos. 24 dys. Three years a soldier in the 6th N.Y. Bat'y. Horse Artillery" and "Almira Wyman Perkins. Died Apr. 28, 1882. Aged 41 yrs., 2 mos. Dull cold marble can never tell her worth." Courtesy of Michael T. Russert.

Library of Congress Cataloging-in-Publication Data

Perkins, George, d. 1890

Three years a soldier: the diary and newspaper correspondence of private George Perkins, Sixth New York Independent Battery, 1861–1864 / edited by Richard N. Griffin.—1st ed.
    p. cm—(Voices of the Civil War)

Includes bibliographical references (p.) and index.

ISBN 157233455X (alk. paper)

1. Perkins, George, d. 1890—Diaries.
2. Perkins, George, d. 1890—Correspondence.
3. United States. Army. New York Artillery. Independent Battery, 6th (1861–1865)
4. Soldiers—New York (State)—Diaries.
5. Soldiers—New York (State)—Correspondence.
6. New York (State)—History—Civil War, 1861–1865—Personal narratives.
7. United States—History—Civil War, 1861–1865—Personal narratives.
8. United States—History—Civil War, 1861-1865—Artillery operations.
  I. Griffin, Richard N.
  II. Title
 III. Voices of the Civil War series

E523.8 6th .P47 2006

973.7'447'092—dc22   2005014132

CONTENTS

ILLUSTRATIONS

FIGURES

MAPS

FOREWORD

CIVIL WAR VETERANS WANTED FUTURE GENERATIONS TO FORGET ABOUT SECTIONAL divisiveness and simply remember the combatants as brave men who demonstrated the most valued trait of Americanism—manliness. Their appeal to American memory bridged sectional lines as both Northerners and Southerners were able to come together after Appomattox by celebrating the courage of the other side. Reunification on these terms resulted in a terrible historical heresy whose insidious influences persist to this day. Rather than understand the military experience of the Civil War as a political contest over the meaning of national citizenship and freedom, many Americans continue to insist that Civil War soldiers were apolitical, that they were merely doing their duty, and that they can only be honored by celebrating their collective courage. Some have even argued that any discussion of politics or social context at National Park Service battlefields demeans the historical memory of those who fought there. These same critics would prefer that battlefields be studied as soulless chess boards of strategy and tactics.

There is no denying that courage was a core value of Civil War soldiers, but it should not be understood as a mechanism that controlled all behavior and thought. Valor in battle derived from a host of complex motivations that were both emotional and ideological. The diary and newspaper correspondence of George Perkins of the Sixth New York Independent Battery reveals how ideas about courage and manliness gave shape and form to political beliefs. *Three Years a Soldier* offers a unique opportunity to understand how ideas about masculinity animated political beliefs among members of the rank and file. Perkins possessed a fierce sense of independence that was at the very core of his identity as a man. He did not take kindly to demanding officers, and he was quick to denounce any martinet who violated the rights of his men. Adjusting to a strict military regime proved difficult for Northerners and Southerners alike, and Perkins was no exception. His gradual accommodation to army life reflected a broader transformation from civilian volunteer to veteran, but his libertarian impulses, tied inextricably to his sense of being a man, did not waiver as the war progressed. It is clear Perkins saw the Civil War through the masculine lens of republicanism.

Autonomy was at the heart of manhood for nineteenth-century Northerners and Southerners. In the North the desire to live free of others connected to a broader vision of a free-labor society in which every man had the right to earn the fruits of his labor and move up the social ladder. In the South, white human liberty depended upon the enslavement of African Americans. Although Northerners and Southerners had conflicting understandings of what it meant to be truly free, their ideas about manliness gave lasting political meaning to why they fought for hearth and home. Moreover, their need to be seen as independent men was not a simple expression of hyper-masculinity. If anything, notions about manliness have deep ideological roots. Perkins, for instance, entered the war as an ambivalent youth without a particularly strong sense as to why he was fighting or the higher ideals behind the cause of the Union. Hardships, death, and firsthand observations of a slave society simultaneously heightened his sense of being an independent man while reinforcing his political commitment to the Union cause of antislavery. After criticizing draft dodgers in the North for their passivity during the summer of 1863, Perkins concluded in a letter to his acquaintance Nathan Wyman: "I entered the service with very little patriotism yet I say truth when I tell you that which I had not at the commencement now I have increased in power. Others I know who enlisted in a fit of bombastic patriotism which finally died out. From nothing I have grown something. I have acquired the name in the battery of 'black abolitionist' nigger lover & c. I have at least learned to be a good republican since my service."

As Richard Griffin explains in his superb introduction, Perkins was not an abolitionist, and he subscribed to the dominant racial attitudes of the day. Yet, one can find in *Three Years a Soldier* that Perkins had grown into a political being who saw the Union cause as the embodiment of his vision of a good and moral society. At the core of that vision stood the citizen soldier who was courageous, dutiful, and an ardent defender of republican virtues. It is not surprising that Perkins, when writing to the *Middlesex Journal*, used the pen name Hoplite, which was the name given to the citizen-soldier of ancient Greece. *Three Years a Soldier* is a powerful book that helps explain how Northerners like Perkins channeled "bombastic patriotism" early in the war into mature political expressions of manly duty, just like the hoplites whom Perkins admired so fervently.

Peter S. Carmichael
University of North Carolina at Greensboro

ACKNOWLEDGMENTS

WHEN MY COUSIN WAYNE PERKINS GAVE ME A LOOSE-LEAF, TYPESCRIPT COPY OF our great-grandfather George Perkins's Civil War diary, I thanked him for his gift, but slipped it into a niche on my bookshelf and did not think about the subject for several years. Eventually, however, I took the battered red binder down from the shelf. I was immediately enthralled and determined to edit the diary with a view to eventual publication. Thus, Wayne's gift led directly to this project. I owe him a great debt of gratitude.

A project such as this cannot be accomplished alone but requires a legion of helpers. The fact that my wife Claire and I lived in Hawaii until the summer of 2002 made me unusually dependent on the kindness and forbearance of family members, friends, and acquaintances living on the mainland. All generously gave their time and valuable assistance at many points along the way.

Wayne's sister, Suzanne Perkins Gunston, immeasurably added to the richness of the record by giving me the original documents in her possession that pertained to our great-grandfather and his Civil War service. These items appear as illustrations in this book. I am indebted to her generosity.

My sister, Nancy Griffin Pallazola, deserves my heartfelt thanks. She lives near Boston, Massachusetts, and thus the many historical and archival resources of that area are much more accessible to her than to me, especially when I lived half a world away. In a sense, she made the project her own and never failed to respond to my questions and requests. She made many trips to the public libraries of Boston and Woburn to research and make copies of important documents. She also accompanied me on research expeditions when I was able to travel back to New England. Her husband Victor supported her in these efforts and cheerfully threaded his way through the piles of photocopied documents that ended up on their living room floor during one memorable visit. I thank them both.

I am deeply indebted to the faculty and staff of the University of Virginia's outstanding annual Civil War conferences. All were unfailingly helpful and generous with their insights and suggestions. The conferences are an excellent blend of classroom presentations, discussions and guided battlefield walks to many areas that are not normally open to the public. I have benefited greatly from them, and I commend the conferences to anyone who wants to gain greater understanding of the war in the East. At the risk of inadvertently slighting someone, I want to specifically thank Professor Gary W. Gallagher, John L. Nau III Professor of the History of the American Civil War at the University of Virginia and organizer of the conferences; Tom Dowd, senior director of program development and his capable and friendly staff; faculty members Robert K. Krick and his son Robert E. L. "Bobby" Krick; Peter S. Carmichael; Keith Bohannon; Steven Cushman; Melissa Delcour; and William J. "Bill" Miller. Bob Krick the elder was generous with his vast knowledge of the battlefields of Fredericksburg and Spotsylvania County, introduced me to the collections at Chatham House (the headquarters of the Fredericksburg and Spotsylvania National Military Park), and put me in touch with historians who helped me with a variety of nagging questions. Bobby Krick shared many insights about the battles that took place around Richmond. Pete Carmichael, who also is editor of this series, was challenging and thought provoking in his emphasis on the political and social aspects of the war. Keith Bohannon enriched the tactical details of the Virginia battles and gave them freshness and immediacy. Steven Cushman, a professor of English, American literature, and poetry, gave me a new way of looking at the Battle of the Wilderness and tracked down a quotation from Homer that appears in George Perkins's diary. Melissa Delcour helped me find Buckton Station at the base of the northern face of Massanutten Mountain, where the Sixth New York caught up with the Third Cavalry Division on September 23, 1864. Bill Miller, a leading authority on Civil War mapmaking, Stonewall Jackson's mapmaker Jed Hotchkiss, and the 1862 Peninsula Campaign, gave me a helpful map of Massanutten Mountain and provided great support and encouragement during the critical early phases of this project.

On one memorable day, while reading an article by Gordon Rhea in *North and South* magazine, I came upon a quotation that sounded very familiar. Sure enough, the citation was from a copy of the George Perkins diary in the collection of Michael T. Russert. Through Mr. Rhea, I got in touch with Mr. Russert, who confirmed that he had another copy of the typescript diary. Mr. Russert was very encouraging and sent me copies of photographs from his collection of George Perkins; his wife, Almira; and George with his friend and battery mate Cornelius Miller. These images appear in this book with his kind permission. I am grateful to both Mr. Rhea and Mr. Russert.

I am grateful to Donald Pfanz and Eric Mink of the Fredericksburg and Spotsylvania National Military Park. Mr. Pfanz searched for references to my great-grandfather's battery in the Chatham House collection. Claire and I spent a particularly enjoyable day with Mr. Mink on a successful hunt for the Federal logistics depots on Potomac and Aquia creeks. Eric also found two unpublished maps in the Chatham House collection that depicted the location of Hope

Landing on Aquia Creek, a facility that is inexplicably missing from the plates presented in *The Official Military Atlas of the Civil War*. As a sort of pièce de résistance, he introduced us to a perfect gem, known as White Oak Museum, which has fascinating displays depicting the camps of Stafford County, Virginia.

Julie Krick prepared the excellent maps in this book. Julie responded quickly to my too-frequent requests for changes and transformed my vague notions about what the maps should look like into clear and attractive final products. I thank her for her patient efforts.

I am also indebted to David and Judy Anderson, both retired U.S. Navy commanders. While Judy was assigned as a student at the Army War College at Carlisle Barracks, Pennsylvania, Dave cheerfully and thoroughly searched the archives of the U.S. Army's Military History Institute for photographs of officers and enlisted men mentioned in my great-grandfather's diary. The images that he found are reproduced in this volume. In his search, he received efficient and friendly support from Michael J. Winey, curator of the Military History Institute, and his able staff. I thank Mr. Winey for his help and Dave and Judy for their help on this project and friendship over the years.

My friend and former colleague William E. Spicer knows Fredericksburg and the surrounding counties like the back of his hand, having grown up there when it was still possible to pick up stray minié balls from the dirt roads. Bill volunteered to take me to some of the less-visited but important spots of the battlefields of Chancellorsville and The Wilderness. So, on one of my regular business trips from Hawaii, he made sure that I saw such sites as where Piney Branch was before it was swallowed by a reservoir, Kelly's Ford on the Rappahannock River, Ely's Ford on the Rapidan, and other interesting spots. At the site of Todd's Tavern, he introduced me to Miss Agnes, a dignified lady who let me know that she, at least, had neither forgotten nor forgiven the Yankees who had despoiled her ancestral lands. I thank both Bill and Miss Agnes for ensuring that I understood the Southern perspective.

On another trip to Washington, I spent an enjoyable and productive day in the company of my friend John J. Patrick. John, a witty and talented researcher, writer, and history buff, drove me around a veritable rabbit warren of streets in the northeastern quadrant of the District of Columbia and into the rural areas of Maryland's Prince George's County, searching for some of the sites mentioned in the Perkins diary. Although we could not positively identify all the places on my list, I did gain a more accurate sense of the lay of the land. I thank John for his companionship and interest in my project.

I am very grateful to Michael T. Meier of the Old Military and Civil Records Branch of the National Archives and Records Administration. Mr. Meier made me feel at home and showed me where to find important documents pertaining to the Sixth New York, the deck logs of the Navy ships mentioned in the diary, and Camp Barry, where the battery went to refit in the summer of 1864.

I am also indebted to Rodney P. Katz of the Library of Congress, the staff of the Harvard University Archives, the staff of the Archives Department of the Woburn Public Library, the staff of Lindenwood Cemetery in Stoneham, Massachusetts, and Jane Cahill of the office of the superintendent of the Boston Public Schools. They were all very helpful and responsive to my requests.

Special thanks go to Mr. Leon Basile of Woburn. Leon was working on his own project dealing with Woburn Civil War soldiers but cheerfully pitched in to help my sister as she worked on my research questions in the archives. I thank him most especially for providing valuable details concerning the Woburn militia and for the discovery of the letters that George wrote to the Woburn town clerk.

I also must thank Lt. Col. Harold Frankel (retired), of the Ninth Regiment, New York Old Guard. The Ninth is the successor organization to the Sixth New York, and Colonel Frankel shared information with me on his effort to find the last resting places of the original members who had mustered into the battery in June 1861.

Without my friends at the University of Tennessee Press, this book would never have seen the light of day. Joyce Harrison and her successor as acquisitions editor, Scot Danforth, were enthusiastic about the project and unfailingly helpful and encouraging. I am particularly indebted to the series editor, Pete Carmichael, and the two reviewers whose advice and suggestions were right on the mark. This book is much better because of their efforts. Monica Phillips expertly copyedited the manuscript and caught all the errors I had missed. Finally, Gene Adair, manuscript editor, shepherded the project over the finish line and patiently answered all of my questions. I don't think I could have had better editorial help from start to finish. I thank you all.

Finally and most important, from the bottom of my heart I thank my wife, Claire. She was unfailingly supportive over the course of this project, never complaining about the many long hours I spent in front of the computer nor objecting to the many research trips we took that were thinly disguised as vacations. But, more than that, she was an integral part of this effort, from the first faltering research steps to the final stages of reviewing and proofing. Claire's love of history is as deep as my own; her research, writing, and editing skills are well honed; and her advice and frequent participation were absolutely essential to the successful completion of this project. To cite only one example, it was she who proved beyond a doubt that George Perkins used the pen name Hoplite. Her breakthrough led to the discovery of all but one of the *Middlesex Journal* letters that are included in this book. I rely on her judgment and am eternally grateful for her love and support.

INTRODUCTION

JUDGING BY THE WORDS ENGRAVED ON HIS TOMBSTONE—"THREE YEARS A SOLDIER"—
George Perkins was proud of his Civil War service and wanted to be remembered
as a soldier and defender of the Republic. George's soldiering began in December
1861, when he traveled to Washington, D.C., in company with his older brother,
James Appleton "App" Perkins, to join Battery K, Ninth New York State Militia
(soon to be redesignated as the Sixth New York Independent Battery). Except
for one brief furlough in early June 1863 to his Woburn, Massachusetts, home,
George served as a private with the battery in the Army of the Potomac for the
entire period of his enlistment and mustered out in December 1864.

When he enlisted, George was a twenty-year-old married man who had
attended Harvard College in 1858 and 1859. Except for a cryptic diary entry noting that he had met a soldier whom he had known "when I was a pedlar," there
is no record of his activities between his departure from college and when he
mustered into the army. Whatever he was doing in this period, it seems he could
not stand aloof from the waves of patriotism sweeping the North, and he followed his brother into the army. As his war diary makes clear, however, George's
decision to join the army did not stem from patriotic ardor or any evident interest
in or aptitude for military leadership. Instead, he embarked on an effort to use
his diary to report and comment on every aspect of military life that came within
his notice, including the leadership qualities of prominent and lesser-known officers of the Army of the Potomac.

With few exceptions, George maintained a daily diary for the entire period
of his enlistment. His diary entries make it clear that his habit was to record
the daily activities of the battery in composition books that he received from
home and sent back periodically for safekeeping. The diary that exists today is
a typescript that a member of the family evidently transcribed from the original
manuscripts. Unfortunately, the period from early June to mid-October 1863 is
missing from this version. Even worse, all of the manuscript diaries appear to

have been lost. So, for example, George's daily thoughts about the activities of the battery during the Gettysburg Campaign cannot be known. The material that remains, however, constitutes a remarkable record of an intelligent, perceptive, and opinionated private soldier's view of the war in the eastern theater.

In addition to his diary, George maintained a prolific correspondence with his family and friends and also wrote numerous letters to his hometown newspaper, the *Middlesex Journal.* Unfortunately, only three of his private letters appear to have survived, these being letters written to Nathan Wyman, who was Woburn's town clerk and a kinsman of Almira, George's wife. Fortunately, however, Woburn's *Middlesex Journal* published forty-one of his letters, essays, and literary efforts between February 8, 1862, and November 12, 1864. Taken together, the letters reveal a perceptive and literate young man who seemed intent on propagating his views on the realities and progress of the war, the state of army leadership, patriotism, and the support the soldiers expected from non-combatants far from the seat of war. It is clear that George wanted his letters to do more than just inform. In the tone and tenor in which they are crafted and in the subjects chosen for elaboration, the letters very clearly indicate a writer who has taken pains to convey the impression of an articulate, intelligent, and educated soldier whose views should be listened to, presumably both during and after the conflict. In other words, it is clear that George Perkins hungered to be an influential member of the community and used the forum of his letters to achieve that goal. The penname Perkins chose for his public letters, *Hoplite,* is significant in this regard, in connecting him to the citizen-soldier of ancient Greece and in solidifying his credentials as one who could take his place as an influential member of the community after his discharge from the army.

The greater part of the *Middlesex Journal* letters offer extended commentary on the day-to-day activity of the Sixth New York Independent Battery. Six of those letters provide information concerning the operations of the battery between the onset of the Gettysburg Campaign and late October 1863, a period for which there are no surviving diary entries. Two of the Wyman letters are also from this period and are valuable for what they say about Gettysburg, the aftermath of the battle, and public issues of the day. Eleven of the letters are really essays on philosophical and religious themes, or report and comment on army organization and leadership. Although some of the letters closely repeat what he had written in his daily diary, others, particularly those that deal with issues or philosophical themes, reflect additional polishing and are clearly meant for a public audience. The distinction between the private diary and the Wyman letters on the one hand and the published letters and essays on the other is profound.

In addition to recounting the experiences and opinions of a bit of a gadfly of a private soldier, the Perkins diary and letters provide a history of the operations of the Sixth New York Independent Battery during the campaigns of the Army of the Potomac from 1862 through 1864. The battery, for which there is no other extant history, served as divisional artillery during the Peninsula Campaign, but was converted to horse artillery shortly afterward and served with the cavalry through the end of 1864. During the time of Perkins's enlistment, the Sixth New York participated in many of the battles and campaigns of the Army of the Potomac. In 1862 it participated in operations intended to counter the Confederate blockade of the Potomac River and McClellan's Peninsula Campaign. Upon its return from the Peninsula, the battery was assigned to the defenses of Washington. This assignment caused the battery to miss the campaign of Second Bull Run, the Battle of Antietam Creek, and the Battle of Fredericksburg. The battery returned to action in the Battle of Kelly's Ford in 1863. Other actions that year included the Chancellorsville Campaign, the Battle of Brandy Station, the Gettysburg Campaign, the Bristoe Campaign, the Battle of Rappahannock Station, and the Mine Run Campaign. In 1864, the final year of Perkins's enlistment, the Sixth New York fought in the Battle of the Wilderness, Sheridan's Raid on Richmond, Early's Raid on Washington, and the Shenandoah Campaign of 1864. Together, the diary and letters illuminate the activities and role of the Federal cavalry and horse artillery during the same period.

✦ ✦ ✦

The diary entries vary widely in character, with some simply recording the weather, the daily routine of drills, fatigue and guard duty, and the meals consumed by the private soldiers of the battery. Some are quite revealing of George's character, his resistance to army discipline and subjection to punishment, and his political, religious, and intellectual views. These entries make it clear that he was often a trial to his officers, especially in camp and when combat action was not imminent. In essence, George's standpoint was republican and egalitarian. He viewed himself as the moral and intellectual equal, if not superior, to the officers in authority over him. He frequently critiqued their leadership qualities and held strong opinions on the proper relationship between officers and men in an army of citizen soldiers. His attitude seemed to be that the army should be, in essence, a voluntary compact between partners in a crusade to restore the Union. Officers should see to the well-being of their men, ruling over them with light hands, and imposing only enough discipline to ensure victory in the struggle. George found the reality of army life, however, quite different from his ideal, and, during extended stays in camp, the arbitrary discipline and pervasive, numbing routine often seemed to cause him to turn inward into depression. Small acts of defiance would follow, as would preoccupation with family troubles, morals, and what he viewed as his sinful nature. On the other hand, at times camp life seemed to release creative energies as he explored philosophy, religion, military strategy and policy, and literary efforts.

From the evidence of his diary, George became much less of a discipline problem whenever his unit took the field or was in action. He wrote lengthy, extremely detailed accounts of the movements of the battery, its approach to and employment in battle, and what he could observe of the operations of Union artillery, cavalry, and infantry units. Perkins first came under long-range cannon fire soon after he joined the army, when the battery became part of the Union concentration on the Maryland side of the Potomac, opposite Confederate positions and fortifications in the vicinity of Quantico, Virginia. This type of war at a distance seems not to have caused him any significant concerns about his personal safety. Instead, his diary is filled with descriptions of the countryside around Budd's Ferry, Maryland; the weather; his first encounter with slaves; artillery duels across the Potomac; and the daily economy of the battery. The reality of war first came home to him in the Peninsula Campaign in the spring and summer of 1862. During this period, the Sixth New York was assigned either to the Artillery Reserve of Brig. Gen. Samuel Heintzelman's Third Corps or to the artillery of Hookers' division of that corps. For most of that period, Perkins was assigned to the wagon trains and thus did not serve with the guns on the several occasions in which they were engaged. He did, however, observe the human, animal, and material debris of the marches and battles and filled his diary with detailed and perceptive accounts of what he saw. Both George and App became seriously ill during the march between Williamsburg and the Chickahominy River. George eventually recovered, but his brother's constitution was not strong enough to withstand the effects of the illness and the almost total lack of medical care and sanitation discipline at that stage of the war. As their illnesses progressed, George's diary entries became more and more spare and focused on the need to get App on the ambulances and evacuated out of the war zone. Ultimately, App was transported to a military hospital in Philadelphia, but by then his sickness was too advanced, and he died there in early August.

In August 1862, the Sixth New York was withdrawn from the Peninsula to the defenses of Washington, where it remained until mid-December. It thus missed the battles of Second Manassas, Antietam, and Fredericksburg. It was during this period that the battery converted to horse artillery, thereby shifting from an infantry support role to operating with the cavalry. Horse batteries typically were armed with three-inch ordnance rifles, in preference to the heavier twelve-pounder "Napoleon" smoothbore gun-howitzers favored for service with the infantry. The other significant difference between the two types of mobile field artillery lies in the fact that all of the horse artillery crews were mounted, whereas, in infantry support units, the cannoneer either marched or rode on the caissons. In the Sixth New York's case, the conversion mainly meant that each of the enlisted members of the battery were issued a horse and the necessary equipments, since the battery had already received six three-inch rifles prior to embarking for the Peninsula the previous April. At first, George was opposed to the conversion, but later he became quite proud of the battery's status and association with the cavalry.

In the aftermath of Fredericksburg, cavalry and horse artillery received a boost from the new commander of the Army of the Potomac. In taking over the army from Ambrose Burnside, his defeated predecessor, Maj. Gen. Joseph Hooker grouped the army's cavalry into a single corps and the supporting horse artillery into brigades, thus creating a potentially powerful, mobile strike force. Previous army commanders had frittered away the cavalry by allowing it to be assigned by squadrons and regiments to headquarters guard, outpost, and picket duties. Consequently, the army had no means of countering the well-led and aggressive Confederate cavalry. All of this changed, at least theoretically, under General Hooker. Hooker charged his cavalry commanders to aggressively seek out the enemy and to seize and maintain the initiative. In these operations, the horse artillery was expected to keep up with the cavalry, contributing its firepower when needed to break up formations of enemy horsemen and to counter opposing horse batteries. Brigading the horse artillery with the cavalry corps enabled the two bodies to train together and become familiar with each other's capabilities, thus building cohesiveness and developing combined tactics. In practice, the horse artillery brigades did not operate as single bodies. Instead, individual batteries were assigned, as needed, to cavalry brigades and divisions. As time went by, the confidence and effectiveness of cavalry and horse artillery climbed. A by-product of this system was the building of an esprit de corps and mutual appreciation, as Perkins's diary makes clear.

George's first real baptism of fire did not take place until March 17, 1863, at the Battle of Kelly's Ford. By then he had become a cannoneer serving in one of the unit's three sections of two three-inch ordnance rifles, and he quickly learned what combined cavalry-artillery actions were all about. The battery took its first combat casualty in that engagement when a cannoneer was instantly killed by a solid shot. Kelly's Ford was only the first of the battery's 1863 battles, however, as the Sixth New York was warmly engaged at Chancellorsville and Brandy Station. In fact, in the latter battle, the battery was essentially put out of action when charging Confederate cavalry got amongst the guns. Fortunately for George, he missed Brandy Station, having returned home to Woburn on a brief five-day furlough. The battery was so damaged by that engagement that it was sent back to Washington to re-equip, only rejoining the army just prior to the battle of Gettysburg on June 28, the very day that Major General Meade relieved Hooker from command of the Army of the Potomac. Perhaps because of its condition, the Sixth New York was held in reserve at Gettysburg and did not see action. After the battle, the battery joined in Meade's pursuit of Lee's Army of Northern Virginia as it retreated to Virginia. From then until the commencement of the Bristoe Campaign in early October, the battery enjoyed an almost bucolic routine of quiet outpost duty in the Virginia countryside. The Sixth New York's employment during the period of the Gettysburg Campaign through the Bristoe Campaign has been reconstructed primarily from six letters that Perkins wrote to his hometown newspaper and two that he wrote to Nathan Wyman. The diary for this period, if he indeed wrote one, has been lost. George's daily diary resumes in late October, after the opposing forces had resumed their places along the Rappahannock and Rapidan rivers, following the Confederate attempt to drive the Federals back to the Washington defenses during the Bristoe Campaign. The remainder of the 1863 diary recounts the battle of Rappahannock Bridge, the Mine Run Campaign, and the army's settling into winter camp on the plains of Brandy Station. Although the Sixth New York was not engaged at Rappahannock Bridge, George left a detailed and fairly accurate account of the battle and its aftermath. The battery was in the thick of the action during the Mine Run Campaign, and the diary's account of General Meade's final attempt to achieve a decisive victory as an independent army commander is also quite detailed and perceptive.

For George Perkins and the Sixth New York, the 1863–64 Brandy Station winter camp began quietly. Routine day followed routine day, with occasional illnesses, cold, and wet and muddy conditions taking their usual toll on George's state of mind. He dealt with the circumstances as best he could by plunging into philosophy and religion, and by writing frequently and at length to his hometown newspaper and to a circle of correspondents. These letters provided the home folks with a steady diet of news about the battery, the organization of the army, and his own activities. In addition, he completed a number of essays on philosophical and religious themes, a poem, and a short play and sent them off to the newspaper. Letters and the occasional package from home flowed the other way and afforded relief from camp routine and a sense of connection with the civilian world he had left behind. One of these packages included a copy of *Caesar's Commentaries,* presumably in the original Latin, as he began translating it into English. During this winter bivouac, the Christian Commission was present and very active in camp, organizing a round of worship services, Bible studies, and prayer meetings. George plunged into these activities with vigor. He met privately with the missionaries and brought members of the battery along with him when he could. He also wrestled with what he considered to be his sinful nature and struggled to discover the path that God wanted him to follow.

As winter slowly and reluctantly gave way to the spring campaigning season, George's diary entries began to report on organizational changes in the command structure and the army's preparations to leave the camps and make another attempt to grapple with Lee's Army of Northern Virginia. The organization of the Army of the Potomac underwent an upheaval with the announcement of the consolidation of infantry corps from five to three on March 24 and Maj. Gen. Philip Sheridan's assumption of command of the Cavalry Corps on April 4. These changes coincided with the arrival of Lieutenant General Grant, who announced that his headquarters would be in the field, and with the Army of the Potomac. As far as Perkins and his battery mates were concerned, the most significant of these changes would turn out to be Sheridan's replacement of Major General Pleasonton as commander of the Cavalry Corps. Perkins's diary merely notes Sheridan's arrival, but the feisty general and his three-star mentor would have a profound affect on the cavalry and horse artillery once the campaigning season got fairly under way.

If the previous year had been a challenging one for the Sixth New York, 1864 did not lag behind. With the rest of the army beginning to position itself for the coming campaign, the battery quit its winter camp on April 16 and reported again for duty to the Cavalry Corps. What followed was a seemingly uninterrupted regime of marching and fighting, known in the aggregate as the Overland Campaign, that took Perkins's battery through the Battle of the Wilderness, Sheridan's daring Raid on Richmond, the return of the Cavalry Corps to the Army of the Potomac on the North Anna line, and the Battle of Haws' Shop. Once again, Perkins made a major effort to document in his diary everything that he saw and experienced. The entries vividly and accurately describe the movements and combat actions of the battery and do a remarkably good job of placing them in the context of the overall movements of the armies. In addition, the wear and tear of almost uninterrupted operations on men, animals, and equipment are clearly described. George also had an eye for beauty, and his descriptions of the Virginia countryside are at times almost lyrical.

Shortly after the cavalry rejoined the main army on May 25, the battery received orders to exchange its serviceable horses for condemned animals and return to Washington, D.C. This action was part of a general reorganization of the army's artillery ordered by General Meade and carried out by Brigadier General Hunt, chief of artillery. The Sixth New York was one of six horse batteries ordered to return to Washington. Those horse batteries that were to remain with the army were to be reduced to two sections of two pieces, one of the sections henceforth to be composed of twelve-pounder Napoleons. Undoubtedly, the fact that the enlistments of a large portion of the original members of the battery were set to expire that summer played a major role in including the battery in the group returning to Washington. On June 4, the Sixth New York and Battery A, Fourth United States, went down to the Pamunkey River and embarked on steam barges. Both arrived in Washington on June 6 and moored at the army arsenal to turn in their artillery pieces. When this was accomplished, the Sixth New York took up residence at Camp Barry. This facility, known as the Artillery Camp of Instruction, was located on the outskirts of the city on the toll road leading toward Bladensburg, Maryland.

The future of the Sixth New York was very much in question when it arrived at Camp Barry. Capt. J. W. Martin, the battery's commander, reported his expected monthly losses to the adjutant general's department for the remainder of 1864 and 1865. The tally was severe enough to cause several options to be on the table, including the disestablishment of the battery and the dispersal of the members with time left to serve to other batteries or the Washington fortifications. Ultimately, the decision was made to retain the battery in service as horse artillery and to recoup its personnel losses with men from the disestablishing

Tenth New York Battery. This action was made easier to achieve by reducing the battery to two sections of two pieces, one of the sections to be of twelve-pounders and the other of three-inch ordnance rifles.

The battery remained at Camp Barry until September 15, when it departed to rejoin General Sheridan, who by this time had assumed command of the Middle Military Division and the Army of the Shenandoah. For George and the remaining old-timers, the Camp Barry time was a welcome break from field service. He continued to be subjected to what he considered to be onerous fatigue and guard duty, strict and unreasonable discipline, and occasional punishments, but these annoyances, plus the omnipresent dust and enervating heat of the capital city, did not prevent him from sightseeing, visiting with friends, and using the services of the lending library established for the soldiers. The routine garrison duty was punctuated by much uncertainty regarding the future of the battery and by several alarums, the most significant of which was the furor occasioned by Jubal Early's raid on Washington. For this occasion, the Sixth New York was plucked from the torpor of life at Camp Barry, re-armed, and sent out to stiffen the northwestern defenses of the capital city. In the event, the battery got close enough to the fighting to observe some of the forts exchange fire with the Confederates and to hear the rattle of musketry, but Early did not seriously probe the Washington defenses, and the Sixth New York returned to Camp Barry and temporarily resumed the garrison routine.

When the Sixth New York quit Camp Barry for good, it did so as a horse battery, albeit diminished in firepower from its previous status, and with a significant number of new members from the disestablished Tenth New York. The march took the reconstituted battery on a trek northwestward through the Maryland countryside to Harpers Ferry. The march was uneventful, but the beauty and prosperity of the area deeply impressed Perkins, and he gave full reign to his descriptive powers in his daily diary entries. Nevertheless, heading back into battle without his trusted friends and with a large number of unfamiliar and untried soldiers seemed not to be to his liking, as a number of diary entries recounted minor squabbles and growing feelings of isolation from his fellows. Finally, after arriving in the Harpers Ferry area, Perkins asked to be relieved of his cannoneer duties, "Having had all the fighting I wanted," and was assigned to drive the lead team on the forge wagon. The remainder of the diary, therefore, is written from the perspective of someone who was no longer a frontline soldier. Despite that separation from the business end of the battery, Perkins's diary entries continued to be very accurate, detailed, and descriptive of the marching and fighting that took place between Sheridan's Army of the Shenandoah and Early's Army of the Valley. The diary describes the aftermath of Third Winchester, the pursuit of Early's forces in the Luray and Shenandoah valleys, Sheridan's retreat toward Winchester, and the battles of Tom's Brook and Cedar Creek. Perkins's descriptions of the beauties of the countryside are again quite lyrical, but it is in his accounts of Sheridan's hard war policy toward the noncombatants, the burning of farm buildings, and wholesale confiscation of livestock and crops that he reveals a growing sense of sympathy with the civilian population and disenchantment with the course of the war. The concluding entries of the diary recount George's final tussles with the military bureaucracy during the mustering-out process and the beginning of his journey home as a recently discharged soldier.

◆ ◆ ◆

Perkins's diary is noteworthy for its silence on his motivation for joining the army. His very first entry, on December 5, 1861, begins with a matter-of-fact acknowledgment that he was on his way with his brother to join Battery K, Ninth New York State Militia. Succeeding entries merely describe his travel and say nothing about his reasons for leaving his twenty-year-old pregnant wife to join his brother's unit at the seat of war. Indeed, it is not until March 16, 1862, that he made a brief notation in his diary that he had received a letter from his father-in-law announcing the birth of his first-born son. It is as if those reasons, his family responsibilities, and the discussions that must have preceded his decision were not of sufficient importance to record. Nevertheless, it seems evident that neither patriotism nor abolitionism played a significant role in his decision to join the army. Perkins himself admitted as much in an August 1863 letter to town clerk Nathan Wyman. He said: "But although I own that I entered the service with very little patriotism yet I say truth when I tell you that which I had not at the commencement now I have increased in power. Others I know who enlisted in a fit of bombastic patriotism, which finally died out. From nothing I have grown something. I have acquired the name in the battery of black abolitionist, nigger lover & c. I have at least learned to be a good republican since my service."

Although the Wyman letter suggests a clear progression from an initial state of indifference to political and racial issues to that of a committed Republican and antislavery activist, the evidence of the diary and letters is not quite so clear. The diary contains very few, if any, clear references to politics or the great issues of the day, and much the same can be said about the early letters to the *Middlesex Journal*. Still, the contrast between the private thoughts contained in the diary and the didactic tone of the majority of the letters to the newspaper is very strong. The tendency to preach becomes quite clear beginning with the letters written around the time of the Chancellorsville campaign, but Perkins's views concerning military leadership and the proper relationship between officers and their men first made their appearance in a letter published in the *Middlesex Journal* issue at the end of March 1862. In a brief paragraph concerning the Massachusetts colonel Robert Cowdin, he noted approvingly that the good colonel treated a private "not as a military machine . . . but as an American citizen fighting for the preservation of his native land." For just over a year after he wrote this letter, Perkins concentrated on his diary and abandoned his public correspondence. During the interval, he participated in the Peninsula Campaign as a wagon driver, lost his esteemed elder brother to disease, and, as a cannoneer, fought in the Battle of Kelly's Ford.

Seemingly, these experiences and those that followed changed his outlook and vastly strengthened his commitment to the cause of the Union, for, when he resumed his newspaper correspondence, Perkins's letters began to feature strong statements concerning the justice of the cause and the patriotic and noble nature of those who had put their own lives at risk and interests on hold by joining the army. But Perkins did not confine himself to celebrating the patriotism of the soldier. He instead began to develop several supporting themes, one of which was to lecture his readers on the cowards and traitors in their midst who prospered under the free institutions of the republic, but who shirked their duty in the crisis and even did all that they could to obstruct the measures needed to defend their country. The *Middlesex Journal* letter of May 30, 1863, contains the first clear statement of this position: "when storms arise and their help is needed ... [they] question the legality of motions for the preservation of that government and hesitate not at treason even to shirk their duty."

Another supporting theme was of the moral superiority of those who had fought for the cause and, in so doing, had put duty before private interest. Perkins appears to have believed that the characters of those who stayed at home were sapped by the very creature comforts they enjoyed, while the characters of those who suffered and endured privations and battle were correspondingly elevated. In his mind, those who had been schooled by war knew best the value of the institutions they had fought to defend and had the courage and sense of duty needed to effect vitally needed changes. Perkins expected that his comrades would carry their dedication and devotion to duty forward into the postwar civil world, with untold benefits to follow for society in general and, indeed, for the world at large. The *Middlesex Journal* edition of July 9, 1864, contains the most developed exposition of this view: "come visit these dirty men at Petersburg who carry muskets and eat fried pork, and if you do not find in these same dirty, dusty, and it may be ragged veterans a new nobility of character such as you have never dreamed of; if you do not see that God by noble instruments is working out here the enfranchisement of the nations. . . . These soldiers, who now are the defenders of our liberty, are in the future to be founders of an order of things which shall make our nation pure and christian-like. And if we gain no other thing by this war, there will be the immense benefit of the superior order of citizens which it will return to us. The blood shed in this struggle will purify not only the nation but the individuals of the nation and mankind all over the world."

Perkins's belief in the moral superiority of the soldier did not, in the main, apply to the officer corps, whether professional or volunteer. His views concerning the proper relationship between men and officers were as expressed in his comments about Colonel Cowdin and were frequently repeated in his diary and letters. Essentially, in his mind, a good officer was effective in the profession of arms but achieved his effectiveness without sacrificing a feeling of fellowship with his men or his popularity in their eyes. This tension between military effectiveness and the assumption of authority over others, on the one hand, and the maintenance of popularity, on the other, drove most officers, in his view, toward authoritarian rule and diminished their manly characters, as it did those of the private soldiers who meekly submitted to their rule. The mere exercise of authority and the privileges associated with rank almost inevitably resulted in diminished character, as compared with the rank and file. Perkins's letter in the February 27, 1864, edition of the *Middlesex Journal* makes this point most strongly: "it is nevertheless true that, as men increase in efficiency as officers, there is a corresponding decrease in their degree of moral excellence. Despotic rule fails not often of soiling the manhood of those who become possessed of it."

The key to Perkins's attitude toward officers appears to lie in his tendency to equate the imposition of discipline, whether on the march or in camp, with the exercise of despotic rule. This habit of mind is frequently seen throughout the diary and seems to be most prevalent when the battery was in camp, where the daily round of muster, stable call, fatigue duty, and the like seemed to have little relevance to the great crusade to save the Union. In George's eyes, the officers grew more remote from the men as they imposed increasingly arbitrary discipline while enjoying privileges and comforts that the men could not approach.

A few officers retained their popularity and George's good opinion as the war wore on, but most did not. Perhaps the best example of one who did is Capt. Walter Bramhall, the second commanding officer of the Sixth New York. From the evidence of the Perkins diary, Captain Bramhall, who was elected to his post by the members of the battery upon the resignation of the first commanding officer, took great pains to assure the comfort and well-being of the men while wielding his authority as battery commander with a light hand. Indeed, Bramhall apparently viewed the members of the battery as constituents as much as soldiers subject to his command. The diary entry of February 22, 1862, notes that Bramhall had paid a lengthy visit to Perkins's tent and, in the course of conversation, had offered to lend him some reading matter. Other entries note his tendency to forgo imposing punishments for various disciplinary infractions, while several recount his unusual efforts to provide supplies for the men and horses. One of the best examples of this tendency took place on October 9, 1862, in the aftermath of a grueling march, in which the Sixth New York, which had not yet been converted to horse artillery, accompanied a cavalry brigade on a raid on Rappahannock Station. Perkins recounts that, as they were returning to camp, Bramhall rode on ahead some eighteen miles to secure food for the men and forage for the horses. Bramhall's official report on the raid (which appears in Appendix A) confirms this action. It is also quite graphic in its description of the wear and tear suffered by the battery in the course of this action and strongly critical of the decision to attach a mounted battery to a cavalry raiding force. In spite of Bramhall's criticisms, the Sixth New York was converted to horse artillery, thus cementing its association with the cavalry, and in mid-December it was sent back to join the Army of the Potomac in its camps around Falmouth. It is possible that Bramhall's candor and attitude did not sit well with his superiors, for he resigned his commission on February 18, 1863, and left the battery after another major effort to get supplies through to his men and animals. Perkins's diary entry notes that Bramhall's explanation was "certain troubles he had experienced lately" and concluded "we lost a brave man, a good captain and withal a perfect gentleman."

Captain Bramhall's replacement as battery commander was 1st Lt. (later Capt.) J. W. Martin, who had commanded Perkins's section of artillery. Perkins's attitude toward this officer was decidedly mixed. An early diary entry notes that Martin was censured, because he sent off a team and wagon for rations on his own responsibility: "Lieut. M. seems to be the only one of the officers, who cares in the least, for the comfort and well-being of the men under his command, and he is the only one that is loved and respected by them." Subsequent diary entries noted Martin's small acts of largess toward the members of his section and fairly frequent visits to their tents. After Martin assumed command of the battery, however, Perkins's opinion of his character suffered a steep decline. He continued to express a high opinion of his soldierly qualities, particularly his skills as an artillerist, but resented his approach to instilling discipline within the battery, particularly when he himself aroused the captain's ire and was subjected to punishment or denied privileges. Thus, when during the 1864 Brandy Station winter camp, Martin had Perkins put on extra guard duty "for singing in the rear of his tent" during stable call, he groused about the injustice but made a note to make less noise habitually. Still later, during the battery's summer 1864 sojourn at Camp Barry, Martin again imposed extra guard duty when he saw him sitting down while standing guard. Perkins noted in his June 26 diary entry that "this was cruelty for nearly all other guards in the camp are in the habit of sitting down, and even the sentinel at h'dqu'rs does. Even if I deserved punishment it ought not to have been so heavy as this. At times hard thoughts and plans of revenge against the Capt. arose but God strengthened me to overcome them."

Perkins also had strong opinions concerning the senior leadership of the army, and, in a series of letters to the *Middlesex Journal,* he did not hesitate to critique the commanding generals. With the conspicuous exception of Maj. Gen. Joseph Hooker, he did not approve of their stewardship of the army. In a remarkable letter printed in the *Journal* of September 19, 1863, he outlined his case for General Hooker and against all of the other commanders, from McClellan to Meade. He excoriated McClellan for mishandling the army and for having a "feeble mind," "not large enough to contain victory." Burnside was dismissed as "an honest and noble man, but incompetent." Meade was described as a "second McClellan." According to Perkins, under Meade the army fought only "when it could not be avoided." He acknowledged that Meade had gained a victory at Gettysburg but insisted it was not due to any skill on the part of the commanding general. Indeed, in his opinion, "the result would have been the same had the army had no commander."

When it came to Hooker, however, Perkins could find only good things to say. He began his treatment of Hooker's tenure by correctly noting that Burnside had left the army in sad shape, with discipline poor and desertions at a level of crisis, and that Hooker's innovations had markedly improved morale and had created an effective cavalry corps out of a dispersed and ineffective auxiliary arm of the service. Perkins went on to deny that Hooker bore primary responsibility for the Chancellorsville defeat and to laud his generalship in keeping the army between the enemy and Washington as Lee again invaded the North. According to Perkins, Hooker had amply proved himself as an able general and a patriot. "Every movement he made was for the advancement of his cause not for the purpose of gaining distinction for himself. He is brave, see Williamsburgh. He is prudent, see Chancellorsville."

This quality of unalloyed approbation for Hooker's qualities is distinctly contrary to modern scholarship, not to speak of contemporary opinion as expressed by Hooker's subordinates, fellow generals, and indeed of the Lincoln administration. Perhaps a clue to Perkins's partisanship can be found in his appreciation of Hooker's political ties to the radical Republicans who opposed the limited war policy espoused by many of the senior officers of the Potomac army, who were conservative Democrats, as well as in Hooker's conspicuous bravery and his treatment of common soldiers. In the same letter, he went on to say, "His men loved him and with good cause. He treated them like men fighting in a sacred cause. He was the true type of a republican general, in battle brave when bravery was needed and cautious where circumspection was called for. He made a quick but careful judgment and . . . pressed the enemy with a fury which seldom failed of accomplishing his object. In camp or on the march he was kind, considerate, just. Always easy of access even a private could obtain justice at his hands. He always returned a private's salute with as much care as he would a general's."

In another letter to the *Middlesex Journal,* published in the August 6, 1864, edition, Perkins explored the subject of courage. As Gerald Linderman noted in his seminal 1987 work on the role of courage in Civil War combat, the code and ideal of courage were at the center of the ethos of the soldier of that era.[1] Those who exhibited courage in battle and lived up to that ideal were celebrated, while those who did not were derided. Linderman also made the point that courage was intertwined with other prominent characteristics of the time, two of the most significant of these being an unabashed religiosity that asserted the close involvement of God in the day-to-day affairs of men and the influence of friends and family on the behavior of the soldiers in the field. These themes are present in Perkins's letter, but he also claimed most soldiers, through constant exposure to death and horrible dismemberment, grew habituated to the prospect that they might be killed and therefore did not dread it, as they would have previously in civilian life.

Still, in Perkins's view, the line between cowardice and courage was very fine, and a trivial circumstance could push most soldiers in one direction or another. Thus, "in many instances the particular part which a single person takes in any battle is decided by circumstances the most trivial, only a slight deviation from which would have caused an action extremely different. Thus on a battle field the extremes of courage and cowardice are nearest neighbors." Perkins also acknowledged a different, and much more rare, sort of courage, one that was not subject to circumstances or acquainted with fear. In his view, that type of courage was "a great gift, and especially in commanders of high rank, for it permits of a coolness and deliberation in action that goes far toward ensuring success. Very few possess it. Gen. Hooker has this physical courage in the highest degree." Given Perkins's partisanship, it should not be surprising Hooker was his paragon of courage, yet his description appears to attribute the general's conduct to an insensibility to fear, not to any schooling given by philosophy or religion. With the exception of this type of natural courage, Perkins attributed the attainment of fearlessness to education and religion. "In this state of fearlessness there are observable two facts, according to the persons possessing or acquiring it. Either it has been attained by an education of the mind into the belief that there is no future, or if there is, none of punishment, else it results from a strong faith in God and a belief in salvation obtained through the atonement of Christ." Perkins's identification of the role of religion is quite consistent with the thesis that faith and religious practice were closely intertwined with combat courage during the Civil War.[2]

Perkins's attitudes toward the blacks he encountered, whether slaves, contrabands, or enlisted in Uncle Sam's service as soldiers and sailors, do not appear to be as clear-cut as his statement to Nathan Wyman that he had acquired a reputation in the battery as a "black abolitionist." What Perkins's fairly frequent references to blacks and the effects of slavery, sprinkled throughout his diary and letters, do portray is far more ambiguous. At the most, these sources show that Perkins was not an apologist for slavery. His political sentiments as a supporter of the Republican Party would preclude that possibility. Nevertheless, the record does not portray a man who roundly condemned slavery as a moral evil, nor does it support the thesis that he was or became an advocate for either abolition or enfranchisement. Further, in neither the diary nor the letters is there a suggestion of black equality with whites or that slavery was connected in his mind in any significant way to the rebellion. To the extent that his standpoint was sympathetic toward the blacks, it was so only in a paternalistic sense that coexisted with what today are clearly understood as demeaning, racist characterizations. In this sense, Perkins's attitudes are far from unusual amongst the Northern armies or society at large, as numerous letters and diaries from the Civil War period confirm. Even some soldier diarists and correspondents who took much stronger antislavery positions than Perkins did were not entirely free from expressing feelings of superiority.[3]

Perkins's first encounters with blacks occurred not long after the battery had settled into its Budd's Ferry camp in mid-December of 1861. The economy of that part of Maryland was based on tobacco, and that industry depended on the labor of slaves to keep it going. Thus, Perkins and his comrades were faced with the "peculiar institution" at a time when the policy of the U.S. government was far from being settled, and in an area whose loyalty to the Union cause was tenuous at best. As a consequence, the men of the battery had no compunctions about stealing fence rails and dismantling abandoned houses to feed their fires, but they, as well as Perkins himself, initially did not seem to know what to make of their interactions with the slaves of the vicinity. It does seem that at least some of the Sixth New York soldiers held strong views about slavery, for the diary entry for December 14 states that Perkins had engaged in an argument with a tent mate on the subject. What the opposing positions were is left unsaid, but the evidence does not support the idea that Perkins espoused radical abolitionist views.

His first recorded close-up view of slaves occurred a mere two days after the argument with his tent mate, when a group of three black children entered camp. The diary entry notes their arrival and records that he and his fellow soldiers were much amused by their "grotesque actions, singing and dancing." On February 6, 1862, a slave visited Perkins and his corporal while they were on picket duty on the shore of the Potomac. The slave, who had brought a primer along with him, belonged to the Widow Mason, who also owned the land on which the picket post was situated. When asked what would happen if his owner knew that he was learning to read, he replied that he would be whipped. When the soldiers asked what would happen next, the slave replied that the whipping soon would be over, and he would get another book. Perkins noted, "This and all I have seen of slavery so far hasn't as yet exalted it in my sight."

Perkins's readiness to find humor in the mannerisms of the blacks he observed was never far from the surface, even after another year had passed. On a rainy and cold night on April 5, 1864, as he sought shelter by the cook fire of a Negro servant during a stint of guard duty, he recorded that he had "a good opportunity for observing the negro character which was not without amusement." Perkins did not say if the cook was wearing an army uniform. Again, on May 25, a large number of slaves belonging to a local landowner congregated around his column when it stopped for a bivouac. He noted that some of the slaves stated that they would leave their owner and accompany the troops when they moved on. In the morning, while the units belonging to the column were waiting for the march to resume, an army band began to play and Perkins wrote that "it was really laughable to see the antics of a couple of darkies. They rivaled in extravagance of action any negro minstrels I ever saw."

He recorded his first observations of black soldiers and sailors in a more sober fashion. On May 22, as the battery arrived at the Pamunkey River after Sheridan's Richmond expedition, he noted the presence of a boat crew of the gunboat *Mystic.* He wrote: "They were darkies and looked very nice in their cool straw hats, blue pants, and spotless white shirts." On June 4, while the battery waited at White House Landing to embark on a steamer to return to Washington, D.C., he spotted some black troops who had just arrived. "I saw some negro troops for the first time who came up on a steamer. They were fine looking men. I conversed with some of them for some time."

Perkins did occasionally express strong sentiments against slavery; however, he apparently opposed the institution fundamentally for its alleged effects on society at large, rather than on grounds of moral revulsion. Indeed, his antislavery stance comfortably coexisted with racist views and expressions. In this attitude and mind-set, he was squarely in the mainstream of antislavery thought.[4] The best example of this belief is found in Perkins's letter in the June 27, 1863, edition of the *Middlesex Journal,* which he wrote after his brief furlough to his Woburn home. After a brief paean to the beauty and prosperity of New England, brought about by free institutions and free labor, he turned to a polemic on the deleterious effects of slavery on the society and economy of Virginia. "To my mind, the *shiftlessness,* neglect, and slovenliness in the appearance of all Virginia communities are but the effect and proof of the presence of slavery. Visit a southern village or even a city, and one cannot help but be struck with the appearance which everything presents of being in the last stages of decay. Fences half fallen down or never completed, doors hanging by one hinge . . . are the common characteristics of all Virginia dwelling places. But in going North, the improvement is almost instantly noticed as soon as the free and fertile fields of the Middle States are entered upon. Habitual sloth gives way to an appearance of energy and industry. Again one sees neat dwellings and listens to the true Saxon tongue undisguised by niggerisms. The line between freedom and slavery is as distinctly marked by customs, language, and popular tone of thought as it ever was by Mason and Dixon's black line across the schoolboy's outline map."

✦ ✦ ✦

Perkins did not use his diary to elaborate on his hopes and plans for postwar life. His diary makes it clear, however, that he intended to overcome what he considered to be serious character flaws and had formulated a plan that he hoped he would be spared to pursue. On his twenty-second birthday, on February 21, 1863, he wrote the following: "I think that in the past year I can see some improvement in myself in that my mind seems to have greatly matured as well as my body. More true manliness I seem to have gained in this twelve-month than in all my previous life. May God grant me another birthday and time to carry out the plans for future life which I have this year formed." If he made these plans explicit, he most likely did so in private correspondence to Almira, other members of the family, or to other friends and acquaintances. Unfortunately, these thoughts do not appear in the only private letters that have been found, so the exact nature of his plans is unknown.

It is clear that Perkins did not find intellectual nourishment in his day-to-day life as a soldier. He did, however, have regular access to books, both in the field and in camp, and liberally sprinkled his diary with notes about what he had been reading and thinking. It seems he was constantly reading, whether in camp or in the field, his choices ranging from dime novels (*Jack Adams, the Mutineer*) and philosophical tomes (*Abercrombie's Mental Philosophy*) to major contemporary authors such as Dickens (*Great Expectations* and *Bleak House*) and Alfred, Lord Tennyson (*In Memoriam*). He received some books and newspapers from home and borrowed others from fellow soldiers or a Washington, D.C., soldiers' lending library. Some few he "liberated" from private Confederate libraries. A shipment from home received on January 7, 1864, included "a lexicon, a 'Caesar' and an English grammar." He began writing out a translation of Caesar less than a week after he received it. It seems a safe assumption that he intended his postwar life to be focused on intellectual pursuits.

Whatever the nature of his 1863 plans may have been, George did not waste much time after leaving the army to launch the career in which he would remain for the rest of his life. After mustering out on December 7, 1864—"once more a free man"—he returned home to Woburn and was hired at a salary of one thousand dollars per annum as principal of Central Grammar School Number 1, starting work on February 27, 1865. As principal, George oversaw a staff of eight, including a music teacher, and was expected also to care for the classrooms. Grammar, or advanced, schools boasted a four-year course of study that would roughly correspond to a middle or junior high curriculum in today's educational system. He remained at Central Grammar School through the 1870–71 school year.[5]

After leaving his job in Woburn, George began work in the fall of 1872 at the Phillips School in Boston. Phillips was a public grammar school, founded in 1844, one of the first public schools in that city to have an interracial student body. He was hired as an usher at an annual salary of $1,700, making as much as $2,000 in subsequent years. By the 1880–81 school term, George had been promoted to second submaster, with a salary range of $1,500 to $1,800. His final promotion to submaster occurred on or before the school year beginning in 1889. Published salaries for this grade level ranged from $1,500 to $2,240.[6] According to an October 18, 1890, article in the *News,* George's failing health had compelled him to retire from active service during the previous year.

Perkins was well established in his postwar career as an educator before he became active in the Grand Army of the Republic (GAR). Records of Burbank Post 33 in the Woburn Public Library indicate that he joined that post by muster on April 14, 1881, and served as junior vice commander in 1882. He was "honorably discharged" from Post 33 on December 20, 1883.[7] Evidently, Post 33 could not accommodate all of the Woburn veterans who wished to participate, for the *Woburn Journal* of January 11, 1884, contained a report that a second post of the GAR would be organized in Woburn and stated that "it promises to start out with a large membership."[8] In fact, less than two weeks later, a meeting was held at Fraternity Hall for the purpose of organizing a new post of the GAR. The inspector of the Massachusetts Department of the GAR called the meeting to order and read a special order from the department commander authorizing the formation of a new post to be known as Post 161. Elections to select the post officers were held, and the name "Woburn Post 161" was chosen by unanimous consent. George Perkins was elected to be commander of the post for the first year of its existence.[9]

After the completion of his one-year term as commander, the records of Post 161 indicate that George remained an active participant in the affairs of the post through August 1890. In that month, Boston hosted a National Encampment of the GAR, with a grand parade, speeches by veterans and politicians, and other public events. Both Woburn posts were present and marched in the parade. It appears unlikely that George was well enough personally to participate in the encampment, but his son, George H. Perkins, was chosen to be a member of the Sons of Veterans staff of the Department Commander.[10]

George Perkins's comrades, colleagues, and students were present in force at his funeral, which was held at Woburn's First Congregational Church on a very stormy Sunday, October 19, 1890. The service featured choral music; prayers, preaching, and scripture readings by the pastor of the church; numerous floral tributes from colleagues, students, and GAR comrades; as well as a reading of the GAR ritual. Thirty members of GAR Woburn Post 161 were present to mark their comrade's passing. The Boston public school system was represented by a large group of masters, submasters, and teachers from the Phillips School, along with several other public schools. Twelve students from the Phillips School class of 1890 and one from the class of 1891 attended the funeral, and the four pallbearers were members of the submasters' club.[11] At the end of his life, George Perkins had indeed become a prominent and respected member of the community.

A short note about the editing process is perhaps in order. In general, I have respected and retained the spelling and grammar of the typescript diary in my possession. In most cases, George Perkins's choices agree both with contemporary and modern-day English usage. As a recipient of at least a partial Harvard education, this is hardly surprising. George's writing, however, did have a few quirks that seem to be uniquely his own. For example, he invariably put a final "h" on place-names ending with "burg." Thus, Fredericksburg is always rendered as Fredericksburgh and Harrisonburg as Harrisonburgh. The town of Strasburg gets the gift of two additional letters. It appears in the diary as Strausburgh, no doubt because it was and still is pronounced that way by the locals. In addition, most likely to speed the writing process, George usually abbreviated the titles of military organizations. Examples are "reg" for regiment and "div" for division. All of these usages have been retained to preserve the kind of shorthand tricks used in the maintenance of a daily diary written, for the most part, in field conditions. I have, however, removed stretches of the diary that record little but mundane and monotonous comments about the weather and the food eaten by the private soldiers of the battery. In so doing, I believe I have not excised any material that is crucial to the historical record. Omitted material is identified and summarized in the introductions to each chapter.

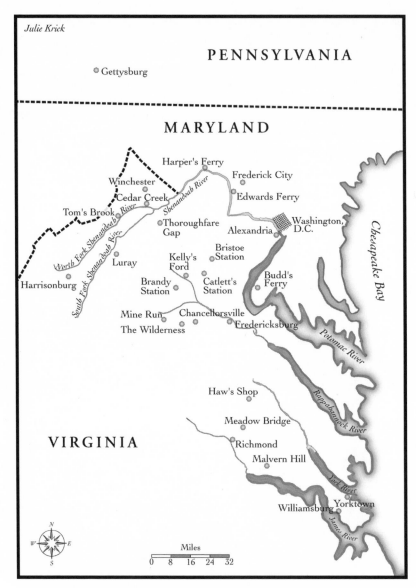

The Campaigns and Camps of the Sixth New York Independent Battery, 1861–64. Drawn by Julie Krick.

The Diary and Newspaper Correspondence of
Private George Perkins, Sixth New York
Independent Battery, 1861–1864

CHAPTER 1

THE STORM OF WAR DRAWS NEARER:
DECEMBER 1861–APRIL 1862

ACCOMPANIED BY HIS OLDER BROTHER, JAMES APPLETON "APP" PERKINS,
George Perkins departed home on December 5, 1861, to join Battery K, Ninth New York State Militia, then temporarily encamped
near Washington, D.C. App and four other men from Woburn had
joined the battery in June during the wave of patriotic fervor that
swept the North, but George held back until App returned to collect
him. George mustered in on December 7, and the next day the battery began to march to Budd's Ferry, Maryland, on the eastern bank of
the Potomac River, opposite Quantico, Virginia. Upon its arrival, the
battery reported to Gen. Joseph Hooker's (Third) Division of Third
Corps, where for the next four months it trained, supplied artillery
pickets, and sparred with the Confederate batteries at Quantico that
were attempting to enforce a blockade of the Potomac River.

George joined the army in the aftermath of several severe disas-
ters for the Union cause in the East, the most notable of these being the
humiliating defeat of Brig. Gen. Irvin McDowell's half-trained troops
at Bull Run on July 21. In the aftermath of this catastrophe, President
Lincoln replaced McDowell with Maj. Gen. George Brinton McClellan,
who was fresh from his success in a relatively minor campaign at Rich
Mountain, Virginia. On July 27, McClellan assumed command of what
would become the Army of the Potomac and set about creating a drilled
and disciplined army out of the disorganized remnants of the Bull Run
defeat. In this effort he had great and immediate success, but, unfortunately for his relationship with the president, he seemingly could not
bring himself to risk the army by using it to crush the rebellion by force
of arms. Eventually, however, McClellan prepared a plan for an offensive to take place in the spring of 1862. This plan involved outflanking
Confederate Gen. Joseph E. Johnston's army in its Northern Virginia

positions by transporting the Army of the Potomac by water to a position near the mouth of the Rappahannock River. From that position, McClellan expected to attack and occupy the Confederate capital or defeat Johnston's army on a field of his own choosing.

Hooker's Division, in its positions along the Maryland shore of the Potomac River, was part of this grand plan, but, in early March, before McClellan could get his forces in motion, Johnston evacuated his forward positions and withdrew his army behind the Rappahannock River, from which position it could more easily defend Richmond whenever the Federal host got under way and from whichever direction it approached.

George Perkins's diary and letters chronicled the desultory war along the Potomac between the battery's arrival in December and its embarkation for the Virginia Peninsula in April. He noted the Union attempts to break the blockade of Washington, the Confederate attempts to maintain it, Johnston's evacuation of his positions along the Virginia side of the river, and the army's preparations to embark for the peninsula.

The diary entries of March 28–31 have been omitted. Little occurred but the regular round of guard duty, drills, and the usual unsettled weather. Perkins filled his spare time by browsing in Charles Dickens's *Household Words* and also began reading a novel of presumably lesser quality entitled *Will Watch, the Bold Smuggler.*

1861

Dec. 5th

Started to join Battery K. 9th New York State Militia in afternoon at 2 o'clock. As I passed through Boston stopped at Gas-Light Co.'s office to see Albert Chittenden, but he was away.[1] Started from Boston at 5½ o'clock on Providence R.R. Took second class ticket, cost $2.00. Appleton was with me, and paid half my fare, between East Woburn and Boston paid no fare. Arrived at Groton Conn., about 10 and in about an hour started on the steamer Plymouth Rock for New York, slept greater portion of the night on a cotton bale, on lower deck.

6th

Arrived in New York about 7 in the morning and having crossed in the ferry boat Jersey City, took the cars on the New Jersey R.R. for Philadelphia. Took notice that the soil of New Jersey was a bright red, or rather a brick-red color. Arrived in Philadelphia at 11 o'clock. During the preceding night fell in with a detachment going to Washington, to reinforce the Mass. 15th Reg. Luckily for Appleton and me, we managed to pass free with them to Philadelphia, and also all the way to Washington. On arriving in Philadelphia, took horse-cars about

5 miles across the city to the Baltimore R.R. The only noticeable thing I saw in Philadelphia, was the white marble door-steps, and white wooden window shutters, and casements. They presented a very fine appearance, stretched the whole length of a very long street. Arrived in Baltimore about 2 P.M., and having changed cars, was drawn across the city, by a team of 8 donkeys, through the famous West Pratt Street, on which occurred the 19th of April riot; towards the close of the afternoon, began to fall in with tents and baggage wagons. Shortly came to Perryville where the whole train of cars was pushed on to a ferry boat, and steamed across to Havre-de-Grace, where was stationed the 4th N.Y. Reg. Splendid scenery, looking up the river, it was the Susquehanna. After about half and hour's more riding came to the Relay house, where we stopped, and I found on enquiry that Cousin Bill Jordan's Reg. was stationed about 5 miles farther on.[2] Arrived in Washington about 7 o'clock, having accomplished the journey in the short space of 28 hours, went to hotel for lodgings, after mailing my 1st letter home.

DEC. 7TH
Eat breakfast of stewed rabbit (which wasn't tom cat) and then went through the principal market. From there went to find the war department, and by mistake stumbled upon the state department, from there went through the grounds of the white house to the war department, where we were directed to go to the head-quarters of the Army of the Potomac to find the whereabouts of Battery K. From there, was told to go to Gen. Bussy's head-quarters, who is chief of artillery.[3] There, learned that the battery was in the city about half a mile east of the capitol. From there, went to the patent office. App. bought for me, on the way, a pair of boots, price $3.00. Saw in the patent office various relics of Gen's. Washington and Jackson. Also saw in the left wing, which has been converted into a hospital for wounded soldiers, a convalescent soldier, and in one of the alcoves a dead one. From there went to the Smithsonian Institute, where I saw various curiosities, pictures, and the library. Went then to see the Capitol, visited the Senate house, and house of Representatives, and there sat in the chair of the Senator Sumner. Joined the battery at their encampment, at sundown; had crackers and coffee for supper. Slept in a tent for the first time but not very well.

DEC. 8TH.
Sunday. Breakfast, coffee and crackers. Battery struck tents and took up their march for Budd's Ferry on the Maryland side of the Potomac, about 40 miles from Washington. Encamped on the road in some oak woods, about 4 miles from V. Coffee and bread for supper, slept cold, being in the open air.

9TH
Coffee and bread for breakfast, then resumed our march, accomplished about 12 miles, and encamped at 2½ o'clock, coffee, bread, and fresh beef for supper, slept under the gun cover, which is made of heavy canvass. The first night of good sleep I have had yet.

3

10TH

Breakfast, coffee and pilot bread. Harnessed and resumed the march; roads horrid bad; reached camping place for the night, about 2 in the afternoon, with all the horses quite used up. Bread, and very fat bacon, fried, for supper, slept in some pine woods, with a blazing fire at my feet, was quite comfortable. This was my first night of guard duty, my hours were from 5–7, 11–1, and 5–7. Kept guard the first two hours, but in the night the corporal of the guard couldn't find me, and so I had the whole night to myself.

DEC 11TH

Coffee, crackers, and fried bacon for breakfast, started on the march at 10 o'clock, and passing over roads the worst I ever saw, arrived at camp at five in the afternoon. During the day, passed by the camps of various regiments, among them, those of the 1st and 11th Mass. The night of our arrival, our baggage wagons went astray, and we had nothing to eat till very late. Very cold all day, and slept very cold all night.

12TH

Coffee, bread and bacon for breakfast. Very heavy frost during the past night. Dinner, potatoes and stewed beans, in the afternoon chopped wood, and cleared the ground for the tents from 1 to 3. We have got nine new Sibley tents for the battery.[4] They are of a circular form, with a place for ventilation, at the top. Pitched 2 of them. Supper, coffee, rice, and hard bread.

13TH

Still colder, did not sleep well last night. Breakfast, coffee, bread, and veal. N.B. Somebody stole the veal in the vicinity of the camp. Asked no questions for conscience sake, it was only about half cooked. Mailed a letter to Myra. Dinner, rice and hardees. Hardees is the name given in camp to hard bread.[5] Supper, coffee and hardees. I helped level the ground for the remainder of the tents, from 11 to 1. Rest of the tents pitched to-day, and we moved into them. Built a fire in ours but it smoked very bad.

DEC. 14TH

Was wakened this morning, by a bustle in the camp, and found that Lieut. Brown's section, with their two guns, had gone away at 5 o'clock to do picket duty along the river.[6] Breakfast, coffee and hardees, and a small piece of cheese, App. having bought a pound last night, costing 20 cts. Heard firing on the river, in the course of the day, learned afterwards that our guns fired a number of times at batteries across the river; dinner, salt beef and hardees. To-day, cleaned the guns and caissons, a very tedious job. Supper, coffee, hardees, and cheese. Guns came back from picket after dark. Had an argument in the tent, with Frank Jones concerning slavery.[7]

Corp. George H. Brown, Sixth Battery, New York State Volunteer Light Artillery. Courtesy of U.S. Army Military History Institute.

15TH

Breakfast, coffee and hardees. While I went to the spring to wash, I missed the nine o'clock roll call, not having heard the bugle. Went to Capt. Bunting, who excused me.[8] Sat down in the forenoon to write, and wrote to Myra, and Mother. App also wrote some letters. All day there has been firing on the river. In the afternoon App went down to the river, and while there, saw the rebel batteries give a few shots. A new battery was also discovered. The federal gun-boat Yankee replied to them, from about 2 miles up the river.[9] Lieut. Bramhall joined the battery.[10] Dinner of stewed salt-pork, potatoes, and hardees. At the morning roll-call the orderly ordered the canoniers to pick up the stones, where the guns were parked. Being Sunday, the men did not do it. Went off for persimmons, but did not get any. Two live oxen driven into camp, for the subsistence of the battery. Coffee and hardees for supper. Spent a very pleasant evening, conversing, reading, and singing.

DEC. 16TH

Slept very cold last night. Heavy guns on the river towards morning, coffee and hardees for breakfast. Did police duty from 10–12. Built a bedstead of pine saplings.

App and I gathered hemlock boughs for a bed. Salt horse and potatoes for dinner. Drill in the manual of the gun in the afternoon, by the whole battery, in which I was omitted. Coffee and hardees for supper. In the evening, 3 little negroes came into camp, and amused us not a little, by their grotesque actions, singing and dancing.

17TH
Slept very comfortable last night, thanks to our new bed-stead. Washed in the forenoon. Beefsteak for dinner. In the afternoon, our battery went on review with two other batteries. Two of our guns absent on picket, didn't make a very good appearance. Lieut. Martin, who was officer of the day, gave me a pass till 5 o'clock.[11] Also visited the camp of the 11th Mass. Regiment, saw James McDonald of North Woburn, who is captain in the 11th.[12] Saw the dress parade of the regiment, and thought they looked very fine. Saw Col. Cowdin, Acting Brigadier General, and also Brig. Gen. Hooker, who reviewed the batteries, he is quite an elderly man, with a very stern looking countenance, and gray whiskers, mixed with red.[13] Saw enough of the infantry service to be more and more thankful, that I am in a battery.

2nd Lt. T. B. Bunting, Company K, Sixth Independent Battery, New York State Volunteer Light Artillery. Courtesy of Massachusetts Commandery, Military Order of the Loyal Legion and U.S. Army Military History Institute.

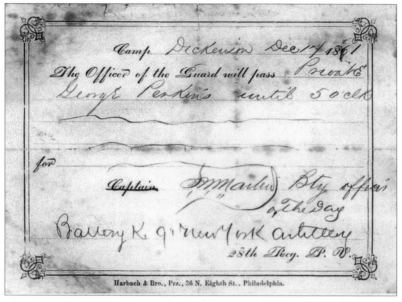

Camp Dickenson pass. Griffin Family Collection.

2nd Lt. Joseph W. Martin, Sixth Independent Battery, New York State Volunteer Light Artillery. Courtesy of U.S. Army Military History Institute.

Maj. J. W. McDonald, Eleventh Massachusetts Volunteer Infantry. Courtesy of Massachusetts Commandery, Military Order of the Loyal Legion and U.S. Army Military History Institute.

DEC. 18TH

Did two hours' police duty, building stables for the horses. Dinner, soup made of fresh beef and potatoes, my ration consisting of half a pint dipper full, with 4 hardees. Bought 10 cts. worth of Apples, both the soup and the apples tasted good. Had a present of half a cranberry pie, which tasted delicious, but which if I were at home, I should refuse, as not being fit to eat. The whole battery went out for drill in the afternoon. Supper of boiled salt beef, and coffee. In the evening, there was very rapid and heavy firing on the river, from the rebel batteries and five steamers that passed. Could see the shells explode in the air.

19TH

Slept cold again last night. Two guns in the third section went out at 9 in the morning for battery drill. On guard to-day. Had bean soup for dinner, and beef-steak for supper. In the afternoon the remaining 4 guns went out for battery drill. Half a dozen men put in the guard house, for refusing to carry logs on their shoulders, to build a stable with.[14] Lieut. Brown returned from Washington. Heavy firing on the river again to-night. The guns of our section go on picket

tomorrow, and I intend to get a pass from the Capt. and go too. On account of
the prisoners in the guard house, I have the privilege of sleeping in my own tent
to-night.

Dec. 20th

Very pleasant last night, moonlight and warm, kept guard from 11 to 1, and
pleasant the thoughts of home prevented it from being tedious. The corporal of
the guard did not waken me at 5 so instead, I went on from 7 to 9. The guns of
our section went off on picket at 4 o'clock, App with them. Applied for a pass
from the officer of the day, but was refused, no passes being given out this day.
Occasional firing on the river, during the forenoon. Pea soup for dinner. Very
heavy firing in the afternoon, thought of App's danger. Got straw for bedding.
The other 4 pieces went out for drill in the afternoon. App returned late in the
evening very tired. In the afternoon a schooner passed up the river, and the rebel
batteries fired over fifty shots at it. Our guns opened on the rebels, and provoked
them to return. Shells burst all around the sand pit, covering the men with sand.
The rebels fired 64 lb. shells and some 96. Lieut. Martin sighted a gun, and
threw a shell right into one of the enemy's camps, and stopped the sound of their
drums. They could hear the rebels swearing as they worked their guns.

21st

Morning cold and cloudy, but sun arose towards the middle of the forenoon,
making it pleasanter. Hardees all gone, had nothing but coffee for breakfast,
found 1 cracker on the ground, which I was only too glad to get. The Captain
begins to stir, and appoints all sorts of duties. The men grumble. Tried to make
me take care of a team of horses; Lieut. Martin spoke in my favor. Bean soup,
without any crackers, for dinner. Detailed to get wood, and lifted too much,
causing bad dreams at night. Rations came in the afternoon. Officer of the day
inspected tents. Said our tent was too disorderly. Forbidden to steal any more
rails, under pain of a court martial.

Dec. 22nd

Slept warm. Had flour dealt out, a quart dipper full of flour to be all the bread
we were to have for 1 day. We mixed it with water, and fired it as griddle-cakes.
It tasted delicious, although we had nothing to eat upon it. Had bean soup for
dinner. Had an inspection in the afternoon, and I took J. A. P.'s place on the caisson. Cold to-day and yesterday, rained in the evening. Felt sad all day, no letter
from home yet.

23rd

Rained all last night, slept very comfortable. Hardees, and coffee without sugar
for breakfast. Rained till about 3 in the afternoon. Griddle cakes again for dinner, didn't set well on my stomach. On guard 3rd relief, my hours 1–3, 7–9, 1–3,
7–9. Capt. more and more strict, caused the drivers and cannoniers to rub down

the horses, which wasn't in the least necessary, very nasty and muddy, altogether uncomfortable. Cleared off, towards night, moon-light during my night-watch.

24TH
Slept very comfortable. No sugar for coffee again, griddle cakes for dinner again. Bean soup for supper. Had a pass, but did not use it. The third section went on picket yesterday. Learned since, that our section when on picket, fired 68 shots, mostly shells. On account of that, the commanders have been forbidden to fire more than seven shells, unless on account of something extraordinary. Lieut. Martin has been censured today, for ordering a wagon off, for rations, on his own responsibility. Lieut. M. seems to be the only one of the officers, who cares in the least, for the comfort and well-being of the men under his command, and he is the only one that is loved and respected by them. The clothing has arrived in camp, and I expect to get my fit to-morrow. No letters yet. I learn that some one has got to go to Washington to get the mail. Gen. Hooker visited our camp to-day. Have had a slight touch of the dysentery, but have now got quite over it.

DEC. 25TH
Christmas, very pleasant indeed, sun shines, and it is very warm, no work to-day, wrote to Myra. Lieut. Martin furnished materials for a dinner to his section, beef-steak, and bread, and plum dough; beefsteak and bread, splendid; but the pudding a failure; they put it into pots to boil, and the puddings burst through on the bottom. App and I took our share of it, and putting it into a fry pan, cooked it in that manner. Slept about all the afternoon. App on the wood-guard. Learned that there was a pontoon bridge, and a fleet, that would soon come down the river and shell out the rebels on the other shore, this is only a report and I cannot answer for the truth of it.

26TH
On stable guard to-day. Beef soup for dinner. Weather growing colder.

DEC. 27TH
Detailed on wood-guard, and worked through the morning. At noon got two letters from home, one from Myra, and one from A.H. Richardson, experienced the most pleasure in receiving a letter, that I think any body ever felt.[15] I trembled all over and fairly jumped for joy. I may fairly set down letters, as one of the greatest pleasures of a soldier's life. Did not work in the afternoon. Stewed beans for dinner. Wrote to A.H. Richardson, Esq. Had a great delicacy for supper, in the shape of molasses and bread, with our coffee. Tried on my new over-coat to-day, for the first time, and found that it fitted better than I expected; got it yesterday.

DEC. 28TH, 1861.
Slept poorly. Griddle cakes and molasses for breakfast. Detailed for guard on the 2nd relief. Very cold but sunny. Fight occurred between two men of the battery.

They were called up before Lieut. Bramhall who after talking to them let them go. Noticed that all the travellers in this section of the country go either on foot or on horseback. Have not seen a carriage since I have been out here. We are going to have regular mails after this, to go on Mondays & Thursdays and some on Tuesdays and Fridays. Griddle cakes again for dinner. Cold all day. Wrote to Albert Richardson.

29TH.

Very pleasant guard last night, stationed over the horses. Sat by the fire all the time. Our section went off on picket at 5 in the morning and do not return until the same time tomorrow morning. Went down in the woods by a brook and had a good wash. Wrote to Myra. Went down to the river. It was a pleasant day and no wind. The prospect was most beautiful. At Budd's ferry the Potomac is about two miles wide. On the other side of the river could see the rebel batteries, and their gun boat named the Page laying at the mouth of Quantico creek.[16] The land on this side I should judge to be particularly adapted to cultivation. The widow Budd's house and outhouses are rapidly being demolished by the soldiers who take away the boards to build huts and floor their tents.[17] They have infantry pickets all along our shore. The scene such as I viewed it today was most pleasant to look upon. Came home through the camp of the 11th Mass. infantry and stopped awhile to listen to their band. They played some old familiar tunes which reminded me of my New England home. When I arrived in camp found that I had overstayed my pass and I expect I shall have to do double guard duty on that account. Nothing but cakes, again, for supper.

DEC. 30TH.

Slept very poorly last night. Heard a rustling in the straw in which I laid, did not know whether it was a mouse or snake. App sick today. He did not attend roll call. Received today from government a pair of pants, light blue, and a pair of boots. Our battery had a drill in the afternoon. Went to see the dress parade of 11th Mass. regiment. A new lot of hardees which tasted quite nice, had them and coffee without sugar for supper. Tomorrow inspection and muster to answer to our names upon the pay roll. All men to be present with all their personal effects at 9 o'clock.

31ST.

Slept cold again. Weather growing colder. Had muster and inspection for pay at 9 in the morning. Had the oath of allegiance and service administered to me by 1st. Lieutenant Walter M. Bramhall, Lieut. Martin and Dr. Moran being witnesses. App is getting better. Received a letter from Myra dated 22d. Wrote to Myra's father and to Myra herself. Spent a very pleasant evening.

JANUARY 1ST 1862. WEDNESDAY.

Hardee, coffee, and fat bacon fried for breakfast. Appleton well and on guard. Very warm and pleasant. Had no fire all day. By far the warmest New Year's Day

I ever experienced. Passed the day in writing and reading. Captain not returned from Washington yet. Heard some rumours of his resignation and that of Lieut. Bramhall. In that case I hope Lieut Martin will be Captain in his place.

Jan. 2nd.
Cold and windy today. On guard the first relief. App went out of camp on a pass. Bean soup again for dinner, but did not eat any. Rumors about to the effect that we should join General Burnside and go up the James River, and also that there would be a general forward movement within a few days. App and I have determined to build a log house for winter quarters. Would we not be in a quandary if when we had just completed it we should receive orders to march.

3D.
Not very well today. Boiled salt pork with hardees for dinner. Had a pass 'till 4 o'clock but did not go out of camp. Received a letter from Myra and wrote in return. App on stable duty all day. Court martial today of those soldiers who refused duty a little while ago. One private also punished by standing on the head of a cask for two hours a day until remission by the commandant.[18] Weather cold but sunny. The ground commences to freeze. Firing on the river. App received a letter from mother directed both to him and me. Felt uneasy and dejected this evening. Sprinkled a little after night fall.

4TH.
Hailed last night, ground very slippery in consequence. Cold and chilly all day. A slight fall of snow in the forenoon. Caught cold last night and have felt chilly all day. Right section down on picket with our lieutenant. Heard that the capt. was sick at Washington. Lieut. Martin visited our tent last evening. Did nothing all day but sit in my tent, shiver and feed the fire. Salt horse for dinner, that is salted beef.

Jan 5th. Sunday.
Rather unwell all day. App on guard. Just one month ago left home to join the battery. Cold all day.

6TH.
Slept well. Light fall of snow during the night. Busy all day. On guard, 2nd relief. Warm biscuit for dinner. Very damp under foot. Got my feet wet which made my cold worse.

7TH.
Better today. Had a pass and went with App over to the 1st Mass. Reg. Saw the Phillips boys and took dinner there, which consisted of cold corn beef with warm potatoes and soft bread.[19] Called at a store on the way home for the purpose of buying some new camp-cooking utensils. Was told to call tomorrow afternoon.

App was appointed commissary for our section this week. Lieut. Clark returned to camp this evening.[20]

8TH.

Slept poorly last night. On stable duty in the forenoon. In the afternoon went to the store according to the appointment of yesterday and learned that the articles had not yet come down from Washington. Took a walk over to Skinner's store. Received no letter yesterday or today, one being due yesterday. Felt concerned for Myra. Ice on the Potomac prevents the usual connection between Washington and Rum Point, and because of this Lieut. Clark came from W. by carriage. Warm throughout the day. A partial thaw took place making the camp very muddy. Forgot to note down that yesterday the 7th I received a pair of buck gloves from the government.

JAN. 9TH.

Rained all last night. Muddy and stormy in the morning. Cleared way at noon. Capt. returned from Washington last night. Wrote to Myra. Very warm all day. No letter yet. Perfectly well. Made some pan cakes for supper. Beef tea for dinner. Our section goes on picket tomorrow.

10TH.

Slept first rate. Got up at 4 o'clock and tramped down to Budd's Ferry. The way very muddy and several brooks to cross. Got down there about daybreak and after placing our guns in the sand pit went into the widow Budd's house or rather what was left of it, the soldiers having pulled about half of it down to feed their fires and for the sake of the boards. After sunrise went along the beach picking up stones. Reminded me of my last trip to Nahant on 4th of July. Spent the day in running about and reading. Had soft bread and a little butter for dinner, or rather for dinner and breakfast combined. I never thought when at home that I should ever snatch so greedily at bread. When I got my bread I was so hungry that I began to eat it scarcely willing to wait for my portion of the butter. App returned to camp at noon and did not come back again although he previously said he would. Laid down on the floor at night with one blanket under and two over me, and slept as sound as a top although there was a window wide open with the wind blowing right on to me. Doubtless if I had done the same thing only two months ago while at home the consequences would have been a very bad cold or a fit of sickness, but now it did not trouble me in the least, in fact I never had a sweeter sleep. Was on guard over the guns from 6–8.

JAN. 11TH.

Was awakened at 5 o'clock and went on guard over the guns for about an hour, when the two guns of "Smith's Battery" arrived and we set off for camp.[21] I was far behind the rest being compelled to carry all our blankets and App's overcoat.

Arrived in camp at half past eight and found that I was on guard again on the 1st relief. Received from government two pr. socks, 2 pr. drawers and two undershirts, both the drawers and undershirts of inferior quality. Very warm all day.

12TH.
Very warm last night with a little rain. Towards morning the war steamship Pensacola went down the river from Washington and the rebel batteries fired quite a number of shots at her, but as I have learned since did not hit her. Could hear the working of her engine quite plainly. She went down while I was on guard from three to five in the morning.[22] Today very fine and warm, I may say actually hot. Had a pass and started out to visit General Sickles' division but stopped in the woods by the way to read "Great Expectations."[23] For the last two days have been troubled with a bile on the back of my neck which is now getting quite painful. App on guard today.

JAN. 13TH, MONDAY.
Snowed all the forenoon. Perley Griffin arrived in camp from home bringing me a small package.[24] My bile very troublesome. In the evening got a letter from Myra dated Jan. 3d & 5th.

JAN. 14TH.
Slept very poorly. Rained all night and part of the day. Very cold. Bile still very bad.

15TH.
Rained most of the day and very cold. Felt quite miserable.

16TH.
Cold but clear. Slept quite well. My bile getting better. Received a letter from Hero, with a letter enclosed from Miss Ransom of So. Reading which contained six postage stamps, she being indebted to me for that amount. Was very much pleased with Hero's letter.

17TH.
Slept cold, App having slept in the commissary tent. Had but one blanket. Bile much better. Weather quite warm. Had a very good dinner, consisting of beefsteak and fried potatoes. Done the cooking myself and am quite persuaded that mother herself could not have done much better. While cooking our dinner the mail came in and I received two letters from Myra. In the afternoon the paymaster came and we were paid off, my pay amounting to $10.83. The mode of paying off is as follows. First all the men are called up and sign their names to two pay rolls. Afterwards they are called up in alphabetical order when the paymaster hands to each man the amount of his pay. The paymaster came into camp in a baggage wagon with two men as guard, with the money in a large

trunk. Received my pay in two five dollar shin-plasters on the U.S. treasury, the rest in silver. Paid App $3.75 which he had loaned me to buy my boots and to pay my fare in the cars. Enclosed five dollars in a letter which Corporal More took with him to New York where he will put it in the post office.[25] I also gave him a half dime to pay for registering the letter. Think that Myra will get the money safe enough. I wish the amount were much greater. Am at present possessed of $2.05. Very heavy and rapid firing on the river late last night. Some of the shells must have burst very near the camp for they shook the ground where I was lying awake in my tent. For supper coffee, hardees and salt beef. App slept with me again last night because it is so damp and cold in the commissary tent.

JAN. 18TH.
Rained during the night. Very damp all day. Rained heavily a great portion of it. Dinner very good again today being beef soup. A very nasty day.

19TH, SUNDAY.
Another nasty and rainy day. Mud four inches deep in camp. Our section on picket. App did not go with the section but staid in camp to do the cooking. I was visited by a doctor belonging to the regular battery who lanced a stye upon my left eye. Rained all day.

20TH.
Another rainy day. On guard first relief. Bought bottle of ink, five cents. Carried some clothes out of camp to be washed, and also my boot to be mended which I had burned. Sent three letters, to Myra, to Hero and to Albert Chittenden.

21ST.
Still rainy but not cold. Stood guard six hours in the night for Harry Budelman for the consideration of 25 cts.[26]

22ND.
Cloudy but not rainy. Clothes fresh from wash, and carried some for App.

23D.
Cloudy but dry. On wood guard. Slept in commissary tent. Had sconse for dinner.

24TH.
Hail and snow. Boiled, sugar cured ham for dinner. On guard the first relief. Roads very bad just now on account of the rain. Two of the baggage wagons only day before yesterday went down to Liverpool point after feed for the horses, a distance of six miles and in returning with a load of 1500 lbs. got stuck, with four horses. Liverpool point is below our camp on the Potomac. Today the Captain sent 40 men on horseback for a load of one bag of corn apiece. Bought an

account book of sutler, price 15 cts. App's clothes came from the wash. In the afternoon it moderated and rained. Lieut. Bramhall returned from Washington where he went four days ago.

JAN. 25TH.

A mixture of snow, hail and rain all night. Guard duty last night dismal and unpleasant. The sun rose clear and pleasant. Warm all day and the snow melted making our tent very damp. Got my boot from the cobbler. Price for mending 75 cts. Washed myself this day. Found on the pair of drawers that I took off, a body louse. Examined well but could find no more, although all day I thought I could feel them crawling over me. Hope to God I shall never have any more. It is a most horrible feeling. Sent clothes to wash. The price for washing clothes here is six cents. If some washerwoman were to come out here, without a doubt some of them would make a fortune in a very short time.

JAN. 26TH, SUNDAY.

A warm damp wind during the night. Sun rose clear and warm. Hardee fried in bacon fat with coffee for breakfast. Beef soup for dinner. Worked on the stable during the forenoon. Wrote to A.A. Chittenden and A.H. Richardson. Very warm all day. Also sent a communication to the Middlesex Journal.

Middlesex Journal, February 8, 1862

Camp Dickinson, near Budd's Ferry, Md.,
Jan. 21st, 1862.

Thinking that doubtless your readers would be pleased to hear from the Woburn volunteers in the 9th Battery, I send you the present communication.

Your correspondent joined Battery K, 9th Regiment, N.Y.S.M., on Dec. 7th, 1861 at Washington, where it was temporarily encamped on the way from Poolsville to join Gen. Hooker's division on the lower Potomac.

At Washington Arsenal four of our guns, six-pounders, rifled "James" cannon were returned, and in exchange we received Hotchkiss' field guns, so that now the battery presents a much more uniform appearance, all our guns being of the same size and make. Our battery now consists of six-pounder rifle cannon, made of bronze and carrying a conical, cap shell of 13½ pounds weight.[27] The advantage of the cap shell consists in the fact that it always explodes at the moment of striking, allowing no opportunity for extinguishing and thus rendering it void of effect. Even if the shell strikes the water it is sure to explode, whereas the water often extinguishes the fuse of a spherical shell.

Since joining the battery, it has been detached from the 9th Reg., and now is called 6th N.Y. Artillery.

In the battery, besides myself, there are four other Woburn boys, viz: J.E. Tileston, J.B. Horne, P.M. Griffin, and J.A. Perkins.[28] J.E. Tileston is our orderly sergeant and enjoys a well deserved popularity. All the boys enjoy good health, although for the last week the weather has been anything but conducive to health, in fact we haven't seen the sun in five days, and it was only yesterday that we were treated to a thunder shower. I doubt whether in Woburn you can boast as much at this time of year.

At present we are camped on the edge of some pine woods about a mile from Budd's Ferry on the lower Potomac. At this place the river is about 1½ miles wide. Opposite the ferry the rebels have erected several batteries containing in all 14 guns, as can be seen with the glass very plainly of a clear day.

Right opposite the ferry, and lying in the mouth of Quantico Creek, can be seen the smoke stack of the rebel gun-boat Page, just peering above an intervening strip of land. Yet although the river is almost lined with batteries, the rebels have not been enabled to entirely stop navigation. It was only a few evenings ago the Pensacola passed down the river while the rebels fired over fifty rounds of shell at her without one of them taking effect. And scarcely a day passes but what they fire at some passing schooner, though I have never heard of their hitting anything.

The duty of our battery consists in doing picket duty on the bank of the river at the ferry, two guns at a time in alternation with those of the two other batteries which constitutes the artillery of this division.

Such is our situation and such is our duty, but as to the probable movements, and the intentions of government, with which I perceive the correspondents of the Boston papers are in the habit of treating their readers, I must confess I am entirely ignorant.

Yours, &c. G.P.

JAN. 27TH.
Very warm all night. Cloudy but warm all day. Looked like snow. Beef soup again for dinner. Wrote to Myra. App slightly unwell so that he was unable to cook. Samuels did the cooking instead.[29] Commenced reading "Lena Cameron; or the four sisters" by Mrs. Grey. Our section goes on picket tomorrow and I have obtained permission of Lieut. Martin to go in place of Fred Wall, who is just now convalescent of a fever.[30] App says he intends to give up cooking as it strains him.

JAN. 28TH.
Sat up last night cooking beef-steak for tomorrow. Warm last night. Got up at 4 o'clock and started down on picket. Was very muddy and once got into the mud over the top of my boot. Arrived at the river just at daybreak and having placed our guns in the sand pit went into the widow's now dilapidated house and took breakfast. For breakfast hardees and butter with tea. After breakfast washed in the Potomac. Clear and warm but cloudy. Could see the opposite batteries very plainly. Wind freshened toward the afternoon. App came down about 2 o'clock. During the afternoon, the rebels fired 4 times, once at the river for no apparent object and

the remainder down at a boat. The boat contained some of our fellows and some hay which they were bringing up the river to a place called Mason's creek, from whence it was to be carted to camp, the roughness of the roads rendering it yet impossible to cart it by land from Liverpool point.[31] They got above the creek and got aground full in sight of the rebel batteries and ourselves. The first shot went under, the second over and the last under again. The line shot very good but the elevation bad. On guard over the guns from four to six in the evening. After I came off guard received a letter from Myra dated Jan. 17th. Received disturbing news of domestic trouble at home. In the evening a steamer came down the river at which the rebel batteries fired quite a number of shots. The shells looked very beautiful as with their bright burning fuse they hurtled through the air, first rising on a curve and then declining until explosion, when it flew into an innumerable number of sparks with a sound like thunder. In looking at the batteries first would be seen the flash of the cannon, then the burning fuse as the shell flew through the air, then as the shell had almost reached its place of explosion would be heard the report of the gun followed by the whistling of the shell. Then comes the flash of the exploding shell followed at an interval of a few seconds by the noise. The noise following the flash at so long an interval quite astonished me. In firing at the steamer one shot struck the bank about 200 yards in front of us without exploding. Another exploded to the left of us scattering the pieces very plainly to be heard as they pattered on the ground still nearer to us. Afterwards App and I spread our blankets in the house and went to sleep right under a hole made by a piece of shell in the roof of the house. They fired quite a number of shots during the night, but one towards morning exploded right in front of the house and I am quite positive that I heard a piece strike on the stones with which the path of the front yard is paved.

JAN. 29TH.
Slept very well. The corporal awoke us at 5 o'clock and having pulled our guns out of the pit we started for camp. Arrived there just in time for the morning roll call. Performed my simple toilet and having eat my breakfast of hardees and coffee went on guard at 9 o'clock on first relief. Early in the morning it was very misty but cleared off bright and fine about 10. App still not very well and looks quite sick and haggard. Quite apparent to me that he has lost flesh lately. Between 11 and 12 went over to the store by the 11th Mass. reg. and bought some tea for App and some pepper for the cook. Beef soup for dinner and very good too. Slept all the time from dinner until I went on guard at 3. For the second time in my life gambled. Never want to feel so miserable and mean again for a much larger sum as I have today for only a few pennies. After playing a whole hour found that I had lost only three cents. With the help of God will never gamble again. Very warm all day, seemed quite like summer.

JAN. 30TH AND 31ST.
Both days rainy, sloppy, and disagreeable. On the 31st, Friday was laid up. Laid abed about all day.

FEB. 1ST. SATURDAY.
Rained all night and about all day. Was occupied most of the day making a bedstead. Heard that Captain Bunting had resigned or else intended to.[32] Leastways he has gone to Washington, leaving Lieut. Bramhall in command. Feel perfectly well again. App bought a bag of buckwheat and we had cakes for super. Received a letter from Myra very cheerful indeed. Wrote to her.

FEB. 2ND SUNDAY.
Reported for duty again and was put on stable duty. A very dirty job to clean the stables. Fine weather again, sun shining brightly. Stable duty lasted about 2 hours. Firing on the river. Finished another letter to Myra. Beefsteak for dinner. In the month of January we have had only five fair days. Washed myself. Looked on the garments I took off but found no more live cattle. The one I found must have been the only one and lately caught. He was a big one. Learned for a fact that Capt. Bunting had resigned. Fellows came to the camp in the afternoon who said that the firing on the river was at the boat and men convoying the feed. Lieut. Martin visited us in the evening. Quite a warm and summer day.

FEB. 3D MONDAY.
When I awoke in the morning it was snowing quite fast, and it snowed all day. On guard 1st relief. Rained quite hard all the evening. App also on guard, 3d relief. Commenced to read "Rutledge" by the author of "The Sutherlands". Borrowed it of Lieut. Bramhall. Snow came about 4 inches deep. In going out to cut wood for our fire I managed to cut my boot. There will probably be an election tomorrow and nothing could be heard today but "vote for this man" or "vote for that". A very disagreeable and dirty day. My feet wet all the time. Kept a large fire all day & kept as comfortable as possible.

FEB. 4TH TUESDAY.
Fair and sunny all day. Had buckwheat cakes for supper. Sat by the fire nearly all day reading "Rutledge" and finished it. Was greatly interested in it. Am not quite certain whether the author is a man or woman but think the latter, although I found quite a number of unfeminine expressions. I also found a new word viz. "promulged". The plot is good but very aggravating. The style although not pure, being adulterated with many useless french expressions, yet is vigorous and very fascinating. Should like very much to have Myra read it and think I will buy it if ever I go home.

FEB. 5TH WEDNESDAY.
In the morning cold and frosty but the sun shone brightly and the middle and last part of the day was very warm and pleasant. Buckwheat cakes for breakfast. In the morning at 9 o'clock there was an election for the post of captain from which Capt. Bunting was discharged. Our senior first lieutenant Walter M. Bramhall was unanimously elected.[33] Rather unwell today. Got another bile on the back of my neck and a stye in my right eye. Shortly after dinner received orders to

take two days rations and with Corporal Antrim go down to the river where the forage had been landed and keep guard over it.[34] Took the rations, my overcoat and a blanket, and tramped away through the mud and snow to the Potomac. Although it felt quite warm on the way, yet when it was reached we found it quite cool and windy. Much a pleasanter post than the ferry. The forage lay in an old fish house about a mile below Budd's Ferry. A little back from the shore is the house of the Widow Mason, who is the owner of the fish house. The view across the river at this point is very beautiful. The fish house had a roof but no sides, and so we rolled up the bales of hay so as to make a shelter. Then wrapping our blankets and overcoats around us, we slept on the hay with a large fire at our feet. Although it was rather cool yet I slept very well, and would have much better had it not been for the bile on my neck.

FEB. 6TH 1862. THURSDAY.

Woke early, washed in the Potomac and breakfasted. Close by the fish house there is a dwelling house or rather a portion of one, for it has been pretty well torn to pieces by the picket of the 11th reg. There is a fireplace in it and the pickets keep a good fire. So the corporal and I went up there, it having commenced to rain quite heavily. While there we were visited by a darkey, a slave of Mrs. Mason. Contrary to common belief he seemed neither to love nor fear his mistress. He had a primer which some soldier had given him, and upon our asking him if he let her know that he was learning to read, he said, "no indeed sah". Then we asked him if she found out, what then. "Get whipp'n den, sah". What then we said. "Why whipp'n, sah, dat's all, when she's done dat it's soon over, an I get anoder book." This and all I have seen of slavery so far hasn't as yet exalted it in my sight. About 11 the relief went up the river, the wind being strong, with apparently only two men on board. When right opposite us the rebel batteries fired 3 shells at her. The first one burst between us and the vessel and I could see the pieces as they splashed in the water. One piece of it flew right over the edge of the house in the door of which we were standing looking at the sport. It could not have passed more than 15 feet over the vessel and I saw one of the pieces strike in the water about 10 feet from the helmsman, in fact it must have thrown the spray all over him. The 3d one went clear over the sloop on to the shore but did not explode. As the vessel kept on they fired 21 shots more, but as she got out of sight behind a point I could not see with what effect. The corporal and I ran out to look for the shell that did not explode but found that a sergeant of the 11th had got ahead of us and dug it out. It must have weighed between 60 and 80 pounds. Now as these large shells cost about 15 dollars apiece, the rebels threw away as much as $350. Toward the afternoon it cleared off and I took a stroll up to the sand pit where our section was on picket. As I went along the shore the waves sounded pleasantly as they lapped the pebbly beach, meriting Homer's epithet of βρυχηθμος ρορτιωγ, many voiced.[35] About half way between the forage landing and the ferry I saw a breast work thrown up about 7 feet high and 30 feet long which was intended for a battery but where I heard there would be a balloon ascension shortly for the purpose of reconnaissance. When I arrived at the ferry I heard that the shots fired at the sloop had rattled quite briskly about the pit, and they had dug out a 32 lb. shot which had scattered the sand smartly about their ears. Asked the orderly sergeant to continue me at this post. Coming back, one of the Massachusetts pickets gave me two pieces of shell which had been fired at the sloop but over-reached and burst on the land. Am going to send it home if possible. The election in camp for junior brevet lieutenant, I learned at the ferry, resulted in the choice of sergeant Robbling on the third ballot.[36] Sunset on the Potomac was very fine indeed. Wind quite high all day. In the evening five schooners went up the river, but the rebels did not fire.

FEB. 7TH, FRIDAY.
Slept warm but restless. Got up early just as a small schooner was going down the river at which the rebels fired 11 shots. Some of the pieces hit within a hundred yards of where I was standing. After the schooner had passed went upon a hill close by and out of a hole where a shell had exploded picked up four pieces. The morning remarkably fine and clear. Wind arose toward the middle of the day. The teams came down twice and took away the rest of the hay. On the first loads sent four pieces of plank up to camp but when I got up there could only find 3. Rode up on the last load top of the hay. Had as much as I could do to hang on. Found the camp muddy as usual. Buckwheats for supper. Finished a letter to Myra.

FEB. 8TH, SATURDAY.
Overslept myself and missed the morning roll call. Morning cloudy. Detailed to clean the stables. With App made a floor of the planks I got yesterday. Boiled potatoes for dinner and buckwheats for supper. Detailed in the afternoon to help make racks to put the harnesses. A little hail and snow about 3 o'clock. Went over to the store and bought two lbs. sugar at 16 cts. Damp and cold all day.

FEB. 9TH SUNDAY.
Warm and sunny. Almost a summers day. Mail came in this morning but no letter for me. On guard, 3d relief. Washed and changed clothes. Pleasant all day.

FEB. 10TH, MONDAY.
Guard duty a cold job last night and this morning. Sun rose brightly. In the afternoon went out on a pass to 1st Mass. reg. Coming home stopped to see the dress parade of 11th. M.V.M. Saw Col. Cowdin acting brigadier. Saw soldiers engaged in making a corduroy road. A corduroy road is made by throwing up dirt and then placing poles and brush upon it. Above all more dirt is thrown and the road is completed. Roads very muddy yet, in one instance got in over ankle deep. Got home about 4½ o'clock, overstaying my pass 2½ hours. Very fine and sunny all day, quite spring weather.

Feb. 11th, Tuesday.
Rapid and heavy firing on the river last night and this morning. Have since learned that 18 schooners went up. No damage done. Cloudy in the morning but sun rose bright towards noon. Snowed at nightfall. Got a pass again today and went over to the 1st. M.V.M. Boiled hominy with butter and sugar for supper. Received a letter from Myra, contents rather disheartening.

Feb. 12th, Wednesday.
Hominy for breakfast. Fried ham for dinner. Wrote to Myra. Received a letter from Hero Nichols with one page from Mrs. Leslie. Received four papers from the editors of the Middlesex Journal one of which contained the communication which I sent on the 26th of last month. Felt rather flattered at seeing my effusion in print. App advised me to continue writing to it. Think I shall at least once more. On stable guard from 9 to 10. At ten had a drill at the gun. Had a drill in the afternoon at taking from the carriage, in other words at dismounting from the gun. While I was engaged in writing to Myra during the afternoon, Lieut. Martin paid quite a visit to our tent. Very fine and warm all day, what they call a spring-fever day.

Feb. 13th, Thursday.
Like the preceding very warm and sunny. Beef steak for dinner.

Feb. 14th, Friday.
Cloudy all day, and somewhat cooler than yesterday. Received a letter from Myra, also another newspaper. On guard, 3d relief. Ball playing in camp. Played draughts.

Feb. 15th, Saturday.
When I came off guard at three o'clock did not go to bed. Started at 4 on picket. Fried crackers and coffee for breakfast, baked beans for dinner. Snow all day 'till 4 in the afternoon. Fall of snow about six inches. Misty about all day. Small schooner loaded with oysters coming up was fired at by the rebels. The frightened captain run his vessel aground and went ashore in his boat. Some of our fellows went aboard and got about three bushels of oysters. Boat came down toward night and got her off, but the pickets had thrown over about half her cargo. Harriet Lane went down and three other small steamers. A very large number of vessels went up and down today. Rebels fired a new kind of shot shaped like a cube. In the evening had a jolly time, singing, dancing, etc.

Feb. 16th, Sunday.
Had a hard time pulling the guns out of the pit on account of the snow. Had eight horses to each gun to draw them to camp. Got to camp before reveille. Had oysters and sausages for breakfast. Wrote a letter to the "Middlesex Journal".

Lieut. Bramhall returned from Washington. Warm and sunny all day. Caught cold last night. In evening played a game of chess.

Middlesex Journal, March 1st 1862

Budd's Ferry, Lower Potomac, MD.,
February 15th, 1862.
To the Editor of the Middlesex Journal.

Dear Sir: —The copies of the "Middlesex Journal" which you so kindly sent, yesterday came safely to hand and were received with much pleasure. None can appreciate news from home better than the soldier, but when it comes in the form of one's own local paper it begets a double interest. And by the time that this communication reaches Woburn your very acceptable presents will probably have been well worn by continued circulation.

Since my last letter to you there has been somewhat of a change in the command of our battery. Our former commander (J.B. Bunting) has left us, whether by resignation or discharge is not known, and we are now under the command of Lieut. W. M. Bramhall. Probably your readers will recognize in him the gallant officer, who in the battle of Ball's Bluff so bravely and discreetly managed the Rhode Island cannon engaged in that fight. Having recovered from his wounds there received, he again joined his corp on the 15th Dec. last. Immediately upon the withdrawal of Capt. Bunting an election was held, in which Lieut. Bramhall obtained a unanimous vote for the captaincy.

In looking over the list of Woburn volunteers contained in the Journal, I perceive that our battery is named as 6th N.Y. Artillery, Col. Stiles. Now being detached from the 9th Regt. we are no longer under the command of Col. Stiles. Our title now reads, 6th N.Y. Independent Artillery, Lieut. Bramhall commanding.

This present communication is written in the widow Budd's house, or rather what is left of it, the pickets being in the habit of pulling it apart according as they want it to feed their fires. Before me spreads the broad Potomac, and the searching breeze blowing across its windy surface, by its severity reminds me of New England's far severer climate. The long range of Virginian hills in the distance, the pine clad summits, relieved here and there by patches of snow, gloomy and barren, present a fine contrast to the bright blue foreground of the river. In front to the left, and running at right angles to the river, a misty ridge of hills is seen, leading to Manassas and the scenes of Bull Run.

Right opposite to Budd's Ferry – which takes its name from the widow's residence – lies Shipping Point, its high bluff furnishing a fine position for the batteries which the rebels have there erected. Beside this battery they have placed other guns planted both above and below, commanding the river for the distance of six miles. The river here being at the narrowest, and also quite shallow on the Maryland side, causes vessels sailing up and down to keep nearly the middle of the river, thus presenting a fine mark.

Until quite lately the rebels were in the habit of throwing scarcely anything except shell, but within a few days it has been noticed that they fire less often and then only solid shot or *empty* shell, from which the inference that will probably be drawn is that there is a scarcity of ammunition among them.

This morning it being the regular turn of our section to do picket duty, at 4 o'clock we started from camp through the thick falling snow for the river and arrived there about daybreak. Scarcely had the guns been placed in position in the sand pit, when the mist, rising for a moment, showed a small schooner beating up the river. The rebels, at the same time perceiving the vessel, paid her their compliments in the form of five shells, whereat the captain leaving the helm in great haste, jumped into his boat with the rest of the crew and rowed ashore. The vessel, being thus neglected, fell away before the wind and finally struck a sand bar about 200 yards from the shore. It again commenced snowing, and the mist hiding the schooner from the view of the batteries the infantry pickets and some of our men went off to her. On going aboard of her our boys found that she was loaded with oysters and bound to Washington. Finally a boat came down the river and towed her off, but not until nearly half the cargo was thrown overboard. N.B. At present all the boys look remarkably cheerful, and the whole building smells like an oyster house.

Taking advantage of the storm many vessels have passed up and down, among the rest the steamship Harriet Lane.

Occasionally the mist lifts, and then the rebels peg away right merrily at any poor schooner who may be caught within range. At one schooner thus caught they threw a shot of a very novel construction. It was solid shot cast in the form of a cube.

The Woburn boys are all well, those in the regiments here encamped as well as those in the 6th battery.

Yours, etc. HOPLITE

Feb. 17th, Monday.
Rained all night. Missed morning roll call, and expect I shall have to do double guard duty as punishment. Finished and sent a letter to the "Middlesex Journal". Saw a large flock of robins this day. Beef steak and fried potatoes for dinner. Compelled to chop green cedar trees down for fire-wood, having been forbidden to take any more rails. At evening roll call Lieut. Martin read official account of the capture of forts Henry and Donelson, together with Gens. Buckner and Johnson, and 15,000 men. Great rejoicing in camp, and guns fired in salute. Rained hard all day. Wrote to Myra.

FEB. 18TH, TUESDAY.
On guard 3d. relief. Punished for missing roll-call yesterday by going on three hours at a time, viz. 12–3. 6–9, 12–3, 6–9. Saw a large flock of robins. Misty and drizzly all day. Fried ham for dinner.

FEB. 19TH, WEDNESDAY.
Guard duty very dismal last night. Rained hard all day. Dreary and sloppy. Slept about all the afternoon. News came of the taking of Savannah.

FEB. 20TH, THURSDAY.
Sun rose bright. At 10 o'clock whole battery had a drill at the manual of the piece. Saw blue birds. Had fried liver for supper. Fine all day and the mud dried up rapidly.

FEB. 21ST, FRIDAY.
My 21st birthday. I am now of age and must depend in the future entirely upon my own exertions for a living. Can it be possible that I shall not live to see another birthday. Received a letter from Albert Chittenden. There is not a vestige left of the snow which fell last Saturday. Wrote to Myra and sent her three papers. Beef steak for dinner. Slept nearly all the afternoon. Fair and sunny all day.

FEB. 22ND, SATURDAY.
Birthday of George Washington, father and preserver of his native country. Raining very hard when I woke in the morning. Received a letter from Myra, and wrote to Hero and A.A. Chittenden. Rice and molasses for dinner. The same for supper. At night Lieut. Bramhall came into our tent and had quite a conversation with me. He offered to lend me some reading matter. Rained all day. Learned today that we were to have new guns made of wrought steel. Firing all day towards Washington which some thought birthday salutes, and some an engagement between the rebels and Gen. Heintzelman's division. Got a bad cold.

FEB. 23D, SUNDAY.
Sloppy, muddy and drizzly. Myra's birthday. Pray God that she may safely see another. On guard, 1st. relief. Post, officers' tents. Washed and changed clothes. Got the magazine which Lieut. Bramhall offered to lend me, name "The Knickerbocker." In the evening, firing on the river. Beef steak for dinner. Countersign for the night was "Springfield." Played chess.

FEB. 24TH, MONDAY.
Rose at four and went down to the ferry. Rode down astride one of the guns. Rained a little at starting. Found some very pretty and peculiar stones on the beach. On guard over the guns from ten to twelve, during which a heavy squall arose accompanied with rain. It rained for a short time only, but the wind

Pvt. Charles R. Vail, Sixth
Independent Battery, New York
State Volunteer Light Artillery.
Courtesy of U.S. Army Military
History Institute.

continued high all day and most of the night, in fact almost a hurricane. One of
the chimneys of the Budd house blew down. Cut some buds off a rose tree in the
garden to send home to Myra. Baked beans for dinner. In the afternoon a row
boat came ashore supposed to belong to the rebel steamer "Geo. Page." Charley
Vail got wet in getting it ashore.[37] Not a shot fired by the rebels all day.

Feb. 25th, Tuesday.
Rose early and returned to camp. Cold but not windy. Got a pass and went with
App to see the trial of the two new Whitworth guns presented to America by
loyal citizens abroad.[38] Took dinner at the 1st. Mass., beef soup and soft bread.
Gun trial at 2½ o' clock, some very fine shots made. They carried a distance of
six miles. Bought a pair of boots, cost $5.00. The legs came as high as my knees.
Letter from Myra and A.H. Richardson. Cold but clear all day.

Feb. 26th, Wednesday.
Very fair and clear in the morning but rained toward night. Steak for dinner
and liver for supper. Received a "Middlesex Journal" from home. Also a "Boston
Weekly Journal" from Albert Chittenden. The boys of our section built a sort of
oven to bake beans in.

Feb. 27th, Thursday.
Fine weather all day and a very busy day for me. In the morning aided in cleaning our gun, carriage and limber, in the afternoon washed and greased a set of

double harness. All this was done for inspection which was to happen next day. Rice and molasses for dinner. Orders read from Capt. Bramhall calling upon the men to clean up and present a soldierly appearance for next day's inspection both in person and in respect to their tents. Busy all day.

Feb. 28th, Friday.
Clear but cold all day. Wrote to Myra. The men, camp, equipments and horses inspected by Major Wainwright at half past one.[39] Presented a very satisfactory appearance. Bean soup for dinner. Rumors about the camp of a move very soon but in what direction is not known. Another rebel battery on the river.

March 1st, Saturday.
Last night very cold and windy. Nevertheless slept warm. Jim Horton in the morning left camp to go to Washington to get more horses.[40] This betokens a move soon. All the surplus ammunition sent away. Had my clothes washed. Fried ham for dinner. In the evening went to Mr. Morgan's tent and not hearing the bugle staid after taps.[41] Was challenged by the sentinel before the officers' tents and not having the countersign run the guard. Fair all day.

March 2nd, Sunday.
Fair in the morning but snowed and hailed in the afternoon. Steak for dinner. Inspection in the forenoon by Lieut. Martin and Clark. At night our section (the Guerrillas) had a snow-ball match with the middle section ("the Israelites"). We got the best of it. Rained in the evening.

March 3d, Monday.
Rained about all night. Drizzled all day and rained very hard in the evening. Played chess in the afternoon. One of the tents was flooded and Griffin slept in ours on the cracker boxes.

March 4th, Tuesday.
Cleared off and froze during last night. Fair and warm all day. App was detailed to go again and try the Whitworth guns. When he got to where they were stationed the order was countermanded and so came back without doing anything. Played chess about all day and in the evening. Jim Horton returned from W. with six horses.

March 5th, Wednesday.
Fair all day. Bean Soup for dinner. Played chess. Heavy firing on the river early in the morning and during the forenoon. Heard that we probably would not be paid off before six weeks from the last of February.

March 6th, Thursday.
Warm and fair all day until just before nightfall when there was a little flurry of snow. Our section went on picket today, but App and I did not go with them. At 10 o'clock in the morning started with the teams and went to Liverpool Point

a distance of 5 miles down the river. On the way passed the camps of the 1st reg. N.Y. Sickles' Brigade, the 2nd, and the 5th.[42] Also passed the headquarters of General Sickles and the encampment of his body guard of French zouaves. Saw some of the zoo-zoos uniformed in a very fancy manner. A red zouave cap with a yellow tassel, a blue overjacket, loose and profusely ornamented with yellow braid; a blue tight-fitting underjacket braided in the same manner and with a light blue sash, or rather swathing, being very large; scarlet trunks full and plaited at the waist coming almost to the ankle, also braided with yellow; white garters. Such is the uniform of the French zouaves, and to my mind too showy to become men, but would do very well for boys. Saw three gun boats at the point viz. Resolute, Island Belle, and Thomas Freeborn.[43] Saw a sailor belonging to the Freeborn and of him enquired for Charley Chittenden who was aboard of her.[44] Sent word to him. Loaded the teams with hay and grain and returned to camp at 3 in the after-noon. Roads very bad, corduroy road half of the way. Beef steak and coffee for supper.

March 7th, Friday.
Fair but cold all day. Received two letters from Myra one in the morning and one at night, also one from Hero. Received a "Middlesex Journal" of March 1st with my 2nd communication in it. Wrote to Myra. Rice and molasses for dinner. Played chess in the afternoon, App just learning. Three of our fellows got put in the 11th Mass. reg. guard house for stealing rails. I with three others and a corporal went over and got them. Capt. Bramhall dismissed them saying, "Boys you musn't do it again." Lieut. Martin reprimanded them not for stealing but for being caught.

March 8th, Saturday.
Very cold last night. Slept badly and caught a bad cold. Went out on battery drill from 9–12. Was reviewed by Major Wainwright. Smith's battery also out in same field.[45] On guard, 3d relief. Been 12 days off guard. Countersign for the night was "Winton". After 4 o'clock roll call had a very interesting manual drill, all the officers present. Captain drilled us a little. Fair and warm all day.

March 9th, Sunday.
Guard duty very pleasant last night. Slept better than the night before. Mounted inspection in the forenoon. For dinner crackers, and ham seasoned with vinegar and pepper. Visited by a private of the 11th reg. whom I knew in Reading Mass. Washed in the afternoon. Fair and very warm all day. Got in a very great perspiration chopping wood. Exceeding warm for March. Towards night heard firing on the river. Climbed a pine tree in the rear of our camp and saw the rebel camps, the Geo. Page and some small schooners all in flames. There was no doubt in camp but that the rebels had evacuated. A horseman from the river said that a boat landed from one of our gun boats and raised the stars and stripes

on one of the rebel flag staffs. Camp all excitement and expectant for orders to march. The storm of war draws nearer. Commenced a letter to Myra. Capt. Bramhall's father in camp.

MARCH 10TH, MONDAY.
1st Massachusetts reg. crossed the river and one or two of the Jersey regiments. Cloudy and rained part of the day. Finished my letter to Myra and sent it by Capt. Bramhall's father. Learned that mail communication with the north had been closed. Commenced a letter to the "Journal". Played chess in the evening. Warm.

MARCH 11TH, TUESDAY.
We have been now three months in this camp. Very warm and fair all day. Battery drill after 9 o'clock, which was witnessed by Mr. Bramhall. Liver for dinner, and beefsteak for supper. Had my hair cut.

MARCH 12TH, WEDNESDAY.
Fair and warm all day. Studied science of artillery for one hour. Section drill under command of the lieut. from 9 to 12. Drill rather poor. Lieut. Martin offered a prize worth $25 or that amount of money to the detachment which shall drill best at the end of four weeks or at next pay. A detachment consists of the cannoneers and drivers attached to one gun. Stewed beans for dinner. Manual drill right after four o'clock. Attended prayer meeting in the park in the evening. Great deal of whiskey in camp.

MARCH 13TH, THURSDAY.
Battery drill from 10–12. Beans (baked) for breakfast and for dinner. Fair in forenoon, but had quite a shower in afternoon. Played chess. Commenced to take lessons in French, M. Tresserra teacher.[46] Heard that 51 steamers passed up the Potomac this day.

MARCH 14TH, FRIDAY.
Cloudy all day. Battery drill in the morning. Rice and molasses for dinner. Played chess. Pitched quoits. French lesson in the evening.

MARCH 15TH, SATURDAY.
Rainy all day. Very heavy showers in the afternoon and evening. No drill. Wrote to Myra. Got cheated out of my baked beans for dinner. French lesson.

MARCH 16TH, SUNDAY.
Fried liver for breakfast. Same for dinner. Cloudy all day. Received a letter from Myra's father saying that a son was born to me on the evening of March 10th at 10 o'clock. Read a yellow covered novel entitled "Duval in Newgate, or the Traitor Jew". On guard, 2nd relief. App also 1st relief. Countersign "Sugar Creek". Very sleepy during the night watch.

March 17th, Monday.
Cold and fair. Section and battery drill in the morning. Slept a great portion of the afternoon. French lesson.

March 17th, Tuesday.
Last night seven of our fellows were out after taps in search of black wenches. One of the neighboring citizens came into camp and complained of them. An extra guard was sent out after them and having caught them put them in the guard house. Our guns got about a mile and a half from camp on the way to Rum Point to exchange our bronze field pieces for iron regulation guns. There it was learned that they had not yet come down from Washington, and so they turned back. Had beans for dinner, but they being only half baked made me quite sick, as also some others. Middle and left sections had a field drill in afternoon. Our section drilled in the manual and dismounting the piece. French lesson. Received "Middlesex Journal" of March 8th.

March 19th, Wednesday.
Fair all day. Battery drill, but I did not go out. Fried crackers for dinner. In the afternoon went to see battalion drill of 11th. reg. Got into a little fight with Addis.[47] At 4 o'clock roll call Capt. Bramhall sent for the commissary and enquired in regard to the provisions. Will probably move tomorrow.

March 20th, Thursday.
Rainy all day. Battery went to Rum Point and exchanged guns. Got wrought iron rifled guns. Smaller bore than our former bronze cannon.[48] Wrote to Hero and the "Journal". Fried crackers for dinner. A very nasty day.

Middlesex Journal, March 29, 1862

ARMY CORRESPONDENCE

Camp Dickinson, Lower Potomac, MD., March 10th, 1862

Mr. Editor: — Feb. 24th, a detail of eight men was made from the 6th Battery to try a pair of Whitworth guns which had been brought down from Washington and placed upon a hill a short distance from the encampment of the Mass. 1st. Some very fine shots were made. The Shipping Point battery, which lays at a distance of five miles from where the guns were stationed, was repeatedly struck, drawing expressions of admiration from the assembled spectators.

While viewing the trial, I stood near to where Col. Cowdin was sitting upon his horse. And here let me bestow my mead of praise upon the Massachusetts colonel, who, through much ill report yet has become the very *beau ideal* of a commander of American volunteers. Col. Cowdin not only exhibits the military knowledge and ability necessary for the welfare of the soldiers under his command, such as becomes a man who looks upon a private not as a military machine, and as such to be used, but as an American citizen fighting for the preservation of his native land. You often read of good military commanders, but when to military ability is added an unbounded popularity, then is found a man fitted to command the Republic's citizen soldiers. Long may he wave.

During the day I had an opportunity of closely examining the Whitworth guns. The axletree of the gun carriage bears the inscription, "Presented to the United States of America by her loyal citizens abroad." They are breech loading, and are very finely rifled, the grooves having a twist of three whole turns from the muzzle to the breach. The projectile was solid shot of a convidal from, 9 inches long, and 1½ inches in diameter.

Since my last, the soldiers of Gen. Hooker's division have been pursuing the usual routine of camp duty with but little variation until yesterday, when the whole vicinity of St. Charles Co. seemed in a quiver of excitement. Late in the afternoon our camp was roused by the sound of cannon and musketry seemingly indicating an action in the direction of Gen. Heintzelman's division. Following the example of many others I climbed a tree, from which could plainly seen the Potomac and sacred soil of Virginia. Far up the river was Indian Head and the position of the rebels' upper battery. In the stream within musket shot lay one of Uncle Sam's gunboats. Shortly a boat put off from her and in a few moments the stars and stripes floated proudly from the same staff that usually held the ensign of rebellion, proving that the point had been evacuated. All the while, heavy smoke from between the ridges of the hills here and there, proclaimed destruction of rebel camps and a hasty retreat. Soon the rebel gunboat Geo. Page is seen wrapped in flames, and a faint sound of cheering from the Mass. regiments saluted the downfall of her smoke stack. Now the schooners that lay close by show that they too have not been forgotten, and send huge volumes of smoke into the sky. Magazines explode throwing the dirt for a great distance around, and a dense smoke rising from the Shipping Point battery and those below, show the destruction of their gun carriages. Cautiously the gunboat makes its way down the river throwing her shells upon the shore and adjacent hills until opposite the mouth of Quantico Creek, when apparently she sends a boat ashore.

Gradually the lengthening shadows wrap the river from our view, but still the sound of cannon tells of the progress of gunboat down the river. All through the night occasional firing testified to the vigilance of our flotilla.

This morning I have learned that the Mass. 1st is to cross immediately. Our camp is all excitement and expectant of marching orders.

March 17th. — I had delayed sending the above because of a rumor which prevailed throughout the camp, that mail communications with the North had been closed by order of the commander-in-chief.

Since the evacuation of the rebels, some of our boys have visited their fortifications. As was supposed, they had evacuated in a great hurry, destroying as much as possible. They have blown up some of their magazines and others partially. They also rendered useless some of their large guns. On the Shipping Point battery was planted an English 120 pounder rifled gun. This monster piece of ordnance weighs over 10,000 lbs. Under it they had made a fire after loading it to the muzzle with sand, but the great thickness of the breach had rendered it impossible to heat it sufficiently to ignite the powder.

At the extremity of the point an exploded gun was found bearing an inscription which states that it burst Feb. 15th. On that day your readers will recall that I wrote a communication to the "Journal" dated at the sand pit right opposite, where, with the two guns composing our section, I was on picket.

It seems also that there were several logs of wood mounted on gun carriages, and covered in canvas, to deceive our balloonists.

Skirmishing parties of the Mass. 1st, and Jersey 5th, have penetrated as far as six miles into the country, resulting in the capture of several contrabands and one rebel soldier from Texas. One man was also found whose throat had been cut by the rebels upon his refusing to accompany them upon there [sic] retreat.

Those of our fellows who have made a visit to the other side, brought various secession relics. One cook has a coffee mill, another a bayonet, and some papers left by a rebel surgeon, another an axe, &c.

In the house on Shipping Point used as a hospital, was found three of our solid shot, two from the Whitworth guns tried Feb. 24th, and one from our guns stationed at Budd's Ferry. It appears from the writing found upon them that all of them lodged in the house, luckily without injury to any of the occupants.

Contrary to general expectations, Gen. Hooker's division still occupies the Maryland side of the Potomac, where for the present we enjoy our *otium cum dig,* without even our usual picket duty to do. As the weather has become more settled and the mud less deep, more attention has been paid to drill lately, and every fair morning there has been an exercise by the battery of manoeuvre, or a section drill.

Situated as the division now is, it can be of direct advantage in the prosecution of the war, and doubtless you will soon hear of a movement in this quarter. The prevailing impression is that the division, after being split up, will be sent to reinforce other portions of the army, and there is a report that this battery will join Gen. Burnside.

Tomorrow we make a march to Rum Point in order to exchange our guns. Instead of our present bronze cannon we are to have rifled iron regulation guns. These pieces are fitted for throwing all kinds of projectiles, thus combining the advantages of the howitzer and field gun.

Rum Point is about five miles up the river and has steamboat communication with Washington.

Since my last a new battery from New York has joined the division.
They have four guns, all of the regulation pattern.

HOPLITE

March 21st, Friday.

I forgot to mention in the record of yesterday's transactions the presentation to
Lieut. Martin of a sword, belt and sash by the members of his section (the Guerillas). Rainy all day. Cleaned guns and carriages and fitted ammunition. Each
gun carries with it in the limber and caisson 200 rounds, 125 case, 55 shell, and
20 canister. In the afternoon went over to 11th Mass. reg. to see Jim Goodwin &
Capt. McDonald.[49] Also called on a Reading fellow in Co. K.

March 22nd, Saturday.

Cloudy all day. Beefsteak for breakfast and dinner. Went to Lieut. Martin's tent
and saw his presents. App weighed the sash (silk) weight 26 ounces, said to have
cost 22 dolls. Read "Dare Devil Dick". French lesson. Received orders from the
captain at 4 o'clock roll call to pack knapsacks and be in readiness for a march.
When we march, he said, we are to have no tents and only one baggage wagon.
Knapsacks to be strapped on the gun and caisson.

March 23d, Sunday.

Fair all day. Pork steak for dinner and supper. Perley Griffin killed the pig. Went
into the woods and had a good wash. On guard, 3d relief. Watch word was not
given to the battery.

March 24th, Monday.

Guard duty quite pleasant and warm last night. App and I packed our knapsacks for the march. Lost my best handkerchief. Set about making a hammock
of a piece of seine taken from the fishery at Budd's Ferry. Pork steak and boiled
potatoes for dinner. French lesson. Troops went down the river, probably from
Washington. Could hear their bands as they sailed down. Fair all day, with the
exception of a short shower just at nightfall. Received a letter from mother and
one from Myra and Mrs. Stevens.

March 25th, Tuesday.

Weather fair. Wrote to Myra and to mother. Battery drill in the morning. One of
the caissons got stuck and was unable to drill with the rest. French lesson.

March 26th, Wednesday.

Weather fair all day. Played quoits. Received the "Journal" of 22nd inst. For dinner beef steak and boiled potatoes. App and I each got an artillery jacket from
the government.

March 27th, Thursday.

Fair and very warm. Beef soup for dinner. In the afternoon the battery went over to the 3d reg. of the Sickles brigade to drill.[50] Coming back one of the caissons broke down and hurt a corporal and two cannoneers. It was a most wonderful thing that they did not all get killed. Broke the stock short off. On wood guard.

April 1st, Tuesday.

Fine and warm all day. Section drill in the morning. One of our caissons got stuck going out. I went as No. 2 on the gun.[51] Stewed beans for dinner. Drill in the afternoon at Manual, dismounting gun and carriage, and slinging the gun, I did not drill there being no vacancy. Received "Middlesex Journal" of March 29th containing my last communication. Wrote to A.H. Richardson. General Hooker was present while we were drilling in the forenoon. The following is the amount of clothing allowed a private of artillery.

Hat & Trimmings	$1.84
2 Forage Caps	$1.26
Uniform Jacket	$5.84
3 Pr. Trousers	$12.00
2 Blouses	$4.30
3 Flannel Shirts	$2.64
3 Pr. Drawers	$1.50
2 Pr. Shoes	$3.88
1 Pr. Boots	$3.33
4 Pr. Stockings	$1.04
1 Overcoat	$9.75
1 Blanket	$2.95
1 Leather Stock	$0.14
1 Stable frock	$0.68

April 2nd. Wednesday.

Fair all day. Washed the guns and caissons. I also helped clean a double harness. Fried ham for dinner and supper. Pitched quoits. Reports in camp that General McClellan had come to review this division. It seems that he went down the river on his way to Old Point. Capt. Bramhall came back from head-quarters and said that we should go this week and that the infantry commenced to embark tomorrow.

April 3d, Thursday.

Very warm all day. Battery drill in the morning, during which I was detailed to guard Lowny who was in the guard-house.[52] He and I went down to the ferry and there saw men from the 11th reg. building a pier for the purpose of embarkation. Saw two steamboats and a schooner going down filled with troops. Saw one steamer and a schooner going up apparently empty. Detailed in the afternoon to mend road. Boots hurt my heels so that I was compelled to take them off and return barefooted. Drill of non-commissioned officers. Very bad headache.

April 4th, Friday.

Warm and fair. Bad blister on my heel and slept very poorly last night because of head-ache. Was detailed to take care of a pair of horses but got excused on account of indisposition. Beef steak for dinner. Battery drill in the afternoon. Lieut. Brown's father in camp. Visited by a Reading man from 11th. reg. Knew him when I was a pedlar. Went over to the 11th on horseback. Found them striking tents and learned that they were to move directly. Came back to camp and learned that we were to move the same night or next day. Received a letter from Myra and answered it.

CHAPTER 2

SICK WITH NO CARE:
APRIL–AUGUST 1862

WITH THE EARLY MARCH WITHDRAWAL OF GENERAL JOHNSTON'S ARMY from its positions around Manassas and the Virginia side of the Potomac River, the rationale underlying McClellan's plan to outflank the Confederates by transporting his army to the mouth of the Rappahannock was made moot. Nevertheless, to General McClellan the indirect approach still had many attractions. He therefore proposed to President Lincoln that he instead land his army at Fortress Monroe, from which position he could push up the peninsula between the York and James rivers and threaten Richmond. Albeit with many misgivings, the president approved the new plan, and in mid-March the Army of the Potomac began filing onto a huge but motley fleet assembled in Alexandria for the purpose. From its positions on the Maryland shore of the Potomac, Hooker's Division and the Sixth New York battery followed in early April to join McClellan's army in its encampments at the tip of the Virginia Peninsula.

What followed was a slow, grinding advance, in which McClellan hoped to wage a meticulous campaign of position, supported by as much field and siege artillery as could be brought to bear and by the large-caliber guns of the Union navy on the James and York rivers. Maj. Gen. John Bankhead Magruder, the Confederate on-scene commander, ably employed his smaller army, playing on McClellan's credulity to make it appear that his positions and forces were much stronger than they were in reality. Nonetheless, Johnston and Magruder slowly fell back from Yorktown, Williamsburg, and other positions until, by the closing days of May, they were behind the Richmond fortifications.

The chaotic battle of Seven Pines, which took place almost within sight of the steeples of Richmond from May 31 to June 1, was more or less a bloody draw, except that it resulted in a change of command on the Confederate side that transformed the nature of the contest between the two armies. President Davis replaced General Johnston with Gen. Robert E. Lee, when Johnston went down with severe wounds, and the new commander began laying plans to attack and defeat the Federal host. What followed was a series of Confederate attacks between June 25 and July 1, known in the aggregate as the Seven Days' Battles, in which McClellan abandoned his attempt to take Richmond and retreated to a secure base at Harrison's Landing on the James River. After evaluating this disaster for Union arms and listening to his commanding general's proposals for renewing the attack, Lincoln lost confidence that anything good could be accomplished with the forces under McClellan's command on the Peninsula, and so on July 30 ordered the army to begin returning to Washington.

The Perkins diary offers a detailed report on the voyage to the peninsula, the army's vast encampments, and the siege of Yorktown. Once the army began its slow pursuit of the Confederate forces, George was assigned to the battery's wagons in the wagon train of Hooker's Division. His account provides many details concerning the marches and encampments from the Yorktown starting point, through Williamsburg, New Kent Court House on the Pamunkey River, to the final advanced positions on the Chickahominy River near Richmond. The main themes of the diary are the slow and laborious progress of the march, the prevailing uncertainty concerning the military situation, the poor food and sanitation practices, the frequent rain and resulting deep mud, and especially the baneful effects of illness compounded by the inefficiency and disorganization of the army's medical department. Both George and his brother App became severely ill on the advance to the Chickahominy and were placed in ambulances, where they apparently languished without medical care or special attention of any sort. App was evacuated out of the war zone, but George remained on duty with the battery until it was withdrawn to Washington with the rest of the army.

The diary entries of June 8–11, 16–25, and July 16–24 have been omitted. Little occurred of note during the June dates. The Sixth New York settled into a dull routine after the drawn battle of Seven Pines on May 31, only interrupted by stints of artillery picket duty. George, parted for the first time from his brother App, pulled guard duty and dealt with some lice he found in his underclothes. He received several notes from his brother, who reported from the hospital that he was feeling somewhat better. During the July period, very little occurred to break the tedium. The numbing routine and the separation from family resulted in feelings of isolation and depression, interrupted only by guard duty, worship services provided by the chaplain of a neighboring regiment, and the reading of *Life and Adventures of Col. Monroe Edwards, Forger.*

APRIL 5TH, SATURDAY.
Slept very little last night. Cook was busy all night cooking for the march. Rose at 3 o'clock and struck tents. Commenced to rain just at day-break and was drizzly all day. Took up march for Liverpool point and arrived there about 9 o'clock. I was wagon guard. Shortly after we got there Osborne's N.Y. battery of four guns arrived also. Found four steamers close in shore, Elm City, Argo, Emperor, and C. Vanderbilt. The Argo is a Boston boat. Steamer Rockland returned from the other side bringing soldiers who had been scouting in Virginia. The soldiers had all sorts of plunder which they had captured, such as, ducks, chickens, pigs, sheep, &c. Saw General Sickles. Liked his appearance very much. Thomas Freeborn also came over from the other side and I sent a note aboard to Charley Chittenden by one of the boat's crew that came ashore. Charley had been left on the other side to take care of some white men prisoners. The Rockland is a Maine boat and I found that one of her crew was acquainted with Nate while he lived in Rockland. Saw a gun for discharging rifle balls. It would discharge 240 balls per minute.[1] Also saw a mountain howitzer or rather as I learned afterward a *boat* howitzer. The Elm City drew up to the dock and I went aboard of her and also a ferry boat named Talleca. Stole some tea from the last named. About dark the 3d Sickles embarked on the Elm City. Listened to their band in the twilight.

APRIL 6TH, SUNDAY.
Slept on the grain in a shed close to the river side, and very comfortably too. Was wakened in the night by the band of the 5th Sickles, which was embarking on the Vanderbilt. Learned in the morning that the 4th S. had also embarked making three in all. Quite a number of steamers came and went during the day. Saw Charley Chittenden. Went over to the camp which 5th Sickles reg. had vacated and got a canteen, a tin cup, a bayonet and some magazines. App got a couple of rubber blankets. Other fellows got other things. About dark steamer Massachusetts brought down two schooners and aboard one of them were embarked nearly half our horses. Slept under one of the caissons very warm.

APRIL 7TH, MONDAY.
At breakfast Johnny Furbush and Samuels had a fight.[2] Other schooner came up to the dock upon which we embarked all the remaining horses except about ten, those were put on board a schooner with the horses of Osborne's battery. Rained in the morning and snowed in the afternoon. Slept in a shed on a pile of tents in company with a lot of Irish soldiers.

APRIL 8TH, TUESDAY.
Slept very warm last night. Rained all day and was very cold. Rest of Sickles brigade got embarked. Was on guard last night but corporal of the guard couldn't find me so I got free. Sent forage off to the schooners. Got wet through and felt very miserable. Just at nightfall the tug Talleca brought down a barge on board of which was put our battery and also Osborne's. Name of barge was "The Wallkill of Newburgh". Quarters very comfortable, had a bunk all to myself.

April 9th, Wednesday.

Slept nicely last night. Coffee in the morning. Anchored all last night in the stream with the rest of the fleet. Started down the river about 7 o'clock. Passed the stone fleet which was anchored in the river in readiness to be sunk if the Merrimac came up the river. Our barge and two schooners loaded with horses were towed down by the steamer Vanderbilt. Drizzly and nasty all day. Anchored all night off St. Marys.

April 10th, Thursday.

Started down the river early in the morning. About noon we got into the Chesapeake bay where it was so rough that the cable of the schooner behind us broke and we left her far behind. The barge rocked very badly, so much so that we were in great danger for some time. I was very seasick. Arrived at Fortress Munroe just at dark and anchored. Rainy.

April 11th, Friday.

Sun rose fair and I early. Quite recovered from my sickness although stomach quite weak. Boiled hominy and sugar for breakfast. Saw the Monitor close by where we were anchored. During the forenoon the rebel steamer Merrimac came down the river in company with others. One of these, probably the Yorktown, came close and took two vessels out very neatly. The vessels around us began to heave up their anchors and scattered rapidly. Two or three of our gun boats and war steamers made their appearance but too late to save the vessels. One steamer went close beside us with the men all at the guns ready for a fight. From where we were anchored could see Hampton and the Rip Raps, on which there were fortifications being erected. About two o'clock the steamer Hero took us in tow and we left Hampton Roads and started up the Chesapeake. As we went along I had a fine view of Fortress Munroe. Also saw the great union gun and the "Lincoln Pill" which were mounted on sand banks close to the water's edge and outside the fort. Threaded our way through a maze of shipping and close beside the Monitor.

A little above the fort the Hero also took in tow two schooners and another barge. Voyage up the bay very fine indeed. About five arrived at the mouth of York river which seemed quite choked up with shipping. Nevertheless after dropping the two schooners and the other barge we managed to thread our way about 3 miles up the river to Ship Point where we anchored for the night. York river is a beautiful place, abounding in inlets and low points, covered in most instances to the water's edge with a heavy growth of pines. The oysters here are most plentiful and large. Saw soldiers wading along and picking them up by hand. All along the river were soldiers, some with tents and some bivouacking. The whole scenery seemed a strange compound of river, steamers, soldiers, and pine woods. Weather fine all day.

APRIL 12TH, SATURDAY.
Sun rose fair and warm. Fair all day. Laid where we anchored last night until dark when a tug carried us a little farther up to a landing. Wrote to Myra. Placed my foot on the sacred soil of Virginia. Saw Jones formerly of our battery, now lieut. in the Connecticut artillery. Visited 50th N.Y. Reg. of Sappers and Miners. Slept aboard the barge. Caught a slight cold.

APRIL 13TH, SUNDAY.
Sent my letter to Myra by Lieut. Jones to be mailed. Took a walk on shore, saw heavy guns, mortars, and siege missiles. Sappers and Miners marched off. Landed our guns and encamped by the side of the water. In course of the day the horses were also landed. Made a tent by raising one of the tarpaulins on a long pole supported at each end by a crotched stick. Learned that where we landed is called Goose Creek, not York river.[3] Saw peach and wild cherry trees in blossom.

APRIL 14TH, MONDAY.
Reveille sounded at 4½ o'clock. Had coffee and the battery started on the march farther up the country. App and I were detailed to stay behind with the baggage. Just after sunrise loaded the wagon and I started with it. Found our encampment about a mile distant. Parked and pitched the tarpaulins in a very orderly manner. Started shortly after nine up the country the [sic] find the Mass. 22nd. reg. After going about 2 miles met App who had lost his way. With him went in search of the 22nd which we at length found after a deal of trouble. They were encamped on a large plain with many other regiments, thousands on thousands, a splendid sight. Saw all the Woburn boys and took dinner with them, beef soup. Coming back saw the topographical engineers at work. Could see the line of rebel batteries and the York River. Saw our vessels fire at their shore batteries and them reply. Felt much better at seeing home faces. Arrived in camp just in time for coffee.

APRIL 15TH, TUESDAY.
Rained a little last night. Washed and changed clothes, felt refreshed. Detailed to dig a trench behind the horses. Fried potatoes and salt beef for dinner. Warm and fair all day.

APRIL 16TH, WEDNESDAY.
Rose at sunrise. Orders that no bugle or drum should sound. Took a walk and visited the house of a woman whose husband is in the rebel army. Gus Crane gave me his pass and I again visited the 22nd.[4] Also visited the bridges being built over a creek just before the enemies entrenchments. Stewed beans for dinner, good. Got back about five. Fried crackers for supper. Very warm. Considerable firing on the outposts.

April 17th, Thursday.
Detailed to take care of a pair of horses. Fed them in the morning and then they were given to someone else. Salt horse for dinner. Artillery of this division was reviewed in the afternoon by Major Wainwright, after whom this camp was named. Firing during the day.

April 18th, Friday.
Very hot. Reviewed by Gen. Hooker.[5] Fresh beef for dinner. Mail this day, but was much disappointed at not receiving a letter. On guard, 2d relief. Guard mounted at 8 o'clock bringing me on from 10–12 and 4–6. Countersign was "tete".

April 19th, Saturday.
Cloudy. Got a pass and again visited 22nd Mass. reg. Got back about dark. Rained a little in afternoon.

April 20th. Sunday.
Rained all last night. Visited the Jersey brigade of Hooker's division. Rainy all day.

April 21st, Monday.
Cloudy and drizzly in the morning. Battery received orders to move. I was detailed as wagon guard and started with the first load, ahead of the battery. Came to the camping ground four miles distant and only half a mile from 22nd.[6] Put officer's tent and other duty. Battery came up shortly after. Commenced to rain very hard, got wet through. Had to pitch tents on ground inch deep with water and mud. Captain gave us a little hay, and I stole an old door, so that App & I were very comfortable although wet through. Quite sick in afternoon.

April 22nd, Tuesday.
Showery all day. Strolled over to the 22nd. App, Johnny Furbush and I built a tent for ourselves. Drew a pint of molasses. Pork stew for dinner. Worked on stable. Very rapid firing on outposts, cause, the enemy sent out two field guns against some of our troops building roads. They fired one shot, when a whole battery, which we had masked, opened on them and drove them back.

April 23d, Wednesday.
Fair but cool. Again detailed for stable duty. Rice for dinner and supper. Saw battalion drill of some regulars, very poor. Witnessed dress parade of 8th N.J. reg., very good indeed. This camp was called "Camp Hall" after Lieut. Hall of Fort Sumter notoriety. Saw him the other day. The whole of this camp has been named Camp Winfield Scott by Gen. McClellan. There are thousands on thousands of soldiers in this one monster camp.

April 24th, Thursday.
Slept poorly last night. Wind from the east. On guard, 3d relief before the officers' tents. Did no night duty so that the guard for this day was only six hours.

Planted some young trees about our tent. Captain also had a great many set all through the camp. Fair. Wrote to Myra.

April 25th, Friday.
Cold and cloudy. Had a pass and visited Dr. Drew in 9th Mass. reg.[7] Went through camp of 22nd who were out on picket. Got back to camp about noon. Beef soup for dinner. In afternoon tried to get out to the advance lines but was stopped. Got a N.H. state button from private in 2nd N.H. reg. Rice for supper. Played quoits.

April 26th, Saturday.
Battery up and ready for the field at 3 this morning in accordance with orders received the preceding night. Rained all day. Mass. 1st and 11th regiments stormed one of the enemy's earth-works last night. Loss small. Captured 18 of the enemy.[8] Laid abed all day.

April 27th, Sunday.
Cold and cloudy all day. My cold much worse. Laid in my tent all day and read "Rosemary". Received a letter from M.C.J. dated March 11th and also one from Hero. Boiled rice for dinner. M.C.J's letter contained a lock of my little one's hair. The letter was directed by Myra and I was much disappointed it did not come from her.

April 28th, Monday.
Fair but cold, wind from the east still. Finished reading "Rosemary". Detailed to fix picket rope and police camp. Section drill in afternoon during which I was detailed to guard feed. Beef soup for dinner.

April 29th, Tuesday.
6th battery was awakened at 4 o' clock, made ready for the field and marched about ¾ mile and there waited near Gen. Heintzelman's quarters for further orders until daybreak, then turned around and returned to camp.[9] Misty in the morning but fair the rest of the day, cool. Beef soup for dinner, salt horse for breakfast. Detailed on digging. Received the 19th letter from Myra dated April 20th. From contents of this letter was led to believe that she had sent some letters which I have never received. Felt much cheered by her epistle. Pitched quoits.

April 30th, Wednesday.
Detailed to clean stables. At 10 o'clock mustered for pay for the months of March and April. Stewed beans for dinner. Slept nearly all the afternoon. Cold and rainy all day. Report that the rebels had evacuated their fortifications. Our battery went on picket, 6 guns and 3 caissons, other caissons to be in readiness if sent for.[10] I was detailed with others to guard camp. Countersign was "Alcola" probably a mistake for "Arcola".

MAY 1ST, THURSDAY.

Rainy and cold all day. Battery got in all safe before six o'clock. Fried crackers for breakfast, stewed beans for dinner. Signed two muster rolls and two pay rolls. Received my pay for the months of Jan., Feb., March and April, 52 dolls. Paid five dolls. for my boots and 25 cts. which I had borrowed. Received Journal of Apr. 26th.

MAY 2ND, FRIDAY.

Turned out again at 2 o'clock and harnessed. I was called to take position as No. 5.[11] Didn't move out of park. App was unwell. Fair and warm all day. Sent a letter to Myra. Beef steak for supper. Sent $45 home by Capt. Carruth, Co. H, 1st Mass. reg.[12] Headache and sick all day.

MAY 3D, SATURDAY.

Fair all day. Sick also this day. Got medicine and advice of a Dr. in the Jersey 7th. Rebels fired a great deal through the day and towards dark at our balloon which went up to take observations.

MAY 4TH, SUNDAY.

Slept very well last night. Rebels evacuated their fortifications during the night. Great jubilee in our camp. had my hair cut "fighting clip", cost 10 cts. Still unwell. Battery started on the advance shortly after noon but I was detailed to stay behind and ride on one of the wagons, they at the time being away after rations. Wagons started (3) about 3 o'clock over the sacred soil of Va. in direction of Yorktown which we reached just after dark, being delayed by the length of the baggage train. Passed the rebel fortifications which seemed to me impregnable to anything we had yet brought to bear on them. Our fortifications were not so near or good as reported. Rebels must have apprehended an attack in the rear. Passed on the road a large shell so placed that any wagon striking it would explode it.[13] Saw many graves of rebel soldiers. Saw in one place vast quantities of flour burning. Being unable to find battery, stopped by night close by the road. Hardees and coffee and went to bed in the wagon. Rained hard all night, but thanks to wagon kept dry.

MAY 5TH, MONDAY.

Stopped last night only 2 miles short of the battery. Coffee and hardees and started early to march again. Made an advance of about a mile where we were stopped by the press of wagons &c. Heard heavy cannonading. Toward night all of the boys came back to the wagon saying that the enemy had captured our pieces after firing away all our ammunition.[14] None injured. Rained hard all day. App and I slept together in the wagon under my blanket, he having lost his in the fight. Bought 2 lbs. bad cheese price 30 cts. per lb. I staid in the wagon all day.

MAY 6TH, TUESDAY.

Fair with cold wind. Raw ham and hardees for fodder. Had a little tea. Our guns were retaken with considerable loss and Williamsburg occupied by our troops.[15]

Learned that Richmond and Norfolk had been taken. Our troops on the advance. 2 of our wagons carried the rations about 4 miles farther on to where we camped for the night and where were one of our guns, one caisson, one limber, battery wagon and forge. All these had not been in the action or else had been brought off for some reason. It was a very pleasant camp on the edge of some heavy woods about 1½ miles from the scene of the battle. Had a small piece of fresh pork for supper but without salt on it. News just arrived at dark of the capture of General Magreeder [*sic*] and 15000 rebels.[16] Great joy and cheers. Our army still pressing on. Slept under the canopy of the sky "cum candescente rore".

MAY 7TH, WEDNESDAY.
Woke up my blankets quite wet with the dew. Packed up and started with the wagons for Williamsburgh. Went through some fine rural scenery, broad green fields skirted by bright green forest and bounded by the James River. Came to a little settlement which had been converted to a hospital. Saw various wounded standing about, one with his upper lip and part of his nose shot away. Laying in the barnyard and apparently thrown down as useless rubbish the amputated leg of some poor fellow. It had on a shoe, stocking and part of a leg to his drawers. Looked white and livid with the exception of the gory stump. Just below where it was amputated it had been pierced by a minie ball. In conversation the steward said that previous to the operation he had suffered a great deal, but was eased very much by it. They gave him ether.

One of the wagons got stuck. Got my heels much chafed because of holes in my stockings. Found a stocking some one had thrown away which I put on and threw my own away. Saw all the fortifications, 7 in number. In rear of the battle field saw them burying 3 dead rebels. Arrived at Williamsburgh at 11 o'clock, 3 miles from last camp and about 16 from Cheeraman's [*sic*] landing.[17] It is a very pretty and romantic village, but with bad streets, quite New Englandish and civilized. Tried to buy something to eat, but was unsuccessful.

MAY 8TH, THURSDAY.
Slept under our canvas. Hot and fair all day. App managed to buy some warm biscuit which tasted very good. Wrote to Myra. Received a letter from Albert Richardson enclosing half a dozen postage stamps, very kind of him. Beans for dinner. App and I washed clothes. Repitched our canvas.

MAY 9TH, FRIDAY.
Smith's div. passed our camp. The whole of the 3d Corps passed. Fair and warm. Beef soup. Visited the camp which 5th Michigan and 37th N.Y. regiments left, and got blankets, tent & c. Ammunition arrived for our guns. Shall move shortly. On wood and water guard.

MAY 10TH, SATURDAY.
Fair and warm. Took a stroll through the town. Got a supper at an old darkey's house by name David Smith, price 50 cts. Oysters, boiled ham and warm biscuit.

Saw William and Mary College, next oldest to Harvard. It is converted into a hospital.

May 11th, Sunday.
Warm. On guard last night 4 hours, no countersign. App bought some butter 60 cts. per lb. and cheese 40. Ginger cakes 25 cts. for 10.

May 12th, Monday.
Detailed to take care of a pair of horses. Weather fair. Washed a secesh shirt that I had found. Boiled beef for dinner. Battery nearly fitted out again, expect to move tomorrow.

May 13th, Tuesday.
Started on the march about 8. Rode for about 2 miles and walked about the same, when I got into the wagon and rode. I was detailed as wagon guard and my horses were given to some one else. Greater part of the way through pine woods and across occasional farms. All along saw evidence of a large army's march, guns and caissons that the enemy had left, dead horses foetid beneath the summer sun, and broken wagons. Stopped about noon at a little church in a small grove and rested 'til 4. Had a good wash. Started on and stopped about 7½ o'clock encamping near to the 2d & 3d brigades of Hooker's div. 1st brigade were left behind at Williamsburgh. Day's march about 17 miles. Very warm and dusty. Pitched my new tent.

May 14th, Wednesday.
Rainy. Very sore from yesterday's riding. Laid abed about all day. News of the capture of Norfolk and Portsmouth.

May 15th, Thursday.
Broke camp about 8 and made an advance through the rain of about 6 miles. Pitched our little tent again.

May 16th, Friday.
Staid in camp all day. Cloudy. Boiled ham for dinner, very good. Received my 20th letter from Myra, date May 4th.[18]

May 17th, Saturday.
Fine weather. On guard, 2nd relief. Colby was on 3d relief and went out of camp, so I did both his duty and my own, thereby escaping all my night guard.[19] Wrote to Myra and to her father.

May 18th, Sunday.
Marched at 9 with frequent stoppages and over a very rough road 'til 5 in the afternoon. Distance about 6 miles. Passed through the little village of New Kent Court House. Very pretty but as usual the roads very bad. Walked all this march.

Camped in some pine woods.[20] Close by were the graves of two rebels, one bore the inscription, S.O. Leslie, 2nd reg. Miss. Died May 9th of Pneumonia.[21] Very hot all day. March very tedious.

May 19th, Monday.
Resumed our march 'till 3½ o'clock in afternoon when we camped in a large wheat field. Place called Baltimore cross roads, 21 miles from Richmond.[22] Saw a flag of truce which came in accompanied by two rebel officers. Like yesterday's march it was very tedious. Rained nearly all day. Received a "Journal" from home. Saw the country house of the son of ex-president Tyler.

May 20th, Tuesday.
Warm and fair. On water guard. Had to lug it about half a mile. App had a turn of the fever and ague last night.

May 21st, Wednesday.
Very warm. Detailed on another team.

May 22nd, Thursday.
Very warm in forenoon with heavy thunder shower in the afternoon. Hail fell as big as marbles and some as big as English walnuts. Our little tent stood the storm well. Fell sick toward night.

May 23d, Friday.
Fair. Very sick with a sort of remittent fever. Orders to march at 4 in afternoon. Staid behind and ambulance came back for the sick.[23] Roads very bad and lost our way. Slept in a barn with some of the 5th Michigan regt. Barn full of rats. Slept very poorly. 5th belongs to Kearney's div.

May 24th, Saturday.
Started early and reached camp about 5 o'clock. Fight between sergt. Fulton and Patten.[24] Patten tied up. Rained hard all day. Still sick.[25]

May 25th, Sunday.
Marched about mile and a half beyond bottom bridge and camped.[26] 14 miles from R. Rode on caisson. Very sick.

May 26th, Monday.
Still sick, App also, with a sort of camp fever. Letter from Myra with picture of my boy. Also one from A.H.R. Found I had caught a kind of itch the night I laid in the corn barn. Just at dark had orders to cook 3 days rations and next day to march with nothing but the battery, officers to mess with the men. No wagons allowed.[27]

May 27th, Tuesday.
Rained all last night and part of the day. Battery didn't move. Sick with no care.

MAY 28TH, WEDNESDAY.
No better. Shower in afternoon. Something to eat this day.[28]

MAY 29TH, 30TH & 31ST.
Cloudy and rainy. Sick all the time. 31st, Battery moved late in afternoon leaving sick behind.[29] App very sick and just over my fever. Baggage wagons recrossed the Chickahominy. Heavy firing.

JUNE 1ST, SUNDAY.
Staid at camp all day. In evening put the sickest aboard some wagons and blankets and I with them got over the bridge and came to camp about 12. Slept in open air. Felt much better this day. Roads horrible.

JUNE 2ND, MONDAY.
Found our wagons close by. App still very sick. Staid here this day and night. Slept in my little shelter tent with Saunders.[30]

JUNE 3D, TUESDAY.
Very warm. Washed and changed. App was carried of to the hospital in the ambulance with two others. Stayed here again this night which was very rainy. Wrote to Myra.

JUNE 4TH, WEDNESDAY.
Drizzly and rainy all day. Longed very much for home.

JUNE 5TH, THURSDAY.
Cloudy without rain. Heavy firing on the right. Been from home 6 months today.

JUNE 6TH, FRIDAY.
Cloudy and rainy. Started and walked up the Richmond and York river railroad to where the battery was camped about 8 miles from Richmond. Two of the baggage wagons came down and took the knapsacks and blankets. A very tedious walk. One of the wagons got upset in the swamp, but luckily my blankets and knapsack were in the other one, so I got them all dry. They arrived late in the evening.

JUNE 7TH, SATURDAY.
Long and I slept last night beneath an old hen pen.[31] Did not sleep very well. In the U.S. service just 6 mo's today. Wrote to Hero and to A.H.R. Heavy shower.

JUNE 12TH, THURSDAY.
Fair. Returned to camp. Jewell returned with me, and I carried his blankets.[32]

JUNE 13TH, FRIDAY.
Was awakened at 2 o'clock and went on picket about 2 miles in advance of our camp. Saw numerous graves of rebels who had fallen in the fights of May 31st

and June 1st. Roads very bad. Outposts visited by Gens. Sumner, Heintzelman and McClellan. Slept in open air, very poorly for it was very warm.

JUNE 14TH, SATURDAY.
Very warm. Spread my blanket over the gun and layed under it all day. On guard 2 hours last night. Returned to camp about 4 in afternoon. Moved the position of camp slightly. Slept in open air last night. Detailed to take care of a horse.

JUNE 15TH, SUNDAY.
Relieved of my horse. Wrote to Myra & Mother. Sent certificates home for App and myself of membership of the battery. Heavy thunder storm in afternoon. Boston Journal received from A.A. Chittenden.

JUNE 26TH, THURSDAY.
Got up early and went on picket in place of Dick Breese who came back sick.[33] Visited acquaintance in 16th Mass. Heavy cannonade on the right afternoon and evening. Returned to camp just at dark. Great cheering among the troops at news of Jackson's defeat.

JUNE 27TH, FRIDAY.
On water guard last night and this morning. Got up at 2 and got water. Had coffee, and battery harnessed up. Did not go out though. Another team of horses to take care of. Busy all the morning. Got a Journal from home. Harnessed again this afternoon and the battery started for the front. The wagons went down to Savage's station and camped the other side the railroad on a hill. I had a spare horse and went with the wagons. Slept in the open air.

JUNE 28TH, SATURDAY.
On guard 2 hours last night. Saw Geo. Cobbett and Cyrus Converse of 22nd M.V. who were with their wagon train.[34] Geo. just recovered from a fever. Borrowed 25cts, and bought a pound of dried beef. Many wagons and wounded passed. Troops also went by toward the rear. Knew not whether it was a stratagem or a defeat, thought the latter. Got orders to move just at night. Started about 8 and got tangled among a vast number of baggage wagons, so that we advanced only about half a mile. Slept under a wagon on a blanket with nothing over me.

JUNE 29TH, SUNDAY.
Saw the battery which lay close by. Visited some deserted camps and got some paper and a variety of other things. There was a large quantity of supplies burned. Visited App who was trying to get his discharge. He was still very weak. Returned to the road and when the ambulance came along got him across the woods and into it. Travelled 'til dark and camped. Geo. Cobbett and Newcomb of Woburn joined us here, took supper and staid with us over night.[35] Slept under my tent. App slept in ambulance. Very warm and dusty all day.

JUNE 30TH, MONDAY.

Slept soundly and rose before sunrise. After advancing about a half mile the ambulance separated from the baggage wagons in order to take a shorter route to the James River, where he and 2 others were to embark for Fort Monroe, being too sick to remain with the battery. Felt sad at parting from him not knowing what might become of him or when I might see him again. Saw Gen. McClellan, Barry and many others at a house by the roadside. Also saw the prince De Joinville. About noon heard heavy cannonading in the rear. Enemy probably following us up. Passed the battery on a high hill and in a large field. Enemy also attacked this hill and were shelled by the artillery upon it and from the gun-boats in the James River. Continued the march and night coming on I found it impossible to lead my horse and also keep up with the wagons, so I tied him to one of them and being very tired got inside. While there horse broke loose and was lost. Stopped for the night about 2 o'clock, and was put on guard for 2 hours. At the end of my turn of guard the day began to dawn and I awoke the sergeant and laid down to get a little sleep.

JULY 1ST, TUESDAY.

Slept a very little last night or rather this morning. Had coffee and hardees for breakfast. Went down to the river which I found close by and there saw steamer Daniel Webster taking in sick and wounded to carry away. Tried to find out if App had gone aboard but could not. Went back on the road in search of my horse but could not find him. Pitched my tent in anticipation of rain. Fair and hot all day. Very dusty.

JULY 2ND, WEDNESDAY.

Rained hard all day. Struck tent and with the wagons regained the battery, which was only a quarter of a mile distant. Got there in a pouring rain and again pitched tent. Feet and legs sopping wet. Have not heard from App or the ambulance and did not know whether he went down the river, was captured by the rebels, or was still somewhere in the neighborhood. The vicinity of the landing became crowded with troops and it seemed to me quite evident that the rebels had got the best of us and we had made a hasty but orderly retreat. Last night slept in a wheat field and this night in a clover field. This vicinity constituted a large and splendid farm the immense crops of which have been destroyed by the presence of the union troops. Thousands on thousands of dollars worth of property have been destroyed.

JULY 3D, THURSDAY.

Rained all last night. Felt sad and thought of home. Early went down to the landing for forage with the wagons, but getting none returned to camp and found the battery harnessed up. Was detailed to drive a team on the forge. App came into camp in the ambulance, having experienced many hardships since quitting company. Unhitched again and put up tent for App and myself to sleep in. Cloudy all day. Firing from the gun-boats. A very busy day for me.

JULY 4TH, FRIDAY.
Rose early, breakfasted off beef steak, (the only good meal I had had for a great while) and harnessing up, marched. Took us from early in the morning 'till 4 in the afternoon to accomplish 1½ miles. Several batteries fired national salutes in honor of the day. Warm and the road was very bad from the recent rain. Quite a different mode of spending independence from that of last year. Bands played in the evening. Saw McClellan again, who passed by our camp.

JULY 5TH, SATURDAY.
7 months from home today. Very warm. Wrote to Myra.

JULY 6TH, SUNDAY.
Very hot. App a little worse.

JULY 7TH, MONDAY.
Very hot indeed. App worse. Washed clothes for App and myself. Changed clothes. In the service of the United States seven months today. App went in the ambulance down to Harrison's landing and embarked on steamer John Brooks, either for home or Fort Munroe.

JULY 8TH, TUESDAY.
Felt very lonely last night because of App's absence. Moved camp at sunrise a distance of half a mile. Scarcely had I got the harness off my horses when orders came to harness again, and we moved again another quarter of a mile and camped in the edge of some woods close by a pond. Very hot. Toward night harnessed and took horses down to water and wash harness. Had scarcely got done when orders came to repair immediately to camp, when the guns went out to fire a salute in honor of President Lincoln who was present at Gen. Heintzelman's head-quarters. Went bathing. Received a letter from A.H. Richardson. On guard, 3d relief.

JULY 9TH, WEDNESDAY.
A little cooler. Had a pass and went to visit 22nd & 32nd Mass. Vols. also Dr. Drew. Saw the Woburn boys in both. Those in the 22nd seemed quite used up, Penny quite sick.[36] Those in 32nd looked fresh as daisies, having just come out. Received a "Journal" from Woburn. Had some nice beans (stewed) in camp of 32nd. reg.

JULY 25TH, FRIDAY.
Section drill at 8 o'clock, went out as No. 4 in left section.[37] Received a letter from mother and one from Zillah, also a Journal.[38] Wrote to Mother. Very hot.

JULY 26TH, SATURDAY.
Very warm. Took a horse out to exercise and went over to camp of 16th Mass. Vols. Section drill again today but I did not go out. Received letter from Myra, date 20th July and one from A.H.R. of 21st. Wrote to Zillah. Heavy shower in the night.

July 27th, Sunday.
Fair. Inspection at 8 o'clock. I had to harness pole team of the battery wagon for inspection, which I had been taking care of for some days already. Wrote to Myra.

July 28th, Monday.
Got a pass and went over to 16th Mass. reg. Had some nice beans for dinner. Saw McCollins, nurse in hospital whom I knew in So. Reading. Wrote to A.H.R.

July 29th, Tuesday.
A fine morning. One of the members of the battery, by name Ira Shay, died during last night of typhoid fever.[39] He was a married man, and a good fellow. In my opinion, he was neglected by our officers. He ought to have been sent home at the same time with App. He was buried at 11 o'clock close by the encampment, the whole company attending the funeral. Services by Rev. Mr. Parker, chaplain of 2nd N.H. Vols.[40]

July 30th, Wednesday.
Very hot. Got rid of my horses and took another pair. Put on stable guard for two days for being late to feeding horses in the morning; cause of my tardiness I wanted to eat some warm griddle cakes. Battery drill, but I did not go. One of the guns broke a pole and finished the drill prematurely. Took a walk over to 11th Mass. reg. Staid to dinner which was very good. Wrote to Myra.

July 31st, Thursday.
Rained all day, yet was very warm. Section drill, went out in my own section. Draw one day's ration of fresh bread. I eat the whole of mine at one meal, and without anything with it. Tasted quite refreshing. Received a Journal.

August 1st, Friday.
Fair and cool. On guard, 3d relief. Received a letter from Myra, and one from brother Sammy. Very much pleased with the latter. The battery got a ration of one lemon apiece. Frank More, carpenter to the battery, built an enclosure and headboard for Ira Shay's grave.[41] Got rid of my horse again.

August 2nd, Saturday.
Fair and hot. Washed guns and caissons, and washed and oiled harness. This duty I very luckily got free from. About 4 o'clock received orders to be harnessed and ready to move at sundown. Shortly after dark we moved and with several other batteries started on what was judged to be a reconnaissance. With us went Hooker's div. and a thousand cavalry. Went about two miles and the whole battery got stuck in the mud. Road was so bad had to turn back. Reached camp about 2 in the morning, quite used up with working to get the caisson out of the mud. I went as No. 7 on No. 1 gun.[42]

August 3d, Sunday.
Reveille did not sound 'till 6 o'clock. Cleaned the mud off my clothes and washed up. Wrote to Sammy. Yesterday wrote to Myra. Rainy at intervals. Religious services at 5 in the afternoon by Rev. Mr. Parker of 2nd N.H. Vols.

August 4th, Monday.
Very warm. Roast Beef for dinner. Signed the pay roll in the afternoon. Just at dark received orders to be in readiness to march. About 5 o'clock started and took up our line of march, through and beyond our line of defences. This was truly a most delightful march. The moon shone brightly and our way lay through some of the most beautiful portions of Virginia, through luxuriant clover fields, by old and picturesque farm houses, and now and then crossing broad strips of forest, dark and faintly checkered by the pale moon beams. As we progressed our march became slower and more silent with frequent stoppages. Our object was to attack Malvern hill from the rear, therefore we took a long and round about path. Finally we turned into a large field close by a large farmhouse shortly after midnight. Here our battery took position with two others and awaited dawn. I was on guard half an hour. Managed to sleep a very little.

August 5th, Tuesday.
Rose at 3 o'clock and continued our march. Just before we got upon the road again and as we were waiting in column close by several infantry regiments, a horseman came galloping by making for the woods. He was pursued by Johnny Furbush who kept shouting, "Kill the son of a b——h" Whereupon several of the infantry let fly at him and wounded the horse. He immediately cried, "I give in," and he was captured. He was one of the rebel cavalry pickets and was not aware of our occupation of the place until too late. When we were within about 3 miles of the hill we heard cannonading in that direction. As we approached nearer began to see signs of the fight. Saw a dead soldier by the wayside and another wounded. Shells began to explode near us. As we entered the field we skirted the hill to the left while on the right one or more batteries of flying artillery were peppering away at the rebels. The rebs replied smartly with, as was afterward learned, only four guns, which were posted on the hill just in front of the house. We laid still for half an hour, when we advanced a little way and came into battery on a little knoll scarce half a mile from the enemy. The infantry and De Russy's battery of napoleons took position in front and to the right.[43] We loaded with case shot, 5 second fuse. Just then the rebels ceased firing and we waited for the smoke to clear up. The infantry continued to advance. Gradually they closed in taking several prisoners and found that the birds had flown. The whole division advanced and occupied the hill. I saw two rebels who had been killed by our shells, one by a piece of shell which entered his left cheek and went out at the back of his head. The other was torn in the back and side. Before he died he begged to be killed to escape the torture he was suffering.

I ate some unripe pears which I gathered close to the house and some of the biscuit which the rebels had left behind. The latter were without salt. Spent the rest of the day trying to keep cool but succeeded very indifferently, it was so very hot. From the brow of the hill there was a fine view of the James and an estuary in which lay two of our gunboats. Slept soundly all night.

AUGUST 6TH, WEDNESDAY.
Rose late. Spent the forenoon lying under a large tree close to where we were parked. Shortly after noon one of our wagons came up with rations and forage for two days. Among the rest there were two days' rations of soft bread. Carried a pair of horses to water at night and got thrown off into a mud puddle. Fell on my side upon a rail. One of our men got shot through the arm while wandering through the woods, his name Hoffman.[44] Had scarcely laid down when orders came to hitch and harness. Waited 'til about 10 when we commenced to march toward the camp by the river road, the same we took on the previous retreat. Arrived in camp just as the bugle sounded reveille. Was so tired and sleepy on the road that I nearly fell off the caisson two or three times. Immediately laid down to try and get some sleep but did not succeed very well. This day I received a blank book from Myra for journal purposes. Quite breezy all day.

AUGUST 7TH, THURSDAY.
Very warm. Laid in my tent all day. Felt very lame because of yesterday's fall. Nice boiled veal for dinner. The orderly sergeant detailed me for stable duty. I told him I felt so lame that I was unable. Just after dark orders came to hitch to the guns and three caissons and report to Gen. Kearney. The guns were placed in a redoubt and the horses and men came back all but the cannoniers of the left section. Received a "Middlesex Journal". Very warm all day.

AUGUST 8TH, FRIDAY.
Felt very lame all day. Got excused from duty. *Very* warm and uncomfortable. Received a letter from Myra, also a Woburn Budget. She sent me some postage stamps and a dollar bill. Visited our guns at the redoubt and bought some cakes and a lemon. Had some lemonade. Artificer West reduced for insulting Lieut. Martin.[45] Capt. Bramhall acting major of reserve artillery and Lieut. Martin commanding the battery.

AUGUST 9TH, SATURDAY.
Much better. Had a good wash and changed clothes. Bill Randolph appointed blacksmith in place of West.[46] I was detailed on his team. Bought a loaf of bread, price 10 cts., weight 1½ lbs. Also bought some lemons. Received 2 mo's pay, viz. May and June. Went rambling off to find some onions and got back to camp too late to give my horses hay. Expect to get stable duty as punishment. Still very hot. In the afternoon 5 doz. bottles whiskey came into camp and many of the men got very drunk. It was a most disgusting exhibition. Three of our men were sent off sick.

AUGUST 10TH, SUNDAY.
Still very hot. Had boiled plum pudding for dinner. At evening roll call had orders to be in readiness to move next day.

AUGUST 11TH, MONDAY.
Rose early and packed my knapsack. All the knapsacks were labeled and put on board a transport. Boiled potatoes and onions in vinegar for dinner. On guard, 1st. relief. Wrote two or three lines to Myra to let her know we were going to move. Order countermanded for this day and we spent the night in the old camp. Had my hair cut and whiskers trimmed.

AUGUST 12TH, TUESDAY.
Cooler. March still delayed. Slept in the open air.

AUGUST 13TH, WEDNESDAY.
Received two letters from Myra and a Journal. Got tidings of brother Appleton's death at the hospital in Philadelphia.[47] The first death in the family.

"Death is the end of life. Ah why should life all labor be! Let us alone. Time driveth onward fast and in a little while our lips are dumb."

AUGUST 14TH, THURSDAY.
Quite cool. Received a "True Flag" from home.[48] A sad and melancholy day for me. Felt very lonely, my mind continually presenting pictures of the many adventures and pleasant days I had so lately experienced in dear App's company. Sad thought to know I never again can see his familiar face, never again with him to enjoy the rapid march, and with him never in company to return to our distant New England home. Can it be possible that my fate will be the same?

AUGUST 15TH, FRIDAY.
Reveille sounded at 2 o'clock and the assembly immediately after. Got orders to move directly, but did not start 'til nearly 8. Finally got off and took the road down the river. Frequent and long stoppages because of the baggage wagons. Made about a dozen miles this day. The march lay through a most beautiful tract of country. Passed through large fields of corn and other grain. I drove the pole team on the forge and had a good opportunity of seeing everything. Scattered all along the road were the planters' residences, most always embowered in a copse of beautiful trees a little back from the road. Passed the court house and gaol of Charles City County. The former is of brick and a very pretty building. It was used also as a church. The soldiery despoiled it of its records and other law documents. The gaol was partly of brick and partly of wood. Would have been a very pleasant day's march, had it not been so long. We did not camp until about 11 at night. Then I had to go a mile and a half to water horses. Finally laid down and went right to sleep. Cool all day.

August 16th, Saturday.

Day opened cool and breezy. Bought some hoe-cake of a darkey at a house near by. Watered and fed horses. Found that my off horse was about "played out". Harnessed and moved forward about a quarter of a mile. Went in battery and unhitched and unharnessed. This bivouac was just by the house of secessionist by name Jordan. He was said to own all the cleared land within 7 miles around. The house was a large brick building well surrounded by trees. In its rear were quite extensive negro quarters. His negroes said he had, i.e., Jordan, been in the habit of supplying large quantities of food to the rebs. One old negress said she had been expecting and praying for us for a whole year. Saw a cotton field for the first time. Also saw sweet potatoes growing. Got some apples nearly ripe from Mr. Jordan's orchard. Gen. Heintzelman made his house headquarters for the 3d Corps. Cold night with heavy dew.

August 17th, Sunday.

Got up at 2 o'clock, fed horses and had coffee. Harnessed and marched. Had gone but a few miles when my off horse gave out. Took the nigh leader and put him on the pole. I saddled and rode the off leader the rest of the day. Crossed the Chickahominy. Just after noon we struck the Williamsburgh road, the same we travelled over on May 13th. Formerly brother App was with me, this time I was alone, to me a sad thought. Toward night camped. On guard, 2nd relief.

August 18th, Monday.

Rose again at 2 o'clock. Had to drive the pole team on the forge, the other driver being sick. Took up our march for Williamsburgh where we arrived about one. Went foraging with Ackerman.[49] Had just got our hands on some geese when the secesh owner gave chase and we had to throw them away. Got supper at a house in the town. Had for supper fried bacon, hot biscuit and butter, and coffee with fresh milk. Price 50 cts. Quite a pretty and modest girl waited on us. Got to camp about 9 at night. Had some good peaches & apples.

August 19th, Tuesday.

Harnessed, hitched and started about 8 o'clock. Travelled all day 'til 7 in the evening when we camped at Yorktown on the bluffs above the river. Had to go two miles to water, so that after watering and feeding, it was between 9 and 10 at night. Passed by during this day's march the scene of the battle of Williamsburgh. Here it was that brother App got the foundation of the sickness that eventually caused his death. Many things during this day's march caused me to bring him to mind. Very dusty roads. Was very tired. Fried bacon & hardees for dinner.

August 20th, Wednesday.

On water guard. Washed harness. Mustered and inspected but for what object could not learn. A very busy day. Shall probably embark from here and go to Acquia [sic] Creek on the Potomac.

August 21st, Thursday.
Slept very poorly last night on account of eating too freely of berry pie just before going to bed. Mailed a letter to Myra. Had a bath in the York river, the water is salt. Bought some ginger cakes. In the afternoon swam the horses in the salt water. A little rain toward night.

August 22nd, Friday.
Rainy in the forenoon but fair in the afternoon. Because I had sent my tent off on my knapsack I got quite a wetting. In afternoon went down to the landing and bought some lemons.

August 23d, Saturday.
Had no horses to take care of. Had quite a holiday, went down to the landing two or three times. Had a good wash all over and changed clothes. Quite cool all day.

August 24th, Sunday.
Heavy rain last night. I crept under a tarpaulin and got only slightly wet. Cold and a very high wind all day. There were white caps to the waves in the river. A small schooner went down. Played bluff and lost $3.75. Pitched a tarpaulin to sleep in.

August 25th, Monday.
On guard last night in place of J. McDonald who was sick.[50] On 3d relief, very cool. Washed guns and caissons. Bought some pickled tripe and various other dainties.

August 26th, Tuesday.
Rather unwell in consequence of what I eat yesterday. Got some powders from the doctor but did not take them. Harnessed and drew the guns down to York-town landing for embarkation. Horses came back to camp for want of transports. Cannoneers embarked. Sent a letter to Myra.

August 27th, Wednesday.
Harnessed and embarked aboard the schooner Josephine G. Collyer of Portland Conn. Lay in the stream the rest of the day and night. Slept on deck, it was rainy and I got a little wet. Bought a novel, "Dick Tarleton; or The Last of his race."

August 28th, Thursday.
Just at sunrise the large black steamer "Peabody" of Baltimore came off and took us in tow with 3 other schooners. Sailed all day and lay at anchor all night. Just at night there was a heavy gale accompanied by rain. On guard, 1st relief.

August 29th, Friday.
Started again early and reached Acquia Creek about noon. Were ordered to continue our voyage and reached Alexandria just after dark. Passed Liverpool Point

and Budd's Ferry. Alas, Poor App, would that he were with me to enjoy all this. The voyage lost half its charm from want of his presence. Also passed Mt. Vernon, residence and burial place of the "father of his country". The scenery between Budd's Ferry and Alexandria is most beautiful, almost like fairyland. The banks are clothed with foliage down to the water's edge with here and there a smiling glade or nook in which nestle white shining cottages. The stream was perfectly alive with steamers and vessels. While we lay at Acquia Creek the boat from our schooner put off and picked up a man who was unable to regain his vessel by reason of the swiftness of the tide, he having gone overboard for a swim. Just below Alexandria is Fort Washington, built of dark blue stone and bristling with cannon. The grounds and lawn between the fort and river were very beautiful and neat. The channel runs right under the guns. It would be difficult even for a Monitor to get by such an obstacle. Cast anchor and lay in the stream all night. Slept on deck again.

AUGUST 30TH, SATURDAY.
Lay in the stream all day and just after dark were hauled up to the dock and after some delay disembarked. I went into the city and bought some bread and pies. After rambling about some time returned to the wharf where we lay all night. On guard, 2nd relief. This was not my regular guard but I shifted with Hadfield, I being on stable guard.[51]

CHAPTER 3

I DON'T LIKE THE PLAN:
SEPTEMBER–DECEMBER 1862

WITH THE REST OF McCLELLAN'S ARMY, THE SIXTH NEW YORK RETURNED
to Alexandria, Virginia, at the end of August. While on the Peninsula it had been assigned to Hooker's Division of Maj. Gen. Samuel P.
Heintzelman's Third Corps. Now, however, it became part of the tug-
of-war between McClellan and Maj. Gen. John Pope, newly minted
commander of the Army of Virginia. President Lincoln's intention was
to strengthen Pope's army by transferring as many of McClellan's forces
as possible to him. After McClellan arrived in Alexandria on August 27,
however, he strenuously objected to this plan, arguing variously that
Pope's location and intentions were unknown, the Confederates were
on the move, and, in any case, it was imperative to retain sufficient
forces under his command to render the capital safe. In the event,
almost the entire Third Corps was forwarded to Pope and fought in
the Campaign of Second Manassas under Heintzelman's command.
The Corps Artillery, however, did not accompany its parent command,
and the Sixth New York was one of the units retained in the defenses
of Washington.

After the Federal debacle at Second Manassas, General Pope was
sent packing and McClellan reassumed command of those parts of the
Army of the Potomac that had been sent to Pope, as well as the rubble
of the Army of Virginia. Heintzelman, found wanting for the last time
in corps command, was given command of the defenses of Washington.
When McClellan marched his army to confront Lee's Army of Northern Virginia at Sharpsburg, Maryland, the Sixth New York was one of
the units assigned to the Artillery Reserve under Heintzelman's command. Consequently, it missed both Second Manassas and Sharpsburg.

During this period, Private Perkins visited and described many
of the components of the system of fortifications that guarded the

national capital. This quiet period for the Sixth New York was inter-rupted only once. In October, the battery participated in a raid on Rap-pahannock Station, together with two brigades of cavalry. The rapid march was quite challenging for the battery, equipped as it was to act in support of infantry and not to participate in cavalry operations. Despite these handicaps and the consequent wear and tear on men, horses, and equipment that the expedition produced, the battery apparently turned in a creditable performance, because its designation was changed to "flying" (horse) artillery. It was equipped with additional horses and equipment from the Washington arsenal to allow it to fulfill that role. Perkins's diary provides a detailed report on the Rappahannock Sta-tion affair and also describes the changes in equipment required by its new role as horse artillery. As the title for this chapter suggests, Perkins initially was unimpressed by this development. Later, however, he became very proud of his battery's association with the cavalry.

With the exception of the raid on Rappahannock Station and the subsequent conversion to horse artillery, many of Perkins's diary entries during this period merely chronicled the daily routine. Thus, the entries for September 24–30, October 11–16, October 28–November 1, Novem-ber 5–9 and 19–26, and November 28–December 4 have been omitted. During these periods, Perkins reported little but the increasingly cold, raw weather as winter approached, his stints of guard duty (some-times in consequence of committing infractions of battery discipline), and bouts of illness. George's position as a cannoneer was cemented on September 28 when he was appointed to the post of Number Five on the number one gun, and on October 31, 105 new horses were brought into camp to enable the battery to function as horse artillery.

August 31st, Sunday.
Harnessed early and took the horses down to where the guns were, and having tied them went into the city with Pearse to get breakfast.[1] Wandered about view-ing the city and finally found a place to get breakfast, price 37½ cts. Had pork steak and potatoes, bread and butter, and coffee. Tasted delicious. Returned to the guns which lay in a street close at the water's edge. Hitched and marched through the city to a field in the environs where we camped. Rained all this time. Our camp was situated just between the city and Fort Ellsworth.[2] Saw two members of 10th Maine reg. and heard from cousin Bill Jordan.[3]

September 1st, Monday.
On guard, 1st relief for being late to roll-call. Went over to the camp of 33d Mass. reg. and found 3 fellows that I knew. Beef soup for dinner. Wrote to Myra. Received a letter from Nate, one from Zillah, and one from mother and Sammy. Received also a "Boston True Flag". Heavy rain just after dark. Battery received

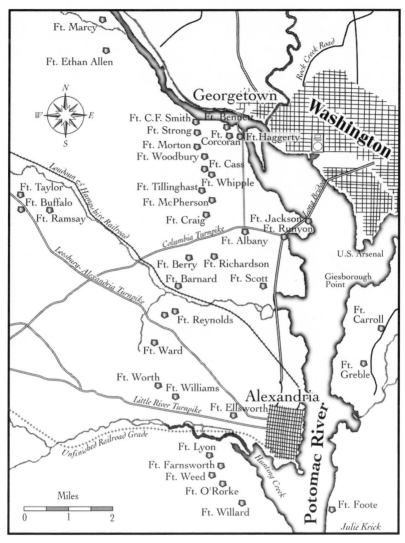

The Virginia Defenses of Washington. Drawn by Julie Krick.

25 new horses. Four men have deserted, two of which were known to be in the Washington city guard house.[4]

SEPTEMBER 2ND, TUESDAY.
Fair again. Battery was mustered for the last 2 month's pay. Got a new off horse for my team. Went into the city. Had for dinner cold roast lamb, potatoes, pickles, bread and butter, and coffee; cost 50cts. Had my picture taken, price 50 cts. Saw the Marshall House where Ellsworth was shot. Saw Bowen of Woburn, also

Dennett, Moody and Bill Cobbett, the latter sick in hospital at Fort Ellsworth.[5] I visited the fort by moonlight.

September 3d, Wednesday.
Harnessed and marched at 8 o'clock. Went through Alexandria and along the river road toward Washington. Reached Arlington Heights about noon where we encamped. A very pleasant march, the river in view the whole distance. Could see the capitol all the way and gradually drew near to it. Passed the end of long bridge and through Fort Runnion up toward the heights.[6] Our camp lay on a little hill close to the river side and directly opposite Washington. From the top of the hill was a fine view of Georgetown, Washington and vicinity. Could see chain bridge, our camp being located half way between that and long bridge. Close by also is the family mansion of Gen. Lee of the rebel army. In the afternoon went up on the heights by Fort Albany to find the 35th M. V., but learned that the Woburn company was not in it.[7] On guard, 3d relief for missing roll call.

September 4th, Thursday.
Fair and cool. Busy all day blacking harness. Received a letter from A.H. Richardson, also a Journal.

September 5th, Friday.
Finished the harness. Nine months away from home this day. Rather down-hearted.

September 6th, Saturday.
Received two letters from Myra and two "True Flags". On guard, 1st relief again for punishment. The officers beginning to feel their oats and in a manner oppress the men. The tenor of Myra's letters rather harassing, showing evidence of mental trouble. Would I were at home.

September 7th, Sunday.
Orders to move between 9 and 10. Took the back track toward Alexandria. Very dusty, so that soon all the horses and men were covered with a thick incrustation of the "sacred soil". Passed through A. All very quiet, being Sunday. J. McDonald fell off a gun limber and was run over by the gun carriage, probably severely injured. Passed by our former camp and Fort Ellsworth. Camped just below Fort Lyon through which we passed.[8] Passed Gens. Hooker's and Heintzelman's headquarters. Fort Lyon commands a beautiful view of the valley containing Washington, Georgetown, and Alexandria. But the chief object is the Capitol which in the distance towers huge and massive. We camped close to what was Gen. Kearney's div. before his death. Our camp lay close to a bridge connecting the city to Fort Lyon across a creek tributary to the Potomac.[9] Run short of bread. I was 9 months in the U.S. service from this date.

SEPTEMBER 8TH, MONDAY.
Washed and changed clothes. One month today have I mourned the loss of a dear brother. I hardly think I can ever forget him. Wrote to mother.

SEPTEMBER 9TH, TUESDAY.
Cool and cloudy. Wrote to brother Nate. Received two "Journals". Drill in forenoon and afternoon. Went in the forenoon but not in afternoon. Pitched tarpaulin it looking like rain. In the afternoon visited 1st brigade Hooker's div. Bread and butter for supper.[10]

SEPTEMBER 10TH, WEDNESDAY.
Drill in morning. Cool and cloudy with a little rain at night. Got a lot of new men detailed from the regiments in Hooker's div. Soup for dinner. Wrote to Myra. Dusted harness. Smashed the fore finger of my left hand. In afternoon harnessed and hitched to limber of the forge, and exercised the horses. Rather unwell this day.

SEPTEMBER 11TH, THURSDAY.
Wrote to Zillah. Harnessed and marched in a heavy rain. Marched about 1½ mile and camped in a peach orchard near to Fairfax Seminary.[11] Slept outside in a pouring rain, yet very soundly for all that. Asked Lieut. Martin to relieve me from driving the pole team on the forge. Said he would. On guard, 1st. relief.

SEPTEMBER 12TH, FRIDAY.
Awoke well wet. Received a letter from Myra. Contents not very pleasing. Got orders to move and harnessed early in the forenoon. Did not move until nearly night when we marched about 3 miles and camped at a small opening in the woods about 3 miles from Alexandria and 4 from Arlington Heights. Went in battery on the brow of the hill commanding the adjacent valley. On the various hills round about are numerous forts. Many troops were encamped in the neighborhood. Slept soundly this night.

SEPTEMBER 13TH, SATURDAY.
Quite warm. Had my side whiskers shaved off.

SEPTEMBER 14TH, SUNDAY.
On guard, 1st relief for missing roll call yesterday. Countersign "Pharsalia". Guard carried loaded revolvers. Heavy but distant firing in the forenoon.[12] Very warm. Night guard tedious.

SEPTEMBER 15TH, MONDAY.
Very warm. Not very well this day. Wrote to Myra.

SEPTEMBER 16TH, TUESDAY.
Sultry and cloudy. Received from government the clothing which was lost in my knapsack viz, 1 Artillery Jacket, 1 Blouse, 2 Shirts, 2 pr. Drawers, 2 pr. Socks. Drew a cap, cross cannons, and figure 6.

SEPTEMBER 17TH, WEDNESDAY.
Cloudy and rainy. Went out of camp without a pass. Visited Fort Albany and the camp which the 39th Mass. reg. had left. Saw only one man of Co. K. whom I knew, his name Ingerson of North Woburn.[13] Also saw a man in 14th reg. whom I knew. By the kindness of corporal of the guard visited the interior of the fort. It was very beautiful and neat. It contained a well and 3 months rations for the garrison. The armament consists of 12 or 15 guns, siege, garrison and field, one 24 lb. Parrott. Got back to camp about 2. Sent the knapsacks away. Received orders to keep 5 day's rations on hand. Probably move soon.[14]

SEPTEMBER 18TH, THURSDAY.
Had a good wash. Very warm. On guard, 2nd relief, for missing 12 o'clock roll call the preceding day. Countersign was Grodnow.

SEPTEMBER 19TH, FRIDAY.
Received a letter from brother Nate and also one from Sammy. The former contained Nate's picture. Also received a Journal.

SEPTEMBER 20TH, SATURDAY.
Borrowed a horse and rode over to Alexandria. Visited 33d. M. Vols. whose camp lay near our old camp of August 31st. Also visited 11th M.V. who were lying near to Fairfax Seminary. Had a very pleasant ride. Had a doctor join the battery and a new ambulance. In my excursion saw Fort Worth which lies near the Seminary and farther advanced than Fort Ellsworth.[15]

SEPTEMBER 21ST, SUNDAY.
Inspection in the morning. Beam's battery was also inspected by Capt. Bramhall acting as major.[16] We made a fine appearance with our new clothes. On water guard for missing roll call the preceding day. Got shaved again.

SEPTEMBER 22ND, MONDAY.
On sick list this day. Had no mail for three days.

SEPTEMBER 23D. TUESDAY.
Well again. Went out on drill as No. 7. A mail but no letter for me. Wrote to brother Nathan, yesterday to Sammy. Taken off my team and took Sergeant Bunting's horse to take care of.[17]

OCTOBER 1ST, WEDNESDAY.
Started about 9 o'clock for Bailey's Cross Roads where Gen. Birney's div. and the reserve artillery of the 3d Corps was to be reviewed.[18] Got into position action

front with four other batteries and directly in rear of 55th reg. N.Y.V. The battery on the left fired a salute and shortly after, Gens. Birney and Heintzelman came riding by. Afterwards the infantry wheeled by battalion front and passed in review followed by the batteries at decreased intervals. It was very dusty and warm. Saw more of the defenses of the Capital. Reached camp again between 1 and 2 with a voracious appetite. Received a Journal.

October 2nd, Thursday.
No drill. Cloudy. On guard 1st relief. No countersign. Capt. Bramhall returned from Rahway where he had gone two days before. He went home to get married.

October 3d, Friday.
Drill. Washed and changed clothes. Rice for dinner. In the afternoon went to Alexandria on horseback. Roads very dusty and the horse nearly throwed me three times. Visited John McDonald in the hospital. On my return visited camp of the 33d Mass. reg. and saw two E. Woburn boys, Coveny and Cogan.[19] Also visited 11th reg. A good breeze all day.

October 4th, Saturday.
No drill. Washed the guns and caissons preparatory to Sunday inspection. Quite windy. No mail. Received no letter this week.

October 5th, Sunday.
Ten months from home. Quite cool but dusty. Inspection. Saw Johnny Sullivan of Woburn.[20] Rumors of moving camp.

October 6th, Monday.
Quite cold last night. Did not sleep very comfortably. Drew nine new horses and a new caisson from the Washington arsenal.[21] At retreat roll-call received orders to harness and hitch. Marched and reached Bailey's Cross Roads about midnight. Unharnessed and laid down to sleep.

October 7th, Tuesday.
Harnessed again at two and after waiting a couple of hours started once more. The force consisted of our battery and a number of cavalry regiments. The country is very hilly but the roads good. The moon was at the full and the sky cloudless. A very pleasant night march. The country along our route was very picturesque. The houses appeared much the worse for the war, many being burnt or otherwise destroyed. About 7 o'clock we arrived at Fairfax where we made a short halt. The town of Fairfax Court House is an ancient but dilapidated little place and at this time swarming with Dutch soldiers and sutlers. About noon arrived in Centreville which is very strongly fortified. Stopped here to feed and rest a little. After resting, the column moved on by way of Bull Run and Manassas Junction. Crossed Bull Run. Very hilly in this neighborhood. Between Bull Run and Manassas Junction there were many fortifications. The road all

along showed the evidence of the late battles. All the houses were dismantled and deserted. At the railroad junction we again stopped for a short rest. The remnants of engines and cars were scattered all around. This neighborhood was very strongly fortified. I saw a house with "Union Hotel" painted on the side, but the "Union" had been painted over. Continued on march until 8 in the evening when we reached Brentville a little town situated on a high hill. Here we unhitched for a short time. The cavalry went a-foraging being short of feed. One of them going into a garden to get hay, the secesh lady of the house came out with a gun and threatened his life. He drew a revolver and the woman drew in her horns. The cavalry fairly swarmed about the stack and in a few minutes the hay had all disappeared. And this wasn't the only one that was served in the same way.

October 8th, Wednesday.
Harnessed at 1 o'clock and moved on. Stopped at daylight to feed and have coffee. Continued the march with frequent stoppages to allow the advance to scour the country until about noon. Marched this day through a portion of the famous Shenandoah Valley. Many of the views were very beautiful, of mingled grove and field, all of them edged by the frame of the blue ridge; which is *blue* indeed. At about noon we had arrived within five miles of the Rappahannock. I learned that the cavalry of our advance had burned the railroad bridge at Shenandoah station, this having been the object of the expedition. Here we turned back and at about 4 camped for the night in a large open field. The battery formed in echelon. The cavalry camped all around us and threw out pickets. Got a lot of nice apples and a persimmon or two.

October 9th, Thursday.
Rose and resumed marching at two. Found more persimmons and a kind of fruit called paupaws (don't know whether I spell it right or not.) They are shaped something like a banana only shorter and thicker. They taste something like a banana also, although not so good. They have large seeds some of which I preserved. Reached Brentville again shortly before noon and halted to feed. While resting here, heard that our cavalry had scattered some of the enemy who hung on our rear and flank. From here we returned to Manassas Junction by a different route from that we came, bearing more to the left and avoiding many hills. Saw at the Junction or rather a little below it the remains of many cars that had been burned, and the car wheels had been left standing on the rails. From here we passed on over the same road we came through Bull Run to Centreville. At the latter place learned that the rebels had sent a large force to flank us by way of Thoroughfare Gap but were deterred by a large force which was turned out at Centreville to meet them. From here the captain rode back to camp (18 miles) to order feed and rations for us, and also to send up the blacksmiths, many of the horses having lost shoes. Here we camped for the night just outside the town. The horses were pretty well exhausted having within 66 hours marched over 100 miles. The men were pretty well used up also. The cavalry gave us great praise

for the manner in which we had followed them, saying they had never had even a flying battery do the like. It was a welcome rest.[22]

OCTOBER 10TH, FRIDAY.
Slept rather late. The wagons arrived early with rations and forage, also the blacksmiths and forge. Borrowed a dollar of Griffin and with him went up into the town to buy some victuals. Bought some pies, cake and bologna sausage, also cider and lemonade. Returned to camp and at 4 o'clock the battery started for camp. Rode part of the way between Centreville and Fairfax with old darkey who was going to the latter place to draw bread for the 13 N.Y. Battery. Some of our fellows tried to steal some chickens on the way but were tackled by a man, woman, and a big dog, quite a laughable scene. Just before entering Fairfax Lieut. Martin halted to view a sham picket fight between two regiments. It was a fine sight. Bought some cider at Fairfax. Reached camp at about midnight. Found a letter from Myra and one from mother waiting me.

OCTOBER 17TH, FRIDAY.
Received a letter from Myra, one from brother Nate and one from Hero, also a paper. Changed my clothes. The left section went out and were reviewed by Gen. Sickles. The whole battery did not go out because the horses were in such poor condition that there were not enough to drag the whole battery. In the afternoon I took a ride over to the 9th Mass. Battery, which lay near Fort Albany. Quite a pleasant little canter.

OCTOBER 18TH, SATURDAY.
On guard, 3d relief. Chas. Morrell formerly of our battery, who fell sick about the same time with brother Appleton, visited camp.[23]

OCTOBER 19TH, SUNDAY.
Fair and cool. Shower in evening. Wrote to Myra.

OCTOBER 20TH, MONDAY.
Cold and blustering in the morning. Took a pleasant canter over to Fort Albany with Ed Marsh.[24]

OCTOBER 21ST, TUESDAY.
Very cold. Washed the carriages preparatory to review the next day.

OCTOBER 22ND, WEDNESDAY.
Very blustering. Rode over to Gen. Sickles' head-quarters with Charley De Voe.[25] Saw the place picked out for our winter quarters. Rode up to Fairfax Seminary, which consists of a number of handsome brick buildings. It was at this time used as a hospital. Besides there were many long, white-washed wooden buildings built on the grounds for the same purpose, also some in the process of building. In one corner of the graveyard were the graves of those who died in the hospital,

a sad commentary on the rebellion. It was a theological seminary and previous to the war had over 250 students. Received a letter from Myra. The battery was reported unfit for service and so did not go to the review.

OCTOBER 23D AND 24TH.
Cold and windy. Got a "True Flag".

OCTOBER 25TH, SATURDAY.
Warmer than the previous days. Wrote to Myra. On stable guard. Got news that we were to be turned over to flying artillery. I don't like the plan.

OCTOBER 26TH, SUNDAY.
On guard, 3d relief. Rainy, windy and very cold. Guard duty very unpleasant. My overcoat got wet through and so did my boots. My post was on the officers' tents. Lieut. Martin reprimanded me.

OCTOBER 27TH, MONDAY.
Stopped raining just after daylight. I took Bishop's horse out and run him bareback 'til my backside was sore.[26] The U.S. inspector visited us and inspected the harness &c. Very cold all day. Built a large fire in front of our tent. Got some persimmons.

NOVEMBER 2D, SUNDAY.
Warm. Distribution of horses. My horse was a very large sorrel, 28th choice.

NOVEMBER 3D, MONDAY.
Reveille earlier than usual. At 7 o'clock started for Washington. Took all the guns and the horses and harnesses of the caissons, cannoniers mounted bareback on their own horses. Went by way of the famous long bridge. Went through the city to the arsenal which is close to the Potomac. There we received new sights for the guns and some new wheels, new harnesses for the team horses, and McClellan saddles and equipments for the cannoniers. Had a good opportunity to view the arsenal, not getting away 'til 4 in the afternoon. Saw there all varieties of weapons from a revolver to a 15 inch mortar. Also saw some old guns taken from the Mexicans and British, also a 12 pds howitzer that was at the battle of Palo Alto, Resaca de la palma, and Monterey. Coming back we paraded through Pennsylvania Av. We passed close by the Washington monument. Very cold and windy, and coming back we had to wait on the bridge the draw being off. There the wind pierced us to the marrow. Returned by way of Arlington, and reached camp about 7 in the evening. Fed horses and got some salt junk and coffee. Found I was on guard 1st relief. Piercing cold.

NOVEMBER 4TH, TUESDAY.
Weather moderated during the night. All received revolvers and belts. The number of mine was 68,749. Made some little alterations about my saddle, so that I

shall be ready for a move. 24 rounds of cartridge were given out to each and we were ordered to load our pistols. Captain's wife visited camp. Orders were read for a review by the Captain the succeeding Thursday.

NOVEMBER 10TH, MONDAY.
Warm once more. Broke camp at one in the afternoon and moved to Arlington. Camped just below Fort Albany near the long bridge and about a mile from Washington. On guard, 1st relief.

NOVEMBER 11TH., TUESDAY.
Very cold last night sleeping on the ground. The captain's wife visited camp. Griffin and I built a bed of oak saplings. Drilled in the afternoon by the captain and his wife in cavalry movements.

NOVEMBER 12TH, WEDNESDAY.
Slept more comfortably. Battery drill in the forenoon and afternoon both, Mrs. Bramhall present. Rations short. Bean porridge for dinner.

NOVEMBER 13TH, THURSDAY.
This camp was named "Camp Lathrop" after the inspector general of 3d army corps. Battery drill in forenoon. Flying artillery drill is much more arduous than that of light battery. In the afternoon Griffin & I took a ride up to Fort Craig to visit his cousin.[27] Beef steak for dinner. Had quite an audience at our drill in forenoon.

NOVEMBER 14TH, FRIDAY.
Battery drill in forenoon, Mrs. Bramhall present. Exercise in the afternoon at jumping horses. My horse is not a very good jumper.

NOVEMBER 15TH, SATURDAY.
No drill. Went down to the Potomac to wash the carriages. Our gun run against a stump and Furbush, who was driving the pole team, was thrown off and came near being killed. Washed and greased my saddle and equipments. On a detail to put up harness racks. A very busy day.

NOVEMBER 16TH, SUNDAY.
On guard, 1st relief. Trial of skill with revolvers with the guard. I did not hit the target, but I made by no means the worst shot. Inspection by the captain at 10 o'clock. Guard duty very dismal.

NOVEMBER 17TH, MONDAY.
Dull and cloudy. No drill in consequence. Visited Fort Tillinghast and saw Wm. Cobbett of 14th M.V. Had some apples from home which were very delicious. Tried to find two of my cousins who were in this reg. but did not succeed. Boiled rice for dinner, miserable stuff. Received a letter from Myra.

November 18th, Tuesday.
Rainy and no drill. Found and visited Fort De Kalb where were my two cousins Edwin and John Henry Smith of Ipswich.[28] Saw numerous other forts in my ride viz. Haggerty, Corcoran, Bennett, Cass, &c &c. Found two acquaintances from So. Reading in Fort Albany. Had a little fight with Leonard about the forge.[29]

November 27th, Thursday.
Thanksgiving. No duty but guard duty this day. First day of my return to duty. On guard, 1st relief. In the morning target practice for prizes. Prizes as follows: 1st, 1 box cigars, won by E. Marsh; 2nd, a five dollar treasury note, to E.M. Rake; 3d, a pair of pants; 4th, one blanket; 5th, one blanket.[30] I didn't hit the target as usual. The officers treated the company to oyster stew for dinner and ale. It tasted delicious. Cousin Edwin Smith from Fort De Kalb came down and took dinner with me. In the afternoon was a sack race for a barrel of apples. Won by A.T. Cole.[31] It was a most laughable affair. A fine day. Quite a Thanksgiving.

December 5th, Friday.
One year from home. It seems a much shorter period, in fact the shortest year I ever remember. Fed and cleaned my horse very early and started for Alexandria to carry his horse to Capt. Bramhall. Went into Adam's Express office. Run my horse a great portion of the way back so that when I got back to camp he was all of a reeking sweat. Rubbed my horse down and soon after it commenced to rain which turned into snow. Snowed all the rest of the day. Bill Cobbett from Fort Tillinghast visited and took dinner with me. Beef steak for dinner. Wrote to Myra. Very cold.

December 6th, Saturday.
Snowed most of the last night, depth about 3 inches. Very cold. No drill or anything but camp duty. Potomac frozen over.

December 7th, Sunday.
Very cold and windy. Visited Bill Cobbett at Fort Tillinghast and got some baked beans, 1st time since leaving Budd's Ferry. No inspection. Letter from Myra and a pamphlet from Sammy.

December 8th, Monday.
Still cold. No drill. Went up to Gen. Heintzelman's headquarters to get the passes. Got a pass to go to Washington and went over with the ordnance wagon to get my barrel and anything else for the battery that might be at the express office. Went over by way of the aqueduct bridge which crosses at Georgetown. The bridge was originally built for a canal since discontinued. Georgetown appeared to me much more of a business place than its neighbor the capital. Got my barrel and brought it home to find it filled with all sorts of delicacies sent from the old Bay State. Found nothing spoiled. Grew warmer toward night.

December 9th, Tuesday.

Weather more moderate. Muddy. Feast day with me. Bill Cobbett and two of his friends from the fort visited and took dinner with me.

December 10th, Wednesday.

Warmer. Most of the snow melted away. Exercised the horses in the forenoon, but in the afternoon was eating my dinner so that I could not go. May get punished. Beef steak and potatoes for dinner. Letter and picture from Sammy. It was a splendid likeness. Rumors prevalent of our joining Gen. Burnside. Wrote to Myra.

December 11th, Thursday.

Fair and sunny, but very muddy. Exercised the horses.

December 12th, Friday.

Quite warm. Ransom visited me. Reported marching order on the morrow.

CHAPTER 4

THE BULLETS BEGAN TO WHIZ
ABOUT OUR EARS:
DECEMBER 1862–JUNE 1863

HAVING MISSED SECOND MANASSAS AND SHARPSBURG, THE SIXTH NEW York next escaped participating in the Battle of Fredericksburg. Ultimately, the battery received orders to report to the Army of the Potomac but did not leave its Washington encampment until the morning of December 13, when the contest along the Rappahannock was just getting under way.

The army that the Sixth New York marched to rejoin was different from the one that turned back the Army of Northern Virginia at Sharpsburg. President Lincoln had at last lost patience with General McClellan's lack of aggressiveness and sacked him on November 7, replacing him as army commander with Maj. Gen. Ambrose Burnside. The new commander acted with speed and decisiveness, promptly moving the army to Falmouth, across the river from Fredericksburg. Unfortunately for the Union cause, poor planning and woefully inadequate command leadership at the highest levels of the army dashed the bright hopes with which the campaign began, and the army suffered another crushing and bloody defeat. By the time the battery arrived at the Falmouth camps on December 18, it was already three days after the army had abandoned its lodgments on the Fredericksburg side of the river and retreated to Falmouth.

Nevertheless, it was not until the failure of the notorious January 19–24 "mud march," with which Burnside had hoped to retrieve the strategic advantage, that the president again relieved the commanding general. This time, he picked Major General Hooker to command the Army of the Potomac.

General Hooker at once began instituting a series of reforms, which markedly increased the morale and efficiency of his army. Two of these changes directly affected the Sixth New York: namely, the creation of a cavalry corps out of the several divisions and brigades that had been previously parceled out to the various infantry corps and grand divisions of the army and the brigading of horse artillery batteries in order to better support the reorganized cavalry. In addition to these welcome organizational changes, the commanding general made it abundantly clear that he expected aggressive action and battle successes from his horse soldiers and their artillery supports. These and other reforms initially seemed to bear fruit in the March 17 battle of Kelly's Ford, in which the cavalry arm showed aggression and stiffness in action against their southern opponents and in the promising beginning of the Chancellorsville Campaign in late April and early May. Once again, however, at Chancellorsville serious command failures on the Union side resulted in another severe defeat at the hands of Robert E. Lee. This time, the Sixth New York did not sit on the sidelines but was in the thick of the action in both battles.

The highlights of this chapter are Perkins's observations and reflections concerning camp life near Fredericksburg, the reorganization of the Army of the Potomac under General Hooker (including the formation of the First Horse Artillery Brigade), the battle of Kelly's Ford, and the Chancellorsville Campaign. After a one-year hiatus, Perkins resumed his correspondence with his hometown newspaper, the *Middlesex Journal,* and freely reported on the activities of the battery and his views on the issues of the day. In so doing, he offered a strong endorsement of General Hooker's leadership and character.

Other subjects covered are the resignation of the battery's commanding officer and his replacement by the senior first lieutenant, as well as a review of the army by President Lincoln. The diary describes the severe winter weather and its effect on camp living conditions, military movements, and the resupply of the army. Perkins describes the efforts to maintain a logistical flow over the extremely muddy roads leading from the Hope Landing base on Aquia Creek. He also reports the use of fatigue details, extra guard duty, and punishments such as spread-eagling on the extra caisson wheel to enforce and maintain discipline. Perkins himself committed various minor offenses against army discipline and was regularly subjected to these measures. The chapter ends with a description of his five-day furlough to Woburn and his return to duty while the battery was involved in the cavalry action at Brandy Station.

George's diary remarks for January 6–10, January 27–February 2, February 10–12, and February 24–March 11 have been omitted. The entries dwelled on the miserable weather, guard duty, occasional artillery drills, and the atrocious roads. The roads evidently were so bad that wagons could not maintain a sufficient flow of supplies between the logistics bases on Potomac and Aquia creeks and the army camps.

Several times George was pressed into service to take his horse to the Hope Landing logistics base to retrieve needed fodder for the battery horses. George also recorded his choice of reading material: *Wagner the Wehr-Wolf,* by G.W.M. Reynolds; *Aurora Floyd,* by Mary Elizabeth Braddon; and *Pirates of the Prairies,* by Gustave Aimard.

December 13th, Saturday.

Started and moved camp at about 9 o'clock. Crossed to Washington by way of long bridge. Waited some time close to the capitol. From Washington we marched over the same road we went a year ago in going to Budd's Ferry. Report that we were going to the same place this time. Passed by the lunatic asylum and toward night camped in the same place we did Dec. 8th, 1861 and where I gained my first experience of camping out. A year ago on this road poor App was with me, now he is not and has returned to original dust.

Slept on the tarpaulin without any cover. Great deal of whiskey in camp. Weather remarkably fine for the time of year.

December 14th, Sunday.

Rose before light and after the usual morning duties continued the march. Was detailed with five others as a sort of advance guard at each house on the road to prevent the boys from getting whiskey. After the battery passed they rejoined the advance. Passed through the little village of Piscataway. Stopped for a short time at a Roman Catholic chapel.[1] The priest was sermonizing, a very fine looking man. He was dressed in a white surplice trimmed with red and yellow.

Camped on a low piece of ground which could not be far from our camp of Dec. 9th, 1861. Weather fine.

December 15th, Monday.

Started again about 9. Marched over poor roads and reached Camp Dickinson, our last winter's quarters. On the way some of the fellows captured pigs. Griffin and I foraged in advance of the battery and at some negro quarters got some corn bread and meat.

December 16th, Tuesday.

Did not spread our tarpaulin the preceding night but laid on it. About 3 in the morning it commenced to rain quite heavily but I slept snugly for all that. Rose early in the morning with wet feet and drenched blankets. Bill and I went foraging and got 5 chickens, which we picked. Three we cooked and saved the other two for another time. Potato stew for dinner. We stole the fowls from a house where they had the small pox. Ceased raining about 10. Recommenced the march immediately after dinner. I was detailed on wagon guard. Roads very rough. Reached Liverpool point an hour before dark and camped where the 5th Reg. Ex. brig. did last year. Very cold during the march.

December 17, Wednesday.
Slept very well last night. Early we saddled and went down to the landing where the battery was put aboard two ferry boats "The Eagle" and "The Star". It took about an hour to ferry us across to Acquia creek which is about 5 miles below Liverpool point. Got off the boat and laid on the shore long enough to draw rations and forage. It was bitter cold and as we commenced to move it began to snow. We moved about 3 miles into the interior of the country and camped for the night close by the Acquia creek and Richmond R.R. Cooked the two remaining chickens and invited Lieut. Martin to sup with us. They were not hardly done enough.

December 18, Thursday.
Slept cold last night. Started again about 9. Roads frozen and very rough. One of the wagons upset. Towards noon began to arrive among troops and at two camped in the edge of some pine woods near to Burnside's headquarters. Close by lay two other flying batteries. We were placed on the reserve. Bloody cold and was on guard. Had a bad cold for three days. Took some medicine.

December 19th, Friday.
Slept very poorly last night, my cold bothered me. Took more medicine. Still very cold. General cleaning up of saddles, harness, &c. Sudden orders came for an inspection and we were inspected by Major Hunt, chief of artillery.[2] No feed for the horses.

December 20th, Saturday.
Colder than yesterday. Fixed our tarpaulin so it would be warmer. Detailed in the afternoon with five others to build a log house for chief of reserve artillery, but as we could get no axes came back again.[3] My cold still very troublesome.

December 21st, Sunday.
The usual Sunday morning inspection, but not mounted. Wrote to Myra. Very cold.

December 22nd, Monday.
Warmer. Washed the guns and caissons. Got a pass in the afternoon and visited the 1st brigade of Hooker's old div. Saw many of my acquaintances from Woburn and So. Reading.

December 23d, Tuesday.
On guard, 1st relief. The right section turned out in a body and logged up Lieut. Martin's tent, I among the rest. Much milder.

December 24th, Wednesday.
Got a pass and rode over to visit 32nd, & 22nd Mass. Vols. in Griffin's Div. Saw all the Woburn boys. Took dinner with Capt. Crane of the 22nd.[4] Saw Gen.

Hooker. Overstayed my pass 4 hours. On guard tomorrow I suppose. Weather still growing warmer.

DECEMBER 25TH, THURSDAY.
Christmas. Quite warm. Helped Kiely build his log house.[5] On guard, 3d relief. Commenced to cut logs for a house of my own.

DECEMBER 26TH, FRIDAY.
Continued working on my house. Took Bob Fowle in as partner.[6] Letter from Myra and one from Sammy. Ordered to pack knapsacks in order to move. Destination by some supposed to be Brook's Station and by others Washington. Still very mild. Looked like rain.

DECEMBER 27TH, SATURDAY.
Did not move. Detailed to work on log house at headquarters. Worked in forenoon but in afternoon went down to the Rappahannock. Saw Fredericksburgh

Capt. John P. Crane, Twenty-second Massachusetts Volunteer Infantry. Courtesy of Massachusetts Commandery, Military Order of the Loyal Legion and U.S. Army Military History Institute.

which seemed but little the worse for the shelling it suffered. Opposite the city the river is very narrow and shallow. Could see the rebel pickets. The bridges (two) were destroyed. Could see on the hills back of the city the rebel earth works. Got back too late for roll-call.

December 28th, Sunday.
Inspection by Lieut. Brown. On guard, 1st relief for missing roll-call yesterday. Got kicked on the foot.

December 29th, Monday.
Quite warm. Did not go out on a pass because of my kick.

December 30th, Tuesday.
Colder. On guard, 2nd relief. Orders came in to hold ourselves in readiness to move at a moment's notice.

December 31st, Wednesday.
Cold and cloudy. A mounted inspection of the battery by Lieut. French of the regular army, also mustered by the pay-roll.[7]

January 1st, 1863 Thursday.
Cold and clear. A very restless day with me. A very poor dinner, viz. desiccated vegetables boiled with salt horse. Wished for roast pork and apple sauce with boiled apple pudding.

January 2nd, Friday.
Warm again. Battery drill in forenoon, Lieut. French present. Poorest drill we ever had. Built a bed. Wrote to brother Sammy.

January 3rd, Saturday.
Very fine. Cleaned and oiled the carriages. Boiled rice for dinner.

January 4th, Sunday.
On guard, 2nd relief. On the officers' tents where only is guard in day time. Consequently did only 4 hours guard duty. Beans for dinner.

January 5th, Monday.
Got a pass from 9-12 but overstaid it 2 hours. On guard tomorrow I suppose. Visited the camp of 1st Mass. Cavalry at Potomac station distance 4 miles. Saw many friends from So. Reading. Weather the finest I ever saw in Jan.

January 11th, Sunday.
Fair again. No inspection. On detail in forenoon to build a forage house. Corneil Miller and I commenced a log house.[8] Worked hard all day. My horse taken sick.

January 12th, Monday.
Continued working on my house. Weather fair.

JANUARY 13TH, TUESDAY.
On a detail in the forenoon for cleaning the stables which were very nasty because of the recent rains. Worked all my leisure time upon my log house. Moved into it although not quite finished. Wrote to Myra's father. Weather fair.

JANUARY 14TH, WEDNESDAY.
Cloudy. On guard, 2nd relief, post the guns. Found enough about my house to busy me all my leisure time this day, principally about the fire-place. Received a letter from Myra. Wrote to Myra.

JANUARY 15TH, THURSDAY.
High wind all day, almost blew the roof off our house.

JANUARY 16TH, FRIDAY.
Rained hard the past night. Letter from Mother and Sammy. Wrote to Mother and a note to Mrs. Macfarlane. Received orders to pack knapsacks and roll our blankets in readiness to move, did not move however. Wrote to Sammy. Quite cold.

JANUARY 17TH, SATURDAY.
Very cold, and kept a blazing fire all day. Did not move this day either. My horse still very sick. Wrote to Myra. Signed the pay-roll for 4 mo's viz. July, Aug., Sept., & Oct. Signed after dark at the 7 o'clock roll-call.

JANUARY 18TH, SUNDAY.
Still cold. No pay this day.

JANUARY 19TH, MONDAY.
Freezing weather. A letter from Myra. Wrote to Myra.

JANUARY 20TH, TUESDAY.
Cloudy. Received orders once more to hold ourselves in readiness to move. Large bodies of infantry moving already. Got another horse to take care of. Just after dark the paymaster, Maj. Webb came into camp and after signing one more pay-roll we were paid for 6 months up to Jan. 1863. I gave $70 to U. Freeman to send home.[9] Detailed with three others to escort the paymaster to the headquarters of 2nd Jersey brigade. As it had commenced to rain and the wind was high it was a very unpleasant job. Paper from home.

JANUARY 21ST, WEDNESDAY.
Rained all night and flooded our log house. Rained all day. Was very thankful we were not called on to march. Paid my debts generally.

JANUARY 22ND, THURSDAY.
Rained all night and all day. Truly dismal weather, just the kind to disgust one with soldiering. Wrote to Myra. Bought some eatables at very high prices.

January 23d, Friday.
Misty and foggy. On guard, 1st relief. Great portion of the army in returning to their former quarters passed by our camp.

January 24th, Saturday.
Fair again. Did some repairing about our house. Went over to the sutler's and bought a dinner of soda biscuit and butter. Wrote to Myra. Considerable whiskey in camp and quite a serious disturbance occurred in the left section. One man got his nose broken. I did not drink. Played chess with Griffin.

January 25th, Sunday.
Fair and sunny. Received a "Journal" from brother John, and three "True Flags" from Myra. Drew from government a pair of pants, pair of boots pegged, and an artillery jacket. I turned in a blouse.

January 26th, Monday.
Fair. Gen. Hooker takes command of the army of the Potomac.

February 3d, Tuesday.
Woke up and found it very cold and trying to snow but did not succeed because of the cold. Letter from brother Nate. Had my horse's hind foot shod, and it was a difficult job. He broke away from me 3 times. Engaged all day in reading "The Children of the Abbey" by Maria Roche. Orders for an inspection next day by Col. De Russy.

February 4th, Wednesday.
Bitter cold all day on account of which the inspection was postponed 'til next day at 11 o'clock. On guard, 1st relief.

February 5th, Thursday.
Commenced to snow about 5 in the morning and continued 'til afternoon when it turned to rain. No inspection because of the storm. Finished reading "Children of the Abbey". Received a paper from home. Wrote to brother Nate. Flapjacks for supper which were a great treat.

February 6th, Friday.
Rained all the previous night and all the day 'til towards night when it cleared off. Letters from Myra and A.H.R. Wrote to Myra.

February 7th, Saturday.
Fair. Detailed to bury horses at headquarters.[10] Fresh bread one ration. Had liver for supper.

February 8th, 1863.
In camp near Fredericksburgh, Va. On guard, 2nd. relief. Inspection of horses and harnesses by Lieut. Martin, the Capt. being absent on furlough. Miller

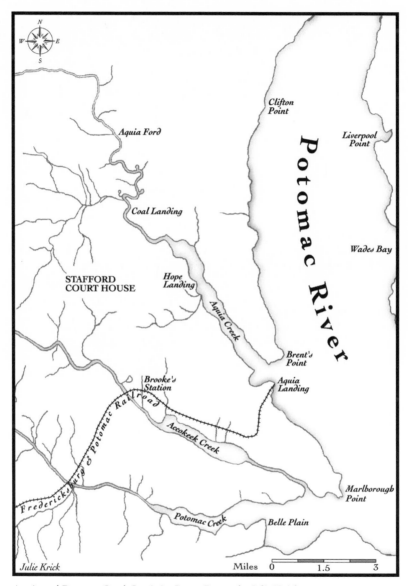

Aquia and Potomac Creek Logistics Bases. Drawn by Julie Krick.

my tent-mate got up a pot-pie for dinner. Visited 11th Mass. reg. in afternoon. Thawed all day, very muddy.

FEBRUARY 9TH, MONDAY.
Warm and runny. Received a pamphlet and some paper and envelopes from home. Mounted inspection by Capt. Robinson.[11] Griffin and I visited his brother

who was clerk in the commissary dept. in Franklin's Corps d'Armee. Roads were horribly muddy. Wrote to Myra.

FEBRUARY 13TH, FRIDAY.
Staid up all the preceding night. Came off guard at 4 in the afternoon. Found Jesse Richardson in camp and he staid with me this night.[12]

FEBRUARY 14TH, SATURDAY.
Kiely did my police duty for me at head-quarters and I got a pass and went with Jesse back to his reg. (2nd Mass.) and also visited 10th Maine. Had a fine time. Jesse got some oats for my horses. Staid with Leonard all night. Saw three of my cousins viz. Leonard and William Jordan, the latter a Capt., and Charley Greene.[13]

FEBRUARY 15TH, SUNDAY.
Rained 'til noon when it cleared off and I started for camp with Jimmy Goodwin and Mr. Rowen both of whom I found down there. Got to camp just in time for retreat. Found a letter waiting for me from Uncle Hero. Wrote to Aunt Lizzie.

FEBRUARY 16TH, MONDAY.
Weather fine. Received orders to gather 11 other cannoniers to pack up and saddle up in order to go down to the vicinity of "Hope Landing" and make preparations for the battery, build a wharf &c.[14] Put my knapsack and blankets aboard the wagon which was to accompany us and we started. A similar detachment from 3 other horse batteries also came along. This move was made in consequence of the four flying batteries being brigaded together under command of Capt. Robinson and in order to the better obtain forage for our horses as we had not been able to get all the forage due us while in this camp.[15] In fact we did not get hay half the time. After advancing about a mile, the wagon got stuck and we were helped out by an obliging teamster. The horses were balky. My horse was put in the team in place of one particularly bad. Shortly after, the wagon stuck again and a man was sent back to camp for another horse, which arriving my horse was taken out and I had him to ride again. I had to lead the balky horse. After this we managed to pull through all other places 'til just before dark when we came to a place where a whole wagon train was stuck in the mud. As there was no possibility of getting ahead that night we camped in a little glade close by the road. Had some coffee and turned in, having just spread a tarpaulin to sleep on and built a large fire at our feet. During this day's march we came across some of Sigel's Corps drawn up in line to be inspected by Gen. Hooker. Distance of march, 8 miles.

FEB. 17TH, TUESDAY.
Woke up about 3 and found it storming. Drew the top of the 'paulin over our heads and bodies, and covered our feet with a poncho, then went to sleep again.

Woke up at daylight and found 3 inches of snow atop of us. N.B. Snow is a very warm coverlid. Snowed all day. We stayed here 'til we had cooked and eaten some stewed potatoes when we saddled up and went on again over the worst roads I ever saw. The lead horses of the wagon got mired once up to their bellies and we got stuck about every quarter of a mile. Finally we got stuck so that we had to send forward for assistance which came in the shape of a man and 2 horses. By this help we reached our destination where Gen. Pleasonton was going to establish his headquarters.[16] Here we came in sight of water, whether the Potomac or some creek I knew not. After waiting here in the pelting storm some time, orders came to leave the wagon and go forward. We turned to the right and went about 2 miles seemingly all the time up hill and through a heavily wooded country until we reached an open field on the top of a high hill where we found the captain with his tent pitched and one man for company. It seems he had come through with 2 wagons by a better road than the one we followed in the space of 3 hours. Never was there a more welcome sight than his face, a good fire, and rations which he had brought. Unsaddled and pitched the tarpaulins. Fed ourselves and horses. Built a large fire (wood in abundance here) and tried to make ourselves comfortable. The guard list was arranged so that each man would stand an hour in the course of the night. After my turn of guard I dried my feet and went to bed, blankets rather wet.

FEBRUARY 18TH, WEDNESDAY.
Woke up and found it had ceased snowing and was raining slowly. Washed and brought water to cook dinner. Half a dozen men were detailed to work on the road, luckily I was not one. Beans for dinner. I was engaged in writing this Journal when the captain sent for us all and telling us he had resigned bid us goodbye and went off. He said the reason of his resignation was certain troubles he had experienced lately. I had not had anything disturb me so for a long time. We lost a brave man, a good captain and withal a perfect gentleman. I was very sorry, as so were all my companions. Rained very hard in the afternoon.

FEB. 19TH, THURSDAY.
Cloudy. Got up quite late, and after taking coffee, saddled up and with three others went down to where we left the wagon on Tuesday. Returned to the hill again with the wagon. About noon another set of men came to relieve us and we set out on our return to camp which we reached about four. The roads were most horribly muddy. Lieut. Robling after an absence of 10 months returned to the battery. Lieut. Martin read Capt. Bramhall's farewell address to the battery at retreat roll-call. Most thankful was I to again return to my little shanty. Wrote to Myra.

FEB. 20TH, FRIDAY.
Cleaned myself and horse. Weather fine. Horse inspection. Did some sewing. Orders to move next day.

FEB. 21ST, SATURDAY.
My 22nd birthday and 2nd one passed in the U.S. service. I think that in the past year I can see some improvement in myself in that my mind seems to have greatly matured as well as my body. More true manliness I seem to have gained in this twelve-month than in all my previous life. May God grant me another birthday and time to carry out the plans for future life which I have this year formed. - - / Weather fine. Rose at five o'clock and packed up. Capt. Bramhall left us after shaking hands with each one. This is the severest loss the battery ever experienced. Started on the march just after daylight in company with 3 other flying batteries. After repeated sticks we managed to reach our camping ground about dark. Pitched ponchos, Griffin, Horne, Miller and I.[17] A letter from Myra, one from Sammy and one from Tim Adams. On guard, 3d relief.

FEB. 22ND, SUNDAY.
Commenced to snow during the night and continued all day. Woke up in the morning and found it had drifted in on our blankets considerably. Cold as Greenland. Built a large fire and by means of that and stirring about managed to keep up the circulation of blood. In the afternoon went to water in Acquia Creek and so warmed up both myself and horse.

FEB. 23D, MONDAY.
Myra's birthday. Would I were at home to honor the day. My little wife is 22 years old and nearly 2 years a wife. God bless my dear wife and preserve her for many more birthdays. - - Weather clear and cold. Miller and I cut logs to build another house. On a detail in the afternoon to put up harness racks. A pamphlet from home with paper and envelopes.

MAR. 12TH, THURSDAY.
Cold. Inspected by Lieut. Woodruffe, Inspector Gen. of the Brigade.[18] On detail to do some ditching.

MAR. 13TH & 14TH.
Cool and fair.

MAR. 15TH, SUNDAY.
Cold and cloudy. Some hail in the afternoon. Wrote to Gil. Adams & cousin Bethiah Kinsman. Went on guard at 6 o'clock, 1st relief.

MAR. 16TH, MONDAY.
While on guard from 12–2 an orderly rode into camp with orders to go out on an expedition at daybreak. Packed and saddled up and moved at daylight taking only the guns and 4 teams to each. I guided the battery to Stafford Court House where we arrived between 8 & 9. I rode over to the 10th Me. and saw my cousins. From there we were led by a cavalry-man over very muddy roads to Hartwood

church which we reached about 4 in the afternoon a distance of 15 miles. Here an escort of the 1st Mass. cavalry awaited us. We fed selves and horses and started on. Marched about 12 miles and reached a small village called Morriceville where many cavalry bivouacked. We unhitched, but did not unharness or unsaddle, fed our horses and laid down to try and sleep but did not succeed.

Mar. 17th, Tuesday.

St. Patrick's Day. Got up at 2 o' clock and fed. Moved on about 12 miles and just after sunrise reached the Rappahannock at Kelley's Ford. Here were about 75 rebs who disputed our passage from rifle pits on the other side. The ford was deep and swift. One of our guns got in position but did not fire. Some of our men dismounted and with their carbines covered the carbineers while they cleared away the felled trees on the banks, then our cavalry charged across the river and drove the rebels but not without a small loss. We captured some 30 or 40 rebels. The whole expedition crossed and we waited while the cavalry scouted. After a while we commenced to move forward when firing was heard at the front and some rebel cavalry made a charge. Our gun and three others went back to an open field while the other two went in battery on the open road and drove the rebels back. Shortly our section was ordered up on the right on the edge of an open field on the opposite edge of which I could see the rebel cavalry in force. We fired and finally routed them. We advanced across the field, now and then taking position, and into the woods beyond, when we heard firing again in front with shouts as if a charge was being made. Directly also the rebels opened with artillery and we were ordered up into position in a large field on our left. The rebel battery of 3 guns were about ½ mile distant and pegged away right merrily at us which we returned with rather poor effect though. Shortly the rebel cavalry charged us on our right and left flanks. Our cavalry support on the right broke and ran. Our gun broke up the charge with a round of canister and they retreated. On the left our cavalry stood firm and as the rebs got within about 20 yards set up a big shout and made a counter-charge. The rebs did not receive them but broke and ran. Our cavalry did not pursue but drew off and we poured in some case shot which completed their rout. After this as our shot began to grow scarce we were compelled to cease firing and for two hours lay still doing nothing, all the while that their artillery played all about us. We lost one man, killed by a solid shot instantly.[19] Finally we received orders to get canister in readiness as a charge was expected. Scarcely had we done this when orders came to limber up in retreat which we did and moved back in good order. The rebs redoubled their shots but to no avail. We reached the ford and crossed. Our gun was put in position to command the ford but as it got dark we limbered up and followed the rest of the guns in retreat. We left the ford at just after nightfall and reached Morriceville about 11 and after feeding laid down for a little sleep, which I managed to get. The object of this expedition was said to have been a raid on Culpepper, but it was found that the rebels were too thick on that road, so Gen. Averill who commanded the expedition determined to go through Rappahannock station and from there to Warrenton and home to Washington.[20] But as we made such poor shots thus wasting our ammunition we were not able to hold our ground or advance so we were obliged to retreat. Lieut. Martin had not yet returned from his furlough and so we had only 2 officers with us. If he had been there I feel that things would have been much different. Thus did we celebrate St. Patrick's Day.

Mar. 18th, Wednesday.
Resumed the march at daylight and about noon got within our outposts where we stopped to feed. Started on and in about 2 hours came in sight of encampment when I was sent to camp to tell the cooks to prepare a hearty meal for the fellows when the battery arrived. Unsaddled and fixed up the shanty. The sight of my little shanty was indeed most welcome. Corneil Miller my tent mate got a box from home and we had quite a nice supper.

Mar. 26th, Thursday.
Fatigue duty. Fair. Played chess. Letter from Myra with news of my parents' sickness.

Middlesex Journal, Saturday, April 4, 1863

Letter from the 6th N.Y. Battery.
Camp Bramhall, VA, Near Acquia Creek Landing
March 26th, 1863
    Dear Editor: —Taking courage from the consideration of the old adage that it is never too late to amend, I once more essay to inform you of the condition and whereabouts of the 6th Independent N.Y. Battery.
    Doubtless you were aware of our movements on the Peninsula the past season from other sources. After our return from that Golgotha, the battery was stationed until the middle of Dec. last, in the vicinity of Alexandria and Washington. During that time quite an important change was made in the complexion of the battery.
    In October, with a large force of cavalry, we assisted in a reconnaissance as far as the Rappahannock, and with such credit to ourselves as to induce the war department to change us to flying artillery. The difference between light and flying artillery lies only in the fact that in the latter the cannoniers are mounted, and the armament is somewhat lighter. Flying artillery is used almost altogether in conjunction with cavalry on reconnaissances, raids, &c.
    While the battle of Fredericksburg was raging, we were ordered down from Arlington, where we were camped for the purpose of drill at flying artillery tactics, as reinforcements for Gen. Burnside. We arrived just in time to be too late, as Paddy would say, and were included among the reserve

artillery of the Army of the Potomac. We were camped near Falmouth for two months, when we brigaded and moved to our present camp, which is situated on the south bank of Acquia Creek two miles from its mouth. Our brigade consists of four more batteries, all regulars but ours, and is termed 1st Brigade of Horse Artillery.

During the past month the battery has experienced an almost irreparable loss in the resignation of Capt. Bramhall, who had commanded us for 13 mos. The battery has lost in him not only an able captain, but also a most sincere friend. He was a thorough artillerist, a *gentleman,* and a kind commander. He was what a citizen soldier should be.

1st Lieut. J.W. Martin now commands, and beyond a doubt will receive shortly his commission as captain. It is reported that Jas. E. Tileston, of Woburn, now 1st Sergeant, will be promoted to the vacant lieutenancy. He well deserves it, for he has always held the arduous office of orderly not only with credit to himself and justice to the men, but also with popularity.

Ours has been a somewhat inactive career for the past four months, which was suddenly broken in upon during last week by an expedition against the rebs., terminating in quite a fight at Kelley's Ford, on the Rappahannock. Our force consisted of about 6000 cavalry, including a small body of the 1st Mass, and the 6th N.Y. Battery. We started from camp with no cassions [*sic*] on the morning of Mar. 16th. Marched steadily until 4 o'clock in the afternoon, when we reached the outposts and stopped to feed without unsaddling. From there we advanced rapidly for six hours, the roads being good, a distance of about 12 miles, and bivouacked for the night: orders not to unsaddle.

Continued the route next morning at 8 o'clock, and after a march of 12 miles, reached the Rappahannock at Kelly's Ford. Here a small body of rebels from rifle pits on the other bank disputed our passage, but after two unsuccessful attempts, our cavalry finally managed to cross in the face of their fire, and compelled them to run. We took here 24 prisoners. They were much better dressed than any I had before seen, and were fine looking men.

The ford is deep and swift, and it took some time to cross, but which being accomplished we pushed on and shortly came upon the enemy, cavalry, on the edge of a large field. It seems they nearly surprised us, and, charging, broke our cavalry. Two of our guns went into action right in the road, and quickly routed the enemy. Whereupon our cavalry forming again, charged, and drove them clear across the field to the woods on the other side. Meanwhile two more of our guns, on one of which I worked, coming into action on the right, finished their discomfiture, and the rebs disappeared in the woods beyond the field. Slowly we made our way across the field, frequently taking position to guard against surprise.

We entered the wood beyond, when shots were heard, then a volley. Directly we heard the roar of rebel artillery, and we were ordered up double quick. Coming up we debouched on the left into a large open field, and took position.

At first we banged away at the battery, but seemingly, with little effect. At length the rebel cavalry gathering courage for a final effort, charged our battery on both flanks. We loaded with cannister [*sic*], and then I had full opportunity to watch the progress of events.

Those on our left came thundering down with drawn sabre, and yelling like fiends, until within about 20 yds. of our support, which setting up a return shout, made a countercharge. Just as the rebels on our left broke before the onset of our cavalry, their retreat hastened by a few case shot, my attention was called to the right, where the enemy were coming down in a compact mass. Our cavalry wavered. The command came to fire, and our gun poured in its iron hail of canister with such effect as to completely break and rout them. They retreated in great disorder.

Our ammunition began to get low, as we only had 50 rounds to each gun, therefore we were compelled to fire only at intervals, till at last we lay perfectly still, serving as a mark for the rebel artillery. Thus we remained for two hours, when came orders to retreat. We limbered up and moved back in good order. The rebels did not think best to pursue, and at nightfall we were all safely back from the ford. The succeeding night we reached camp again, and the sight of our "shanties" was quite pleasant to our returning eyes.

This is claimed to be the greatest cavalry fight in which the Army of the Potomac has been engaged. In many instances happened hand to hand conflicts, and many were wounded by the sabre. Casualties in the battery—one man killed, a native of N.Y.; one wheel stove by a round shot, and two or three horses lost or killed.

HOPLITE

Sat. 28th March.

Rainy. Played chess. Wrote to Myra. Played cribbage. Did not hear stable call in the morning and was put on guard for late attendance at the same. Letter from Aunt Lizzie and one from my wife. The former contained picture of my aunt and my cousin Martha. The latter brought news of my father's probably mortal illness. Troubles never come single handed. I asked Lieut. Martin for a furlough and he said it was impossible unless I could induce some one, who had the promise of one, to give way in my favor. Frank Mann promised if the case were as urgent when his furlough came due he would do so.[21] God bless him for a generous youth.

29th Mar. Sunday.

Cold and clear. Inspection by Lieut. Martin. I had to harness and hitch a pole team for the occasion. Jesse Richardson of 2nd Mass. reg. visited our camp. Came off guard at 6. Wrote to Myra.

MAR. 30TH, MONDAY.
Fair and sunny. Brigade inspection by Capt. Robinson, brigade commander.
Fatigue duty.

MAR. 31ST, TUESDAY.
Commenced snowing during the night and snowed or rained all day. Wrote
to Aunt Lizzie. Telegram from home of father's sickness. Showed it to Lieut.
Martin who told me no more furloughs were to be granted. I never shall see my
father again probably. If it were possible to desert I would.

APR. 1ST, WEDNESDAY.
Fair. On guard.

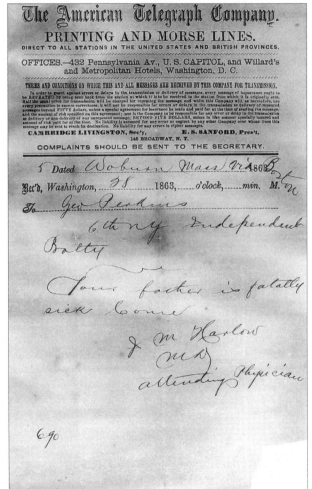

Telegram from
home. Griffin
Family Collection.

Apr. 2nd, Thursday.

Came off guard at 6. Drew two pair of socks.

Apr. 3d, Friday.

Very warm and sunny. Not very smart all day. On detail to load rations into the wagon at headquarters. Guns went off with the non-commissioned officers for target practice but were forbid by Gen. Pleasonton.

Apr. 4th, Saturday.

Cold and windy. Got a pass but did not go out of camp. Lay abed most all day. Order for review next day by President Lincoln.

Apr. 5th, Sunday.

Reveille at 4. Got up and found it snowing, in consequence of which the review was postponed. J.R. Furbush went home on a furlough and I accompanied him to the landing in order to bring back his horse. Sent home a blanket and pair of spurs by him. My horse fell down, threw me off, and rolled on me. Fortunately it did not hurt me, which was remarkable.

Middlesex Journal, Saturday, April 18, 1863

Letter from the 6th N.Y. Battery.

Camp Bramhall, VA, Near Acquia Creek Landing

April 5th, 1863

Dear Editor —The fifth of April and snowing. You would hardly believe it of the "sunny south," would you? I doubt whether New England has experienced a more inclement season than has fallen to the lot of the Army of the Potomac this winter, nothing but one series of snow and rain, and then snow again, accompanied by the muddiest roads in all christendom. And now, just as one was beginning to expect some alleviation of mud and wet, down came four inches of snow. Therefore in self defense I am driven to inflict myself on you and your readers.

Yesterday orders were received from superior headquarters for a grand review of the Army of the Potomac by President Lincoln. Consequence was that the entire camp became a scene of bustle and preparation, for harness and saddles must be washed, oiled and blacked, steel and brass work polished, guns and carriages cleaned, and a multitude of other business incident to every review or inspection be performed. It takes a great deal of work to keep a battery looking well. But the snow has caused all this preparation to be thrown away, and now, instead of waiting perhaps with chattering teeth on some bleak field for Uncle Abe to take a flying glimpse at us, I am sitting in my little "shanty" writing to the *Middlesex Journal.* Father Abram will be compelled to postpone the grand review indefinitely.

The season is much later this year than last. A year ago the army had already commenced the campaign some time. Doubtless Gen. Hooker had contemplated some move before this, as a short time ago an order was issued forbidding new furloughs, which three days back was countermanded. This storm will still further detain the army in its winter quarters.

Since the late expedition to Kelley's Ford, we have lapsed again into the quiet routine of camp life, disturbed only now and then by a review or occasional drill, when the weather is fair.

Our camp is situated in what would be called in summer a most romantic spot, but soldiers, looking more to material considerations than to romance, "don't see it in that light." Camp Bramhall, so called after our late captain, is situate half way down a large hill, on the top of which are our pieces, guard house, picket, &c. At the bottom of the hill is a deep ravine, with a chrystal, swiftly flowing brook. The other side the ravine rises steeply again, the steep hillside clothed thickly with shrubs and trees. To the right the ravine winds far away until hid among the hills, while to the left it opens on a beautiful view of Acquia Creek. This is the season of foliage and verdant grass would constitute a view of surpassing beauty, but the soldier, considering the depth of mud, the length and steepness up which he must carry all his water, pronounces it very disagreeable camping ground.

In the vicinity can be found quite a variety of game, including coon, possums, quail, partridges and even a few wild turkey. We have been here now above several weeks.

Beyond a doubt there will be a movement . . . I will take the first opportunity to write you.

HOPLITE

APR. 6TH, MONDAY.
Fair and sunny. Rose early and prepared for review. Started at 7 o'clock with the whole brigade and reached a large field near Falmouth about 9. Here was reviewed the whole of Gen. Stoneman's corps, consisting of our brigade and a great many regiments of cavalry. President Lincoln and Gen. Hooker were also present. The cavalry made a fine show. There was one regiment of lancers. The President reviewed all the troops, then they passed in review, afterwards at double-quick. Uncle Abe looked very pale, thin and careworn. He appeared preoccupied and paid but very little attention to the troops.[22] After the review I asked permission of Lieut. Martin to visit the 22nd Mass. reg. but was refused. On the way back Griffin, Horne, & I stopped in camp of brigade headquarters of 1st Brigade, Hooker's old division. Overtook the battery again just before it reached camp. Took supper and had just got into bed when I received orders to go over to headquarters on guard, which I did.

APRIL 7TH, TUESDAY.
Completed my guard duty. Stole some flour and sugar from the commissary dept.

Apr. 8th, Wednesday.
Fair. Received as punishment 7 days fatigue duty for leaving the column when returning from the review. Letter from Myra containing 10 dollars. On fatigue duty at headquarters.

April 9th, Thursday.
Fair and very warm. On fatigue cleaning the carriages, then sent to headquarters to build corduroy road. Orders for muster the succeeding day.

April 10th, Friday.
Fair. Cleaned our caisson and policed the park. Mustered by Major Robertson. Very warm all day. Signed the pay-roll for Jan. & Feb.

Apr. 11th, Saturday.
Still very warm. Received 2 months pay viz. Jan. and Feb. On detail to do some digging. Paid wash bill 85 cts. Bought 3 oranges 15 cts. Orders for review next day.

Apr. 12th, Sunday.
Fair and warm. Policed the park. Harnessed for review, which was scarcely done when orders came to move next day. Went down to Acquia Creek landing and had my picture taken, also hair cut. Bought some eatables. Wrote to Myra and sent the picture home. On guard, 2nd relief.

Apr. 13th, Monday.
Reveille at one o' clock. Orders for moving were countermanded. The other batteries of the brigade moved. Warm, and sunny. Letter from Gil Adams. Furbush returned from his furlough bringing me a letter from Myra. Fair and warm.

Apr. 14th, Tuesday.
Police duty. Warm and sunny.

Apr. 15th, Wednesday.
Equinoctial gale. Rained hard all day. Ordered out to search for a strayed horse. Went to Stafford and saw Jesse Richardson and my cousins. Completely wet through. Lieut. Martin gave me some whiskey when I got back. Changed my clothes and went to bed. An awful storm. Wrote to Myra.

Apr. 16th, Thursday.
Cloudy but no rain. Read "Abednego the Money Lender". Two negroes were whipped on their bare backs for stealing whiskey by order of Lieut. Chapin of battery M, 2nd regulars.[23] He staid in our camp because of alleged sickness when his battery moved. Sickness was probably drunkenness. Lieut. Brown went in his place. While in our camp he was drunk most all the time. Orders to be ready to move at a moment's notice.

Apr. 17th, Friday.

Fair. Read "Montezuma". Received by mail Capt. Bramhall's picture.

Apr. 18th, Saturday.

Sunny and very warm. Commenced a communication to the "Middlesex Journal". On guard, 1st relief.

Apr. 19th, Sunday.

Very hot. Took some salts to cleanse my blood, having quite a number of boils upon my legs and thighs. Had a good wash. Came off guard at six o' clock. Finished my letter to the "Journal".

Middlesex Journal, Saturday, April 25, 1863

Letter from the 6th N.Y. Battery.

Camp Bramhall, VA,

April 19th, 1863

Time rolls away and is gathered among the shades of the past; men die, nations rise, flourish, and hasten to their decline, and yet, no matter what has been preceding history, mankind never evinces so much surprise as at the nature of present passing events. And although no subject so convulses and occupies the general mind now as the progress of the great rebellion, yet beyond a doubt the time will come when the present crisis will be commented upon without even the accompaniment of wonder or interest. Humanity always finds more attention to bestow upon a mere finger cut, so it only be in the present, than upon disease and death in the past.

At this point in our nation's history, while the din of battle is in our ears, and the groan of the wounded patriot assails us from the hospitals in our midst, while we see the battlefield and its concomitant horrors, while bereaved parents, silent, mourn their martyred offspring, and broken-hearted wives mourn the wreck of their young happiness: while we experience at our very hearthstones all these dire evils of civil war, our attention is directed only to them. But when this war with those of years agone becomes a matter or chronicle, then will men, thinking of their own troubles as we do of ours, turn with casual remark, from records of the great war and delineations of its bloody battles to the more interesting topic of Joan's illness, or Darby's unsuccessful speculations in trade. 'Tis always thus. The present swallows up the past, and oftentimes the future.

This self conceit of present time, then how does it mar the patriot's glory and rewards of generous self abnegation! Who falls struggling in behalf of this native land against false demagogues and misled followers, what glory, what honor should not be his! This in the present is always conceded with warm enthusiasm, but when glorious deeds are viewed far down the vista of past days, enthusiasm degenerates to praise, and sometimes to forgetfulness. What then are the allurements of glory, if its deeds so soon come to be looked upon with indifference! Surely the selfish spirit of mankind would prompt them to choose rather present comfort and safety to evanescent fame, and it is so. Such being the case, how much nobler are they, who, disregarding personal glory and unmindful of present safety, oppose their bosom in the strife from a conviction of duty and a love of country! Too many there are who mistake a thirst for distinction and glory for the purer feeling of patriotism. Let us strive to believe that of the former class there is a goodly portion of the republic's armies.

These thoughts, dear editor, were induced by a controversy on the progress of the war and the calibre of our soldiers, to which by accident I became a listener. If they are somewhat disjointed doubtless it is owing to the fact that in course of time the soldier's mind begins to partake of the wandering tendency to which his bodily motions so soon become subservient.

The review of Stoneman's Corps, which was postponed by the storm of Apr. 5th, took place the succeeding day. The column was formed at 7 o'clock and the brigade moved to a large field in the vicinity of Falmouth passing on the way through the camp of the 16th Mass. Vols. Here after the usual amount of waiting we formed in line, brigade front, and the flank battery, Co. M, 2d Regulars, unlimbered to pay the customary salute. Over the vast plain as far as the eye could reach were stretched long lines of cavalry, while directly in rear of us, their red pennons fluttering in the breeze, were drawn up the only lancers in the service, the 6th Pennsylvania cavalry. They were a fine sight, and their subsequent movements proved them to be as finely drilled.

The national salute was fired and the review commenced. As the President reviewed the regiments each band in turn played some national air. It falling to our lot to be the last, we had something more than an hour to sit in our saddles in the position of attention. At last Uncle Abram came riding by surrounded by a troop of general officers, Hooker on his right and Stoneman on the left. It almost dazzled one's eyes, the gay caparisons and splendid uniforms. The President looked very thin and careworn and much preoccupied, scarcely seeming to notice the troops. Afterwards forming in column of sections we passed in review and lastly at double quick, after which the review was dismissed and we again reached our camp just before dark.

The weather has been very fine latterly and in consequence we had received orders to move on the 13th, which was at the last moment countermanded. The remainder of the brigade nevertheless moved, and as has since been learned, in the direction of Kelley's Ford and Rappahannock station. With them went all the available cavalry of the army with the exception of Gen. Pleasonton's brigade. Our battery is under marching orders and another day perhaps may see us en route to join the brigade. Since the departure of the last expedition, which is supposed to be the prelude to a general movement, the equinoctial storm usual to this season has happened, so swelling the river as to somewhat delay the intended crossing.

As the case now stands our forces are stretched along the river from Kelley's Ford to Rappahannock station, now and then shelling the rebs as they show themselves on the other side. Within a week something will probably be done. The infantry are in readiness to move with eight day's rations. "Fighting Joe" evidently intends to push things through.

HOPLITE

APR. 20 & 21ST.
Cloudy. Bought some flour for griddle cakes. Had orders to move to Potomac creek bridge.[24] Packed up and started at 10 o'clock. I had a spare horse and so could carry all my "duds". On detail to strike and pitch officer's tents. Camped in the valley close to the bridge close by Pleasonton's division to which we were attached. Visited camp of 11th Mass. Vols.

APR. 22ND. WEDNESDAY.
Cold. Jimmy Goodwin and some others from 11th Mass. Vols. visited me. Lieut. Martin forbade Miller and myself to use our little tent. Miller went into a wall tent with the 1st Sergeant and I into a shelter of canvas with Kiely and Ward. Raised my bed off the ground.

APR. 23D, THURSDAY.
Rained hard and cold. Lay abed and read.

APR. 24TH, FRIDAY.
Cold and rainy. Letter from Cousin Bethiah. Tent blew down.

APR. 25TH, SATURDAY.
Fair and sunny. Washed and blacked my saddle, cleaned gun and caisson for inspection. In afternoon visited 22nd reg. M.V. and saw Penney and Cobbett. A pamphlet from home containing paper and envelopes and some pictures. On guard, 3d relief.

APR. 26TH, SUNDAY.
Fair and sunny. Mounted inspection by Lieut. Martin. Read "Mrs. Haliburton's Troubles". Divine service in the afternoon by a chaplain, band accompanying. Came off guard at sundown.

APR. 27TH, MONDAY.
Very warm. Battery drill in the forenoon. Orders to move next day but one. Wrote to Cousin Bethiah.

APR. 28TH, TUESDAY.
Dull and cloudy. Battery drill in forenoon. Rain in afternoon. Wrote to Myra. Orders to move next day for which preparation was made, getting grain, &c. The

whole army of the Potomac commenced to move. Two "Journals" from home. In this camp just a week.

Apr. 29th, Wednesday.

Reveille at 4 o'clock. Packed up and started shortly after daylight. Passed by Falmouth which is a prettily situated little village in a gorge between two hills. Continued along the highlands as I thought keeping near to the river. Shortly after noon reached Hartwood church where we parked and proposed to stay for the night. Had a good dinner of ham and eggs, the latter being obtained by bartering coffee and sugar with the inhabitants. Had got our tent pitched and bed made when orders came to report to Gen. Pleasonton at U.S. Ford. We took the back track for about two miles and then turned in the direction of the river. Our way was blocked by a long train of wagons and ambulances. Night found us 4 miles from the ford, so we parked for the night. Lieut. Martin rode forward and reported to Gen. Couch, not being able to find Gen. Pleasonton. Pitched tent again. Rained in afternoon.

Apr. 30th, Thursday.

Rained during the night. Started at 7 o' clock for U.S. Ford. Delayed all day by wagon trains so that we only advanced 2 miles in the whole of the day. Drizzly all day, but cleared up toward night. Camped for the night on some high ground but not in sight of the river. Gen. Hooker camped in the same field with us. Glowing account reached us of affairs at the front. It seems by some mistake in giving the order we were altogether wrong and instead of being here should have been on the Rapidan River.

May 1st, Friday.

Got up at 2 o' clock and saddled up, taking all the grain on the horses and carriages. Left the wagons and spare horses behind. Crossed U.S. Ford by a pontoon bridge. The river here is about 400 feet wide. It took 19 pontoons to make the bridge. Banks very steep on both sides the river. Advanced through the woods at right angles from the river a distance of about 4 miles to Chancellorsville. This village consisted of 2 or 3 wooden houses and one large brick house at the crossing of two roads. This was Maj. Gen. Slocum's headquarters. Saw 6 - 32 lb. rifle guns same make as ours. Saw my two cousins Leonard Jordan and Charley Greene, who were on provost guard duty at Slocum's headquarters.[25] Parked in a large field near the brick house. Unharnessed, fed, and watered. Gen. Hooker came up and made the house his headquarters. The house and its vicinity was swarming with aides-de-camp and officers from General down to Lieutenants. Gen. Stoneman's supply mules came in and it was said he had gone to make a raid in the rear of the rebs. Very warm all day. About two o'clock the troops began to move with great regulation and in good spirits. Saw parts of 2nd, 5th, 11th, 12th, and 3d Army Corps. Saw Generals Hooker, Slocum, Howard, Sickles, Meagher, and many others. About 3 a partial engagement took place principally on our side by Sykes div. regulars. Batteries fired and were responded to, musketry firing mingled with the roar. Artillery advanced on a double quick. The engagement lasted about an hour when our line was ordered to fall back which it did. All the troops from the front said that we drove the enemy more than a mile, but for some good reason or other were ordered to fall back. The fighting was very sharp while it lasted. We harnessed and hitched shortly after it commenced and were in readiness to move. The fighting ceased all but some artillery practice and the wounded commenced to arrive at the brick house which was converted into a hospital. I saw a great many myself. Just before dark we were ordered off and went to the rear in the direction of the Rapidan and Rappahannock a distance of about 2 miles. Parked in a little glade in the woods, fed, and watered. Took a little of something to eat and lay down to get a little sleep, but without unharnessing. Shortly after orders came to unharness which we did and then returned to our blankets. Pitched no paulins. Fine all day.[26]

MAY 2ND, SATURDAY.

Slept finely during the night and was aroused just before dawn to hitch up. Saddled up and then was ordered to take the pole team on our caisson, its usual driver having his head stept on while laying asleep. Shortly after fed and watered but without unharnessing. Moved a distance of about ¼ mile in the direction we came and again parked, but did not unhitch. Could hear the army cheering and occasional shots at the front. Very fine and warm. Moved a similar distance and stopped. About 3 o'clock we were ordered off and going back to the brick house, went up the plank road leading to Culpepper. Advanced about ¾ mile and turning into a narrow path to the left soon reached an open field surrounded by woods.[27] Laid here to feed and groom, and saw meanwhile a rebel reg. 23 Ga. which had been captured by Berdon's sharpshooters.[28] Started off shortly with our two guns in the advance without caissons and entering the woods went on about half a mile when we turned back, cavalry also. The road was so narrow that we had to unlimber just to get round. Returned to the field just as the sun was setting. We were put in battery facing toward the woods out of which we had just come. Scarcely had we done this when musketry was heard in the rear and our infantry came running in. We faced about and then the bullets began to whiz about our ears. All the batteries in the field opened, ours also. Our horses frightened by the sudden firing got excited and a portion of them were lost, mine among the rest. The caisson horses ran away and overturned the gun limber scattering the ammunition on the ground. We continued to fire very rapidly until the rebels retreated and we were ordered to cease firing. Tried to make things straight and partially succeeded. I lost all my blankets, overcoat &c. Went out to a deserted battery wagon in front of the pieces and found an overcoat and blanket. Twice during the night there were engagements which kept us awake and in readiness to fight. This fight was very sharp while it lasted. I thought at one time that the rebs would get us all. We lost one man killed and 3 wounded.[29] We fought after nightfall.

Bvt. Maj. Gen. John C. Tidball, U.S. Army. Courtesy of Massachusetts Commandery, Military Order of the Loyal Legion and U.S. Army Military History Institute.

May 3d, Sunday.

Limbered up just at daylight and moved off to the left and rear, passed the brick house and halted in the large field close to U.S. Ford. Very heavy fighting all the morning, the rebels attacking desperately. They tried to follow up their success of the preceding night's flank movement. A great portion of the artillery fell back to the ford. This flank movement of the enemy was a sore thing for us resulting almost in a defeat. Gen. Pleasonton was highly pleased with our battery. We finally drove the rebels with great loss. We lay here all day with harness on in readiness to move. I went across the river with 24 others for grain and rations. Hard fighting at the front all day. Reported capture of Fredericksburgh heights by Gen. Sedgwick's corps. Pitched tent for the night. On guard, 2nd relief.

May 4th, Monday.

A large fire in the direction of the rebel lines. A rebel flying battery came up the river as near as the ford as possible and shelled the heights on the other side. One of our men was killed in camp with forge, wagons &c on the other side the river.[30] After throwing a few shells they left before our guns could open on them.[31] I afterwards learned that our cavalry captured them. No fighting in this neighborhood but heavy firing in the direction of Fredericksburgh. Lay here all day until towards night when we crossed the ford and camped close by Tydbauld's flying battery.[32] Rations for four days given out. Very warm.

May 5th, Tuesday.
Woke up at 2 o'clock and harnessed. Marched back to Falmouth where I learned that the 6th Army Corps had been beaten back across the river from Fredericksburgh after taking the heights. Watered and fed at Falmouth. While we lay here some of our troops threw a few shells across the river in order to test whether the rebs were there in force or not. Started back again, as was said, to go on picket at Kelley's Ford with 2 or 3 regiments of cavalry. As we passed by U.S. Ford saw a host of wagons coming down. It was said Gen. Hooker was taking two Corps' from the main army to join to the 6th, and again try to retake Fredericksburgh. Stopped to rest at Hartwood church and then proceeded. Shortly after it commenced to rain and it came down in torrents so that about 5 miles from Hartwood we were impeded in our course by a small stream which had become so swollen as to render it impossible to cross. All this was done in the short time of 2 hours. Camped right in front of the brook and pitched our tents in a pouring rain. On detail to pitch officers' tents. Drank some warm coffee and went to bed with wet legs and feet and damp blankets, but thankful that I had a shelter for my head. Very warm first part of the day. Letter and picture from F.W. Adams.

May 6th, Wednesday.
Rained all last night. Slept very poorly owing to my wet feet and legs. Rose at daylight, fed, and harnessed up again, it still raining. Unharnessed again after waiting about half the forenoon. Rained most all day. Laid here this day. Cavalry crossed the run.

May 7th, Thursday.
Rained most all night. In the forenoon went across the run foraging for pigs. Called at a house where we, Kiely & self, remained on guard while the owner went to look after his cattle. When he came back invited us to take dinner. Had bread and butter, fresh milk, and peach sauce. Tasted delicious. Shortly after returning to camp received orders to return to Falmouth and report to Gen. Pleasonton. Arrived at our old camp near Potomac Creek bridge shortly after dark. Found the army all in their old camps but in readiness to move again with 8 days' rations.

May 8th, Friday.
Rained during the night. Fed and watered and then moved to the vicinity of our old camp when we were in the reserve. Camped close by the old camp. Joined our brigade again. Cloudy all day. Wrote to Myra and received a letter from her with a picture of my son. Talk about going to the peninsula again. Preparations for refitting the battery. Appointed No. 2. Received 12 new men from 5th U.S. regulars. Had dinner for first time in 10 days.

May 9th, Saturday.
Very warm. Drew new horses and saddles. Washed and changed clothes, 1st time in three weeks. Inspection at night by Lt. Martin. Visited by J. Goodwin.

May 10th, Sunday.

Hot. Visited friends in 11th Mass. reg. and took dinner there. Bought some pickles. Went on guard for 2 hours in place of a regular who returned to his reg. All of them returned and we received in their place some vols. who had been dismounted and doing guard duty at Acquia Creek landing.

May 11th, Monday.

Very warm. Fatigue duty and water guard.

May 12th, Tuesday.

Very hot. Moved with rest of the brigade to the vicinity of Brook's station. Camped in a pleasant field on the edge of the woods and on high ground. Plenty of wood and beautiful water. Letter from Gil Adams. Built a bed of pine poles. Report that we were taken out of 1st Brigade Horse Artillery and attached to Gen. Pleasonton's cavalry division.

May 13th, Wednesday.

Very hot. Wrote to Myra. Put up harness racks. Drew from government 2 pr. drawers and 2 pr. socks.

May 14th, Thursday.

Rained in the night and during the day. Letter from Myra containing her photograph.

Middlesex Journal, Saturday, May 23, 1863

Letter from 6th N.Y. Ind'pt Battery.

Camp at Brook's Station, Near Acquia Creek VA,

May 14th, 1863

Mr. Editor: —Gen. Hooker has fought a brilliant battle. Whether it may prove of more advantage to us than the rebels is doubtful, but it has shown one thing, I think, most conclusively, viz: —that we have at last found the general to command the army of the republic.

It is useless now to go over the ground in search of who was wrong and who was the cause of the failure of the late attempt. Gen. Hooker can not be looked upon as responsible for the failure. As far as his plans and superintendence went no fault can be found. There is a point beyond which human foresight and human wisdom ceases and may be of no avail. *This* at least is true, that "fighting Joe" held the army more in hand and conducted it with more system, more order, than has any other general to whom has been entrusted the command of the army of the Potomac. If, as has been reported, it is true that Stonewall Jackson has been killed, added to the immense slaughter that the rebels must have suffered in their attempt to turn our right wing, then indeed has not the battle of Chancellorsville been barren of benefit to our side.

In the fight of Saturday night and Sunday morning the rebels must have suffered to a degree only equaled by the slaughter at Malvern Hill.

Our battery was in action for a short time at dusk on Saturday night. Previously we had been lying well to the rear, it not being customary to bring flying Artillery into a general engagement, but late in the afternoon of that day we were ordered up in conjunction with a force of cavalry to attack the rear of the rebel left wing which was well nigh separated from the remainder of their line of battle. Advancing well to the right we were wedging ourselves in between their left wing and the rest of their forces, when, shame to tell, our right, which had been entrusted to the care of the 11th Army Corps, broke before the desperate attack of the rebels and fled in great confusion. This turned our purpose from offence to defence, and falling back to our line of battle, the battery took position. Scarcely was this done than terrified masses of infantry came rushing through us in panic stricken confusion, then the rebels appeared on the edge of the woods pouring in volleys of bullets which whistled by our ears in a tone anything but musical. Coming from the cover of the woods they attempted to form on the edge of the field for a charge. At this time the sun had set and the new moon first rising shed but a dim light on the fight so that the rebels arrayed beside the woods looked but a long line of shadows. The word *"fire"* echoed along the line and simultaneously from the throats of twelve pieces a tearing storm of canister swept down the foe. Vainly they *struggled* to *withstand* the storm and shortly retired, but still the iron hail tore through the woods until by no possibility could there be a living enemy within its nearest borders. Then the welcome order came to cease firing and with dripping brows we had opportunity to observe the condition of affairs. We had lost in the engagement one killed and four wounded. The horses of one caisson terrified by the cannonading had run away and quite disabled it. Some of the cannonier's horses also had broken away from their holders and got lost, and among these, mine. Directly upon the conclusion of the fight Gen. Sickles and Pleasonton rode through the battery and were greeted each by three cheers with three more for Joe Hooker.

The edge of the woods must have been piled with dead rebels.

We laid here in position all night called now and again to the guns by infantry fighting in the woods to the front.

At daybreak we limbered up and moved to the rear, reaching U. S. Ford, about 8 o'clock. Scarcely had we got off the field when the fighting was renewed with greater violence then ever. From the position of our artillery at this place I feel certain that the rebels must have been slaughtered dreadfully, for out of the woods they had to march up a little slope at the top of which were entrenched as many as light twelve pounders as could be worked. So that after suffering from our musketry they must have been literally mowed down by the deadly fire of canister from these. In fact it is said, that the rebel dead laid so thick here, that upon recovering the ground our infantry fired upon them thinking them a line of battle lying down for some crafty purpose. After leaving the field we laid in the vicinity of the ford two nights and then started up the river to do outpost duty at Kelley's Ford. This we were prevented from reaching by a violent thunderstorm which so flooded a run necessary to be crossed in the route that we were obliged to camp 17 miles short of our destination. Staid there 2 days and were ordered back to Falmouth where returning we found the army across the river and in their old quarters. Since then after diverse flittings we have settled down at this place, 4 miles from Acquia Creek landing.

HOPLITE

May 15th, Friday.
Cool and sunny. Read "Marguerite De Valois" all the morning. Got a pass and borrowed a horse to go to Stafford. My horse's back was sore else would have taken him. Got thrown from my horse going over but did not hurt me luckily. Visited my cousins in tenth Maine reg. Also saw cousin Leonard Boody who was in same reg.[33] Got back just at water call. Journal from Woburn.

May 16th, Saturday.
Cool. Wrote to Myra. Cleaned saddles. Went on guard at 7 o' clock, 1st relief.

May 17th, Sunday.
Very warm. Wrote to Miss Hoskins.

May 18th & 19th.
Warm. Visited camps of 1st Mass. Cavalry & 22nd Mass. infantry. Took dinner with Geo. Cobbett, boiled ham and soft bread.

May 20th, Wednesday.
Washed clothes and the "Flying Eagle's " stockings, the latter looked nice. Wrote to Myra.

May 21st, Thursday.
Second anniversary of my wedding. Warm. Wrote to Myra and received a letter from her. Applied for furlough.

May 22nd & 23d.
Fair and hot. Went on guard at 7 o' clock, 2nd relief.

Middlesex Journal, Saturday, May 30, 1863

Letter from 6th N.Y. Ind'pt Battery.

Camp Pleasonton, Near Acquia VA.,

May 1863

The summer sun glows more with fervid ray, bringing in its train dust, sweat, thirst. Southern summer seems to spring at once from the loins of father Winter without the intermediate change of spring, whereas you of New England rejoice in all the joyness of budding flower and springing blade. The glare of day immediately succeeds to nightly shade, no delicious dawnings, no pleasant twilights. Virginia may be a very good place and well adapted to soldiering, but for christian habitation none can equal our northern homes. Doubtless a natural prejudice has some influence in the thought, yet in all my wanderings have I never seen a spot so complete in beauty, comfort, or healthfulness with my far New England dwelling place.

The army of the Potomac once more pauses to breathe itself after its recent struggle. The troops look finely and appear more as though war were their business than at any previous time.

In passing through the camps of Hooker's old division the Sunday succeeding the battle of Chancellorsville, I noticed the extreme order and discipline evidently habitual. But a few days previous this division had borne the brunt of a heavy battle and yet so soon everything had settled again to its usual neat appearance. The men neat, clean and fresh, their camps cleanly polished, and the rank and file turning out promptly with bright faces, glittering weapons, polished boots and clothes guiltless of one speck of dust to the usual Sunday morning inspection. I remember last summer it appeared to take more than *one* week for the morale of the Army to recover the effects of a great battle. Is this improvement due to the new commander, or to the fact that the army is growing more accustomed to its avocation, and the improvement is the consequence of habit.

Let us hope both. Certainly Gen. Hooker has handled the grand Army with more skill than his three predecessors, and there is no reason why the mass of the Army should not improve by experience as well as individuals.

What then are the deductions to be made from the late battle. Not truly as some of the hastily judging editors of metropolitan papers would say that Hooker is a failure, the Army demoralized, etc., etc., but as follows.

1st. It is not always necessary to give the rebels advantage of fortifications when we fight them.

2d. When they do assume the offensive they are sure to suffer as overbalancing a loss as we do when we attack their fortifications, thus proving our light artillery in field positions equal to their heavy artillery behind fortifications.

3d. Gen. Hooker is possessed of prudence and judgement as well as valor.

4th. The army being in good spirits and discipline so immediately after a great battle that this battle cannot be looked upon in the light of a defeat.

If it were necessary, the Army could have continued the fight many days longer, for never yet did the army keep in so good spirits and fighting trim, even when the troops had returned to their old quarters they were jubilant at the reception of orders to be in readiness to move again with eight days rations.

Although the campaign thus far has not been a complete success neither can it be termed a failure. If it has the effect to keep the rebel Army of Virginia in its present position, it has not failed of benefit.

Doubtless shortly the long talked of draft will take place, for the Army much needs it. Numerous two year regiments and some of the nine months' have gone home. The army has been more than decimated and is scarcely large enough to take the offensive again. By an occasional paper we hear of the progress of events at home, news of copperhead conventions, treasonable outpourings, &c.

There seems to be considerable questions whether the north will submit to a draft or not. As a general thing people seem disposed to give too much weight to the expression of a few cowards. It is shameful to own that there are citizens who as long as everything goes on smoothly are content to enjoy the benefit of a free government, but, when storms arise and their help is needed to protect the institutions under which they have flourished and enriched themselves, then question the legality of motions for the preservation of that government, and hesitate not at treason even to shirk their duty. They are cowards and deserve not the boon of freedom. They try to gild it with the name of free speech, the maintenance of their holy rights, &c., but the true reason, if it were only truly told would be cowardice.

This party, copperheads so called, and it (2 words obscured) the name of party, is the refuse of *all* parties. Is a man a traitor at heart, is a man a coward and fears he may be drafted, such men are copperheads. Their tether is very short. Let the army of the Potomac decide by vote what should be the fate of copperheads, and summary would be their punishment.

God save the United States.

Our battery still occupies its old camp in vicinity of Brook's Station, which has since been named "Camp Pleasonton" in honor of the Gen. Commanding 1st Division of cavalry. Furloughs have been forbidden in this Corps. Doubtless there will soon be some raids to write you of.

HOPLITE

May 24th, Sunday.
Fair and warm. News of great successes in southwest by Gen. Grant. A quire of paper from home. Came off guard at 7 o' clock.

MAY 25TH, MONDAY.
Cool and cloudy. Brigade arrangement of flying artillery broken up. Battery M. 2nd U.S. went into Maryland and E. 4th U.S. to Dumfries. Our battery directed to report direct to Gen. Pleasonton. Got a lot of boards and some canvas from the deserted camps and improved my own tent, made table &c. News of capture of Vicksburgh by Gen. Grant.

MAY 26TH, TUESDAY.
Cool. Rode over to Stafford Court House to see my cousins and found they had moved with Gen. Slocum's headquarters to the vicinity of Brook's Station. Went there and found them camped within 2 miles of our camp. Took dinner with them. Got back just at water call. Shaved.

MAY 27TH & 28TH.
Fair and warm. 28th had boiled pork and greens for dinner. Read "A Strange Story". Wrote to Myra and A.A.C.

MAY 29TH.
My furlough of five days went in for approval to Gen. Pleasonton. Visited Gen. Slocum's headquarters and borrowed 7 dollars of cousin Leonard Jordan.[34]

MAY 30TH & 31ST.
Very warm. Furloughs not returned, fear I will not get it. On guard, night of 31st.

JUNE 1ST, MONDAY.
Warm. On fatigue duty. Tied to Caisson wheel because I refused to do more than my fair share of fatigue duty.[35]

JUNE 2ND, TUESDAY.
Very warm. My furlough came in, approved, contrary to my expectation. Made preparations and left camp at 10½ o' clock in company with two others likewise going home on furloughs. Griffin went to Acquia Creek landing with me in order to carry back my horse. Started from landing in steamer "John Brooks" at 1 o' clock. My 4th time on the Potomac. Once more enjoyed the magnificent scenery of that great river. Saw again Mt. Vernon, Fort Washington &c. Arrived at Washington about 5 o' clock. Saw 29th reg. N.Y.S.V. returning home their period of enlistment being completed. Bought ticket at cor. of 6th St. and Penna. Avenue to N.Y. by way of Harrisburgh. In cars made acquaintance of an infantry and likewise a cavalry man. Baltimore we left at 9 o' clock. Arrived in Harrisburgh shortly after midnight where my cavalry friend left me. Changed cars. Slight headache. Reached Easton shortly after daylight. Remaining portion of this route was through a very beautiful portion of Penn. Saw Bethlehem, Lebanon, Lehigh valley. Infantry man left me at Easton. Arrived at N.Y. about 1 o' clock, bathed, shaved, hairdressed, boots blacked &c. Felt like a civilized man

once more. Visited Barnum's museum, seeing the curiosities, Tom Thumb &c, 25 cts. well spent. Very near to my darling, only 12 hours more. Stopped to performance in the afternoon. Started on boat Commodore at 5 o' clock for Boston, by way of Providence. Arrived in Boston about 6 in the morning.

JUNE 4TH, THURSDAY.

Went directly across the city to Lowell depot. While I waited there saw some of my Woburn friends, who came in on the cars. Deck Hart gave me a pass on the cars to Woburn on my telling him I had no money. Started for Woburn on 7

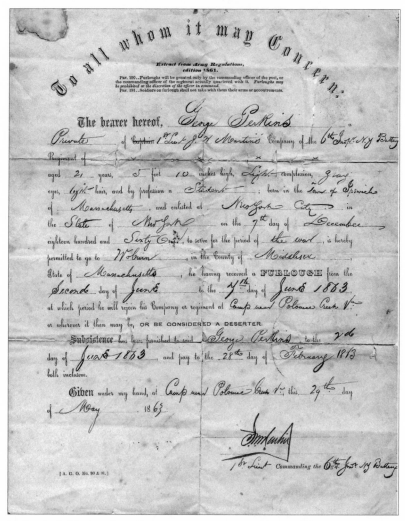

Furlough. Griffin Family Collection.

o' clock train. On arrival at E.W. saw first A.L. Richardson. How beautiful everything looked in its springly beauty, but its principal beauty was that here was my home. Found the family at breakfast, took them by surprise. Myra seemed glued to her chair, while mother with a scream rushed at me and soon had me in her arms. After first greetings were over had a chance to look more carefully and was immediately struck with my wife's improved appearance. She looked *positively beautiful*. My boy I found thriving and something to be proud of. Staid at home all day. At dusk with Myra visited Mr. & Mrs. Adams, very pleasant.

June 5th, Friday.
The day and night of June 4th was truly one of the happiest of my life. Once more I clasped in my arms the warm form of my wife, felt her fond caresses and experienced the tenderness of her affection. Saw for the first time my son, beautiful, bright and healthy. God render me truly thankful for this great happiness. Rose late. Started for Boston in 8½ o' clock train to find out if it were possible to get my furlough extended. Saw quite a number of military authorities, the Adjutant General &c. Learned that it was impossible to get my furlough extended. Called at the office of the U.S. Sanitary Commission in Kingston St. and got an order for soldier transportation for my return. Had my ambrotype taken (in uniform) on Hanover St. Went out to Charlestown to see Brothers Nate and John and families. Arrived there at dinner time and took dinner. They were greatly surprised. Sarah gave me pictures of herself, John and Cally. Left at 1½ o'clock in order to reach home again in 3 o' clock train. Bought a black hat $2.50, a pair of cannons and No. 6. At dusk hired a team and took Myra with me on a short visit to Uncle Hero and Aunt Maria. Saw also Mrs. Leslie and Mr. Bancroft. Had a drink of warm, new milk. Got home again about 10. A very busy day indeed.

June 6th, Saturday.
Another happy night. Got a team early in the morning and with Myra and G.H. visited her father's aunt at N. Woburn. Staid to dinner at her parents'. Mrs. Pratt & Miss McFeely came in to see me. The latter had grown quite pretty. Came down through the centre, stopped at Knowlton's and had an ambrotype taken, for which I forgot to pay. Called on Nathan Wyman. Got home again about dark, found brother Nate there. A very pleasant day.

June 7th, Sunday.
Another happy night. Spent the day with the family. In afternoon father, John, Nate, Sammy and myself went over to the cemetery to see brother Appleton's grave.[36] In evening made a short visit to Mr. McFarlane. A happy day.

June 8th, Monday.
Furlough expired. Bid Sammy goodbye in the morning before he went to work, & John and Nate at 10. Much moved. I feel my brothers love me. Myra sad at my near departure. Dear wife, how I longed to remain with her. I could only drive

back my own tears and try to sustain her courage. Commenced to rain heavily about noon which prevented my sisters from accompanying me into Boston as they had intended. Father and Myra went down to the depot with me in the rain. At 3 o' clock once more bid my wife and father goodbye and started again for the seat of war. I was glad to see that Myra was not so much depressed this time as at our last parting. God grant our separation be short.

Bought my through ticket from B. to Washington by Old Colony route, price $8.76. Called on Mr. Chittenden for a few minutes. Left Boston at 5½ o' clock. Reached Fall River before dark and embarked on Steamer Metropolis. Saw on steamer one of my old college class-mates, J. Read.[37] Slept soundly and reached N.Y. about 7 in the morning. Had to wait 'til 10 for outward train on N.J.R.R. In the meantime had breakfast, got shaved, &c. Reached Phila. about 2 and started again at three. Arrived at Baltimore about dark. Saw in the cars a corporal's guard who had 4 deserters handcuffed together in pairs. Were dragged through Baltimore by horses and started for Washington about 8 o' clock. Reached W. at 10. Went to a hotel for the night and paid for lodgings for myself and another fellow of 5th Conn. Vols. who had no money. Very warm all day.

Acting Assistant Paymaster John Read, U.S. Navy. Photo courtesy of Massachusetts Commandery, Military Order of the Loyal Legion and U.S. Army Military History Institute.

June 10th, Wednesday.

Very warm. Got up about 6½ and hurried down to the boat. Reached Acquia Creek landing about 12 and took cars for Brooks Station where I got off. My 5th Conn. friend left me, he belonging to the 12th corps. Walked to the old camp a distance of 2 miles and found the battery absent on a reconnaissance. Turned in to the tent with Griffin. At nightfall three of our fellows came in from the battery and told of a desperate fight in which the battery had been engaged. Two of these fellows were wounded. One of our guns had bursted.

June 11th, Thursday.

Looking back over the time of my furlough I have come to the conclusion that these have been the four happiest days of my life. How beautiful and bright seemed my happy New England home. How much of grace has my darling gained by her accession to the honors of maternity. My God I thank thee, I have once again seen my home and embraced my kindred. I feel now that I can with a better heart do my soldierly duties, and if it be my chance to fall I can be more resigned than I could before this. My only wish for safety is for my wife's sake. God bless my dear wife and prosper my young son.

Very warm and flies beginning to be very troublesome. Was given two horses to take care of. Received a towel, a blank book, a paper, and envelopes from home which had been sent before my furlough. A letter from M.C.J. Wrote to Myra. Fired and cleaned my revolver.

June 12th, Friday.

Very warm. Slept late. Wrote to Myra. No news from the front. Felt very anxious. Heard that the battery had been almost disabled.

Middlesex Journal, Saturday, June 27, 1863

Letter from 6th N. Y. Ind'pt Battery.

Camp Pleasonton, Acquia VA,

June 13th, 1863.

Happy, bright New England! How green your fields, how pleasant, how little showing evidence of a mighty war! How joyous the landscape smiling beneath a temperate sun, not as here withering under the fervour of almost torrid heat! All the extended country greets the returning soldier with hearty though silent welcome, and seems to justify to him his home prejudice so firmly cherished beneath the far Virginia skies. The air blows differently, and with quiet happiness one seems to inhale long draughts of life.

And here, too, is freedom. It may appear a little bombastic, yet verily it seems as though the air, the fields, the streams proclaimed the fact. To my mind, the *shiftlessness,* neglect, and slovenliness in the appearance of all Virginian communities are but the effect and proof of the presence of slavery. Visit a southern village or even a city, and one cannot help but be struck with the appearance which everything presents of being in the last stages of decay. Fences half fallen down or never completed, doors hanging by one hinge, dilapidated barns, ragged "mokes" of all sizes, styles, genders, and shades, are the common characteristics of all Virginian dwelling places. But in going North, the improvement is almost instantly noticed as soon as the free and fertile fields of the Middle States are entered upon. Habitual sloth gives way to an appearance of energy and industry. Again one sees neat dwellings and listen to the true Saxon tongue undisguised by niggerisms. The line between freedom and slavery is as distinctly marked by [. . .] customs, language, and popular tone of thought, as it ever was by Mason and Dixon's black line across the schoolboy's outline map.

How pleasant then, once more to revisit one's native Northern home, after an 18 mos. sojourn with the Army of the Potomac. Its beauty, its quiet prosperity, and in fact all the characteristics, which so distinguish it from this thriftless Southern land are but still further causes of pride: pride in my citizenship of the "old Bay State," and descent from the Puritan fathers. I doubt if any F. F. V. of them all feels a more genuine pride of his cavalier descent than I in my citizenship in the commonwealth.

I fancy I have been guilty of something akin to sentiment thus far, and if it should prove unpalatable to you or the readers of the "Journal," the remedy is easy, for *you* not to publish it, and for *them,* in case you do publish it, not to read it. Still I think a little might be pardoned me, for my provocation is great.

My late five days of furlough fled with winged speed.

While I have been absent in Massachusetts the battery has managed to get into the severest fight it has ever experienced. On my arrival at Camp Pleasonton, June 10th, I found the battery absent on some expedition up the river with a large force of Cavalry. That night two of our fellows came to camp wounded, and with news of a fight somewhere in the neighborhood of Bealeton (I am not positive as to orthography) Station, on a railroad the other side the Rappahannock. Their news, which was not very ample, showed a loss in the battery of some dozen wounded, and two or three killed, and that the battery was almost completely disabled by loss of horses. One gun had bursted, but luckily with injury only to the rebels. It seems that the rebels in charging managed to get right in the midst of the battery, when a hand to hand conflict ensued, our fellows using their revolvers with some effect. And now you know as much as myself with regard to the affair. As soon as the battery returns to refit I will write a more particular account.

The Army of the Potomac have changed their quarters from plain to forest in deference to old Sol's summer rays. It now occupies a much larger space then when in winter quarters, being scattered from Hartwood Church to Port Royal. One Corps is across the river in the plain below Fredericksburg, and one is at U. S. Ford.

The country, which has been occupied by the army during the winter, has been so stripped that it presents the appearance of a desert, and in many places has been burnt over, so [much] so that it reminds one of the tract of country in Asia Minor that the Greeks called Katakekaumene.[38]

The army appears settled for the season in summer bowers, and there is no certainty what a day may bring forth.

Yours, . . . HOPLITE

CHAPTER 5

I ENTERED THE SERVICE WITH VERY LITTLE PATRIOTISM: JULY–OCTOBER 1863

AFTER A SEVERE MAULING SUFFERED IN THE JUNE 9 BATTLE OF BRANDY Station, the Sixth New York was sent back to Washington to recover its losses in ordnance, horses, and equipment. Because of this necessary detour, the battery did not rejoin the army until June 28, the same day that President Lincoln relieved Major General Hooker—Private Perkins's favorite general—with Maj. Gen. George Gordon Meade. Lincoln had lost confidence in General Hooker, and, for his part, Hooker seems to have been convinced that the administration was unwilling to properly support him with the troops and freedom of action he deemed essential.

The Sixth New York was present at Gettysburg during the battle but was kept in reserve and not engaged. After the battle, the battery participated in the pursuit of Lee's army back to Virginia, being engaged only once in a minor affair near Shepardstown, Virginia. From July until the middle of September, the battery was mostly employed on detached service with cavalry commands on outpost duty guarding the flank of the Army of the Potomac. Meade's advance from the Rappahannock to the Rapidan, in which he occupied Culpeper on September 13, spelled an end to this quiet period for the Sixth New York. With Gregg's cavalry division, the battery followed in the army's wake on September 16 and remained encamped at Culpeper until September 26, when it retraced its steps behind the Rappahannock and reported for duty at Catlett's Station near Warrenton. When Lee's army advanced across the Rapidan on October 10, thereby initiating the Bristoe Campaign, the Army of the Potomac abandoned its advanced positions and ultimately retreated as far as the vicinity of Centerville before reaching a strong defensive position. Perkins told the story of the Sixth New York's participation in the Bristoe Campaign in a letter written on October 23, which is presented in the next chapter.

It seems likely that Private Perkins did not maintain a diary during this period. If he did keep one, it has been lost. He did, however, pen a series of letters to the *Middlesex Journal,* as well as at least two to Nathan Wyman, the town clerk of Woburn. To Wyman, he complained that he had had little time to write, being always on the move, and had anyway been unable to procure a supply of ink. Whatever the challenges he faced in finding time and writing materials, it is evident that he deemed it essential to keep up his public correspondence.

Some of the newspaper articles are paeans to the bucolic countryside in which the battery was assigned to outpost duty, but others were obviously intended to educate the home folks about the nature of the duties performed by the cavalry and horse artillery and one in particular to defend the reputation of General Hooker.

George Perkins to Woburn Town Clerk Nathan Wyman
Bivouac near Middletown, Md.
July 11th 1863
My Dear Nathan

I at length find an opportunity to send you the information which you desired of me and which you will find enclosed. I started once previously to write to you and was interrupted by a sudden order to march.

Am in good health and spirits and hope to remain so at least long enough hear from you in answer to this. You will excuse pencil writing as I have used up all my ink and can get no more. Since my return from furlough I have had but little chance for writing being continuously on the move. We have traversed a considerable portion of Virginia, Maryland, and Penn. We were present at the battle of Gettysburgh although we did not get into the fight in actuality. We were ordered in three times but very fortunately common light batteries were found at the last moment who went instead. They did not wish to send us into a general engagement as being flying artillery we had more horses to risk and a light battery would do just as well. From Gettysburgh we came to this place by way of Frederick starting on the 5th. We are now situated on the Hagerstown turnpike midway between Frederick and Boonseboro. Yesterday we lay at the latter place, but for some reason or other were ordered back to this place and here we came. We are at present under command of Gen. Gregg.

Middletown is a pleasant little town and apparently prosperous having 3 churches and two hotels. One of these taverns rejoices in the name of "National House" the other in the sounding title of "Liberty Hotel". To call Middletown a city would be more ridiculous than to bestow the same name upon Winchester Mass. The town is in the midst of a small and fertile valley which is very appropriately named Pleasant Valley. Between it and Frederick, which city is about 8 miles distant lies a range of hills called the Kittoctin Mts. Bounding the valley on the other side is the range called South Mountain and a portion last fall's battle was fought within this valley. Night before last we camped within half a mile of the battle field of Antietam and close to the village of Boonesboro. The portion of Maryland which we have been occupying for the last few weeks comprises the most beautiful farming country I ever saw. As far as the eye can reach stretch immense fields of wheat which the farmers are just beginning to harvest. With the harvest it is impossible but what the presence of a large army should do a great deal of damage. The country presents a cheering contrast to the neighboring state of Virginia where all seems desolate and going to ruin. Frederick City is the smallest and prettiest city I ever have seen, very compactly built and containing about 9,000 inhabitants. The famous 7th N.Y. Vols occupy this latter place. I might fill many pages with descriptions of places we have lately visited but not to weary you I will for the present close presenting to Mrs. W. and yourself the best respects of Yours Truly, Geo. Perkins.

Middlesex Journal, Saturday, August 15, 1863

Letter from 6th N. Y. Ind'pt Battery

Little Georgetown, Near Thouroughfare Gap, VA,

Aug. 5th, 1863.

Dear Editor: —It would be useless for me to attempt as your correspondent, to give as news what has already become historical. The campaign in Maryland and Pennsylvania, its object, incidents, and completion have already for a long time furnished topics for conversation, argument, remark. Therefore let me rather dilate upon the few things worthy of remark which came within my cognizance. A private soldier scarcely can attempt to carry on a prompt and interesting correspondence with a literary journal, most especially amid the activities of a campaign such as we have lately been undergoing.

My last I think was dated from Fairfax C. H., early in the month of June, and shortly after my return from furlough. Since that time we in common with the rest of the army, have visited Pennsylvania, by way of Edward's Ferry, Frederick, Taneytown, Gettysburg, and again nearly retraced our steps by way of Berlin, Leesburgh, Centreville, Warrenton.

Behold us now located at this village (said village comprises two houses and a brick church), of Little Georgetown, and close to Thoroughfare Gap, in company with 2d Brig., 2d Div., C. C. A. P., commanded by Col. Huey. Our object appears to be to guard against a rebel raid through the gap upon our R. R. communication with Washington. We have been here ever since Aug. 1st, and appearances do not as yet denote any prospect of a move.

As to the continuance of our stay in this vicinity, it would not be a very unpleasant duty were it not for the irregularity of the mails, for as letters are the soldier's chiefest enjoyment, when any thing causes an interruption to the reception of letters, then he begins to be dissatisfied and desirous of a change nearer to headquarters, or at least to some place where communication is more direct. If it was not for this draw back I should be content to stay here the remainder of the summer.

The extraordinary coolness which has heretofore been our portion to enjoy, has at last given place to the heat of ordinary Virginia summers, and somewhat reminds us of the extreme heat which tortured us the last summer upon the peninsula. Fortunately the nature of our present duty does not compel any very violent or long-continued exertion, and consequently just now we are in the enjoyment of a luxurious laziness, which is doubly increased by the nature of our position. The country hereabout is a succession of hills and valleys, the latter green with the heavy growth of grass which the war has not spared hands to cut, and in pleasant relief to the white hill-tops shining beneath the beating sun. How pleasant then, these days of almost white heat, to seek the hilltop and there stretched out within the shade of some broad tree to lay half dreaming, or absorbed in lazy contemplation, watch the sunshine parching the whitened fields. The distant hillsides belted with dark pines, varying in shade according as the sun is clouded, or again shines forth, and in the valleys the long lines of green following the water courses, here and there enlarging into a grove about some old stone mill. Occasionally a farm house gleaming whitely from out its surrounding shade trees, suggesting of coolness and comfort. These constitute the features of a landscape, which, seen from beneath a spreading tree as one lies extended with half-closed lids, inspires a feeling of inward enjoyment which to appreciate must be experienced. Or if one feels inclined for more active pleasures a short walk leads to hillsides where one may pick blackberries unsurpassed in size, flavor, or plenty. The abundance of blackberries in this vicinity is perfectly immense. An hour suffices to fill a waterpail, and blackberries in every style, "au natural," or "a la sucre," are become a daily dish with us. And then as the sun declines comes the daily bath in some swift flowing stream. This, though last, is not the least of our pleasures, for the luxury of cleanliness after the recent restrictions thereupon during the late campaign, is doubly appreciated. So you will see that at present we are in the enjoyment of arcadian pleasures which are by no means less pleasing because of the hardships of the Pennsylvania campaign.

Of news of the Army of the Potomac, I can give you none as we have been so long separated from the main body on outpost duty that probably more is known at home on that head than here among us. Gen. Meade's headquarters are reported to be at Germantown, six miles from Warrenton.

When Lee's army fell back across the Potomac, Gregg's division of cavalry to which we have been attached for some time lately, made a movement across the river at Harper's Ferry. On the afternoon of July 15th, we arrived in the vicinity of Shepardstown, Va., where we laid till the succeeding afternoon, when we were attacked by the rear guard of the rebel army. At this place we captured 3600 lbs. of bacon, 2 ambulances, and quite a body of prisoners. On the afternoon of the 16th, as we were lying half asleep, we were aroused by picket firing, which in a short time became quite a fight. The rebels attacked our dismounted cavalry skirmishers beyond a belt of woods in our front, but were unable to drive them when reinforced from a line of stone wall which they maintained as our line of defence. From where we were stationed could be plainly heard the yells of the rebs as they charged the wall, and the counter-shout of our fellows in reply. Finally they brought up six pieces of artillery to aid them, but were unable to accomplish their object then. The first Penn. Cavalry which had obtained the name of being the best skirmishers in the Army of the Potomac, have more than maintained their reputation. To those six pieces we replied with but two, holding six others in reserve. These last six pieces were so posted that had the enemy made their way through the weeds they would have been exposed to a most merciless enfilading fire from three points. For several hours we stood to the pieces in readiness to give them a reception should they have made an opening through our skirmishers, but at length the approach of night put an end to the fighting. By persons engaged this was said to be a very smart cavalry fight. That night we fell back to Harper's Ferry along the river. On the way our caisson ran off the road into a ravine 15 feet deep, where it laid bottom side up, the pale horses on their backs and their driver under them. Luckily neither the driver, horses, or caisson were injured. After three hours hard work, we managed to right it, and just as the sun was rising we reached the little town of Bolivar, which is situated upon the heights just above Harper's Ferry, in a pouring rain. Here your correspondent managed to get a breakfast at the house of a German resident quite in civilized style, and I can assure you after a night of such toil and fatigue it was by no means unwelcome.

From there to this place, we in conjunction with cavalry have covered the rear of the army, which laudable occupation we are also now engaged in.

HOPLITE

Middlesex Journal, Saturday, August 29, 1863

Letter from 6th N. Y. Ind'pt Battery

Warrenton, VA,

Aug. 20, 1863.

Dear Editor: —The summer wanes finding us, if anything, a trifle farther from Richmond than the close of last season's campaign. Once more here come cool nights and days of not quite scorching heat. The army of the Potomac occupies nearly the same line which was established a month ago. Nothing of interest transpires except now and then the capture of a few guerillas. The army has quite recovered the fine condition in which it quitted its quarters about Falmouth in the month of June, and is fully prepared for operations offensive or defensive.

The battery left Thoroughfare Gap on the 13th inst., and with regret, for a pleasanter neighborhood it has never been our lot to occupy. On Thursday the 13th, we broke camp in a pouring rain bidding farewell almost with tears in our eyes to all the comforts of veal cutlets and veal soup, new potatoes, blackberries, milk, &c., and took up line of march in the direction of Warrenton where we arrived about noon. On the way two of our wagons broke down which much increased the pleasures of a wet march by the privilege of jumping into the mud and getting them out. This was accomplished only by the loss of 12 bags of grain, enough to feed all the horses in the battery once and a half. While we were on the road the clouds broke and the sun came out with force, apparently increased by its previous restraint.

Warrenton is quite a beautiful city or rather was. Many of the private dwellings are elegant and surrounded by spacious grounds. Large shade trees line the streets and furnished a coolness in quite refreshing contrast to our heated ride as we entered the town from the pike. As we looked down the vista of the shady street and pleasant dwellings my mind, induced by the resemblance to Woburn's Pleasant St., went off into a sort of dream of home and home scenes which was suddenly dispelled by the loud tone of command echoing down the column "forward — trot — march." Closing up in compact column once more we found ourselves upon the hard Pike which lay stretched before us in a dreary line of white.

Leaving Warrenton we took a south west direction which at length brought us at the end of a 6 miles march to Sulphur Springs on the Hedgeman River, or as it is called on some maps north fork of the Rappahannock.

At intervals along the road from Warrenton to the Springs were camped portions of the 6th and 3rd Corps.

Sulphur Springs has apparently been before the war a resort for pleasure and health. There are still standing the remains of a large hotel which our troops destroyed by fire last year while the army was falling back for the second battle of Bull Run. Here are the headquarters of Maj. Gen. Birney commanding 3rd Corps. The hotel and its numerous outbuildings, all built of brick and painted a pale straw color, form a semi-circle. Within this semi-circle and in the rear of the buildings lies a beautiful lawn containing the Sulphur Spring in an octagonal spring house, and a beautiful pavillion fitted up for bathing purposes.

From curiosity I tried some of the water of the spring and was well satisfied of its sulphurous properties. As soon as one gets within 6 yards of the spring he is assailed by the sulphurous exhalations and if he stops to take a sniff at the water in his cup previous to drinking, it well nigh overpowers his inclination to drink. While drinking there is no perceptible bad taste but immediately upon removing the cup from one's lips there is experienced a flavor similar to the smell of sulphuretted hydrogen. This water kept in a canteen one day reminds one very forcibly in its smell of rotten eggs.

Some of our fellows got here several silver forks marked "Fauquier White Sulphur Springs." Why they should be called "white" I know not. The water is of a bright violet hue.

We camped on a high hill just beyond the river where we found our other section which had been separated from us about a fortnight. Here also laid Mackintosh's brigade of cavalry which contains the 1st Mass. Col. Huey's brigade, to which we had been previously attached, was dismembered here, part remaining with us, and part going to Warrenton Junction in which vicinity was then Gen. Gregg's headquarters.

At this place we remained two nights after which we returned to Warrenton and occupied our present camp. We have been here since the 15th.

As we returned by the springs I had an opportunity to hear Gen. Birney speak in a farewell address which he was making to one of the regiments about to leave his command. This is only one of quite a number of quite a number of regiments which have left the army of the Potomac, among them the 1st Mass. Infantry.

Have they gone to Charleston? Time will show.

We have lain in the present camp just long enough to give the battery a thorough cleaning for the fist time since leaving Falmouth. Our tents are pitched in a strip of oak woods at the edge of a field in which are parked the pieces. As I now sit I can see the carriages shining in their coat of olive and black paint, and the harness, which, lately oiled and blacked and with brightly polished brasses, presents to the eye of an artillery man a sight of neatness not often seen in the midst of an active campaign.

Were we to be inspected now I make sure that the verdict would be greatly in our favor.

Last evening I rode over to the camp of the 1st Mass. cavalry and learned that they had just returned from out post duty near Warrenton and Orleans. They had lost a patrol of a corporal and [f]our privates which had been gobbled up by a force of infantry and cavalry in the vicinity of Orleans.

Yours, HOPLITE

George Perkins to Woburn Town Clerk Nathan Wyman

Geo Perkins
Warrenton, Va., Aug. 25th 63
My friend,

Yours of the 20th inst. received. I scarce can remember from what place my last to you was dated but I think it was at Middletown Md. Since our sojourn at that place we have traversed many miles and seen many new places until at last we have settled down in this vicinity. With the exception of occasional trips to Sulphur Springs and elsewhere for a day or two at a time we have been almost stationary. We are very pleasantly camped and in a comfortable and healthy neighborhood. We are only a short half mile from Warrenton. Night before last there was a great blow out in the town given by Gen. Meade's staff comprising a ball and concert. The high born dames of Virginia did not disdain to honor our officers with their presence and it is reported that it was a merry time. I have speculated a considerable on whether they had any supper at this same ball. If so it must have been rather costly. Chickens not ½ grown are worth in this goodly town of Warrenton $1 per pr. and everything in proportion, pies 50 cts, potatoes $2 per bush., in fact a man must be a Croesus to live even. As for us we make a levy upon the neighboring farmers for any thing they may have and we fancy, and we pay them neither in gold or notes federal or confederate. Consequently for soldiers we have been living very high making all the meals we can from the different combinations which can be made of green corn, veal, fresh pork and Uncle Sam's rations.

I am in unusual health and am much stouter than when I was at home last. Soldiering agrees with me finely and I have at length got so used to it that now I do not in the least regard what when I first came out I should have thought the greatest privations and hard ships. Do the boys in the 39th seem to be pretty well satisfied? Strange to say we have not been any where in their vicinity since they have been out and so I could not see them.

The war goes bravely on and I think we are safe in thinking that one more season will completely crush the rebellion. If it had not been for the riots at the north I think the rebs. would have been played out *this* season.

To my mind it appears totally ridiculous the manner in which they are now carrying on the draft. It is nothing but a farce the way in which they refuse men concerning whom it can be found there is anything the matter —even so trifling as a sore finger almost.

The drafted men ought to be with the Army of the Potomac now in order to make a forward movement early in the next month. One good whipping administered to the rebels of the Army of Virginia would do more towards subduing the south than the possession of Charleston & Chatta-nooga. But although "Old Abe" may be true and honest, still my judgment can not allow that he is over skillful or prompt.

As you say I may be proud of having belonged to the Army of the Potomac, yet the motive which prompted to this I may not boast of. But although I own that I entered the service with very little patriotism yet I say truth when I tell you that which I had not at the commencement now I have increased in power. Others I know who enlisted in a fit of bombastic patrio-tism which finally died out. From nothing I have grown something. I have acquired the name in the battery of "black abolitionist" nigger lover & c. I have at least learned to be a good republican since my service.

Yours & c. Geo. Perkins

Middlesex Journal, Saturday, September 5, 1863

Cavalry Corps, Army of the Potomac

By Hoplite

In the daily newspapers or in any of the public notices of passing events it is surprising that there is so little mention of this valuable arm of the military service. Our infantry and artillery are praised collectively and by detail, and yet beyond a casual mention of the increased serviceability of the cavalry, or a notice that at such or such a place occurred a cavalry fight, nothing is heard in relation to their excellence and discipline, their courage and dash, which since the beginning of the war has steadily increased until now Uncle Sam can boast of as effective cavalry as is at present possessed by even the best disciplined army of Europe. —No one attempts to portray the extent, the character, and the multifariousness of their duties, to praise their performance of them or their neglect. A better field is found, it is thought, in the exploits, the endurance of infantry.

Unless one can be present among and become a portion of the cavalry corps he is unable to form any adequate idea of what is performed by them. Infantry may and really do accomplish a deal of hard work but only with great intervals of rest, whereas cavalry are always busy. At any time when the rest of the army are enjoying a period of rest, perhaps after some great battle, the cavalry corps is condemned to ceaseless activity. —Even now while the infantry are only occupied by what may be required by their personal comfort, their cleanliness or ease, the cavalry are daily in the saddle making long reconnoisances, scouts, or patrols. And in these many expeditions occur cavalry engagements of more or less magnitude which do not always find their way into the papers and in which oftentimes are performed deeds of daring that need only to be related to be admired.

An immense area of country contained in the segment of a circle the ends of which rest on Harper's Ferry and Falmouth is continually patrolled by cavalry, and it is by no means seldom that the enemy's cavalry is met therein and is able to carry away no matter for boasting from any such collision.

And beside there are the occasional expeditions within the enemy's lines which often result in something more than skirmishes. Thus much without our lines, within there are the regular outposts to be maintained which, though not as dangerous yet are fully as arduous duty. It may look very pretty and statuesque on some fine summer's day to visit the advanced pickets and view each trooper on post as he sits motionless on his horse, his carbine upright upon his thigh and his finger upon the trigger, but picture to yourself that same soldier amid the rains of Autumn or the snows of Winter, sitting silent and still longing for the expiration of his two hours when at last he will have the privilege of motion, then you will have a very slight idea of one of the hardships of a cavalryman. An infantry picket can in most of cases warm his blood by walking his beat, but not so the mounted outpost who, situated in the corner of some remote field, must sit still as an equestrian statue resolved all to eyes and ears. It would occupy a much larger space than could possibly be spared for this little article to chronicle even the many duties of the cavalry corps.

They do all these things and there is a necessity they should be done, yet Gen. McClellan thought in the summer of '62 he had enough for all purposes. Since then the cavalry corps has been more than tripled. Have we not found work for it? And yet he is the general whom so many laud for judgment, for ability.

Now we have a cavalry force such as ought not to shame any nation under the sun to own. The rebels own our superiority in more than one cavalry encounter.

To whom or to what is this improvement due? To Gen. Joseph Hooker!

From a disorderly and poorly disciplined rabble of mounted men whose only earthly benefit seemed to be as orderlies for generals or as a careless kind of picket guard, he converted them into a well-disciplined and organized corps. He infused into them some of his own pluck and mettle, and they became the cavalry which since so many times have proved their prowess on rebel squadrons. Well may Gen. Pleasonton be proud of his command. Poor "old Joe Hooker," that after reducing this grand chaotic mass, the army of the Potomac, to comeliness, to regularity, to efficiency, he should have his head lopped off just as the crowning glory of his career was apparently within his grasp.

Honor to the brave in misfortune? But courage: it yet remains for history to say whether Joe Hooker was right or wrong, whether justice or malice, envy and fear removed him. But in any case it can but redound to his credit, his inspiration of the cavalry corps, which, first manifested upon the 17th of March, of this present year, at Kelley's Ford, has still shown itself throughout the many battles of this eventful campaign. The battles of Brandy, Aldie, Emmettsburgh and many others are the pride marks to which the Cavalry Corps, Army of the Potomac, may ever point. Alas that the noble man who so aroused this latest excellence should fall so far from obtaining his just due.

Middlesex Journal, Saturday, September 12, 1863
Letter from 6th N. Y. Ind'pt Battery
Near Germantown, VA,
Sept. 6th, 1863.
Dear Editor. —Once more amid the affairs incident to a change of camp and preparation for a grand inspection, I find time to direct a few words Woburn-ward. On Sept. 3d, a battery of horse artillery arrived at Warrenton, where we were then lying, to relieve us from our detached duty with Col. Macintosh's brigade of cavalry. We were ordered to report immediately

to headquarters 1st Brig. Horse Artillery, Maj. Robertson. This order was received with extreme regret both by the men and officers of the battery, and by the commandant of the cavalry brigade to which we had been attached. On our part, we had been treated with great kindness by Col. Macintosh and we had seemed to suit him.

By a late order commanding the substitution of mules for horses for draught purposes throughout the Army of the Potomac there remained in his brigade quite a number of horses to be turned in to government. Those horses were for the most part magnificent animals and in splendid condition, in fact I never before had seen so many beautiful horses collected together in one place. Anxious to keep his command in the best possible order Col. Macintosh turned them over to our battery receiving from us in return as many horses the refuse stock of the battery. So that in return for our worn out hacks and horses effectually "played out" by the Penn. campaign we received some of the finest animals in the Army of the Potomac.

It is easily imagined his disgust and our regret at the reception of marching orders from Gen. Pleasonton. It is possible though that we may return shortly as both Col. Macintosh and Capt. Martin are exerting all the influence they possess to bring such event about.

The evening previous to our departure from Warrenton, something unusual to the quiet life of the battery happened in the way of a serenade by the band of the 1st R. I. Cavalry. This was only one of the many instances manifesting the esteem in which the 6th N. Y. was held by our commander.

Through dust and heat we made our way according to orders to the vicinity of Germantown and here have joined once more our comrades of the 1st Horse Artillery Brigade. Since we have been away two more batteries have joined it, making in all six. There has also been formed a 2d Brigade under command of Capt. Graham, U. S. A.

Germantown is situated upon the Orange and Alexandria R. R., two miles beyond Warrenton Junction. Why it should be called a town is hard to tell. There is no village for miles around and only a scattered house or two and some remnants of lone chimneys to prove this district was ever inhabited. Gen. Meade's headquarters are but a short distance from here.

We are camped on the edge of some thin oak woods, the pieces parked in the open field outside. Our camp is in the shape of a parallelogram with one end open and resting on the field, very comfortable and pretty, yet wanting in the soldier's chiefest necessary, water. We have to go nearly a quarter of a mile for it and very brackish it is too. I never saw a neighborhood so destitute of springs. There are only two in a circuit of several miles.

We have been here now three days all of which time has been spent in constant labor. Infantry have accomplished their work when they have laid out their camp and thoroughly policed it. Not so with artillery. There are many more details numerous and laborious which occupy the first days of a new camp. Cleaning the carriage, harness, saddles, and equipments; erecting harness racks; making a picket for the horses, and many other duties of regulation and improvement are among the artillerist's occupations.

Such have been our late employments and at length we begin to settle down to the quiet monotony of usual camp discipline.

To-morrow there is to be a grand inspection of the whole brigade by Gen. Hunt, Chief of artillery.

All the Woburn boys are well and prosperous.

Yours, HOPLITE

Middlesex Journal, Saturday, September 19, 1863

For the Middlesex Journal
Army of the Potomac
By Hoplite

It will scarcely be possible on so broad a subject to present all the things worthy of notice in a short newspaper article, yet if some of the most salient points are presented, and if one entirely new is eliminated it will not have been entirely useless. Many years will not elapse ere the army of the Potomac will furnish subject matter not merely for short articles, news items, anecdotes, & c., but for numerous volumes of history and story. The events which now look trivial and excite but little remark by way of their commonness and frequency will then furnish subject for disquisition and matters for many works of numerous volumes. Courage, daring, patriotism, endurance, and the thousand and one soldierly virtues which latent by this war have been aroused and which now are accepted as a matter of course, will then be dilated upon to the full measure of their deserts. Perhaps then reading some author's masterly production on those or similar subjects we shall wonder to ourselves "are these events of but now and which we thought so common-place, and are they really so extraordinary! Why it rivals the account of the American revolution and the current stories of the heroism of our forefathers!"

Previous to the present war the greater portion of the nation were quite ignorant of what extent was the military and naval power, or took it for granted that it compared favorably to other armies and navies. Or if they knew our inferiority they did not imagine it one tithe so great as it really was. Buried in the pursuit of arts and appliances which are the concomitants of continued peace and prosperity the American people had for so long a time neglected the science of war and its practical applications that at the outbreak of this rebellion it is not to be wondered at that we were found almost defenceless. The smallness of the military power greatly surprised the nation. But when the first shock of wonder and surprise had passed the belief in the native power of the nation began to assert itself. The rebellion was deemed foolhardy in the extreme and it was thought the Government had but to stretch forth its hand to immediately crush it. This very belief itself whether just or not bespoke the strength of the nation. Reverses came and the strength of the people arose to meet the occasion.

At the commencement of the war troops were raised and according as they were needed stationed at different points. Gradually a cordon of armed men grew upon the southern bank of the Potomac having as its centre to be defended the city of Washington. The battle of the first Bull Run proved this mass not to be an army.

Geo. B. McClellan took command and the fall and winter of 1861 were spent in drilling, augmenting, and organizing the forces which were called the army of the Potomac. In the succeeding spring at Yorktown for the first time the armed defence of the Capital, then turned to the channel of offence, presented the appearance of an army. This army though poorly organized accomplished the famous peninsula campaign, thanks to their native worth not to any genius on the part of its commander. Success followed our arms even up to the very walls of Richmond.

> "*There* is a tide in the affairs of men
> Which taken at the flood leads on to fortune."

The flood tide of success had carried the Army of the Potomac to within five miles of the rebel capital and there conquered their army of defence with only three fifths of our own forces. The mind of the union commander was not large enough to contain victory and the fighting portion of the army bivouacked on the battle field of Fair Oaks while the remaining two fifths remained on the other bank of the Chickahominy. It would seem as if fortune disgusted at the refusal of her choicest gifts took alarm and deserted the union arms. What was possible the first week of June grew less possible as that month progressed and towards its end gradually impossible until the close of June and opening of July found in full retreat the army to which only a short month before all things were possible.

From that time disaster seemed to pursue the army of the Potomac until it culminated in the invasion of Pennsylvania and Maryland. At Antietam and South Mountain the collective bravery and patriotic fury of the union army, combined with the talent of the corps commanders, hurled back across the Potomac the invading columns in dire confusion. Again the feeble mind of the commanding general let slip the golden opportunity and the rebel army was permitted slowly to retreat toward Richmond until finally it intrenched itself upon the heights above the city of Fredericksburg.

Gen. McClellan was dismissed and with good cause.

Next the command was thrust upon an honest and noble man, but incompetent. The defeat at Fredericksburg and the failure of his second attempt by reason of the inclemency of the weather at length obtained for him what repeated solicitation did not avail, his relief. Maj. Gen. Hooker succeeded to Burnside.

At the time this general took command the army was in a deplorable condition. Discipline was poor and desertions began seriously to impair its effectiveness. The government paid the army and gave it to Joe Hooker. In two months what a change! From out of a chaotic and turbulent mass of armed men Gen. Hooker reconstructed the army of the Potomac, gave to it vitality, restored discipline. Desertions became rare. The cavalry corps which had previously been only an adjunct of the army he inspired and it became the body which now defers to no arm of the service. All this with great labor and in the short period of two months. —Confidence grew apace and at the opening of the present campaign the bodily condition, the discipline, and morale of the troops were the best they had ever been. The battle of Chancellorsville was fought without absolute victory to either party. Who can point to one instance of bad generalship on the part of Joseph Hooker during the battle? Was it not one proof of the commanding general's genius that immediately after this battle there remained more order and discipline than the army had ever possessed for weeks succeeding any previous engagement? The discharge of two years and nine month's troops greatly diminished the army and the enemy once more turned his mind to the favorite scheme of invasion of the North. Gen. Hooker moving his army on an inner circle between the enemy and Washington watched him closely, all the while beseeching reinforcements from the defenses of the capital to allow him successfully to cope with the invading rebels, undue fear or official envy refused them. Taking advantage of his authority as commander of the army of the Potomac he ordered the evacuation of Harper's Ferry and the forces there to reinforce his, and moved steadily forward upon the flank of the invading column. On June 28th he was relieved and Maj. Gen. Meade, then commanding the 5th Corps, was appointed in his place.

As Burnside incompetent was maintained in command against his own desire, so was Hooker most able of all the army commanders relieved contrary to his wish when upon the eve of making his greatest movement. Appearances would seem to say that there is weakness somewhere in the administration of the war department. The continued interference from Washington with even the most trivial affairs connected with the army of the Potomac is a well known fact. Hooker said with justice that during the day he fought the enemy two hours and the government the remaining twenty two. It was sufficient to render abortive the genius of a Napoleon.

Thus the army lost its most able commander. What general can point to a fairer record throughout his soldierly career. At the commencement of the war he held the rank of Lieut. Col. From thence he has risen to be a major general by the simple force of merit. Steadily has he won his way upward wasting nothing on personal glory or the desire for advancement. He has proved himself not only an able general but also a patriot. Every movement he made was for the advancement of his cause not for the purpose of gaining distinction for himself. He is brave, see Williamsburgh. He is prudent, see Chancellorsville. As a soldier he was everything the army of the Potomac needed, as a man the devotion and respect of his old division (2nd Div. 3rd Corps) proves his excellence. His old command were as much attached to him as were the French army to Napoleon. Let but Joe Hooker ride down the line and speak but one word of exhortation and they were ready to follow even into tougher places than they were really called to go. His men loved him and with good cause. He treated them like men fighting in a sacred cause. He was the true type of a republican general, in battle brave when bravery was needed and cautious where circumspection was called for. He made a quick but careful judgment and when that judgment was for assault pressed the enemy with a fury which seldom failed of accomplishing his object. In camp or on the march he was kind, considerate, just. Always easy of access even a private could obtain justice at his hands. He always returned a private's salute with as much care as he would a general's. To speak of it in the mildest strain how were they mistaken when they relieved Gen. Hooker! yet in the midst of natural disappointment at being relieved when apparently about to win his greatest glory we see his patriotism rising superior to all personal feeling. He asked to be returned to active duty. All honor to "*Old Joe,*" and though he may not possess the full mead of glory he otherwise would have earned, yet "Fighting Joe" and "Hooker's old division" are a portion of American history.

Gen. Meade took command and once more the army has relapsed into the same inanity which characterized its first campaign, only fighting when it cannot be avoided. One victory has been gained, but little glory did that bring to him because the result would have been the same had the army had no commander. At the battle of Gettysburgh as at Malvern Hill the victory was due to the bravery of the troops and exertions of the corps commanders. For four days the army laid in line of battle at Hagerstown and received no orders to attack. On the fifth the enemy had fled. Again was a signal opportunity lost. Gen. Meade has thus far proved himself a second McClellan. Now the army of the Potomac lies quiescent hoping for good news from the south and almost distrusting their ability to again whip the rebels.

GERMANTOWN, VA., Sept. 11, 1863.

Middlesex Journal, Saturday, October 3, 1863

Letter from 6th N. Y. Ind'pt Battery

Culpepper, VA,

Sept. 26th, 1863.

DEAR EDITOR. —I snatch a few moments from the inevitable bustle consequent on a contemplated move to scribble you of our whereabouts and condition. We are camped just without the town of Culpepper and in the immediate vicinity of the reserve artillery. A pleasant open knoll in a glade of the woods contains the pieces while a neighboring apple orchard gleams with our new shelter tents. Before us runs a dingy red stream of water called

Mountain Creek, in our rear a hill which rises to the broad plains of Culpepper now resonant with the locomotives shrill whistle and the rumblings of innumerable army wagons. Culpepper is now the depot for commissariat and ordnance stores of the army of the Potomac. It must have been previously a manufacturing place as several brick factories are still standing. It is much more of a business place than Warrenton yet much inferior to the latter in the way of beauty and pleasantness of station. It must seem quite bewildering to the ordinary inhabitants the bustle and turmoil which the little town has suddenly acquired, all its streets echoing the rattle of huge trains of subsistence stores, the shouts of teamsters, the braying of mules, the clatter of horses, and jingle of sabers and accoutrements. Occasionally a long train of artillery thundering along the streets and shaking the windows in their frames causes the citizens to look forth with renewed wonder at the extent and auxiliary power of the union army.

Since rejoining the brigade, as had been foreseen, we have been pestered with reviews and inspections innumerable by officers of all grades and branches of the service. —Twice have we been inspected by Gen. Hunt, chief of artillery, once at Germantown and but two days ago in this place. As I have before mentioned we have received shelter tents to be used in place of the tarpaulin which previously we had been using as tents. A tarpaulin is made of heavy canvas totally impervious to rain, twelve feet by fifteen in dimensions. Our paulin sheltered from six to nine individuals. Their original purpose was to cover the carriages and harness as protection against the weather. At the first inspection by Gen. Hunt orders were given to restore the paulins to their original use and draw shelter tents for the men. We all grumbled but that availed nothing against military authority, and now behold us domiciled together in parties our only cover one thickness of common heavy factory cloth. They look bright, pretty, and picturesque as I had an opportunity of observing a few nights ago while pacing up and down the hillside on guard, viewing their shimmering whiteness beneath the cold moon, but remembrance of their exceeding dampness in a Virginia storm quite spoiled my appreciation. A soldier grows immensely practical.

We moved from Germantown the morning of the 16th and although the distance to this place is only 15 miles it took us two days to accomplish it. Our tardiness was caused by immense wagon trains which blocked the roads for many miles rendering progress necessarily very slow. Crossed the Rappahannock at Beverly Ford on a bridge composed of eight pontoons, passing close by the site of the 39th Mass. Vols. Camp which they had vacated only that morning. We bivouacked for the night on the plains of Brandy and I was enabled to view the scene of the cavalry fight of June 9th in which our battery was served so roughly.

The next day we made Culpepper and the present camp. During that day's march we passed the residence of John Minor Botts the famous union man.[1] Maj. Robertson halted the brigade and in company with the other officers visited him. He lived (J. M. B.) in a magnificent domain of 9000 acres. His dwelling built in a heavy English style of architecture seemed the abode of all comfort and delightful ease. Doubtless the officers were well satisfied with their visit as they returned with smiling faces and moist moustaches. From Brandy to Culpepper were many traces of Stuart's cavalry, and the edge of nearly every patch of woods showed the remains of their camps.

In this vicinity occurred quite a series of fights immediately upon the withdrawal of Lee's Army from the line of the Rappahannock. Many of the dwellings are deserted and of some there only remains a cellar and a few standing posts to mark their site. The army of the Potomac have had a sufficiently long apprenticeship to be able to totally dismantle a building in the very shortest possible space of time. And in truth it seems a trick well worthy the famous Ravels to see with what dexterity and swiftness a dwelling house and barn is converted into beds, stools, and refuge. Only a short distance from here is a little hamlet consisting of a brick dwelling and several wooden cottages. At the retreat of the rebels and the approach of our cavalry the inhabitants of the wooden houses all fled to the cellar of the brick dwelling for refuge. Rebel sharp-shooters bursting the doors ensconced themselves therein and worried our approaching forces exceedingly. Our artillery was turned upon it and shortly gave it the appearance of a house of card board. The walls were pierced in many places. An old man and a boy were killed and one female wounded. Some of our fellows upon visiting the house saw the latter, her wound being upon the head. Truly war must be a very unpleasant thing to the inhabitants of the country where it is waged!

Yesterday came a sudden order to be ready to move at a moment's notice. To-day everything is ready. Grain is packed from the caisons and nothing scattered about except for minutely use. We may be compelled to start before I finish this article. The movement appears to be to the rear rather than to the front. But in what direction it may be it hardly excites curiosity. Those days have long since passed by for the soldiers of the Potomac army.

It is wonderful how little is done from honest motive, how much for policy. There has lately appeared in the army of the Potomac a circular in relation to a testimonial for Gen. McClellan. A private's subscription thereto is limited to 10 cts., a captain's $1. Is it possible that this has been proposed from any healthy esteem? The general opinion seems to be no. To me it appears like a seeking to destroy the prestige of the government in the minds of the soldiers. The Gov. expressed a plain disapprobation of this man. It does not look much like a good citizen's deed this striving to awaken for him a new popularity. Some hint that this testimonial, instead of lining Gen. McClellan's pocket, goes into the exchequer of the opposition to overthrow the administration that deposed him. Leastways it looks scarcely honest.

HOPLITE

129

Officers of U.S. Horse Artillery Brigade, Culpeper, Virginia, September 1863. Capt.
Joseph W. Martin is seated on a chair, second from left. Courtesy of Massachusetts
Commandery, Military Order of the Loyal Legion and U.S. Army Military History
Institute.

Middlesex Journal, Saturday, October 10, 1863

For the Middlesex Journal.

Thought.

We live to learn. We learn how much there is to learn, and how little
we really can learn. Every day as it passes one with another brings new
thoughts, new ideas, new perceptions. And this is not only true in regard to
all material affairs, but more especially in regard to the ethics of daily life.
As early in life one begins to think upon such subjects it is generally the case
that the youthful mind imagines distinctive lines between good and bad, and
between especial temperaments than later obtains in the same mind. A person is esteemed all bad or all good according as his general disposition seems
to point and this positive distinction seems to satisfy, neither does the mind
appear to question the possibility of a different grading from that which we
are accustomed to accept. These distinctions in the youthful mind are as
often the result of individual or popular expressions of belief from without as
the moral impressions upon the mind itself. What our neighbors, or friends,
and the world say is the true value of a person's morality and ability is very
apt to influence our own decisions and most especially in youth to consti-

tute the basis of our own belief. Gradually as life unfolds our perceptions themselves we begin to perceive the numerous shades betwixt good and evil, between excellence and inferiority. The old established lines gradually fade and we at length begin to perceive the great graduated system which harmonizes the Universe. We see the little good here that somewhat redeems the evil and there pity the evil that sullies the face of great goodness. We see that even the lowest have some redeeming point, the noblest some fault, and that between these two extremes are many shades of excellence. Truly we cannot help but feel shocked at seeing the immense wickedness of which man is capable and really commits, but a small portion of the word's wickedness is comprised in acts. The thoughts, the intentions of human beings oftener contains a certain measure of wickedness than is ever perpetuated in performance. Fortunate is he who, rising to a higher perception of life, can at the same time with seeing the bad search out the good, who learning of another's depravity by his frequent acts yet can give him credit for the occasional repentant thoughts and vain yearnings for goodness and innocence, which to him are unattainable. The tenor of a wicked life, is generally self evident, but who shall know the frequent longings, trials, and struggles for a better life which often accompany the lowest in crime but which we only now and then catch glimpses of in some beautiful and unexpected act of kindness or burst of feeling! Then let us not wholly condemn the bad because they are bad in the main, but believe them capable of much good although perhaps it may not at first appear evident upon the surface. For in reality badness and goodness are in the being, and doing only a sometime proof thereof.

So numerous and so nice are the shades between good and evil, that who can draw the line! Is it not correct philosophy when on perceiving any of these mental peculiarities to refrain from precise judgement, taking all things as they are? Only God is judge because only he can see the whole of man's inward life. Man looking at only violated acts can scarcely ever be correct.

Thus these higher and broader perceptions vouchsafed to man with his opening life ought to beget charity. And charity is the only thing which can reconcile man to the revelations which daily come to him of his own humanity. Therefore selfishly, if one were able to reason thus in regard to his feelings and then adopt the result of his reasonings, man should adopt charity, for would it not be to his own spiritual advantage? But man is only too apt to be determined by external evidence. Internal feeling he will allow to be no proof. And yet what inconsistency! What man does not judge himself by his motives, will allow to another only the benefit of his acts! Truly in judicial judgement we can ask no more than a verdict from the consideration of acts alone, but in the matter of charity does it not become man, who is made in the image of God, to take into consideration something beyond mere acts? For though acts bespeak the preponderance of the mind, yet as in republics the rights of the minority are carefully regarded, so the minority of the mind which is not allowed so frequent proof by act should have its right as well. That right is charity.

How as one grows into this superior mind-life does the great capacity of humanity for good or evil surpass all former *conceptions*. The same that is capable of a holiness, a purity of purpose and action, only less than that of Deity itself, is alike capable of a wickedness most appalling. Each day recognizing the many phases of human life and human purposes we are always happening upon something before unheard and un-thought of. And although authors may say there is nothing new under the sun and dilate on the sameness of human nature the world over dwelling upon usual wickedness and usual worth, still there will always remain depths of the human character as yet unsounded, which in the long ages to come will remain to excite surprise, pleasure, or disgust according as they are gradually brought to the surface. The human mind even of the shallowest subject possesses intricacies of, and each can only judge of another's capabilities by his own, oftentimes very different. This thought upon thought is the sublimity of thought.

The subject is broad yet we should take heed lest from a broad foundation we should carry the consideration of it to too fine a point. We should beware lest, as some German author has said, thought may become too thinly refined until nothing remains but vague imaginings like some broad western thoroughfare which gradually degenerates from highway to cart path, thence to a woodland foot trail and finally runs up a tree. The human mind is near enough to its divine constructor in character to present a subject broad enough and deep enough for profound thought or for argument fine drawn to the utmost tenuity. Fortunate then is that thoughtful man who stops short of the fine, perhaps that lay beyond human ken contenting himself with the beautiful and useful knowledge to be gained from a more superficial examination. He saves himself a deal of vexing thought which begets only disquiet. For the subject thus carried out is as baleful to the one who entertains it as the olden mania of Alchemy and the search for the philosopher's stone.

There are many to whom all these perceptions are denied, or similar to one who in daily life sees certain features yet takes no note thereof and if questioned is quite ignorant, so these things constitute a part of daily life yet make no impressions upon their minds. Man is apt to slip along through the ordinary duties and actions of daily life unthinking and unheeding anything but the accomplishment of the object immediately at hand. He does not see, or if he sees to care, that even the most ordinary things have a philosophy attached to them which it is worth enquiring out. And yet it is far from being unpleasant, this looking behind the veil of daily action to see the course of thought, emotion, impulse, which constitute the inner life. Not that each separate thought can be noted, but that the occasional glimpses of a thought here and one there, and the exercise of the perception necessary to fill the hiatus, make up a pleasure of the highest order.

"The proper study of man is man."

The study of the philosophy of the human mind as shown in its properties and peculiarities is not only productive of much pleasure, but of much
lasting benefit. Though it may not beget a trust and firm faith in the Creator,
yet to the man who considers carefully it must satisfactorily prove the immortality of the soul. It would be useless here besides being quite trite to go into a
lengthened argument to show this proof, for many learned men have already
gone over this ground. The design of this article is to state a few facts placing only an index, as it were, to chapters in the book, and all will be accomplished that is designed, if it should lead only one person to the consideration
of the chapters which the few remarks may serve as indices. The philosophy
of matter seems more generally to attract attention and yet in interest the
philosophy of mind far transcends the former.

> HOPLITE
> Catlet's Station, Va., Sept. 30th,
> 1863.

Middlesex Journal, Saturday, October 17, 1863

Letter from 6th N. Y. Ind'pt Battery

Hartwood Church, VA,

Oct. 8, 1863.

Dear Editor: —As you will perceive by the dates of my various epistles, the
6th Ind. N. Y. Battery has a sort of roving commission. Since my last we have
seen a variety of different places.

On the 25th ult., we were inspected by Gen. Humphrey chief of Gen.
Meade's staff, making the sixth inspection we had undergone in the course of
a fortnight.[2] The next day with great pleasure we broke camp, having been
detached to Gen. Gregg's division of cavalry, and ordered to report to him at
Rappahannock Station. On our way thither we had an opportunity of seeing some of the proofs of the cavalry fight during the late advance from the
Rappahannock to the Rapidan. For several miles along the railroad we met
with the bodies of dead horses, and an occasional grave. This fight from all I
am able to gather seems to have been much severer than the papers generally
reported. The 1st Mass. Cavalry were engaged and lost some men. A participator mentioned to me that it was the most exciting affair he had enjoyed
since he had been in the service. For the rebels after contesting the ground
for a mile or two, at length turned to run, when it began to partake of the
character of a chase. The rebels put their horses to their utmost speed. Close
in their rear charged our cavalry and flying artillery. On both parties went
at headlong speed, thundered through the little town of Culpeper awaking
the usually silent streets to the clank of sabres and din of hoofs, and causing
the citizens to look forth from their houses in dumb amazement and with

pale faces. Down to the Rapidan hurried the rebels pell mell and scarcely had their main body got across when our horse batteries coming up at a gallop, obliqued into line and were in action before the rebels could reform their scattered squadrons. But the other side of the river was fortified and held by infantry. Of what avail was the light armament then present, and therefore we were compelled to content ourselves with the ground already gained.[3] But to return to our muttons as the French say.

About noon on the 26th, we arrived at Rappahannock Station, and Captain Martin having reported to Gen. Gregg received orders to report to Col. Mackintosh, then lying at Catlett Station with his brigade.[4] Catlett Station is nearer Washington than the Rappahannock by nine miles. As we continued our way down the railroad I noticed that all the infantry guard had been removed which had been stationed there previously. They together with the 12th Corps had been sent to reinforce Rosecrans. In their place Gen. Gregg had been entrusted with the safety of the R. R., and his division of cavalry was stretched along from Manassas Junction to the Rappahannock.

Arrived at Catlett we as usual turned our attention to the subject of beds, & c: Close by were the remnants of a house, and in an incredible short space of time all had not only board beds, but also one-story cottages, average height from plate to the ground 2½ feet. We were very comfortable. The house from where we obtained our material was the same one from which Gen. Pope promulgated his famous headquarters-in-the-saddle order.

Close by Catlett station the railroad crosses Cedar run by a considerable bridge. Our camp was situated upon an elevation commanding this bridge and a large tract of open country beyond it in the direction of Warrenton Junction. We remained here just a week during which time we were once alarmed and turned out to harness up in consequence of a cavalry officer being shot by a guerilla in the vicinity. It turned out to be nothing serious, and after remaining in readiness all the afternoon we unharnessed and returned to our quarters.

On Saturday the 3d inst., we were relieved by infantry from the 6th Corps, and artillery from the reserve. Immediately packing up we prepared to evacuate but not without some glances of regret at our comfortable little shanties. These before they were hardly cold of our presence were occupied by our relief, Battery H, 1st Regulars. —About noon four of our pieces started for Bealton, leaving our section, Lieut. Wilson commanding, to go elsewhere. Just at night fall we started off in company with the brigade which I learned had passed into the command of Col. Sargent, of the 1st Mass. Cavalry. After following the railroad as far as Warrenton Junction we struck off to the left and marching at a rapid rate reached a small place called Elk Run, about 10½ o'clk.

Bivouacking there for the night, the next morning we continued the march and arrived at this place about two in the afternoon.

We are now on the extreme outposts of the left flank of the army 15 miles from the main body. Hartwood is about four miles from U. S. Ford, and 12 from Kelly's. And this same ground which is now the extreme left flank, last winter was the right. The 1st Mass. Cavalry did picket duty here all winter.

The building from which this vicinity takes its name lies at the upper portion of an extensive open tract of country several miles in extent. The building is built of brick and of it the bricks only remain, the soldiers having removed every particle of wood work for their own purposes, and should there be any troops stationed in this vicinity during the next winter, not even the bricks would remain. In rear of the church are many graves, only distinguished as such by slight mounds, and an occasional rock at head or foot. In many places the graves have been trampled even with the remaining earth by the picketing of horses. As death little respects the soldier, so he in return pays little reverence to death. The church is plastered inside with various designs, hieroglyphical and otherwise. Prominent above all the rest is a very fine charcoal sketch, representing the 16th Penn. Cavalry charging upon the rebel infantry which is in full retreat. In the foreground on the right is seen the charging squadron, on the left the retreating and confused enemy. In the background union artillery is in action, throwing shells at a prodigious rate. This was done by a lieutenant of the 16th Penn. Cavalry, who was stationed here with a company on outpost. It was done at early dawn. He had just finished it and was laughing at it with the greater portion of his command clustered around him, when a body of rebel cavalry charged up to the door and took them all prisoners. That was an entirely different matter. The sketch shows evidence of considerable talent. The lieutenant was cashiered for his carelessness.

We probably shall not be here much longer as something is on foot, I know not what.

HOPLITE

Middlesex Journal, Saturday, November 14, 1863

By the Camp Fire
by Hoplite
"Nunc est bibendum,
Nunc est pulandum terra"
sings Horatius Flaccus.[5]

How at times does a certain collection of words haunt a person's mind and ever falling from his tongue beget a sort of mental fever. Sometimes it is a phrase, a sentence, a distich. Dwelling consistently in his mind and on his tongue every change in its sound is rung, and every different possible meaning is searched out. This in childhood begets fanciful and laughable names for familiar objects, in later years oftentimes is in the foundation of trains of thought more or less valuable and interesting. I remember during the first engagement in which it was my luck to bear a part that I was ever repeating to myself the chorus of a certain ballad just then coming into vogue, and always since that mention of the battle calls to my mind the ballad and vice versa. The chorus occupied my attention until crowded out by the press of other matters or replaced by another. Thus these words from Horace, haunting me for a certain space I began to look about for the wherewith to make the intruding sentence pay for its keeping. Therefore the toll which I will extract from it shall be a new and exceedingly free translation and an adaptation of it to present circumstances. These fair October days, possessing the very essence of life enjoins that translation to be, "now let's drink long draughts of health, now let's spurn the earth with springing foot." To enjoy the beauty of these days none has such opportunity as the soldier. Springing from his lowly bed to the piercing bugle note, rendered doubly ringing by the frost pervaded breeze, from beneath his blankets jumping at once into the open air; he lays the foundation for a day of healthy enjoyment. The invigorating air causes the blood to circulate merrily and dashingly, health tingles in the farthest vein. It seems to me that if those house-dwellers, to whose lungs the morning brings nothing but unpleasant surprise, could turn soldiers, they would draw something else beside melancholy reflections from the fading of the year. Doubtless may authors have written many prosy things upon the decline of the year, the fall of the leaves, the withering of the grass, and correspondingly laud the opening bloom of spring, drawing from the former dismal comparisons upon the closing of life, from the latter hopeful visions for the future; but a more careful consideration from the standpoint of common sense and experience must needs tell a different story. It is a well known fact that Fall is the most healthful season of the year, Spring the sickliest. The atmosphere of these autumn days, like rich wine, puts strong life into the veins and joyous imaginings into the mind. The sun seems nearer and to hang about one a very atmosphere of light and joyness. The air intensely rarified shows outlines wonderfully distinct of objects at extreme distance. The sky clear or dotted here and there with fleecy and quickly shifting flakes, presents scenes of chaste and cold beauty, to be insensible of which one must needs be soulless indeed. The trees have put on their autumn colorings and in Virginia where the mingling of evergreens and deciduous growth is so fine, the effect of October's approach is indeed beautiful. Red, purple, yellow, green, combinations in plots, patches, strips, flanked perhaps in the distance by the sober russet of a huge pine forest or the glittering of some silver winding stream, such scenes varied by every variety of combinations yield not the palm even to the growing life and opening freshness of young Spring. And with Autumn's still beauty there comes withal such overflow of animal life! It is an intense enjoyment itself the mere possession of existence. No melancholy thoughts there, no dismal forebodings, all is free, buoyant as the air we breathe. Hail happy Autumn!

All these sights and feelings the soldier experiences more especially from his closer intimacy with nature. From the nature of his profession delivered over to many hours of idleness nor allowed the pleasures of civilized life to occupy his attention, he needs must come to an appreciation of all the beautiful and healthful which surrounds him. It is just the present weather that brings out to the full extent the careless joviality of camp life. As the shades of evening begin to gather, the flickering camp fires shimmer among the sturdy oaks each surrounded by its merry throng of blue-clad soldiers. The joke passed from lip to lip and "the sounding aisle of the dim woods" ring with hearty laughter.

Antics strange and boisterous are cut oftentimes more vigorous than graceful. Loud arguments are held upon every debatable subject under the sun. And as the evening wanes grown quieter they indulge in home reminiscences and anecdotes with intervals of silence in which no doubt home loves and home hopes prevail.

The circle which shortly before was all activity with boisterous mirth, perchance now sits in silence around the crackling blaze each mind bent upon its separate errand. Thus ends, with cheerful sport and thoughts of home three days spent in healthful habits. The bugle rings out upon the stilly night air "tattoo" notes which at intervals reaching from every copse and dingle then sinks and dies upon the ear among the distant mountains. Once more the silence of the night is broken by solemn sounding "taps" and then all is still. No sound remains except the clank of sabre scabbard as some lonely sentinel turns on his beat. The fires glimmer and the lines of snowy tents shine lonely beneath the Autumn moon. Thus ends the soldier's day.

CHAPTER 6

A SHARPSHOOTER CAME VERY NEAR TO
BRINGING ME DOWN:
OCTOBER–DECEMBER 1863

AFTER A FOUR AND ONE-HALF MONTH GAP, PERKINS RESUMED WRITING
his diary on October 23, 1863. On this date, the battery was ensconced
in a camp near Sulphur Springs, Virginia, about ten miles southwest
of Warrenton on the Rappahannock River. After the Bristoe advance,
which had taken the Army of Northern Virginia from the Rapidan to
Bull Run in five days of heavy campaigning, Gen. Robert E. Lee began
returning south on October 17 and completed his withdrawal behind
the Rappahannock River on October 20. Along with the rest of the
Army of the Potomac, the Sixth New York retraced its steps and two
days later resumed its former position along the Rappahannock.

Gen. George Gordon Meade resumed the offensive on November 7, attacking and capturing an exposed Confederate position on
the northern side of the Rappahannock at Rappahannock Bridge and
another four miles downstream on the southern side of the river at
Kelly's Ford. As a consequence of this Union success, Lee once again
withdrew his army behind the Rapidan River. On November 26, Meade
began another offensive, attempting to flank Lee's army out of its positions by advancing his entire army across the Rapidan at Jacob's Ford,
Germanna Ford, and Culpeper Mine Ford. Lee countered by massing
his forces behind a strong defensive position behind Mine Run, a minor
tributary of the Rapidan. Finding Lee's position too strong to be carried, Meade withdrew across the river and went into winter camps at
Culpeper Court House and Brandy Station.

This chapter begins with a letter that Perkins wrote describing
the Bristoe Campaign of early- to mid-October and outlining the battery's part in that action. The Rappahannock Bridge affair and the
Mine Run Campaign also receive detailed treatment. Although the
battery was not engaged, Perkins had an opportunity to observe at close

range Confederate prisoners who were taken captive at Rappahannock Bridge and conversed with several. The battery was heavily involved in the Mine Run Campaign, and the diary provides many details of the advance, the action at Parker's Store on the left flank of the army, and the retreat across the Rapidan. In addition, during the few days in which the battery was not on the move or engaged in battle, Perkins used his pen to enter the realms of philosophy and religion.

Camp near Sulphur Springs, Va.
Friday, Oct. 23rd, 1863.
    Fair and cold. Wrote a communication to the Journal. Beef Steak for dinner, first fresh meat in a fortnight.

Middlesex Journal, Saturday, October 31, 1863
Letter from 6th N. Y. Ind'pt Battery
Near Sulphur Springs, VA,
Oct. 24th, 1863
Dear Editor: —As your correspondent I felt somewhat obliged to write you of the stirring events in which we have been engaged for the past few days, and sooner than this, but the being in the saddle every day and a great portion of every night has precluded every opportunity for the discharge of said obligation. And I think my duty to yourself and readers is discharged fully by this seizure of the first opportunity which has been afforded me to write for many days. But first allow me to call the attention of such as may have read my by-the-way scribblings in the "Journal" to a certain fact, and to make some sort of excuse therefore. I have noticed in the printed copies of nearly all my communications mistakes of grammar and punctuation more or less laughable. I take this opportunity of freeing you from all blame on the score of mis-printing, and of satisfying my own vanity which can not suffer it to be believed that those mistakes occurred from ignorance. From a long-continued habit of careless writing, which was adopted for ease and rapidity in the execution of the many exercises incident to a school life, I find that my handwriting presents at all times somewhat of a hieroglyphical appearance and must in some instances puzzle the printer. And the appearance of one's handwriting is not improved by the situation the soldier is compelled to adopt within the narrow limits of a shelter tent, seated upon the ground with knees almost in his mouth or a posture equally uncomfortable. Is my excuse valid? Then in future let the Journal readers seeing any laughable or improper construction in communications from Hoplite, give me the benefit of a remembrance of my unfortunate chirography. A combined sentiment of justice and self-esteem prompted this apology. Has it been too lengthy?

Doubtless before this will have reached you all the particulars of the late movement of the army of the Potomac will have been made public but as no correspondent accompanies Gen. Gregg's Div., perhaps I may make known some special movements not unworthy notice in your columns.

Our section of artillery with the Cavalry brigade to which it had been attached, left Hartwood Church for Culpepper, upon the 10th inst., by way of Kelley's Ford. At noon of the 11th, we reached the plains of Brandy, where the first intimation of the recent retreat met us in the shape of rapidly moving columns of wagons, ambulances, artillery, &c. At the same time receiving new orders from Gen. Pleasonton, we turned back and reaching the Rappahannock at Beverly Ford, reached Sulphur Springs toward nightfall. What a contrast to our last visit. —When there before, the walls of the old hotel echoed to the rattle of the drum, the clang of martial music, the loud word of command, the rattle and clash of sabre. The green lawn then looked greener by the contrast of blue coats, white gloves, and polished boots. Now our column clattering along the stony pike awoke strange echoes about the building, the old place seemed to look with surprise upon the invaders, and as the rear of our line passed up the road, relapsed into a relieved silence returning to its gradual process of fading and decay. We camped some distance up the road toward Warrenton, and next morning were joined by the other brigade and the remainder of the battery which had come up the other side the river from Culpepper.

About noon of the 12th, we had moved still farther toward Warrenton and had just unharnessed when once more the bugle sounded "boot and saddle" and at the same time came the rattle of small arms and the boom of cannon from the direction of the river. All the afternoon our brigade laid in readiness and listening to the music at the front. At length just before dark, we were ordered up but too late. The enemy had effected a crossing and were pouring down to the river in heavy columns. Four of our pieces were ordered to the rear at double quick and the other two going into action merely to create a little delay, delivered a few shots and then limbering up, followed at a full gallop. They soon overtook the remainder of the battery and together we all clattered along pell mell over the roughest road I ever remember. Our way lay toward the rail road midway between the river and the Warrenton Branch. Reached Fayetteville about midnight, which place is distant from Bealton about four miles. There we staid all night without unharnessing and it was bitter cold. Next day about the middle of the afternoon we commenced the retreat, and as we proceeded, I found that we constituted the extreme rear guard. Just after dark we overtook portions of the 2d Corps in a large plain situated between Warrenton and Warrenton Junction. From there we continued the march across the fields always keeping to the West of the railroad until we reached the vicinity of Auburn, where we camped in a large field about midnight. During this night march, the infantry who had

preceeded us, had kindled numerous fires along their route of march probably in order to deceive the enemy into the belief that the army had camped
there, whereas the main body was far in advance. It was a beautiful sight this
cordon of fire stretching far away into the darkness. As we mounted each
swell of the landscape, new lines of fires unfolded to the view, until it seemed
we never were to reach the end of them. Neither did they seem to stretch
forward in a straight line, but to curl round from our right to the rear and
front, hemming us in by a fiery semi-circle. In every instance these fires were
made from the cornshocks just harvested and standing in the fields.

The next morning, 14th, we had just breakfasted and hitched up as the
day was breaking, when a lively picket firing in front and to the right electri-
fied us and immediately we went into battery. The cavalry threw out skirmishers to the woods a half or three-quarters mile distant and soon found the
enemy, at the same time we perceiving him through an opening in the woods
passing down an adjoining field in column dosed him with a few percussion
shells and made several admirable shots. This we continued for sometime,
worrying them not a little and paying the compliment of an occasional shot
to some smart firing which was going on in the woods to our right. We were
not annoyed except for an occasional shot from a sharpshooter, none which
happily did us any injury although I have been told one horse was wounded
in the 1st Mass. Cavalry which was in the rear supporting the battery.

About the middle of the forenoon we were withdrawn and advanced
about two miles to the vicinity of St. Stephen's Church, four miles from
Catlett Station. There we went into battery commanding a long valley.

As soon as we had formed this second line their battery and a portion
of the 2d Corps which had been holding the enemy while we executed this
movement fell back on a double quick followed by the rebels. Again we
opened upon them making the valley too hot for them, when they penetrated
to a house situated in a little niche in the woods and on a slight elevation to
our left half a mile distant. Upon this house and opening we concentrated
our fire and soon they went back much faster then they came. I could distinguish their grey clothing very plainly with the naked eye.

In the intervals between the firing there was ample leisure for observation and we could see at the near extremity of the valley a heavy column of
the enemy passing to the right, but they were out of range. Gen. Warren of
the 2d Corps who was looking at this column with his field glass from the
centre of the battery was heard to give it as his opinion that it was the rear
guard of Lee's army which we had brushed against. Meade's rear guard was
fighting Lee's rear guard. From here we fell steadily back with the 2d Corps
and reaching the R. R. but a short distance from Catlett continued on toward
Bristow. We had got close upon this latter place when a hot firing was heard
in that direction. It proved that A. P. Hill's Corps coming through Thoroughfare Gap had tried to cut us off. The firing grew more distinct as we

came nearer and at length we debouched upon the large plain about Bristow Station which was the scene of the conflict.

I have seen many pictures of battles but nothing to grand and terrible as this. The whole scene was spread before me like a panorama. Through the immense field ran the railroad, on one side of which were long lines of the rebels firing with inconceivable rapidity. Far down the plain and on the right our infantry had found a double line of battle under a terrible fire. Just as we came upon the scene this line was being compressed by an oblique movement to the left on the double quick. Rapidly the long line swung around and with a shout became stationary. The shout, the roar of firearms, the long lines of grey and blue, the wreaths of smoke spit forth from the shining tubes, at intervals along the line the waving of the battle flags, the roar of artillery from the rear of each line playing over the heads of the combatants, the plain dotted numerously with the fallen, constitute some of the most salient points of the scene which I have neither the talent nor inclination to arrange into an impressive description of the late battle at Bristow. But these points which at once burst upon my view even now as I remember them causes the blood to bounce in my veins. It was an intensely thrilling sight. We did not get into action immediately but cutting across the edge of the plain under a shower of bullets halted in column in the woods. Shortly returning to the edge of the field we took position when it was evident that the rebels had been beaten back into the woods at the other extremity. Upon their showing themselves again we opened upon them and drove them back and our infantry charging into the woods captured five pieces of artillery.

After this all was silent for the space of an hour during which I had leisure to view the field of battle. Far out on the plain where once had been the line of battle laid many a poor fellow but one short hour before strong and hearty. The ambulances went out to bring them in. As I mounted the gun to get a better view I could hear their cries of agony and entreaties for water. As I looked the thought rose hard within me "and shall men who cause these things shall they be tolerated, and can this union be reconstructed as it was with *such* men its accepted members?" That sight of one short moment was to me a greater argument against the peace cry of the "Union as it was" than all the folios that copperheads might write in its favor.

About dark we were aroused by the opening of a rebel battery upon our left flank but which was soon silenced by two batteries of 12 pounders, which opened upon it. But for a short time they threw the iron and gravel about our ears with total disregard for our comfort. Luckily no one was hurt. Shortly after nightfall we withdrew in the direction of Centreville where we arrived about 1 o'clock. About a mile from the battle field we met the 5th Corps which had come to reinforce us. As they moved along without even a whisper or the sound of a footfall it seemed like a column of spectres rather than union soldiers.

When the army reached Centreville it seemed to me as if the army formed a line of battle the left resting on Wolf Run Shoals. On this flank was posted Gen. Gregg's division with our battery. When the army advanced again we covered the rear as formerly until the 21st, when advancing through Thoroughfare Gap (when by the way I saw the boys in the 39th, the 1st Corps being stationed there) through New Baltimore and Washington we reached this place half way between Warrenton and Sulphur Springs. We now hold the right flank I think. All the Woburn boys are safe and in good health.

HOPLITE

OCT. 24TH, SATURDAY.
Rained hard all the preceding night. About noon came an alarm and we harnessed up and took down our tents, the cause our pickets had been driven in by the enemy. Toward night unharnessed again and pitched tents whereat I was much pleased as it was cold and rainy. Received two letters from Myra and one from H.A.H.

OCT. 25TH, SUNDAY.
Cold and clear. Wrote to Myra. Sent home a volume filled with my diary. Picked some delicious persimmons. Beef steak for dinner.

OCT. 26TH, MONDAY.
Cold and fair. Occupied most of the day in boiling pork. Received letter from Aunt Lizzie. Wrote to Miss Moulton. On guard, 3d relief. Veal soup for dinner.

OCT. 27TH, TUESDAY.
My horse got loose and strayed away and I went off on horse-back in pursuit of him. Went to Warrenton which looked cold, dismal and deserted, far different from its appearance last August.

OCT 28TH, WEDNESDAY.
My horse returned to camp minus his halter lead. The battery drew 28 new horses. Had a little muss with Cloyston. Sergt. Miller who had been captured at the Brandy Station fight in June returned to the battery.[1] Wrote to Aunt Lizzie. Fair.

OCT 29TH, THURSDAY.
Very warm. Cleaned and greased the harness and equipments. Received letter from Myra. Read Tom Hood's "Up the Rhine".

OCT. 30TH, FRIDAY.
Wrote to Myra. Baked beans for dinner. Read "Jack Ariel". In the evening held a great argument with Horton on Foreign Intervention.

OCT. 31ST, SATURDAY.
Rained heavily during the preceding night and part of the day. Mustered by Capt. Martin for pay for the months of Sept. & Oct. Commenced an article for publication.

NOV. 1ST, SUNDAY.
Very cold in the morning but warmer toward noon. "Boot and saddle" about 10 o' clock and we moved our camp about ¼ mile nearer to Warrenton in the angle of some woods on very high ground. A very warm situation. Kiely and I put up our tent with a wall and built a bed of boards brought from the other camp. A very busy day. Matters seemed to portend some movement whether backward or forward impossible to judge.

NOV. 2ND, MONDAY.
Very warm. Wrote to brother Jacob. Received a letter from cousin Bethiah enclosing two pictures. Was much disappointed at not receiving a letter from Myra.

NOV. 3D, TUESDAY.
Very warm indeed. Wrote to cousin Bethiah. Visited 1st Mass. Cav. Had a good wash all over in the brook, first time for three weeks. Rations run short, had to buy hard bread, price 6 cts. per lb. Received letter from M.C.J., a blank book from home for Journal, and a Middlesex Journal. Still no letter from Myra. Fear one or more may have miscarried.

NOV. 4TH, WEDNESDAY.
Still very warm. Occupied most of the day in reading "Jack Adams, the Mutineer" by Capt. Caramier. My horse grown so lame that I could not ride him. Wrote to Myra. Received a letter from Myra enclosing picture of herself and Georgie. On guard, 1st relief.

NOV. 5TH & 6TH.
Fair and warm. Wrote to Myra 2 letters. Read "Abercrombie."

NOV. 7TH, SATURDAY.
Windy yet warm. "Boot and saddle" about 12 o' clock and after forming the column took up the line of march toward Fayetteville by the same road on which we went on the 12th ult.[2] Shortly before we reached Fayetteville overtook the wagon train of the 6th Corps going the same way. Just before we reached Bealton could hear cannonading and musketry. Camped for the night in the large plain about Bealton Station. Rode another horse and led my own, the latter being very lame. As we came in sight of Bealton the long lines of baggage wagons stretched across the plain in serpentine windings, the sun shining on their white covers presented a very picturesque sight. We finished cooking our beans. Slept on the paulin.

Nov. 8th, Sunday.

Cloudy in the morning. Just after breakfast my attention was attracted by a column of rebel prisoners coming from the front. There were about 2000 among them many officers. They looked in good condition and well dressed. They seemed to be mostly deficient in shoes. I saw one poor fellow with bare feet blistered. They seemed in good spirits. One seeing some negroes among the onlookers enquired if they were native Americans. They were of Ewell's Corps and consisted of 5 regiments. I told one he would have good winter quarters. He said, "I *done* built my quarters already." They were under escort of cavalry. I noticed that the buildings at Bealton Station had been burned down probably by the rebs, and the railroad track torn up. A great many of these prisoners had on new jackets and some new suits throughout. All sorts of reports rife, such as that our army was flanking the rebs at Kelley's Ford &c. During the day I saw various other squads of rebels which as they came in were halted here and receiving one day's ration were marched off toward Washington. They seemed eager to get the victuals. I talked with some of them quite a long time and learned that they were engaged in building winter quarters when attacked. They were taken by surprise, our fellows getting between them and their bridge and cutting it adrift. Many of them were driven into the river. I saw one of the rebel artillery men. The battery was from Louisiana and consisted as he said of 2 parrotts and 2 three-inch Dahlgrens. We captured in all about 3000. Bitter cold all day. About four in the afternoon we harnessed up and after feeding and getting supper we started on after the wagon train toward the river, following the railroad. On the way Lieut. Clark had a man arrested for selling some of our fellows whiskey. Reached the vicinity of Rappahannock Station at about 9 o'clock and camped for the night. Looked like snow.[3]

Nov. 9th, Monday.

Passed a very poor night. Cold but fair. Letter from Myra, but an old one which had miscarried, one from Sammy, some stationary, a Harper and some papers. Wrote to Myra. Went to the river to water and noticed that the rebels had made extensive fortifications. Snowed just a trifle and we went to bed.

Nov. 10th, Tuesday.

Reveille before daybreak. Coldest day yet. Took up line of march toward Fayetteville where we arrived about noon.[4] Saw Capt. Robertson on the way. Could see the Blue Ridge in the distance covered with snow which had fallen in the night. The mountains looked as if made of burnished silver. Kiely and I doubled up with Tileston and Miller and put up a paulin.[5] Camped in some heavy pine woods, very warm.

Nov. 11th, Wednesday.

Very cold and clear. Moved directly after stable call a distance of about two miles nearer to Sulphur Springs and camped in some thick oak woods.[6] Pitched paulin and closed it up warm and tight. A very warm camp.

Nov. 12th, Thursday.

Much warmer. Very fair and pleasant. Wrote to Myra. Wrote an article for Journal. Begin to like my new horse which I received two days before in place of Bunting who had fallen lame from the grease heel.

Middlesex Journal, Saturday, November 21, 1863

Letter from 6th N. Y. Ind'pt Battery

Near Fayetteville, VA,

Nov.12th, 1863

Dear Editor: —Once more the coming frosts have retreated before the warm attack of the broadly glowing sun and we enjoy a return of the Indian summer. Old Sol floods the fields and purple woods with golden beams, and the morning airs bereft of their icy edge breathe health and comfort. No longer is the soldier's attention solely occupied with plans for the retention of animal heat, and your correspondent again finds himself at liberty to indulge his own garrulity and inflict his composition upon your readers. We have been undergoing an exceedingly cold snap. For several days previous to our flitting from Sulphur Spring rumors of movement in every imaginable direction were rife, but not until the morning of the 7th inst., was any of them realized.

Upon that day about the middle of the forenoon much to the consternation of our mess who were engaged in the laudible [*sic*] occupation of stewing beans, "boot and saddle" sounded and soon we were in the saddle. Being determined not to lose our beans, the water was drained off and enveloping them in several thicknesses of grain bags we tied them upon a caisson postponing the completion of the cooking until the first halt. Forming column of march much more speedily than usual, the brigade moved swiftly off in the direction of Fayetteville, by the same road on which we made our very precipitous march upon the 12th of the preceding month. Arriving near that place about the middle of the afternoon we could distinctly hear cannonading in the direction of Rappahannock Station. Continuing the march to Bealton, where we arrived just previous to night fall, the sound of the fighting came more plainly to our ears, the sound of cannon intermingled with the rattle of musketry. Slowly the cannonading proceeded with a desultory fire of small arms until gradually swelling to a full battle chorus, the fight seemed to cease with one tremendous volley of small arms. We bivoucked [*sic*] upon the plain at Bealton. Darkness settling down upon the broad extended fields enveloped the monstrous wagon trains and their guards bringing with it a rising and a cutting wind. Searching about the bare plain, we found just wood enough wherewith to cook our coffee and beans, and the latter tasted none the less excellent for their two doses of cooking, and that we had been without eating from early dawn until after dark. Rumors more or less extravagant kept arriving from the front, but all seemed to concur in the point that we had whipped the rebels.

The night was spent alternatively between my blankets and the fire, not that my blankets would not keep me warm, but Wax, my bed companion, would persist in pulling them off me.

Morning came colder than ever, and soon it was possible to learn the true state of affairs. We had attacked the rebels at Rappahannock Station, flanked them and cut off their retreat across the river. Our batteries aided by flanking columns of infantry had destroyed their pontoon bridge and on this side some 2000 men had fallen prisoners to the prowess of the veteran 6th Corps. I saw these prisoners as they were marched to the rear and will acknowledge they were very fine looking men. They were nearly all comfortably dressed being deficient chiefly in foot covering. Yet I did not see but one bare-footed. Poor fellow, I could not but pity him, for the soles of his feet were blistered and bloody. In conversation with one of them belonging to the 57th N. C. Regt., I learned that they belonged to Ewell's Corps, and that they had been engaged in building winter quarters at the time of the attack. It was a complete surprise to them. I saw a member of the Louisiana battery which our fellows had captured, who told me that the battery consisted of two Parrott guns and two 3-inch Dahlgrens, all captured from us at Winchester. But I think he must be mistaken in regard to the latter as the U. S. does not use the latter for land purposes. They must have been 3-inch Griffin guns sometimes called regulation guns.

The army advanced across the Rappahannock at Kelly's Ford capturing at the latter place some 300 more of the rebels. Gregg's division of cavalry remains behind at Bealton all that day being engaged at its old occupation of covering the rear. Just at dark all the baggage train having moved toward the river we followed and camped about half a mile short of the river. Bealton is distant from the river about three miles. The cold still increasing. There we remained two nights and one day. While camped there we watered at the ford and could notice the increase to the fortifications which the rebels had made while they had possession of the river this time. On both sides to the right and left stretched long lines of earth works comprising rifle pits, redans, and redoubts, innumerable. Some of our fellows saw the graves of those fallen in the engagement. It was very brisk while it lasted. Leaving at this place on the 9th, the succeeding morning we made a retrograde movement and halted near the little town of Fayetteville. Remaining there one night, we, next day, advanced two miles to this place, where we have been ever since. Gregg's division now pickets the rear of the army from Falmouth to Waterloo a distance of some 50 miles. Up to to-day the weather has been very cold, but now it is much more endurable. On the morning of the 10th marching from Rappahannock Station to Fayetteville we were only too glad to walk leading our horses by the bridles. The preceding night there had been a slight fall of snow upon the Blue Ridge and their white summits viewed from the lowlands looked indeed beautiful but "shivery." Their tops seemed as if clad in burnished silver.

Isolated as we are from the rest of the army it is utterly impossible to learn of the current of events. We needs must content ourselves with the belief that we are contributing our portion to the success of the movement now taking place. Whatever it is it seems to excite but little remark and yet it is not impossible that it may prove the greatest success of the season. As usual all sorts of rumors prevail, some saying that the advance of the Potomac army is now beyond the Rapidan, others maintaining that it is about to fall back once more to the line of the Rappahannock. Whatever is done must be done soon as before long the winter rains will set in, wherein are greater reinforcements for Lee than thousands of soldiers.

HOPLITE

Nov. 13th, Friday.
Very warm and pleasant. Wrote an article for the Journal. Had my hair cut and beard trimmed. No mail.

Middlesex Journal, Saturday, December 5, 1863

By the Camp Fire
by Hoplite
We were encamped among a thick growth of young oaks. It was early evening. The cold November wind went rushing through the tree tops. Their wide arms swaying and creaking in the breeze, complained loudly in the tempest. From out the darkness here and there, throughout the whole extent of the wood, glimmered huge watch fires. The whirling wind ever now and again would catch the bright sparks and send them eddying and twisting far to leeward, until they one by one disappeared in the surrounding darkness. Each fire possessed its circle of soldiers engaged in earnest conversation, or cheerful mirth. From one fire came the sound of political discussion hot and earnest, from still further points rolled on the evening breeze, the jovial chorus, or sentimental ballad.

Two days previously the battery had been filled to a serviceable condition, by detached men from the several regiments, comprising the 1st Brigade of the 2d Division Cavalry Corps. Among these men, was one, a German, from the 1st R. I. Cavalry. On that night, he with several others stood before the glowing fire made from huge logs of green oak, enjoying its genial warmth and listening to the progress of conversation among us. Gradually he himself was drawn into the current of talk and finally engrossed it entirely. The subject was the utility of worshipping the deity. He acknowledged the presence of a great first cause, and yet doubted whether prayer to that cause benefited the one praying. He contended that events would happen equally in a given order, no matter what prayers were made, therefore that prayers were useless. His knowledge of English was so imperfect that it was altogether impracticable to argue with him with any degree of satisfaction. Yet his conversation was so pleasing that I lingered by the fire far into the night listening to him. I propose to relate a tale which I heard upon that evening, and which he told as a casual incident, closing with a question as to what he was to believe in connection with it. I can hardly hope to succeed in putting it before the readers of the Journal in as pleasing a guise as it was delivered to me, for his simple and elegant, though often ungrammatical language, told his story in most attractive style. Indeed I felt an interest in it, told there by the blazing logs and usual camp accompaniments, such as I have never experienced before in the perusal of even our most successful romanticists. The story is a personal experience and undoubtedly true.

I was pursuing a course of study at the University of Bonn. At different times I had met and become acquainted with an officer of the line stationed in the vicinity. Acquaintance soon ripened into friendship, and in Germany friendship is something more than a term. Some necessary duty separated us and for several months we saw nothing of each other. One evening as I was sitting with my companions at our pipes and beer, my friend came hurriedly into the room, and with much agitation told me that he must see me alone. I took him to my own room and locking the door, entreated him to calm himself, and inquired the cause of his disturbance. His gaze seemed to be fixed upon a pair of dueling pistols which, with a student's affectation, I was accustomed to keep exposed above my mantel shelf, and the sight seemed to affect him most unfavorably. He shivered as with ague. Growing calmer after a lapse of time, he spoke fearfully and with deep sorrow. "I know not why it is, but I must tell you the deep seated grief which I now retain gnawing at my heart. I have a very dear family, and a kind father, but, I know not why I can tell you what I cannot tell my own parent. I am a murderer."

"How," said I; "you a murderer? It is impossible." For he had always been with me one of the most generous and impulsive of human hearts.

"It is indeed so. It happened as follows: we were playing at billiards, my friend and myself, when between us rose an altercation. I insulted him, which he as quickly returned. I challenged him to fight with pistols. We immediately repaired to the dueling-ground and after a harmless exchange of shots my adversary affirmed himself to be satisfied and that he bore no resentment. I also said that my malice was satisfied. I lied. I cherished hatred in my heart. Some days afterward my friend and myself were present at a hunt. We were posted, each at his appropriate position, he number seven, I number two. The beaters go within to stir up the game. In the excitement of the chase we change our places. I found myself at the bottom of a deep ravine across which ran the road. I hear a rustling upon the bank above. My former adversary appears in plain sight and alone. My former hatred surges up from the depth of my bosom. Quick as the flash of hatred which flies across my mind I raise my rifle and fire. I am a murderer."

As my friend arrived thus at the catastrophe of his sad story, he swooned quite away, and lifting him upon my bed I applied what remedies I could read-

ily command. At length he recovered and then I attempted to soothe his excitement. I knew his excitable disposition, and feared a predisposition to insanity. I questioned him as to whether all this might be some terrible hallucination. Taking from his pocket the process at law by which he was acquitted from willful murder, I saw he had alleged he thought his adversary to be a deer and thus had escaped the punishment of his crime, for no living witness was present. At length I was enabled to restore him to comparative calmness, and then he told me of his daily torments. Even my pistols caused him to shiver for they reminded him of his dreadful crime.

After that we became inseparable companions, brothers, in fact. Together we served three years in a western expedition, he as captain, I as private. Always we maintained our love for each other, and it made me happy to know that in the recurrence of his phrenzied fits I alone could soothe him. Our friendship "passed the love of woman."

At length returning to our native state I persuaded him to leave the service and retire to seclusion and the enjoyment of his wealth, for he was rich. Soon he became almost an inmate of my father's house. He grew to love my father and yet feared him. One day after a long talk with my father, he came to me with the old terror depicted on his face. "Your father is a terrible man. He knows that I am not as other men are. He reads my secret. Go into him and learn of him what I am." Complying with his wish, I went to my father and asked what he thought of the captain. "I think him a noble young man, but rather peculiar. He either has some great secret trouble, or else is somewhat crazy." My father said thus and going to my friend I told him his suspicions were incorrect. Finally I quieted his terrible excitement and things went on as before.

Having occasion to go a journey of some days, I returned two days behind my intended time. I found a letter from the captain desiring if I arrived home before seven that night to call at his lodgings. I looked up at the time-piece. It was seven and ten minutes. I rushed down the street with all speed only to learn at his lodgings that he had left for Coelen in the 7 o'clock express. I obtained a fleet horse and forced him to his utmost speed, only to arrive at the next station in season to see the rear of the train just disappearing from view. I learned from the station master that a person which answered to the description of my friend had indeed been on the train. On the next hour's train I followed him to Coelen, where I arrived about 11 o'clock. At the Golden Fox I learned that the captain had retired for the night, I requested to be shown to his room. I found the door locked and could not gain admission by the loudest knocking. Unwilling to make any disturbance and being sure of reaching him in the morning, I requested another bed, and retiring was soon asleep. At 5 o'clock in the morning I arose and going down stairs found that he had again escaped me, by taking the train at two for Coblenty. I followed as soon as steam transportation would allow. Enquiring at the various hostelrys of Coblenty I soon found the one at which he had stopped, and found that after returning from the purchase of a rapier, he had *again gone out. I searched for the shop at which he had bought the weapon and found that he had also bought a complete officer's outfit, even to the boots and mantle. My heart sank with dread. I wandered aimlessly about the city, stopping every now and then at the hotel to learn if he had yet returned. At length, just outside the city gates I perceived a crowd upon the walk. I shivered, for I knew well what I should see when I should approach. At length I gathered courage and at once realized my worst fears. On the pavement laid my unhappy friend. Coming through the city gates he had spread the magnificent mantle which he had just bought, broad upon the ground and shot himself through the breast. His officer's mantle was his shroud. Sadly I performed the last duties as his friend, for indeed, he was very dear to me although a murderer. He had suffered the full measure of punishment for his crimes upon earth. Can we hope it was ended with his death?*

Such was the story of my German friend, and the manner as well as the place of telling ensured breathless attention. For some minutes after the conclusion of his tale, the fire crackled without a sound to mingle with its roar save the rush of the wind through the bending boughs. Each one made his own moral which was none the less useful that it was unspoken.

The relator first broke the silence by remarking, that thus evil deeds always bring accompanying punishment, but that all the theories of future reward or future punishment were but theories after all.

I did not stop to argue the question, but quietly resolved to give the story to the Journal readers, for them to judge of the obvious moral.

Fayetteville, VA,
Nov. 13th, 1863

Nov. 14TH, SATURDAY.
Still warm with rain in the evening. Played cribbage the only game of cards which really is interesting to me. Finished reading "Abercrombie's Mental Philosophy" and wrote out my opinion of it. Wrote to Sammy and to M.C.J.

Nov. 15TH, SUNDAY.
Rained heavily all the preceding night and early this morning. Cleared off about the middle of the forenoon. Cleaned the carriages. In the afternoon the battery together with the whole brigade went out to witness the punishment of two deserters from the 3rd Penn. Cavalry. After forming the brigade into line the sentence was executed. Their heads were one half shaved and then each was branded upon the left hip with the letter D 1½ inches long. After which they were followed down the lines bareheaded with the band playing the rouge's march. They looked very comical with one half their heads bald, and what hair they had was quite long. One was quite a young man and of light complexion, the other darker and much older. The younger one seemed to take his punish-

ment much more to heart than the other. They received a dishonorable discharge from the service. Received a pair of Wristers from home, very pretty, and a lead pencil. Was much disappointed at receiving no letter from home. Wrote to Myra. Weather raw and cold. Sent home my opinion on the "Mental Philosophy."

Nov. 16th, Monday.
Raw and cold. Washed and changed clothes, almost freezing my toes in the operation. At night went to a neighboring house to buy some milk. Paid 25 cts for 3 pints. Wrote again to Almira. Rumor that the succeeding day our section was going to Warrenton on detached duty. Our pickets in that direction had been annoyed greatly by guerillas and it was proposed to take our section to within 1½ miles of Warrenton and when the guerillas attacked, to shell Warrenton under pretense of firing at them. Warrenton was supposed to be the hiding place of all these guerillas.

Nov. 17th, Tuesday.
Fair and warm all day. Still no mail. At 5½ o' clock our section harnessed up and in company with two squadrons of cavalry took up line of march in the direction of Warrenton. I had two offers from fellows in the other section to go in my place, but I would not accept it. About 2½ miles from camp we arrived upon the top of a small eminence where two roads met and about one mile from Warrenton.[7] We placed the guns in position bearing upon the town and waited for Mosby and his guerilla band. The wind had arisen since sundown and it was bitter cold. I laid down in a paulin but could get no sleep because of my cold feet. Had to get up and warm them by walking about and put on another pair of stockings.

Nov. 18th, Wednesday.
Returned to camp before daylight without having heard or fired a shot. A very lazy day. In the evening visited my friends in the band of the 1st M.C. Very warm.

Nov. 19th, Thursday.
Still very warm. No mail yet and I began to feel unusually gloomy. For some days my mind had been dwelling upon the subject of morals and religion, but could come to no satisfactory frame of mind upon the subject. Commenced to read the testament carefully.

Nov. 20th, Friday.
Fair. Wrote an article for publication on Knowledge. On guard, 1st relief.

Nov. 21st, Saturday.
Rainy all day. Read Gospel according to Matthew and wrote my thoughts upon the same. In the afternoon there was an alarm and we harnessed up. Guerillas had made an attack upon our wagon train and captured about 20 mules and two

or three men. The cavalry got out very quickly and pursued them. Took back the men and some of the mules and several guerillas.[8] Felt much pleased when orders came to unhitch and unharness. No mail.

Nov. 22nd, Sunday.

Fair again, but quite cold. Finished a letter to Myra. Potato stew for dinner. Read the "Acts of the Apostles."

Nov. 23rd, Monday.

Reveille at 5 o'clock. Boot and saddle and moved away with the whole brigade about 9 o'clock.[9] Made Bealton before noon where I saw that the R.R. had been rebuilt. There were several wagon trains lying there and tents up for contra-bands who were at work upon the R.R. Weather very fine. Crossed the railroad and proceeded due east along what had been a very good road but then much out of repair. There was a telegraph along the road and two places where wires branched off toward the river. About two we halted distant from Bealton about 5 miles. At first not knowing when we might move we cooked, but afterward remained there all night. Morrisville was not far distant.[10] All sorts of rumors rife. It appeared to be a general movement of the army.[11] Pretty cold.

Nov. 24th, Tuesday.

Reveille before daylight. Started shortly after sunrise, direction still east and southerly. Passed through a little village and about noon by a brick mill and certain houses called Patterson's Mill. Rainy all day and quite cold. Very dismal marching. Shortly after noon reached the Rappahannock at Ellis' Ford. Here there is quite a settlement. The banks are high on both sides. The river is broad and rapid and came one half way up my horse's sides. Noticed on the south side a field where they had been making hay at this season of the year. Con-tinued marching right out from the river for about a mile when we counter-marched and returning about ½ mile camped for the night near some houses.[12] Got into camp just in time to pitch paulin, clean horses and get supper before dark. Rumors that the movement had failed and we were going back to the old place.[13] A very unpleasant day's march.

Nov. 25th, Wednesday.

Heavy frost during the night. Reveille before daylight. Harnessed and hitched about sunrise and after waiting until about 11 o'clock unhitched again and went into camp. Fair and sunny all day. Occupied the most of the afternoon in boiling some pork and cabbage. Pitched paulin again.

Nov. 26th, Thursday.

Thanksgiving. 2nd in the service. Reveille before daylight, and harnessed up. Lay in readiness 'til about 10 o'clock. Received official notice of victories in the west and intimation that we were expected to whip Lee tomorrow.[14] Moved out towards the Rapidan along a thickly wooded road, arriving at Ely's Ford about noon. The banks of the river are very high and the landscape was very beautiful basking beneath the glowing sun. The second brigade crossed first and after they had massed themselves on the opposite heights it was indeed a fine sight. Their equipments glittered in the sun and the signal flags flashed here and there. We crossed between 1 and 2 p.m. and the column commenced to move shortly after. Ely's Ford is much shallower than any I had yet crossed. We forded in the form of a crescent going down stream and then up. We moved to the right through heavy woods and just before nightfall halted for an hour. Again moving on we crossed three plank roads and just as night came on could see across some woods into a field beyond which were apparently infantry. Moved straight out at right angles with the plank road, bearing shortly to the left through a thickly wooded country. This vicinity is called the wilderness. Continued the march 'til about 8 o'clock when we halted in a large field, and unharnessed. Passed just after dark a little village called Rose Mount.[15]

Nov. 27th, Friday.
Continued march at daylight still through unfrequented woody roads, but gradually bending round to the right so as to make a detour. About 10 a.m. we again reached the Orange C.H. and Fredericksburgh plank road about 4 miles from where we had crossed the previous night. Here was the head of the 5th Corps coming up the road in column. Went up the plank road in advance of the infantry and about noon found the enemy at an opening near a place called Whitehall. Brisk skirmishing took place between our cavalry and the rebels when we drove them, losing only two men wounded, whom I saw as they were brought to the rear. Shortly after they opened with artillery when the right section was ordered up and opened in reply. In about 15 minutes the column moved up and we advanced across the plain where the fighting had been. Halting here some time, shortly we advanced through the woods beyond to a little knoll in the road with the woods in front. One piece went into battery right in the road and the other piece on the left. We could see the rebels run, backward and forward across the road about ¾ mile in advance, and between them and us our skirmishers. We went to firing upon some artillery which opened upon us from the left of the road. They made some fine shots at us hitting just in front of the pieces and exploding. The pieces of shell flew all about our ears but luckily hurt none. They threw once at us what appeared to be a cubic piece of iron. The left section opened on the right and front and we limbered up and advanced down the road about ¼ mile and went in action again. We could now see the rebels quite plainly and the fire waxed warm. A sharpshooter came very near bringing me down as I was tending the piece. They opened again from the left and threw the shell all around us but luckily hurt none. One shot entered the ground about 4 feet from me and scattered the dirt all over me. Fortunately it did not burst. It dug a hole large as a bushel basket. The fighting in front was very furious and shortly

our fellows brought in some prisoners who turned out to be infantry from A.P. Hill's Corps. Gen. Sykes of the 5th Corps came to the front. Our ammunition gave out, the two pieces having fired 3 chests full. We limbered up and another section came up to relieve us. The "dough boys" of the fifth Corps came up and relieved the cavalry. Battery E 1st Ohio took our position and it was reported lost 5 killed in as many minutes. We returned to the first field passing the 5th Corps in column coming up.[16] This was the smartest fight I had been in, but felt less apprehension than in any previous engagement. It was perfectly wonderful that none of us were hurt. We lay in the field at the rear 'til dark, occasional artillery firing at the front. Kiely and I had a good wash and had just got supper ready when we had to move again. We put our coffee in canteens and victuals in our saddle bags. The whole brigade moved with us to the point where we first struck the plank road in the morning. Passed wagons on the road, and where we camped for the night was the 1st Corps. Saw Irving Foster, A.H.R., and Linscott and had quite a chat with the former. They moved up to front shortly and we unharnessed. Scarcely was this latter done when a shot or two was heard and we had to hitch up again. Waited an hour and had just got half unharnessed again when some more shots were heard and again we hitched up. No more disturbances occurred but remained harnessed all night. Lay down before the fire and pulling the blanket over me slept tolerably. A hard day's work.

Nov. 28th, Saturday.
Unharnessed after daylight. Commenced to rain. Pitched paulin and boiled some beef. About noon the rain ceased and at the same "boot and saddle" sounded. Harnessed up and the whole brigade started toward the Rapidan crossing the plank road and following an exceedingly narrow and muddy road which forms an acute angle with the plank road toward the river. The way lay most of the way through thick woods. At a small opening near a house I got a few cotton heads which had still remained in the field, the first I had ever seen. Some of the other fellows got leaf tobacco which was drying in an outhouse. Towards night we arrived in a large field through which runs the Culpepper & Fredericksburgh plank road. Trains were coming and going between the front and rear. We camped in the edge of the woods and pitched the paulin. Unharnessed and unhitched. Marched about 4 miles.[17]

Nov. 29th, Sunday.
No forage for the horses so the whole battery went out foraging. We came across a drove of small pigs and charged them. Ran them about 'til they were tired out when I dismounted and caught one. Kiely stuck him and I took him back to camp. Shortly after the rest of the fellows came straggling in with forage and all sorts of trash. Some had chickens, pigs, potatoes, cabbages, onions, all sorts of other stuff. About 11 A.M. we harnessed up and crossing to the other side of the field took position on the knolls, 2 guns in a place. It seems the rebels had

come down in force on the pickets at the place from whence we had come the preceding day and surprised their camps creating great havoc. The 3rd Penna. Cavalry were badly cut up. They came in about noon their horses and selves all bespattered with mud. They had run their horses all the way.[18] We took up our position on a hill close by a deserted house, some negro quarters and some barns. It was very cold. I went into the house and found remnants of costly furniture, a library &c. The owner must have been an educated and wealthy man. A dirty white flag flaunted from one on the chimneys. The house had been used as a hospital at the battle of Chancellorsville. The fellows went into the negro huts and I among the rest. We found many articles laid away which had evidently belonged to their master. I took for my own use a good pair of mittens and an all wool vest. Also some tobacco and a couple of dippers. The others took all sorts of articles, blankets, counterpanes, clothing &c. Some even took the poor darkeys' victuals. After dark the battery was massed but did not unsaddle. Lay down in the paulins, and almost froze to death. Very cold all day.

Nov. 30th, Monday.
Still very cold. The whole brigade returned to its camping grounds of 3 nights before which I found was called "Parker's Store." Went in battery on the field facing toward the East. Shortly after 2 pieces were taken away and went into battery facing up the plank road, and 2 down it. All around the field lay evidences of the rebel charge, dead horses, &c. In a building lay two of our dead dragoons. Toward night an alarm arose that the rebels were coming down with three regiments and one piece of artillery. The other piece in our section fired 4 shots at a long range, but the rebels did not make their appearance. It turned out that fifty rebs had charged the barricade in the road. At night our pieces were moved near to the house and built large fires burning boards from the house and a deserted army wagon. Very cold all day. The firing at the front seemed to recede from which I judged that we had beaten the enemy or else they had fallen back. A very cold and dismal day indeed.[19]

Dec. 1st, Tuesday.
Nearly froze during the night. Slept only about 2 hours, alternating all night long between the fire and my blankets. We did not unharness. The horses had no feed the preceding night nor this morning. Our wagon was sent out for forage with a squadron of the 1st Mass. Cav., and returned with corn on the ear, some pigs already dressed, and a barrel of flour. It was divided out among the battery. Lay here all day in position. Towards night the wind rose and it became bitter cold. About the middle of the afternoon the 1st Brigade of Hooker's old division came down the plank road and camped close by. Saw some fellows in the 1st Mass. infantry. Unharnessed just at dark. About 8 o' clock we harnessed up again and shortly a heavy column of infantry commenced pouring down the road. The army of the Potomac was falling back. The 2nd and 3rd Corps came

down the road. We came down the road in the rear of the infantry. We started about 2 A.M. of the—

2ND DEC. WEDNESDAY.

The column moved very slowly and it was bitter cold. All along the road in the woods the infantry ahead had built many fires. Of these I took advantage, for riding ahead of the battery I would dismount and sit beside some fire until it had passed when I would ride ahead again. Arriving at the road on which we had crossed the three plank roads we turned to the left and again to the left on reaching the Culpepper plank road. Passed through the field where we had waited all day of the 28th ult. for the rebels to attack us. Proceeding beyond there for about 2 miles we turned to the right into the woods and at the end of three miles came out upon a large open plain which borders upon the Rapidan. There is quite a settlement upon the south bank and a building which I judged to be an iron foundry. The land is very high on both sides the river here, and the ford I heard called by some Germania Ford, by others Culpepper Ford. When we came down to the river they were busy taking up one of the pontoon bridges. We crossed on the other which was composed of 8 pontoons. We proceeded straight up the hill which is very steep and waited in the plain above. There lay several batteries and quite a large quantity of infantry and some baggage wagons. After we had just gotten something to eat the pieces without caissons were ordered back to the hill overlooking the ford and went in battery. After waiting about two hours a couple of squadrons of rebel cavalry showed themselves in the plain on the other side and we fired a half dozen shots at them. The shots were very poor having too much elevation. Towards night I went down to the ford to water my horse. Everything was deserted and still, a contrast to the bustle and crowd which was there only a few short hours previous. About 4 P.M. the right and centre sections moved off about 1½ miles from the river and went into camp, leaving the other section on picket at the ford. Got feed once more for our horses and a chance to rest for ourselves. A dismal day and night's work.[20]

3D DEC. THURSDAY.

Once again the sun returned with grateful warmth quite different from the cold rays of the two previous days. Managed to wash my face and hands again. For breakfast fried fresh pork and fritters without any "rising" in them. About 9 o' clock boot and saddle sounded. Unharnessed again without moving out of camp. Lay here all day.

DEC. 4TH, FRIDAY.

Aroused about 1 o'clock to move which we did immediately. Advanced about 3 miles and apparently in a direction up the river. Halted at the junction of two roads and parked in an open field without unharnessing. Lay and shivered by a camp fire until daylight when we unharnessed. Spent the day in dozing and trying to make up for last night's short rest. Rations getting short. Nothing but a little flour and some boiled beef which furnished just one meal and which was all we had this day.

DEC. 5TH, SATURDAY.
Cloudy. Rations came up and were greeted with a shout. Received the back mail, the first time I had heard from home in 5 weeks. Received four letters from Myra one of which contained 2 pictures. Received also a worsted cap and scarf from Myra, the latter which I sold. A letter also from H.A.H. Pitched the paulin as it looked like rain.

CHAPTER 7

THOUGH HE SLAY ME, YET WILL
I TRUST IN HIM:
DECEMBER 1863–APRIL 1864

With Gen. Robert E. Lee's Army of Northern Virginia bivouacked in winter camps on the southern side of the Rapidan and Meade's Army of the Potomac ensconced in its own around Culpeper Court House and Brandy Station, the war in the East entered a quiet period. For the army as a whole and the Sixth New York in particular, the dull routine of camp life was interrupted only by several minor alarums and excursions during February. The most prominent of these events was the February 6 reconnaissance in force across the Rapidan, ordered by Maj. Gen. John Sedgwick, who was in temporary command of the army in the absence of Gen. George Gordon Meade. Other actions took place in early February in favor of a push up the Virginia Peninsula by Maj. Gen. Benjamin Butler and at the end of February in support of the unsuccessful Kilpatrick-Dahlgren raid on Richmond. The purpose of both of these excursions was to release Union prisoners from the Richmond prisons and, in the case of the latter, to capture officials of the Confederate government. The Sixth New York participated in none of these affairs, but they at least provided grist for the camp rumor mill and for Perkins's diary.

With the above exceptions, both the Union and Confederate armies seemed preoccupied with staying warm, well fed, and well supplied in their winter camps. A religious revival swept both armies, and, in the case of the northern side, the Christian Commission was very active in the Brandy Station camps. Bible studies, worship services, and small group meetings were the order of the day. Whenever the weather permitted, the torpor of camp life gave way to inspections, drills, and more inspections. A number of social and quasi-social events also occurred, including balls, dinners, races, and grand reviews, at which at least the officers and their wives who had made the arduous trip down from Washington were entertained. Occasionally, the men also were indulged in entertainment. Perkins relates that the First Brigade Horse Artillery built a barnlike structure for social events, the most notable of which was an evening varieties program of music and dancing.

The March 9 promotion of Ulysses S. Grant to the grade of lieutenant general and his appointment a few days later as general in chief of the Union armies presaged major changes to the Army of the Potomac that would drastically alter the nature of the war in the East. Grant decided to make his headquarters with the Army of the Potomac and arrived permanently at the end of March. Following his arrival, plans were made for a spring campaign focusing on engaging and defeating Lee's army in the field, and, on March 24, the component corps of the Army of the Potomac were reduced from five to three, the latter measure being effected by transferring divisions from the disestablished corps to their new commands. Another action, one that would prove to be especially significant for the Cavalry Corps and the associated horse artillery batteries, took place on April 4, when Maj. Gen. Philip Sheridan replaced Maj. Gen. Alfred Pleasonton in command of the cavalry.

This chapter opens with the Second Brigade Horse Artillery relieving the First Brigade Horse Artillery from duty with the Cavalry Corps of the Army of the Potomac. The Sixth New York Independent Battery then went into winter camp at Brandy Station. The bulk of the diary deals with the daily routine of camp life. Perkins and his mates spent much time and effort logging up their tent and making it warm and comfortable. He fell ill several times and had to seek medical attention. He recorded that a doctor prescribed a roast onion to be bound on his ear as a remedy for a severe earache. The winter weather made it difficult to conduct drills and reviews, but December saw two notable reviews, one put on to impress visiting Russian naval officers and another by Generals Meade, Henry Hunt, and Robert Tyler. The daily maintenance of the camp continued throughout this period, however, with due attention paid to the gathering of firewood and gravel, care of the horses, and fatigue and guard duty. Perkins was able to enjoy occasional respites by visiting other regiments and by entering wholeheartedly into the activities of the Christian Commission.

The diary entries for January 1–5, 14–20, January 28–February 2, February 13–16, and March 29–31 have been omitted. George's remarks for those dates simply and tersely record the fluctuating weather patterns, the omnipresent mud, and the continuing round of camp chores and drills, relieved only by the occasional Bible class and work on his translation of Caesar's commentaries.

Dec. 6th, Sunday.
Reveille before daylight. We were relieved by the 2nd Brigade and took up march for Brandy Station where we arrived about noon, distance about 6 miles but roads very rough. Another mail and received another letter from Myra, and one from Bethiah, also several newspapers. Very cold and windy all day. Reports of being relieved and returning to the brigade of horse artillery.

Dec. 7th, Monday.
Somewhat warmer. Wrote to Myra. Pitched paulin.

Dec. 8th, 9th, 10th, 11th.
Cold and windy. Wrote to Myra. 11th moved a distance of about 2 miles toward the Rappahannock and by Brandy Station. We had been relieved from duty with the cavalry by the 2nd Brig. H.A. We rejoined Maj. Robertson on the edge of some oak woods. We had to clean the brush away for a park and a picket. Received 2 letters from Myra, one of them old. Got one also from Miss Moulton. Pitched paulin.

Dec. 12th, Saturday.
Rainy and disagreeable all day. Engaged most of the morning in cutting oak logs for a house. Cut 5 and dragged them up by a mile. Then we went over to the deserted camp of the 1st Brig. H.A. [sic] with a wagon and got logs enough to build the whole of our shanty. A very hard day's work. My right ear began to grow very sore.

Dec. 13th, Sunday.
Rained heavily during the night and at intervals during the day with strong wind. My ear very painful. Went to the doctor at sick call who prescribed a roast onion to be bound on. The other fellows worked hard and got the logs up and fireplace built. Wrote to Myra.

Dec. 14th, Monday.
Ear still very sore, excused from duty by the Dr. The other fellows continued working on the house, finished mudding the walls and fireplace, stretched the paulin and closed the ends. A very fine day but wet.

Dec. 15th, Tuesday.
My ear continued painful and I was excused from duty by the Dr. The other fellows finished the chimney and in the afternoon all of a sudden the battery was ordered out with the rest of the army to be reviewed by the Russian Naval Officers who had just come out from Washington for that purpose.[1] The battery did not get back 'til some time after dark, and had a tough time in the cold and mud. I congratulated myself on escaping it. Received a letter from Myra and a Middlesex Journal. Our new house quite a palace.

Dec. 16th, Wednesday.

My ear much better. The Dr. marked me for light duty. All sorts of reports rife that the army was about to fall back to Fairfax. Built our bunks. Kiely and I split ours out of a large oak tree into shingles. Our house very warm and comfortable.

Dec. 17th, Thursday.

Rained heavily all the preceding night from which our new *palace* shielded us well. Rained nearly all day and as my boots were very poor I kept in the house nearly all day. There was some clothing drawn but unfortunately no boots. Wrote to H.A.H., also a piece for the "Journal" on circumstance.

Middlesex Journal, Saturday, December 26, 1863

For the Middlesex Journal
By the Camp Fire
By Hoplite

Man in the abstract and as represented by philosophers, is a creature as far different from the every-day man, the creature of circumstances, as is present humanity from the magnificent specimens of imagination which painters and sculptors deal out to us from canvas and from the block. The artist in his study strives to portray an ideal excellence, not the objects of common and daily life. In each as it comes before his gaze he searches out its few, mayhap its only, excellence of form or of color, and fixes upon his memory. Then with his collection of excellencies he finds one ideal whole of beauty beyond comparison, like to the child who with his toy blocks, divisions of a house, builds one complete house.

The artist in his masculine masterpiece of Antinous from this one seizes the depth and beauty of chest, from that the narrow loins, and still farther from another the Jove-like head and ambrosial curls, until, were each component part of this beautiful and magnificent whole again returned from whence it came, 'twould indeed be difficult without the sculptor's collective genius to reconstruct the beauty which but ere now so delighted us. So also philosophers constructing mental humanity for a model wherefrom to issue to the world their analysis and observation do not portray the earthly, the actual man, and consequently their speculations are only good upon supposition, as, if so and so be so, then the result must be so and so. Philosophy of humanity can have no certainty and each specimen of mankind must have to a certain extent a philosophy of his or her own. Some very general deductions are all that can be made from mankind as a race. Further all is guess-work and conclusions unjustly made, general from confined consideration and too narrow premises. By circumstances even the same individual is swayed so that what once was a just estimate of his own powers and a probable view of his future line of action becomes a mere hypothesis, oftener quite wrong indeed. As day by day passes some property of the mind, or quality, becomes more prominent by cultivation or less so by disuse. The mind which to-day is thus, in a half year is as different oftentimes as that of two different persons, and that too, without any ground for the imputation of variableness or instability. Such a change is very likely to take place in case of a change in association or removal to a different scene in life. In considering the mode of action in any certain case the determination can rarely be just from the fact of the inability of each one to know the peculiar mental circumstance affecting his neighbor, for unseen and mental circumstance conduce as much to the formation of lines of action as any apparent outward inducings. I cannot now remember Tennyson's beautiful line on "circumstance," yet if I could would here repeat them not only as fine poetry but as true philosophy.

How do the daily happenings of life sway our spirits and influence our mood for good or evil, to joy or sorrow.

Some long forgotten strain of music soars in our soul remembrance of some sweet happiness of the past and again those moments are lived over. The remembrance and the association reminds us of our mode of thought then, and perhaps by comparison with that of the present prompts to nobler efforts in the occupation of life. Thus this circumstance improves and elevates the soul which else had plodded on the way it was going. Even if the remembrance only lead to momentary improvement still much good has been obtained, for by a series of such reminding circumstances the general tone of the mind may become elevated to a higher standard.

The murmuring wind among the trees about our childhood's home, the glancing ripple of the

> "Little brook that loves to curl
> O'er matted trees, or ribbed sand,
> Or dimple in the dark of rushy cover
> Drawing into its narrow earthen urn,
> In every elbow and turn,
> The filtered tribute of the rough woodland."

A familiar song, a word, a joke, all in themselves constitute circumstance which sways the wind if not to different lines of action at least to different modes of thought. Circumstance is happiness or woe, and the many gradations of human feeling between. Philosophy too often leaves out of the account circumstance, and is therefore too often incorrect. Let each man then make his own philosophy, and he not only obtains greater correctness but also a benefit by thus knowing himself which knowledge of books or the material world can never equal.

Brandy,
Dec. 17th, 1863.

DEC. 18TH, FRIDAY.

Rained during the night and cloudy all day. Read "Noctes Ambrosianae" all day long. Letter from Myra. Commenced letter to the Journal. Had some magnificent stewed beans for dinner.

Middlesex Journal, Saturday, March 5, 1864
For the Middlesex Journal
By the Camp Fire

The research of learned men has unfolded an infinity of knowledge useful and interesting. And yet the infinity of facts ascertained together with the further knowledge which from those facts has been deducted, is but as a straw from the still more infinite haymow of the universe. Such use of the word infinite doubtless will appear somewhat paradoxical and extravagant, but extravagance of expression, has for many years been conceded to be the American's birthright. Not only is this true of a searcher after truth in a general way, but also of him who makes any special art or science his study. Beyond a doubt Lewis Agassis, has long ere this found out that his poor life is all too short to explore even the half of the natural mysteries which so far have been his study. If not then there is at the first one great fact which he has not as yet discovered. How does this knowledge of the littleness of the human mind in general affect mankind? This is a question which each person must answer for himself, looking carefully at the emotions of his own intellectuality within and judging carefully of those of others without. The greater portion of the human family does not perceive their ignorance. Whether the old distich,

> "Where ignorance is bliss
> 'Tis folly to be wise."

could be quoted here with wisdom, each one must judge for himself.

Seeing one's own ignorance, the determination to arise therefrom would seem to be one of the two following. First, as that I do not know is always sure to overbalance that I do know, what use is there working toward an end which I can never reach! I therefore will know all is easily known and productive of sordid, tangible benefits. All else is useless and weariness to the soul. Or second, seeing the immense field of knowledge, awaiting my search, and knowing that it would yield much profit as well as pleasure I will increase my stock of knowledge as far as possible. Which of these determinations he will adopt, each one will decide from his own temperament and accustomed habits of thinking. Which determination is best admits of more argument than appears evident at the first consideration. Action upon the former is not without a certain portion of earthly comfort and mental ease.

As with the miser, who possessing much treasure yet ardently longs for more, so the scholar possessed of a certain amount of knowledge still is harassed by an uneasy feeling in regard to the many things he has left unlearned. This disquietude ignorance escapes. The unlearned by their little knowledge are blinded to the universe of truth which always awaits their investigation. The less is known the less is knowledge sought, but increase in wisdom begets increase of desire for it. Ignorance by its blindness to the immensity of knowledge obtains freedom from anxiety.

Knowledge is power. In ancient times a knowledge of natural causes and natural effects, and from the former how to produce the latter, was very often productive of temporal power. A knowledge of human nature and the springs of action is social power. By it popularity is gained, friendship retained, admiration and emulation stimulated. Knowledge of books, closet knowledge, is scholarly power, it leads to the high places in the world of letters.

But knowledge of one's self is a power like to God's. As man was created in the similitude of the Deity the consideration of this heavenly handiwork must bring him nearer to God, the maker. Buried in the depths of a subject so profound he must with awe and reverence acknowledge the immensity and divinity of Him who created this perfect structure, man. By such consideration man brings himself the nearest possible to the mighty architect of his being, and makes the nearest approximation to His attributes. Man knowing well himself then can look down from a pinnacle of celestial power second only to God's. For self-knowledge is celestial and God-given.

Who shall put limits to the commencement or to the termination of wisdom. Before reason ascends the throne of human intellect the bodily senses are acquiring knowledge. In the other direction the patent facts of the universe lie stretched far beyond the limits of human existence. In life man, like the shipwrecked mariner who feels only the pressure and dampness of those water drops which immediately press against his person, only perceives and learns those facts which are nearest his existence. Beyond stretches the immensity of knowledge, in the bare contemplation of which his mind loses itself.

Knowledge, and especially of self, approximates to the Divinity. Is not excellence sought after by even the most material? As immortality is superior to mortality, selfishly then is not man judicious in making advances, be they never so little toward immortality, the state of excellence? Who chooses knowledge obtains for himself a treasure superior to gold, superior to bodily enjoyment; which makes him a god and powerful for all time. The boundaries of humanity and divinity are but shortly separated and knowledge bridges the chasm.

"Knowledge is power."

HOPLITE
Brandy, Dec. 17th, 1864[2]

Dec. 19th, Saturday.

Frost during preceding night and ground frozen all day. Spent most of forenoon chopping wood. Oyster stew for dinner.

Dec. 20th, Sunday.

Very cold all day. Completed our door of canvas on a wooden frame, and closed up the end closer. Chimney smoked somewhat. Wrote to Myra.

Dec. 21st, Monday.

Still cold. Wrote off "The Minstrel's Return", and sent it home to the Journal. In default of boots drew a pair of shoes which were too small for me. Quite a musical assembly in our house in the evening.

Middlesex Journal, Saturday, January 23, 1864

The following song was sent to us by our correspondent "Hoplite." He says—"I have taken the pains to collate it from dictation and reduce it to correct verse. It gains much in the singing, as it is adapted to very beautiful music. I never saw or heard it before in any collection of songs whatever. It is sung with much applause to guitar accompaniment."

The Minstrel's Return.

The minstrel returned from the war
With spirit as buoyant as air,
And thus on his tuneful guitar
He sings in the bow'r of his fair;
He sings in the bow'r of his fair.
The noise of the battle is over,
The bugle no more calls to arms,
A soldier no more but a lover,
I kneel to the pow'r of thy charms.
  Sweet lady! Dear lady! I'm thine,
  I bent to the magic of beauty;
  The helmet and banner are mine,
  But love calls the soldier to duty.
The minstrel his suit warmly pressed,
She blushed, sighed, and hung down her head,
'Til conquered she fell on his breast
And thus to the happy youth said;
And thus to the happy youth said:
"The bugle shall part us, no, never,
This bosom thy pillow shall be,
'Til death tears thee from me forever,
For faithful I'll perish with thee."
  Sweet lady! Dear lady! & c.
But fame called the youth to the field,

His banner waved high o'er his head,
He gave his guitar for a shield
And soon he laid low with the dead;
And soon he laid low with the dead.
While she o'er her young hero bending
Received his expiring adieu.
"I die while my country defending,
"With heart for my lady-love true."
   "Oh Death! Then she cried, I am thine,
   I'll tear off the roses of beauty;
   The grave of my hero is mine.
   He died true to love and to duty."

Brandy VA,
Dec. 21st 1863

DEC. 22ND, TUESDAY.

Very cold. Left section commenced to build the stables. We tried to remedy the fault of smoking in our chimney, but did not succeed. Got permission to go out of camp and visited the 39th M.V. near to Kelley's Ford. Went a very round-about way to find them. Passed through the field where we had the fight on the 17th March. Saw all my friends in the regt and my horse made very good time back to camp trotting nearly all the way. Reached camp shortly after retreat and after eating supper went almost immediately to bed. Received a Journal.

DEC. 23RD, WEDNESDAY.

Slept very poorly during the night and got up feeling very sore and disagreeable. Received orders to prepare for work on the stables when the assembly was sounded and we were ordered to prepare for review. I had scarcely cleaned my horse when "boot and saddle" sounded and we got ready. Which done the order was countermanded on account of the weather and we unsaddled again. It clearing off fine almost immediately the order was given again and we saddled up. Did not start from camp until 2 p.m. Formed brigade front, Capt. Martin commanding brigade in absence of Maj. Robertson. The whole reserve artillery was reviewed by Gens. Meade, Hunt, & Tyler. It was dismal cold and one of my feet nearly froze. Got to camp just before dark. Went to bed immediately after dark being quite ill. A very irksome day.

DEC. 24TH, THURSDAY.

Could not do my guard duty being ill. Felt feverish. Went to Dr. and got excused from duty and received some cathartic pills. Felt miserable and feverish all day. Soaked my feet in warm water and changed clothes. Much whiskey in camp.

DEC. 25TH, CHRISTMAS.

Clear and cool. A ration of whiskey dealt out to the battery. Much drunkenness and jollity in the camp all day. Felt no better. For dinner had 2 apple dumplings.

DEC. 26TH, SATURDAY.
Worse. Excused by Dr. from duty. Took pills and salts. Eat nothing all day. Orders for the monthly inspection. Lay abed portion of the day. Paid off.

DEC. 27TH, SUNDAY.
Better yet weak. Excused from duty. Inspection in park by Maj. Robertson. Settled my debts and put $5 in the tent fund. Bought a bottle of pickles. 1 qt. 75c. Wrote 2 letters to Myra, and sent a letter already written to M.J. Boiled potatoes and pork for dinner. Rainy nearly all day.

DEC. 28TH, MONDAY.
Rainy and very muddy. Marked for light duty. Drew a pair of boots, sewed. Potato stew for dinner. Wrote to Myra.

DEC. 29TH, TUESDAY.
Still gloomy, muddy and rainy. The mud is the deepest in this camp of any place we have ever been in.

DEC. 30TH & 31ST.
Rainy most of the time and the mud got very deep. Mustered by Major Robertson for 2 mo's pay. Wrote to Bethiah.

Middlesex Journal, Saturday, January 16, 1864

Brandy Station, VA,
Dec. 31st, 1863
Dear Editor: —
"Man proposes, God disposes."

Many days before this I had proposed to myself to send to you the particulars of the advance over the Rapidan, and, in fact had filled two sheets in commencement of a letter, when illness came in the way to its completion, and until now has not permitted a continuance. Fearful then lest I may be tedious upon a subject now so old I will only append a short summary of the aforesaid events. The advance was made in several columns, it being guarded against, lest any column should outstrip the other. Gregg's cavalry division constituted the extreme left column which crossed the Rapidan at Ely's Ford, at noon on Nov. 26th. Taking a south-east course straight out from the river toward the rear of Fredericksburgh and Spottsylvania C. H., we bivouacked that night some 13 miles from the Rapidan. The next morning continuing the same course for some hours we then turned sharp to the right and shortly after noon reached the Fredericksburgh and Orange C. H. plank road, which we had crossed the preceding night before dark, only four miles below. Here we found the 5th Corps in column awaiting us to take the advance. Our whole column wheeled into the road in front of them and moved on slowly. The road was straight and broad. The cavalry formed in broad platoons filling the whole road as far as the eye could reach.

It was a bonny sight. Advancing about 4 miles to a church called New Hope, the enemy was at length found, as was proclaimed by some smart firing at the front. The column halted in the road to await conclusions. The noise of the fighting swayed hither and thither, now forward, now backward. There seemed to be an open field at the front. Ever and again would come to our ears the well-known scream, which the rebels use in action, as their skirmishers pressed back by ours, rallied with their reserve. Aid-de-camps momently dashed down the column or orderlies with written orders in their hand. Occasionally the skirmishing party at the front would be strengthened by a squadron from some regiment in the column. The firing had died away, and the column was once more in motion, when suddenly came to our ears the report of cannon, then immediately the whistle of a shell and its bursting in the woods 50 yards to the right. The column again halted and the right section went off at a smart trot. In a few moments we heard the sharp, piercing crash peculiar to their calibre and rifling, and in expectancy we awaited events. Shortly the whole column moved up and we entered upon a large open space which had been the scene of fighting only 30 minutes before. Even the fire was still smoking in the middle of the road where had been the post of the rebel picket which had just been driven in.

On the further side the field close up against the woods and on a little knoll, were our other two guns in battery and firing over the trees at the rebel artillery beyond. Gen. Gregg's aide riding up for another section, off we went without the caisson, pell-mell along the road into the woods, our support following close behind. Arrived at a little knoll in the road where the trees were somewhat less thick, we went into action, receiving orders to fire to the left of the road. Right before us again about a dozen rods, rose another little hillock and beyond that stretched the road in a straight line for nearly a mile, when it disappeared from view, taking a short bend either to the left or right. Just beyond the second hillock an open field stretched far away to the left. From the further extremity of this field their artillery opened upon our two pieces hardly before we could get loaded. All around and about us they dropped their shell which exploding threw the ground and iron about our ears in a manner unpleasantly suggestive. Most of their shells struck about a rod in front of the pieces, exploding almost at the instant of striking. To this storm we replied as fast as possible, aiming at the smoke of their guns. Continuing thus for sometime the left section was brought up and went into action on the right. This was altogether too hot for the rebels, and they soon withdrew their artillery.

All this while brisk skirmishing was going on about a quarter of a mile in front of the guns, and where I stood in the middle of the road could be seen either skirmish line as they swayed backwards or forwards, and the blue wreath of smoke as they puffed from the shining barrels. As far as I could see down the line of the road a rebel on a gray horse was constantly riding backwards and forwards across it.

Limbering to the front we quickly gained the second knoll and went into battery again distributing our shell with strict impartiality along the whole length of the rebel line. Our skirmishers gained ground. At length the rebels bring forward two pieces almost in the same place as before. Knowing the exact distance from having previously gone over it they made beautiful shots. They stirred the dirt under our very noses, which vexed us as they did not seem to mind our practice in the least. The rebels grew bolder and pressed our men harder. Prisoners are brought by the pieces, and we open our eyes when we see the knapsacks and bayonet sheaths. *We were fighting infantry!* The cavalry who are dismounted skirmishing in front, bravely stand to their duty till they are pushed back from want of ammunition. While we distribute a few rounds of case shot among the rebel "doughboys" to keep them quiet, two more regiments came up and deploy coolly and steadily to relieve our tired fellows on the skirmish line. They push the rebels back until their artillery transfer their fire from us to the advancing line. Just at this moment our ammunition fails, and regretfully we limber up, yet stand waiting the coming of another section. Our fellows losing their artillery support, are again pushed back a little, while the rebel artillery again pays its devoirs to us. How the shells did rattle around us, tearing the ground up all about. I looked back on the road and my eye caught a joyful sight. The road was alive with bayonets. The 5th Corps had come up and were deploying into line of battle. We were relieved by an Ohio battery of light 12 pounders, and went to the rear. The rebels still kept up a furious cannonading. Although we had been under their fire two hours, not a man or horse was hurt, but scarcely had our relief got into position before five men were hurried to their last account by the explosion of one shell. Was it Providence or was it chance?

We did not stop in our rearward progress until we reached the place where in the morning we had struck the plank road. Here there were some houses and what had once been a store. The vicinity was called Parker's Store. We halted there for the night just as the 1st Corps was passing on their way to the front. That night we were disturbed by the guerillas thrice. The succeeding day we proceeded 4 miles further to the rear to the vicinity of Wilderness Tavern. On the 29th, the two regiments, which were left behind at the store to keep the communications open, were surprised by rebel cavalry and rather roughly handled. One of Buford's brigades relieving us at the tavern, we returned to the store next day, where we remained until falling back, which commenced on the 1st of Dec. As we rode across the street in front of the store my eye fell upon dead bodies lying on the floor, and some undefinable [*sic*] feeling prompted me to look upon them. There they laid, poor fellows, one of them was shot through the head. 'Twas not a fascinating sight those frozen forms. "Killed in a cavalry dash," yet who shall know how many hearts in northern homes mourned for them, none the less fondly and none the less despairingly, that on their shoulders shone not the gold lace of military rank. Some sad life cherishes itself in bitter repining no less for him, who lies there having lost his life in a simple cavalry foray, which neither fame nor the paper will fix in remembrance, than for others more numerous, who have fallen in the battles of this war. Folks shudder when they read the summaries of great engagements, and pass lightly over the item in their daily paper of "—killed—wounded, in such, or such a cavalry skirmish." It does not affect them, but oh! the world of sadness it must bear to some. It does not come home to the mass of the people because they can not experience that great shiver of terror which comes to them from the great southern battlefields.

Death is none the less hideous thus, alone, stiff and frozen in an empty barn, than among thousands others on some hotly contested field. Let not then the sympathies of those at home be alone for the dead patriots on the battle fields, but then let them once at least call to mind the lonely killed.

After night fall on Dec. 1st, the army commenced to retreat, pouring down the broad road in one mighty stream, that made a roar on the heavy planks like the flow of a current. Even before the head of the column reached our post, I could hear it as the dash of a mighty waterfall. At daylight we fell into the extreme rear of the column, and at noon we were safely across the Rapidan, no pursuit being attempted.

Dec. 12th, we were relieved from further duty with the cavalry by a battery of the 2d Brig. H. A., and we returned once more to reserve. We now are situated about 2 miles from Brandy Station, and between that and the Rappahannock. As yet we have been treated to only three inspections, quite moderate you will say to the manner in which they dosed us at Culpepper in the middle of the summer. The fellows have all completed their shanties and spacious habitations many of them are I can assure you. They were built at cost of much hard labor, for the wood was distant and of oak. Your correspondent rejoiced with four others in the possession of a magnificent mansion, 11 feet by 9, and 7 feet in altitude. According to the custom of soldiers we have named this spacious palace, "Hotel Egalite," to be erudite and stylish, and at the same time to be republican. The edifice proper has been completed a fortnight, but the fireplace and chimney were not sufficiently tutored to their duty until a day or two ago, for the smoke like that in Mrs. Bouncer's attic *would* come down. We take a deal of comfort in more ways than one. I hope to send you scribblings of a better quality in future, as I expect nothing less than inspiration from these walls which must get classical in the course of three weeks. All the boys are well.

HOPLITE

JAN. 6TH, WEDNESDAY.
Frozen hard. On detail putting up brush fence. Commenced an article for Journal.

JAN. 7TH, THURSDAY.
Cold with a keen breeze. In A.M. was detailed to go with wagons to get gravel for stable. Went down to the Rappahannock at Beverly Ford and still farther down

the river but could find no gravel so came back without any. On this side the river the rebels had built a great many breast works to command the ford. Got back just in season for my dinner. Received a lexicon, a "Caesar" and an English grammar from home by mail. Seemingly a very short day.

Jan. 8th, 9th, 10th.
Pleasant cool days. The 10th went down in the woods with C.H.M., and chopped a load of wood. Received a letter from Myra telling of her illness. Read some in the Caesar.

Middlesex Journal, Saturday, January 23, 1864

For the Middlesex Journal
By the Camp Fire
[Scene in Hotel Egalite, near Brandy Station, VA, Jan. 8th, 1864. Present Sergeant Master, Guidon, Wax, and Hoplite.][3]
Wax—The question, which now agitates the assembly, is what shall be for dinner. —Beans, or no beans! That is the question!
Guidon—There he goes again. No sooner is his breakfast finished than his mind takes up the subject of dinner. Alas! What gluttony.
Wax—And why not? In such a dearth of subjects for interest as must invariably be the case in the soldier's life, why should not the matter of meals be an important one?
Sergeant Master—Let me assure you, Cornelius, that the subject of gastronomy, the consideration of which with us has degenerated to "what shall be for dinner" and the slight cookery which results from a decision thereon, has attracted great attention in all ages of society.
Hoplite—Very aptly said, Jimmy. Man's gluttony equally with all his other sensualities has occupied a great space in his life. —Cookery has thriven faster than the true religion, and tastes have been and are as diverse as the various doctrines of salvation. In ancient times beyond a doubt, gastronomy had arrived at a pitch of perfection such as never has been attained since. Emperors at ruinous rates sent to distant portions of the globe—perhaps only to furnish some unusual dainty such as the tongue or roe of a certain fish. Birds and fishes were introduced alive at the dinner table, killed in some prescribed manner to preserve a certain peculiar flavor, and immediately cooked. Fabulous sums were spent sometimes on one article of food such as would astound even the most extravagant cooks of the present day.

Neither was gastronomy neglected in the middle ages, except perhaps in Saxon England. And at the present day has not the business of caterer become a science? Nor is it a science that is devoid of a higher element than sensuality. There is needful a sense of the beautiful which if it is not poetical, yet begets for the eye, a pleasure that speaks as well to the mind as the body.

Attention to methods of cookery can not always be termed gluttony. He is a glutton, who careless of quality, rejoices in quantities of common and poorly cooked food, but it is not unbecoming the character of a temperate man to have a care that his food is good and well cooked. Beyond this, again comes the gluttony, the every care of which is not to lose one titillation of the palate, and the invention of some new provocative to appetite. There is the gluttony of vulgarity, and the gluttony of gentility, and between the two, lies the wise man's careful temperance that inclines to neither. There is no need of imputing Wax's very normal interest in his victuals to the score of gluttony.

Sergt. Master—Truly even gluttony is not without a certain portion of benefit at least to others than the entertainers of that failing. Man's appetite encourages the agriculturist to perfection in the cultivation of his produce, and by consumption furnishes the spur to the mariner for the bringing of luxuries from beyond the sea. The preparation necessary to place these delicacies, domestic and foreign, before the epicure in their most enticing form extends employment to others. And thus do even the vices of one portion of mankind give a livelihood to another. "It's an ill wind that blows nobody good."

Wax—All of which is a plan in my favor, that I may not be called a glutton, is it not?

Hoplite—Most assuredly.

Guidon—Behold me then, morally at your feet. Wax, I beg your pardon.

Wax—My son, thou hast it. *Pax vobiscum.*

Sergt. Master—But to return to our muttons as the French say. What shall be for dinner? Shall it be beans?

All—It shall.

Sergt. Master—Baked or stewed?

Guidon—Baked.

Wax—If so be as how a dutch oven can be borrowed whereby baking can be accomplished.

Hoplite—It's a whack, as very pertinently remarked Cornelius, the centurion.

Sergt. Master—"Or words to that effect." Ah's me! Baked beans! "A dish I do love to feed upon." Methinks I see them smoking enticing, garnishers of the Sunday table! You are indeed the very prop and cornerstone of Yankee land. But the white livered mass, which we are obliged here to content us with, is about as much like the browned and crispy beans of New England as—as—as

Guidon—"Hyperion to a satyr?"

Wax—Shakespeare!

Hoplite—Those same satyrs, that Shakespeare would have us believe to be so ugly, were not as bad as they are portrayed. Some of them at least, have even made pretensions to gentility. One engaged in a musical contest with Apollo in a cave of Phrygia. Poor fellow, he was worsted and Phoebus Apollo flayed him alive, which was indeed shocking, considering the prejudice which is generally maintained in favor of an intact cuticle. Certainly a creature thus alive to the power of music, and to some extent an adept therein could not have been so entirely repulsive.

Guidon—Talking of music, suppose Jimmy, you favor us with something light and pleasing.

Wax—Yes. Let us have the "Spanish Retreat."

Hoplite—Or rather the last original.

All Three—Hear! Hear! The last original!

Sergt. Master—(Taking guitar.) Well as you like. (Sings to guitar accompaniment.)

> Soldiers let us merry be,
>> Life is short, pleasures fleeting
> Let us never chary be,
>> When thus together meeting
> By the watch fire's ruddy glare,
>> Of healthful mirth as light as air.
> Longer marches may await,
>> Weary hours bestriding,
> Rising early, riding late,
>> But ne'er from duty hiding.
> Future toll ne'er shall scare us,
>> Future danger ne'er deter us.
> Fill high the jovial bowl
>> And pass it right merrily—
> Enlivener of the soul!
>> Pass it, pass it cheerily.
> Ruby wine to thee we drink,
>> In thee all weary woes we sink.
> Let's then forget war's alarms,
>> Turn to other, gentler thoughts,
> Wine has many sparkling charms
>> Waiting only to be sought.
> Wine! Red Wine! Hurrah for wine,
>> Care soothing produce of the vine!
> *(Applause)*

Guidon—A pleasing fiction of the imagination it is, Jimmy, to represent the soldier as drinking wine, but it would be much truer to nature if you had made it commissary whiskey. But I suppose something must be allowed for poetic license. What poet ever sung the praises of "Old Rye" or "Jersey Lightning."

Hoplite—Whiskey and wine may both be very good in their way, but to obtain a draft of the true life elixir that sends the blood singing through all your frame, and conveys a sense of pleasure even to the ends of your toes, you should have accompanied us in our gravel-seeking expedition, to Beverly Ford. The route at first skirted the huge plain of Brandy. Across its broad surface the wind came nippingly though lightly, its edge somewhat softened by the bright morning sun. The slight depth of snow crunched under our swift feet. My eye wandered far over the plain which glistened whitely beneath the sun's rays, a plain of shining silver. Far to the South and East rolled up into the frosty air the steam from a train passing on the railway. What beautiful shapes the smoke warped itself into, beautiful blue wreaths momently disappearing into the crispy air. The morning breeze brought a bodily enjoyment of the scene.

Turning sharp to the left in the direction of the river, the teams struggled through a narrow belt of oaks where the ground was thickly strewn with brush. I feel certain that those mules can go through places with loaded wagons where horses would balk with empty ones. For draught purposes, mules are much the more superior animal I think.

At length free of the woods, we came out upon a range of hills overlooking the valley, through which runs the Rappahannock. On every knoll to the right and left, as far as could be seen, the rebels had built redans to command Beverly Ford, and the river. Far up to the left and north, the valley stretched until it gradually expanded into a snow clad plain. As a background and relief to this picture, a belt of dark pines intervened between the plain and mountains. The Blue Ridge looked truly magnificent. Rising from out a gloomy forest of pines, the ridge towered boldly far away from us northward, its blue sides and pinnacles bound here and there with plots of silvery shining snow. —For the last six months have we, as it were hovered in the very shadow of those mountains, and I have seen them in all their phases, but not one so grand as this winter view. At the close of the long summer days, I have sat and watched the sun's red light, as it faded out behind their hazy heights. Each ridge and towering mountain was as distinctly outlined in purple mellowness against the ruddy evening sky, as though some godlike limner had drawn them on the fading day. I have seen the lightning of the gathering storm play about their lofty tops lighting their sombre brows with fierce fitful glares, which faded as the storm clouds rolled down the piney sides. I have seen the Ridge in all its moods, but none so beautiful as that of yesterday. "The cloud capped towers, the gorgeous palaces—

Sergt. Master—When did you say you would be down?

Hoplite—Hey, what? Down? Where?

Sergt. Master—Why you were getting so far up into the clouds that I began to doubt very much whether you would ever get down again, leastways in season to get any of these beans for your dinner.

Wax—Haw, haw, haw!

Guidon—Speaking of beans, did you taste any of those beans which some of the fellows foraged the other side the Rapidan, as small as peas?

Sergt. Master—I did, and they were indeed delicious. Did not our brigade do some excellent foraging in that expedition. I nearly experienced an apoplectic fit with laughing to see how affairs fell out while we laid in position at Parker's Store. One wagon, you will remember, was sent out foraging with a squadron of cavalry. In a few moments we heard some shots from the vicinity of the pickets and it was laughable to see the dragoons lurking about that nearest house skurry [*sic*] around for their horses, mount, and dash for the main body. Shortly after two of our fellows came galloping in saying that a party of guerillas has attacked the wagon. For a few moments all was bustle and there we were ready to receive them. We stood to the guns. Before long the party returned and then we learned that the shots were accidental by our own pickets. There were no end of jokes cut upon the two fellows who saw a guerilla party in the smoke of three carbines.

Wax—There seemed to be plenty of victuals of all kinds, except bread stuff. One old farmer had nine hogs killed and dressed in an upper chamber. Our foraging party took possession of three of them. No matter what scarcity of food thereof may be in the rebel army, there never seems to be any among the citizens of Virginia. It never appeared to me that we were going to subdue the rebels by starvation, although the newspapers have so much to say on the subject. I only speak from my own observation, it may be different farther South.

Guidon—Well I am inclined to believe that we are able to whip them without calling in the aid of starvation, and it is not altogether impossible during the coming season. If not ———

[Bugle sounds water call without. *Exeunt omnes.*]

JAN. 11TH, MONDAY.
Still cool and pleasant. Bought a gold pen from C.H.M. price $1.50. First day of cooking by the company cooks.

JAN. 12TH & 13TH.
Fair days freezing at night. Threatens rain. Wrote to Myra each day and sent home C. H. M.'s picture. Commenced to write out a translation of Caesar.

JAN. 21ST & 22ND.
Warm and sunny. Wrote to Myra. Completed translation of first book of Caesar. Letter from Myra.

JAN. 23RD, SATURDAY.
Fair and sunny. Got a pass and started to visit the 39th M.V. but learned they had moved when I had got half way there. Went over to see Johnny Sullivan in 9th Mass. Battery. Agreed with him to have a box sent from home to me in his name, as they can get boxes more readily in his battery. Roads very muddy. Dumplings for dinner. A letter from Myra and one from Bethiah. Wrote to Myra.

24TH–27TH JAN.
Very warm and sunny, so that we kept no fire in the tent. Brigade monthly inspection. Letter from H.A.H. containing picture. Wrote to the "Journal."

Translation of Caesar's *Gallic Wars*. Griffin Family Collection.

Middlesex Journal, Saturday, February 6, 1864

Brandy Station, VA,

January. 29th, 1864

DEAR EDITOR: —The depth of winter finds the army of the Potomac comfortably settled and in better quarters than any preceding winter. This immense plain of Brandy is completely beset with log cabins, built for the most part of split oak logs. Already the extensive forests, which have for years embroidered the edges of these fields, have begun to melt before the legions axes in the hands of sturdy soldiery, and the sun to shine through belts of timber which but one summer ago withheld its beams from their roots. Many acres of ground have thus been cleared, and should the army maintain its present position until the opening of the spring campaign, instead of being encamped upon the edges of this plain it will hold a position nearly in the centre of it. Even now regiments and brigades, which in the first days of December encamped in the midst of thick woods, stand far out upon that plain surrounded by stumps, the continuations of which once have furnished cabins and firewood. Every soldier becomes an adept in the handling of an axe. Slim city youths, who once did flourish the yard-stick with graceful elegance rejoicing in lily hands and smoothest shirt front, in one winter of Uncle Samuel's service learn to swing an axe with wonderful vigor and precision.

As yet wood is plenty—and so is mud. Every man insane enough to ask for a pass and use it, runs a fearful risk. For if he sets out on foot it is a matter of extreme good luck if he ever returns out of the vast and deep sloughs of mud which everywhere pervade this vicinity. And if he goes mounted he thereby entails upon himself an exhausting job to clean his beast upon returning. Only by dint of continual ditching and corduroying is the camp maintained in a habitable state. The stables are floored with split logs to keep the horses feet out of the mud. Owing to this and the mildness of the weather heretofore the horses are in excellent condition, and being little used when they do get out prance and chafe until they are almost crazy with their desire to run. When the column for water breaks up to seek the various watering places along the stream, then always ensues such a snorting, and plunging, and kicking of heels as sufficiently proves whether or no they have good care. In truth I believe the battery possesses as fine animals as can be found in any organization of the army of the Potomac.

At the commencement of the winter there was a rumor afloat that the army was about to fall back as far as Fairfax, but nothing is heard of it now and all goes on as quietly as though a few miles in our front there was not the best appointed army of the confederacy so called. The reenlistment of veterans is going on at a rate quite unexpected. In fact so many have reenlisted and gone home on furlough that Gen. Meade, fearful of weakening the army too much, has issued an order forbidding furloughs for reenlistment until those already home shall have returned. The first corps, to which the 39th is attached, have recently moved from their position near Kelley's Ford, to the vicinity of Culpepper. It must have been quite disagreeable as most of the regiments had already completed their shanties. Before they moved the line of encampment for the army was as follows: on the extreme right sixth corps, extreme left first corps, right centre third corps, left centre second corps, reserve artillery at the rear of right centre near Brandy Station. The fifth corps guards the railroad. Gregg's cavalry is the other side the river at Warrenton, and the remainder of the cavalry corps at the front in the vicinity of Culpepper and Stephensburgh.

The organization of and mode of warfare used by all armies have always differed more or less according to the nature of the country, the climate, and the state of improvements of the nation. The organization of the Potomac army may not be an uninteresting subject, as doubtless it is the most perfectly organized and conducted of the armies upon this continent, perhaps in the world. It is composed of five infantry corps, (formerly seven) one cavalry corps, a reserve artillery corps, a signal corps, and an engineer brigade. Each infantry corps is composed of three divisions of sundry brigades,

and about five batteries of artillery. Each corps is commanded by a Maj.
Gen., divisions by Maj. or Brig. Gens., each brigade by acting or actual Brig.
Gen. The batteries in each corps are consolidated into a brigade commanded
by an artillery field officer. The artillery in a corps is subject to the direct
order of the corps commander, and only in special cases to that of division
or brigade commanders. Formerly the artillery was apportioned among the
division. The cavalry corps consists of three divisions of two brigades each.
To each brigade of cavalry is attached a horse battery under command of the
brigade commander. The reserve artillery is commanded by a Brig. Gen.,
and is divided into brigades of four or more batteries each. The horse artillery of the army consists of two brigades, one of six, the other of five batteries.
Both of these brigades take their turn at being detached with the cavalry.
The brigade not with the cavalry is attached to the reserve artillery.

The signal corps is attached in small parties to the suite of commanding
generals. The engineer brigade, formerly of two regiments and one battalion,
now one regiment and a battalion, is commanded by a Brig. Gen. and has the
care of the pontoon train.

Thus the army of the Potomac is so classified that any portion of it
which may be needed is where it can be reached with the least possible delay.
This organization renders it easier to bring the troops into action, quicker to
march them, and more convenient to them.

Each infantry corps is distinguished by a badge worn upon the cap and
displayed upon the various divisions and brigade battle flags. The badge of
the first corps is a full moon, second a trefoil, third a lozenge, fifth a Maltese
cross, sixth corps a cross I know no name for, with the projections plain and
of equal length. The corps flags are a Greek cross upon a light ground, the
number of the corps in the centre of the cross. The different divisions of each
corps are distinguished, 1st, 2d, 3d, by red, white and blue of their respective
corps badges. Each brigade has its battle flag, triangular in shape. The division flag is rectangular, that of the corps swallow-tailed. In battle these flags
facilitate movements and render it easy to find the several generals. In the last
fight at Bristow the use of these flags was fully demonstrated. The lines of
battle stretched far across the plain. At regular intervals along the line waved
the brigade battle flags, while everywhere in the hottest of the fight hurried
the division and corps flags.

Said Gen. Warren to the trooper that bore his flag "*Wave* that flag, hold
it high up that they may know where I am," and immediately ordered an
advance. It was a grand sight to see those long lines hurrying forward to the
charge, their banners waving high above there [*sic*] heads at a slightly forward inclination. It did not take long for that one veteran division to clear the
field of gray-backs.

Although the army is not now of the huge proportions which it has
been at some former periods, yet it is in as great a state of efficiency as it has

ever been. The health of the soldiery is most excellent, the discipline good, their spirits confident. They have come to look on war as their trade, and having become already skilled in their trade its details are attended to with scarce an effort or remark. The enemy is neither dreaded or despised, and battles are looked upon as a matter of course, and not as a frightful bugbear always haunting the future. The truth is, old soldiers are accustomed to believe themselves going into battle only when they hear the bullets beginning to whistle about their ears, and then they get in so quick that they can't afford time to indulge fear. For many times whole corps find themselves massed or marching in the immediate vicinity where actions are going on and take no part in them. So the veteran always trusts to his good fortune to keep him out of a fight until he is fairly in. This insensibility to apparently impending battle has a good effect upon the recruits in an organization, for the new-comer seeing the nonchalance of their older brethren in arms persuade themselves to a similar conclusion as to the probability of going into action; nothing influences so much as example.

"A little leaven leavens the whole lump." With armies this is especially true. Thus with as small a proportion of as one third veterans to two thirds recruits the army looses but little of its efficiency. Fortunately by the recent reenlistments there is a great prospect that the army of the Potomac will retain many more than enough of its present stout soldiery to maintain its veteran character after the influx of raw recruits about to result from the last call. In fact the discharge during the summer of troops whose time may expire will not very sensibly diminish the army. This appears to me the only result sufficiently adequate, which has yet arisen from the paying of such large bounties, that we have thus far been unable to maintain in the field substantially veteran armies.

Yesterday occurred the regular brigade monthly inspection for January. It was a warm and sunny morning. The several batteries appeared upon the plain nearly simultaneously each in columns of pieces. They formed rapidly into line according to a previous alignment of guidons. It must have been a fine sight viewed from some one of the surrounding knolls to see that long array of cannon stretching far out toward the centre of the plain, their muzzles even as if dressed by mathematical line. The brigade commander's bugle from the centre of the line but faintly brought the orders to the ears of those upon the flanks. The brigade appeared in excellent condition. After inspection, wheeling into column of batteries, the brigade passed in review twice, executing for nine times in succession that most difficult of artillery manœuvres, a battery wheel. Returning to camp we congratulated ourselves upon our safe recovery from the mud, yet viewing with rueful faces our encrusted horses, harness, carriages. But we encourage ourselves by saying it is all counted in the "three years or during the war."

HOPLITE

FEB. 3RD, WEDNESDAY.
Cold and windy all day. Commenced an article for the Journal entitled "Old Boots and Shoes." No letter from Myra.

FEB. 4TH, THURSDAY.
Fair and sunny. Kiely went into the woods with me to help me cut logs for my stable. Letter from Myra telling of barrel sent.

FEB. 5TH, FRIDAY.
Slept very poorly. Laid the floor to my stable; couldn't complete it for want of a pick axe. Two letters from Myra with play bill and account of play. Went over to 9th Mass. Battery to see if barrel had come, found it had not and that they expected express matter succeeding day. Continued article for Journal entitled "Old Boots and Shoes."

FEB. 6TH, SATURDAY.
Rainy. Finished article for Journal and commenced translation of second book of Caesar. Disappointed at not getting the barrel. Heavy firing in the direction of Culpepper and the Rapidan, and just at nightfall musketry.[4] All sorts of rumors rife. Finished the stable.

Middlesex Journal, Saturday, April 16, 1864

For the Middlesex Journal
Old Boots and Shoes
by Hoplite
As within the limits of an apartment each article possesses some musical tone which breathes in unison with corresponding chords that may be produced by some instrument and reciprocally those articles when struck elicit a corresponding tone from the instrument, so in human life circumstances, persons, objects, cause a vibration of the corresponding chords among the heart's emotions. All things whether material or otherwise have a music which awaits only an awakening touch. With individuals the extent, to which their heart music has been awakened, constitutes their measure of joy or sorrow. How luckless they whose life plods on in daily round of discord and un-tuneful living. From their existence is withheld all harmony, which is happiness, all soul awakening, which redeemeth man from the punishment of original sin. On the other hand they, who have found the corresponding tones without, which waken within life's finest music, have obtained the nearest approach to the fruition of immortality possible below the skies.

Not only persons and circumstances, but also simple objects awaken emotions of various quality and tendency. All know how the heart is stirred by the sight of familiar home objects seen after a period of separation. Thus only in an inferior degree is it with other objects from the favorite haunts of former days down to worn and discarded pieces of wearing apparel. There seems not much of interest or poetry in a pair of old boots or shoes, and yet setting before us those last retired from active service what memories may they not arouse. How rejoiced we looked upon their new and shining surface reflecting that at least for a certain period in the future we were to be protected in our understanding. They seemed a vast capital in leather better to possess than cash, but as they began rather pointedly to remind us of the fact that they were new some doubts arose as to our actual excess of good fortune. Coming down through the days in which they passed from new to worn, from worn to useless, how many thoughts, hopes, and passions have those boots born witness to. In them we have trudged long miles of pleasure and of duty. The same which perhaps had dripped with muddy blood from a wound caused by some glancing axe, had tripped gaily along the floor in time with whirling music. They remind of the time when side by side they stood still bloody against the wall most patiently awaiting our return to active service, a mute imploration to the surgeon's skill for our recovery, as also the glare of lights, the glassy floor, the heat, the murmur, the sweep of female robes, the glancing eyes and twisting fans, black dress coats and white vests, and all the accompaniments of the evening assembly. They remind of the midnight haste which sought the physician for loved relative in distress, when, though at other times their indoing was a work of time and strength, they came instantly on without loss of strap or bruise of finger. Their soles attest the daily journey to school or place of business, perhaps each week's nocturnal visit to the maid we loved with its midnight return. Such a day we stood in them with joy, on such another our cup of sorrow seemed full even to the overflow; in all, those boots were their gathering associations of joyness and of woe, reminders in the future of the unreturnable past. Thus each pair has its separate history, if written perhaps as eventful as that of many men and objects which now possess a great circulation. And the general tenor of each pair's associations compared with that of others, affords much room for reflection and improvement. Then it would be a plan not entirely devoid of benefit to preserve each pair of boots or shoes when unfit for use, putting into the leg of each a paper inscribed with the special emotions of the wearer at different times, general deductions therefrom, and a general principle gathered from these deductions. The general principles of the different pairs at any time compared together will show the wearer's progress in life or deterioration, and furnish exact knowledge of the direction in which improvement is needed. They would be a very superior kind of diary, inasmuch as the classification of subjects would render references much easier. For does not one write a diary for reference?

Man's character and situation in life is as broadly told in the boots he wears, as in the matter of head coverings and gloves. To the gentleman it is as necessary that his foot be as well clad as his back.

Taking a position at the corner of some street in a populous city look well at the boots and shoes of the passers by. As we reach the curbstone on our way to take place of observation we are assailed by the ever present newsboy, who thrusting his bundle into our face at the same time stuns us with the name of the paper he would have us buy, although it may be very plainly read upon the papers in his hand. As we buy a paper we observe his shoes and notice they are as slipshod as his general appearance. Newsboy is as well manifested by his feet as by his face and bundle. Taking position with back against the plate glass of the apothecary's window we turn just in season to see a pair of boots approaching of sturdy dimensions, a faint pretension to polish, broad soles and still broader heels. They come down upon the sidewalk with a clack that speaks well for the propelling muscle of the limbs above. Following the continuation of drab up, we find that those boots are true indications of the man within them, a farmer. While we have been occupied in making these observations as he halts irresolute upon the curb stone amid the passing throng, a shoe approaches, the character and movement of which proves instantly the possessor. Square and homely and made for comfort, yet nicely polished, it approaches with firm even tread, 23 inches from step to step. It needs not a glance at the blue garments above to tell it is one of Uncle Samuel's veterans. Close behind him follows a pair of boots of the same characteristics but with the heels ornamented by brazen spurs. It is a light dragoon. Next comes a boot which fairly puzzles us. From its neatness, fit, and polish, we say clerk, but looking higher for confirmation we see military pants, blouse, and forage cap. We look at his boots and white face and think he is a counterjumper. We consider his dress and say an officer. Just as he hurries out of sight we notice his arms swinging to and fro and then we know he is no soldier. We ask the newsboy still yelling at our elbow what the uniform means. "Do yer mean that cove what's just goin down-street? Oh he's one of the independent fire-eaters, b-longs to first battalion rifles." A city soldier. A brace of gaiters stout but neat speaks the business man. A pair of boots with extremely long and square toes come rambling by and we think he must be an Englishman even before we notice his funnel shaped silk hat. A schoolboy runs by with boots run over to one side and toes white with constant coasting. A pair of pattens come clinking along, a Dutchman. A pair of huge rubber boots stumble past, it is a country express man.

The fashion of boots has varied as extensively as headdresses and wearing apparel. Ancient sandals were the only things used to preserve the feet from contact with the ground, simply wooden soles bound the feet by straps much in the fashion of the skate straps of the present day period. The colder weather of more northern regions induced an improvement in the way of untanned leather. The Dutch to this day, because they are slow in improvement and because of the moist nature of their soil, still preserve a reminder of the ancient sandal in their wooden shoes. Coming down through the middle ages all sorts of changes were wrought in shapes of shoes. Once breeding was proved by the length of boot toes, as also once by the height of heels. Boot toes were once worn so long as to necessitate some contrivance for holding them up when in motion, and as now the chinese lady takes pride in the curtailed proportions of her feet, so then French noblemen rejoiced in shoes with toes so long they could not walk with them. With hoops also came in high heels, and truly the ladies attained much apparent dignity by the increase of their height and surroundings. Gradually hoops and high heels died out together, the latter being last retained by the English sailors in their low cut gala shoes. Again upon the introduction by Eugenie also came high heels, both welcome fashions to short and undignified females. At the present day fashions of shoes are as various as the people that wear them. If one preserved all his old boots and shoes how easy might he trace the path of fashion and his own fancy.

Neither are those portions of our covering, which often wander among the slops and filth of earth, wanting in a certain portion of poetry. The ladies, bless them, are not ignorant of this and do not leave the world entirely in the dark as to a pretty foot looks in a neat gaiter. In fact I think that subject has inspired more than one youth to admiration and the perpetration of rhyme. Is anything more needed than given a youth of moderate genius, pretty feet of pretty owner, and necessity for adjustment of skates?

Boots and shoes awaken both music and poetry. Should we despise them because it is in an inferior degree, and perhaps never discovered?

"All things ripen toward the grave,"

shoe leather amongst the rest. Respect them for the service they have rendered and when past their time deliver them to the retirement of the garret, nor barter them to the old-boot man for the scanty pence which will affect neither our wealth nor poverty.

> Brandy VA,
> Feb. 1864.

Feb. 7th, Sunday.

Cloudy in the morning but fair at night. Went to divine service at the tent of Christian Commission. Text: "Prepare to die." Was not much attracted, preacher dull and prosy. Commenced to read Chas. Reade's "Very Hard Cash." Visit from J. Sullivan.

Feb. 8th, Monday.

Fair. Johnny Sullivan came over and told me my box had come. Went over with Wilson in ordnance wagon and brought it back.[5] Everything all good and sweet. Pleased more with it as a proof of my darling's love and forethought. Felt no great appetite for the nice things but was very happy to have them. Only ten more months of separation and in which my only tokens shall be her letters and such occasional dear remembrances as this. God bless her.

FEB. 9TH, TUESDAY.
Fair and cool. Wrote to Myra. Continued translation. Enjoyed the goodies from home. Received a Journal.

FEB. 10TH, WEDNESDAY.
Fair and cold. On detail and went to the Hazel river with a wagon to get some poles. A very pleasant expedition.

FEB. 11TH, THURSDAY.
Quite cold, ground frozen hard enough to bear horses. Mounted cannoniers' drill. Commenced letter to Journal. Letter from Myra written at So. Reading. A rumor prevalent in camp that the government was going to send 5000 men to California to bring back overland 20,000 mules. None but veterans whose time was only 6 mo's or shorter to be taken. Felt an inclination to go myself. Quite an excitement in camp about it.

FEB. 12TH, FRIDAY.
Fair and cool. Drill at the manual of the piece. Finished letter to Journal. Went out in woods for a load of fuel. Received a letter from M.C.J. Determined not to answer it. Felt sleepy all day.

Middlesex Journal, Saturday, February 27, 1864

Brandy Station, VA,
Feb. 13th, '64
Dear Editor: —A southern winter is like an intermittent fever, the wintry weather prevails only at intervals. Once more the frost has bound the mud, and stinging winds again striduously hurry by these canvas dwellings, playing shivering tunes upon the projecting logs at all the corners. Firewood is once more at a premium; axes are dulled and again dulled, and the log chimneys, in which erewhile the flame had nearly died out, again send columns of dense smoke eddying down the wind. Doors of canvas strive to imitate the closeness of misers. Soldiers go about their daily duties with briskness complimentary to the season. The present cold season seems all the colder from the preceding very mild weather. Still with these alternations of cold and warm the winter which only a short while ago seemed so large a capital of comfort, gradually melts away, and shortly the season will be with us of marches and of battles, of motion and of action. The army has not quite stagnated in its present quarters. On the 11th a reconnoissance [*sic*] in heavy force was made across the Rapidan, by one of Kilpatrick's brigades and a portion of the 2d corps. The former crossed the river at Culpepper Ford, capturing the entire picket at that place. Thence they scoured the

whole country on the right flank of the enemy, but toward Fredericksburg. The infantry crossing higher up fell upon the enemy in force and had an engagement resulting on our side of the loss of about two hundred. The enemy engaged were principally of Hood's division. All sorts of rumors were rife as to the object of the movement, but the true one was probably to learn whether the enemy still occupied their position in front of us, which was found to be the fact. Some would have it that the object was a diversion in favor of Gen. Butler, then moving up the Peninsula upon Richmond. All day long we could hear the cannonading, and as night closed down the pattering of musketry when our fellows re-crossed. It sounded like a brisk engagement, and was quite a relief to the monotony of camp life. At one time the firing was so brisk that the belief began to grow of a general engagement. Various rumors more or less absurd came in from the front, while the action was pending. In fact rumors as ridiculous and remarkable as any ever circulated in northern cities since the war began prevail on all occasions of battle, at the distance only of two or three miles from the scene of action. And when the army is in camp all sorts of stories are always creeping round as to some movement, expedition, or change about to take place. At present the favorite story is in regard to an expedition which the government is about to send out to California, to return overland with 20,000 mules. It is reported that 5000 men are to be recruited for that purpose from among those soldiers who will have only six months to serve, or less after the coming first of May. They are to receive $45 per month as pay, with complete equipment, to be sent out to San Francisco by water, and return with the mules over the plains. It creates quite an excitement, and if the government were to undertake any such thing, there would be found a plenty who would be willing to join it. Such a journey presents many attractions to the material of which the army is now composed.

Drilling is now the order of the day: battery drills, section drills, detachment drills, manual of the piece, in fact in too great variety to entirely suit. All day long the plain echoes to bugle calls of batteries at drill. When the weather is warm it is rather pleasant than otherwise, but when one's toes emulate the frigidity of icicles in the stirrups, and the chill wind sweeping across the fields conveys the sensation to the face as of one cutting steaks therefrom, men begin to question the utility, and grumble at the insensibility of officers. And truly, not to make any especial charge, it is a necessary portion of discipline, a certain degree of insensibility and hardness of heart among officers. This is hard to be believed by those at home, who cherish for the most part an exalted idea of the relations between soldiers and their officers, but it is nevertheless true that, as men increase in efficiency as officers, there is a corresponding decrease in their degree of moral excellence. Officers, who join the army with qualities which at first win the esteem of all under their command, as their reputations grow lose their popularity.

Despotic rule fails not often of soiling the manhood of those who become possessed of it. It is most natural. And yet there are men who are benefited in this total abnegation of their own mind, men, who feel it a labor to exercise their own judgment and who enjoy the sleepy vacuity of mind consequent upon the needed deference to their officers' will, thought, judgment. "A soldier has no right to think, only to obey," is the military maxim, and, though it may make good soldiers, makes but very indifferent men.

HOPLITE

FEB. 17TH, WEDNESDAY.
Blustering and very cold all day. Slept very coldly preceding night because of the cold. Battery E, 4th U.S. artillery of our brigade went to Washington to refit and were replaced by I, 5th regulars.

FEB. 18TH, THURSDAY.
Still very cold. Wrote on translation of 2nd book of Caesar. Wrote to "Risible." Disappointed in my expectation of a letter from Myra.

FEB. 19TH, FRIDAY.
Still cold. Wrote some on my poem. Letter from Myra. Wrote to Myra.

Capt. James M. Robertson, commanding First Brigade Horse Artillery and staff, Brandy Station, Virginia, February 1863. Captain Robertson is seated on a chair, second from left. Courtesy of Massachusetts Commandery, Military Order of the Loyal Legion and U.S. Army Military History Institute.

Feb. 20th, Saturday.

Warmer. Monthly inspection for Feb. in the forenoon by Capt. Martin commanding the brigade in absence of Capt. Robertson.

Feb. 21st, Sunday.

Clear and comfortable. My 23rd birthday. I can hardly realize that I am so old. Seems as though I were a boy yet. I only bring myself to an approximate realization when I call to mind that I have a wife who is an adult, and a boy nearly two years old. A year ago was spent hugging the fire in a snow storm. Betwixt now and then what changes have I not passed through, of place, of person and of heart. I feel that I am a somewhat better man than a year ago and yet so little that it were scarce worth while to boast of it. I try to hope that there will be more the coming year. Letter from Myra.

Feb. 22nd, Monday.

Clear and fair. Washington's birthday. Spent the whole day in the woods getting fuel. On my return to camp crushed my 2nd finger on the right hand so badly as to force the blood from under the nail. Fear I shall lose the nail. Received a notice from home of the formation of a High School Association. Wrote to Myra. Long walk in evening.

Feb. 23rd, Tuesday.

Myra's birthday. I hope she will not be compelled to spend another birthday so far apart from him who loves her best. The day was so sunny and beautiful that I was tempted to ride out. Went up the road to Culpepper. Roads very good and even dusty. Troops scattered all along the R.R. This is the first time I went into Culpepper although during the past summer we lay near the town a week. It is a dirty place. The 14th N.Y. reg. from Brooklyn was doing provost duty there, they wore a pretty uniform, red pants & cap, and red trimmed jacket. I saw the Col. and his wife riding out, she wore a Col's shoulder straps.[6] Arrived just in time to witness the last part of a review of the 1st Corps by Gen. Newton.[7] There were many ladies present in ambulances and on horseback. Culpepper is distant from Brandy Station about 5 miles. Got home at 2½ p.m. Added a few lines to my poem.

Feb. 24th, Wednesday.

Fair and warm. a.m. had a long talk with Mr. Stockwell of the Christian Commission in our brigade, and was considerably moved thereby. In evening went to Bible class. Felt rather unwell all day.

Feb. 25th, Thursday.

Cloudy. Paid off for the mo's of Nov. & Dec. Deduction from my pay of 71 cts because of overdrawing my clothing account. Had a picture taken singly, and one with Kiely, neither very good. Paid $1.50 for a battery memorial in lithograph. Paid my debts. Borrowed $5.00 of L. Devoe, 5 of Armstrong, and 5 of Tileston. Went to church in the evening.

Feb. 26th, Friday.

Fair and warm. Prayer meeting in evening and minister tried to persuade me that I had experienced religion. Did not feel convinced it were so quite, nevertheless prayed. Thought it proof of insincerity that it took so great an effort to pray. Am sure I have a conviction of sin to some extent, although not a corresponding sense of Jesus' loveliness and the redemption he works for all sinners. Felt much disturbed alternating now and then with a ray of satisfaction. Whatever may be the result of my thoughts I don't think I can ever again relapse into my old life of utter wickedness. God help me, I believe was my truly sincere prayer as I retired this night. —Capt. Martin ordered me to be put on guard for making a noise (singing) in the rear of his tent at morning stable call, he being in bed and disturbed thereby. This seemed to me most unjust, for it were time he were up. Nevertheless did my duty without complaint. Mem. —To endeavor to make less noise habitually. 3rd Relief. Disappointed at no letter from Myra.

Feb. 27th, Saturday.

Still fair and very warm. A portion or the whole of the 6th Corps and some cavalry went out on some expedition, probably reconnaissance. Very sleepy all day for want of sleep the preceding night. Had my picture taken in a group of 20 others at Mr. Calhoun's request, bible class teacher. Poor pictures. Read Tennyson much during the day, and especially "Maud." "Maud" is indeed a poem full of fire, pathos, and extreme poetical feeling. No letter from Myra yet.

Feb. 28th, Sunday.

Fair and warm. Went to chapel in the morning and evening. Sermon on the war by Mr. Stockwell. Two long letters from Myra, received with much rejoicing and unusual pleasure. Conversation with Mr. S. who said he thought me converted and that I might aspire to be a minister of the Gospel. Cannot concur in either opinion.

Feb. 29th, Monday.

Cloudy. Mustered for pay for mo's of Jan. & Feb. by Maj. Robertson. Finished a letter to Myra. Bible class in afternoon, studied 15th chap. John.

Mar. 1st, Tuesday.

Rained all preceding night and nearly all day. A little snow toward night. All sorts of rumors prevalent about the 6th Corps and Kilpatrick's cavalry.[8] Wrote on translation. Sermon in evening by Mr. Ferris.

Mar. 2nd, Wednesday.

Fair. Sloppy underfoot. Wrote on translation. Sermon in evening by Mr. Ferris.

Mar. 3rd, Thursday.

Fair and warm. Wrote on translation. Bible class in afternoon by Mr. Ferris. Sermon in evening by Mr. Stockwell.

MAR. 4TH, FRIDAY.

Fair and warm. Wrote an article for the Journal. Bible class in afternoon to Mr. Stockwell.

Middlesex Journal, Saturday, March 26, 1864

Army Correspondence
Brandy Station, VA,
March 4th.[9]

Dear Editor, —Broadly shines the sun on Brandy. The sere fields stretched vast and wide, bask enjoyingly beneath his rays, and the soft ground seems absolutely to drink in the flooding brightness. Turn we everyway, and our eyes meet the glistening whiteness of canvas roofs. Each hillside boasts its crowning habitations, each valley and ravine its white dwellings and blue-clad population. Every way over broad tracts of land, studded with stumps and low lying brush, camps, beautiful in the distance by the purity of the dwellings and their regularity, grow upon the vision. The hills that close the horizon gleam with tents, and closer by, but overlooked by reason of their nearness, regiments and batteries lie thickly scattered. The army of the Potomac, gnawing steadily upon the edges of the plain, has made it nearly double its former extent. Camps, formerly hid from each other by heavy belts of oak wood-land, now stand apparently in the same field; and even beyond sight, the sound of drums and bugles comes to the ear, which was not so before. Soldiers, that in December cut their fuel so that its bulk would fail to cumber their doorways, now are compelled to go two and three miles for it. A large army in winter time is a wonderful corrosive to a wooded country, and were the Potomac army to be quartered for about three winters in the famous Virginia wilderness, it would be a wilderness no longer.

The winds of March, tempered by a Southern sum, blowing softly, have dried the mud so lately prevailing, and the roads for a season have been even dusty. Taking advantage of the pleasant weather, your correspondent made a visit to Culpeper during the past week, on the occasion of a review of the 1st Corps. It was truly a delightful ride. The scenery, the invigorating morning air, the undefinable joyous feeling which seems to penetrate through all one's frame, feeling the bounding, springing animal that beneath us so spirited yet swerves to the lightest touch, all combined to intoxicate. Joshua, to which name answers the animal wherewith Uncle Samuel has for a period endowed me, seemed to enjoy the time equally with his rider, and though rather too large to be graceful, yet felt as graceful as the lightest, curving his long neck and introducing into his gait as minute and numerous steps as any fancy dance of the stage. Anywhere out of the army I feel conscious we would have provoked gazers and many uncomplimentary remarks, for occasion-ally yielding to Joshua's apparent desire, which was mine as well, away we would go at a furious gallop, Josh performing the locomotory portion of the partnership, and your correspondent indulging in an accompanying screech rather more forcible than elegant. Nor did we stop until Joshua's distended nostrils and steaming flanks enjoined prudence and economy of horse flesh. In the army they are used to such sights and nothing surprises. Anyone who has not felt the intoxicating feeling that sends the blood rushing through every vein and flushes the face with fire as beneath him he feels the noble steed gather his powers at a bound, responsive to his rider's will, has yet one more great pleasure in reserve.

The road for the greater part of the way stretches along the railway taking in Brandy Station. The station presents the appearance nearly of a large inland town, and were there buildings instead of tents would quite. Along the railroad are built huge sheds, much like freight depots in the North, some boarded and some with canvas roofs. Everywhere laid large piles of grain and rows of pork barrels. Boxes of hard bread piled high, reached the altitude of two-story buildings. From every direction across the plain wound long trains of white covered wagons all converging toward the station, until entering into some of the of the narrow streets made by the innumerable Sibleys, they were lost to sight in this village of subsistence. Passing swiftly by and dodging in and out among some few outlying tents, and enfilading many columns of army wagons going and coming, the road stretched white and wide far before me, — on the right the plain, on the left the railroad. For four miles Josh, at length somewhat sobered, jogged along allowing ample opportunity for the enjoyment of the sunny scene. Far upon the right the plain was closed by the usual boundaries of woods and tents over and beyond which rose the Blue Ridge bold in purple mellowness against the blue sky. A slight haziness, which capped the mountain heights but made the effect more beautiful nor caused the least indistinctness that, like the illusion veils that ladies wear, making the face behind more fair, toned the scene to a beauty and color so fair and pleasing that the eye glutted not with gazing. And even the mountains followed on as though to accompany the progress, nor ever seemed more distant. Beyond the railroad stretched the encampments of the 3d corps, set in a wilderness of stumps.

At length passing all encampments and piercing a strip of woods a hill received me. Culpeper beyond gleamed brightly in a nest of the hills.

> "Far beneath a blazing vault,
> Sewn in a wrinkle of the monstrous hill,
> The City sparkles like a grain of salt."

It seemed as if the woods just passed had been the boundary of two far different countries, behind it sunny, broadly smiling plains, but here a land of lofty hills and lowliest valleys. Culpeper shone like a gem upon the face of day, its two steeples just redeeming it from sleepiness. Joshua seemed to think he had nearly reached the extent of his journey, for he pricked up his ears very knowingly as we paused lazily to view the scene before entering the valley in front. But the distance unwound itself double its apparent length before we reached the town, from the unevenness of the road between.

How did its distant view belie itself, when arrived within its streets, we found a dirty shabby little village, made all the shabbier from its contrast with the spruce dresses, the scarlet pants and caps, and shining buttons of a Brooklyn regiment doing provost duty therein. Joshua switched his tail in derision. The whole length of the main street traversed and the hill beyond surmounted, the roll of drums and blare of bugles came borne upon the air, and dashing through the next valley and breasting an opposite hill the parade was reached. I had missed the inspection and already a portion of the corps had passed in review. The corps was passing in column of divisions of regiments (two companies front). It was a sight can only be appreciated by experience. The long lines stepped forward at a swift pace as though as the impulse of but one will, and preserving always the same distance from division to division with a precision wonderful to be seen. Let home guards boast of prize drills and the 7th N. Y. Militia, but I feel positive that regiments marched by me on that day whose precision might be envied even by the "immortal Seventh." As they topped the hill to gain the table land, where the reviewing general was stationed, first appeared the streaming standards, and then the glistening bayonets just above the bronzed faces of the Union veterans. The level gained, some lines, just a little disordered in mounting the slope, at the word of command shivered for a moment like a ribbon in the wind, then straightened out almost to a mathematical line and swept by with even step. An observer stationed close at the extremity of the lines could see the brass plate on every cartridge box, so even was the dress and so well was it maintained. With scream of fife and deafening roar of drums, each flag dipped to the reviewing officer, and not a few of them showed the marks of battle. It was a grand, a thrilling sight. And those men who constituted on that day, this military pageant, had been where cannons roar and bullets whistle thick. Their occupation is not all of show. Those shining rifles had more than once been blackened and heated in the midst of furious battle. Those lines, so long, had once been longer, before smitten by the battle's tempest, and perhaps ere long would be shorter still. After the review the 1st Maryland Battery staid to give an exhibition of its state of drill to Gen. Newton and numbers of ladies who were present.

Learning that the camp of the 39th Mass was still five miles distant in the direction of Slaughter Mountain, courage and time began to fail me, and turning backward, Joshua re-measured his former course toward Brandy.

Long before this will have reached publication doubtless all the particulars of the late combined movement of cavalry and infantry will be fully known. The facts as they can be known at present seem to be that the 6th Corps made an advance movement in light marching order to the vicinity of Madison C. H. on the enemy's left. Beyond it a picked brigade of cavalry under Gen. Custer penetrated almost to Charlottesville, destroyed several mills, and surprising a camp of the enemy blowed up six caissons. Shortly after this movement had commenced Kilpatrick with his own division and some additional regiments crossed the Rapidan much lower down and marched straight out between the rebel right and Fredericksburg, no doubt with the intention of making a raid on Richmond and releasing the union prisoners. The movement on Madison was a feint to cover Kilpatrick's advance on the other wing; when last heard he was at Spotsylvania C. H., sixty miles from Richmond. The 6th Corps and Gen. Custer's brigade have returned to their former quarters. Let us hope that Gen. Kilpatrick will succeed on his daring errand. As usual all sorts of rumors more or less improbable are afloat, many of them taking color from the prevailing hopes and wishes. The army still maintains a cheerful humor and the enemy is looked upon as sure to be whipped during the coming campaign.

The guerrillas, which formerly pestered the army's communications from the vicinity of Warrenton and New Baltimore, thinned by the late capture by Gregg's cavalry, no longer are even troublesome. All the Woburn boys flourish and wax amazing fat.

Yours, &c.,
HOPLITE

MAR. 5TH, SATURDAY.
Fair and warm. Wrote a letter of introduction to brother John for Mr. Stockwell. Bible class in P.M., Mr. Ferris. Letter from H.A.H. The battery memorials arrived. Wrote a few lines on my poem. On guard, 2nd relief.

MAR. 6TH, SUNDAY.
Fair. Church in morning and evening. Letter from Myra which I answered.

MAR. 7TH, MONDAY.
Fair. Visited by Brown of . . . .
A long and hard day's work. Much disappointed at no letter from Myra. Commenced to read Dickens' "Bleak House."

Middlesex Journal, Saturday, March 19, 1864

Army Correspondence
Brandy Station, VA,
March 11th, 1864.
Dear Editor, —As swiftly as shifts theatrical scenery, has changed the sunny skies and softest winds, for leaden clouds and descending rains. The fair face of Brandy is clouded once more, and the fields, which but a short while since smiled back to the sun with reciprocal joyousness, now stretch mist-clad

and growing apparently but half their former length. The skies seem to lower close upon the earth, and the nearer horizon shuts out the farther hills and boundary of woods. Dense mist and falling rain shut in the view. All is dreary, dismal, waste, and wild. Even the horses, poor brutes, stand drooping and depressed beneath the downfalling flood, and penetrating mist, occupying the least possible space, and striving as if to creep within themselves. Everybody and everything seems to have a most determined attack of the blues. The roads have nearly returned to their primitive state of mud, ponds exist, and little streams run brawling by where once no moisture was. Brightly glows the fire in every soldier's chimney, and every hut presents a doubled charm by the inclemency without. Now is the season of letters, of reading, and of songs.

Inclement weather, drives man within himself for recreation and for occupation. It is the time for searching thought, and naturally induces meditation. It is a sign, man is vapid and thoughtless when he acknowledges to ennui. What springs of employment man has within himself if he would only search. It is by thought, and belief induced thereby, that man makes himself; and the outer circumstances of life, his contact with his fellow men, his education, are but the polishing touches to a work already done en actualiter. Insanity filled with excess of thoughts and ideas, fears not solitude. Why should the solvent mind dread it more? Solitude continual induces a morbidity and rustiness of thought. But whether is worse the narrow round of thought circumscribed by continual solitude, or the vapidity that always shuns reflections? Besides, man being naturally socially disposed need exercise no extreme exertion to avoid excess of loneliness. His endeavor should rather be the other way to avoid inanity and frivolity. Nor is a habit of thought a task, save to a certain degree. When once warmed we fit to the traces with wonderful facility. Then comes the pleasure. The world of thought! How boundless, how sublime, how pleasing! The slightest thing in nature by the power of thought occupies a beauty, and pleasure-giving power before undreamed; and works of art are appreciated with a zest ever freshening with their consideration. In walks about the fields each tree and twig and joyous bird seen thro' the thoughtful man's means of vision, the brooding skies, the flowering meadows, the tints of distance and the brightness of nearness, beget within an exquisite deliciousness of enjoyment that is a pleasure as apparent as any of sense. There penetrates from without the subtle essence of beauty absolute, and from within arises the happy grateful sense of His goodness, who possessing to himself the power to make whatever his will might wish, yet in love immeasurable hath made all things so lovely, that all their loveliness may not be learned, only for us. The pleasure and need of thought can never be narrated.

The winter seems lightened of one-half its weight, as also men's mind. All sorts of arrangements for comfort and pleasure and improvement have ripened into fullness. With the opening of Spring come many rumors which in their variety, beget as great a variety of theories as to the commencement and conduct of the ensuing campaign. Even the old fear is not wanting, and there are some who say Lee meditates another invasion, others even that he is now within the limits of Maryland. You will at once perceive that army rumors not always take counsel of probability. These rumors are one source of the army amusement, which for the rest is made up of balls, races, reviews, &c. The officers of the 1st Brigade H. A. have built and dedicated to amusement a log building about 20x40. It is used for a club house, an arena for sparring exhibitions, and shortly will be for the performance of an amateur minstrel troupe. Not half a dozen rods from where stands this club house, is located another institution of the brigade, viz., the tent of the U. S. Christian Commission, which serves as a chapel. Here has been divine service since the early part of the winter. The labors of the Christian Commission, throughout the army have been highly successful, and really it seems that, had the U. S. expended the money it has wasted on incompetent and lukewarm chaplains, as judiciously, it would have been a great saving to the U. S. in the quality of its soldiers.

Near by our camp, are the encampment of the famous Vermont brigade which won such honors at Fredericksburg and else where. It is composed of five regiments, each very large in comparison with most the other regiments in the army of the Potomac. At a review a few days since, it appeared on the field as many as 3,500 strong. Many times I have seen whole divisions reviewed which could boast no more. It was a fine sight and well may the Green Mountain State be proud of her favorite brigade. Most of the men seemed recruits, and yet after the usual ceremonies of review were over, they deployed into line of battle, and made a charge with as even a line, and as much earnestness as though all were veterans. With a shout and prolonged yell the line swept heavily forward, a shivery sight of blue, and bristling bayonets. I can compare it to nothing save when in summer the noonday sun retiring behind some cloud, the shadow swiftly sweeps the ground surmounting everything, coloring all. Once seen, one can well appreciate the dread that soldiers have to face that glaring line, seeming about to sweep everything before it. The brigade stretched nearly a mile in length.

I shivered involuntarily.

Uncle Abram and the conquering Ulysses are now at army headquarters, and is reported will review the army as soon as the weather will permit. And the rumors of movement may not be altogether without foundation, in fact, for to-day has arrived the order to put the artillery in thorough order to take the field. Well *allons mes enfans,* we will not rust.

Yours, &c. HOPLITE

Mar. 13th, Sunday.
Church in evening. Hurt my sore finger again. Read "Bleak House" nearly all day. Visit from Johnny Sullivan and friend. Mr. Ferris's farewell sermon in evening, subject, "The Judgment."

MARCH 14TH, 1864 (WINTER QUARTERS, NEAR BRANDY STATION, VA)
Fair but cool. Bible class in afternoon, and sermon in evening by a Mr. Barnard
from Vermont. In forenoon very busy at arranging ammunition in the chests.
Continued "Bleak House." Was made very happy at receiving a long letter from
Myra. Commenced a letter to her. Had a long talk with Kiely on religion. Was
invited by some of the fellows to make an elocutionary address on occasion of an
entertainment about to take place. Agreed to it. On guard, 3rd relief.

MAR. 15TH, TUESDAY.
Warm in morning, flurry of snow about noon and cold at night. Finished letter to
Myra. Bible class in afternoon, and sermon in evening by Mr. Barnard. On guard,
through which I escaped helping to clean the carriages. Received Journal.

MAR. 16TH, WEDNESDAY.
Fair and cold. On fatigue. The carriages were all painted. Read "Bleak House."
Bible class. Sermon in evening. Wrote to Myra.

MAR. 17TH, THURSDAY.
St. Patrick's day. First anniversary of the fight at Kelly's Ford. New harness for
the battery throughout drawn and the old turned in. Nearly finished "Bleak
House." Went to see a review of a division of the 6th Corps close by. Saw Gen.
Sedgwick and quite a number of ladies.[10] A magnificent sight. Sermon in the
evening by Mr. Barnard. Kiely and I went into his tent after services to ask some
questions. It did me much good, and it pleased me much to find Kiely concerned.
Prayed.

MAR. 18TH, FRIDAY.
Fair but very windy. After helping to mount the chests received my pass for 24
hours to visit the 39th and started for Culpepper on Joshua, where I arrived about
noon. Found that Sergt. Brown had already gone up to Mitchell's Station. A very
windy ride. Took dinner with some of Brown's friends in a house and left Joshua
with them. About 3 P.M. went into Culpepper to the station and got the Provost
Marshall to sign my pass so that I could ride up on the cars. The town seemed to
be rather lively. About 5 miles beyond C. passed some regular cavalry regiments
camped by the R.R. and probably doing outpost duty. Reached Mitchell's station
about 5 P.M. It is no village, only a few houses and a station. The brigade commander of the post had his headquarters near to the R.R. I found the 39th and
the whole brigade packed up and under arms because of an alarm. It was said
that Stuart had crossed with cavalry at Raccoon Ford. Was much pleased to see
all the Woburn boys in Co. K, and they appeared to be glad to see me. Put up
with Irving Foster and Barrett.[11]

MAR. 19TH, SATURDAY.
Still quite cold. The excitement all subsided. Found that the reg. was camped
close under Cedar and Slaughter Mts. where was the scene of fighting in 1862.

They are two wooded peaks rising abruptly from the plain only separated by a very slight declination of land between. They looked like twin hills joined as were the Siamese twins. The reg. underwent an inspection which occupied all the morning. Their appearance was very creditable. They seem to be under very strict discipline, stricter than I should like. They had erected a very beautiful chapel which I visited. Started to return home about 4½ p.m. Stopped at Culpepper with Brown and had supper. Reached camp about 8½ and reported to Capt. Learned that the fright had extended throughout the whole army and that our battery had been harnessed up. Found also a letter awaiting me from Myra.

Mar. 20th, Sunday.
Fair and windy. Sermon in morning and evening by Mr. Barnard. Bible class in afternoon. Started to write a letter to Myra but could not; I felt so gloomy.

Mar. 21st, Monday.
Fair and cold. Brigade drill, and review by Gens. Meade, Pleasonton, Sedgwick, and Hunt. The brigade looked finely and manoeuvered beautifully. I did not go out, but was detailed for guard at headquarters to permit another man to go out. Felt very gloomy all day. Managed to continue on my letter to Myra, but did not finish.

Mar. 22nd, Tuesday.
Cold. Occupied most of the day in the woods getting a load of fire wood. Got a fine load of white oak. In unloading it I managed to fall off the wagon, making a somersault but only bruising my leg a little. A very fortunate affair that I did not hurt myself seriously. Finished my letter to Myra, and wrote to father. On guard, 2nd relief. Commenced to snow just before nightfall.

Mar. 23d, Wednesday.
Snowed nearly all night, depth 8 inches. Fair and warm during the day, eating the snow away fast. Wrote to John. Exercised somewhat in mind in regard to religion. Went to Bible class and meeting in the evening. Prayed for the first time with sincerity. May God help me in the way I have chosen and which I believe to be the way of salvation.

Mar. 24th, Thursday.
Warm and the snow melted almost entirely away. On fatigue duty shoveling snow and piling grain. Visited by Mr. Farrington. Bible class in afternoon. Wrote a little on the translation. A long letter from Myra, and very encouraging. May God bless her and make her happy for the light she has shed over my life. And may God enable me to become worthy of her and her love. Chapel in the evening where Mr. Farmington officiated in absence of Mr. Barnard. Spoke and prayed and enjoyed the meeting very much. Afterwards stopped with Mr. Farrington for a while. During the evening the minstrel troupe gave a performance in the club house.

Mar. 25th, Friday.

Cloudy, and heavy rain at night. Did not feel very well or cheerful. Wrote a letter to Journal. Bible class in afternoon.

Middlesex Journal, Saturday, April 2, 1864

Brandy Station, VA,
March 25, 1864.

The tenth day after the ides of March. The month that slipped on us almost unawares, so quietly and mildly it came, now blusteringly reminds us that March is the month of winds and bids fair to go out like a lion in realization of the old saying. We are but just rid of the deepest snow that has fallen here this winter. The army is in a state of waiting. Each short period of pleasant weather begets prophecies innumerable as to the commencement, objects, and direction of the coming campaign. Reviews and inspections multiply, which are the infallible signs of movement. Preparation is everywhere. —Trains are repaired, wagons painted, and all organizations equipped to the very extremity of serviceability. The army is in excellent condition, health, and spirits. Each day adds to its numbers, and by the time the Potomac army takes the field it will be as perfectly organized and in as perfect a state of efficiency as American skill and military ability can make it. The Lieut. General is present here, which everybody takes as a presage of coming activity. What does not a man's reputation achieve for him even in untried fields. The veterans of this army who have felt the influence of so many generals and experienced their policy and ability, look with calm confidence toward this captor of 90,000 men and hundreds of cannon, a vastly different feeling to the enthusiasm that for more than a year followed McClellan to be so thoroughly disappointed. It is really pleasing and encouraging to perceive the trust which the army of the Potomac now reposes in their new commander, and which grew even before his coming. If Gen. Grant has the confidence in this army which the army has in him, then it seems that there must be accomplished the great deeds which the whole nation has looked toward it to perform. Report has maintained steadily now for several months that the 11th and 12th Corps are coming back, and now even another corps is added to the story. But whatever may be the additions to the army the opinion everywhere prevails that the coming season will see active service here and hard fighting. —Which belief is far different from that universally obtained early in the winter, for then it was thought that this army would be but a make weight, fighting only when it might be necessary to make a diversion or to retain a force in front of us, while the chief work would be done in the vicinity of Chattanooga and like vital points.

Doubtless Gen. Grant will inspect and review the army. Everything is held in readiness with that expectation, so that it may take place at a moment's notice. On the 21st inst., the 1st Brig. H. A. was reviewed by Gens. Meade, Pleasonton, Sedgwick, and Hunt. After the review they rode through our camps, a perfect constellation of military stars. What portraits

I have seen of Gen. Meade are very indifferent. He is spare built, though not what is called slim, medium heighth, sits very erect in the saddle, and is of a very austere countenance, his whiskers of an iron grey, with mustache and imperial. Very military in appearance indeed. In inspecting the various batteries he had an appearance of one inspecting and not going through a mere form, and after his return to quarters could undoubtedly give an exact account of the condition of the organizations he had been reviewing. All generals do not have this appearance, but rather one of getting through a disagreeable job at the fastest pace possible. A gallop is the usual rate of reviewing. The batteries of the brigade were in splendid condition and made a beautiful appearance, so that he spoke very flatteringly to Capt. Robertson, brigade commander. All the carriages had been lately painted, new equipments and harness drawn, and the horses were in good condition. The movements performed were wheeling from and into close column and marching brigade front at a trot.

Found an opportunity the past week to visit the Woburn boys in the 39th. Arrived late on the afternoon of the 18th at Mitchell's Station, and found the whole brigade under arms, in consequence of a scare which extended throughout the whole army. Stuart was reported to have crossed at Raccoon Ford with a heavy force of cavalry. —Their camp is most beautifully and neatly situated right at the foot of Cedar mountain within about two miles of the advance picket line. Mitchell's Station is about six miles beyond Culpepper. Cedar and Slaughter mountains in the vicinity are twin hills which rise abruptly from the plains, partially wooded and connected by a strip of land but slightly less elevated than the hills themselves. These two hills have been already rendered celebrated by the battles which took place there in '62. Beyond the hills but a very short distance is the Blue Ridge.

Halfway between Culpepper and the station are camped several regular cavalry regiments, which are doing outpost duty on both flanks of the infantry pickets. All the Woburn boys are flourishing, and the most of them begin to make calculations as to their return. Battery's time is out in June.

HOPLITE.

Mar. 26th, Saturday.
Cloudy, cold and rainy. Wrote to Myra. Bible class in afternoon. Chapel in evening where happened a very unpleasant affair through Antrim, who took exception to loaning the tent to the officers for a collation.[12] Prayed, and especially for him. Fear it was not in a Christian spirit.

Mar. 27th, Sunday.
Fair and warm. A very interesting Bible lesson this day on Mat. 5th. Discourse in evening and prayer meeting. Spoke. Commenced a letter to H.A.H. A very pleasant day. The battery drew 24 new horses, the first lot we have had for a long time. Detailed to take care of one, a bright sorrel.

Mar. 28th, Monday.

Fair and warm. Finished letter to H.A.H. and wrote to Myra. Bible class in afternoon and sermon in evening. Prayed and felt more sincere in this prayer than ever before. Felt quite happy afterward as one who had been enabled to do his duty. This and preceding day quite a large body of troops joined the army from Washington and Harper's Ferry, mostly heavy artillery. Army being reorganized by Gen. Grant for a vigorous campaign. Army enlarging rapidly. The Corps overturned and the army formed into three Corps only under Gens. Hancock, Warren and Sedgwick.[13]

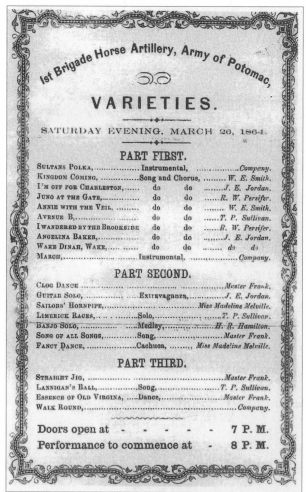

Variety show program. Griffin Family Collection.

April First.
Cloudy and rainy. Commenced to read "Trevlyn's Heir" by Mrs. Wood. Bible class in afternoon. Finished translation of 3rd. Book of Caesar.

April 2nd, Saturday.
Snow and rain very cold all day. Finished Mrs. Wood's novel in which was so interested could not wash my face even 'til night. Bible class in afternoon. Letter from Miss Moulton of a very whimsical character. Cold a little worse. Did *not* go to church in evening. Much disappointed at no letter from Myra.

April 3rd, Sunday.
Rainy. Felt unwell all day, results of my cold. Did not go to church in morning or Bible class. Church in evening. Prayed and spoke. Experienced much pleasure in this prayer. Kiely and I went in to speak with Mr. Barnard. Prayed again, Kiely also. No letter from Myra.

April 4th, Monday.
Rainy and a little snow. Wrote to Mr. Stockwell. Kiely and I went out in the rain and picked up a small load of wood in a deserted camp. Captain put me on guard at headquarters for forgetting to take my nose-bag off my horse. Posted on the wagon train 2nd relief. Letter from Myra.

April 5th, Tuesday.
Rainy and cold all night, but had shelter by the negro's cook fire. Felt indifferently well because of my cold. Had a good opportunity for observing the negro character which was not without amusement. Commenced a letter to Myra. This must be the equinoctial storm I think because it hangs on so long. The equinox was on the 20th March.

April 6th, Wednesday.
Rained nearly all night. Finished letter to Myra, and sent it enclosing $10 that I had borrowed of Griffin, also a picture of Kiely. On fatigue at headquarters. Cut wood and aided in the preparations to settle in camp a Capt. Cranford who came to the brigade for Commissary from the 1st Corps. Had to gather chips to make a path, and helped in putting up a brush fence and his tent. After I got home late at night was ordered to clean my horse. Tried hard to maintain a Christian spirit toward the Capt. in spite of his severity to me. Church in the evening, and had reason to believe that God poured the Holy Spirit upon me. Blest be God for his mercy and loving-kindness. I felt as if I could sufficiently thank him. Went in to speak with Mr. Barnard on the doctrine of salvation before the time of Christ.

April 7th, Thursday.
Fair and warm. Wrote to Myra. Bible class in afternoon. Letter from Myra and one from mother. Was again detailed for guard at headquarters in continuation

of punishment. Felt that I had no anger toward the Capt. My post was on the wagon train. Early in the night the officers' club house was burnt, set on fire.

April 8th, Friday.
Still pleasant. Finished my guard duty. Order came in for our brigade to relieve the 2nd with the cavalry. Christian Commission also ordered to take down their chapel tent, signs of a movement. Met there in the evening perhaps for the last time. Felt sad and prayed. Mr. Barnard's discourse was on Christian life. 20 cavalrymen arrived at the battery, detached from Gregg's division to fill us up.[14]

April 9th, Saturday.
Awoke in the morning and found it raining hard, which continued all day. Wrote to Myra and to Bethiah. Bible class in afternoon. A very dismal day.

April 10th, Sunday.
Fair. Was unable to attend church in the morning because of fatigue duty. Bible class in afternoon. Church in evening. Felt very unsettled as if God's face were turned from me. Did not feel the usual joy in prayer.

April 11th, Monday.
Fair. No mail because the freshet had carried away the railway bridge over Bull Run. Bible class had a picture taken for Mr. Barnard, a very good one. Washed and oiled saddles and equipment. A very busy day.

April 12th, Tuesday.
Warm and sunny. Letter from Myra. Polished bridle. Church in evening. Still felt the want of the usual pleasure in prayer. Felt very unhappy and more than ever convinced of my low nature. Still in it all I never once thought to retrace my steps. "Though he slay me, yet will I trust in him."[15]

April 13th, Wednesday.
Warm and sunny. Literally wasted this day doing scarce anything. Bible class, and sermon in evening. Went to see brigade drill of some infantry in an adjoining field, a fine sight.

April 14th, Thursday.
Fair and warm. Brigade reviewed by Gen. Sheridan commanding cavalry corps.[16] Mr. S. is quite a young man. Commenced to read "John Marchmont's Legacy" by Miss Braddon. Chapel in the evening. Spoke. Orders to move tomorrow at 8 o' clock. Made the necessary preparations. Kiely and I determined to separate from Miller and Tileston and use shelter tents.

April 15th, Friday.
Cloudy. Reveille at daybreak. Packed up and got started from camp about 9 o' clock. Had spent 4 mo's and three days in this camp. Took up line of march in the direction of Rappahannock Station. Passed by the headquarters of the

reserve artillery. Crossed the river at the old place by a bridge formed by 9 pontoons. Went straight down the R.R. and camped for the night at Bealton. Portions of the 5th Corps lay along the R.R. The 50th N.Y. Reg. of Engineers had a beautiful camp enclosed by an abattis, and the entrance stockaded.[17] Pitched a paulin with Kiely and four others for the night. A raw and damp wind all day. The march was very pleasant, consisting of only about 7 miles. Yet from disuse the saddle tired me even for that short distance. Continued reading Miss Braddon's novel.

APRIL 16TH, SATURDAY.
Rained all night. Reveille at daybreak. Marched immediately after feeding in a heavy rain. Went down the R.R. passing encampments of regiments, that were guarding the R.R., at short intervals. At Germantown we struck sharp to the left upon the road on which we retreated from Fayetteville October last. Shortly we arrived at the road between Warrenton and the Junction which we had travelled so frequently before. About half way between these two places we came upon the cavalry outposts of Gregg's Div., and uncomfortable they looked sitting motionless in their saddles while the rain poured down drenchingly. Although we had been marching all day in the rain and I was wet through overcoat and all, still I thought their job more dismal than mine. Passing the picket, we came up with the reserve, and shortly arrived at the camp of the 2nd. Brig., where we left Batt. A. We continued on to Warrenton where we halted in the main street while the Capt. reported to Gen. Gregg. The town looked dismal enough in the pouring rain. Saw a number of females gazing on us from the windows as we passed. How comfortable the houses looked. Turning out of the town a short distance we camped for the night on a hill nearby the 1st. Penn. Cavalry. Kiely and pitched our shelter tent against a fireplace which had been left from an old torn down shanty. We built a fire and managed to make ourselves tolerably comfortable. Was put on guard because the orderly thought I was absent from the morning roll call. Proved to him that I was there and he gave me credit for it as my regular turn. A very tough day's march.

APRIL 17TH, SUNDAY.
Cold and cloudy. Moved at 7 o' clock to another position nearer the town where we camped on the side of a grassy hill. Tore down the camp of the regular battery which we had relieved, and built beds &c for ourselves. Put up our shelter tent and built a bed. Felt miserable and dirty all day, the miserable red clay almost an inch thick on everything. Went to church in the evening in what had once been a court house. Text—Fight the good fight of faith. Lay hold on eternal life. Not a very eloquent preacher. The audience was large. Felt tired and went to bed early.

APRIL 18TH, MONDAY.
Fair and sunny. Cleaned carriages and harness. Had to wash a harness, the driver being sick. On fatigue, burying horses &c. A very busy day. Maj. Robertson & Capt. Graham visited the battery bringing a mail. Letter from Myra containing

a picture of brother Appleton, and a photograph of myself. Gave the letter to Frank Bliss.[18] There was a review of Gregg's div. by Maj. Gen. Sheridan, which was interrupted by a reported advance of the rebs. The 2nd Brig. went out with the right section of our battery as far as Sulphur Springs and accomplished the stupendous feat of capturing *one* (1) rebel. The section returned early in the evening. —Visited Walton and my friends in the band of the 1st Mass. Cav. They were quartered quite comfortably in the 2nd story of a brick barn. Church in the evening, prayer meeting afterward. Prayed.

APRIL 19TH, TUESDAY.
Fair and sunny. Wrote to Myra. Drill at the piece which I escaped, having a team to take care of. Read Tennyson and took a long nap. A very lazy day. Received pay for Jan. & Feb. Paid my debts with the exception of $5 to Griffin and $5 to Smith De Voe.[19] Church and prayer meeting in the evening.

APRIL 20TH, WEDNESDAY.
Cloudy and exceeding cold for this season of the year. Wrote some on my poem. Read Bible, Tennyson and Caesar. Went into Warrenton and bought the last three sheets of paper in the town for 5 cents. Bought a bottle of ink for the very moderate sum of *20 cts.* Church and prayer meeting in evening.

APRIL 21ST, THURSDAY.
Cloudy and cold all day with a little rain. Packed up right after stable call and about noon our whole brigade left Warrenton. Moved over the old road in the direction of the Junction. Had an opportunity for the first time of seeing our new Brigade commander, Gen. Davis.[20] A very smart and young looking man. Moving by the 2nd Brig., we camped near to Turkey Run and about 3½ miles from the Junction. Camped in the middle of a grassy field, a very pleasant and dry situation. Put up a picket. Although our march was only about 3½ miles, still I felt very tired at night. Kiely and I pitched our shelter tent and raised a bed of the flattest rails we could find. The cavalry camped around us in all directions, so that the whole division was very closely massed. Saw Gen. Gregg.

APRIL 22ND, FRIDAY.
Fair and quite warm. Cleaned the carriages and equipments, put up harness racks, and polished my bit, a very busy day. In afternoon received a large mail, letter from Miss Moulton & H.A.H., two papers from Charlestown, a magazine and two papers from Woburn. Commenced a letter to Myra. Drew a blouse. Rumors of a forward movement immediately.

APRIL 23D, SATURDAY.
Sunny and breezy. A beautiful day. Finished letter to Myra, and read a great deal. Four days' rations of coffee and sugar dealt out to us. This looks like a move. Rumors that the rebels were going into Maryland again. N.B. Sent $5 in the letter to A. On guard 1st relief.

April 24th, Sunday.

Fair and very warm. The reg. of cavalry camped nearest to us broke camp and went on picket, it was reported, to Morrisville. Mounted inspection by the Capt. Received a letter from Myra and three pictures. Felt very lazy all day. After retreat there was a prayer meeting, which was interrupted by rain. Prayed.

April 25th, Monday.

Rained nearly all night. Cleared off in the forenoon and became very warm. On fatigue. Wrote to the Journal. Visited friends in 1st Mass.

Middlesex Journal, Saturday, May 7, 1864

Army Correspondence
Turkey Run, VA,
April 25, 1864.
Dear Editor: —Fair Spring has come again with fickle face, at one time smiling with wreathed smiles, anon weeping fertilizing tears that gladden dry earth in the bearing of its

"Lovely freight
Of overflowing blooms, and earliest shoots
Of orient green, giving safe pledge of fruits,
Which in wintertide shall star
The black earth with brilliance rare."

The fields and the hillsides rejoice the eye with their bright new mantle, and one can never weary of gazing, remembering the whitened hardened aspect so lately prevailing. The oak woods seem sprinkled with a fine powder of living green. The glad sunshine, not as yet possessing any distressing or enervating power, shines as well into the hearts of men as upon the spreading fields. Men feel their lives springing as the grass, feel the joy of living, that to breathe and move are pleasures. Men joyously hail the coming spring, though perhaps insensibly to themselves, not naming the emotions within them, and feel their hearts grow in breadth. Their life grows verdant with the springing grass.

Above the earth hangs changeful skies, deeper blue built upon by fleeting structures of finest hues, here long strips of frail brown with empurpled edges through a space of azure overlap upon a ragged mass of smoky cloud, beyond which swell long waves of golden red, the gildings of a fitful sunbeam; far down the horizon, at an opposite point, heavy dun spots of storm shut out the blue, ever shifting and moving, at one time growing into a presage of coming showers and again melting into mere vaporous spots upon the fair day. Swift shadows shift across the fields, to be succeeded by pouring sunshine. Fair April, fickle as fair, coming to us perhaps in sadness, always wreathes the heart in gladness. She brightens hope and freshens life. Misanthropy dwells in cities and between brick walls never to have felt his life bound within at Spring's glad presence. Nature, with a subtlety that cannot be fought against, because intangible and imperceptible, conquers insensibly, and he who loves not life the dearer, and feels it more gladsome when he sees the earth waking from her wintry sleep to don her lovely living robes, and feels not a freshened spirit with freshened nature, is indeed unhappily framed and fit only for a jailer's life, sere and yellow, within dark walls and behind prison bolts and bars. The rare radiance of the earth testifies to God's love and the beauty of his character.

For us the campaign has commenced. —Moving from winter quarters at Brandy Station on the 15th inst., the 1st Brig. H. A. scattered in all directions, each battery to join their respective brigades. We with battery A, 4th U. S. A., moved to join Gregg's division, then lying at Warrenton. Passing down the river as far as the Rappahannock Rail Road bridge, we crossed, and continued the march that day down the railroad, as far as Bealton. Next morning reveille awoke us to the reality of a heavy rainstorm and a long march. Harnessing early the route was continued down the track as far as Germantown, where, turning short to the left, we soon struck the main road to Warrenton. All along the railroad were the camps of the 5th Corps, which had been occupied all winter in guarding the line of communication. The camp of the 50th N. Y. engineer regiment, arrested every eye as a model camp for elegance and convenience. Situated upon the slope of a hill that had once been wooded, it was entirely surrounded by an abattis, the entrance way stockaded and ditched. It reminded me of the illustrations of Robinson Crusoe's plantation, in DeFoe's tale.

We found the first brigade of Gregg's division camped in and around Warrenton, and the second about three miles out of the town toward the Junction. After some miles of weary plodding through the red mud and pouring rain, we at length halted in the main street, awaiting an assignment to camp. Dismounting I strove to warm my feet by stamping up and down the flagged sidewalk, ruefully speculating as I considered my splashed garments whether they would ever return to their natural color of blue, or always retain their then British hue of scarlet, for the soil in this portion of the State is of a bright red, and when applied to anything in solution gives a shade similar to red ochre. In fact my clothing had acquired a color the exact shade that I remember my father's house to be at the back. Camped that night on a hill just outside the town. The succeeding day we moved our camp nearer the town, and laid very near the winter quarters of the battery which we had just relieved. —There we remained until the 21st, when we removed to this place. While we remained in Warrenton nothing of importance occurred save a review by Gen. Sheridan. This was interrupted by an alarm that a rebel brigade of cavalry were in the valley between Warrenton and the Ridge. The parade being at once dismissed, the 2d Brig. with the right section of our battery was ordered out to make a scout. The expedition went as far as Sulphur Springs, and from thence sent out across the river, dismounted skirmishers to Jefferson, a distance of about four miles. They returned the same night, having, with their force of nearly 3000 men, accomplished the stupendous feat of capturing *one* (1) rebel, who was at home on furlough and for the purpose of getting a horse.

It is one of the schemes of the rebels to improve their cavalry force, that when any cavalryman is dismounted by any chance of war to permit so many days of furlough in which to procure a new horse, which if not accomplished then he is obliged to join some infantry regiment. And it appears that our own government is about to take similar measures, viz.: if any man is found to neglect or abuse his horse he is to be turned over to some infantry regt. and his horse given to another. Still let the Government take all the precautions of that nature it may, if it uses the cavalry to the same extent and in the same manner as during the preceding season the loss in horses will undoubtedly be great. It is not an uncommon thing for cavalry to march several days and nights with but very short intermissions, and across scores of miles without a mouthful of food. Many times I have wondered that they endured it as well as they do. Besides a rider, saddle, and equipments are no light load, averaging at least 200 lbs.

Warrenton has always been eminently of a secession sentiment, although remarkably quiet whenever occupied by our forces. There is no doubt but what it is a resting place and harbor for guerillas when our lines are without the town. During the past winter every citizen in the place was compelled to answer to his name morning and night, which no doubt has prevented much information being afforded to the guerillas from within the town. Yet for all the precautions within and watchfulness upon our lines here, a young lady, daughter of the rebel Governor Smith, was enabled to escape through them with all her personal property. And the pickets upon the outposts have had no lazy duty during the winter. Continued vigilance has been the price of safety. Nearly every night firing is heard at some post, sometimes a combined attack, but oftener a crawling upon the picket in darkness to pick him off unseen. But two nights ago two pickets were shot dead upon their posts by stealthy cowardly assassins. They will shoot a man just to get his boots. It is nothing short of murder for it helps on their cause not one whit. Although they may kill a picket still they make no impression on the line, for it but keeps the reserves more widely awake. The most watchful picket in most situations can thus be picked off.

It is whispered that the reason for vacating Warrenton was because that the officers of the division held too frequent council with the gracious ladies of the town, and General Gregg is said to have remarked that all his officers knew, the women of Warrenton knew. Be that as it may the ladies of the town received our officers very generally, and when, on the 21st, our brigade passed through the main street, in column of march, the doors and casements were crowded with females, who at least pretended that they were sorry that their friends of the shoulder-straps were leaving them.

At present the whole division lies camped midway between Warrenton and the Junction, three miles from each place. It is only about a mile from here that we had an engagement last autumn. The division is very closely massed whether for any more definite purpose than convenience to forage is not known. The fields and the edges of the woodland glimmer white with shelter tents. Our brigade has lately received a new commander in the person of Brig. Gen. Davies, lately promoted from a colonelcy. He is a very young man of a dashing and assured appearance. Everybody seems to have confidence in him and all seem to think the brigade fortunate both in brigade and division commander. And here let me say a just word in favor of Gen. Gregg. People in reading the dashing and often rash enterprises of Kilpatrick gradually come to forget Gregg, less showy but more sure. No one ever yet read of a duty tardily or slackly performed by him, no one ever read of any movement made abortive by the poor execution of the part assigned to him. Wherever he has been ordered to be at any given time there he has been promptly no matter what the intervening obstacles. Gen. Gregg has character, ability and confidence, and his men have confidence in him. This reciprocal confidence between commander and commanded is the first requisite for success. It is a dreadful feeling to go into battle doubting the ability of one's commanding officer to handle his men.

The division is larger now than it has been for a year and in better condition. In fact I have reason to believe that this division has had better rations during the past winter for both men and horses, than we in the reserve artillery and near to the headquarters of the army. The first Massachusetts has received its new battalion and all the regiments are more or less recruited, to such an extent in truth that there are men to the number of a full regiment in our brigade who are not mounted. Every one looks forward with confidence to the coming campaign, and all tired of inaction, anticipate stirring movements with pleasure. As usual imagination and rumor are at work. All sorts of stories are rife as to the direction of the coming campaign and the especial part of this division in it. First there is the usual story of a Maryland campaign. Next there is a rumor to this effect, that there is collected at Brandy Station forty days rations and Gen. Grant is shortly to close communication with Washington thus saving a corps to guard the R. R. Then a vigorous forward movement is to be entered upon, with Brandy Station as the transient base of operations. Whatever is done it seems ought to be commenced shortly, as the weather is good and the roads settled. It is to be hoped that his vicinity to Washington will not neutralize Gen. Grant's genius.

The returning sun again multiplies reviews and inspection. Every day sees a review of some kind. A great amount of labor is thus consumed for no purpose but show. Steel bits and everything that admits of a polish are subject to a constant friction, and the wood-work on the carriages is washed and washed again until they imitate the tidiness of livery getable hack. Harness is washed, brushed, blacked. A day or two in camp breeds a drill. Add to these the regular camp duty and it will be seen that we are not allowed to rot in laziness. Still this is not without its benefit. Days spent in labor fly faster and the boys begin to look smilingly as they see their days of service "grow less by degree and beautifully small."

Yours, HOPLITE

April 26th, Tuesday.
Fair and cool. Section drill in the forenoon. Slept nearly all the afternoon. Commenced a letter to Myra.

April 27th, Wednesday.
Sunny with a cool breeze. Section drill under Lieut. Wilson.[21] Finished letter to Myra and commenced one to Mother. Received two papers by mail. Prayer meeting, very interesting. Spoke and prayed.

April 28th, Thursday.
Very cold and chilly, quite in contrast with the previous weather. Finished letter home. Section drill. Officers getting very strict, kept Vannett tied on the spare wheel which he was relieved from by order of the Dr., else he would have been kept there six hours longer.[22] Much indignation about it. The officers getting very unpopular.

CHAPTER 8

THE REGULARS WORKED THEIR
PIECES BEAUTIFULLY:
APRIL–JUNE 1864

GEN. ULYSSES S. GRANT KICKED OFF HIS CAMPAIGN IN THE EAST ON
May 4, 1864. In contrast to previous years, this time all of the Union
armies were expected to conduct simultaneous offensives, thus making it impossible for the Confederate government to shift its forces to
meet a crisis in one of the theaters of operations. As events transpired,
however, it proved more difficult than anticipated for all the Union
armies to carry out successful, mutually supporting operations. Consequently, William Sherman's army in Georgia, Benjamin Butler's along
the James River, Nathaniel Banks's Red River campaign in Louisiana,
and David Hunter's efforts in the Shenandoah Valley all proceeded
essentially independently with varying degrees of success and failure,
leaving the Army of the Potomac to conduct an unsupported, grinding
slugging match with the Army of Northern Virginia known as the
Overland Campaign, which began in the Wilderness on May 5 and
ended in the trenches around Petersburg in the summer of 1864.

Between the Wilderness and Petersburg, the two armies fought
a series of bloody battles at Spotsylvania Courthouse, the North Anna
River, and Cold Harbor. Always, however, Grant and Meade (who still
commanded the Army of the Potomac) kept marching south and east,
trying to get around Lee's right flank and force him to fight outside of
his entrenchments. Each time, the Confederate leader successfully par-
ried Grant's thrusts, but, in so doing, gave up vital ground that could
not be recovered.

The Sixth New York's part in this drama was bound to that of
the Cavalry Corps and its combative leader, Gen. Philip Sheridan. The
horse soldiers entered the campaign carrying out the traditional roles of
cavalry: screening the main army from attack, conducting reconnaissance to determine the enemy position, and clearing the enemy away

from the route of advance of the infantry corps. During the Battle of the Wilderness, the cavalry performed these roles with mixed success, but Grant sided with Sheridan in a dispute with Meade over the employment of the cavalry corps. Meade wanted Sheridan under his control and very much in a support role, while Sheridan insisted he be allowed to function independently as a mobile strike force.

As a result of Grant's decision, Sheridan took the entire cavalry corps and supporting horse artillery away from the main army and launched it on a raid toward Richmond. Sheridan's action forced J.E.B. Stuart, his Confederate counterpart, to follow with most of his cavalry. From the Union perspective, the greatest success of the raid was the mortal wounding of Stuart in an action at Yellow Tavern outside of Richmond. Nevertheless, Sheridan's adventure cost the Army of the Potomac dearly in its battles with Lee, depriving it of operational and tactical flexibility and forcing it to use infantry formations to discover the whereabouts and intentions of the enemy.

After a brief respite to rest men and horses at Harrison's Landing on the James River, Sheridan's force rejoined the army along the North Anna River, crossed the Pamunkey River, and fought in the Battle of Haw's Shop. This brutal, largely dismounted action pitted Sheridan's troopers against the Confederate cavalry, now under Maj. Gen. Wade Hampton. While this battle raged, the Potomac army completed its crossing of the Pamunkey River and the Army of Northern Virginia settled into new fortifications along Totopotomoy Creek. Haw's Shop was the last action that the Sixth New York participated in as part of the Army of the Potomac, for shortly thereafter it was relieved from duty and sent back to Washington to turn in its artillery pieces and be reorganized.

The chapter begins with the opening actions of Grant's 1864 Overland Campaign and ends with the Sixth New York's receiving orders to return to Washington, D.C. Major actions covered in this chapter include the Battle of the Wilderness, Sheridan's Raid on Richmond, the movement of the Cavalry Corps to the James River for rest and resupply, its return march to the army, and the Battle of Haw's Shop.

April 29th, Friday.

Cool and sunny. Fed hay immediately after reveille roll call, by which I at once knew that we were going to move. Packed up and started off about 9 o' clock with the whole division. Went down the R.R. passing on the way very many laborers in the woods getting out R.R. ties. Bearing gently to the right we intersected Warrenton main road and struck into the road through Germantown which we had travelled twice before. Continuing which we soon arrived at Bealton where we stopped and watered. Crossing the R.R. there we took the same road to Morrisville which we used in the advance across the Rapidan last fall. It was reported that we were going to take just the same route as then, but as the 5th Corps still lay along the R.R. with no signs of moving, I thought not. Just before reaching Morrisville we turned off the road to the right and soon arrived at Kelley's Ford where was a pontoon bridge already laid for us. Stopped to get some water for the detachment, and in catching up nearly used up my horse. The bridge was built with ten pontoons, which were made of canvas stretched over wooden frames. The bridge was the weakest I had ever crossed. We proceeded straight from the river toward Stevensburgh about 3 miles passing the camps which the 1st Corps had occupied early last winter, and when I had visited the 39th. Camped for the night in the midst of a large field with cavalry all about us. Could see in the distance other camps, and hear the roll of drums. The 2nd Corps was camped not far off. We could not be above 4 or 5 miles from Brandy Station to the south and east.[1] We had probably come here to await the concentration of the army for a forward movement. Kiely and I did not pitch tent.

APRIL 30TH, SATURDAY.
Cloudy. Moved the battery but a short distance to the edge of the woods. Made a picket, put up harness racks, pitched tents, cleaned harness and carriages. The Capt. seemed bent on keeping us at work. Gradually he is growing unpopular, a general shout this day saluted the fatigue call. A very busy day. Mustered for pay for March & April. Disappointed in receiving no letter. No rails handy and Kiely and I had to make our bed on the ground.

MAY 1ST, SUNDAY.
Fair and warm. Wrote to Myra. Letter from Myra and one from mother. Wrote to M.C.J. Prayer meeting in evening, which was quite pleasant. Prayed and spoke.

MAY 2ND, MONDAY.
Fair and warm. Battery drill in the morning, the best for many months. Gen. Davies was a spectator part of the time. All the brigade was out drilling. Read Tennyson nearly all afternoon. Letter from Myra.

MAY 3RD, TUESDAY.
Cool but fair. Reveille before daybreak. Column moved about 9 o' clock, with a pontoon train in the direction of the Rapidan. We soon struck the road on which we returned from the Rapidan last fall. Passed by the camps of an infantry brigade, then the fork of the road which leads to Germania Ford. Shortly turned to the left through the woods and about noon camped in a little opening in the woods three miles distant from both Ely's Ford and Culpepper Ford. Pitched shelter. Visited friends in first Mass. Cav. Liver for supper.

MAY 4TH, WEDNESDAY.
Got up about midnight and harnessed. Moved out between 2 and 3 by very good roads and in the grey of the morning reached Ely's Ford where was already a pontoon train. Our section without caissons crossed with the 6th Ohio Cav. as

advance and climbing the high hill took position to protect the laying of the bridge. Just as we reached the top of the hill, where a broad road led back from the river, I heard four carbine shots, and the rebel picket fires were still burning. Here we remained until the whole division had crossed when we went down the road. Five of the rebel pickets were taken. We followed down the road and soon found it to be the road on which we lay all day previous to the fight May 2nd, 1864 [sic]. Had a chance to see the battlefield of Chancellorsville after the lapse of a year. Was surprised at the extent of the earth works which our army had thrown up. The debris of the fight still remained, old knapsacks &c. All the houses had been torn down, and the Chancellor house burnt, a mass of brick ruins. We halted for a time at Chancellorsville as was said for the infantry of the 2nd Corps to come up. All about were the graves of men and horses, and fragments of shell. I picked up a piece of shell and a piece of a man's skull as a relic. Continued out straight across the plank road by another plank road for about three miles when we turned sharp to the right on a broad sandy road and continuing on about a mile halted about noon at a large field. Watered and fed twice. Lost my haversack on the road with all my rations. Did not miss that so much as my knife, fork and spoon. About 5 P.M. we returned to the corner of the plank road where was a large open field and a dwelling house. Going back on the road to the extremity of the field we took position on the rising ground and went into battery. Back of us about a half mile were the infantry pickets. The story ran that we were trying to trap Hampton's rebel legion of cavalry. Just at nightfall managed to wash for the first time that day. Had some coffee and lay down on the paulin without unsaddling. A very pleasant day's expedition. A little skirmishing by the cavalry was reported to have taken place toward Fredericksburgh.

May 5th, Thursday.
Night passed without an alarm. Roused up at 4½ A.M. Fed, watered, and got breakfast before daylight. Spilt my ink which was quite an untoward event. Gen. Sheridan came up with the 1st Div. Cav. Saw Gen. Custer, a very young looking man with a fanciful dress. He wore a brown velvet jacket with a broad collar turned over. About noon we moved out and again marched up the road to the right. Halted awhile in the field we lay in the preceding day, and then proceeded up the road still farther. Saw a rebel soldier by the roadside under guard with his wife and child. Probably had deserted from rebels and living in this region had taken his wife with him. She had been crying. The baby was in arms. Watered at the same stream as yesterday, which is called Piney Branch. Continued up the road for about a mile passing on the left a church and at length came to where 4 roads met with a few buildings there. This place is called Todd's Tavern. Found here a brigade of infantry of 2nd Corps. Just after we had halted there, the 3rd Div. Cav. came in on a road from the left and then we learned that they had been fighting the rebs all morning and had been driven back. Our div. relieved them and they went to the rear. Shortly fighting commenced right in our front and

on left flank. The left section of our battery went way out to the front and went into action. The fighting for a time was desperate, but our brigade drove them fighting splendidly. The wounded came in fast from the front. Toward dusk the firing ceased and we watered and unharnessed.[2] Lay on the paulin. All day it was very warm. According to the way I looked at affairs we established this day our line fronting Gordonsville, the whole cavalry corps on the left flank, and the 2nd corps on the right next to us. All things seem to prosper so far.

MAY 6TH, FRIDAY.

Got up and harnessed about three o' clock. Moved back about daylight about 40 rods to another opening and took position on a rising with the right section on a knoll to the front and left. Shortly heavy musketry firing commenced far up on the right with occasional artillery fire. It sounded deadly. The pioneers pulled down a log building at our right so as to afford nothing to aid the rebels in getting range on us if they came out on us with artillery. The musketry on the far right continued without intermission for two hours very heavy. About noon an outbreak occurred nearer to us and shortly our section was ordered up. It appears that Gen. Custer with his cavalry lay next to us on the right, and him the rebel cavalry had furiously attacked hoping to break through. Our section was ordered to report to him as for some reason his own batteries were not at hand. We went up to the cross roads in a northwesterly direction we went at a quick trot down the road which was through a thick oak forest. We were accompanied by a company of cavalry as escort. All along the road were thickly strewn the evidences of the passage of infantry the preceding day in the shape of blankets, knapsacks, clothing, &c. At intervals along the road were detachments of cavalry to preserve the connection between the two cavalry divisions. In one place I saw some of the Michigan cavalry armed with Spencer's seven shooters. About a mile down the road we debouched on the left upon a field dotted at intervals with young pines. We came upon cavalry in line behind a knoll. The rebels had opened with artillery just before we got out of the woods. Waiting a moment behind the cavalry, we then went through and beyond them upon some high level ground. Took position about 40 rods to left and front of them. The rebel battery immediately turned their fire upon us, as I afterward learned killing a man on the other piece at the first shot. We replied as fast as we could, but their fire was terrible, having 4 pieces against our two. Before us a short distance the grassy field ended, then came a ploughed field, a rail fence between. The other side the ploughed ground were planted the rebel pieces, distant about 1400 yds. The ground sloped up in front toward the rebels and just this side the slope laid our skirmishers close to the ground, the line a semi-circle with the bow toward us. In the hollow to the right and front, lay a regiment of cavalry all mounted. We fired out both limber chests nearly when a battery of four pieces, part of B. & L., opened on the rebs from our right and rear. The other piece of our section had been disabled by a shell which got stuck in it halfway down, and taken to the rear. For about 15 or 20 minutes our gun had to bear the fire of four, and it grew very hot. When B. & L. opened, our piece limbered to the rear and went back to take position on the left of the regulars. Then I learned the extent of our damage, two killed, Cripps & Brennan, one wounded, Sergt. Turner. Sergt. Turner's leg was shot off below the knee and was amputated at the knee joint.[3] In our detachment three horses (cannonier) were killed and one wounded so he had to be killed, besides two slightly wounded. In our new positions we remained until in all we had fired over a hundred shots. The regulars worked their pieces beautifully, as if only at drill. We were sent back to the rear just as the Johnnies began to run. Just as we left the field the regulars fired a whole volley at the rebs, which must have hastened their departure. Went back at a slow walk to our old place near the corner. This is the hardest artillery fire I have ever been under. At first I was somewhat flurried but overcame it at last. All the time we were in action I thought of whether I was prepared to die. Tried to be resigned to God's will if I were to die, fraid I didn't thoroughly succeed. But I think that my shrinking was only the natural dread of youth. Before we left the field I helped to bury the two dead. I prayed for the souls of Cripps and Brennan. Cripps thought that during the winter he had experienced a change of heart. I trust that it was so. In this action I got more exhausted than at any time previously in my life, for we were not full handed and it was hard work running up the gun. Besides the thirst caused by the gunpowder was awful. The concussion caused by the gun had a very bad effect upon my chest, and my ears were stunned so they rang. The Gen. thought we had been very efficient. Had a good wash which freshened me up greatly. While we were occupied in this fight our brigade had a little fight with the rebs also. Stuart's cavalry had been trying all day to break through our lines upon the wagon trains, but we were too much for him. About half after four we with the rest of the brigade moved down the road again toward Chancellorsville, passing battery M in position on the road. Halted for the night at the corner of the plank road, and each section took separate positions. Had a hearty supper of hardees and fried pork, with a cup of strong coffee. Went to sleep on the paulins and slept soundly for I was very tired.

May 7th, Saturday.
Rose at 3 o'clock and packed up. Remained saddled and harnessed all night. Good news from the front, and the bands played the national airs. Gave my horse a good grooming and myself a good washing. Felt emphatically played out. Had some fried beef for breakfast of the toughest kind. Horses now for two days on half rations of grain. News from the rear not so encouraging as at the front. Remained here until shortly after noon when our brigade moved up the old road again and halted on the knoll a little short of Todd's Tavern where we had been in position once before. Remaining there a short time a heavy fire of musketry broke out on our left and we went into position a little to the rear and left commanding some broad fields. Our gun fired only one shot as we were afraid of hitting our own men. The musketry firing was terrific; we drove them

at length and Brown's section advanced a good distance and commenced firing. Our brigade band was ordered up and commenced playing. The 6th Ohio cav. did prodigies of valor as so did all of our brigade. The firing ceased toward dusk and all of a sudden just after sunset broke out a good distance up on the right. The rebels tried hard by a sudden dash to break through but did not succeed. Our fellows beat them back at every point. After dark when the fight was over I went up to a house close by, and found the yard and house were crammed with wounded. Our cavalry are not to be beaten. The battery was massed for the night about ten o'clock, we fed, and had supper and went to bed on the paulins. While Brown's section was in action one of his pieces broke its stock in the recoil. The artificers stayed up all night to make a new one. Very hot all day.

MAY 8TH, SUNDAY.
Got up about three o'clock. Although I was on guard, was not called up at all. Saddled up and lay in park 'til daybreak, when we moved close up to the Tavern and found infantry had arrived. The fifth Corps passed off to the left towards Spottsylvania C.H. Saw Cobbett and Merriam in 22nd M.V. and Capt. Tay of the 32nd.[4] Gens. Grant and Meade and Sheridan were at the house early in the morning. Saw Gen. Williams A.A.G. of the Potomac Army.[5] The 2nd Corps came up and formed in line of battle directly in front of us. Gens. Grant and Meade went down the road toward Chancellorsville. All was bustle and movement preparatory to a battle. So far it appears we had had the advantage. It was very hot. Second Corps came down from the right and formed a line of battle right in front of where we were lying. Todd's Tavern which had been the left of the line now became the right. Our troops appeared to be massing farther out on the left and to be fortifying here. Very little firing along the line. We remained here 'til about 2 P.M., when the whole division went down the road again passing by the way 2500 rebel prisoners and the headquarters of the army in a farm house. Passed near the church the whole of the reserve artillery harnessed up. Long trains of wagons were rattling to and fro. Crossing Piney Branch, we turned short to the left into a bye road through the wood which brought us out into a large field where was parked an immense wagon train. Stopped to water and went on, regaining the main road. On the main road with us was a train of ambulances going the same way. It was a sad sight to see men there wounded in every manner. Coming to the corner at the plank road instead of turning to the left we kept right on the other way which led to Fredericksburgh. Shortly encamped for the night on the right. Unhitched and unharnessed. Relished my supper heartily. A very hot and fatiguing day. We are evidently getting the best of the rebels rapidly. All sorts of rumors were prevalent as regards the movements of other armies.

MAY 9TH, MONDAY.
Rose at 3 and got in column on the plank road toward Fredericksburgh. The whole cavalry corps seemed to be massed and getting in column to make some

Capt. Cyrus Tay, Thirty-second Massachusetts Volunteer Infantry. Courtesy of Massachusetts Commandery, Military Order of the Loyal Legion and U.S. Army Military History Institute.

movement. Saw a portion of Burnside's Corps. Reports of a great raid &c. At length about 9 A.M. we moved off, our section in the rear of the whole column with the 6th Ohio. We went down the plank road toward Fredericksburgh until at length we came to some of the rebel defenses used in the winter of 62–3. They consisted of redans commanding the road and a line of rifle pits. About four miles short of F. the road forked and we took the right hand thus avoiding the city. We marched along rapidly through a level table land pleasantly wooded and with pretty dwellings. Shortly the column threw out flankers and we continued our path. At length about noon we came to where a road turned sharp to the right in a direction south of south-east. Telegraph poles were set along this road and it was said to be the direct road for Richmond. Just at the turning of the road the way ran through a beautiful and broad valley. All the cavalry formed to the left of the road in the open field and marched down the slope of the hill and into the valley in column of squadrons, while we marched in the road. It was a glorious sight, the far stretching, verdant valley, fading away in the hazy distance into broad low pasture lands and above winding away to the south, a river of beautiful green brinked with sombre pine. And then the long even lines of cavalry obliquely descending the slope showed boldly blue against the summer green. Over all hotly shone the sun. My eye could not tire with gazing. The whole column watered in the swiftly flowing stream that wound its way through the valley. During the afternoon the route lay through a very beautiful and highly diversified country abounding at intervals in beautiful farms and farm houses. All along the road were strewn every kind of army clothing which the cavalry found too burdensome to carry: new overcoats, blankets, jackets, &c. A great many cavalry horses gave out along the road which were left and the equipments destroyed. Passed on the right a small brick church with the following inscription "Massaponax Church, July 4th, 1859", and next passed through a river called Ta Creek at a place called Thornbury where was a mill. The cavalry took great quantities of flour out of it. Shortly the flankers commenced skirmishing and continued at intervals for some time. At length the rebels ambushed and suddenly fell upon our rear. They were in force enough to drive the rear guard back upon the column. A panic ensued. The pack mules being driven off at a gallop increased the confusion and at length Gen. Davies coming to the rear and seeing our pieces in danger of capture, ordered us away as quick as possible. Our pieces moving away at a trot increased the panic, and the brave 6th Ohio, which two days before had proved themselves heroes almost, took to flight and crowded against our pieces in the narrow road entirely hindering further progress. Their colonel tried frantically to rally them. At length one squadron made a sort of broken line and received the rebels. At the same time Col. Taylor rallied his men into line, and the 1st Mass. took position on the opposite side of the road. The rebels were checked just in time, for they had got up to the rearmost gun and one rebel was captured near enough to have put his hand on the piece. It was a most disgraceful affair, but resulting from a surprise. Going through a small field we took position on the right of the road in a ploughed field. Scarcely was this done when a gun opened far up on the right and at first we were in doubt whether or not it might be one of our own pieces. Our doubt was answered almost immediately, for they threw a shell directly at us. We turned our gun toward it and soon shut it up. But the firing on the right was getting hotter, to which we responded by some well directed shells. Then the rebel piece broke out again in a different place. We paid attention to that, and in fact alternatively we paid our compliments to the artillery on our left and the cavalry on the right, til we had fired about 45 rounds from each gun, when with a parting salute we limbered to the rear and took out. The rebel artillery did very poor shooting. We continued up the road for a part of the time at a trot. The country became more wooded. I grew so sleepy I scarce could sit in my saddle. Found a bag of flour which I strapped on the limber. At length about midnight we debouched upon a high and cleared field where we camped for the night. Far away to the south could be seen the flames of burning storehouses and rebel provisions, the work of our advance. I found we had halted on a high hill underneath which ran the North Anna River. Went down to the river to water and to get cooking water. A hearty supper and went to bed. Unhitched and unharnessed.[6]

MAY 10TH, TUESDAY.
After scarce two hour's sleep, was aroused to saddle up. This was scarcely done when musketry was heard from the direction we came, and a shell came hissing over us. We quickly went into battery and replied. The firing grew nearer,

was driven off again, and at length ceased. Leaving the left section in position the rest of the battery went over the ford. One of the rebel shells came down in Gen. Sheridan's headquarters killing two horses. The North Anna at this point is about as broad as the Rapidan at Ely's ford. It ran here between very high banks, and was heavily shaded to the edge by very high trees. There was a mill here and a dam. The ford took its name from the dam, and is called Beaver Dam Ford. I found that the whole force had stopped there for the night. The column was so long that the advance got into camp before dark, while we of the rear not until midnight. Know that there were at least 3 brigades with Gen. Sheridan in command on this raid. Whether the other two brigades had remained behind or were with us I could not ascertain. Think they remained behind.[7] Getting into column the south side the river we moved on. A short distance on passed about two hundred muskets which we had captured the preceding night and spoilt. About three miles from the river we struck the Gordonsville R.R. at Beaver Dam Station. Our advance had reached here the preceding night and destroyed the building and the R.R. for a great distance. We also burned much provision stored for the rebel army, said to be 7 days' rations for their whole army. When we came by the fire was still burning. There lay smouldering huge piles of meal and scattered charred remains of bacon. Gen. Custer had destroyed large stores of meal, coffee, sugar, bacon, salt, &c. I saw two locomotives which he had destroyed besides as many as a hundred cars said to have been loaded with rations. The station consisted of several fine brick buildings all of which were destroyed. At the time Custer attacked there were released about 300 prisoners which the rebs were conducting to Richmond.[8] We continued our march in a south easterly direction all day through a beautiful but thinly settled country. Just beyond the station saw a dead rebel face upward toward the sun, giving proof that our advance had met with some resistance. The sun was burning hot and the clouds of dust suffocating. Halted about noon for an hour to feed horses and ourselves. During the forenoon crossed the small stream the Little River. Continued our course all the afternoon in the same direction without any interruption and about 5 P.M. arrived at the South Anna. In the morning we could faintly hear Custer fighting the rebels in our rear. It was reported he had captured the gun that opened upon us the preceding day, and with it another.[9] Before crossing the South Anna we halted and watered and foraged some corn from a neighboring house. It was the very pattern of a Va. Mansion and the owner must have lost much. A very large barn full of corn was taken away, besides what the soldiers fancied from the house, bacon, potatoes, flour, preserves, kettles, &c. I was satisfied with corn sufficient for two feeds for Joshua. We crossed the river on an excellent bridge and advancing about 1½ miles camped for the night at Goodale. Unharnessed and unhitched. Kiely and I cooked some flapjacks for ourselves without any rising.

MAY 11TH, WEDNESDAY.
Slept very poorly owing to the lead-like quality of my supper. Got up about 3½ A.M. and immediately saddled up. Moved out with apparently only our own bri-

gade in a direction about South East. Marching about five miles we came upon the R.R. at Ashland station and the cavalry immediately proceeded to destroy it, burning culverts &c. They captured a rebel mail &c. We went into battery in an adjacent field and a few shots were heard. Very soon we limbered up and took out by the road we came for a short distance when we turned short to the left by a road the guide board of which showed it to be only 17 miles from Richmond. After winding around in a general westerly direction we soon came upon a main road running S.E., and along which a heavy column of our cavalry was moving. We halted to fall in their rear. I afterward learned that the 1st Mass. Cav. or rather one squadron of it got used rather roughly at Ashland Station after we left. For stopping to make a little destruction to the R.R. and Telegraph, a company of infantry stole upon them and poured a murderous volley right into them. It broke them, but they re-forming charged but could not do much being mounted, for the rebels took refuge in all sorts of nooks and crannies. The one squadron lost about 40.[10] After greasing the carriages we continued on behind the column that had passed for several miles and at length halted in a large open field shortly after noon. On the way we crossed a small stream which was said to be the Chickahominy, though I am not certain it was that stream.[11] At a house by the way I foraged enough corn for another feed for Joshua and found an Andrew's & Stoddard's Latin Grammar which I took. About 2 P.M. artillery firing was heard in our front a short distance, and also in our rear much nearer. All sorts of rumors more or less absurd were afloat. Shortly we moved on again by a good road in an easterly direction and crossed a railroad. At this crossing there was a little square building with the inscription "Glen Allen Post Office."[12] The other side the railroad we formed a line of battle to the rear and remained so until the second brigade fell back and formed a line right in front of us, when we fell back through a strip of woods and formed up in some large open fields, while in the direction we were going there was some very smart firing. Shortly news came down that Gen. Custer had captured 2 guns from the rebs whereat there was great cheering.[13] A storm suddenly arose and poured down with great violence so that my overcoat was wet through. Just before dark the column got started on the road again and then halted. It rained all night at intervals, nevertheless at one halt a little longer than usual I lay down on a board about 8 inches wide and got asleep, and dreamed of home I think. The column moved very slowly, halting at one place to put wounded in the wagons and ambulances. We were getting very near to Richmond. We crossed quite a considerable stream by a high bridge. The road became a turnpike. During the night two blank reports were heard which I afterwards learned to be from the explosion of torpedoes laid by the rebels. —Daylight of the 12th found us just past some town or other and about to turn to the left. Sharp firing in the advance. Going to the left we at length came upon some broad fields newly planted where the whole force appeared massed. Made coffee. It rained heavily occasionally. At length the fighting seemed to come nearer and to hem us in on three sides. We were only two or three miles from Richmond, and infantry had come out to stop our course. I began to feel a little alarmed. At length the fire got more furious and the rebs opened from two pieces of artillery. They pressed on and our battery went into action each section in a separate place. We were stationed on the flank close to some woods and where the rebs seemed to be pressing hotly. We opened fire on them with shell and at length drove them off. At the same time I perceived that the other parts of the line had been equally successful. Slowly our whole force passed away to the east over a high hill and we were withdrawn a section at a time. As we passed down the hill into a low lying valley, at the east I noticed fortifications which were said to be the extreme rebel left at the siege of Richmond in '62. Along the valley lay the railroad which our men were destroying as we passed. Here also ran the Chickahominy, a swift and dirty stream. We crossed it on a bridge which Gen. Custer had hindered the rebels from destroying by desperate fighting at the same time as we were fighting.[14] Crossing into the low lands beyond, we halted for a short time seeing the evidences of the late fight in the dead horses and breastworks &c. There were some dead men also, but I did not see them. Here we made coffee. And when the whole brigade had crossed, it moved in from the river about a mile and halted near the little town of Mechanicsville. Some firing occurred here. About dark the column moved on halting occasionally to allow time to forage the country. Got enough corn to feed Josh twice. At length we camped for the night in a wheat field about 9 P.M. Turned in beneath the paulin, joyful to find opportunity for sleep.[15]

May 13th, Friday.
Rained heavily nearly all night and woke up to find it still raining. Rose about three and saddled up. Between 8 & 9 we moved off S. E. by E. along a narrow road our brigade taking the extreme advance and our section going in advance of the remainder of the battery. Passed the 1st division on the road and thus found out that the whole of the cavalry corps was on this raid. A little before noon we came upon the York R. and Richmond R.R. near Dispatch Station. Close by there was a deserted steam saw mill probably belonging to the rebel government. Crossing the R.R. we soon struck the road on which our army had marched up the peninsula two years before. Instead of turning to the left we turned to the right once more facing Richmond and halted. Went for some corn but could get none. Our fellows here captured a rebel who had been detailed to work at the saw mill. Close by here was the place where my brother Appleton had left me to go to the hospital. What would I not have given to have had him by me still! But it is wrong to indulge such thought. At length we got some corn. By a mistake our section went over the Chickahominy with two regiments that were sent there on picket. We came back again and unharnessed for the night. Bottom's Bridge was a frail plank structure which shook fearfully beneath the pieces.[16] Everything here looked very natural but deserted. The old camps of '62 were distinctly visible. Scouting parties were sent out to White oak swamp and elsewhere. A very wet and gloomy day.

May 14th, Saturday.

Slept soundly and for a wonder was allowed to sleep all night. Rations ran out and had to fall to making Indian cakes of meal foraged on the route. About 9 a.m. the column moved over Bottom Bridge, our brigade on the advance, and the right section on the advance of the brigade. After crossing the bridge the column turned short to the left by the same road as we took when in '62 we crossed the same bridge. Saw a portion of the old fortifications, a redoubt right across the road &c. Passed the large house on the left which was the hospital where Appleton lay sick two years ago. All these scenes brought him forcibly to my mind. God rest his soul. Also saw the path through the woods to the right which Appleton and I took to strike the road on which the army was retreating, and to get him into an ambulance. Farther on passed the situation of our first camp on the Richmond side of the Chickahominy. Shortly we struck on to the road on which the main body of the army retreated to Harrison's Landing. Next passed over the White Oak Swamp by the same corduroy bridge as on the retreat. Was pleased on this day's march to fall in with Lieut. Flint Wyman who was one of the 300 prisoners whom we had released at Beaver Dam Station, but whom I had not before seen because he had kept with another division on the march.[17] Passed by the site of the action at Glendale, and some of our fellows scouting through the fields came across the skulls and bones of men who had not been buried after that action. As we advanced through the woods saw the church and road to the left where we struck this road on the reconnaissance to Malvern Hill in August of '62. As we approached Malvern Hill saw evidences of the fight in quantities of trees with tops broken by artillery fire. At length we came upon the hill. All looked green and deserted. Several guns were heard which were said to be from a gunboat shelling our column taking us for rebs. It ceased shortly, I suppose upon or fellows signalling. We did not stop upon the hill but went straight over it by the old road toward the river and down the hill. Could see the gunboats in the river. We continued down the river by the Harrison's Landing road for about three miles when we turned in toward the river and halted right on the bank. The bands played merrily. Foraged some fodder from a neighboring barn. Parked close to the river's edge and camped for the night. Watered in the river near by and just as we got down to it a gunboat went swiftly up the river with the black muzzles of its '64 pdrs yawning upon us. Looking down the river two or three miles I could see a great cloud of transports lying close to the other side which was Butler's depot. Towards dark went down to the river and had a splendid wash from head to foot. Changed clothes. Lieut. Wyman and one of his men, a fellow prisoner, took supper with us, and was going to stay all night, but they were ordered to report to the provost marshal of our division to get transportation to Washington. Wrote a note to Myra and one to Mother for him to mail so as to relieve their anxiety. Pitched paulin. Cloudy all day and occasional squalls of rain.

Lt. Luther F. Wyman. Courtesy of Massachusetts Commandery, Military Order of the Loyal Legion and U.S. Army Military History Institute.

May 15th, Sunday.

Rained a little during the night, but sun rose fair. Fried pork and corn cake for breakfast. Went down to the river and had a bath. The river looked beautiful, brinked to its very edge with bright green. Put up a picket. Drew rations for ourselves and horses which were ferried across the river from City Point to a landing a little above us on the river called Haxall's Landing.[18] Wrote to Myra. In the afternoon a very heavy thunder shower. Prayer meeting in the evening. Prayed.

May 16th, Monday.

Rained during the night, but fine in the morning. Took a bath in the river. Put up harness racks, and reduced the park to small intervals. For a wonder did not clean the pieces although the drivers washed harnesses. Joyous news from the different armies. Drew more grain, and strapped it on the caissons. Greased the axles. Move doubtless tomorrow. All sorts of guesses as to our destination. Could hear heavy artillery practice in the direction of Butler's army all the forenoon, and at one time volleys of musketry.[19] In the evening I went to the brigade commissary's to bring over some hard bread. The candle, which I had left burning, set fire to our tent and spoiled half of it. Very warm.

MAY 17TH, TUESDAY.

Cloudy and cold all day. Had a bath. About 9 A.M. we harnessed and hitched and started off in the direction of Harrison's Landing with the rest of our div., but had scarcely got a mile from camp when we turned about and returned to the same place. Kiely got a lot of potatoes and pork which the brigade commissary had left not having transportation. Kiely and I went into a paulin with Horton, Roth and Whitney.[20] Had a potato stew for dinner which tasted delicious. Detailed for guard, 1st relief. Had just been posted after retreat roll call when "boot and saddle" sounded from Gen. Davies' headquarters, and packing up immediately we moved out just after dark. Took a direction apparently straight back from the river to the N.E. Moved on at a good rate until the column appeared to have got lost in the depths of a great swamp. The travelling was awful. We blundered on until toward morning when a fog coming up obscured the moon and made it as dark as Erebus.[21] Within about an hour of dawn we halted in an open field to await daylight. A tedious night's march. Felt so sleepy I scarce could sit in my saddle. Josh getting nearly "played out."

MAY 18TH, WEDNESDAY.

Morning found us unrefreshed and thoroughly exhausted. We continued our way for some distance through narrow and tangled bye-ways, once more counter-marching for quite a little distance, and about ten A.M. we arrived at a point which I recognized as having seen before. We were on the road which we had pursued in Aug. of '62 on the retreat from Harrison's Landing. We struck that road about six miles from Charles City C.H. and where we had camped on the first night of the retreat. Passed by the brick house where we had lain all of one day in position, and arrived at the Chickahominy. A portion of the 2nd Brig. had been here before us to build a bridge. The river here is divided and forms two streams, one of which we had to ford, but a bridge was over the other. Since last seeing this the rebs had built a breastwork for two guns to command the road. We halted immediately after crossing, unharnessed and fed. Our mess got a hearty meal of fried pork, boiled potatoes, and coffee. As we lay here a violent thunder shower occurred accompanied with hail which thoroughly saturated my overcoat. That over we saddled up again and lay for some time in readiness to move, while the other divisions of the corps crossed the river. At length about 4½ P.M. we moved off in a direction N.E., crossed a small stream near a mill, a tributary of the Chickahominy. Our division alone seemed to go by this road. The way lay for the most part through low land and densely wooded. Passed a white church at the junction of 4 roads, where the columns of the other divisions appeared to join ours. At length just after dark went into camp at some cross roads. Pitched paulin as it rained occasionally. Got a hearty supper of fried pork and tea, and went to bed well tired. A tedious 24 hours' march.

May 19th, Thursday.

Slept 'til daylight when we rose, fed, and cleaned, and got breakfast. About 8 o' clock harnessed up, which was scarcely done when recall was blown and we stretched the picket rope and unsaddled again. Remained here all day, as some alleged, awaiting rations which were to come up to the "White House" on the Pamunkey, as others said, because the other batteries some of them got stuck in the mud. Pork stew for dinner. On detail to pitch tarpaulin for the officers, in doing which I got pretty wet by a heavy thunder shower that came up. Rained heavily for some time. A detail went out to forage which got a little corn, and shame to say robbed the citizens of much property. One fellow came back with some false curls, another with a woman's night gown. Slept nearly all the afternoon. Pitched paulin again just before dark and went to bed early. A long day.

May 20th, Friday.

Reveille before daylight. Neglected to go to reveille roll call for the first time in a number of weeks and suppose I was checked for extra guard duty. Sun rose trough a heavy mist. Just after daybreak got in column in a northerly direction and started by muddy and wooded road. Crossed the York River R.R. as I thought not far from Tunstall's Station. At a short halt at the junction of some road was pleased to see Gen. Davies reprimand some of our flankers for plundering the houses in their way and made them give up their spoil. I saw an accordeon, a flute, a whip, a hunting horn &c. Passed a small and very prettily appointed white church which I entered. Found a couple of Sunday school books lying in the pulpit inscribed "Hopewell Sunday School." At a short halt we made Kiely lay down beneath the gun-limber and when we came to move he fainted from the effects of the heat. We got him into an ambulance and I rode beside it for the remainder of this day's march. Halted about 2 P.M. on a little knoll at a short distance from a place called Cold Harbour. Had a hearty dinner of fried eggs and flapjacks, foraged on the road. Remained there over night. For supper had a stew of potatoes and chicken. Rations ran out this day. Kiely got quite well. I had feared it was sunstroke. A party went out foraging, for which I was detailed, but a driver went in my place. Very hot all day.

May 21st, Saturday.

Harnessed and hitched about 3 A.M. and then lay down on the ground to sleep 'til daylight. At daylight got breakfast of fried pork, coffee and the remains of our crackers. Feed for the team horses but none for those of the cannoniers. All sorts of talk prevalent as to why we were lying here. A fair prospect of going hungry. This day was the third anniversary of my marriage. What a way to spend it! It is some comfort to think it is the last one will be spent thus. I wonder what Myra's thoughts are in regard to it. Heavy firing in the extreme distance, most probably from the army of the Potomac. Remained here all day, and it seems to me was the longest day in the service. The sun blazed all day with unclouded ray. Towards nightfall unharnessed and grazed the horses in default of oats. A foraging party sent out, Wax among them. Cooked our last victuals in the shape of a potato stew. Rations now overdue a whole day. Pitched paulin as it looked like rain. Foragers returned bringing abundance of victuals, meal, poultry, flour &c.

May 22nd, Sunday.
Reveille before daylight. Got up about 3 a.m. and plucked some chickens. Corn cake and molasses for breakfast. Column got in motion about daylight on the same road as we came by. Rode a good distance of the route with a friend in 1st. Mass. Band. When we reached the R.R. we turned up it to the East in the direction of White House.[22] Arrived at the latter place about noon, which instead of being a white house was a mass of charred ruins. Saw the Pamunkey for the first time, which here is quite broad but shallow. A gunboat, the Morse, a wooden one, lay here with several transports laden with rations and forage.[23] One division had arrived one day before us and were camped in the large fields about the landing. Camped and drew five days' rations and forage. Bathed in the river. Wrote a short note to Myra, which I entrusted to a sailor of the Morse to mail for me. Saw her commander, who wore major's strap with an anchor in the middle between the two leaves. He was styled Lieut. Commander.[24] Also saw a boat's crew of the gunboat Mystic.[25] They were darkies and looked very nice in their

Babcock's ship USS *Morse*. Courtesy of Massachusetts Commandery, Military Order of the Loyal Legion and U.S. Army Military History Institute.

Comdr. Charles A. Babcock, U.S. Navy, commanding officer of USS Morse. Courtesy of Massachusetts Commandery, Military Order of the Loyal Legion and U.S. Army Military History Institute.

cool straw hats, blue pants, and spotless white shirts. One of the divisions crossed the river on the R.R. bridge. The firing yesterday was from Custer who had gone up to the South Anna to destroy a bridge.[26]

MAY 23RD, MONDAY.
Reveille before daybreak. Had scarcely time to get breakfast when off we went to cross the bridge. With the rest of the cannoniers I was detained at the dock to get forage. Went aboard the steamer Helen Getty where there was a sutler and spent my last 20 cents for a few molasses cakes. A first Lieut. of cavalry accosted me on the boat offering to give me a good breakfast and money beside to sell some goods for him. I declined not having opportunity, but this compliment to the honesty of my appearance quite flattered me. Many soldiers would have made him repent his trust. Had to take a bag of corn across the bridge on my horse. The bridge had evidently been destroyed, and was patched up for the occasion very loosely with boards &c.[27] The bridge is about ¼ mile long and about half

the distance tressel work. The brigade formed and halted on the other side and watered. I went back to the bridge to get some rope out of a net lying there. We lay here 'til 10½ A.M. when all being across, we took up line of march the 2nd Brig. being in front. At first we held a direction North East through a very pleasantly diversified country, but at length turning at right angles the course ran North West. The roads were deep with a bright yellow sand, but owing to the recent rains no dust arose. Got very sick in the course of the day. Felt so poorly that I was unable to sit my horse and rode on the caisson for the last 8 miles of the march. Shortly after noon we passed through the shire town of the county, viz. King William C.H. It was a pleasant place yet with the usual dilapidated appearance of southern towns. Fences were in ruins and grass grew in the stable yards. There was a large wooden house with a verandah which appeared to be a hotel. Quite a collection of ladies were sitting there to see the column as it passed. A great many horses gave out on this day's march owing to the extreme heat and the marching without water. Gen. Sheridan actually *wasted* horses by using them such. There was not the least necessity for the horses to go without water. At a distance of about 10 miles from K.W.C.H. we came to quite a little village, the name of which as it sounded to me is Aylettesville. It had evidently been a manufacturing place, for there were quite a number of large brick buildings in ashes with quantities of ruined machinery lying about, a steam engine &c. It was said these buildings were destroyed by Kilpatrick on some one of his raids. At this place there was a pretty little church, wooden and painted white, inscribed St. David's P.E. Church 1859.[28] Just outside the town we turned off the road upon the estate connected with a large house and camped for the night. On the piazza to this house sat two ladies, one quite young and dressed in white. It looked like home. I think *young* ladies ought to wear white a great deal. Gen. Sheridan made his headquarters in the front yard of this house. Just as we got into camp I felt worse than ever and could scarcely muster strength to unsaddle, but which at length accomplished I lay down on some rails. All day long could just hear in the distance a desultory cannonading, but just about sunset it grew plainer and very heavy. There must have been a heavy engagement in the army of the Potomac. It sounded terrible even at the distance we were from it, so fast and furious was it.[29] God send the victory to the side of right and liberty. Ate no supper. Spread the paulin. This day I felt the heat more than any day of the raid previously.

MAY 24TH, TUESDAY.
Reveille before daybreak. Felt a little better but by no means well. Harnessed up at sunrise. Came near being dismounted, for they were going to put my horse in a team. But they found another instead. Moved off a short distance where we parked in a field and unhitched to water. Our division took the advance of the column and our brigade of the division. Our course all day lay in a north west direction and we made a very long day's march. The weather was intensely hot. Passed through two villages, the last of which was called as near as I could find out Edewood. About noon halted for about half an hour, and again about

3 o'clock. My horse nearly gave out. Could scarcely get him along when we camped. Lieut. Wilson and six of our fellows were at the head of the column all day to pick up horses. Got 4 horses and 3 mules. We must have marched as much as 25 miles this day. Our column drove a scouting party of rebs before it all day. They were evidently watching our movements. At intervals during the day we could hear heavy firing as was thought at Hanover Junction or a bridge over one of the branches of the Pamunkey.[30] In the morning it seemed in a north west direction, when we halted for the night in the *south* west so that in this day's march we had nearly gone around the fighting. In the morning and for a few miles of the march I felt miserable, but as the day wore on the pain left me and I felt only rather weak. At night was able to eat a hearty supper. Bathed thoroughly in hopes to get a good night's sleep. We camped for the night near a large farm house quite in northern style. As we passed it I noticed Capt. Harper of Davies's staff on the porch making himself agreeable to a lady. She was smiling and talking, and seemed not at all displeased at the presence of the "Yankee". It was said she was of union sentiments. Roads getting dusty. All day the route lay through a sandy level, and for the most part wooded with here and there an opening for a farm. All the cultivated fields seemed planted with corn.

MAY 25TH, WEDNESDAY.
A heavy shower during the night. Luckily we had pitched a paulin. Slept poorly because of the heavy griddle cakes I had eaten for supper. For a wonder we were allowed to sleep 'til daylight. This place was called White Chimney Tavern from the fact that the house had five white chimneys and had once been a tavern. It was now inhabited by a widow lady by the name of Young. It had once been a very large farm and even now there were many acres under cultivation and quite a number of slaves remaining on the estate. Some of them expressed a determination to leave their mistress and go with us. While we lay harnessed up waiting for the head of the column to move out, the band played and it was really laughable to see the antics of a couple of darkies. They rivalled in extravagance of action any negro minstrels I ever saw. About 10 A.M. we moved out, our brigade being the extreme rear of the column, about two miles back on the road we had come, when we turned to the right in a direction due west. After about five miles a long halt was made. Marching 8 miles we reached the Fredericksburgh & Richmond R.R. at Chesterfield Station. The R.R. seemed in running order, but apparently not used. All about lay empty boxes where probably rations had been served out to the army. Saw here one solitary infantry straggler, and shortly after crossing the R.R. came upon baggage wagons going south in the direction we could hear firing. Was astonished to find no outposts of any kind, and our rear and flank apparently unprotected. News very scarce. All I could learn was that the army was pressing steadily forward and was already across the North Anna.[31] Saw some of the infantry we had recaptured at Beaver Dam on their way back to their regiments at the front. After crossing the R.R. we turned toward the north and after advancing two miles were halted for some time to build a bridge. Which

completed, we camped for the night in a large field near Corps Headquarters, the whole division together. Some of our wagons, forge, &c. joined us. Received a mail first time in 3 weeks, three letters from Myra, and one each from Mother and Mr. Farrington, and 3 papers. Rained heavily at intervals during the afternoon. Marched only about 12 miles this day. Weather quite cool.

MAY 26TH, THURSDAY AND MAY 27TH, FRIDAY.

Reveille at daybreak. Morning opened cloudy and rainy. Drew additional rations and prepared for further marching. Reported that we were about to return to the White House to establish a base of operations at that place. About noon the whole division moved back on the road we had come for some distance, while the column formed. Arrived at Chesterfield Station we found the 1st Div. of the 6th Corps awaiting us with a large wagon train. We halted here for awhile and I went a little distance from the battery to find my cousin in a Conn. reg. When I came back I found the battery had moved. I caught up and was about to mount when Lieut. Wilson shouted to me to stop. He asked me why I had left the battery and said he had more occasion to speak to me than any other in the detachment. I replied he had no more occasion to speak to me than others, but that he *did* speak to me more. He ordered me to walk, which I did for some three or four miles. Some bitter thoughts arose at his injustice, but I prayed God would enable me to stifle revengeful feelings, and partially succeeded. We took the same road as we had come from the Pamunkey. In front of our division was a pontoon train, and it was said in rear of us the infantry followed. Passed the road leading to White Chimney Tavern just before dark and about 8 P.M. halted for an hour to feed and make coffee. Continued marching all night at a very rapid pace. Sometime during the night we turned off to the south from the previously travelled road. We travelled rapidly halting but seldom. Felt but little sleepy. Dawn found us still travelling and as we thought close upon the Pamunkey. About 8 o'clock we halted in a large open field where we watered and got breakfast. Washed for first time in two days. Skirmishing and slight artillery firing about 9½ A.M. About noon we moved slowly across the river on a bridge built from 8 canvas pontoons. They were also just completing laying another below the first composed of 10 pontoons. The Pamunkey is quite narrow here and appeared very high. I conjectured this to be Newcastle Ford.[32] Crossed, the whole division formed in a large plain the farther side. One division was already out of sight and one remained the north side of the river. About 5 P.M. we went down to the river to water, when I saw that the first division of the 6th Corps had come up with us. They must have made excellent marching. After coming back we unharnessed and camped for the night. Our mess had a present of some fresh pork, which was for supper. Had a complete wash from head to foot. Felt rather poorly. Very hot all day.

MAY 28TH, SATURDAY.

Reveille at daylight. Harnessed and hitched. Watered and grazed the horses. Felt very poorly. Was just able to finish washing a shirt when the column commenced to move. I rolled it up wet and packed it on my horse. Took a southerly direction which a negro said led to Richmond and Cold Harbor. After advancing two or three miles we again halted in a large open field. Shortly shots were heard in front and our brigade mounted up and formed. Presently our section was ordered up and went in battery a little in advance of a house on the right, all the while a smart fire going on in the woods in front. Before us stretched a ploughed field, the road running along it to the left with woods on the other side of it. To the right of the ploughed field the woods stretched nearly to the woods in front. Through an opening beyond this point the field stretched away to the right in the form of a gulf. In the edge of the woods in front and on the road was a house, all around which as we came up the skirmishers were firing. Our position was about 250 yds. from the woods in front. At the edge of the woods the 10th N.Y. Cavalry were drawn up in line as support to the skirmishers in the woods. We were ordered to fire over their heads into the woods. Capt. Martin ordered to fire 3 sec. fuse and 3 deg. elevation, and looked at the shell himself. We fired and horrible to say it exploded right over the 10th N.Y. The shell was good for nothing and not to be trusted. That fuse ought to have carried three times as far. The shot wounded one man and several horses. The fellows of that reg. talked hard against us. Before firing again we limbered up and advanced to within 50 yds. of the woods. As we took this new position the mini bullets whistled thick around us, one struck the limber wheel right in front of me. The musketry was terrific only about a hundred yds. in front of us. We opened and fired slowly, being short of ammunition. The rebels opened with two or three guns but made overshots. We fired our limbers all away and were relieved by Brown's Section. We went to the rear near the house where the caissons were, and where Clark's section had been firing over our heads. By the way their first shot came right over our gun and struck in the ground only 20 feet in advance of us. It came near to killing Kiely. Cause, damp cartridges, which hanging fire depressed the piece. We filled up with ammunition and took position where Clark had been, he being now about to relieve Brown who had finished his ammunition. Just as Clark got engaged the enemy opened a heavy cross fire of artillery which damaged his section greatly. After he had used up all his ammunition, our gun being the only one which had any ammunition went down and went in alone. Here we remained without any damage until we had fired all our ammunition when we were relieved by a section of A 4th. We went about two miles to the rear where we massed in a little field on the right. Then I learned the extent of our damage, one man probably mortally wounded, viz. Loud, two men with a leg amputated, viz. J.R. Bunn and Corp. Oliver, three wounded by bullets viz. McCluskey, W. Johnson, Pageatt.[33] One wheel was stove up, and several horses killed. Lieut. Wilson's horse was killed by a shot while he was on him. After we had got out I had a good wash and a hearty supper, and felt very lively and fresh. This was the hottest musketry fire I have yet been under. It is wonderful some of us were not hit by them. Pageatt was wounded by a minie when his limber went down to carry ammunition to Brown's section. Gens. Gregg & Davies I saw close by during a portion of the engagement. The rebels for the most part made overshots and made it so hot about the house that they had to remove the hospital farther to the rear. One of Gen. Gregg's aids was killed. This fight will doubtless be called the Battle of Hawe's Church as that place was about a mile or so to the rear of the scene of engagement.[34] I was cooler in this engagement than ever before. As we were about to go in I prayed God to strengthen my trust and I feel that he answered my prayer.

May 29th, Sunday.

The preceding night we marched with the whole division farther on the left flank of our army for the infantry came up and relieved us and threw up earth works. I saw friends in the 16th Mass. and 1st. Heavy Art'y. Morning opened cool and sunny but the wind soon died away. We laid abed 'til an hour after sunrise. Got a hearty breakfast and watered the horses in the Pamunkey at the bridge where we had crossed which was only about a mile from where we lay. Saw that the wagon trains had crossed the river and probably the main body of the army. Saw near the bridge a great many contrabands, mostly women, who had run away from their masters. Busy nearly all day in washing the rest of my clothes. Sent some things away by Fuller who left the battery to go home but who returned at night, there being no communication with Washington. His time of service had expired as well as that of three others. No fighting all day.[35] A good breakfast and dinner. About 4 P.M. saddled up and moved off the east. Moved about a mile and a half and camped in a large field on very high ground. As when we crossed the Rapidan the whole cavalry corps covered the left flank. Cool all day.

May 30th, Monday.

Harnessed before daylight. Found we were camped on a broad plain partly cultivated along the northern edge of which ran the road, the forest and heights running all around the other sides. In the edges of the woods were several houses and among them that of the owner of this vast estate. There were several brick storehouses and outbuildings here, from one of which I got quite a quantity of black beans. In the day of its prosperity this must have been a magnificent plantation. About the middle of the afternoon we unharnessed, and our mess cooked a pot of the beans. They were scarcely done when a smart firing was heard in the woods in front and the brigade in front of us saddled up and moved up out of sight. We harnessed up and lay for about an hour in the same place, during which we sent and received a mail. No letter for me. About 4 P.M. our brigade moved off to the left and east into a road which gradually curved around until it ran southeast. Advancing along it about a mile and a half, we halted for a short time in an open field on the left, hearing fighting at length which gradually ceased, while directly ahead of us a considerable distance there was evidently an engagement going on with the infantry. Just before dark we again moved up the road in the direction of Richmond and about 9 P.M. halted for the night at some cross roads 14 miles from Richmond. Here were breast works built by our men to protect the extreme left. On our way up this road we passed quite a number of beautiful residences and a large brick tavern called Old Church Tavern. Near by was the Old Church, a pretty little Gothic structure of brick, and painted white.[36] Passed the 1st Div. on the road. Felt rather languid all day.

May 31st, Tuesday

Reveille before daybreak. Had to go a long distance to water. Occasional cannonading at the front.[37] Just before noon the whole brigade fell back to our preceding position on the south side of the road and unharnessed. Our mess had just time enough to cook a dinner of boiled potatoes and fried pork when boot and saddle sounded and we found that a battery of the 2nd brig. H.A. had come up to relieve us. We moved up a little past the brick tavern, passing the two batteries which were to serve with the 2nd Div., and turned to the right.[38] On this road was Sheridan's Headquarters and there we halted a few minutes. Then proceeding through the woods we came out upon the plain where we had lain nearly all the preceding day. Was surprised to find it so near. Parked very near to our former position and at the same time the other batteries of our brigade commenced to arrive. Pitched paulin. Very hot and dusty this day. Washed and changed my clothes.

June 1st, Wednesday.

Did not rise 'til an hour after daybreak, quite a relief to our former fashions. Washed all my clothes. The 18th Corps came up from the White House as reinforcements. They had been with Butler the other side of the James. Saw Brig. Gen. Martindale, who turned me out from the shade of a tree where I was washing.[39] All sorts of stories in camp about going to Washington, breaking up the battery &c. An inspection of horses. It appears that an order was really received for us to turn over the best of our horses to the other batteries in our brigade, receiving unserviceable ones in return, and to return the detached men to their regiments. We to go to Washington, for what purpose it is not clear. All day long an immense wagon train was passing towards the front.[40] About 4 p.m. boot and saddle sounded and the whole brigade moved about half a mile to the edge of the field, a position not near as good as the one we had. Read piece of an old volume of the French Revolution nearly all day. The various reports and conjectures circulating about camp as to what was going to be done with us made me feel very unsettled. It seems to be settled we are to go to Washington.[41] The report was not wanting even that all the recruits to the battery were to be discharged at the same time with the first men, viz. 20th June. I do not expect it.

June 2nd, 1864

The sun rose clear and hot. Lay in this place all day. The other batteries of the brigade took our serviceable horses and those of Battery A., giving us in return their condemned ones. We turned over also our wagons and a few cannoniers' equipments. Altogether quite a busy day. Heavy firing and musketry at the front all day. A heavy shower at nightfall.

JUNE 3RD, FRIDAY.

Harnessed up about 7 A.M. and such a looking lot of plugs were never seen collected into one battery. All the detached men were sent away, some to their regiments and some to join other batteries in the brigade. Some of these men had been with us nearly two years. There remained about 95 men. All of the men detached *from* our battery returned. Started for White House about 10 A.M., the whole of the brigade going part way with us. Our route ran nearly due east through a wooded country and over a sandy road. Battery A. had 11 horses give out on the way, luckily we not one. Met a brigade of infantry of the 18th Corps going to the front. About the middle of the afternoon we struck the road we had pursued when going to the same place a fortnight before. About 3 P.M. arrived on the monstrous plain which lies about White House landing. It was crowded with a motley mixture of troops, wagons, prisoners, hospitals &c. We halted in column awaiting a transport but found we could not have one 'til next day. Went into park close by the landing and unharnessed. Here lay some of the Ohio militia out for the period of 100 days. Begged my dinner of them. I went down to the bank to view the busy scene. The narrow river was crowded for a great distance with transports and steamers of all kinds, motionless and moving. Many vessels were unloading at temporary docks all the varied supplies which a great army needs. At one place a steamer was taking a load of "contrabands" all shades, sizes, and sexes. The Christian and Sanitary commissions each had a boat, and tents pitched upon the land. A gun boat lay close to the R.R. bridge. A locomotive and stock to open the R.R. lay on canal boats in the stream. Cloudy all day. I visited some rebel prisoners, about 800 in number, among whom there was a woman said to rank as 1st Sergt. in a battery. She was a dirty looking specimen. She did not talk very nice either.

JUNE 4TH, SATURDAY.

Harnessed and hitched about daylight and moved down to the wharf. Battery A. embarked first on a steam barge named United States. After they had loaded and left the wharf, another drew up named I.B. Mollison on which we loaded our battery. The boat was so small we had to send the carriages unlimbered down into the hold. I took opportunity to boil some pork while the battery was embarking. I saw some negro troops for the first time who came up on a steamer. They were fine looking men. I conversed with some of them some time. We finished embarking about 4 P.M. and upon trying to move off found the boat was aground. A small tug dragged us off and away we went down the river. The Pamunkey is much larger than I had expected, but very crooked. Passed gun boats at different points as we went down, and occasionally met vessels coming up. Just about dark we made West Point at the confluence of the Pamunkey and Matapony, and in company with another boat, that had overtaken us from

White House, anchored for the night. It commenced to rain quite hard and as night closed in really poured. The shelter on the boat was very scant. I lay down on the deck beneath an awning with the certainty almost of getting wet through before morning.

June 5th, Sunday.

As I had expected I was routed out by the rain and sat up nearly all night in the engine room. Toward morning the rain ceased. At daylight we tripped our anchor and continued our way down the York. About 7 o'clock arrived at York-town where we stopped to enable the skipper to buy some provisions, and to hand over to custody a fellow who had secreted himself in the coal hole of the boat with the intention of getting to Washington and deserting. As the day wore on the weather cleared up. Shortly we got upon the Chesapeake Bay which fortunately was very smooth. All day we steamed across it, the shore in sight on our left but on our right view was bounded only by sea and sky. So near of a hue were they that it was difficult to tell where one merged into the other. We met and passed numerous transports and steamers, and an occasional gun boat. Saw the S.R. Spaulding.[42] Toward night we entered the mouth of the Potomac, and passed Point Look out. We continued 'til after sundown and then running close in to shore, anchored for the night.

CHAPTER 9

HALF OF THE FEMALES IN WASHINGTON SEEM TO BE COURTESANS: JUNE–SEPTEMBER 1864

On June 3, the Sixth New York arrived at White House Landing on the Pamunkey River to embark for Washington. This was the same day that Grant executed a disastrous frontal assault against the Confederate earthworks at Cold Harbor. While George and his battery mates were enjoying a scenic cruise on the Pamunkey and Potomac rivers, the army they had left behind remained hunkered down, exhausted, in their Cold Harbor positions. Grant, however, now convinced of the folly of directly assaulting the earthworks in his front, was busily planning his next move.

The essence of Grant's plan was to keep the Confederates looking in other directions while the Army of the Potomac quietly disengaged from the Army of Northern Virginia and made a wide sweep across the James River to assault Petersburg and its nexus of railroad lines. If this plan were properly carried out, Lee would be forced to come out from his prepared earthworks and move into the open, where he could be engaged and destroyed.

The job of keeping Lee distracted was entrusted to Maj. Gen. David Hunter and Maj. Gen. Philip Sheridan. Hunter's orders were to march up the Shenandoah Valley with the objective of destroying its railroads; then, when that had been accomplished, he was to move east across the Blue Ridge Mountains to threaten Richmond directly. Sheridan's assignment was to take his cavalry west to smash up the railroads west of the capital and join the victorious Hunter. With Petersburg taken and all of the remaining railroads feeding Richmond destroyed, the Confederate government would have run out of time and strategic options.

Unfortunately for the Union cause, each of these movements, after good beginnings, failed to achieve their objectives. Hunter, stymied by Lt. Gen. Jubal Early in front of Lynchburg, retreated across

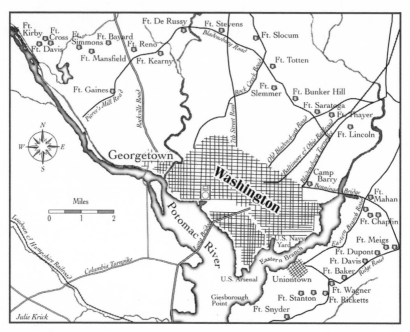

Maryland Defenses of Washington. Drawn by Julie Krick.

the Alleghany Mountains into West Virginia, leaving the Valley free of Federal forces and open to the Confederates for whatever use they might care to make of it. Sheridan thrust westward, in accordance with his orders, but Maj. Gen. Wade Hampton, with nearly equal numbers, pinned him at Trevilian Station with a fierce cavalry contest that lasted two days. With Hunter hightailing it for West Virginia, the possibility of linking the two forces, as originally planned, was gone for good.

Grant and Meade, on the other hand, successfully disengaged from Lee and executed a brilliant flanking move across the James River, moving to threaten a lightly defended Petersburg before Lee could get there. At the key moment, however, the Federal on-scene commander, impressed by the obvious strength of the Confederate works and not realizing how few soldiers opposed him, paused just long enough for Lee's army to file into the earthworks and bar the door. After another series of costly assaults, the opposing armies settled into a regimen of trench warfare that lasted until the following April.

With the Shenandoah Valley empty of significant Federal forces, Lee felt free to order Jubal Early to drive north with his small Army of the Valley. He rightly believed that this action would cause great anxiety in the Federal high command for the safety of the capital. With a presidential election in the offing, the administration could not afford to take such chances, and Lee expected that the threat of Early's army in the lower valley would result in a thinning of the forces facing him in front of Petersburg. When Early crossed the Potomac on July 6, burning Chambersburg and rolling over a Federal blocking force at the Monocacy River, that is exactly what happened. Grant was compelled to release the entire Sixth Corps to defend the capital. On July 11, Early arrived in front of the northwestern forts ringing Washington, but the native strength of the fortifications and the arrival of the Sixth Corps made it impracticable for him to mount a serious attack, and he withdrew across the Potomac and reentered the Valley.

When the Sixth New York arrived in Washington on June 6, it turned in its ordnance and commenced a lengthy sojourn at Camp Barry. This facility, named the Artillery Camp of Instruction, was used to receive and administer field artillery batteries that needed to be reconstituted and refitted. With the hard service it had seen and the imminent release of a good portion of its experienced soldiers, the Sixth New York certainly fell in that category. As the diary makes clear, the ultimate disposition of the battery was for a time uncertain, with options on the table ranging from disestablishment, conversion to an infantry support battery, and reconstitution as a smaller horse artillery battery. In the event, the artillery bureaucracy chose to fill up the depleted ranks of the Sixth New York with officers and men from another New York battery that was being disestablished, retaining it as a horse artillery battery and sending it out to join Sheridan's new Army of the Shenandoah.

Much of the diary for this period deals with day-to-day life at Camp Barry. Highlights include descriptions of the camp, various attractions of the city, the future of the battery, and preparations to take the field. The Sixth New York left camp for a short time when Early's army appeared before the Washington defenses but soon settled again into garrison routine. As the title of this chapter suggests, George was impressed by the large numbers of prostitutes who plied their trade in the city, but he seemingly contented himself with the more refined cultural resources of the town, including the soldier's lending library, the botanical garden, and the artwork adorning the Capitol. He also kept tedium at bay by writing several lengthy letters to the *Middlesex Journal*.

The entries for August 16–23 and 26–28 have been omitted. These dates contain the usual jottings about the weather, run-ins with Captain Martin, guard mounts and inspections, as well as George's reading list. This latter included *Con. Cregan* by Charles James Lever, *The Life of the Chevalier Bayard* by William Gilmore Simms, and *Journal of a Residence on a Georgia Plantation* by Fanny Kemble.

June 6th, Monday.

The sun rose hot and clear. We continued our voyage. At 11 A.M. we arrived at the Washington Arsenal and found the steamer on which Battery A. had sailed was just being unloaded. This morning's sail was indeed delightful. It hardly appears possible to me that the Hudson can be more beautiful than the Potomac with its green-clad banks and smiling plantations. Passed Budd's Ferry and noticed that there had been some buildings erected since last seeing it. It reminded me of brother Appleton forcibly, and I found that yet the tender regard for his loss and sad remembrance of his person had not died out into commonplace. May God rest his soul. —The earthworks of the Shipping Point batteries still remained. Passed Mt. Vernon which looked indeed beautiful amid its nest of green foliage. On arriving at Washington Griffin and I jumped ashore and went up into the Arsenal. At length after looking around for some time, we went up a little way into the city and got some dinner at a boarding house, boiled beef, ham, cabbage &c. and it tasted delicious. Had a glass of ale. Returned to the Arsenal just in time to assist in unloading the pieces. That accomplished we lay around in the yard until the Capt. returned from the city where he had gone to report. We then formed in column and marched out of the Arsenal with all of our traps on our backs and halted just without the Arsenal gates on 4½ St. Battery A. camped on the grass at the edge of the road and we took possession of the loft of a government stable close by. Just as we started from the Arsenal a heavy shower came up which wet me through. While at the Arsenal I noticed that they were shipping heavy guns and mortar shells, probably for the siege of Richmond. —I with a dozen others went up into the city to get supper at the Soldier's Rest. This institution is a place where they furnish meals and lodgings to soldiers whom it is not possible to supply in a more regular manner. It is a long wooden building right in the rear of the R.R. depot. It is provided on the ground floor with seven long tables and will accommodate about 800 at once. On the second floor are the sleeping accommodations which I was unable to see. The tables were laid with tin plates and crockery bowls, with pails of hot coffee at regular intervals along the board. In each plate was a third of a loaf of bread and a slice of meat. The coffee was the best I had tasted for many days.[1] Returned to the barn about 9 P.M. It seemed good to be once more in the midst of civilization. Slept poorly because of the closeness of the stable.

June 7th, Tuesday.

Rose late and went back to the Arsenal. Battery L. 5th U.S. Art'y came down with their horses from Camp Barry to remove our pieces for us. We loaded our baggage on their wagons and with them returned to Camp Barry. Passed through the city and across Penna. Avenue. The city was teeming with hospitals. Camp Barry lies at the N.E. of the Capitol on the slope of a hill and can accommodate more than a dozen batteries.[2] It has a large entrance gate over which the inscription "Camp Barry, Artillery Camp of Instruction." The stables are all together at the lower end of the camp, are very substantial wooden buildings and look much like a village of rope walks. Higher on the hill are the barracks for the men, two storied and white washed. On the side of each barrack toward the city there is a piazza its whole length. In the midst of the camp there is a large white building for the post commandant. The pieces are parked right in front of the barracks of their respective batteries at close interval. In front of the commandant's quarters was a parade ground for guard mount &c. We took possession of barrack No. 5 situated half up the hill. The interior economy is as follows. Ground floor east end is cooking department with door in the end. Next the staircase with door opening on the piazza. Next dining room for battery with long tables and benches. Next officers' quarters with corridor running from dining room to door at west end. On both sides the corridor were sundry rooms for officers, 1st Sergt., officers' mess &c. On the second floor are the sleeping quarters for the men. The bunks are double and in three tiers, foot toward the passage way down the centre of the building. The central passage way is about ten feet wide and that between the bunks five. There are plenty of windows and the room is well ventilated. Altogether they are very comfortable and healthy quarters. Dimensions of building about 20 x 60 feet and will accommodate between 130 and 140 men. Kiely and I took a top bunk on the front side. Went down to the Soldiers' Rest for my dinner. Changed clothes. There seems to be a great deal of ceremony hereabouts, at guard mount &c. All the other batteries, four in number appear out on parade with jackets, polished boots, white gloves, and shoulder scales. The guard duty is very heavy. Order for us to draw new clothing, and until it came we were to take no part in camp duty with the other batteries. Ordered a new suit throughout. Although it was quite a hot day it seemed quite cool in the barracks.

JUNE 8TH, WEDNESDAY.
Early reveille. Went down to the Soldiers' Rest for breakfast. Washed the carriages, which was quite a long job there were so few of us. Wrote to Myra. Quite cool all day. Washed clothes.

JUNE 9TH, THURSDAY.
Very warm and hot. On guard, 3rd relief, countersign "Exeter". Signed the payroll for March and April but owing to some misunderstanding did not receive our pay. Tileston received his commission as Lieut. in the battery. News of Sergt. Turner's death.[3] Wrote to mother and H.A.H. Received a letter from mother and blank book from Myra. Was surprised at receiving no letter from the latter. Her burnt finger must have become more troublesome. Clothing arrived. Felt very languid all day. Read Tennyson's "In Memoriam".

JUNE 10TH, FRIDAY.
Sunny, but with a cool wind. On fatigue, cutting wood &c. Drew a new suite of clothes, which fitted well but were of poor quality. On detail at headquarters with two others to put up a flag for the purpose of a review which took place in

the afternoon. Received pay for the months of March and April. Paid my debts. Took a walk as far as the capitol in the evening.[4]

June 11th, Saturday.

Quite cool. Received a pass for all day and about 9 a.m. went into the city. Bought some photographs of Gen. Gregg and went away down beyond the president's house to the medical directory to find out where my cousin John Greene was. Learned he had returned to his battery the 1st of June. Bought Scott's "Lady of the Lake" and left it in an ambrotype saloon. Shaved the beard off my chin and upper lip. Had two pictures taken, one before shaving, the other after. Visited the Capitol, which appears more magnificent on each successive view. Went into the gallery of both houses of legislature. In the senate they were debating some question in regard to the Indian Fund interest. In the house two members from Penn. and Ill. were having a nice little quarrel between themselves. Was much pleased with a beautiful picture of the Pilgrims on board the Speedwell at Delfthaven and with the bronze door to the hall of Representatives. Got back to camp at 5 p.m. thoroughly tired. No letters yet from Myra. My tramp in the city exhausted me exceedingly. Washington abounds in dust.

June 12th Sunday.

Fair. Wrote to Miss Moulton, to Mr. Farrington, and to Myra. Did not feel very well all day. Attended church in the evening at the camp chapel. A.M. Gilbert of the Christian Commission preached. I was introduced to him. Wrote to the Journal.

Middlesex Journal, Saturday, June 25, 1864

Army Correspondence
Washington, D.C.
June 12, 1864.
Dear Editor: —The changes of a soldier's career are various and extensive, and yet none as sudden and unlooked for in the history of the 6th N. Y. as this last, which has removed us in a trice from the banks of the Pamunkey and the seat of war to Washington and civilization. Your correspondent writes almost from within the shadow of the capitol with the din of a populous city coming to his ears, borne upon the fitful summer breeze. To him the morning sun no longer shines over broad fields, flecked with the little tents that shelter the Potomac army's veterans, but glares hotly on white-washed hospitals and barracks, or reflects from the shining roof of the neighboring city. The returning Sabbath finds us within the sound of church bells, not as lately in battle array awaiting the enemy. We have been here now about a week, and have become nearly accustomed to the quietness of our new life. No cannon sounds, or if it does, only in salute, and without the swiftly following shriek of shell to which our ears had been so accustomed. Everything

is done precisely and methodically, no hurry, no "boot and saddle" to rouse one to the realization that we are before the enemy, or pattering of musketry as grim war springs his dead rattle along the battle line. Here the sun pours less hotly, and the dust circles less thickly. Quiet and comfort and rest are ours, after nearly three years of incessant action. How long it may last there is no possibility of learning.

It would take many pages, and more columns than you would be willing to occupy, to relate in any manner more than casual the part we have taken during the movement of the army from the Rapidan across the Pamunkey. We have been in frequent engagements and made many long marches. Many days have been passed in activity so continual as to prevent even the morning ablutions. Still, through it all the men have been cheerful and confident. All feel that the enemy has had a dreadful drubbing at the hands of the army of the Potomac. Under success, the army has done harder work and retained more of discipline than ever before. Half the exertions could not be obtained from it through having done much less fighting provided it had been unsuccessful. To ensure future success, it is eminently necessary to possess it in the present. Grant has proved himself a great general inasmuch as he has apparently handled the monstrous army now before Richmond with as much ease as the lesser thousands with which in the preceding campaign he whipped the more numerous enemy six times within the short space of twenty days. He is the great military genius which the war has developed for us. The army feels it to be so, and now, when going into action, strikes with all its might, never fearing of the result. Proficiency in drill, and confidence in the commander are the first requisites for efficiency.

The 2d Cav. Div. crossed the Rapidan at Ely's Ford in the gray of the morning of the 4th ult., being the advance of the left flank of the army. While the battle of the Wilderness was being waged the entire cavalry corps was massed at and near Todd's Tavern to protect the left flank and rear. Several times the rebel cavalry strove hard to break through upon the trains, but got most roundly thrashed. At one time, the enemy having made a rush against Gen. Custer, that Gen. sent to Gregg to borrow a section of artillery until he could bring his own up. Our section went up and fell into the hottest artillery fight we were ever in. Description can never portray justly the manner in which shot and shell shrieked about our ears. For the space of an hour and a half the rebels played upon our two guns with the concentrated fire of four. Still we stuck to our position and have reason to think the "Johnnies" felt our fire, as they changed the position of their pieces several times. After the engagement the Capt. and a Lieutenant of the rebel battery were found dead upon the field, whether killed by our fire or the battery that relieved us, could not be determined. We were relieved, after two hours hard fighting, by Batt. B and C, 2d U. S. Artillery. In this engagement our section lost two killed and one mortally wounded. Just as we were relieved, the rebels "took out," and as we were leaving the field we heard a volley sent from the whole battery to hasten their retiring footsteps. At different times the rebels engaged our brigade near Todd's Tavern, but luckily with no further damage to us, save the breaking of the stock of one of our pieces. In one night our artificers supplied a temporary stock of hewn oak which made a very passable substitute.

On the morning of the 9th, the Cav. Corps started upon the raid, the particulars of which all have no doubt read long ere this. It fell to the lot of our section, together with the 6th Ohio Cav., to form the rear guard. About the middle of the afternoon our rear began to be harassed by Fitzhugh Lee's brigade of rebel cavalry. At length, just about dusk, they made a rush so unexpectedly upon the rearmost squadron of the 6th Ohio that it broke in considerable confusion. Here was a military anomaly. The very men who two days before, at Todd's Tavern, had fought like tigers, and piled the rebels in heaps before the muzzles of their carbines, now ran like sheep. But they were surprised, for no one thought the party in our rear more than one or two squadrons on a scout. As it was they caused quite a stampede of the pack animals, and drove the rearmost squadron in upon our pieces. We being in a narrow road and between woods could do nothing. Things appeared rather misty for a short time, and your correspondent began to make serious calculations upon how long it would take Grant to capture Richmond and thus relieve him from the prison he saw awaiting, but shortly Col. Taylor formed the 1st Penn. right across the road and checked the rebs while we hurried off to a small eminence a short distance ahead and opened fire. At one time in the melee a rebel officer penetrated as far as our hindmost piece, saying, as he attempted to mount a horse he had laid hold of, "This piece is mine." One of our cannoniers shouted in return that he didn't see it, and, in default of a better weapon, struck him with his fist. Some one seized the officer and took him off the field. The rebs opened with one piece of artillery, which was very poorly served, and which we silenced as soon as it opened and caused to change position several times. The whole brigade formed for action, and repulsed two attacks, not continuing the march till long after nightfall. That night we made Beaver Dam Station, near the North Anna, where was destroyed a large amount of rebel provision, two locomotives, and many cars. There was also recaptured about 300 prisoners taken from the army of the Potomac in the battle of the Wilderness, among whom was Lieut. Flint Wyman, of the 39th M. V. The next morning we were shelled upon the ground where we had bivouacked by the same gun as had troubled us the night before. This was a little too impertinent to be borne, and Gen. Custer very quietly took away their troublesome little pop-gun. That night we made the South Anna, from where, the following day, several expeditions were sent out to destroy the railroad at different places, all of which were successful. At Ashland a squadron of the 1st Mass. Cav. lost heavily in an encounter with a battalion of rebel infantry. From thence we continued our course until within two miles of Richmond, when we were attacked on three sides by the Richmond home guards and a portion of Stuart's cavalry. We beat them off after a brisk fight in a pouring rain, and made an opening across Meadow Bridge to Mechanicsville. The sound of our guns must have echoed in the very streets of Richmond. Taking a roundabout course, we reached the James by the old road through White Oak Swamp and over Malvern Hill.

Our return to the army was marked by no particular incident save the hanging of a few stragglers by guerillas. The corps crossed the Pamunkey on the R. R. bridge, by the White House, and marching through King William and Queen's Counties, joined the army again near Chesterfield Station. One night's rest only was allowed us. The army marched by the left flank, and the cavalry corps took the extreme left to cover the laying of the pontoons on the Pamunkey near Newcastle. Close behind us came the 6th and 2d corps. About mid day of the 28th the rebels fell upon us near Hawes' Church, and the 2d division, together with Custer's brigade, stood the brunt. It was hot work, one of the most desperate cavalry fights of the war. The fighting was done in some heavy timber, both sides dismounted. Our battery had six men wounded, two suffering amputation. They got a cross fire on us, their shots centreing right between the pieces and crossing each other at right angles. We also had one wheel stove. This was our last action, for three days after, the artillery of the corps was relieved by the 2d brigade, and our brigade went to the rear.

Since then another battery with ours has been dismounted to furnish horses for the remainder of the brigade. In return for our serviceable horses, which it is not boasting to say, were in as good condition as any in the army, we received just enough condemned ones to drag the battery to the White House.

At the same time all the men detached to us from the cavalry and infantry were sent back to their regiments or to other batteries in the brigade. This diminished the battery nearly one half, so that now we number only about 95 men. At White House we shipped for the Washington Arsenal, where we arrived on the 6th inst.

From thence the battery that accompanied us was sent to one of the forts in this vicinity to do duty as heavy artillery. This fate had been ours except for recommendations from Gens. Meade and Hunt to the Artillery Bureau to remount us. But previous to doing thus, we must receive a large number of recruits, as, in a short time, by the discharge of old men, the battery will diminished to about 69 men. By the first of July, all the Woburn boys but your correspondent will be at home. J. E. Tileston, late 1st Sergt., has just received the commission of Lieut., now so long his due. He commenced his career as commissioned officer possessed of much popularity among the men. The best wish that can be offered for him is, that the possession of power may not diminish his manhood, as is too often the case!

HOPLITE

Middlesex Journal, Saturday, June 25, 1864

Washington, D.C.

June 12, 1864.

Camp Barry, Artillery Camp of Instruction, is situated about one mile northeast of the Capitol, on the southern slope of a small hill. Seen from Capitol hill it presents the appearance of a village of large cottages rather than of Government barracks. Each house is capable of accommodating a battery. The buildings are two stories in height, about 60 feet long, and with a plaza extending along the whole south side. All brightly shine in purest white. The barracks are arranged one over another on the hillside, with a very commodious and more pretending building in the centre of the encampment for the post commandant. The camp is arranged for 15 batteries, though there are but five here now. In front of the commandant's quarters and lower down the hill is the parade ground. At the foot of the hill are the stables which are long, low, whitewashed buildings grouped together as if a party of ropewalks in consultation. On the right and west runs the turnpike to Bladensburg and Baltimore. Before us the road stretches away obliquely to the right until it disappears, broad, white, and dusty, in the foliage that surrounds the Capitol. Turn whichever way one may the low, black, roofs and whitewashed walls of hospitals meet the gaze. Washington appears to consist chiefly of public buildings, hospitals, and government corrals. The inhabitants chiefly subsist by working for and swindling the government, and swindling the soldiers. Pies are a staple commodity. A person speaking of Cincinnati said that every second man one met was a pig. So in Washington every second house is a barber shop, and the remainder restaurants.

Washington is a monstrous humbug. The pubic buildings alone save it from an appearance of poverty. It is situated within a natural ampitheatre of hills and upon low ground. On the heights which encircle the city are the defences which have cost so much labor and expense. All along the ridges, fortifications thickly cluster, and each point particularly prominent has its flag and staff that shows the situation of a redoubt.

This chain of forts is perfect on both sides of the Potomac. On the south they take in Alexandria, on the north Georgetown. Just below the city a large creek empties into the river, and the Point thus formed by the confluence is occupied by the arsenal. About a half mile up the creek is the navy yard. This creek is called Anacosta. Right opposite to the arsenal is Giesboro Point, the situation of the cavalry bureau it looks like a city of ropewalks. At convenient situations within and without the city are the numerous hospitals. As all the hospitals and government wooden buildings are whitewashed, and as the city is in great part composed of hospitals and other government buildings, Washington has a distressingly new appearance. Of a sunny day the glaring white of the surrounding buildings fairly dazzles one's eyes, moreover as but few of the streets are paved great clouds of dust prevail during dry intervals, so that the capital of the nation is decidedly uncomfortable.

We have been enjoying a state of supreme laziness since arriving at this place, having no horses to care for and camp duty being unimportant. This state of affairs has rendered it possible for all to visit the notable places of the city, which opportunity has not been disregarded. But having now for over two years been in the habit of mounting a horse to go any distance over a quarter of a mile the men find it tiresome to walk even the short distance necessary. In my next I shall probably be able to inform you of what disposition is to be made of the battery. Report says that Capt. Martin upon offering his resignation was not listened to, and was promised men from other batteries to fill his own up. The government has lately been breaking up a number of light batteries and sending the men into forts. The number of horse batteries in the Potomac army has been reduced from 11 to 7 and infantry batteries in like proportion. It is more than probable that we shall be remounted as a horse battery after having been filled up by men from other batteries, and after a short session of drilling be sent to the front again. The recommendations from the army and the high opinion in which the battery appears to be held by the chief of artillery are very flattering to our soldierly pride, yet we feel that we have in part earned them, having been continually in the field and at the front now for three years and taken part in 15 engagements.

On the 20th, twenty nine men received their discharges at expiration of service. All the Woburn boys will be at home by the first of the ensuing month save "Hoplite," who will not return much before Christmas. Lieut. Tileston will probably return with the rest.

The most of our boys, who were wounded in the early part of the campaign, are in the hospitals here and doing well. It was but to day that a wonderful instance of what human flesh can endure was afforded. On the 28th of May, in an engagement near Hawe's Church, Va., a man detached from the 1st Mass. Cav. to the battery named Loud, was struck in the right shoulder by a shell which carried away a great portion of it, and about an inch of his collar bone.[5] The chief surgeon of the cavalry corps gave his case over as hopeless, and would not dress his wound. Surgeon Wood, of the 1st Mass. thought otherwise, and dressed it.[6] To-day, three weeks only from the reception of his wound, this man ran the guard at his hospital, and after searching for some time, managed to find the battery, and took breakfast with us. Verily, flesh and blood are an admirable combination. And in fact it is wonderful to see the patience and endurance under suffering which are the characteristics of or soldiers in hospital. In visiting our poor wounded comrades, I have been enabled to see a considerable of these characteristics, and those very men now in the field seem to feel most the hardships of the campaign, and mayhap now and again complain, when laid low in hospital by grievous and painful wounds, seem to attain to a beauty of character one would hardly deem possible. Resignation, cheerfulness, loving kindness toward brother soldiers in misfortune, patience, endurance, hopefulness, are the characteristics that mark the wounded soldier in all our hospitals.

In every hospital and every ward, there are cases of men suffering from the most dreadful wounds, and yet one is surprised at the quietness prevailing. Very few groans are heard. And another fact worth noticing is that soldiers who have once suffered from wounds and returned to their commands, are much better soldiers than before. But I will not trespass.

Yours, HOPLITE

JUNE 13TH, MONDAY.
Fair and cool. Stayed in camp all day. In the evening Billy Conger and I went to a cemetery nearby but could not get in, it being after hours.[7] Felt very shiftless all day.

JUNE 14TH, TUESDAY.
Went off early in the morning to the city, leaving my jacket at a house on my way to be altered. Went through the capitol from front to rear and saw some statutes &c which I had not seen before. Went down the avenue to get shaved and as I was coming back met Colcord of the Invalides who was my schoolmate formerly.[8] Turned round with him and went down to the market where we had some dinner. The Washington market is altogether of a different style from the large markets in Boston. It is not a building, but simply an immense roof supported by stone pillars and here the produce dealers sell their stuff, all seeming to be petty hucksters rather than regular dealers. From thence we went to the public garden. This is a small place but well repays a visit. There are several greenhouses, in which there are many tropical plants, a banana tree with fruit. There seemed to be a profusion of fuchsias of every color. They were indeed beautiful. This contains a large variety of rare and beautiful plants.[9] Went into the capitol again when we met Griffin and Horne. Visited the Senate again and Colcord pointed out to me some of the most prominent, Wilson, Sumner, Johnson, Harris, Trumbull, Chandler. Saw the famous painting "The Storming of Chapultepec". Saw the Congressional Library which is truly magnificent. From the Capitol we took the cars up to the White House. Entered the reception room which looked much as I remembered it 2½ years ago, but the carpet appeared much worn. Next we visited the Smithsonian Institute which appeared much increased since my last visit. The building itself is very beautiful being built of very dark brown stone and in a beautiful style. The [sic] was a surgical lecture in progress while we were there. Returned again to the Capitol where Colcord left us. We stopped to have some ice cream and then returned to camp well tired. Detailed for guard 1st relief. Quite cool all day.

JUNE 15TH, WEDNESDAY.
Much warmer. Countersign for the night was "Reynolds". Washed all over and changed clothes. Got my jacket, which fitted quite well. Monthly inspection in afternoon. Received an old letter from Myra dated 23rd May. Feel somewhat concerned at receiving none of a later date. Wrote to Myra. Prayer meeting in evening. Prayed.

June 16th, Thursday.
Windy and dusty. On fatigue duty, chopping wood &c. The whole fatigue was sent over to the post hospital to do whitewashing. Whitewashed all day and managed to splash some lime into my left eye which caused considerable pain. Whiskey was supplied, but drank none.

June 17th, Friday.
Sun rose red and hot. After breakfast and before 9 a.m. the boys had a boisterous time in the dining room, singing, dancing &c. Received a pass and went out into the city with Jimmy Drake. Went through the rotunda of the capitol just to see my favorite picture. Bought some guitar strings in the Avenue for Frank Jewell and then went into the Smithsonian Institution.[10] Spent most of the time in the library, picture gallery, and among the statuary. From thence we went up to Judiciary Square hospital to visit Joe Oliver who lost his foot in the fight near Hawe's Church. He looked nicely, and was well advanced in his recovery, his wound having healed. Stayed quite a while talking with him. He was cheerful and hearty. While we were there Capt. Martin came in to see him. I was amazed to see the neatness and cleanness and order of the hospital. It is like all the other hospitals about Washington, whitewashed and of a single story. The buildings consist of a long building as corridor, on to which are built the wards for the sick at regular intervals, thus affording good chance for ventilation. From there we went down through 4½ St. to the Stanton Hospital which lies north of the capitol. Buner looked very poorly, evidently being in a gloomy state of mind. He looked like one worrying himself into his grave. Got to camp about 4 p.m. ravenously hungry. During the day we called at the soldiers' free library but could get no books, it not being office hours. No letter yet from Myra. Talk seemed to point the way that Capt. Martin was going to stay with us and maintain the battery organization. Very hot all day.

June 18th, Saturday.
Fair. Detailed for extra fatigue and went to the hospital to whitewash. Finished in the forenoon. Slept a good portion of the afternoon. Letter from Myra. Commenced a letter to Journal. Griffin and I took a walk toward evening and in going across a field near a house was stopped by a guard. We chaffed him a little. Went to prayer meeting. Prayed. Corneile gave me some clothing.

June 19th, Sunday.
Lay abed late. Loud who was so badly wounded and had been lying in the Emory Hospital for three weeks came over to visit the battery. This is a most wonderful case of recovery as he had at first been given over by the corps surgeon. He bids fair to have the use of his arm although having lost an inch of his collar bone, it being carried away. In the morning Griffin and I went to a Catholic church not far off. It was a very spacious edifice and made of brick.[11] The interior was beautifully decorated. The exercises I could not understand much of because in Latin and pronounced in a droning sing song style. The sermon was quite

ordinary, although from the size of the church I could not hear much of it being in the gallery. The singing was splendid, in part by a prima donna hired at a great price. The exercises seemed very little like worship. Got back about 1 P.M., but found no dinner, none having been cooked. Slept a great part of the afternoon. Went to church in the evening.

June 20th, Monday.
Very hot. Early in the morning the fellows had quite a crazy time of it, dancing, singing, &c, the last together. The barrack was in a great bustle all day because of the fellows going away. They did not get off 'til about 4 P.M. when after reciprocal they left the battery not without some sadness on both sides.[12] The barrack seemed very lonely after they had gone, and especially at the supper table. Griffin and I took a walk after retreat. On guard, 2nd relief.

June 21st, Tuesday.
Very hot all day. Wrote to Myra. Temperance meeting at the chapel in the evening, Maj. Hale presiding. Drew shoulder scales.

June 22nd, Wednesday.
Still very hot. Whitewashed all day, in the afternoon the dead house. Had a good wash in the evening. Went to prayer meeting at the chapel.

June 23, Thursday.
Suffocating hot. Griffin and I went into the city on a pass. Went first to the patent office which interested me not as much as I had expected. The office is a magnificent one. Took dinner at the Soldiers' Rest, boiled ham and bean soup. Went into the Capitol grounds to sit. On the way back came through the rotunda to look at my favorite picture. Took a book out of the Soldiers' Free Library on 6th St. This is quite an institution and comprises about 2000 vols. It is also used as a reading room. On arriving at camp found Mr. Davis there with whom had quite a talk. He gave me a picture of himself. Mounted guard for first time with the other batteries.

June 24th, Friday.
Intensely hot. Received a letter from C.H.M. Could do nothing all day scarcely for the heat. Prayer meeting in the evening.

June 25th, Saturday.
Still exceedingly hot. Wrote to C.H.M. Letter from Myra. It appears to me this weather is warmer than any I have yet experienced. On guard in the park. Read 4th Book of Caesar.

June 26th, Sunday.
Still very hot. While on guard from 5 to 7 in the morning Capt. Martin saw me sitting down and ordered the Sergt of the guard to keep me on from then until 1 P.M. It was exceedingly tiresome duty and my neck got burned badly. This was

cruelty for nearly all other guards in the camp are in the habit of sitting down, and even the sentinel at h'dqu'rs does. Even if I deserved punishment it ought not to have been so heavy as this. At times hard thoughts and plans of revenge against the Capt. arose but God strengthened me to overcome them. I forgive the Capt. How by God's help one can do anything! In looking into my heart although I cannot find any absolute love for Capt. Martin, still I can honestly say I cherish no hard feelings. Thank God for it. A short shower during the afternoon. Felt so poorly I did not go to church. Meant to have gone to the Capitol.

JUNE 27TH, MONDAY.
Quite cool. On fatigue. Wrote to Myra and received a letter from her, also a Journal. Detailed to headq'rs to aid in collecting from the empty barracks the stoves and pipe and storing them. Quite a violent storm toward night but which lasted but a short time. It hardly laid the dust. Drew "David Copperfield" and "Little Dorrit" from the library. 27 new men joined us from the 10th N.Y. Battery. More are to come. Comparatively a comfortable day.

JUNE 28TH, TUESDAY.
Quite cool all day. Wrote to Myra. Played chess with Griffin. In afternoon got a pass and went over to Emory Hospital, and stayed for some little time. As I was going by the Lincoln Hospital they were bringing in wounded from the front. Poor fellows, they looked sadly.

JUNE 29TH, WEDNESDAY.
Still very pleasant. A very lazy day, reading, sleeping and playing chess. Letter from Myra, and one from Mr. Farrington with picture. On guard, 2nd relief.

JUNE 30TH, THURSDAY.
On guard all day at stables. Read and finished David Copperfield for the 3rd time. Countersign for the night was Vicksburgh.

JULY 1ST, FRIDAY.
Much warmer. On whitewashing detail at Barrack No. 7. Did some washing.

JULY 2ND, SATURDAY.
Fair with shower in afternoon. Received a pass but did not go out. Wrote to Myra and to Journal. Commenced "Little Dorrit". Letter from C.H.M. A very lazy day indeed.

Middlesex Journal, Saturday, July 9, 1864

Army Correspondence
Washington,
July 2d, 1864.
Dear Editor: —Once more the temperature admits a return to old habits, and your correspondent essays a line or two for your information. Was there ever at any time such hot days as composed the last week of the last month?

It hardly seems possible that there can be sufficient degrees on the Centigrade thermometer to mark the heat under which for a few days we have suffered. And now after the receipt of a few showers that the atmosphere has somewhat cooled, how pleasant to be able to sit without the perspiration gathering in great drops to form minute rivers of hot water ever running and scorching! If life were to be composed entirely of such days as the 24th and 25th ult., it were a burden scarcely worth possessing at any price.

Feeling thus the stress of the weather as we do, laying here idle and all the appliances for soldierly comfort close at hand, how must they feel it who much farther south and exposed all day and every day to the full beating of the southern sun still face the enemy in the entrenchments near his capital. Oh, you at home who move about airily and thinly clad, who carefully choose the shady side of the street as you saunter to your place of business in your linen duster and hat of straw, who look with eye of jealousy upon the one speck of dust that may chance to light upon your varnished boot, who frequent apothecary shops to sip the cooling soda, and sit upon the portico of your hotel to chat the news over, wondering why the army of the Potomac does not finish up "this little job," come visit these dirty men at Petersburg who carry muskets and eat fried pork, and if you do not find in these same dirty, dusty, and it may be ragged veterans a new nobility of character such as you never dreamed of; if you do not see that God by noble instruments is working out here the enfranchisement of the nations, has the life you have led amid brick wall and safety, sapped out the existence of those qualities which mankind look to mankind to possess for the elevation of the human standard. None but one who has been a soldier can fully understand what the men, who comprise our armies, are doing for their country. There is not a man in our armies that face the enemy but suffers more than those in civic life think it possible for man to suffer and do. It is not one season of hardship or battle, that happens at intervals of rest, but it is always fighting always enduring. The day's battles are succeeded by the night's march. Day after day men lay at their arms in line of battle and in a blazing sun without the privilege even of washing themselves. The dust gathers in layers upon their bodies. It would shock you, my dear madam, to have one of these dingy veterans enter your parlor, or sleep in one of your snowy beds, but yet these are the men that are guaranteeing to you the preservation of all these comforts.

The men of our armies not only are going to preserve the nation against rebellion but elevate the nation in moral excellence. It is usual for people to talk of the immorality and evil influences of a soldier life. Whatever may have been and is the character of other armies, morality and good habits are the marked characteristics of those now in the field. When after the end of this war our soldiers are returned to civil life, they will improve society. The great reason of improvement in many is that great opportunity is afforded them to think which the bustle and attractions of home life tend to prevent. Many acquire habits of personal cleanliness which they never had before. At home it is quite frequent to hear religion ridiculed and scoffed at. I have been in the army now nearly three years and do not remember one instance of such. It has been the habit in our extreme enlightenment to sneer at, as weakness, any exhibition of the softer emotions of the heart. It is not so in the army. Companionship in danger and hardships breeds tenderness of heart, and I have seen the hardy soldier that had faced the enemy in many hard fights and laughed at cold and heat and marches, burst into a passion of tears at parting from his comrade. Rough men acquire womanly tenderness and compassion toward their sick and wounded companions. Bayard Taylor says rightly

> "Ah, soldiers to your honored rest
> Your love and glory bearing,
> The bravest are the tenderest
> The loving are the daring!"[13]

These soldiers, who now are the defenders of our liberty, are in the future to be founders of an order of things which shall make our nation pure and christian-like. And if we gain no other thing by this war, there will be the immense benefit of the superior order of citizens which it will return to us. The blood shed in this struggle will purify not only the nation but the individuals of the nation and mankind all over the world. God grant that the glory of the coming day may dawn upon the eyes of the present generation!

All of this grew out of the hot weather. Now to return.

The days jog lazily on about equally divided between guard duty and whitewashing. At the latter we are rapidly becoming experts having whitewashed the post hospitals and some of the empty barracks. We have received 27 men from the 10th N. Y. Battery which has for a month been garrisoning Fort Craig. With them came a Lieut. Church.

Capt. Martin went home yesterday on a furlough of ten days. As usual all sorts of rumors prevail, some of them of the most extravagant. The most probable course seems to be that we shall get horses shortly and go immediately to the front, for in the recent movements, the horse batteries have been rather roughly handled. Pennington's battery of our old brigade got pretty well cut up near Gordonsville, losing 47 men and several caissons. Gen. Sheridan's last raid was not as successful as it might have been notwithstanding newspaper correspondents. Since last writing two other batteries (infantry) have come into this camp to fit out and drawn their horses, guns, & c. It seems rather strange that they should come after us, and get fitted out first.

HOPLITE

July 3rd, Sunday.

Fair and hot. Read and slept. Did not go to church. Did not feel very smart. On guard, 2nd relief.

July 4th, Monday.

Hot and sunny. A very quiet day much like Sunday. Finished my turn of guard duty. Also finished "Little Dorrit". Found it not up to the standard of his other pieces, being in many places prosy and highly exaggerated. Battery C. 5th U.S Art'y 17th N.Y. left the camp. Much drunkenness prevalent. Drew 84 horses, enough for a four gun mounted battery. Received position of No. 2 on No. 4 gun.

July 5th, Tuesday.

Very warm. Harnessed and hitched, and took the battery down to the arsenal to turn in, receiving in exchange 4 light 12 pdrs. Luckily I was left behind which enabled me to do my washing. Was on fatigue, cutting wood, &c. We were unable to get any ammunition, so great had been the demand. Wrote to C.H.M. 3rd Maine Batt. and F, 4th U.S. went away.

July 6th, Wednesday.

Fair and warm. Paid off for the months of May and June at the raised rate. But as the revolver which I lost was deducted I received only 11.50. In the afternoon went down to the arsenal where we filled the chests with ammunition. On guard in the park 3rd relief.

July 7th, Thursday.

Fair and hot. Finished my guard duty. All the horses shod. Five months only to serve. In the evening played billiards for first time in 4 years.

July 8th, Friday.

Very hot. On fatigue. Felt tired and languid all day. Received my pictures from home.

July 9th, Saturday.

Quite cool. Received a long letter from Myra enclosing pictures of herself and son. Wrote to her. Went down to the Capitol grounds to hear the band play but was disappointed. Sat for about an hour enjoying the shade and then returned. On guard, 3rd. relief. Letter from Griffin.

July 10th, Sunday.

Hot again. Finished my tour of guard. 1st Me. Battery and L 1st Ohio went away afternoon. Church in evening. Wrote to Myra.

July 11th, Monday.

Very warm. On fatigue cleaning stables &c. Orders to pack up in forenoon. Hitched up to fit harness. Orders to move at 8 p.m. Moved about 7. I packed up my new uniform and one or two other things and left them at a house near the camp by the name of John Beartruff.[14] Received one day's ration. Took up line of march by the straight road down by Swampoodle.[15] This street is H. Street. The streets were crowded with spectators, mostly ladies. Turned down 6th St. then into D. St., then into Penna. Avenue. There seemed to be considerable excitement in the city. We proceeded straight out the avenue across the bridge and through Georgetown. At the latter place we turned off the main road to the right and pursuing a northwesterly direction about 10 P.M. arrived at the little village of Tennalleytown and halted just behind it on an open space in rear of Fort Reno. Tennalleytown is a pretty little village with one tavern. The houses for the most part are white cottages embowered in trees. Here we halted awhile to report and then went back a quarter of a mile and parked. Returned to the fort again and unhitched, but did not unharness. This was scarcely done when we had to hitch again. Lay down to sleep about midnight.

July 12th, Tuesday.

Rose shortly after daybreak. It seemed very strange not to have any horse to care for. I found the fort right in front of us and that the rifle pits were not 3 rods from us. A regiment of invalids occupied the rifle pits near us and a N.Y. Heavy Art'y reg. the fort. The country to the left in front is most beautiful, being open farm lands with the land under cultivation. Several forts were in sight. The landscape from the hill is beautiful. There was skirmishing going on to the right of the fort in the direction of Fort De Russy with an occasional artillery shot. To the right and east the country was much more uneven, had apparently been woodland. I could see the puffs of smoke from the rifles. Washed in a brook in front of the fort. The battery unharnessed but almost immediately harnessed up again. The people in the nearest houses appeared excited, some of the women crying. It appeared to me I could fight here as long as a drop of blood or a breath was left me. The day was very hot and would have been unbearable but for a slight breeze. Saw the 2nd Mass. Cav. —Fort Reno is a thoroughly built fort and contains 11 barbette guns mostly 24 pdrs smooth bore, and 3 casemate.[16] Besides there are a number of embrasures for light artillery. There are also two small mortars. There is one 100 lb. Parrott and several of about half that calibre. There are two bomb proofs within, and a well. The ditch is broad and the abattis strong. Lay near the fort 'til noon when we moved back about ¼ mile and parked in an open field. Lay there all the afternoon. Found an abundance of blackberries. Toward night the musketry became quite brisk in the directions of Forts Stevens & Lincoln. Could see the forts reply. They made (the rebels) a desperate attack which was repulsed. Unharnessed after dark and had just got laid down when we had to harness up again. Rained a little in the afternoon.

July 13th, Wednesday.

Slept soundly all night. The right section under command of Lieut. Wilson went out with the cavalry to reconnoitre. It seemed as though the rebels were retreating. Toward night troops began to arrive, part of the 6th Corps and the 19th. Saw the 29th Maine reg. in which my cousins were, but from a number of causes saw none of them. Our section returned having followed the enemy as far as

Rockville, a distance of 7 miles. The cavalry didn't behave very well. Two more batteries came up from Camp Barry. Troops came up from the city (19th Corps) and bivouacked all about us. The rebels certainly retreating.

JULY 14TH, THURSDAY.
Fair and very dusty. The infantry moved off in the direction of the river and one battery the opposite way. We lay in this spot 'til the middle of the afternoon and I occupied the most of the time in reading the memoirs of Count Grammont. At length orders came to return to Camp Barry and we harnessed up and started off east by a cross road in the direction of Fort Stevens. Passed through a beautiful glen and a small stream on which was a stone mill. Crossed the head of 14th Street and passed the Mt. Pleasant Hospital where many wounded soldiers came out to see us pass. From here a ravine on the right afforded a beautiful view of the city and the Capitol. Arriving at 7th Street we proceeded down that street toward the city a short distance and then taking a southeasterly course by the Campbell and Finley Hospitals reached Camp Barry about 5 P.M. I went up into the city to get some supper and found the 3rd div. of the 6th Corps at the depot having just arrived from Baltimore. There were some Mass. regs. going home.

JULY 15TH, FRIDAY.
Hot. Because I did not stir quickly enough upon Lieut. Clark's command was tied between the wheels for 8 hours, from 5–1. Luckily there was a good breeze. Slept all the afternoon. On guard at night 3rd relief.

JULY 16TH, SATURDAY.
Cool. Finished my guard duty. Wrote to the Journal. Received letters from Myra, Bethiah, and C.H.M. Five batteries of the 6th Corps came into camp, making 13 in all. Discipline growing very strict and the officers more unpopular than ever.

Middlesex Journal, Saturday, July 23, 1864

Our Army Correspondence
Washington,
July 16, 1864.

Dear Editor: —The rebels have made a raid into Maryland. Yes, you know that. Now they are off again with all their booty. You know that too.

Perhaps it will be something new to let you know what part the 6th N. Y. Battery took in repulsing the enemy. But previous to doing so, it would be advisable to premise one or two facts. On the 4th inst., we drew 84 horses from the Government corral here, they being the number requisite in the fitting out of a mounted battery of four guns. The succeeding day our battery of six guns, three inch rifles, were turned in at the arsenal, and we drew in exchange four light twelve-pounders, smooth bore. The latter are bronze, the former steel.

In one of my former letters it was explained to your readers the difference between mounted and horse batteries, but as that was some time ago, it will not be amiss to repeat it. Mounted batteries have three teams to each carriage, and the cannoniers either march or ride upon the ammunition chests of the limbers and caissons. They are used in conjunction with infantry. Horse batteries have three teams to each carriage, light twelve-pounders, four, and the cannoniers are mounted, and ride in rear of the guns [*sic*]. The caissons of the rifled guns have one less ammunition chest in horse batteries than in mounted. Horse artillery is used with cavalry. From which explanation it will be understood that we have been made a mounted or infantry battery of four guns.

At the first knowledge of the crossing of the Potomac by the rebels, one battery left this camp to go to Harper's Ferry by rail. As the rebels drew nearer to Washington, other batteries were sent out to the line of the city fortifications and their places in this camp replaced by others, quickly to be equipped and mounted. At length, in the afternoon of the 11th, Capt. Martin not yet having returned from his furlough, we were ordered out to Fort Reno in command of Lieut. Clark. As we passed through the city just at dusk, it was possible to perceive that the excitement in the city was very great. The sidewalks and doorsteps on Sixth street were crowded with ladies, who expressed their approbation of our mission by the waving of handkerchiefs. The sight of so many fair dependants upon our valor had no dispiriting effect. Passing down the whole length of Pennsylvania Avenue, and through Georgetown, we made an abrupt turn to the northwest and pursuing this course for about three miles, entered the little village of Tenallytown. Just without the northern edge of this town is Fort Reno, and we halted for the night close up to the earthworks. All about us laid the infantry like so many logs of wood wrapped in grey blankets, for it was ten P.M. before we halted.

The morning sun opened to us a view of our position. Immediately before us was the fort and its straw-colored barracks, with the threatening black muzzles of its armament peeping just over the works and through the embrasures. To the right and left in winding courses the rifle pits stretched, filled with infantry. Beyond the fort and to the left the country spread finely, rolling and highly cultivated. At intervals, the shining gravel and tall flag-staff showed more distant works, beyond which the pine trees blue stretched far away into the horizon. A goodly sight and wearied not the gazer.

> "All seemed as quiet and as still
> As the mist slumbering on yon hill."

But hark! Far away to the right and north a faint report of firearms is heard. Hurrying to the right and northern face of the fort, what a different sight meets the eye. As far away as can be seen, the land stretches up to meet the pine-clad heights in deep ravines and high hills. Four miles away Fort

De Runy [*sic*], and from behind an intervening point of woods the flagstaff of Stevens rises high in the air.[17] Directly in front of these the skirmishing is going on. The puffs of smoke from the two lines can be plainly seen. The firing gathers volume, and then with a heavy boom the forts open.

All day long a desultory firing is kept up, with an occasional shot from Fort Stevens, when just after sunset it merges into a prolonged rattle. The rebels made a last and violent effort to force the works. The heavy guns in the fort saluted them in volleys. After two hours fighting they themselves were forced back by the veterans of the sixth corps, and the fire slowly died away. All this while we had been lying in readiness to move to any point. Early in the morning of the succeeding day the right section of our battery made a reconnoisance [*sic*] as far as Rockville, with about a thousand cavalry, the odds and ends of different regiments recently mounted. Rockville is seven miles without the fortifications, and the greater portion of that distance was accomplished at a gallop. Arrived at the town, our section took position commanding a fork in the road, and the cavalry charged into it. They were repulsed in confusion by the rebel rear guard, and fell back behind our pieces in so disorderly a manner as to afford us no support. Whereupon our guns were limbered to the rear, and the section withdrew although having seen not one rebel. The cavalry were dreadfully frightened, affirming that the enemy were 30,000 strong in the town. The whole expedition returned to Tenallytown toward night again, which place the battery did not leave until it returned to this camp in the afternoon of the 14th instant.

Tenallytown is a pretty little village, composed for the most part of white cottages, and as each house is well shaded by ornamental trees, presents quite a romantic appearance, far otherwise than its name would seem to indicate. It is situated on the Rockville pike, about three miles from Georgetown, and five from Washington. It has a Post Office and a hotel.

During the evening of the 13th the 19th corps commenced to arrive, and the next day began the pursuit of the rebels with two divisions of the 6th corps.

Late in the afternoon of the 14th, we started to return to Camp Barry, taking a road that ran directly east across 14th and 7th streets. This road ran through a beautiful glen musical with brook and waterfall, with an old mill and a farm house just peeping from out a leafy nest. A rustic suspension bridge joined the opposite banks of the stream. Standing upon this swinging structure to gaze at the battery halting to water the steaming horses, it was a picture worthy to be commemorated on canvas. Crossing the top of 14th street, and by the Mount Pleasant Hospital, where crowds of convalescent soldiers stood to see us pass, showing every possible variety of maiming, we came to where a ravine opened up to the right a magnificent view of the Capital. It surprised me to find there was a point from which the city appeared so actually beautiful.[18]

> "Tis distance lends enchantment to the view
> And robes the mountains in their azure blue."

Thus the capital. All of its low wooden dwellings, and dirty purlieus were indistinguishable, and the city shone out a perfect picture beneath the still afternoon sun. The distant blue of the Alexandrine hills toned to a softer shade by the nearer line of the river that wound about the city a narrow strip of azure, was a fit background to the bossed green and white of the city, that circled the Capitol like jewelled setting to a shining opal. Our road from thence laid south easterly by Finley and Campbell hospitals, and a length about nightfall, after our arduous (?) and dangerous (?) campaign of three days we arrived in Camp Barry without the loss of a man—*except* a bag of pork, which unfortunately dropped off a caisson on our outward march. We try to persuade ourselves that we did an immense deal of good, but cannot quite succeed. Leastways here are the facts, and your readers can determine for themselves.

There happened one incident worth reporting. While we laid near Fort Reno a guard was posted on the pike to prevent such as had no passes from going to the front. On trying to pass this guard who was a hundred days man, he burst forth as follows. "Why *can't* you keep cool? There is no occasion for excitement. Why don't you keep cool like me?" All this with the most protecting air imaginable. We "caved" and came to the conclusion that it could not be possible we had ever seen a fight before.

Now that the rebels have come and gone, it will be worth while to mention the state of feeling in which the city was during their presence. It seemed to me that there was an amount of fear greatly above the cause. Men moved restlessly about the city, and feverishly searched the faces of any passing column of soldiers. The ladies were much excited and apprehensive. At one house on our route they were out in the road giving water to the soldiers as they passed. One lady was so nervous and trembled so that she scarce could ladle the water from her pail into the tumbler, and yet she would not retire within doors. She said she had been doing it all day long in the dust and heat. And I doubt not their white faces, their tears and their tremblings, braced more than one stout heart to the conflict. As to the arrangement of the troops, that was carried on in a very orderly and creditable manner. A great body of the citizens were armed, and aided in manning the trenches, so that on our return through the city it looked almost deserted.

This raid has proved beyond a doubt that there are many secession sympathizers yet in the city. One rebel flag was captured in the city in process of construction, and many young men went out to join the raiders. Our fellows saw one citizen of Washington lying dead near Rockville and who had been fighting in the rebel cause. Near by where we were stationed there was a large house, the owner of which was engaged in fabricating a rebel flag while the fight was going on at Fort Stevens, as was learned from her negro laborer.

By this time the rebels are safely across the Potomac, having accomplished the most successful and best paying raid of the war. The 6th and 19th corps are after them, but too far behind I fear to reach them.

HOPLITE

July 17th, Sunday.

Very warm. On fatigue getting water and carrying wood. Went to the Catholic church in the morning to hear high mass. Came out after the sermon. I noticed that both times I had been there the burthen of the discourse was the necessity of preparation for death and the horrors of an unprepared state. The singing was magnificent, especially a solo by a basso. Went to church in the chapel in afternoon and evening. Commenced a letter to Myra. A battery went out from the camp to fire over Anacosta Creek where two soldiers had drowned and their bodies had not been regained. Whether they raised the bodies I did not hear. There was a funeral of a fireman at the cemetery nearby, a procession of firemen in a brass band. Discipline growing steadily tighter. Three more men made spread eagles on the spare wheels.

July 18th, Monday.

Very warm. Finished letter to Myra. Wrote to Griffin. Drill at the piece in forenoon. Commenced a piece for publication.

July 19th, Tuesday.

Very warm. Did some washing. Continued article for publication. Received a pass and in afternoon went into the city to exchange my library book. Took out a history of Switzerland. Went in to see Joe Oliver and found him doing finely. Loitered a short time in the Capitol grounds and in coming back passed through the rotunda as usual to see my favorite picture. Went on guard, 3rd relief. Packed my box.[19]

July 22 pass. Griffin Family Collection.

July 20th, Wednesday.
Very hot. Countersign for the night was "Sharpsburgh". Finished guard duty. Closed up my box and directed it. Felt languid all day. Read History of Switzerland. Thermometer 96 in doors.

July 21st, Thursday.
Third anniversary of the first Bull Run. What a change in the country since then! On fatigue, got water, dug gravel, &c. Letter from M.C.J. Quite cool.

July 22nd, Friday.
Cool. Mounted drill in forenoon. Drove swing team on our gun. A very poor drill. It was so dusty we were almost blinded, and so returned to camp very soon. Received a pass in afternoon and went down to the city to change my books. Drew out two viz: "Potiphar Papers" and "The Caesars" by De Quincy. Drake and I sauntered up and down the Av. looking at the pictures. Rested a short time in the Capitol grounds, then returned to Camp going through the Rotunda. Long letter from Myra.

July 23rd, Saturday.
The night was so cool that I had to get up and put on more clothing. The coldest night I ever remember in the month of July. Sent my box. Occupied nearly all day in preparing for inspection. Had the pole team on the caisson to harness and ride to the watering place where the carriages were washed. Washed the harness and oiled it. A very busy day. Letter from Corneile and Mr. Farrington. Very hot all day. On guard.

July 24th, Sunday.
A very cold night. The countersign was "Coal Harbor".[20] I went the grand rounds with the officer of the day in the middle of the night which consumed two hours and spoilt my sleep. Quite warm all day. During the grand rounds we caught one sentry asleep and another sitting down. Took both of them to the guard house. Read the "Potiphar Papers". Church in the evening to a new preacher, Mr. Bonwell.

July 25th, Monday.
On fatigue, cleaning stables &c. Rained heavily during the day and preceding night. Wrote two letters to Myra. In evening went with Billy Conger to visit Mr. Bonwell and had a prayer meeting by ourselves. Quite a happy one. Mr. Bonwell is member of a church I had not heard of before, viz: "United Brethren in Christ", very similar to Methodists. I borrowed of him Bunyan's "Holy War".

July 26th, Tuesday.
Fair and sunny again. Received a pass and in the forenoon visited the Catholic cemetery near camp. Found it very neat and pretty, with a very unique chapel

built entirely of cedar poles, in the shape, as the lodge keeper told me, of an ancient Jewish tabernacle.[21] In afternoon went into the city and returned the "Potiphar Papers" and took out "John Brent" by Theo. Winthrop. Spent the most of the afternoon in the Capitol grounds. The half of the females in Washington seem to be courtesans and these grounds their resort. Got back about supper time. Received my picture from home. Rumors of the rebels again in Md. Went to temperance meeting in evening. Quite interesting, three speakers.

JULY 27TH, WEDNESDAY.
Finished reading "John Brent", and must confess it not equal to the expectations I had formed of it from reading the author's first writings in the Atlantic. Wrote to Miss Moulton. Mounted inspection by Lieut. King of Bat'y A., 4th U.S. Art'y, inspecting officer for the brigade.[22] The inspection was very rigid. On guard, 3rd. relief.

JULY 28TH, THURSDAY.
Very warm. Finished my tour of guard. Countersign "Malvern". Read De Quincy's "Caesars". Letter from Myra.

JULY 29TH, FRIDAY.
Very hot. On fatigue getting water &c. Washed my clothing. Wrote to Myra. Felt very languid. Think this camp not a very healthy place. Visited Mr. Bonwell in the evening and had a social prayer meeting. Did not experience as much pleasure as the previous time.

JULY 30TH, SATURDAY.
Very warm. Finished article for Journal entitled "Courage". In afternoon went into town on pass. Prayer meeting.

> *Middlesex Journal,* Saturday, August 6, 1864
>
> Courage—Extremes Meet—The line betwixt life and death is drawn with so little distinctness in these days of horrible deaths and wounds, that the latter seems in a great degree to have lost its terrors, although men are in no way better prepared to die than formerly. Familiarity with death, although it does not breed contempt, yet begets a certain amount of insensibility to it and want of fear. Soldiers, from the habit of seeing men killed, dead, and dying of horrible wounds, come to regard death somewhat in the commonplace and passionless manner with which other momentous events of a lifetime are esteemed. That is, their importance is recognized, but they excite no overwhelming interest or anticipation. In times of peace and in civil life, dread of death is the night-mare of many minds, and even where dread is wanting through unreflection, still, when thought does come, there is the involuntary shrinking that tells the unnamed fear. Soldiering in the case of most persons conquers this great dread, but in those, whom this fear does not leave, it becomes a thousandfold stronger. Thus in the accounts that are

given of the most fearful battles, side by side with each other are the records
of most distinguished heroism and most arrant cowardice. The excitement
and carnage of a battle field beget no middle emotion. Their effects are either
the most reckless daring or the most shameless cowardice. And in many
instances the particular part which a single person takes in any battle is
decided by circumstances the most trivial, only a slight deviation from which
would have caused an action extremely different. Thus on the battle field the
extremes of courage and cowardice are nearest neighbors. Repeated instances
are not wanting of men who have sedulously shunned the field of action,
oftentimes at the expense of their soldierly reputation, but once in where no
choice was left, have done their duty manfully and to challenge admiration
and emulation. A major in the cavalry corps of the Potomac army had long
been the jest of his men for the extreme care with which he sought the rear
on the occasion of every engagement. At length he found himself in line
of battle at the head of his battalion, with a smart picket firing going on in
front and the prospect of an immediate engagement. He is reported to have
turned from blue in the face to pale, and thence through nearly all the colors
of the rainbow back to white again. He quaked in his boots. His battalion
shortly was ordered to advance. He assayed to turn over the command to his
senior captain, and suddenly recalled some urgent business to the rear. The
commanding officer of his regiment, who was well aware of the position of
affairs, stopped him as he was hastening to leave the field and peremptorily
ordered him to rejoin his command. The time came to charge. The bullets
whistled thick and for a space the Major could scarce sit his horse. One of his
subordinates let fall a few words in derision of his want of pluck. Here was
the circumstance that changed him from a coward to a brave and efficient
officer. Drawing his sabre, which erstwhile had remained in its scabbard, he
drove his spurs into his horse's sides, and, dashing forward led his battalion
to the charge twice the length of his horse in advance. And when it came
to sabre cuts none did more execution than he, all the while cheering on his
men. Ever after a fight had no terrors for him, and instead of being noted as
a coward his example was cited as that of one of the bravest officers in the
service. In his case the dread was worse than the reality, and his dread was
all his cowardice. Is it not almost always the case that dread constitutes the
greater part of cowardice, and that in very few cases is it the want of audacity
and the capacity to do brave deeds? Perhaps this is a fine distinction, but still
it seems quite just.

It must not be inferred that all cowards can be made brave men, but
that many men, who are cited as wanting in courage are in reality able to be
as brave as the bravest. Possibly this man, had the circumstances of his first
engagement been different, had the sarcasm of his subordinate been wanting, might have proved himself as thoroughly a coward as the most dastardly.
And these instances are not infrequent in our armies. Men esteemed as
milk and water characters in civil life, have proved themselves heroes and

the pluckiest bruisers of the prize ring, and who would stand up and take an indefinite amount of punishment from the fists of their antagonists, have sadly disappointed upon the battle field the expectations of their comrades, who were their former admirers. In many cases the formation of these characters upon the field of action has been the result of slight circumstances at the time unnoticed.

Still, apart from characters such as these, that are moulded by their surroundings and the circumstances into which they fall, there yet is the bravery that knows not fear, but it is most uncommon. This is a great gift, and especially in commanders of high rank, for it permits of a coolness and a deliberation in action that goes far toward ensuring success. Very few possess it. Gen. Hooker has this physical courage in the highest degree. No danger disturbs him, and in action no approaching peril disconcerts his train of thought. At the 2d battle of Malvern Hill, just as our forces had arrived on the hill from the Glendale road, the enemy was vigorously shelling the entrance to the broad field that covers the whole top of the hill. Just within the gate were Gen. Hooker and staff, mounted. He was conversing at the time with a person, evidently a newspaper correspondent. A shell came whistling over and buried itself in the earth but a few feet from his horse. The gravel thrown up by it fell all about their persons. The correspondent turned white in the face and was evidently very nervous. Hooker did not so much as turn his head to see where the shot struck, nor even interrupted the sentence he was then speaking, but continued without a movement, as though there was not within a few feet of him a missile, the explosion of which would be very likely to hurry him into eternity. And the whole tenor of his conduct has shown this insensibility to fear. What may not our country lose some day by this brave man's exposure of his person in the execution of his duty? No General can we spare less.

Courage, whether native or acquired, and our soldiers are courageous, together with familiarity with death, robs it of the greater portion of its terror. In peaceful life, moral and superstitious feelings surround death with terrors, and men fear it from dread of what may come after. A soldier in time comes to overlook that consideration entirely, or, if not, is content to trust himself in the hands of his Creator, while his fears all have reference to the pain he may suffer in the separation of material from immaterial. He dreads not so much what may come after death as the actual fear of dying.

On the battlefield death and life are strangely mingled: here the most active life, and there death in its most horrible aspect. Side by side lie dead men and those so nearly dead it would be difficult to trace the existence of life. The two extremes of humanity are here so near, not separated by a hair's breadth, that men cease to dread the one which always before they had feared intensely. But if there is one thing above another which a soldier longs for in death, it is for some kind and known hand to soften his last hours, to know he will not remain to rot above ground. This is a prejudice that has possessed mankind ever since the ancient days, when men believed that the spirit of an unburied body was doomed to roam the earth with all entrance to Elysium denied. To preserve himself from such a fate, the reward due a tyrant, a matricide, and wholesale murderer, Nero, committed suicide at the brink of the grave which he had dug for himself. And, when in meditation the mind dwells upon the subject of christian burial, to the soldier it does not seem a dreadful thing to be followed to the quiet cemetery in funeral procession. He does not look upon a funeral so sadly as before his service as a soldier. For he remembers the time when death seemed dreadful only from the manner and place of suffering; when himself in danger his longing desire was but to die away from those scenes.

Close by Camp Barry there is a large cemetery, in which there are frequent burials. A few days ago a fireman was buried under the auspices of his comrades. As the long procession wound its way along the road that skirts the camp, the band stirring soft echoes by a plaintive march, it did not seem a sorrowful sight, as I remember to have esteemed such only a few short years ago. Knowledge of and familiarity with death works this change.

In this state of fearlessness there are observable two facts, according to the persons possessing or acquiring it. Either it has been attained by an education of the mind into the belief that there is no future, or if there is, none of punishment, else it results from a strong faith in God and a belief in salvation obtained through the atonement of Christ. In the former case, what dreadful agony comes with the occasional glimpses through the rents in the dark veil of their doubt. In the latter, what quiet vigor and calm hopefulness there is to ensure the performance of arduous and most dangerous duties. Our army reverences them. God gives them.

> HOPLITE
> Washington, D. C.
> July 30. "64"

JULY 31ST, SUNDAY.
Still blazing hot. Inspection in morning. Wrote to C.H.M. Church in afternoon. On guard at night.

AUGUST 1ST, MONDAY.
Very hot. Finished my guard. Countersign, "Stillwater". Finished "The Caesars" and was much pleased with it. It is written in plain, unadorned, yet elegant English. Wrote to Myra. Commenced Bunyan's "Holy War".

AUG. 2ND, TUESDAY.
Was aroused at two A.M. by a great bustle in the barrack and the order was to harness and hitch which was done. Three batteries moved out but with the rest we remained harnessed 'til shortly after daybreak when we unharnessed again.

Felt so sick all day that I was unable to do my fatigue duty. Allbright gave me a dollar for harnessing his team.[23] At night went to bed quite sick with headache and pain in my loins. Drew a pair of boots, 2 pr. Socks and a haversack. Shower.

Aug. 3rd, Wednesday.
Quite cool. Visited the doctor, but got no medicine. My head ached badly all day. Finished the "Holy War". Paper from Miss Moulton. Went to bed quite sick.

Aug. 4th, Thursday.
Still sick. Finished reading "Daisy Burns" by Julie Kavanagh. Did no duty all day. Wrote to Mr. Farrington.

Aug. 5th, Friday.
Still unwell. On guard all day at the guard house on the prisoners. A sad sight. It presented a wonderful mixture of the disgusting and the comic. Felt a little better toward night. Disappointed at receiving no letter from Myra. Hot again. Military burial at the cemetery.

Aug. 6th, Saturday.
Much better. On fatigue. Great bustle in camp and preparations to move which came to naught. Drew 68 horses from Battery K. 1st U.S. Art'y, also some saddles, but returned them. Heavy rain in morning. Reports of going out on the upper Potomac with the cavalry. Sketched "Rutledge" for the second time and like it less than the first time.

Aug. 7th, Sunday.
A day of bustle. Drew baggage wagons and an ambulance. At length the bustle died away and we went back to the old routine. Drew our scales again which we had turned in the day before. Very hot. Read Theo. Winthrop's "Cecil Dreeme" through with unqualified delight. Think it the freshest modern novel I have seen for three years. Mem. To buy it sometime. Studied artillery a little. Wrote to Myra, and received a letter from her as well as one from Tileston and H.A.H.

Aug. 8th, Monday.
Quite cool. Went to Dr. in morning. Section drill in forenoon. Acted No. 6.[24] Missed drill in afternoon, therefore to be punished by fatigue. Wrote to Myra and Mr. Davis. A slight headache.

Aug. 9th, Tuesday.
Very warm. Billy Conger and I being requested to conduct funeral services over the deceased child of a poor woman nearby, went over for that purpose. Poor woman, her lot is hard, living in a small tent and her husband a soldier in the 7th Mass. battery, being in Arkansas.[25] The worst of the case was that the member of the Sanitary Commission who brought the coffin and was to carry the body

to the grave, would not stop for any services but marched off with the body and did not wait for the parent to get into her carriage. Poor woman, how I pitied her! Billy Conger gave her $5. Drill at the piece in the afternoon. Letter from C.H.M. Went on guard at night, 2nd relief. Countersign, Ontario. Fried eggs for dinner.

AUG. 10TH, WEDNESDAY.
Finished my guard duty. Very hot. Letter from Myra, with good news. At night Conger and I visited Mrs. Huntley and I gave her some clothes to wash. Coming back we called on our new minister.

AUG. 11TH, THURSDAY.
Hot and dusty. Review at 9 A.M. by Gen. Howe.[26] Formed in battery, then wheeled into column of batteries to pass in review. Wheeled into line again and then drilled a little. Got back to camp about 11 A.M. Letter from Myra. Wrote a letter for Mrs. Huntley.

AUG. 12TH, FRIDAY.
Still warm. Disappointed in getting a pass. Nevertheless in afternoon went down to the library and got two books, viz: "Life of Chevalier Bayard" by W.G. Simms, and one vol. of Queechy. Letter from Mr. Davis.

AUG. 13TH, SATURDAY.
Hot. Was helping clean the carriages when I was ordered off to go to George-town with 3 others to get a couple of our fellows there in gaol. Found them at "Forrest Hall" on High Street. After much delay got them and started back. Both ways we rode in the horse cars. Took dinner at the Soldiers' Rest. Got to camp about 2 P.M. Just at nightfall there came up a heavy storm accompanied by thunder and lightning. The lightning struck our stable and killed one man, Robert Seaman, one of the men from the 10th N.Y. Battery.[27] Wounded one horse also. The bolt struck Seaman fair in the breast and killed him instantly. Prayer meeting in the evening.

AUG. 14TH, SUNDAY.
Warm with heavy shower in afternoon. Foot inspection at 9 A.M. Funeral services over Seaman's body by Mr. Tomkins in the chapel at one o'clock, after which he was taken to the Soldiers' Cemetery at Arlington escorted by 8 mounted men, a corp'l and a bugler. I was one of the escort. Our gun was used as a hearse, being fitted with a platform for the coffin upon the top. The coffin was draped by the American Flag. We went by way of Georgetown and the Aqueduct bridge and passed and met many hearses containing soldiers. It was very hot when we started but when we arrived at the grave it poured down heavily. Luck-ily I had carried a poncho. The Arlington estate has been turned into a cem-etery and many thousands are buried there. The graves are numbered for future

reference.[28] Mr. Tompkins said a short prayer over the grave. In coming back my horse nearly ran away with me as I was mounting after getting a drink. Got back just in time for retreat. Battery K left camp to join the cavalry.

Middlesex Journal, Saturday, August 20, 1864

Our Army Correspondence
Washington, D. C.
Aug. 14, 1864.

The summer hastens to its fall, yet, like the old Roman empire, that retained all its glory long after the culmination of its power from the sheer force of what it had been, the heat of the season remains undiminished. Men shun the sun, and hide within their barracks. All activity seems accomplished under protest. Vast clouds of dust widely brood, or by the casual wind wheel and circle high in air. All objects become aged. The pinched blades of grass bow to the ground beneath their dusty load, and all nature has donned a robe most dingily white. All is parched and seared white and powdery. A train of half a dozen wagons raises a cloud of dust equal to a division of cavalry.

A man suffering from hunger has beautiful visions of most enticingly set tables. So in the depth of summer, amid dust and glaring sunshine, and parched fields, how freshly to the mind rise the pictures of bracing autumn. We remember how furiously ran the blood in every vein, how the sun seemed to pervade the atmosphere, not shine through it, and the very air seemed redolent of life and hope. The glorious beauty of the woods bathed in late dews enters into every scene. The great enlivener of all these pictures is joyous, spontaneous life; what contrast to dusty, heat-enforced quiet.

A familiar scene rises before me. The glinting rippling waters of Horn Pond. How closely its carpeted edges hang above the wave, and above the stately oaks sway gently in the breeze. The island seems set upon the waters, not in them. If any one can read, if any one can do anything beside dream, as stretched idly on the grass one watches the smiling pond with its passing shades and fitful little squalls, Tennyson is the companion which ought to be taken along. The scene, the breeze, seem to creep into one's frame like a bodily delight through the finger tips and half-closed lids. Thus memory gilds the present with happy thoughts, and hallows the past.

But Camp Barry, what a step from cool waters and quiet scenes to whitewash, heat and dust! Washington still holds us though, as it would appear, upon sufferance only. Twice since last writing have we essayed to leave this camp, and twice have we failed. The first time was upon the occasion of Mosby's attempt to catch a wagon train near the Point of Rocks. The latter happened four days ago, when upon the arrival of the 1st Division of cavalry from the Potomac army, we were ordered to fit out immediately to go up the river with them. In preparation thereto we drew horses and equipments from a battery here at second hand, but for some reason almost immediately returned them. Then it was said we were going to be fitted out entirely new, since when last report nothing. We have retained our full allowance of wagons and an ambulance, which would seem to indicate that we are actually about to move. As it is, we have settled down again into the dull routine of camp life. The lazy waters have engulfed us again, and the summer hastens on.

On Thursday, 11th inst, all the artillery in this camp was reviewed by Gen. Howe. There are six batteries, viz:

> A, 4th U.S. Artillery
> E, 2d   "   "
> L and M, 3d   "   "
> 16th Mass. Battery
> 6th N. Y.
> C, Independent Penn. Battery.

The heat beat and poured, and dust flew thickly. The brigade got into line about 9 A.M., and were immediately reviewed by the General, now chief of artillery and successor to General Barry. We wheeled into column of sections, and after passing in review again wheeled into line. The parade dismissed, several of the batteries staid to exhibit their proficiency in drill. Had it not been for the dense clouds of dust which rose upon every wheel or quick movement, it would have been a pretty sight, this exhibition of every variety of artillery tactics at once, here a battery getting into action, there another limbering up, wheels, countermarches, movements in echelon, by battery, by section; but such a thing as pleasure was impossible with an atmosphere at 100°, and dense with dust.

Danger exists not only on the battlefield. Of this an instance occured [*sic*] in the battery but last night. Just at sunset a heavy shower came up, accompanied by severe lightning and thunder. One bolt descended into our stable, killing instantly one of our guards, by name Robert Seaman, a citizen of Orange, N. J. The fluid entered through one end of the stable, shattered several joists, and after killing Seaman, went down the stable, skipping thirteen horses, and struck down the fourteenth. An exceedingly eccentric course and impossible of explanation. Seaman was struck fair upon the breast. The current ran down his body and both his legs out at the boots, making very perceptible holes in the latter. The only marks left upon his person were a slight abrasion of the breast and the singed hair along the track of the electric fluid. He leaves a wife and several children. The burial will take place this afternoon, with military honors, at the Soldiers' Cemetery at Arlington. His hearse will be the gun, which so many times in life he had handled, and worked, and polished, by means of a platform fitted upon its upper face. May God rest his soul.

Of news there is none. Washington is stagnant since the adjournment of the legislatures. Troops come and go in endless succession, where from and where to is hard to tell. Some of the hundred days men are already going home. Our columns seem to be pushing on down the valley, and before long no doubt we shall hear of a fight in that direction. Every day increases our force acting against Early.[29] A division of cavalry from the Potomac army is already pressing after him, which in conjunction with Averill's command, makes a cavalry force of about 8000.[30] For all the failure at Petersburgh every thing looks encouraging.

Gen. Gregg commands Grant's cavalry, and a noble and capable commander he is.

HOPLITE

Aug. 15th, Monday.
Warm. Wrote to Myra. Thirteen of the old fellows received their discharge and went home.[31] Police in the afternoon, cleaning stable. Went on guard at night, third relief, countersign "Falmouth".

Aug. 24th, Wednesday.
Fair. Received a pass to go to Arlington, and having borrowed a horse rode down to the Provost Marshall's office to have it approved and thence through Georgetown across the Aqueduct bridge, to Fort Corcoran and found that the 6th Mass. Vols. which I was in search of had moved away two days before. Turned around and came back immediately. Fell in with a pleasant middle aged man with whom I had quite a chat as we rode along, principally upon the moral influence of the army. Drew "Rasselas" from the library by Sam'l Johnson. Letter from C.H.M. containing picture of his younger sister and letter from H.A.H. It is now a fortnight since hearing from Myra. Something the matter. Battery drill.

Aug. 25th, Thursday.
Cloudy. Battery drill. No letter. Finished Fanny Kemble's Journal. Wrote letter for Mrs. Huntley. Went on guard at night. Read "Rasselas" and was much pleased. It contains much philosophical discussion.

Aug. 29th, Monday.
Fair and cool. Battery drill. Three fellows discharged.[32] Read "Daisy Chain" all day.

Aug. 30th, Tuesday.
General cleaning up for muster. Scrubbed the barrack and cleaned the carriages, &c. Finished "Daisy Chain" and think it one of the best domestic novels I ever read. Read "Gervase Castonel" by Mrs. Henry Wood, a very poor affair. Went on guard at night. Weather cool.

Aug. 31st, Wednesday.
Finished guard duty. Grand muster and review of the whole garrison by Gen. Howe, which took nearly all day. The General found much fault. I was mustered at guard house. No letter from Myra. Not heard from her now for three weeks. It is hard to keep up my spirits so. Prayer meeting.

Sept. 1st, Thursday.
Fair and cool. On fatigue. A very quiet day. Felt dispirited at not hearing from Myra in so long. Wrote to H.A.H.

Sept. 2nd, Friday.
Received pass for the day and went into the city. Went to the library and drew "Beauchampe" by W.G. Simms and "A Health Trip to the Tropics" by N.P. Willis. Took dinner at the Soldiers' Rest, beans, pork, and bread. Saw a lot of substitutes that came in by rail. In afternoon went over to the Smithsonian Institute for the purpose of looking through the library, but unluckily it was not open. Looked at the paintings and statuary and came away. Passing through town stopped at an iron foundry to see them work and was quite interested. Think of all the mechanical trades I have seen, should prefer to be an iron or brass founder. Saw a prisoner break away from his guard in the street, but he was speedily caught. Visited the public garden. Not so many flowers in bloom as at my former visit, but some very fine roses. The banana tree was doing finely and I could note the progress since my last visit. Stopped in the Capitol grounds for a little while and came through the rotunda to see my favorite picture. Got to camp just before supper. No letter. Prayer meeting in evening.

Sept. 3rd, Saturday.
Cloudy all day. Cleaned harness and pieces for Sunday inspection. The Capt. furnished rotten stone and chamois leather to polish the pieces. Quite a busy day. Went on guard at night, 3rd relief. Countersign was "Williamsburgh."

Sept. 4th, Sunday.
Rained heavily in the night. Finished my guard duty. Finished reading "Beauchampe" and think poorly of it in plot, finish, and morals, especially the latter. By God's help was enabled to withstand the greatest temptation that had yet assailed me since my resolution to live a Christian life. It was to go to the theatre to see some of the actors who were my favorites in old times. Thank God for his mercy and his answer to my prayer. Church in the evening. 16th Mass. Batt. and a section of Batt. A; 4th U.S. left camp as was said to go to N.Y.

Sept. 5th, Monday.
Cloudy and cool. On fatigue. A lazy day. Read "Home Influence" nearly all day.

Sept. 6th, Tuesday.
Rainy and cold all day. Lay abed and read nearly all day.

Sept. 7th, Wednesday.
Fair and pleasantly warm. Just three months to serve. Battery harnessed up about 9½ a.m. and went down to Jackson Square with B't'y L. & M. 3rd U.S. Art'y where at noon we fired a salute of 100 guns in honor of the capture of Atlanta. Saw Gen. Howe and Gen. Harding. This took place right in the midst of the city. Finished "Home Influence" for the 2nd time and was surprised to

find it somewhat tedious. The moral is excellent. Went down to Furbush's and had fried eggs for dinner. No letter from Myra, 4th week.

SEPT. 8TH, THURSDAY.
On guard all day. In forenoon review of all the batteries by Gen. Howe and inspection of non-commissioned officers. Rained gently in afternoon. Read "Health Trip to Tropics". A very heavy weight of unhappiness at my heart at Myra's silence. Can it be the mail is tampered with?[33]

SEPT. 9TH, FRIDAY.
Cloudy in morning, fine afternoon. On fatigue. A comparatively lazy day. Wrote to Corneile.

SEPT. 10TH, SATURDAY.
Cloudy and rainy in the forenoon but cleared up at noon. Washed harness. Received pay for July and August. Went on a pass into the city and sent $28 home by express, bought some little necessaries and ate quite a lot of trash. Wrote a note to Myra and mailed it myself. Got home shortly before retreat. Went on guard in the park, 2nd relief.

SEPT. 11TH, SUNDAY.
Rainy part of the day. Felt sick all day from eating so much stuff yesterday. Finished my guard duty. Much drunkenness in camp. Lay down at 5 P.M. and fell asleep. Did not thoroughly wake 'til morning of—[34]

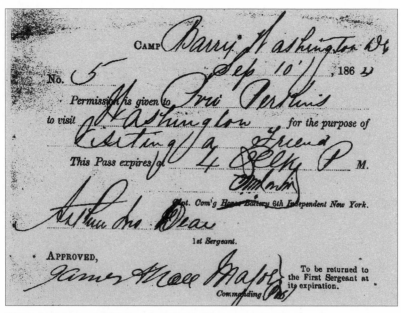

September 10 pass. Griffin Family Collection.

SEPT. 12TH, MONDAY.
Rainy and cloudy. On fatigue. Went for water to Capitol Hill. Ate much trash during the day. In the afternoon was detailed to go to the corral, corner of G. and 22nd Streets and draw horses to fit us out as a horse battery. I forgot to mention in the record of yesterday that the remainder of the 10th N.Y. joined us 31 in all. Capt. Martin received orders to fit out immediately in order to join Gen. Sheridan.[35] On arrival at the corral we learned that it contained no horses but that we must go to the cavalry depot at Giesboro Point to get them. Returned to camp riding down the avenue in a horse car. A hard day's work.

SEPT. 13TH, TUESDAY.
Fair and cool. Details sent off to get horses and to change two of our brass guns for 3 inch rifles, but luckily I escaped from both.[36] Washed all over. Wrote to Myra.

SEPT. 14TH, WEDNESDAY.
Rainy. Letter from C.H.M. Wrote short letter to Journal. The horses were assigned, mine a little black with two white hind feet, and evidently unused to being ridden. He is very obstinate and tedious to manage. A busy day.[37]

CHAPTER 10

BURNING BARNS IN EVERY DIRECTION
MET OUR SIGHT:
SEPTEMBER–DECEMBER 1864

The Sixth New York left Camp Barry on September 15 to join Sheridan's Army of the Shenandoah. With President Lincoln's approval, Grant had assigned the diminutive general to command a field army that ultimately consisted of the Sixth and Eighteenth Corps plus two cavalry divisions. As Grant phrased it, Sheridan's objective was to follow Early's army "to the death." As important as this change was, the consolidation of four military departments with responsibilities for this area into one was perhaps as significant. The former arrangement had fostered division and confusion in the high command and resulted in no one apparently knowing the enemy's location or intentions. Now, one general officer in whom Grant had confidence would be responsible for both the administrative structure of the area and its primary fighting force. Moreover, that officer had clear and simple orders and had been provided with sufficient force to accomplish his mission.

The backdrop for these changes was Grant's growing awareness of the sensitivity of the government to the security of the capital, especially in an election year that many pundits agreed was likely to result in a change of administration. In addition, Grant had come to realize that the Shenandoah was more important than he had previously supposed. Without lowering the significance of the main efforts against Lee in the Richmond-Petersburg area and Johnston before Atlanta, Grant appreciated the importance of the railroads, granaries, and livestock of the Valley in sustaining Lee's army and the Confederate government. If Early's army could be smashed and the resources of the Valley could be removed from the board, Confederate resistance would be that much harder to sustain.

Perhaps the main reason why President Lincoln was in imminent danger of not being reelected was the frustration of the public with the costly campaigns being waged by Grant and Meade against Lee's army and by Sherman against Johnston's army in the western theater. Both efforts were apparently barren of decisive results, and the lengthening casualty lists fed a peace movement that was grist for the mill of the president's political opponents. It was therefore essential, from both political and military viewpoints, to reverse the slide into stalemate and wrest back the strategic initiative in a convincing and obvious way. Stalemate only worked in favor of the Confederates and the Northern peace movement, since success for the South could be defined in terms of survival. For the North, it was essential to crush the rebellion before war weariness made it impossible to carry on the contest.

Perkins's diary and his letters to the *Middlesex Journal* report on the marching and fighting of the 1864 Shenandoah Valley campaign. Highlights include the battery's march from Washington to Harpers Ferry, the march up the Valley to rejoin the cavalry, and subsequent operations in the Shenandoah and Luray valleys. Perkins describes the aftermath of the battle of Third Winchester and the battles of Tom's Brook and Cedar Creek. He also unsparingly details the cost to the civilian population that resulted from Sheridan's scorched earth policy, in which hundreds of barns and other structures were burned and thousands of head of livestock were driven off. In doing so, he reveals a degree of sympathy for the war's victims that is in sharp contrast to his earlier expressed sentiments about the rebels and their cause.

The final entry of December 12 was written after the author had been mustered out and relates a visit to a former battery mate in Rahway, New Jersey. The entries for October 28–31, November 2–5, and November 14–20 have been omitted. Those entries report the increasing frequency of inclement weather, George's culinary activities involving beef heads and brains, fatigue duty, and continuing correspondence with friends and family. George also reported that he laundered his own clothing and commented that he hoped it would be for the last time.

SEPT. 15TH, THURSDAY.
Fair and warm. Much confusion and bustle consequent on preparations to move. Was ordered to take team but it was shortly after taken away again. Wrote to C.H.M. About 3 P.M. boot and saddle sounded and we harnessed up. All the carriages had 4 teams to drag them, and there were two caissons to each of the 12 pounders. We didn't get started 'til about 4½ P.M. Went up Maryland Avenue, down Pennsylvania Avenue, a short distance thence through by-streets to Georgetown. Turned up High Street, passed through Tenallytown and camped about a mile beyond just after dark. Had considerable trouble in getting water for the horses.[1]

Sept. 16th, Friday.

Reveille just before sunrise. Got *en route* about 8 a.m. Just as we got on the road one of the axles to the battery wagon broke down. After a march of about 4 miles we made a short halt and then continuing about 4 miles more halted just outside of the village of Rockville. Here the battery wagon and forge caught up to us. I had a pair of spare horses to lead all day. We passed through R— and halted about 8 miles beyond on the top of a high hill with a beautiful watering place for the horses in a large creek nearby.[2] Rockville is quite an extensive village and very pretty withal. It has three hotels and there are quite a number of elegant brick residences. In fact in Maryland there are many more brick country homes than at home. Ate much fruit, peaches, apples, &c. For supper an "olla podrida" of potatoes, cabbages, chickens, &c, which some of our fellows had foraged. Rations scarcely sufficient to sustain life. Fair and cool. Pleasant marching.

Sept. 17th, Saturday.

Up and moving at the usual hour. Potato stew for breakfast. Sun rose warm and pleasant. This and yesterday's march was through a pleasantly diversified country with many pretty cottages by the way. The landscape really smiled and the atmosphere seemed lambent with health and beauty. Passed through Clarksburgh, a small town with one tavern. It seems to me that a tavern here is maintained by a smaller population than at home, probably owing to the fact that there are no railroads and therefore all the travel is on the turnpike. At length about noon we arrived at the top of a large hill at the foot of which was the town of Hyattstown. It is beautifully situated in a valley between two high hills. The main street runs diagonally up the hill and in fact there is but one street. The white houses peeped out from their surrounding trees giving the finishing touch of civilization to a landscape as beautiful as I had ever seen. We halted just outside the town for the column to catch up. From thence we continued the march over much the same kind of country and passing through the pretty little village of Urbanna and halted for the night on the banks of the Monocacy near a bridge which was destroyed. All day long we had been marching in sight of the Sugar Loaf Mt. and at Urbanna we struck the road on which we had gone from Edwards Ferry to Frederick in June 1863. Boiled potatoes for supper. A very pleasant day's march.[3]

Sept. 18th, Sunday.

Sun rose clear but with a cool wind. My little horse went into a team and I got another black one for the day. This day's march was one of the pleasantest I ever made through a most beautiful country. Every mile or two developed some new landscape and I spent all day in a state of admiration. We crossed the Monocacy by fording and passed by Monocacy Mills and through Buckeystown. Just beyond the latter we halted. Here was a station on the Balt. & O. R. R., and we drew some rations.[4] I ate as many peaches, which I got in a neighboring orchard, as I could, in fact got thoroughly sated with them. At length we arrived at the range of Catoctin Mts. and passed over them into Pleasant Valley. Far to our north and right as we climbed the hills we could just descry the spires of Frederick. Descending the other slope of the hills a magnificent sight spread out before us, a broad smiling valley running far away to right and left bounded at the farther side by the Maryland continuation of the Blue Ridge. Right straight before us there seemed to be a meeting of three great ridges, one of which I knew to be Loudon Heights. To the gap between these our road seemed to tend. Just at the foot of the Catoctin range we passed through the pretty village of Jefferson. The people were going to church as we passed. Much bread &c was bought on this day's march. About the middle of the p.m. we passed through Petersville and halted early about 4 miles from the gap in the Mts.[5] Here I had a little muss with H. Brunt in relation to our horses.[6] I was in the right but still did wrong to maintain myself. It would have been more Christianly to have given in. God forgive me. The thought came up if I kept thus offending Him how could I expect Him always to forgive. I dare not think. I pray Him to return me once

Bvt. Lt. Col. Rhett L. Livingston. Courtesy of Massachusetts Commandery, Military Order of the Loyal Legion and U.S. Army Military History Institute.

more to home life where I may gather help and strength from companionship with Christians. It is hard to do right among a crowd of evil doers especially with my temperament. —Bread and milk for supper. Put up paulins as it looked like rain and actually did rain a little.

Sept. 19th, Monday.
Reveille at daybreak. Slept poorly. Soft bread and fried eggs for breakfast. Continued march and passed through Knoxville at which place we struck the Potomac. Continued up the river to Sandy Hook, a little distance back from which we camped in a valley between South Mt. and Maryland Heights, and right under the latter.[7] All through this valley were the trains of the army and we reported to Res. Brig. Horse Art'y. Capt. Livingtone.[8] There were 3 batteries here, viz. M — 2nd, C & E — 4th, and C — 3rd. Saw some of our old boys who left us on the peninsula. —Sandy Hook and Knoxville are both very dirty little places and crowded with wagon trains &c. The latter place had once been a manufacturing town but the mills are now unused. Pitched paulins &c, and went into camp. Chicken soup for supper. Wrote to Myra. Felt rather lonely living thus with strangers and most of them Dutchmen. Went to bed early.

Sept. 20th, Tuesday.
Fair and warm. Wrote to Mr. Davis. Our battery was reinforced by 25 dismounted cavalry.[9] Mutton soup for dinner. A very lazy day. Turned over my equipments and took the lead team on the forge to drive, a pair of greys. This was of my own seeking, having had all the fighting I wanted. Went on guard 1st relief. Orders to move at daylight.

Sept. 21st, Wednesday.
Reveille before sunrise. Breakfast and harnessed my team which came rather awkward for the first time. Broke camp at daybreak and went through Sandy Hook and up the river. The fog hung so low that the prospect was not very extensive. Crossed the Potomac on the new R.R. bridge. The town as we passed through it seemed dirtier than ever. Halted and parked on Bolivar Heights.[10] Watered in harness & cleaned the horses. Found time to wash and eat some bread and butter. Found that I had left my haversack behind with cup, rations, &c. Sun getting higher burnt off the fog, and I was able to see the view which is indeed magnificent. 'Tis useless to attempt to describe it. The narrow gorge of the river and the craggy woody heights, the village and the tents all combined to make a very picturesque picture. We lay on the hill 'till about 4 P.M. when the train arriving which we were to accompany and about a battalion of cavalry, we started on by the same road as we pursued going to Shepardstown a year ago. But instead of turning to the right we kept the pike. About 2 miles out passed through Hallstown which consists of a half dozen houses and a R.R. store house.[11] In this vicinity was a line of earthworks evidently thrown up by our army which was very complete, having rifle pits, redoubts and abattis in

beautiful style. Our march lay through a beautiful and well cleared country. The trees were all oak and in the woods there was no underbrush but a beautiful green sward. The style was worthy of a nobleman's park. Ever on our left the Blue Ridge seemed to follow us with its mottled green and black sides. About sundown we entered Charlestown, outside of which there were some rebel earthworks. It is quite a large town, larger than Warrenton, and looked as though it had been very aristocratic. It contains many nice buildings. Saw the vicinity of John Brown's execution. The people seemed to live there still and I saw quite a number of ladies on the street and two dressed in a very recherché style. There was a garrison of infantry. Just beyond the town we went into park and performed the usual duties. On fatigue and had to go for water a distance of half a mile and didn't get back 'til very late. The pike was very dusty. Charlestown is about 8 miles from Harpers Ferry.[12]

SEPT. 22ND, THURSDAY.

Rose before daylight. Started off promptly stopping to water on the road in harness. We kept the main road in a S. W. direction and after about 2 hours' march came upon a pretty little village, by name of Smithfield. Just before entering the town we met a regiment of cavalry who were taking 7 stands of captured colors to the rear. The colors were for the most part red or white, the union of the flag being different color from the ground work, with ten or a dozen stars disposed in the form of an X. One was very ragged and one I could make out was of the 36th Va. reg.[13] Just beyond the town we quitted the pike and took a more westerly course. Shortly we came to a covered bridge over the Opequon Creek. Crossing it and a little tributary we halted in a field beyond for the train to get up. Here I found time to wash and eat breakfast. About an hour's march brought us to a little village with several large grist mills. It was called Mill Creek. Just beyond the village we struck the Martinsburg and Winchester pike.[14] Between the two places it was 22 miles. From there to Winchester the country was bare and desolate and bore evident marks of war in dilapidated buildings, broken fences, &c. Dead horses lay thick along the road. Just before we got into W. in a little strip of woods, there were evidences of a very smart fight, some 2 or 3 dozen graves, dead horses, and the trees were marked with bullets. In the field beyond, a caisson had been blown up and there were more graves. We passed through the city about 4 P.M. Winchester is quite a large and substantial city, as large as Alexandria. It contains many nice buildings and I was surprised to see so large a city set right down in the fields as it were. About a brigade of the 6th Corps garrisoned the town. As we passed through the main street we saw a great many wounded, and I noted one poor fellow with his leg just amputated being brought out of one operating room. We camped just beyond the town in the field which I afterwards learned was the battlefield. Dead horses lay all about and completely scented the air. At short intervals along the road I could see where troops had formed into line of battle by breastworks of rails &c. One peculiarity of the valley over the rest of VA. is that it is very stony and stone walls abound. Saw quite a number of females riding horseback along the route, and this I have noticed is the custom even in Maryland for all ages and sexes to ride horseback. In the country a carriage is seldom seen, but ladies ride about on horses, sometimes two on one poor nag. On the heights about W. there are some extensive earthworks, some of them so old as to be grass grown. Our advance said to be beyond Strasburgh. Very dusty.[15]

SEPT. 23RD, FRIDAY.

Moved out on the pike southward with a small escort of cavalry. About 1½ miles out passed through the village of Kernstown. For three miles out of W. I could see evidences of the running fight which had taken place, dead horses, a blown up caisson &c.[16] Passed through Newtown about the middle of the forenoon, which is quite a large town and unlike the generality of Virginian villages was quite cleanly. About noon reached Middletown, a small dirty village, and five miles beyond arrived at Strausburgh. Here were hospitals and a few infantry. The march thus far had been very monotonous and through a very barren country. Everywhere were the desolating evidences of an army's march. We halted just outside the town on the road to Woodstock, and again returning through the town took a road to the S. E. said to lead to Front Royal.[17] Ate much fruit. Our route lead us along the edge of the north fork of the Shenandoah for some distance, on the opposite bank of which the mountain rose abruptly. At length we forded it near an old railroad bridge, as I thought, of the Manassas Gap R.R.[18] The bridge had been destroyed, but the magnificent granite abutments still remained intact. After we had crossed the river we took our way for some distance along the railroad bank. The rails had been torn up and many of them bent. About 4 miles from Strausburgh we reached what had evidently been a station on the R.R. and found the 3rd Div. Cav. in camp with Batt. B. & C. We parked and unharnessed.[19] Went to water and as soon as we got back "Boot and Saddle" sounded for the whole div. Took our route apparently right up the mountain. 'Til long after midnight we continued our march over the roughest ground I had ever seen. Our course lay mostly up hill. Nearly lost the column once. At length we came to the south fork of the Shenandoah and crossed. Here was a sight I should have admired had I not been so tired. We came upon the river which is here very broad and shallow and with a swift current, at a grassy and flat field. Far across the rushing water shone a blue and flickering signal fire. Across its blaze occasional horsemen rode, giving it with the flickering line of light across the rippling stream a very weird appearance. Just across the ascent of the mountains again commenced by a road cut in the side of the hill. This road we came nigh to missing. It was very narrow and steep. At one place the forge of B. & L. had fallen over the precipice, and there as we wound our way up I could see far below me by the pale rays of a candle the group of anxious faces, the overturned forge, and one man, the lead-driver, who had been crushed in the fall, making faint movements with his hands. It wasn't pleasant. We continued marching over and into the heart of the mountain 'til after midnight, when we camped in a very mixed manner. We did not feed the horses, but lay down immediately and slept. This night's march was one of the most tiresome I had made owing to the roughness of the road and its steepness. In all we marched this day about 35 m.

Sept. 24th, Saturday.
Rained during the night a little. On waking I found we were camped in a tableland high up in the mountain. Fed and harnessed and started off immediately. Our course lay all day through valleys and over high wooded ridges. It was very hard on the poor horses. The most of the way was pretence of a pike. N. B. All *made* roads in Va. are called pikes, although most of them have no gates. These mountains are mentioned on the map as Manhattan Mountains and one little valley we crossed as Fort Powell Valley.[20] Shortly we emerged into quite a large valley in the middle of which was situated the charming little village of Luray. It was an elegant sight, this smiling little valley with its gem of a village whose white walls and church spire adorned it greatly. The town is situated on a little eminence in the middle of the vale. We passed by the scene of some stout cavalry fight, as many saddles and carbines and articles of clothing were scattered about.[21] About the middle of the valley we halted and I found that the whole of the 3rd Div. Cav. were there. I saw quite a number of our old fellows who left us on the peninsula and went into D. of the 2nd. While we were halted here a member of one of the Michigan brigades brought a live sheep over and gave it to us. We slaughtered it instantly. Toward sunset we moved out with the Michigan Brigade and shortly struck a splendid pike leading toward the gap. All day we had been marching toward Thornton's Gap which showed in the ridge as if gouged out with a chisel.[22] Just at the base of the mountains we again crossed the Shenandoah. I was mistaken in thinking the river we crossed near Strasburgh to be the Shenandoah. It was some tributary or else the stream made some very devious windings. Where we crossed it at the Gap there had been probably a very nice bridge as the abutments remained to testify. About dark we halted about a mile up the mountain and after lying in column for about ½ hour we turned round and came down again. We had to unlimber to turn around. Got into camp about 8 P.M. and after feeding horses and selves turned in. Fried mutton for supper.
—This day's march, although hard travelling, was truly pleasant to me. Such exquisite scenery I had never seen before. It alternated between most beautiful valleys and sublime mountains. In one place the smiling mead, in another the wooded peaks. The mountains looked as though draped in a flowing mantle of green and brown. I often neglected my driving to gaze at them. One peculiarity which was a most beautiful effect is that a misty wraithlike cloud would come floating along, grow darker and shade the ground. It would discharge its rain

while at the same time on the tops of some mountains there would be the most glorious sunshine. It would sometimes rain at a distance of 200 or 300 yds. while not a drop would fall on us. But I will not attempt to describe. I picked up a sabre near Luray which was probably lost in action.[23]

Sept. 25th, Sunday.

At an hour or two after dawn we again moved up the mountain to cross. On the exact summit of the mountain there is a house, from whence the view of the valley was splendid. But I was surprised to see another range of mountains at a distance of about 8 or 9 miles. On looking at the map I found I had got quite confused in my reckoning, that instead of going east from Luray through Thornton's Gap, we had really come southwest after crossing the Manhattan Mts., and had crossed once more into the Shenandoah Valley. I wonder I didn't think of this while crossing the river for the last time. Just at the foot of the Gap we halted near the town of Newmarket. This town appeared the most prosperous of any I had yet seen. We stayed there about 2 hours giving Frank Mann and I a chance to boil some mutton. Some of our wagons went to join a train going to Harper's Ferry and with them went 7 of our boys, having been discharged.[24] We marched through the town about 1 p.m. and took a pike running a little east of south following the course of the ridge.[25] The ladies seemed to be considerably interested in us, some of them sitting in their doorways in full toilet. The most of the remainder of this day's march lay along side of the pike rather than on it. We passed quite a number of infantry stragglers who said the 8th Corps had passed about the middle of the afternoon. We camped about 9 p.m. Fed my horse, myself on mutton, and turned in very weary and sleepy.

Sept. 26th, Monday.

Reveille at 3 a.m. Came near losing one of my horses but fortunately found him. As we formed in column for the march I found we were near a town, which I found to be Harrisonburgh. This is really a *nice* city and much nicer than anything I had before seen in Va. There were three rebel hospitals in the city which had fallen into our hands. About a brigade of the 8th Corps lay here. On the outskirts of town there are many elegant country houses. Shortly after passing Harrisonburgh we turned off the pike to the left and made towards the mountains. Marched all the forenoon through a pleasant country and over a rough road. The battery wagon turned bottom side up and the pole driver was thrown under his horses, seriously injuring him. About noon as we were watering our horses at a run I heard skirmishing in front.[26] At a mile distant the column debouched upon the top of a grassy hill where a section of K. & C. Battery were in action already. Beyond the country dipped and then rose to meet the mountains. We parked on a hill and waited. Presently the Johnnies could be seen very plainly and then our line of skirmishers advancing across a sort of swale or field indentation of the woodlands. Our fellows advanced steadily, both lines exchanging shots the while. The rebs kept the edge of the woods. Another row burst out in another quarter farther to the left and raged especially severe for a short time. One section of rifle guns went into action against these last and fired quite a number of shots. At length our fellows apparently drove them and all was quiet except an occasional stray shot. The ambulances went down. All was quiet for some time when the Johnnies seemed to wake up and they drove the skirmishers back a short distance. After that the line remained undisturbed the rest of the day. The forge fell back a short distance and joined the wagon train, and then at dark again joined the battery. Unhitched and unharnessed. While the battery was in position the drivers of Forge and Battery Wagon went out with the wagon to forage for corn. We got but little on account of the lateness. Mutton soup for supper. On guard 1st relief.[27]

SEPT. 27TH, TUESDAY.
Rose before daylight and harnessed up. Fried mutton for breakfast. The line seemed the same as at the previous nightfall. Our battery went into position in its old place, but the caissons B. W. & F. remained standing in the same position as they were in during the night. All sorts of rumors were prevalent of all sorts of colors. Went down to the river on a venture and filled some canteens. Also washed first time in two days. The Shenandoah here is very rapid and a beautiful stream. Mutton soup for dinner, to get the water for which I had to go over a quarter of a mile. All the forenoon I could see our line in the lowlands very distinctly, but not the rebs. About 1 P.M. a brisk firing opened far up on our right and it seemed as if the rebs must have got a slight advantage, as our whole division went some distance to the rear and left and formed again, our battery taking position on an eminence. We lay here about 2 hours and I managed to get a good bundle of hay for my horses out of a neighboring barn.[28] While we lay here in position with cavalry formed up on all sides of us, Gen. Custer came riding through, and immediately cheer after cheer rent the skies, for he had just been promoted from commander of our brigade to Averill's division.[29] N. B. We were attached to the Michigan brigade on the 24th inst.[30] Custer looked the very beau ideal of a dashing cavalry general as he went cantering by with his floating yellow ringlets streaming behind, and his lithely elegant figure well set off by his rich brown short jacket and bright scarlet cravat. His somewhat fanciful attire looked completely in character and not as though put on for show. He looked so easy and dashing, and withal young and interesting that I did not wonder his old comrades cheered him. Besides he is as brave and able as he is good looking. As he rode by, he took his slouch hat off and shook it in the air. —From this position we moved about dark about 2 miles farther to the rear and camped for the night. Right above us towered the high peak which is the southern extremity of the Manhattan Mts. Far to our right and rear I could see what I judged to be the rebel camp fires on the side of the Ridge. Just across the Shenandoah from our extreme advance and just behind our advance skirmish line there was quite a town which I learned to be Port Republic.[31]

Sept. 28th, Wednesday.
Reveille at 3 a.m. Breakfast and harnessed up. Supply train came up with rations. N. B. We have been better supplied with rations this march than on any other that I remember. We lay here in harness 'til well into the afternoon when we moved back to our old position of yesterday on the Shenandoah and the rifle pieces went into position on the brow of the hill. I could see our skirmishers advancing in the fields below, but they found nobody. Our guns fired one shot and shortly after limbered up and we went into camp right on the hill.[32] —A very tedious day. I noticed that in this part of the country there was more sugar cane cultivated than corn.

Sept. 29th, Thursday.
Rose as usual at 3 a.m. There was no forage for the horses but luckily I had saved a little corn for mine. Shortly after daylight we harnessed and the whole brigade moved to the rear about a mile, where we turned around and came back. We paused on the top of the hill a couple of hours and then more cavalry joining us, we crossed the river and its north fork.[33] We passed through Port Republic which is a neat little village with one church. We continued our march along the mountains, gradually bearing to the right and west. At length we crossed the middle fork of the river and halted upon the high ground on its west bank. All along the progress of our march was marked by flames and smoke as the cavalry burned barns and mills, and of the latter there were many. Felt gloomy and lonely. Lying here about two hours, when we resumed our march it became evident what the delay was for, for burning barns in every direction met our sight. All barns containing forage were set afire. An immense amount of property must have been destroyed. Besides all the horned cattle and sheep were driven off. The cavalry said that 2000 horned cattle and sheep were collected. This nearly pays off what the rebels captured from us at City Point a short time ago.[34] All the afternoon our course kept bearing to the right until the Blue Ridge which in the morning had been on our left now was on our right. We were returning in the direction of Harrisonburgh. Just at night we struck a pike which we followed nearly due north for about an hour when we crossed what I judged to be the north fork of the Shenandoah and entered the beautiful town of Mt. Crawford.[35] All about lay the infantry. We had rejoined the army. Just beyond the town we camped in a ploughed field. Mt. Crawford is about 8 miles from Harrisonburgh.

Sept. 30th, Friday.
For a novelty we were allowed to sleep 'til daylight. Harnessed and hitched in about 2 hours & moved off in an easterly direction about a mile and camped on the top of quite a hill. I suppose we were on the army's left flank. Managed to get a good wash and changed my clothes, first time for 2 weeks. Spent the rest of the day in foraging hay, corn &c. As it looked threatening we pitched a paulin and brought straw from a neighboring barn for a bed. A very busy day. Reported that the infantry fell back.[36]

Oct. 1st, Saturday.

Rained heavily all night. Lay abed nearly all day. Did nothing else save forage for the horses. Toward night went with Benward and got a sheep just as the cavalry were driving them to the rear.[37] On guard as orderly for the officers. A tedious day. Rained nearly all the time.

Oct. 2nd, Sunday.

Sun rose misty. Splendid fried mutton for breakfast. Boot and Saddle about 9 a.m. and the wagons went to join the trains. Could hear skirmishing in the front. One of our rifle guns went into position on a high knoll in front and fired a few shots. About the middle of the afternoon we went about a mile to the rear where we lay in park until we could see the skirmishers engaged on the hill we had just left. About 4 p.m. we moved back about 2 miles farther, reached the pike, and went into camp after dark.[38] Had to go 1½ miles to water and outside the pickets.

Oct. 3rd, Monday.

Reveille at 4 a.m. Harnessed and moved just after daylight about ½ mile to the front and lay in harness an hour. Then we moved off toward the ridge in a northeasterly course marching over very rough roads. At length we halted and the battery went into position on a high hill while we with the wagons went a short distance to the rear in a field near a barn. Here were a flock of sheep and our mess immediately seized one and dressed it. We were just getting our supper when we had to move. We continued our course and suddenly we found ourselves on the same hill we had occupied on the 27th when we fell back from Port Republic. Lay harnessed up 'til nightfall when we unhitched and unharnessed. It had been raining spasmodically all day and now it came down in torrents. By the time we had watered and pitched a paulin and built a fire I was wet through. Nevertheless we boiled a pot full of mutton and rather late at night lay down on hay without any covering and slept soundly with feet to the fire.

Oct. 4th, Tuesday.

Harnessed at daylight. Three of our old men went home discharged, among them Frank Mann with whom I had been messing since leaving Sandy Hook.[39] Felt somewhat sad. Dried all my blankets & c, washed my dirty clothes, and did a number of small jobs so that the day was pretty well occupied. Pitched paulin again at night. As far as I could make out it appeared as though our brigade were stationed here to hold the left of our line, which I judged to rest on the high mountain which forms the commencement of the Manhattan Mts. At night could see our signal lights on its very highest pinnacle. Fair all day.[40]

Oct. 5th, Wednesday.

Harnessed about daylight but unharnessed again right away after breakfast. For a week now the horses have had to depend upon foraging for their maintenance, and owing to the abundance of green corn and hay have lived very well. They have had all the hay they could eat of the best quality. Took opportunity to wash all over. About the middle of the forenoon quite a large body of cavalry passed our camp going to the left. They passed gaily with bands playing. There must have been two or more brigades of them. Wrote a letter to Myra. Quite warm all day.

OCT. 6TH, THURSDAY.
Shortly after daylight we harnessed up suddenly and the whole brigade took up column of march on the road back to Harrisonburgh which place we reached about 9 A.M. There we joined more cavalry. I was struck by the different appearance of the town from what it was when we first advanced through it. It looked weary, out-at-the-elbows, and dispirited. The several confederate hospitals seemed still to be full of wounded. Just the north side of the town we left the pike on our right and took a very rough and stony road that ran along the base of the North Mts. Our course all day long lay up the valley northeast. There was no trace of infantry. I suppose the main body of the army had been gone a day or two. It rained occasionally and was cloudy and misty all day. At length marching steadily we reached a small village on a hill, by name Timberville.[41] Here we camped for the night and found plenty of forage for the horses. This day's march was very wearing to the horses owing to the roughness of the road. During the whole of our stay in this valley, we were in a very rocky country, a peculiarity directly contrary to what prevails on the other side of the Ridge. Limestone abounds and I saw several kilns. Along the route of this day's march the habit of burning barns and granaries and mills was continued. Great columns of smoke everywhere rolled heavenward and obscured a distant view. Great flocks of sheep and cattle were also gathered from the poor farmers and driven off. It was a sad sight. Famine needs must follow in the winter it seems to me. When we advanced the valley looked smiling, beautiful and peaceful. Now everything looked weary and war-worn. Fences all down, barns burnt or torn to pieces, and *everything* plainly showed what had passed. At times during the day I could see the mountains that bound the valley on either side. The valley seemed not more than 8 or 10 miles wide. —Out of the immense flocks that the cavalry had gathered anyone was permitted to choose what he pleased. We had had so much mutton that I would not take a sheep. Somewhere in the neighborhood of our camp the boys found a quantity of "Apple Butter" which I tasted for the first time. It is made of sweet apples and cider and tastes quite pleasant. Booth's time out and he relieved from duty.[42]

OCT. 7TH, FRIDAY.
Two months more to serve. Rose at daylight, harnessed, hitched and watered. Continued march in same direction and *everything* was a continuation of yesterday, barns, cattle and all. About the middle of the forenoon passed through Forestville which to me looked like a forlorn village cast away up on a rocky lee shore. Four miles beyond there is another little village, the name of which I did not learn. As we passed a house near here with its barns all in flames, it gave my heart

a twinge to hear and see females weeping. —The horrors of war. About noon we came in sight of the pike and a R. R. Here also I saw infantry marching. Again turning off to the left we pursued a road parallel to the pike and at a distance of two miles crossed a shallow stream and halted on the hill beyond. The little town of Edenburgh could be seen on the pike from here. After a delay of about 2 hours, the column moved off in the direction of the pike, but I remained with the forge on which they were mending the broken axle of one of our caissons. While we lay in that place we could hear occasional firing in the rear. When the axle was mended we started off in the direction of the pike which we struck at the little town of Edenburgh. Here I saw a R. R. which must be the Manassas Gap R. R.[43] At the point where the R. R. bridge over the stream had been destroyed was one piece of Battery K in position. Moving along the pike northward about 2 miles, we camped for the night on a high hill by the roadside. A brigade of the 19th Corps was so far behind that we camped just as they were passing. Booth and three others left the battery with their discharges. These are the last before my own and Jewell's. Pleasant and warm all day. March about 20 miles.

OCT. 8TH, SATURDAY.
Rose before daylight and shortly moved out still retreating. About 4 miles from Edenburgh passed through the town of Woodstock which is considerable of a place. At the southwest corner of the place our cavalry had fired a barn which bade fair to burn half the town. It was terrible to see the white faces and tearful eyes, and hear the loud weeping of the women. Just outside the town our two rifled guns went into position while the rest of the battery went into position. Passing on about 4 miles farther we halted and again the battery went into position. I could hear occasional shots far back. By and by a heavy engagement opened on our right and lasted 'til night. The cannonading was quite severe.[44] Just before sunset Lieut. Church took the caissons, forge and battery wagon down the pike and parked just within the infantry lines. We could not have been more than a mile or two from Strausburgh. Just before we halted we passed over a portion of the pike that afforded a weird night scene. The road shelved round and down a mountain. On our right the pine-clad hill rose steeply, while on our left far below us were the infantry fires along the ravine. Dark shadows passed and repassed before the fires and the bustle of an encamping army came to our ears in the pauses of a fitful wind. All day long it had been so cold as to necessitate an overcoat, and toward night the wind rose 'til it was bitter cold. Wood was scarce, and so after watering and tying my horses to a large stone, I lay down in a paulin and slept nathless the cold. Just before going to bed I had supper of mutton broth, and made some tea for Lieut. C.

OCT. 9TH, SUNDAY.
Fed before daylight and started back on our tracks. Joined the battery about a mile from where we left it. Lay there about an hour and got breakfast. The rebels woke up in the same quarter as the fighting had been yesterday. Imme-

diately we moved up on the hills to the right of the pike. I had just time to see the preparations for a fight, to see the rebel line and ours, and see the batteries open, when we were ordered back to join the wagon train. Just as we struck the pike again, the rebels showed themselves and skirmishing commenced about a quarter of a mile from us. We went back on the pike about two miles and parked with the train. For two or three hours the fighting seemed quite severe. We lay still all day doing nothing save to cook and eat. After dark we moved out to Woodstock with the whole headquarter train. On the way passed 4 rebel guns which had been captured during the day. They were all 3 inch rifles and U. S. manufacture. They were dragged by the poorest and scraggiest specimens of horses I had ever seen. The harness was all assorted, odds and ends, anything to get along. Some of them had 4 horses, and some only 2. One had two mules. One had been dismounted and carried off in a wagon I was told, but I did not see it. When we arrived at Woodstock I learned that we had driven the rebel cavalry over ten miles, and they had run in the most disorderly manner leaving wagons, ambulances, forges, and more guns along the route. We captured in all 11 or 12 guns and they chucked one more into the river. It was a most complete victory for our cavalry, and we captured about all their horse artillery. We reached Woodstock about 10 P.M. and found the battery encamped near the town. Fed and went to bed.[45]

Oct. 10th, Monday.

Reveille before sunrise. Awoke to a very raw morning. Heavy frost on the ground. At daybreak, moved back again to within about 4 miles of Strausburgh and went into camp on a hill. In the P.M. went over to the neighborhood of the Ridge to forage hay. Just as I was leaving with my bundle I heard some shots and afterward learned that the guerillas had made a dash. Whether they did any mischief I did not hear. On guard, 1st relief.

Oct. 11th, Tuesday.

Fair and warm. Finished my guard duty. About 1 P.M. harnessed up, and the whole division moved back through Strausburgh and camped on the bank of the north fork of the Shenandoah about 5 miles from the town. As we passed by Fisher's Hill there was an opportunity to note the fortifications and I did not wonder that Early had chosen this place to make a stand. About 3 miles north of the town we found the army encamped. It seemed to me as though Sheridan intended making the Cedar Creek his line of defense in case the rebels should receive reinforcements. —Our camp was in the midst of a little valley and close to the river. Not two miles from us was the northern extremity of the Manhattan Mts.

Oct. 12th, Wednesday.

Lay in camp all day for a novelty. Cloudy and rainy. Pitched a paulin. Mess with Dresher.[46] Went across the river for hay but got only cornstalks. There was a fish weir in the river which the general had repaired. Mutton and cabbage stew for dinner.

Oct. 13th, Thursday.

Rainy during the night but morning opened windy and cold. Went across the river foraging, but after going 3 miles and a whole mile outside the picket line, turned back and took a bundle of cornstalks together with a nose bag full of corn in the ear. About the middle of the afternoon a sudden cannonading arose on the right, apparently where we had crossed Cedar Run two days before. The whole division saddled up and moved off to the right. The B. W. and F. [battery wagon and forge] followed with the wagon train. The train moved off to the west and just at sundown parked upon a high hill over which ran the turn-pike. All about were trains of wagons and ambulances, hospital tents, troops, & c. On the brow of the hill at the front were troops in line and batteries in action. The fighting was not very brisk. I could hear the cavalry fighting on the extreme right and it was reported that Custer had taken more artillery. I went to find my cousins in the 19th Corps and found that not one of them was with the regiment, —Charley Greene having been wounded at Winchester, and had been amputated as to his thumb. Just after dark the train started on again going westward and about a mile out found our div. already gone into camp. It seemed to me that our div. took up a position on the right flank of the army. Watered and fed, and went to bed.

Oct. 14th, Friday.

Reveille at two o' clock. Harnessed and hitched, but lay in the same place 'til the middle of the afternoon, doubtless in readiness for a flight. Then we moved a few rods into another field and went into camp. Stretched paulin.

Oct. 15th, Saturday.

Cold and windy. Wrote to Myra. Had the dumps all day. Just at dark the section of 12 pdrs. went out on a raid or reconnaissance with a heavy force of cavalry taking 5 days' rations. Capt. Martin went. Charley De Voe started for Harper's Ferry after the mail. This was by Lieut. Clark's orders, the Capt. refusing to do so before he left. No mail in a month and no letter from Myra in 10 weeks.

Oct. 16th, Sunday.

Windy and sunny. A lazy day. About the middle of the forenoon our section came back together with the whole force which had gone with it. They had been as far as Front Royal and came back without seeing a rebel. The fellows came into camp looking black and dusty. Wrote to Bethiah.

Oct. 17th, Monday.

Routed out at 3 A.M. by an attack on our pickets by a guerilla force. Harnessed and hitched and lay thus 'til daylight when we went into camp again. Occupied all the forenoon in washing clothes. Slept all afternoon. Fair and warm all day. This day was one of the Indian summer, beautiful and healthful.

OCT. 18TH, TUESDAY.

At morning water call went out 3 miles into the country after apples with Churchill. Crossed Cedar Run and came up with the reserve picket. As we came back, met Gen. Custer and Staff who were going out doubtless to visit the pickets. I had a better view of him than ever before, and was struck by the extreme brightness of his yellow hair which he wears long in ringlets. He looks quite old in face in comparison with the remainder of his appearance. Wrote a letter to the Journal. Cleaned camp for inspection.

OCT. 19TH, WEDNESDAY.

Another morning alarm which turned out to be an attack in earnest. Volley after volley was heard from the right and afterwards from centre. Shortly the whole division filed off to the right while we went to the rear (B. W. & F.) with the wagons and joined the division train. About an hour after daylight the battle began to rage fiercely and soon it seemed that the rebels were driving our forces. Stragglers began to appear and report disastrous news with loss of artillery & c. The train moved off by a side road that ran parallel with pike and in about an hour we heard no more of the battle. The train moved rapidly and in about 2½ hours we made Winchester and parked near the pike at its northern extremity. All of the army trains accompanied ours. Soon news came of a turn in the battle and the success of our arms. Our retreat with the wagon train had been very rapid and we had accomplished the whole distance in about 2 hours. —Toward night the sound of cannon again came from the direction of Strausburg. We lay north of the city 'til about sunset when we moved back again through the town apparently intending to return to Strausburg, but just south of it we turned about and returning, parked in the same place as at first. Got to bed, such as it was, about midnight. The horses remained harnessed all night.

The *Middlesex Journal* and *Woburn Townsman*
Saturday, October 29, 1864

Our Army Correspondence
Strausburgh, VA,
Oct. 19, 1864

Dear Editor: —The October sun rises glorious and grandly from its bed behind the ridge, to shine mellowly and health-giving over this valley, long time so famous. The buoyant days so longed for while suffering beneath the enervating summer glare, have come. The hazy space beneath the skies is lambent with health and joyousness. One seems almost to see the health giving essence as it floats on the breeze. Hoar frost hath begun to paint the woods. The nearer forest spreads out decked in gorgeous hues, while farther on the landscape melts into smoky blueness that clothes the mountain bases. The very atmosphere seems to possess brightness, and to envelope all objects, not hang upon them. The sounds of army life come to the ear with a mellowness that this season only giveth. They come floating slowly through the breeze as though but the echo of some still more distant noise. The season's atmosphere rounds the rougher angles of sound, as it were, and brings it to the ear softly and creepingly. Softly blowing gales breathe health and joyousness. Movements are made more brisk, and gracefulness of action, save of the fashionable invalid order, is promoted. Life, that seemed newly born when fair April powdered the woods with living green, and had e'erwhile languished through the sultry summer months, now receives fresh vigor. The mind gains equal tone with the body and lifts grateful praise to Him who behind nature is the renewer of all life. Man takes a fresh lease of existence, and should of immortal life. Body, mind and soul, how intimate is their connection, and how is the welfare of the latter influenced through both the former.

Returned from a three mile ride to Cedar Run, your whilome [*sic*] correspondent somewhat intoxicated by the air of an exquisite October morning, as doubtless your readers have already perceived, attempts to write up the log since last accounts at Washington early in Sept. It would take much larger space than you would feel willing to concede to make, by any degree a detailed account of our wanderings since leaving the Capital on the 15th ult. A scrap here and there must therefore suffice.

Our march to Harper's Ferry was indeed pleasant, and from it I was enabled to gather more of the real character of the Maryland country than ever before. On the lower Potomac it partakes on a great degree of the shiftless appearance of seceded Virginia, whereas in these more northern portions comfort and plenty and neatness seemed very general. From Washington to Sandy Hook the country is of a pleasantly diversified and pastoral character, abounding in beautiful views of quaint old villages and smiling landscapes. I will only mention one and that the little town of Hyaltstown [*sic*], a gem hidden in a hollow.[47] We came upon it suddenly from the top of a high hill. Far below, and running part way up the opposite hillside, reposed the quiet little town, its painted and white washed buildings here and there lined and shaded by the then unfaded green. It looked too nice to be reality and have a name. The charm was loosed when we were able to make a nearer inspection, for it looked like Goldsmith's deserted village in the first stages of its decay.

We arrived at Sandy Hook, on the Potomac, on the 19th, after a very leisurely executed march, the whole distance being about 58 miles. At this place we remained just long enough to hear the all-day roar of the battle at Winchester, when we started down the Valley to join the cavalry and relieve Battery D, 2d U. S. Art'y.[48] The night of the 21st, we made Charlestown, next day Winchester. At this latter place we encamped for the night right upon the battlefield, and amid its freshly rising odors. The city swarmed with wounded, and everywhere in the green fields that surrounds it, the debris of battle could be seen, and still sadder evidences. Dead horses dotted the sward, a broken or blown up caisson here and there, the little enclosure of rails containing wounded, heaps of fresh earth with simple head-board made from a cracker box, traced the track of the hurricane of war. Occasional and simple funerals anon came from the hospitals within the city, with slow step and muffled drum, to show that not yet had ceased the results that flow behind the glory-giving steps of War. This was a victory for us, and how the northern pulse jumped as they read of it from the papers. They did not mourn, for sure our enemy suffered more than we. The killed of ours were not many.[49] But, Ah's me! many's loved one wept out his life in bloody tears. Victory is glorious, but to estimate it justly the prostrate men that heap its course must be seen.

The succeeding day we passed on the turnpike going south of Kernstown, Newtown and Middletown, halting for a short space at Strausburgh. From the latter place we moved out to the east about 4 miles, and joined the 3d Div., of cavalry. Strausburgh is a small town upon the north fork of the Shenandoah, and is situated just at the point where the valley materially narrows by reason of the jutting out from the main range of the Blue Ridge, of a short range, which is laid down upon the map as the Manhattan mountains. Winchester had been chosen by the rebels for their first stand, because of its already fortified position. The position at Fisher's Hill, near the town of Strausburgh, was chosen, doubtless, because of the narrowness of the valley at that place, and the consequent security of the flanks which rested upon opposite ranges. The distance from mountain to mountain is not more than 6 or 7 miles.

We had reported to the 3d Div., and had sufficient time to unharness and water the horses, when, most unwelcome sound, the bugle blew "to horse." It was just night-fall. We marched that night 'til within two hours of daylight, over the roughest, stoniest roads which I believe exist in America. Our course was straight up and through the mountains. By the fitful, struggling moonbeams we could now and again discern the nature of our course which daylight, I make no doubt, would show to be most picturesque. At one time we struggled across the broad and rapid river led on by a glimmering signal fire that shone from the further bank, immediately to ascend the mountain by a steep, shelving road that went up, up, seemingly for miles. How many dangers we escaped in the dark was never known, or how many precipices our carriage wheels shunned perhaps only by an inch. Once as we climbed the mountain side by a diagonal shelf that only courtesy would call a road, we passed a dismal picture. A traveling forge had fallen off the road into a declivity of about 15 feet, dragging with it is six horses and three drivers. It was a weird though sickening sight. The sickly glare of two or three candles that seemed struggling with the heavy and still night air, and the sounding rush of the river flowing below and behind us were concomitants of a scene as strange as any ever novelist described.

The group of men around holding their horses by the bridle just came within the circle of light the centre of which was the form of a man who had been crushed in the fall. There he laid, his pale face doubly pallid under the candle's sickly ray, and making no movement save a convulsive working of his hand. I shuddered as we passed and plunged into the gloom higher up.

I will not be tedious by attempting to describe the sunrise in the mountains, which was gorgeous in the extreme. The succeeding day we had passed the series of ranges that constitute the Manhattan mountains, and emerged into the lovely valley of Lewray [*sic*], which is contained between them and the Ridge.[50] The full beauty of this valley pen scarce can describe. It is an alternation of waving fields, green groves, gay meadows, and intersecting brooks, the whole enclosed in a beautiful mountain rim that seemed to hem it in on all sides. The mountain ridges themselves are most beautiful, the hugest of crags draped in a mantle of variegated green and dark brown. It is no figure of speech to say *"draped"*, for the mantle of forest seemed to rest on the peaks, and flow down to the valley in most graceful folds, owing to the innumerable smaller offshoots of the mountain. The valley smiled through tears that day. Small smoky clouds would float and gather along the mountain tops, and pass before the gazer like a thin veil, at the same time discharging their moisture without touching him, although it rained quite heavily not a dozen yards distant. It only made the hills look more lovely, like ladies' faces seen behind illusion veils.

At times dark, threatening clouds would shadow half the valley, rain fall in the other half, while on the distant mountain tops dwelt the serenest sunshine. Within the midst of the valley, upon a gentle knoll, civilization had placed the finishing charm, in the shape of a pretty village from which the whole valley had taken its name, Lewray. The whole scene smiled before us as we descended the mountain side, yet beautiful as it was, War's dreadful fingers had been here before us. Everywhere torn fences, dead horses, scattered saddles, sabres, and carbines, and occasional graves, proclaimed the southward surging contest.

After driving the rebels down the valley, the cavalry corps recrossed the mountains at a point farther south and emerged into the Shenandoah Valley at the town of Newmarket. From thence southward laid our route along the turnpike as far as Harrisonburg. This place contained many rebel wounded, as I judged from the grey-clad and placarded cripples that seemed quartered there. From H. we took a course about southeast, and rounding the southern extremity of the Manhattan mountains, came out upon the south fork of the Shenandoah river, where the village of Port Republic is situated upon its opposite bank. Here we struck the rebels once more and had quite a severe skirmish, but could do nothing, as they had infantry to defend their rear, which was passing through Brown's Gap to the east side of the Ridge, while we had left ours at Harrisonburg, some eight miles distant. As Sheridan had thus driven them out of the valley, our forces went no farther, except a small body of cavalry to Staunton, to destroy some rebel ordnance stores. But I will not trespass upon your columns further. Perhaps another letter will be able to tell your readers of the fall back to this place, which is four miles north of Strausburgh and fourteen miles south of Winchester.

Yours, &c., HOPLITE

OCT. 20TH, THURSDAY.
Soon after daylight moved back again to the south side of town, where we could water the horses. Trains commenced to go toward the front about the middle of the forenoon, but we did not get in motion 'til afternoon. Reports came in of great success to our arms and capture of prisoners and artillery. Our march was very slow owing to the length of W. train, the whole of the 6th Corps train being in front. At Newtown the train doubled up on the pike so as to go in two lines. This was for safety against guerillas. About a brigade of infantry was our guard. At Newtown we found the army hospitals. The town was crowded with wounded. We passed a train of wounded among whom was one of our battery. We reached Middletown after dark and parked about ½ mile south. We found the army had taken its old position with the exception of the cavalry which was in pursuit of the fleeing rebels. We had captured all their wagons, artillery and many prisoners.

OCT. 21ST, FRIDAY.
Fair and very warm. We lay in park 'til near the middle of the forenoon, and I improved the opportunity to visit Sheridan's headquarters and see the trophies of our victory, which had been of the most complete description. There were parked in a row about 50 pieces of cannon and many caissons. Besides there were 300 mules & horses, many wagons, ambulances, rifles, and all kinds of munitions. There were also about 1100 prisoners. —We had totally routed the rebel army and taken not only all our own cannon back but nearly all theirs beside.[51] —About noon we moved about a mile to the east of the pike along the road on which we had been encamped on the 12th and 13th. Shortly the whole division joined us and we camped in an open field.

OCT. 22ND, SATURDAY.
Very cold and windy. Occupied nearly all day in making a beef's head soup. In the engagement of the 19th one of our fellows, named Ancony, had his hand taken off by a rebel shell.[52] Charley Oliver's horse was wounded.

OCT. 23RD, SUNDAY.
Cold all day. Wrote to Myra.

OCT. 24TH, MONDAY.
Cloudy with some rain. Moved tent to front of battery. Busy all day, but accomplished nothing. Letter of thanks from the President to the army read out at roll call.

Oct. 25th, Tuesday.

Fair and sunny. Horses without grain now for two days. Wrote to Mother.

Oct. 26th, Wednesday.

Fair and warm. Train came up and with it Charley De Voe bringing a large mail. I received 13 letters and 6 papers, and a package of paper. The horses got feed again after being 3 days without. Fighting in Luray Valley.

Oct. 27th, Thursday.

Rainy and cold all day. Wrote letter to Journal. Wrote also to Myra. Put on guard for missing morning roll call.

Middlesex Journal, Saturday, November 12, 1864

Our Army Correspondence

Middletown, VA.

Oct. 27, 1864.

Dear Editor: —Like storms that come and go across the face of Ocean, so battles stir the current of an army's life. Engagements, large or small, excite more remark and occupy attention for a longer time among the civil community at home than among those who have been actual participants in the struggle. Soldiers forget surprisingly quick the dangers to which they have been exposed. And so the late battle and glorious victory near this place has already become a stale subject to the soldiers of the Middle Military Division. Perhaps your readers may find a little interest in the relation of how a battlefield looks at the rear, as they have already many times read descriptions of how it seems at the front. Your correspondent has before this written to you his impressions gathered amid the blaze and glare of the contest, and now is able to present things as seen a safe distance behind the line of battle.

Two divisions of the cavalry corps had covered the right flank of the army in its position on Cedar Creek, previous to the battle of the 19th inst. Early on that morning we were roused from our blankets by an imperative summons from the bugle to "boot and saddle." Shortly after which could be heard volleys of musketry. This caused no alarm as everybody knew Custer to be on the extreme right, and we were all the more undisturbed that he had but two mornings before entirely frustrated a similar attack upon his pickets. It appears that this was but a feint on the part of the rebels to cover their flanking operations on our left. About daylight they came down in heavy force upon our left flank, and made desperate pushes to gain a position in our rear on the pike. The firing grew terrific and ever seemed to edge round to our left. The cavalry disappeared upon the extreme right, while the wagon trains gathered thick about the pike hastening to quit the vicinity of the battle. With one of those trains duty called your correspondent to go. For many minutes we awaited opportunity to move out in the direction of Winchester, the avenue of movement being all choked with ambulances, forges, wagons, &c. All the while the battle seemed to surge nearer and nearer until its outer waves began to reach us in the shape of wounded and stragglers. As it came our turn to move out I almost began to think the battle would reach us, for looking back the fields were thickly dotted with the fleeing forms of our broken soldiery. The 8th Corps had entirely broken up and was seeking the rear in great disorder. Small bodies of cavalry here and there yet stood firm and managed to detain many of the flying infantry. As we filed into the woods in the direction of Winchester, I took one last look and judged we had been quite soundly thrashed. As we made our way along by-lanes, through orchards, across ditches, and crashing over half-torn down trees, stragglers overtaking us gave out most dismal stories of captured men and artillery, while every now and then a loaded ambulance or limping wounded man bore testimony to their truth. At first we moved so slowly that even the wounded went by us, and for a time the battle seemed to gain ground upon us. As the long column of wagons straightened out, we moved more swiftly until at length our walk changed to a trot, and then to a gallop. Every now and again a short delay would occur as some unfortunate wagon broke down, and then the whole train would close up again leaving it to its fate. Small trains would occasionally attempt to enfilade the main column and then would occur the most extraordinary jamming. Oaths were plenty, and threats of shooting. Whips snapped and lashed violently. All was hurry and crush, with an occasional smash. Yet with all nobody was hurt. In two hours the whole of the immense train reached Winchester and parked at its northern extremity, having made a progress which was indeed wonderful for wagons. From Cedar Creek to W. it is about 14 miles. Toward noon we lost all sound of the battle. About the middle of the afternoon as we valiant soldiers in the rear were leisurely getting our dinner the boom of cannon rang out again fiercely from the south. At night came the news of our wonderful and unexpected success. So thorough a defeat to either party in the east had not happened since Bull Run. The rebels threw down their arms, and each man ran his own way.

As far as the condition of his army would permit, Gen. Sheridan pursued the enemy, collecting arms, prisoners, and artillery at every step. Two days after the fight the open field in front of Gen. Sheridan's headquarters, was crowded with the captured armament and equipments of Early's army. Guns, caissons, ambulances, prisoners, horses, mules, small arms, were all jumbled together in a strange confusion, the fruits of victory. Of a certainty, the rebels must at least receive reinforcements of artillery before they attempt to face us. It is reported that prisoners have stated a section of artillery to be all that Early now has of that arm of the service. My comrades in the battery are loud in praise of the cavalry who on that day actually charged lines and columns of rebel infantry, repeatedly. Some claim that the fortune of the day was turned by their means. And in sooth everybody unites in their praise.

On the field of battle they charged hither and thither, and like a sharp sword blade, cutting whichever way they turned. Our battery lost but one man, whose hand was taken away by a rebel shell.

The army has again settled into its old position, its front along Cedar Creek, and its left flank resting on the Shenandoah. Perhaps it may again be a battlefield. Our div. (the First) holds the extreme left, while Custer, I am told, still occupies the extreme right. Power's, lately Averill's division, are said to be in the Luray Valley to prevent flanking by way of Front Royal. Cannonading was heard all day yesterday in his direction, the cause of which has not yet transpired. The picket line of the whole army extends a distance of about six miles.

In the whole of the campaign which commenced with the battle of Winchester, no general has won more praise than Custer, and in this last fight he has fairly doubled his laurels. He is a great favorite and everybody claims that he has nobly earned the second star on his shoulder. He seems to possess all the fire and courage of Kilpatrick, but infinitely more judgment. In personal appearance his is the very model of a dashing cavalry officer. His figure is slight and elegant and he sits on his horse most gracefully. His costume is a dark red velvet cavalry jacket, with pants of a light drab. His long yellow hair flows out from beneath a broad brimmed hat, and streams in ringlets far behind him as he rides along at a swift canter. His features are strongly marked and pale. His voice is heavy yet musical. The members of his old brigade always cheer him when he passes, and he always returns the compliment by waving his hat above his head. No wonder he is admired when to graces of person he adds excellence of mind. When he lifts his hat his fair complexion and hair, and finer contour of head give him the look of a young Apollo.

Space does not permit a description of our falling back from Mt. Crawford to this place. It was accomplished by the groans and tears of an impoverished community. Fires are dreadful viewed singly, but pen cannot describe the terrible effect of a whole landscape in flames. Not a barn escaped that contained the least portion of grain or forage. The property destroyed must amount to millions. As Sheridan burnt all the barns and fodder, so, doubtless to prevent the poor cattle from starving to death the coming winter, he drove them all off. Perhaps it was to shut off all supplies to the rebel commissariat, as some say, that he did this. In the general conflagration part of the town of Woodstock was fired by accident. It happened as we were passing through. I shall never forget the scene. Families turned out of house and home hurried down the street to escape the flames, fathers and mothers with arms full of helpless children, and others hanging on to their garments. Terror stamped every countenance. Thus the terrors of war reach beyond the battle field. Let your readers be thankful they live so far from the actual scene of conflict.

HOPLITE

NOV. 1ST, TUESDAY.
Got permission to go out of camp and took a ride over to 19th Corps. None of my cousins had yet returned to their regiment. After some running about I found the regiment to which Wilbor Kimball belongs, but did not see him as he was out of camp washing. Lay abed in the afternoon.[53] On guard, 1st relief.

NOV. 6TH, SUNDAY.
Warm again. Took a ride over to the 38th M. V. and saw Wilbor Kimball. It appeared to me he looked younger than when I saw him several years ago. Rainy toward night.

NOV. 7TH, MONDAY.
Rainy all day. Felt shiftless.

NOV. 8TH, TUESDAY.
Finished tour of guard duty. Rainy and cloudy all day. About the middle of the forenoon "boot and saddle" sounded and we harnessed up. Watered and fed in harness and finally just at nightfall went into camp again. An unpleasant day.

NOV. 9TH, WEDNESDAY.
Still cloudy and rainy. Lay all day in expectation of moving. Once partly harnessed to have a review but finally concluded not to have it. All the infantry pickets withdrawn. Wrote to Myra.

NOV. 10TH, THURSDAY.
Reveille at 4 A.M. harnessed and hitched and about 8 o'clock moved out on the pike with the whole division. Found that the infantry had all gone. The other side of the pike could see the 3rd Division also in motion. As we halted there I took a look at the mountains and they were indeed beautiful. They appeared like burnished copper seen through a pink veil. We got upon the pike at Middletown. All about the town were evidences of the late fight, dead horses, graves, houses pierced with shells &c. &c. the positions of the fight were pointed out to me and houses which our battery shelled to drive away sharpshooters. At Newtown we found the infantry garrison and pickets had not been removed. A mile north of that place we found the army camped in two lines and Gen. Sheridan's quarters at a large stone house. We struck off the pike there and made our way across the fields to the left of the infantry line and in a S. E. direction. Camped in the middle of an open field on very wet and soft ground. We went to water still farther to the S. E. and found what had once been a plank road running north and south. This was probably the direct road between Winchester and Front Royal. Along it was encamped Powell's div. of cavalry or a part of it. Pitched paulin and made bed with cedar boughs. Received a mail, 2 letters from Myra, one from Mr. Davis and one from "the boy", also two papers.

Nov. 11th, Friday.

Fair and warm. A very busy day. Put up harness rack. Built bunks. Put up picket. Dug sinks. Just at nightfall heard quite a severe musketry fire in the direction of Newtown.

Nov. 12th, Saturday.

Reveille at 4 a.m. got breakfast and fed horses, and then harnessed up immediately. Struck tents. The battery moved out in the direction of Newtown, but the forge, battery wagon & c. remained behind. The wind rose 'til it became bitter cold. About dark the battery returned and we pitched tents again.

Nov. 13th, Sunday.

Still very cold and windy. Everything was a repetition of the preceding day. The battery came back at nightfall having made a reconnaissance as far as Middletown. Went on guard at night, 2nd relief, and I never stood a colder tour of guard.

Nov. 21st, Monday.

Reveille at a.m. Fed, breakfasted and harnessed. Moved about 8 a.m. in the direction of Winchester. Marching about 2 miles, we halted at the little town of Kernstown and went into camp in a grassy field just outside heavy oak woods. It was cloudy all the morning and commenced to rain just as we had got our tent up. Nevertheless we built a sod fireplace and chimney in our tent, in the doing of which I got wet through. Rained heavily all the evening. When we broke camp in the morning the cavalry did not go with us but the whole division took apparently the road to Front Royal. One section of battery C. & E. 4th U. S. went with them. I did not feel sorry that we had left this camp although we had built our log house, for it was so very muddy as to be uncomfortable. The rebels were reported to be retreating up the valley.

Nov. 22nd, Tuesday.

During the preceding night the weather became freezing cold and very blustering. Occupied nearly all the forenoon in chopping firewood. Grew colder as night approached. Only two weeks to serve.

Nov. 23rd, Wednesday.

Slept coldly. This day much colder than the preceding. Could do nothing scarcely but hug the fire. Put up harness rack. Exercised horses at water call. Toward night returned to old camp. Cavalry all came back from their scout. Weather moderated considerably just at nightfall. Mail came in bringing a letter from Myra and one from Bethiah with picture.

Nov. 24th, Thursday.

Cold but not windy. Wrote to Myra and to mother.

Nov. 25th, Friday.

Much warmer and pleasant. Wrote to Griffin. Went on guard at night 3rd relief.

Nov. 26th, Saturday.

Finished my tour of guard. Only one more for me before my time is out. Cloudy all day and rained toward night. Horses had hay for first time in six weeks.

Nov. 27th, Sunday.

Fair and sunny but mud very deep under foot. Wrote to G. F. Mann. Orders to pack up in readiness to move. On fatigue, but duty very light.

Nov. 28th, Monday.

Reveille at 4 A.M. Breakfasted and hitched up immediately. At daylight the cavalry moved out to the front while we moved back to the vicinity of corps headquarters for safety while they were gone. Owing to a balky horse in one of the swing teams, the forge came near to getting stuck in the mud. We camped in an apple orchard close to Kernstown and only a short distance from our camp of a week before. Cloudy but warm. No rain.

Nov. 29th, Tuesday.

Most extraordinarily warm and pleasant, almost a summer's day. Took a ride to the 19th Corps and visited Wilbor Kimball whom I found on fatigue duty building fortifications. Took dinner with him. The works which the army had made here are of the most thorough description. They were very nicely built and very strong. The troops had not as a general thing gone into winter quarters. The 5th N. Y. Battery was building some very nice stables. Got back to camp about 2 P.M.

Nov. 30th, Wednesday.

Pleasant but with a high wind. Wrote to Myra. Letter from Myra, her last to me in the army.

Dec. 1st, Thursday.

Fair and warm. Although rations were due the preceding night, we did not get them 'til this night. Many of the fellows had been without food for 24 hours. A division of the 8th Corps passed our camp going in the direction of Winchester, reported to be going to Petersburgh. Among it I found an old acquaintance, John Damon, of Reading, and had quite a talk with him. Had not seen him in four years.[54] Went on guard at night 3rd relief. My last tour of guard I trust in the army.

Dec. 2nd, Friday.

Did not feel very well at my stomach all day. Lt. Church ordered two hours extra guard duty for not grooming my horse. Mem. No tyrants over me after four more days! Cloudy all day and commenced to rain about middle of afternoon. Grew cold and windy again toward night.

Dec. 3rd, Saturday.

Cloudy all day. On fatigue but had scarcely anything to do. Packed up in expectation of moving, but did not. The 3rd div. of the 6th Corps went back on the pike probably to join Grant's army. Cleaned harness. Just at night our division came in from the raid upon which they had been absent and a great many of our fellows got sheep. The division had brought in three or four thousand beeves, sheep and swine. Our mess got a sheep, very fat and young.

Dec. 4th, Sunday.
Harnessed immediately after breakfast and returned to our old camp. All of our house was yet standing and we once more occupied it. Jewell left for home, his time out.

Dec. 5th, Monday.
Cold all day. An irksome day, apparently 48 hours long. Although rations were due the preceding night, still we did not get them 'til after taps of this day. Capt. Martin had to raise a muss to get them. Made my supper off boiled beef alone. This was my last day of service.

Dec. 6th, Tuesday.
Turned over all my equipments after morning stable call preparatory to being mustered out. About 10 a.m. took my mustering-out rolls over to division head-quarters, and found the commissary of musters, Col. Parnell, had gone to Winchester. Saw his clerk who showed me that my rolls were wrong and gave me a blank set. Went over again at 4 p.m. with the new rolls and found he had not yet got back. Was told to come in the morning.

Dec. 7th, Wednesday.
Went over to headquarters about 9 a.m. and was told to come again in an hour, which I did. Was then told that Col. Parnell would do no more mustering as he was about to turn accounts over to a Capt. Gordon of the 2nd Cavalry. Was told to call at 3 p.m. [O]n calling at that hour, the clerk told me to come again in an hour and a half. At five p.m. called and waited about an hour when Capt. Gordon came in and signed the papers and I was once more a free man. Owing to the delays this day was one of the uneasiest of my whole life. Fair and warm.

Dec. 8th, Thursday.
It came up cold during the night and this morning opened so frosty as to freeze the water on my hair while washing. About 9 a.m. the wagons being ready, I bade adieu to all my comrades and officers, and started for home after three years service as a soldier. God be praised for his protecting care. The ride to Stevenson's Depot was a very cold one. I drove John's (the negro) six-mule team a part of the way. Stevenson's Depot, the terminus of the W. & P. R. R. R. is about five miles north of W. and is in a little clump of oak woods. The depot of stone had been burnt and stood roofless. Huge trains of wagons gathered thick about the track loading forage and subsistence supplies. Got my R. R. transportation at the office of the A. O. M. by showing my discharge, and then learned no train went out 'til

1:15 P.M. I was surprised to see that they had not started to build any buildings at the depot. About 1:30 P.M. the train started over a little the roughest R. R. that ever was built. The ties were laid on top of the ground and rails spiked to them. As we rode along I noticed that the road formerly had been made in a novel manner, having instead of rails long heavy planks with a binding of iron for the wheels to run upon. It took us nearly two hours to get to Harper's Ferry. Arrived there, we went to Gen. Stevenson's headquarters and received our order upon the Q. M. for transportation over the B. & O. R. R. upon showing my discharge.[55] I saw three of the General's staff, and was struck by their stylish appearance, one in particular, who was, I think, his A. A. G. At the Q,. M.'s office I got another order, sealed, on the ticket master of the R. R. for transportation to Washington. The ticket master gave a written order on the conductor and then made tracks for the cars which were standing on the track ready to start. I was very fortunate to catch them as they were much behind the usual time. Just as I was getting into the cars saw Frank Rombach who had horses and was evidently Woodruffe's orderly. The cars were very full and I was compelled to get into a baggage car which was already crammed full of convalescents and furloughed men returning to their regiments. In fact each man possessed about 2 square feet of room and we were so mixed up that really I wasn't positive which were my own legs. After many and long delays we at length arrived at the Relay house, time about midnight. When I got out of the cars I was more dead than alive for the cold was intense and the wind came through the car cuttingly. Lay in the Relay House 'til four A.M. when the Washington train came along and off we went again.

DEC. 9TH, FRIDAY.
Arrived at Washington just at daylight and immediately hurried down to Furbush's establishment.[56] Stable call was just sounding in Camp Barry. I roused up Furbush and had breakfast, ham and eggs. I was half famished only having eaten 2 hardtack for 24 hours. After breakfast rode down town with Furbush. Left Furbush and went up on H. St. to Maj. Taylor's to get Bounty and pay. After lying around in the cold for about four hours I got it and made a straight line for Maryland Avenue. Bought hat and socks. Met Furbush and friend coming and went back with them to Central G. H. They went in and I waited outside. Got tired of waiting, went in and bought pants, collars and neckties. Took warm bath. Hurried toward Camp Barry. Bought a pair of fine boots next door to F's. Dressed up and hurried back to Depot but found I was too late. Went down to Exchange and took room for the night. Went down to Ford's theatre to see Miss Maggie Mitchell play Fanchon. Acting just passable. Saw two old faces beside hers. I do not think I did wrong, will consider the point and talk with Myra. I think I can do my duty and fear God, and also go to the theatre. When I am convinced otherwise will not go. I do not think this night's amusement estranged me from God. When I came out of the theatre it was snowing fast with two inches already on the ground.

DEC. 10TH, SATURDAY.

Slept poorly. Got up at daylight, dressed and hurried to the depot. Found I was half an hour late for the train I wished and took the 7:30 A.M. train. At Baltimore walked across the city and found no train went out for Harrisburgh 'til 3 P.M. took some breakfast and waited in the Susquehanna Hotel. I was surprised and shocked to be accosted by two or three small boys with, "Want to see the ghals?" Gave a poor woman some money, also a little girl who came through the cars begging. Got started from Baltimore at 3 P.M. and reached Harrisburgh about 8. Found I could not continue my journey 'til the following morning. Went to the theatre and saw J. B. Roberts as Carwin. Was convinced of the wrong tendency of theatre going. Lodged at the Farmer's Hotel.

DEC. 11TH, SUNDAY.

During the night managed to get up in my sleep and smash three panes of glass, bruising my knuckles and costing me $1. Got up in time to take the morning train for N. Y. Reached Elizabeth about 3 P.M. where I go out of the cars. I waited in a hotel near the depot until the 6 o'clock train came along from N. Y.

Cornelius Miller
and George Perkins.
Courtesy of Michael T.
Russert.

on the Phila. R. R. which I took and arrived in Rahway very shortly, the distance being only 5 miles. Found that Corneille was not at home, but was very kindly received by his parents. At 9 P.M. I went down to the depot where I saw Conger and Thorne. On the arrival of the train I saw Corneille, also his fiancée. Went down to her house where I was introduced to a Miss Lainy and Mr. Woodruffe and stayed for about an hour. Returned to his house and turned in after one of the most fatiguing days for a long time. Corneille seemed in good health and was dressed quite richly.

DEC. 12TH, MONDAY.

A very busy day though cold. Corneille fitted me out in a citizen suit and we went all over Rahway. Saw a great many old members of the battery and made a great many new acquaintances. Visited and made the acquaintance of his half cousin Laura Miller, whom I that night took to Elizabeth to hear John B. Gough lecture. Corneille and Miss Martin went, also Miss Lainy and Mr. Woodruffe. Had a very pleasant time, supper at the hotel, &c. subject of lecture was "Eloquence and Orators." It was a very pleasant evening although not very instructive. Thought he caricatured the pulpit orators too much to be entirely reverent toward God. Got back about 10 P.M. and spent a short time with Miss Martin.

APPENDIX A

AFTER ACTION REPORTS

The following eight after action reports provide detailed information on the role of the Sixth New York Independent Battery in the following events: the Battle of Malvern Hill, the Expedition to Rappahannock Station, the Battle of Kelly's Ford, the Chancellorsville Campaign, the Battle of Brandy Station, and the Gettysburg Campaign. All of the documents provide important information or perspectives missing from the diary.

The reports can be divided into two groups. One group relates to actions that were not covered adequately in the diary, either because of a gap in coverage or because Private Perkins was not well placed to observe the activities described in the reports. The second group adds the perspectives of officers with command responsibility to the detail provided by Perkins's diary.

The first group includes Malvern Hill, Brandy Station, and the Gettysburg Campaign. Captain Bramhall's Malvern Hill report provides details of the activities of the battery during the final phase of the Seven Days before Richmond. During this period, Private Perkins was not with the battery and did not witness its participation in the movements and actions associated with the final act of the Seven Days. During the Brandy Station battle, Perkins was on furlough and did not rejoin the battery until it returned to camp. Thus, the after action reports submitted by General Gregg, who commanded the cavalry force to which the battery was attached, Captain Martin, who commanded the battery, and Lieutenant Wilson, who commanded a detached section of the battery, provide the only detailed information concerning the role played by the Sixth New York. The battery was so roughly handled at Brandy Station that it was detached for refitting and did not rejoin the army until just before the Battle of Gettysburg. Captain Robertson's report confirms the Sixth New York was present with his First Brigade Horse Artillery during the battle, although not engaged, and was detached to join Gregg's Second Cavalry Division shortly after the battle. Because of the June–October 1863 gap, the diary is silent concerning this period.

The second group includes the 1862 Expedition to Rappahannock Station, the Battle of Kelly's Ford, and the Chancellorsville Campaign. The

Expedition to Rappahannock Station was important for the Sixth New York because it was apparently instrumental in the decision to convert it from a mounted battery, with a primary focus on infantry support, to horse artillery assigned to cavalry operations. Captain Bramhall's report is explicit in describing the wear and tear suffered by a mounted battery engaged in a quick strike cavalry operation. Similarly, the reports concerning the Battle of Kelly's Ford and the Chancellorsville Campaign supplement the diary's detailed description with the perspective of its commanders.

PENINSULA CAMPAIGN–SEVEN DAYS' BATTLES

JUNE 25–JULY 1, 1862

CAMP NEAR JAMES RIVER, VA., July 5, 1862.
CAPTAIN: I beg to submit for your consideration the following report of the movements of this battery since its departure from Fair Oaks, on the 28th ultimo:
At 6.30 p.m. the 28th ultimo I reported, by order of Brigadier-General Heintzelman, commanding Third Army Corps, to his headquarters at Savage Station, coming into position in the immediate vicinity. At 6 o'clock the next morning I was ordered to follow the column then moving down toward the White Oak Swamp Bridge. I marched that day to a point about 2 miles beyond the bridge, halting for the night near general headquarters. The following morning I moved forward to the position of General Hooker's division, and receiving from that general an order to continue the march toward the James River, I followed the column, arriving at noon in the place upon the bluff near the river then occupied by the Artillery Reserve, reporting, as directed by General Hooker, to General Porter. At 3.30 p.m., by order of General Porter, I moved back upon the road up which we had come and came into battery upon ——— Hill in a position to command the same road, co-operating with Lieutenant Ames' battery in our front and on the right, a battery of 10-pounder Parrotts and Captain Osborn's battery of four 3-inch guns on our left, with a support of two regiments of General Morell's division distributed among these several batteries. I remained in this position until the next morning, July 1, at 6 o'clock, when, by order of General Porter, I took up a position to the right of the road up which the army had marched 200 yards in front of a wood, to command either of two approaches which intersected on the side of the woods on which we lay. I was instructed that our pickets were a short distance in advance in the wood and upon both roads, and that if attacked they would retire through the wood, and emerging at the junction of the two roads, fall back upon the main line.

At about 7 a.m. the pickets, having been attacked, fell back rapidly, and in a few minutes the fire of the enemy fell among us and passed over our heads. Our pickets having retired in order and in the manner indicated I immediately opened fire upon the woods in front and on the right, firing at first the Hotchkiss case shot with 2" fuses. For a few minutes the enemy manfully withstood the fire, advancing and firing. At this time the firing from my battery was very rapid being at the rate of two shots a minute from each piece. That it was effective I am induced to believe from the fact that after about five minutes the enemy's fire ceased almost entirely. Upon this we gradually increased the range and lengthened the fuses until we reached the 5" fuse, using both case-shot and shell, but mainly the latter, and scattering our fire Generally through the woods. At this time, too, I used, for experiment's sake as much as for any other reason, a half-dozen percussion shell (Schenkl's percussion) which we had found and appropriated at Fair Oaks. The result was a perfect success, every one bursting, though some of them fell upon soft meadow-land. Our fire now grew very slow and deliberate, being maintained by order of and in the manner prescribed by Brigadier-General Griffin, in command at that point.

At about one hour after opening fire, being ordered to report to Brigadier-General Heintzelman, we ceased firing, and moved from our position to that indicated by yourself, near General Heintzelman's headquarters. From that time until the present the battery has taken no part in any movement beyond retiring, on the morning of July 2, with the corps of Generals Sumner and Heintzelman to the plain immediately upon the river, from where, by your order, we moved yesterday to our present camp.

I have to report but one casualty among my men, that of Private John H. Vennett, slightly wounded in the leg by a fragment of a shell while the battery was moving from one position to another. One man is still missing, but I hope yet to recover him, he having been known to have gone in advance with the wagons.

It affords me much gratification to testify to the gallant and spirited conduct of my officers and such of my men as were well enough to accompany the battery. Exposed as they had been for five days to almost uninterrupted fatigue, hardship, and privation, with little or no rest and almost nothing to eat, they were always ready to meet their duties, which they performed with alacrity, cheerfulness, and I may say success. I beg to refer particularly to the case of Private William R. Colby, an intelligent lad of twenty years of age, who, having become separated from the battery when near White Oak Swamp Bridge, volunteered his services to Captain Porter, of the First Massachusetts Battery, and served gallantly during the battle of 30th of June, as testified to by Captain Porter in a note which I have received from him.

The main damage which I have sustained during this movement has been to my horses, of which I have lost 9 on the route; one only from a positive injury, the rest having dropped in harness during the last day's march, utterly incapable of being moved. I was already short in the number of my horses before starting, and until I can have time to rest those which I have (95, of which only 80 are effective), and to recuperate their strength by care and sufficient food, I cannot undertake to move my battery any considerable distance.

An equal degree of prostration exists among my men; out of 138 present there being but 108 fit for any duty. My loss in equipments, implements, and accouterments has been but slight, and can doubtless soon be replaced. With rest from too onerous duty, regularity, and sufficiency of food I believe that in a short time I shall be able again to report the battery in as effective a condition as ever.[1]
I have the honor to be, very respectfully,

> W. M. BRAMHALL,
> Captain, Commanding Sixth Independent N. Y. Battery.
> Capt. G. A. DE RUSSY; U.S.A.,
> Commanding Reserve Artillery, Third Army Corps.

EXPEDITION TO RAPPAHANNOCK STATION

OCTOBER 6–9, 1862

HEAD QUARTERS, RESERVE ARTILLERY 3RD CORPS, October 10th 1862. MAJOR. [Maj. H. W. Brevoort, Assistant Adjutant General, First Division, Third Corps][2]: I beg to submit the following report of the participation of my Battery in the recent Expeditionary movement commanded by Col. Davies.

Pursuant to orders from Head Quarters I reported with the Battery to Brig Genl. Bayard Comdg Cavalry Brigade at 11 P.M. on Monday the 6th inst. at Bailey's Cross Roads. The command marched from this rendezvous at 3 O'clock the next morning, moving forward to Fairfax Court House, when a halt of half an hour was made, thence proceeding to Centreville at which place we arrived at about 12 M.

We remained here until 3 P.M., resting and obtaining forage for the animals. At that hour the march was resumed, one Brigade of Cavalry and one piece of artillery taking the advance, the balance of the Battery moving with the other Brigade of Cavalry. Our course lay through Manassas Junction, at which place we halted a half hour when we pushed on to Brentsville by a circuitous route to the left, arriving at that place at about 8:30 P.M. We rested until 12:30 A.M. when we again took up the march, moving steadily until 7 A.M. when we halted to feed the horses and men. After a rest of about a half hour we again moved on, this time proceeding by the Warrenton Road through Bristerburg Church towards Bealton.[3] Our march was rapid and steady. During all this period since leaving Centreville I had kept our place with the advance, moving of course at a more rapid gait than the main column and traveling a greater distance in Scouting upon the different divergent roads. By 8 A.M. of Wednesday I was forced to relieve the piece which had accompanied the advance that morning's march, the Excessive fatigue rendering the horses unable to keep up. During that day's march I was compelled to relieve three different pieces for the same reason. By 9 A.M. I began to observe Exhaustion in many of my horses, but Still hoped to keep up and accomplish the distance to our destination without retarding the rest of the force or occasioning any change in the movement. At this time we had marched a distance of 60 miles in 30 hours, with only such intervals of rest as I have specified. It was not therefore in the least degree Surprising that my horses were beginning to tire, indeed it was a wonder to me that Such had not before taken place. From this hour Every Succeeding mile traveled only made matters worse, until finally when within five miles of Rappahannock Station two of my teams fell from Exhaustion and many others were Staggering in the harness. I was [unreadable word] to think of proceeding further even had the object of our mission been a peaceful one, but under the circumstances when it was more than probable that the Battery would be required to assist very materially in covering our return, it was only too apparent to my mind and to my Company Officers with whom I conferred upon the subject, that it would be impossible for us to perform that duty without running the greatest risk of losing our pieces one by one. I accordingly reported this condition of affairs to Col. Davies Commanding the Expedition and declined to be accountable for any mishap which might occur to the Battery if we were compelled to proceed further. Owing to these representations on my part and to the fact that he had received ~~reliable~~ intelligence which he deemed reliable to the effect that the Property which we were to capture had been removed across the Rappahannock some days previous, the Colonel Commanding, after sending forward a detachment to proceed to the point (Rappahannock Station) reversed the column and we set out on our way back about noon. We marched as far as Bristerburg Church that afternoon and bivouacked for the night. Shortly after arriving at a halt one of my horses dropped dead from Exhaustion whilst the rest were in a deplorable condition.

We marched the next morning at 2.30 O Clock, moving towards Brentsville by a road to the east of the one which we had gone down on, arriving at Brentsville at about 9½ O Clock. Our forage being all consumed we remained long Enough to obtain forage, fed, and at about 11 A.M. resumed the march, proceeding by the direct and Short route to Manassas. The manner in which the Battery marched during the homeward journey attested only too well to the damaging effects of the Excessive marching it had done, and also to the wisdom of the course adopted in returning even as late as we did. Had we been pursued by the enemy in any force I could have done nothing further than make a desperate defence without the Smallest probability of being able to retire in face of the face of the pursuing forces. Had that occurred I should doubtless be obliged to now to report the loss of the Battery in place of its pre-sent unsatisfactory conditions, which is but a few removes from that misfortune.

Before reaching Centreville (at which place I suppose the Battery arrived at about 5 P.M.) I left instructions with Lieut. Martin my senior 1st Lieut., to halt at Centreville and remain there until Sufficiently rested to come on to Camp without any further injury to the horses, whilst I would proceed to Camp and forward Supplies to him. Upon arriving in Camp at a late hour last night I immediately dispatched to him the few remaining horses in Camp and a proper supply of forage and rations for his men.

Of course it will be impossible until the Battery returns to Camp, to correctly report its condition and I can only Say that when I last saw it, it was totally unfitted for field duty. It occasions me much regret to be compelled to make Such a report for before the movement my Battery was in fine condition and Excellently qualified to perform any duty which comes legitimately within the Scope of a mounted Battery, and you may well believe it to be a Source of exceeding regret to me to See it reduced to such a deplorable condition. My men, though worn out with fatigue, (having been obliged to walk much of the way) can of course Soon recuperate, but in the matter of horses I shall require Either considerable quiet and rest or a large number of new ones.

I beg to express my acknowledgements to Col. Davies Commanding the Expedition for the consideration he Showed to my Command, regulating all his movements with a view to the relief and benefit of the Battery as far as was consistent with the duty he had to perform.[4]

> I am Major
> Very Respectfully
> (Signed)   W. M. Bramhall
> Capt. 6th Indpt. N. Y. Battery.

BATTLE OF KELLY'S FORD

MARCH 16–18, 1863

CAMP OF 1ST BRIGADE HORSE BATTERIES, NEAR ACQUIA CREEK, VA, March 19th, 1863

LIEUT: I beg to submit the following report of the participation of my battery in the recent expeditionary movement commanded by Brigadier-General Averell:

Pursuant to orders from headquarters Cavalry Corps, dated March 15, 1863, my battery took up its march from camp near Aquia Creek at daybreak on the morning of the 16th instant, but owing to the fact of the guide having mistaken the road, I did not reach Hartwood Church until 4 p.m.

Upon my arrival there, I reported to Colonel Curtis, and received an escort to Morrisville, which place I reached at 11 p.m.

We halted, fed the horses, and moved forward with the column at 4.30 a.m. of the 17th instant, arriving at Kelly's Ford at about 6.30 a.m.

Upon arriving at the ford, skirmishing commenced between the cavalry pickets of the enemy and our advance. The enemy here making a very stubborn resistance to our crossing, I was ordered to advance one piece into position, with a view to cover the axmen who were employed in removing the obstructions to the ford, which being accomplished, our cavalry advanced to the ford. After one or two attempts, a crossing was effected and the enemy driven in all directions, some 30 prisoners being taken, together with horses and equipments.

At this time I brought one more piece into position, to cover the crossing of the main column, which, being effected, my battery went forward, piece by piece, over the ford, one squadron of cavalry carrying over the ammunition by hand, which was necessitated by the depth of the water. We then moved forward, and our advance came up with the enemy about half a mile from the ford.

At this time my right section was ordered forward, and, after advancing a short distance, the cavalry became engaged with the enemy, who were in force. Owing, however, to the narrow and extremely muddy and impracticable condition of the road, I could bring but one piece into battery, sending the others to the rear. The enemy now appeared in such force as to momentarily check the advance of our cavalry, which, however, soon rallied, and drove them from the woods, their left flank being turned by our cavalry on the right, with which was posted two of my pieces, commanded by Lieutenant Clark, and which did good execution. The enemy were driven across the plain in the greatest confusion.

At this time I received an order from Lieutenant Rumsey to bring my whole battery into position into the open field from which the enemy had been driven. This order I executed at once, calling in the two pieces which were posted with the cavalry on the right, as also the two pieces which were with the reserve. I formed my battery in line, and moved forward with the cavalry to the woods at the farther extremity of the plain, where we formed in battery to receive the enemy, who was expected to make a charge. At this point, by command of Lieutenant Rumsey, I left two of my pieces with the reserve, their ammunition being nearly exhausted.

After a brief delay, we again moved forward in column of pieces, with the cavalry skirmishing as they advanced for about a mile, and came into battery of four pieces in a large open plain on the left of the road. At this point we received from the enemy the first intimation that our farther advance would be opposed by artillery. They opened a fire with shot and shell upon our column as it came up the road, having three pieces in position commanding the road, consisting of two 10-pounder rifles and one 6-pounder gun. On their extreme right was posted another section of their artillery, which was not used, being probably held in reserve to check our farther advance.

Having already expended one-half of my ammunition, I had remaining 150 rounds when I entered this field, and could only fire, therefore, at long intervals, deeming it prudent to reserve my fire for the opposing columns of cavalry, and at long and uncertain ranges upon the enemy's artillery, as it was evident they intended to charge us at once.

In this conclusion we were not at fault, for the enemy soon appeared in force in our immediate front, extending from the right to the left of the road, with the evident object of driving in the supports on either flank of the battery. As I observed this, I opened upon them with shell at about 1,500 yards, and at a distance of, say, 1,000 yards with spherical case, continuing it until they arrived at about 400 yards, when, obliquing my sections to both flanks, I opened on them with double-shotted canister with great effect. Our cavalry at this moment charged the lines of the enemy, driving them back in confusion, when I immediately changed the direction of my fire to the enemy's artillery. It now became evident, both from the statements of wounded prisoners and other sources, that the enemy were being largely re-enforced both by artillery and cavalry. We, however, maintained our position for about an hour, replying at intervals to their artillery, which was most advantageously posted and commanded every approach by the front and flank, their cavalry being at the same time masked by the woods on either flank of their batteries, which kept up a constant and harassing fire upon us, to which, however, I could only reply occasionally, thinking it prudent to reserve a supply to cover the recrossing, should it be necessary to do so. Upon receiving an order from General Averell to fall back, I limbered up, recrossed the ford, and placed two pieces in position on the opposite bank to cover the crossing of the remaining columns, sending the balance to Morrisville with a regiment of cavalry, the First Rhode Island. The recrossing having been effected without loss, in conformity with orders I proceeded to Morrisville, where the column halted until daybreak, when we returned to camp via Hartwood Church.

As regards the loss of the enemy, I have no means of determining, but from my own observation I should say that it far exceeded ours, their prisoners saying also that they suffered very heavily.

As to the effect of this affair upon the morale of our cavalry, it only strengthens my belief in their superiority and efficiency over that of the enemy, as was clearly demonstrated in each encounter.

I beg to tender my acknowledgments to the staff and officers of General Averell's command for the courtesy and consideration shown to me and my command, it being the first occasion on which my battery has ever had the opportunity to maneuver with cavalry, and they were, therefore, perhaps in some respects deficient in the requirements of this branch of the service.

I have to report the following casualties: One man (Private Richard Paxton) and 2 horses killed; 2 sets of horse equipments unavoidably lost; 1 wheel for 6-pounder carriage badly damaged; 1 sponge-bucket and 2 handspikes lost; 6 sponge-staffs broken; 3 felling axes loaned to cavalry and not returned.

	Rounds.
Ammunition expended:	
Hotchkiss canister	32
Schenkl percussion shell	90
Hotchkiss shrapnel	100
Hotchkiss shell	25
Total	247.

I am, lieutenant, very respectfully, your obedient servant,
GEO. BROWNE[5], JR.
First Lieut., Comdg. Sixth Independent N. Y. Horse Battery.
First Lieut. C. F. TROWBRIDGE,
Acting Assistant Adjutant-General.[6]

HEADQUARTERS SECOND CAVALRY DIVISION,
March 20, 1863.
GENERAL: I have the honor to report that, pursuant to instructions received from
you, I left the main body of this army on the 16th instant, for the purpose of crossing
the Rappahannock River and attacking the cavalry forces of the enemy, reported to be
in the vicinity of Culpepper Court-House, under the command of General Fitzhugh
Lee. My orders were to attack and rout or destroy him. To execute these orders, I was
directed to take a force of 3,000 cavalry and six pieces of artillery. Accompanying the
orders were several reports containing information of the operations of rebel cavalry
north of the river, in the vicinity of Brentsville, the force of which was reported from
250 to 1,000, with at least one piece of artillery, and I was directed to take every precau-
tion to insure the success of my expedition. As a precautionary measure, I requested
that a regiment of cavalry be sent to Catlett's Station, which is the key-point to the
middle fords of the Rappahannock, to throw out from thence pickets in the direction
of Warrenton, Greenwich, and Brentsville. My request Was not granted, and I was
obliged to detach about 900 men from my force to guard the fords and look out for the
force alluded to in the information.

The battery ordered from near Aquia Creek made a march of 32 miles on the
16th, and joined my command at Morrisville at 11 o'clock that night, with horses in
poor condition for the expedition. Small parties of my cavalry had been sent, two to
four hours in advance, on all the roads and to the fords, to mask the approach of my
main body from the enemy's scouts.

On the night of the 16th, the fires of a camp of the enemy were seen from Mount
Holly Church by my scouts, between Ellis' and Kelly's Fords, and the drums, beating
retreat and tattoo, were heard from their camps near Rappahannock Station. Rebel
cavalry appeared in front of my pickets on the roads leading west during the evening
of the 16th.

Lieutenant-Colonel Curtis, First Massachusetts Cavalry, was left at Morrisville
to take charge of all my cavalry pickets north of the Rappahannock, who directed
Lieutenant-Colonel Doster, Fourth Pennsylvania Cavalry, with 290 men, to start from
Mount Holly Church at 4 a.m. on the 17th instant, and drive the enemy's pickets toward
Rappahannock Station; to go thence to Bealeton, and, finally, to station himself at Mor-
gansburg and communicate with a picket which would be established at Elk Run and
with Curtis' force at Morrisville. These orders were executed, and the enemy driven out
of that section.

At 4 a.m. I set out from Morrisville with a command of about 2,100 men, made
up as follows: From the First Brigade, Second Division, Colonel Duffie, 775; from the
Second Brigade, Second Division, Colonel Mcintosh, 565; from the Reserve Brigade,
Captain Reno, 760, and the Sixth Independent New York Battery, Lieutenant Browne
commanding. Kelly's Ford was selected for the crossing, because the opposite country

was better known to me than that beyond any other ford, and it afforded the shortest route to the enemy's camp.

The head of my column arrived at the ford at 8 a.m. The crossing was found obstructed by fallen trees, forming an abatis upon both banks, which, defended by 80 sharpshooters, covered by rifle-pits and houses on the opposite bank, rendered the crossing difficult. Two squadrons were dismounted and advanced under shelter of an empty mill-race or canal, which runs near the bank of the river, whence a brisk fire was at once opened, under which an attempt was made to cross by the advance, which failed. Two subsequent attempts of the pioneers met with the same fate. During this time a crossing was attempted one-fourth of a mile below, but it was found impracticable, owing to the depth of the stream and the precipitous character of the banks. After half an hour had passed in endeavors to cross, my chief of staff, Maj. S. E. Chamberlain, who had immediate charge of the operations at the crossing, selected a party of 20 men, and placed them under the command of Lieutenant Brown, First Rhode Island Cavalry, with orders to cross the river and not return. Lieutenant Brown obeyed his orders; the abatis was passed, and 25 of the enemy were captured.

Two pieces of the battery had been unlimbered, but I hesitated to open them until all other means should fail, as I did not care to give the enemy sufficient warning of my advance to bring him to attack me while astride the stream.

The First Brigade was immediately crossed and placed in position, followed by two pieces; then the Second Brigade, the remainder of the battery, and the reserve. The stream has a very rapid current at the ford, and was about 4 feet 5 inches deep. The ammunition was taken out of the limbers and carried over in nose-bags by the cavalry. The crossing was not effected without loss. My chief of staff, Major Chamberlain, fell with a dangerous wound in the head; Lieutenant [John P.] Domingo, Fourth New York Cavalry, was seriously wounded, and Lieutenant [Henry L.] Nicolai, First Rhode Island Cavalry, killed; 2 men killed, and 5 wounded; 15 horses killed and wounded.

My command was drawn up so as to meet the enemy in every direction as fast as it crossed, and pickets pushed out on the roads running from the ford.

From what I had learned of Lee's position, and from what I knew personally of his character, I expected him to meet me on the road to his camp, and I could not object to such a proceeding, as it would not make it necessary for me to march so far to a fight. My horses would be fresher and the chances of battle be more nearly equalized.

The horses of my command were watered by squadrons, and at 12 m. I moved on, with the First Brigade in advance. Looking toward the west from the ford, one sees half a mile in advance a skirt of woods on higher ground, around the right of which may be seen an open field. It is about one-fourth of a mile through the woods. When the head of my column reached the western edge of this timber, the enemy were discovered rapidly advancing in line, with skirmishers in front. I immediately ordered the Fourth New York to the right, to form front into line and advance to the edge of the woods and use carbines; the Fourth Pennsylvania to the left, with the same orders, and a section of artillery to the front to open fire. Sent to McIntosh to form line of battle on the right of the woods; Reno to send three squadrons to act as a reserve to the right, and one squadron up the road to support the center, and one section to the right with McIntosh.

The Fourth Pennsylvania and Fourth New York, I regret to say, did not come up to the mark at first, and it required some personal exertions on the part of myself and staff to bring them under the enemy's fire, which was now sweeping the woods.

They soon regained their firmness, and opened with effect with their carbines. At this moment I observed two or three columns of the enemy moving at a trot toward my right. I immediately went to the threatened point, and found that it was a question which should obtain possession of a house and outbuildings situated there. McIntosh soon decided it by establishing some dismounted men of the Sixteenth thereabouts, and the section of artillery soon opened with splendid effect. The right was then advanced into the open field beyond the house, and the enemy's left attacked by McIntosh and Gregg. Duffie in the meantime had formed the First Rhode Island, Fourth Pennsylvania, and Sixth Ohio in front of the left, and the enemy were advancing to charge him.

Perceiving his want of support, I called to Reno for three squadrons, and we went to the left at a gallop, while Duffie advanced in splendid order and charged the enemy. The gallantry of Duffie had, perhaps, made him forget to leave any portion of his command as a support, excepting the Fourth New York. Two squadrons of the Fifth United States rushed across the field, while Mcintosh came in on the left flank of a fresh rebel column, and the enemy were torn to pieces and driven from the field in magnificent style. Had it been possible to reach the enemy's flank when Duffie charged with the Fifth United States or Third Pennsylvania, 300 to 500 prisoners might have been captured, but the distance was too great for the time, the ground was very heavy, and the charge was made three minutes too soon, and without any prearranged support.

A little reorganization was requisite before advancing farther. It was necessary to form my line again and get stragglers from the Fourth New York and other regiments out of the woods behind, to assemble the sections of the battery, bring up the reserve, and give orders with regard to the wounded and prisoners. These duties occupied me half an hour or more. In advancing from the field we had won, I found the ground impracticable on the left of the road, by reason of its marshy condition. My left was, therefore, rested on the road, and the advance given to a squadron of the Fifth, under Lieutenant Sweatman. After advancing in line of battle three-quarters of a mile, driving the enemy before us through the woods, with the artillery supported by a column upon the road, we found ourselves through the woods and in the face of the enemy, drawn up in line of battle on both sides of the road half a mile in front. It became necessary to extend my line to the left as soon as possible.

The enemy opened two field-pieces upon the road with precision, and advanced upon both flanks with great steadiness. They were at once repulsed on the right. The squadrons to form the left were shifted from the right of the road under a terrific fire of shot, shell, and small-arms, and the enemy in superior numbers bore down on my left flank, arriving within 400 yards of the battery while it was unlimbering. Lieutenant Browne, commanding the battery, assisted by my aide, Lieutenant Rumsey, soon got two or three pieces playing upon them with damaging effect, and a general cavalry fight ensued on the left. We never lost a foot of ground, but kept steadily advancing until we arrived at a stubble-field, which the enemy set on fire to the windward, to burn us out. My men rushed forward, and beat it out with their overcoats. Here the enemy opened three pieces, two 10-pounder Parrotts and one 6-pounder gun from the side of the hill directly in front of my left. No horses could be discovered about these guns, and from the manner in which they were served it was evident that they were covered by earthworks. It was also obvious that our artillery could not hurt them. Our ammunition was of miserable quality and nearly exhausted. There were 18 shells in one section that would not fit the pieces, the fuses were unreliable, 5-second fuses would explode in two seconds, and many would not explode at all. Theirs, on the contrary, was exceedingly annoying. Firing at a single company or squadron in line, they would knock a man out of ranks very frequently. As soon as the enemy's heavy guns were opened, his cavalry advanced again on my right, strongly re-enforced. They were repulsed with severe loss by Walker, of the Fifth, and McIntosh. McIntosh and Gregg pushed on to their left flank until they came to the rifle-pits, which could not easily be turned. Their skirmishers again threatened my left, and it was reported to me that infantry had been seen at a distance to my right, moving toward my rear, and the cars could be heard running on the road in rear of the enemy, probably bringing re-enforcements.

It was 5.30 p.m., and it was necessary to advance my cavalry upon their intrenched positions, to make a direct and desperate attack, or to withdraw across the river. Either operation would be attended with imminent hazard. My horses were very much exhausted. We had been successful thus far. I deemed it proper to withdraw. The reserve was advanced in front and deployed to mask the battery, which was withdrawn, and the regiments retired in succession until the ford was reached and crossed without the loss of a man in the operation.

The country in which these operations were conducted is level and open, and had the ground been firm would have been eminently fitted for a cavalry fight.

The principal result achieved by this expedition has been that our cavalry has been brought to feel their superiority in battle; they have learned the value of discipline and the use of their arms. At the first view, I must confess that two regiments wavered, but they did not lose their senses, and a few energetic remarks brought them to a sense of their duty. After that the feeling became stronger throughout the day that it was our fight, and the maneuvers were performed with a precision which the enemy did not fail to observe.

The enemy's first attack was vigorous and fierce, and it took about an hour to convince him on the first field that it was necessary for him to abandon it. Between his first grand advance and his final effort there were several small charges and counter-charges which filled up the time.

I ought to mention that in front of the first wood there is a deep, broad ditch, along which runs a heavy stone wall, which served as a cover for my carbineers, but which was impassable for cavalry except around the right flank and where it was broken down in the center, and this impeded my operations somewhat. In the second field the enemy's cavalry force was superior to mine, but it was constantly repulsed, and when I withdrew my command it was with unabated confidence in our strength as against cavalry. I hoped that they would advance, but they made no demonstration worthy of notice, even while I was withdrawing my command.

The officers and men of the battery performed their arduous duties with alacrity.

Whatever of success may have attended this expedition, I am greatly indebted to the vigorous and untiring efforts of my staff, Maj. S. E. Chamberlain, First Massachusetts; Captains [Philip] Pollard and [Alexander] Moore, of General Hooker's staff, and Lieutenants [Charles F.] Trowbridge and [William] Rumsey; but to those officers and men of the command who exhibited the unflinching courage which attends a settled purpose, my thanks are especially due. For distinguished gallantry I beg leave to call your attention to the names of Maj. S. E. Chamberlain, my chief of staff, and Second Lieut. Simeon A. Brown, First Rhode Island Cavalry, who first reached the opposite bank. Colonel Duffié was conspicuous for his gallantry; his horse was shot under him. Colonel McIntosh, who had been left ill in camp, joined me at 1 a.m., at Morrisville, and showed during the day that he possessed the highest qualities of a brigade commander.

Captain Reno, whose horse was wounded under him, handled his men gallantly and steadily. Lieutenant Walker, of the Fifth, by his readiness and resolution, did much to repulse the enemy on our left in the second field, when the battery was threatened.

To avoid repetition, I would respectfully call your attention to the names of the killed and wounded, officers and men, in the inclosed list, as deserving of especial notice for distinguished gallantry. Several others had their horses shot under them, and nearly all performed their duty in a manner which cannot be surpassed for coolness and daring.

I inclose list of casualties, of which the aggregate killed, wounded, and missing is 80.(+)

Of the enemy, his force was reported by the prisoners first taken as five regiments, commanded by Brig. Gen. Fitzhugh Lee. Subsequently prisoners reported that he had been re-enforced, and that Major-General Stuart was present. His equipments were inferior, but his horses good. Many of his sabers were manufactured in Richmond. From all the sources, I can estimate the enemy must have left 2 officers and 68 men killed and seriously wounded on the field. If twice as many slightly wounded escaped, his loss in killed and wounded must have been over 200, and his loss in horses must be certainly as great as that of men. I think the above may be an overestimate, but it is made by combining carefully the reports of officers who were in different parts of the field, and who report from observation. The enemy's loss in prisoners was 47; 15 more are reported, but as yet I am unable to account for them.

I inclose a list of paroled prisoners, who are included in the 47. I inclose also tabular statements of losses of my command and of the enemy. I am compelled to believe that the reports of some officers respecting their losses have been carelessly made out, and that they may have been guided in their statement of numbers by the amounts for which they are accountable.

I believe it is the universal desire of the officers and men of my division to meet the enemy again as soon as possible.[7]

> I am, general, very respectfully, your obedient servant,
> WM. W. AVERELL,
> Brigadier-General of Volunteers, Commanding.
> Maj. Gen. D. BUTTERFIELD,
> Chief of Staff, Army of the Potomac.

HEADQUARTERS LEE'S CAVALRY BRIGADE, March 23, 1863.
SIR: I have the honor to submit the following report of an encounter on the 17th instant between my brigade and a division of enemy's cavalry, certainly not less than 3,000 mounted men, with a battery of artillery. My first intimation of their approach was in a telegram received at 11 a.m. on 16th, from headquarters Army of Northern Virginia. At 6 p.m. scouts reported them at Morrisville, a little place 6 miles from Kelly's Ford. At 1 a.m. another report informed me that the enemy had encamped at that place, coming from three different directions.

I that night re-enforced my picket of 20 sharpshooters by 40 more. I regret to say that only about 11 or 12 of them got into the rifle-pits in time for the attack of the enemy (owing to an unnecessary delay in carrying their horses to the rear), which commenced about 5 a.m. The force in the pits, under Capt. James Breckinridge, of the

Second, behaved very gallantly, holding in check a large force of the enemy, mounted and dismounted, for an hour and a half, killing and wounding 30 or 40 of them. I also ordered the remaining sharpshooters of the brigade, under that very efficient officer, Major [W. A.] Morgan, First Virginia, to move from their camps by daybreak to a point on the railroad where the road turns to Kelly's, half a mile from the railroad bridge and 3 from Kelly's, and the rest of the command was ordered to be in readiness to move at the shortest notice. At that time a force was reported to be at Bealeton, supposed to be their advance guard, and it was uncertain whether they would attempt to cross at Kelly's, the railroad bridge, or move on toward Warrenton.

The report that enemy's attack was made at Kelly's never reached me; and the first intimation I received from that point was at 7.30 a.m., to the effect that they had succeeded in crossing, capturing 25 of my sharpshooters, who were unable to reach their horses. I moved my command at once down the railroad, taking up a position to await their approach, ordering my baggage wagons and disabled horses to the rear, toward Rapidan Station. Some time elapsing, and they not advancing, I determined to move upon them, and marched immediately for Kelly's. First met the enemy half a mile this side of ford, and at once charged them. Their position was a very strong one, sheltered by woods and a long, high stone fence running perpendicular to my advance. My men, unable to cross the fence and ditch in their front, wheeled about, delivering their fire almost in the faces of the enemy, and reformed again, facing about under a heavy fire from their artillery and small-arms. The Third in this charge was in front, and First Lieut. [Bernard] Hill Carter, jr., was very conspicuous in his behavior. From that time it was a succession of gallant charges by the various regiments, and once by the whole brigade in line, whenever the enemy would show their mounted men, they invariably falling back upon their artillery and sheltered dismounted skirmishers. Their total advance was 2 miles from the ford. At that time my artillery arrived, and they were driven back, recrossing the river about 7.30 p.m., with us in close pursuit.

My whole command acted nobly; sabers were frequently crossed and fences charged up to, the leading men dismounting and pulling them down, under a heavy fire of canister, grape, and carbine balls. Had I my command in the order it arrived in this enervating section of country, and not weakened by the absence of four squadrons on picket, guarding a line stretching from Griffinsburg, on the Sperryville turnpike, to Richard's Ford, and by the large number of horses unfit for duty by exposure to the severe winter, with a very limited supply of forage, I feel confident the defeat of the enemy would have been changed into a disorderly rout, and the whole brigade resupplied with horses, saddles, and bridles.

Commanding officers of the detachments from the various regiments engaged mention in their reports as deserving especial attention—

In the Fifth: Private William J. Haynes, Company F (badly wounded); Private A. R. Harwood, Company E; Private Henry Wooding, Company C (especially commended; seized the colors when the horse of the color-bearer was shot, and carried them bravely through the fight); Sergeants [John W.] Morecocke and [George B.] Ratcliffe, and Private George [W. E.] James, Company H. In the Fourth: Captains [W. B.] Newton and [Charles] Old, Lieutenant [J. D.] Hobson, and Adjutant [Peter] Fontaine (seriously wounded). Sergeant [W. J.] Kimborough, of Company G, deserves particular notice; wounded early in the day, he refused to leave the field. In the last charge he was the first to spring to the ground to open the fence; then dashing on at the head of the column, he was twice sabered over the head, his arm shattered by a bullet, captured and carried over the river, when he escaped, and walked back 12 miles to his camp. Lieutenant-Colonel [William H.] Payne, commanding, also mentions Privates Joseph Gilman, J. R. Gilman, Poindexter, Redd, Sydnor, Terry, and N. Priddy.

In the Third: Captain [William] Collins, Company H; Lieuts. [Bernard] Hill Carter, jr., and John Lamb, of Company D; Lieutenant [H. W.] Stamper, of Company F; Lieut. R. T. Hubbard, jr., Company G, and First Lieutenant [J. W.] Hall, of Company C (was twice wounded before he desisted from the charge, and when retiring received a third and still more severe wound, and was unable to leave the field). Adjt. H. B. McClellan is also particularly commended for his gallantry; also Acting Sergt. Maj. E. W. Price, Company K; Private [C. A.] Keech, Company I, and Bugler Drilling. Sergeant [G. M.] Betts, of Company C; Privates [W. W.] Young, Company B; [F. S.] Fowler, Company G, and [J. T.] Wilkins, of Company C, died as became brave men— in the front of the charge, at the head of the column.

In the Second, the commanding officer reports that where so many behaved themselves with so much gallantry he does not like to discriminate.

In the First: Captain [C. F.] Jordan, Company C, and Lieutenant [R.] Cecil, Company K, specially commended for reckless daring without a parallel.

As coming under my own observation, I particularly noticed Col. T. L. Rosser, of the Fifth, with his habitual coolness and daring, charging at the head of his regiment; Col. James [H.] Drake, of the First, always ready at the right time and place; Col. T. H. Owen, of the Third, begging to be allowed to charge again and again; Lieut. Col. W. H. Payne, of the Fourth, unmindful of his former dreadful wound, using his saber with effect in a hand-to-hand conflict, and the imperturbable, self-possessed Major Breckinridge, of the Second, whose boldness led him so far that he was captured, his horse being shot. Col. T. T. Munford, of the Second, I regret to say, was president of a court-martial in Culpeper Court-House, and did not know of the action in time to join his command until the fight was nearly over. I also commend for their behavior Captain [W. W.] Tebbs, of the Second, and Captain [C. T.] Litchfield and Lieutenant [G. W.] Dorsey, of the First; also Maj. W. A. Morgan, of the First.

My personal staff—Major [R. F.] Mason, Captains [J. D.] Ferguson and [S.] Bolling, Dr. J. B. Fontaine, and Lieutenants [H. C.] Lee, [G. M.] Ryals, and [Charles] Minnigerode—rendered great service by their accurate and quick transmission of orders and by their conduct under fire. Surgeon Fontaine's horse was killed under him, and my own was also shot, but through the generosity of Private John H. Owings, Company K, First Virginia Cavalry, attached to my headquarters, was quickly replaced by his.

The conduct of Couriers Owings, Lee, Nightengale, and Henry Shackelford deserves the highest praise.

The enemy's loss was heavy. Besides leaving a number of his dead and wounded on the field, he carried off a large number on horses and in ambulances. We captured 29 prisoners—1 captain, 2 lieutenants, and 26 privates. My own loss was 11 killed, 88 wounded, and 34 taken prisoners, making an aggregate of 133. In horses, 71 killed, 87 wounded, 12 captured, making aggregate loss of horses 170.

Among the killed I deeply regret to report Major [J. W.] Puller, of the Fifth, and Lieutenant [C. S.] Harris, of the Fourth, both gallant and highly efficient officers—a heavy loss to their regiments and country.

In conclusion, I desire especially to state that Maj. Gen. J. E. B. Stuart joined me before the fight commenced; was on the field the whole day; assisted immensely by his sagacious counsels, large experience, and by his usual daring and conspicuous example in turning the fortunes of the day in our favor. We share with him the anguish and deep grief felt at the loss of the noble Pelham, of his staff, an officer of the brightest promise for the future.

Major [Lewis F.] Terrell, of General Stuart's staff, beside being active on the field, assisted the gallant [Captain James] Breathed in the management of the artillery. Captain [Harry W.] Gilmer, Twelfth Virginia Cavalry, a volunteer for the occasion on the major general's staff, I also commend for his marked bravery and cool courage. I append a recapitulation of my loss.[8]

> Very respectfully, your obedient servant,
> FITZ. LEE,
> Brigadier-General, Commanding.

CHANCELLORSVILLE CAMPAIGN

APRIL 29–MAY 4, 1863

NEAR FALMOUTH, VA., May 9, 1863.
CAPTAIN: I beg leave to submit for your consideration the following report of the participation of my battery, the Sixth Independent New York, in the recent movements and engagements of this army:

In accordance with orders from headquarters First Division, Cavalry Corps, I marched from camp, near Potomac Bridge, on the 29th ultimo, at 6 a.m., with instructions to report to Brigadier-General Pleasonton at Grove Church, on the road leading from Hartwood Church to Morrisville, Va. I had hardly unparked the battery, however, when the order was changed so as to specify Hartwood Church instead of Grove Church.

At 4 p.m. (about one hour after I had arrived at Hartwood Church), I was ordered by the brigadier-general commanding to report to him with my battery at once at the United States Ford. I succeeded in getting the battery about 200 yards on the road leading to the ford, when, finding it impossible to proceed farther on account of the road being completely blockaded by the wagon and artillery trains belonging to the Second Army Corps, then en route for the ford, I left instructions with Lieut. George Browne, jr., my first officer, to push ahead with the battery as fast as possible, while I went forward to find General Pleasonton, if possible, and report to him the reasons of my delay. I arrived at Major-General Couch's headquarters about 9 p.m., but was unable to find any trace of General Pleasonton's whereabouts. Colonel Carroll, commanding a brigade in the Second Army Corps, advised me to encamp for the night as near to the headquarters of the Second Army Corps as possible, and report my position by letter to him, stating to me that he was in command of the pickets on General Couch's front; that General Pleasonton could not arrive there without his knowing it, and in case he did arrive he would immediately inform him where my battery was. I accordingly returned, and found, to my great disappointment, that the battery had been unable to advance more than 100 yards from where I left it. It was now 11 o'clock at night; my animals had been without food or water and in harness since 5 o'clock in the morning, and the road being no clearer than it was five hours before, I deemed it useless to make any further attempt to proceed, and accordingly went into park, reporting by letter to Colonel Carroll.

At daylight the next morning (30th ultimo) I was again moving, but it was 5 o'clock in the afternoon before I came in sight of the river. From the immense transportation and artillery trains which occupied the road and the fields bordering thereon, waiting an opportunity to cross, I saw immediately that it would be morning before I could get a chance to cross. I accordingly rode across the river, and reported to Major-General Couch. He told me that he did not know where General Pleasonton was, but that he had heard a rumor that he had crossed the river at Kelly's Ford, in advance of the Fifth, Eleventh, and Twelfth Corps. Still, of this he was not assured officially, and he therefore advised me to remain on the north bank of the river, and await further orders from General Pleasonton.

Upon this advice. I encamped on the bank of the river, and remained there until 2 o'clock on the morning of the 1st instant, when Captain Kennedy, of General Pleasonton's staff, reached me with the news that the general's headquarters were at Chancellorsville, and directed me to report there as soon as I possibly could. I immediately moved forward, and reported to General Pleasonton at 6 a.m. By his directions, I remained near his headquarters until 3 o'clock that afternoon, when I moved down the road leading to Ely's Ford, on the Rapidan, and encamped for the night with the remainder of the First Cavalry Division.

The next morning (2d instant) I had the battery harnessed at daylight, but until 3 p.m. the day was spent resting the command and gradually moving nearer to the front. At that hour (3 o'clock) the entire command was ordered out to pursue the retreating enemy.

Proceeding to the brick house at Chancellorsville, occupied by the major-general commanding as his headquarters; thence along the road (known as the Plank road) running in an easterly direction from the house about a mile, and turning from that into a road on the left side, I moved forward until I reached a large open field, where, by General Pleasonton's order, I formed the battery in line, and remained long enough to feed and groom the horses. Across this open field the Third Army Corps was moving in line of battle, while, in the woods and undergrowth beyond, the sharp musketry and artillery firing told plainly where the enemy were. In about three-fourths of an hour I was ordered forward with the cavalry, two pieces without caissons being placed in advance, under Lieutenant Browne. The remaining two sections marched directly in the rear of the Eighth Pennsylvania Cavalry. The column had hardly advanced 300 yards, however, before very rapid firing in our rear and vehement cheering, which I recognized too well as being from the enemy, was heard, and in a moment afterward I met the advance of our column returning, and received an order to reverse the battery and return to my former position. This was a slow undertaking, owing to the narrowness of the road, which necessitated the unlimbering of the carriages and reversing each portion of the carriages by themselves. Having accomplished this, I moved rapidly back, reported to the brigadier-general commanding, and by his orders formed the two sections of my battery in battery, bearing on the woods running at right angles with the road on which we had but a few moments before advanced, the remaining section (Lieutenant Browne's) being formed in battery on the woods in which we had just reversed. The front of the battery was shortly afterward changed to the right, the pieces thrown forward en échelon, and Lieutenant Browne's section brought into position on the right of and about 50 yards distant from the remainder of the battery.

The scene before me was one of indescribable confusion. The Eleventh Army Corps was panic-stricken, and the pack trains, ambulances, artillery carriages, &c., belonging thereto were rushing to and fro, many of the carriages without drivers or teamsters. Not more than 250 yards from the battery there ran a line of fence, and behind this appeared a line of infantry, but in the fast-increasing darkness it was impossible to tell whether they were our own or the enemy's troops. Lieutenant Clark asserts positively that he heard them say, "Do not fire on your friends," and these facts, combined with another, that they carried a flag, which, if not the American colors, was certainly very nearly the same as it, deterred me from opening fire upon the line.

On reporting these facts to the brigadier-general commanding, he ordered me not to open fire until I received orders from him, he in the meantime sending his aide-de-camp, Lieutenant Thomson, to ascertain the true state of affairs. I was not, however, compelled to wait for his report. He had hardly disappeared in the darkness before a bright line of fire and the sharp rattle of musketry told us who were in our front. Almost simultaneously came the order from the brigadier-general commanding to me to fire, and the engagement opened in earnest.

It is useless for me to attempt to describe the heat of the action or the difficulties under which the battery labored in maintaining its position. The brigadier-general commanding, from the exposed position which he kept throughout the action, in the center of my battery, saw it all, and it would only be wearisome to tell him what he saw as well as myself.

The fire of the enemy was very vigorous and well maintained. I trust that of my battery was equally so. The guns were served with great difficulty, owing to the way in which the cannoneers were interfered with in their duties. Carriages, wagons, horses without riders, and panic stricken infantry were rushing through and through my battery, overturning guns and limbers, smashing my caissons, and trampling my horse-holders under them.

While Lieutenant Browne was bringing his section into position, a caisson without drivers came tearing through, upsetting his right piece and severely injuring one of his drivers, carrying away both detachments of his horses, and breaking the caisson so badly as to necessitate its being left upon the field.

At the conclusion of the action, which lasted about an hour, Randolph's Rhode Island Battery, of light 12-pounders, took up position in front of mine, and, by General Pleasonton's instructions, I moved my two sections to the left of the position occupied by Lieutenant Browne's section.

In this position I remained until a little after daylight in the morning (3d instant), when, by General Pleasonton's order, I withdrew the battery to a position behind the headquarters of the major-general commanding, and from thence moved to the United States Ford. Before leaving, however, I went to headquarters to see if it was practicable to take a limber and bring off the body of the caisson which I had been obliged to leave on the field, but seeing that a battery belonging to the enemy occupied the position I had just left, I regarded it as hardly feasible.

I remained at the United States Ford, on the south side of the river, until 2 o'clock on the afternoon of the 4th, when, by direction of Captain Tidball, Second U.S. Artillery, to whom, by order of General Pleasonton, I had reported with my battery, I moved to the north side of the river, and encamped about a mile from the ford.

I should here state that, owing to the loss of horses and men, with the permission of the brigadier-general commanding, I had reduced the battery to two sections, believing that four guns, with full detachments and good horses, would be capable of doing better service than six guns badly horsed and imperfectly manned, and on the afternoon of the 3d sent the remaining section to the north side of the river, where my wagons, &c., were encamped.

At 2 o'clock on the morning of the 5th instant, I received orders from Captain Tidball to march to Falmouth, and arrived there at 11 a.m. At 12 m. I was ordered to report to Col. B. F. Davis, commanding Second Brigade, First Division, Cavalry Corps, and with his column marched to Deep Run, arriving there at 6 p.m.

I remained at Deep Run until 2 p.m. on the 7th instant, when I was ordered to Potomac Creek, where, on the 8th instant, I was ordered to report to First Lieut. A. C. M. Pennington, Second U. S. Artillery, commanding First Brigade Horse Artillery, and reached the brigade camp about 1 p.m. on that day.

In the engagement on the 2d, and in the shelling of our wagon camps on the morning of the 4th instant, I have the following casualties to report:

> May 2—killed, 1 (Private Luther P. Hilvety); wounded, 4 (Privates Patrick Gaynon, Thomas R. Hunt, Noah S. Laing, severely, and Edward Hart, slightly).
> May 4—killed, 1 (Private Herman Sanders).
> Loss in material—1 caisson, 1 set wheel harness, 15 sets horse equipments, 17 horses (killed, wounded, and missing).
> Ammunition consumed—150 percussion-shell (Schenkl), 127 case shot (Hotchkiss), 62 canister (Hotchkiss), and 339 cartridges.

It is impossible to make any particular mention of the conduct of my command. My chiefs of sections (Lieutenants Browne and Clark and Sergt. James E. Tileston) behaved with great gallantry and coolness while under fire, and while on the march their labors tended greatly to promote and maintain the efficiency of the battery. The enlisted men of the command were under the immediate eye of the brigadier-general commanding throughout the action, and a few flattering words which he spoke to them while the engagement was progressing were sufficient to assure me that he was more than satisfied with the conduct of all of them. I feel certain that when the next struggle comes they will not be found wanting.

In conclusion, captain, I beg leave to return my sincere thanks to the brigadier-general commanding for the uniform kindness and courtesy with which myself and my command were treated during the operations of the division. It was owing entirely to his exertions and to those of his staff that my battery was kept so well supplied in everything necessary to its sustenance, and the fact that six hours after it had arrived at its original camp it was ready again for service as a full battery speaks highly for the forethought and attention which he paid my command while it was a participator in the late operations of the Army of the Potomac.[9]

I have the honor to be, very respectfully, your obedient servant,

> J. W. MARTIN,
> First Lieut., Comdg. 6th Indpt. N. Y. Battery Horse Artillery.
> Capt. A. J. COHEN,
> Asst. Adjt. Gen., First Div., Cavalry Corps.

BATTLE OF BRANDY STATION

JUNE 6–JUNE 9, 1863

HDQRS. SECOND AND THIRD CAVALRY DIVISIONS, June 12, 1863.
COLONEL: I have the honor to submit the following report of the operations of the Second and Third Cavalry Divisions in the engagement of the 9th instant:

Agreeably to my instructions from Brigadier-General Pleasonton, commanding corps, on the afternoon of the 8th instant I moved the Second and Third Divisions from their camp near Warrenton Junction to the vicinity of Kelly's Ford. At this point I found Brig. Gen. D. A. Russell, with 1,500 infantry and a battery of horse artillery. This force, which was designed to take part in the operations of the ensuing day, having been reported to me by Brigadier-General Russell, I at once made every preparation for crossing at daylight on the following morning. The Second Division, Col. A. N. Duffié commanding, was ordered to be at the ford at 3.30 a.m. and to cross in advance, in order that it might move at once upon Stevensburg. A late start from camp and an unexpected difficulty in following the direct road to the ford on the part of this division delayed the crossing of my advance until between 5 and 6 o'clock. The enemy offering but slight opposition, in a very short time the entire command was on the south bank of the river.

In compliance with my instructions to establish the left of my line at Stevensburg, I directed Colonel Duffié to move with the Second Division to that place: General Russell with his infantry to proceed directly from Kelly's Ford to Brandy Station. With the Third Division I started to Brandy Station, taking a road west of that occupied by the infantry (about 5 miles). While crossing the Rappahannock, the artillery firing on the right was evidence that General Buford was already engaged with the enemy. Couriers from General Pleasonton, commanding corps, gave me the same information, as also that he had met the entire cavalry force of the enemy. I pushed on rapidly, and, after marching about 5 miles, overtook the rear of Colonel Duffié's division, and there had a dispatch from him that his advance was at Stevensburg. Turning to the right from this point, I pushed on for Brandy Station and toward the firing in front. Another dispatch from General Pleasonton, informing me of the severity of the fight on the right and of the largely superior force of the enemy, determined me to direct Duffié's division also upon Brandy Station. Colonel Duffié having sent me a dispatch that his advance had reached Stevensburg without encountering the enemy, I sent forward an order to push to Brandy Station, but at a point about 3 miles from the station I came upon the rear brigade of the Second Division, and, in order to get the whole force at once to Brandy Station, I again sent to Colonel Duffié to follow with his division on the same road that the Third Division was following. I would thus have my entire command in hand. When the head of the Third Division arrived near Brandy Station, it was discovered that the enemy were there in great force.

The country about Brandy Station is open, and on the south side extensive level fields, particularly suitable for a cavalry engagement. Coming thus upon the enemy, and having at hand only the Third Division (total strength 2,400), I either had to decline the fight in the face of the enemy or throw upon him at once the entire division. Not doubting but that the Second Division was near, and delay not being admissible, I directed the commanders of my advance brigade to charge the enemy, formed in columns about Brandy House. The whole brigade charged with drawn sabers, fell upon the masses of the enemy, and, after a brief but severe contest, drove them back, killing and wounding many and taking a large number of prisoners. Other columns of the enemy coming up, charged this brigade before it could reform, and it was driven back. Seeing this, I ordered the First Brigade to charge the enemy upon the right. This brigade came forward gallantly through the open fields, dashed upon the enemy, drove him away, and occupied the hill. Now that my entire division was engaged, the fight was everywhere most fierce. Fresh columns of the enemy arriving upon the ground received the vigorous charges of my regiments, and, under the heavy blows of our sabers, were in every instance driven back. Martin's battery of horse artillery, divided between the two brigades, poured load after load of canister upon the rebel regiments. Assailed on all sides, the men stood to the guns nobly. Thus for an hour and a half was the contest continued, not in skirmishing, but in determined charges. The contest was too unequal to be longer continued. The Second Division had not come up; there was no support at hand, and the enemy's numbers were three times my own. I ordered the withdrawal of my brigades. In good order they left the field, the enemy not choosing to follow.

Retiring about 1 mile south of the station, I again formed my brigades, and discovered the Second Division some distance in the rear. Hearing that General Russell had gotten up to General Buford's left with his infantry, I moved my command in the direction of Rappahannock Bridge, and soon united with General Buford's left. On the hills near Brandy Station the enemy had artillery posted, the fire of which they directed upon my line in this new position. A few guns well served were sufficient to prevent any advance in that direction. When engaged with the enemy at Brandy Station, cars loaded with infantry were brought there from Culpeper. Before they could quite get to the station, I sent a party to obstruct the rails. Finding a switch above the station, they reversed it, and thus prevented the cars from running into my command.

The field having been well contested and the enemy being re-enforced with infantry, which could be thrown in any force upon us from Culpeper, I received orders from Brigadier-General Pleasonton to recross my command at Rappahannock Ford. The Second Brigade, Second Division, covered my crossing. I got my command entirely over without being molested by the enemy. When the last man had crossed, the enemy displayed a regiment in front of the ford. I directed a regiment of the Second Brigade, Second Division, to re-cross and offer them fight. This they declined, and the regiment quietly returned to this side.

In this engagement the loss of the Third Division was very severe. Three field officers (2 regimental commanders) were wounded and missing, 2 line officers killed, and 15 wounded; 18 enlisted men killed, 65 wounded, and 272 missing. Of these last many were killed and wounded. The division captured from the enemy 8 commissioned officers and 107 enlisted men and 2 colors (these taken by the First Maine and First Maryland). The field on which we fought bore evidence of the severe loss of the enemy.

The Third Division behaved nobly, and where every officer and man did his duty it is difficult to particularize. I would, however, mention Col. P. Wyndham, First New Jersey Cavalry, commanding Second Brigade, and Col. J. Kilpatrick, Second New York, commanding First Brigade, who gallantly led their brigades to the charge, and throughout the entire engagement handled them with consummate skill. Colonel Wyndham, although wounded, remained on the field, and covered with a portion of his command the withdrawal of the division. Capt. J. W. Martin, commanding Sixth New York Battery of Horse Artillery, did most excellent service. His sections were charged by the enemy's regiments on all sides. Two of his pieces disabled and one serviceable fell into the hands of the enemy, but not until 21 of his men were cut down, fighting stubbornly, and nearly all of the horses killed.

Although the loss of these pieces is to be regretted, still, the magnificent defense of them establishes in the highest degree the soldierly character of the officers and men of the battery. The serviceable gun was spiked before the enemy got it. All the regiments of the Third Division were engaged, viz: First Brigade, Col. J. Kilpatrick commanding—Tenth New York Cavalry, Lieut. Col. William Irvine commanding; Second New York Cavalry, Lieut. Col. H. E Davies, jr., commanding; First Maine Cavalry, Col. C. S. Douty commanding. Second Brigade, Col. P. Wyndham commanding-First New Jersey, Lieutenant-Colonel Brodrick commanding; First Pennsylvania, Col. J. P. Taylor commanding; First Maryland, Lieut. Col. J. M. Deems commanding.

Colonel Duffié reports that his division met a regiment of the enemy at Stevensburg; that his advance engaged and defeated it, capturing 1 officer and 57 men, and that his advance was thus engaged at the time he received my order to follow the Third Division, and hence was unavoidably delayed in coming to my support. Colonel Duffié reports the good conduct of his troops when engaged during the day. The loss in the Second Division was: Enlisted men killed, 4; wounded, 12; missing, 13.

I cannot close this report without favorably mentioning my division staff officers. Surgeon Phillips; Major Gaston, First Pennsylvania Cavalry; Capt. H. C. Weir, assistant adjutant-general; Capt. J. W. Kester, First New Jersey Cavalry; Capt. E. A. Tobes, acting commissary of subsistence; Lieuts. W. Phillips and T. J. Gregg, Sixth Pennsylvania Cavalry, employed in transmitting my orders, proved their efficiency in the highest degree.

Major Gaston and Captain Tobes were captured, but the former escaped his captors.

Lieutenant [Clifford] Thomson, aide-de-camp to General Pleasonton, who accompanied me, having tendered his services on my staff, performed the duties of an aide, and in a most excellent manner. Accompanying this is a list of casualties in the two divisions.[10]

> Very respectfully, your obedient servant,
> D. McM. GREGG,
> Brigadier-General, Commanding.
> Lieut. Col. A. J. ALEXANDER,
> Assistant Adjutant-General, Cavalry Corps.

NEAR FAIRFAX COURT-HOUSE, VA., June 20, 1863.
LIEUTENANT: I beg leave to submit herewith the report of the part taken by my battery (the Sixth Independent New York) in the late movements of the Cavalry Corps of this army.

In accordance with orders, dated headquarters First Brigade, Horse Artillery, June 6, I reported with my battery to Col. Thomas C. Devin, commanding First Cavalry Division, at Brooke's Station, and marched with Col. B. F. Davis' brigade, of that division, to Hartwood Church, arriving there at 3.15 o'clock on the evening of the 7th instant.

At 6.30 o'clock the march was resumed, and at 4 p.m. I arrived at Warrenton Junction, and, in accordance with orders from headquarters Cavalry Corps, reported for duty to Brig. Gen. D. McM. Gregg, commanding Third Cavalry Division.

On the 8th instant, at 1.30 p.m., I marched in rear of Colonel Kilpatrick's brigade to Kelly's Ford, and went into park at 8.30 p.m.

At 3.30 a.m. 9th instant, the battery was harnessed, and at 6 a.m. commenced crossing the ford, under the following assignment of pieces: The right section, without caissons, commanded by First Lieut. M. P. Clark, in advance, following the lead regiment of Colonel Wyndham's brigade; the left section, under command of Second Lieut. J. Wade Wilson (also without caissons), in front of the rear regiment of Colonel Kilpatrick's brigade, and the two guns of the center section, with the column of caissons, marching between the two brigades.

The march from the ford to Brandy Station was pursued without extraordinary incident until we reached a point a few hundred yards distant from the station, when a shot from the advance section and an order from General Gregg to form at once in position was sufficient notice that we had come upon the foe. The enemy had a battery in position on an eminence close to a house which was occupied by their commanding general as headquarters, and from this battery poured a heavy fire on the section under Lieutenant Clark. They made no reply to the section under my own immediate command, and did not withstand the combined fire of the two sections more than a quarter of an hour. The distance from the advanced section to the enemy's battery was about 800 yards, and from the center section about 1,000 yards.

While the guns were engaged, an aide-de-camp from Colonel Wyndham, commanding the advance, reached me with an order to report to him immediately with the two guns I was commanding. I told the officer that I had been posted in the position I occupied by General Gregg's orders, was firing under his immediate directions, and I should consequently remain there until I received other orders from him or his superior in authority.

A few minutes after this, an order from General Gregg reached me to cease firing, and report with the two guns to Colonel Wyndham without delay. I did this as soon as I could, urged to a greater rapidity in the execution of the movement by the fact of receiving three separate messages from Colonel Wyndham to "hurry up." The aide who brought me the order to report to Colonel Wyndham told me that I would receive my support from him, but seeing none of our troops on the advanced position, which Lieutenant Clark already occupied with one piece (the remaining one of his section being temporarily disabled), I sent two separate messages for my support, and in reply received word that they were already on the way and would be at the position before my guns were.

During the entire time, however, that I occupied this position I saw no supporting force, and had I not been so hotly pressed by the enemy I should have taken the responsibility of withdrawing my guns to where their safety would have been insured, nor would I have ever allowed the guns to be so much exposed had I for a moment supposed that they would be sent there unsupported. I understand that the support was ordered, but it is certain that it never took the position assigned it. Immediately on arriving at the position where Lieutenant Clark was engaged with his remaining piece, I formed the section on his right, and immediately commenced firing at the house which I before mentioned as having been occupied by General Stuart as his headquarters, and which was completely surrounded by a dense mass of the enemy's cavalry. Almost simultaneously the enemy commenced their attack by repeated charges on the guns, but it was not until they had been twice repulsed that their efforts were successful, and I am confident that even then they would have been discomfited had their final charge not been made almost simultaneously front and rear. It took but one round of canister shot from each piece to repulse their charges, and could I have reversed my pieces in sufficient time on their last effort to have given them a round before they were in the battery, they should never have taken the guns—there, at least. Once in the battery, it became a hand-to-hand fight with pistol and saber between the enemy and my cannoneers and drivers, and never did men act with more coolness and bravery, and show more of a stern purpose to do their duty unflinchingly, and, above all, to save their guns; and while the loss of them is a matter of great regret to me, it is a consolation and a great satisfaction to know that I can point with pride to the fact that of that little band who defended the battery not one of them flinched for a moment from his duty.

Of the 36 men that I took into the engagement, but 6 came out safely, and of these 30, 21 are either killed, wounded, or missing, and scarcely one of them but will carry the honorable mark of the saber or bullet to his grave.

The three guns lost were so disabled by bursting, wedging, and spiking that their possession was of no benefit to the enemy for the remainder of the engagement, and the ammunition (fuse shell and case shot) which they took with the guns was rendered useless by the destruction of the fuses belonging to them. All this was accomplished in less time than it takes to write it, but it was complete and effectual.

Finding that it was futile to do more than had been done, I made my way to where I hoped to find the general commanding the division, my object being, if possible, to secure sufficient force to recapture the guns (and I believe, from the character of the enemy's fighting, that it could have been done with little loss), and to assist in their recapture I intended to take up three of the caisson limbers to bring off the guns with (the horses belonging to the guns having all been either killed or wounded) if the effort was successful, and, if it was attended with no success, I felt assured that I could fall back with the limbers as safely as could the assisting force. After fifteen minutes' unsuccessful search, I returned and found that our forces were falling back on the road leading to Berry's Hill, and I accordingly moved my caissons and the remaining portions of the two sections to that point, and left them under the charge of Lieutenant Clark, while I went to the headquarters of the corps to report my disaster to Captain Robertson, corps chief of artillery.

The operations of the left section were conducted solely by its chief, Lieutenant Wilson, and from all sides I hear nothing but high encomiums on his excellent management of his command and of the gallantry of himself and his men. The reports of his operations and of those of Lieutenant Clark from the time he took the advance until I joined him on the field, are herewith inclosed.

At 3 p.m., in accordance with orders from the general commanding the division, I crossed the Rappahannock at the station ford, and remained in camp until 7 a.m. on the 10th, when I marched with the division to Warrenton Junction, remaining, under the order of the general commanding the division, until the 13th instant, when I reported to your headquarters for duty with the brigade.

I have the honor to report the following casualties: 8 wounded and 13 missing. None known to be killed.

Amount of ammunition expended: 122 rounds Schenkl percussion shell. 126 rounds Hotchkiss case shot, and 15 rounds Hotchkiss canister. The working of the ammunition used was excellent. The only fault to be found was in the paper fuses used with the case shot, and their inaccuracy, it seems, cannot be remedied. The percussion shell was in this case, as I have always found it, true to its reputation. I want no better projectile in my chests. The loss in matériel, I regret to say, is great, and consists, in part, as- follows: Three 3-inch rifled guns, carriages, and equipments complete, 3 sets double lead harness, 2 sets double wheel harness, 24 lead traces, 15 wheel traces, 16 sets horse equipments, and 20 artillery horses.

I beg leave to tender my sincere thanks to the general commanding the Third Cavalry Division for the uniform kindness and forbearance with which he treated myself and my command during the short time I was acting under his orders; and to Captain Weir and his entire staff, and to Lieutenant Thomson, aide-de-camp to the general commanding Cavalry Corps, who accompanied the left wing of the advance, I am also sincerely grateful.

Of the conduct of my chiefs of sections—Lieutenants Clark and Wilson and First Sergeant [James E.] Tileston (acting)—I am deservedly proud. They are well fitted to command men of the caliber and stamina such as those who fought so nobly and so heroically at Brandy Station on the memorable June 9.[11]

> I am, sir, very respectfully, your obedient servant,
> J. W. MARTIN,
> Captain, Comdg. Sixth Independent New York Battery.
> First Lieut. J. H. BELL,
> Acting Assistant Adjutant-General.

CAMP NEAR FAIRFAX COURT-HOUSE, VA., June 21, 1863.
CAPTAIN: In obedience to your order, I assumed command of the left section of the Sixth Independent New York Battery at Warrenton Junction, Va., on June 8, and con-tinued the march thence toward Kelly's Ford, within a mile of which we bivouacked for the night.

On the morning of the 9th, pursuant to orders from General Gregg, through Captain Martin, I detached the two caissons, with corporals, and with the two pieces reported to Colonel Kilpatrick, commanding the First Brigade of General Gregg's divi-sion of cavalry, and was placed as support to the rear guard of the column, marching in front of the rear regiment of the First Brigade. The march was continued without inter-ruption and with great rapidity up the road on the south side of the Rappahannock.

At about 10.30 a.m. rapid cannonading was heard at the front, and almost immediately thereafter an order was received to pass the two pieces from the rear to the front of the First Brigade. Leaving the main road to the left by obliquing to the right, I sought a position on the slope of the ridge which stretched from the former residence of Colonel Thorne, deceased (now the headquarters of the rebel General Stuart), toward the Rappahannock, and bending to the rear.

At this time the fight for the possession of the house was very spirited. To reach the position sought, I was compelled to cross a morass, several immense ditches, and a fence, all of which was accomplished without accident, and the section went into action and opened a vigorous fire with Schenkl percussion on a column of rebel cavalry pushing rapidly from the right toward Thorne's house, on my left and front. The firing was rapid and effective, producing much confusion in the enemy's column. Perceiving this, and pursuant to an order from Colonel Kilpatrick, I limbered to the front, and advanced upon the moving column some 150 yards, and again went into action, effectively delaying and disconcerting the enemy's concentration on their own center, near the Thorne house.

Again, pursuant to orders from Colonel Kilpatrick, I limbered to the front, and sought a position on the crest of the hill behind which the enemy was rapidly massing to force back the advance of Colonel Kilpatrick upon the house. Before reaching the crest, however, a halt was ordered by Colonel Kilpatrick, and soon after a retreat from that position, which was executed without panic and in admirable order. The enemy, perceiving the retreat, charged furiously up the hill and through the section 50 yards in rear of the pieces, charging desperately on the cavalry, some hundreds of yards in the advance of the pieces in retreat. The capture of the section seems to have been thought accomplished by the enemy, and the rebel line wheeled into column and pushed rapidly by the flanks, with the intent to turn the right of the First Brigade, leaving, as they supposed, a sufficient force to secure the guns.

At this time was displayed the heroism of the section, and valor of which any command and country may be justly proud. In reversing, one of the gun limbers was nearly capsized, one wheel being in the air and the axle nearly vertical. Perceiving this, I ordered the cannoneers to dismount and restore to its position the limber. We were surrounded by a squad of rebel cavalry, firing with carbine and pistol. The order was scarcely needed, for the cannoneers had seen the peril of their gun, and, anticipating the order, had dismounted to restore it, and, with revolvers in hand, they defended the gun as if determined to share its destiny and make its fate their own. The bearer of a rebel battle-flag was shot by Private [Sylvanus] Currant, who would have recovered it but for the great difficulty of approaching the colors with a lame and skittish horse, upon which he was at the time mounted. The flag was taken by the First Maine Cavalry. The column of rebel cavalry was rapidly moving toward our right, or rather left, as we were in retreat, and the section moved in the same direction in parallel line in column of pieces, stopping now and then to throw a few shell in the column, and again seeking safety in retreat, until we reached the woods, when the pursuit ceased. Not knowing the whereabouts or fate of the remaining two sections of the battery, I reported to General Gregg, who ordered a continuance of the retreat until we reached a large open field, where I was ordered to report to Colonel Taylor (then, by the wound of Colonel Wyndham, in command of the Second Brigade), with whom I again returned to the front, crossing the Rappahannock road and passing to the right of the position occupied in the morning; then, obliquing to the left and rear, I went into battery and action on a line of cavalry and artillery behind a ridge which masked them partially from view. My ammunition becoming exhausted, I was relieved by Battery M, Second U.S. Artillery, and recrossed the river at Rappahannock Station. I then went into battery near a fort, to command the road leading to the ford. Some rebel cavalry appearing, I opened fire, and by a few well-directed shots, caused them to retire into the woods.

The section was in action at eight different times during the day, and the accuracy of the fire secured the commendation of the generals commanding both brigades and divisions of cavalry, while the conduct of the men was in the highest degree creditable to their valor and skill as soldiers and artillerists.[12]

> I am, captain, very respectfully, your obedient servant,
> J. WADE WILSON,
> Second Lieut., Comdg. Section, Sixth Ind. N. Y. Battery.
> Capt. J. W. MARTIN,
> Comdg. Sixth Independent New York Battery.

GETTYSBURG CAMPAIGN

JUNE 28–JULY 31 1863

HEADQUARTERS FIRST BRIGADE, HORSE ARTILLERY, August 22, 1863.
SIR: I have the honor to submit the following report of the operations of the First Brigade, Horse Artillery, since June 28:

On June 28, I reported with my brigade—consisting of Lieutenant Pennington's battery (M, Second U.S. Artillery), Elder's battery (E, Fourth U.S. Artillery), Heaton's battery (B and L, Second U.S. Artillery), and Captain Martin's (Sixth Independent New York) battery of horse artillery—to General Pleasonton, commanding Cavalry Corps. In obedience to instructions from General Pleasonton, two batteries (Pennington's and Elder's) were detailed, and left camp at daylight on the 29th, to report for duty with the Third Division, Cavalry Corps. These two batteries have been on duty with this division since that time, and make their reports through its commanding officer.

At 8 a.m. I was ready to move with the remaining two batteries (Heaton's and Martin's), but owing to the road being blocked with troops and wagons, I was unable to move until 4 p.m. After marching about 2 miles, was joined by Captain Daniels, commanding Ninth Michigan Battery, who reported to me, and was assigned to my brigade by order of the general commanding Cavalry Corps.

Continuing the march, I arrived at Middleburg, Md., at 2 a.m. the 30th, when I fed, and rested my command until 9 a.m., and then marched to Taneytown, arriving at 4.30 p.m., and remained encamped at the latter place until 11.30 p.m. July 1, when I marched, and arrived near the battle-ground of Gettysburg at 5.30 a.m. on the 2d, and reported to the general commanding the Cavalry Corps, and by his direction held my batteries in reserve near the battle-ground until nearly dark, when, by his direction, I moved back about 2 miles on the Baltimore pike, and encamped for the night.

On the morning of the 3d, I again moved to the front, and occupied the same ground as the day previous, and, by direction of General Pleasonton, I reported to Brigadier-General Tyler, to assist him with the Reserve Artillery. While out with General Tyler examining our lines, with a view of selecting points for artillery, the enemy opened fire with all his batteries, and we returned to our commands. Finding that the reserve occupied a very exposed position, it was ordered to fall back to where it could get cover from the fire of the enemy. While executing this move, General Tyler's horse was shot and killed under him. From the extreme heat and over-exertion, General Tyler received a sunstroke, which prostrated him for the time, and he turned over the command of the entire reserve to me.

Soon after this (about 12 m.), there being an urgent demand for rifled artillery, and having no other at my disposal, I sent forward the battery of horse artillery (Ninth Michigan) commanded by Capt. J. J. Daniels, who reported to General Newton, and was placed in position by him, where he remained, doing good execution, until the close of the battle.

Captain Daniels' loss in this engagement was 1 man killed, 4 wounded, and 23 horses killed. Captain Daniels bivouacked for the night on the field where he had fought. Captain Daniels in his report of this engagement (a copy of which report I herewith inclose) does not particularize any officers or soldiers of his battery, but speaks of all in terms of the highest praise for their coolness and steadiness under fire. Captain

Daniels and the officers and men under his command deserve all the more credit, as this was the first time his battery had ever been engaged.

General Tyler having recovered so as to resume his duties, about dark I moved back on the Baltimore pike with my two remaining batteries to the camp occupied by me the night previous, and was joined by Captain Daniels on the 4th.

I remained here until 10 o'clock on the 5th, when I marched, and arrived at Creagerstown at 10 o'clock the same evening.

Marched from Creagerstown at 9 a.m. the 7th, and arrived at Middletown, via Frederick City, at 10 p.m.

On the 9th, I moved forward to Boonsborough, where two more of my batteries were detached—Captain Martin's (Sixth Independent New York) battery to General Gregg, Second Division, Cavalry Corps, and Lieutenant Heaton's battery (B and L, Second U.S. Artillery) to General Buford, First Division, Cavalry Corps. These two batteries have been on duty with these divisions since that time, and make their reports to these headquarters. Having but one battery remaining with me, by direction of General Pleasonton I reported to General Tyler to assist him with the Artillery Reserve should it be called into action, and remained with it until our arrival at Berlin on July 15, without anything happening worthy of note.

On the 16th, Lieutenant Williston, commanding Battery D, Second U.S. Artillery, and Lieutenant King, commanding Battery A, Fourth U.S. Artillery, each with four light 12-pounder guns, were assigned to my brigade, and ordered to be equipped as horse artillery. Horses were procured at Berlin on July 19, but equipments could not be obtained at that place.

With the three batteries, Williston's, King's and Daniels', I marched from Berlin at 6 p.m. July 19, and arrived and encamped near Warrenton, Va., on the 25th, without anything transpiring worthy of note.

On the 30th, the last of the equipments were received for the two light 12-pounder batteries, and on the 31st they were completed and ready for active field service.

Great credit is due to First Lieut. J. H. Bell, of the Sixth New York Cavalry (the only officer on my staff), for the efficient manner in which he has performed the duties of acting assistant adjutant-general, assistant commissary of subsistence, and acting assistant quartermaster, not only in procuring horses and supplies of all kinds for the batteries which were held in reserve, but also for procuring and forwarding horses and other supplies to those on duty with the different cavalry divisions.[13]

> Very respectfully, your obedient servant,
> J. M. ROBERTSON,
> Captain Second U.S. Artillery, Commanding Brigade.
> Capt. A. J. COHEN,
> Assistant Adjutant-General, Cavalry Corps.1.

APPENDIX B

WOBURN MECHANIC PHALANX

When my cousin Wayne Perkins gave me a copy of our great-grandfather's diary some years ago, one of the first questions I had concerned Battery K, Ninth New York State Militia, and its successor organization, the Sixth New York Independent Battery. Why did George Perkins, a resident of Woburn, Massachusetts, choose to enlist in a New York artillery outfit? One obvious reason, as the first entry in his diary documents, was the fact that his older brother, James Appleton "App" Perkins, was already a member of the battery, having joined up in New York City in June 1861. But this answer begged the question, why did App join this unit? When I began researching the question, I found to my surprise that he did so along with four other "Woburn boys": John R. Furbush, Perley M. Griffin, J. B. Horne, and James E. Tileston.[1] What would induce a group of men to travel to New York City to join a New York militia organization when Massachusetts units were being activated and making preparations to move to Washington to defend the country? In fact, why did the Woburn boys not join their own hometown company, known as the Woburn Mechanic Phalanx?

These men were in a New York regiment due to the politics and history of the militia movement in the prewar period and the early days of the Civil War. The Woburn Mechanic Phalanx had had a checkered history since its founding in 1835. According to the *Middlesex County Journal* of September 24, 1870, and the *Woburn Journal* of October 2, 1885, the Phalanx originated when three Woburn men—John Wyman, Charles L. Moore, and John C. Martin—attempted in 1835 to organize a militia company in their hometown. The Massachusetts General Court duly authorized the formation of the company, and Lt. Gov. Samuel T. Armstrong approved the measure in July of the same year. A month later, Adj. Gen. H.A.S. Dearborn ordered Martin to enlist forty-five "free white able-bodied citizens of proper age to perform military duty." Either there was insufficient interest to maintain the company at strength, or the rigors of militia drill did not appeal to the good citizens of Woburn, for the Phalanx disbanded only four years later.[2] Fortunately for the patriotism and good name of the community, the unit reactivated a year later, in 1842. At this time, the Phalanx assumed the designation of Company G, Fourth Regiment, Light Infantry, Third Brigade, First Division,

Massachusetts Volunteer Militia. In 1855, it retained the Company G designation but was reassigned from the Third to the Fifth Regiment.[3]

The reactivation of the Phalanx was preceded by an 1840 act of the Massachusetts General Court that reorganized the militia system and attempted to put it on a systematic footing. The legislature directed that all able-bodied white male citizens between the ages of eighteen and forty-five (with certain exceptions) "shall be enrolled" in the militia. The act further specified that the *active* militia would henceforth consist of "volunteers or companies raised at large." Finally, it stated that the volunteer militia would consist of companies and officers.[4]

If called to active duty the Phalanx was expected to join its parent regiment, the Fifth Massachusetts Militia. Unfortunately and unaccountably, given the momentum building toward secession, the Phalanx once again disbanded in 1860. This time, its charter was revoked and transferred to Natick. The reported reason for this action was the apathy of its members.[5] The cause can only be speculated; nevertheless, the Phalanx did not attempt to reform until three weeks after the fall of Fort Sumter, on May 4, 1861. On that date, a meeting was held in Woburn in which a decision was made to reactivate the company. An article in the *Middlesex Journal* of that date reported that Furbush, Horne, J. A. Perkins, and Tileston were part of a group of eighty men who signed enlistment papers for the rejuvenated organization.[6] Unfortunately for their honor, patriotism, and hometown pride, the members of the Phalanx found it much easier to reorganize and resume drilling than to maintain the integrity of the unit as a component of the Massachusetts militia.

The history of the attempted reactivation of the Woburn Mechanic Phalanx was recounted in 1871 in a series of articles in the *Middlesex County Journal.*[7] The officers of the reactivated Phalanx offered their organization to Governor Andrews four days after the reorganization meeting on May 8, 1861. By that date, however, it was already too late to join the militia units being pushed forward in response to President Lincoln's April 15 proclamation of a state of insurrection and call for 75,000 militia.[8] As the Massachusetts adjutant general's report for 1861 confirms, the state began activating its regiments the same day, with the Third, Fourth, Sixth, and Eighth infantry being ordered to muster on Boston Common. The Fifth Regiment followed on April 19 and departed for Washington, D.C., the next day.[9] Thus, there was no immediate need for the services of the Phalanx. Accordingly, the governor ordered it to return to Woburn to await orders. This was not the response the organizers had hoped for and, apparently, cooling their heels at home at the time of crisis was not acceptable to the men, for many began looking for other regiments to join. One of these quests was recounted in an article in the *Woburn Weekly Budget* of June 21, 1861. This report stated that a group of men from the Phalanx had gone to Yonkers, New York, to enlist in other units. The *Budget* further stated that D. B. Coffin, Peter Cormick, John R. Furbush, James W. Goodwin, Thomas Hooper, J. A. Perkins, John S. Rogers, James E. Tileston, and Joseph S. Wyman had joined Company K, Ninth New York State Militia.

Thus, when the Phalanx did receive orders on June 28 to join the Sixteenth Massachusetts Volunteer Infantry Regiment, many of the eighty men who had signed enlistment papers on May 4 were no longer available. On July 4, the company clerk responded to the order by reporting to the adjutant general that two officers and twenty-five men had joined the Fifth Massachusetts Militia, about fifteen had enlisted in New York and other regiments, and the remainder had voted to remain at home to await the return of the others in hopes of going out later as a unit. In response, the governor ordered the Phalanx to disband and return its arms to the arsenal.[10] Despite this rebuff, the Phalanx subsequently successfully reorganized and served as a unit in the Civil War. Nevertheless, it is clear that its ambiguous status in May and June of 1861 was the cause of the dispersal of significant numbers of Woburn men to other organizations and, specifically, of the presence of the Perkins brothers in the Sixth New York Independent Battery.

NOTES

INTRODUCTION

1. Gerald F. Linderman, *Embattled Courage: The Experience of Combat in the American Civil War* (New York: Free Press Edition, 1989), 83–84.
2. Ibid., 102.
3. Mark Grimsley and Todd D. Miller, eds., *The Union Must Stand: The Civil War Diary of John Quincy Adams Campbell, Fifth Iowa Volunteer Infantry* (Knoxville: Univ. of Tennessee Press, 2000), xviii.
4. Ibid., xviii–xix.
5. *Woburn Town Report, 1865,* 18; *1870–1871,* 23.
6. *Boston School Committee Report, 1872; Boston Manual of Public Schools 1880;* and *Boston Directory, 1872–1873, 1876, 1880–1881,* and *1889.*
7. "Roster of Burbank Post 33, GAR, 1867–1903," Glennon Archives, Woburn Public Library, Woburn, MA.
8. *Woburn Journal,* Jan. 11, 1884.
9. "Minutes of Meetings, Jan. 23, 1884 to November 12, 1888," Records of GAR Post 161, Record Book, Glennon Archives, Woburn Public Library, Woburn, MA.
10. *Boston Evening Record,* Aug. 11, 1890, and *Boston Daily Globe,* Aug. 13, 1890.
11. "The Perkins Obsequies," *News,* Oct. 25, 1890.

CHAPTER 1.
THE STORM OF WAR DRAWS NEARER: DECEMBER 1861–APRIL 1862

1. *Massachusetts Soldiers, Sailors, and Marines in the Civil War* (reprinted by American Civil War Research Database, Historical Data Systems, at http://www.civilwardata.com; hereafter cited as cited as *Mass. Sol.*). Albert Ames Chittenden, a twenty-year-old clerk, enlisted on September 15, 1862, as a corporal and mustered into Company A, Massachusetts Forty-fifth Infantry. The Massachusetts Forty-fifth Infantry was one of the nine-month militia regiments raised in response to the call of August 4, 1862. It served in the Department of North Carolina. Corporal

Chittenden mustered out on July 7, 1863. On July 16, 1864, he was commissioned as a second lieutenant into Company H of the 100-day Massachusetts Sixth Infantry and was mustered out on October 27, 1864. During its term of service, the Sixth Massachusetts was assigned to the defenses of Washington south of the Potomac River and guarded Confederate prisoners on Pea Patch Island in the middle of Delaware Bay.

2. *Report of the Adjutant General of the State of Maine* (hereafter cited as *Maine*) and *The Union Army: A History of Military Affairs in the Loyal States, 1861–65,* vols. 1–2 (Madison, WI: Federal Publishing Co., 1908), accessed at http://www.civilwardata. com. William P. Jordan, a thirty-year-old from Portland, Maine, enlisted on May 3, 1861, as a first lieutenant and was commissioned into Company C, Maine First Infantry. He mustered out on August 5, 1861, at Portland and enlisted on October 5, 1861, as a captain and was commissioned into Company C, Maine Tenth Infantry, on the same date. (The First Maine Infantry was a two-year state militia outfit but was mustered into U.S. service for only three months.) The Tenth Maine left Portland on October 6, 1861, and arrived in Baltimore on October 9, 1861. On November 4, 1861, the Tenth Maine left Baltimore for Relay House, Maryland, where it served as guard for the Baltimore and Ohio Railroad until February 27, 1862.

3. Mark Boatner, *The Civil War Dictionary,* rev. ed. (New York: Vintage, 1991), 47; *The War of the Rebellion: A Compilation of the Official Records of the Union and Confederate Armies,* 128 vols. (Washington, DC: U.S. Government Printing Office, 1880–1901), vol. 5, p. 5 (hereafter cited as *Official Records*; unless specified, all citations are to series 1). "General Bussy" was Brig. Gen. William F. Barry. Major General McClellan appointed Barry chief of artillery of the Army of the Potomac when he assumed command of the army. Barry served as such through-out the Peninsula Campaign. The *Official Records* contain Barry's report on his stewardship as chief of artillery as well as McClellan's report, which confirms that Barry held that post.

4. Boatner, *Civil War Dictionary,* 700; John D. Billings, *Hardtack and Coffee: The Unwritten Story of Army Life* (Lincoln: Univ. of Nebraska Press, 1993), 46–48. Billings states that the Sibley tent was modeled after the teepee of the Plains Indi-ans. It was eighteen feet in diameter, twelve feet high, and held a dozen men. It went out of field service in 1862 because it required too much transport to move.

5. Billings, *Hardtack and Coffee,* 113–19. Hardtack was a plain biscuit made of flour and water. It formed a major part of the soldiers' diet in the Army of the Potomac. Billings states that most of the hardtack was baked in Baltimore and shipped to the army in sixty-pound boxes.

6. Frederick Phisterer, *New York in the War of the Rebellion, 1861–1865* (Albany: J. B. Lyon Co., 1912); *Report of the Adjutant General of the State of New York,* vols. 1–5, accessed at http://www.civilwardata.com (hereafter cited as *NYWR*). George Brown Jr. enlisted June 15, 1861, at New York City as a corporal. He was promoted to second lieutenant September 7, 1861, and to first lieutenant February 20, 1862. He was mustered out June 21, 1864, at New York City.

7. *NYWR.* Frank J. Jones enlisted June 15, 1861, at New York City as a private. He was discharged for promotion on March 5, 1862, and commissioned second lieutenant into Company L, First Connecticut Light Artillery.

8. *NYWR.* Thomas B. Bunting enlisted on June 15, 1861, at New York City as a captain. He was discharged on January 23, 1862.

9. *Dictionary of American Naval Fighting Ships* (Washington, DC: Dept. of the Navy, 1968), 8:n.p. *Yankee* was a screw steamer of 328 tons, 146 feet in length, and a beam of twenty-five feet seven inches. It was armed with two thirty-two-pounders. *Yankee* took part in the abortive Fort Sumter relief expedition and evacuated the Norfolk Navy Yard.

10. *NYWR.* Walter M. Bramhall enlisted June 15, 1861, at New York City as a second lieutenant. He was wounded October 21, 1861, at Balls Bluff, Virginia, and promoted to captain January 23, 1862. He resigned February 3, 1863.

11. *NYWR.* Joseph W. Martin enlisted June 15, 1861, at New York City as a private. He was commissioned on June 20, 1861, promoted to captain on June 8, 1863, and mustered out February 15, 1865, at Harper's Ferry, Virginia.

12. *Mass. Sol.* James W. McDonald, a thirty-three-year-old leather manufacturer of North Woburn, enlisted June 13, 1861, as a first lieutenant and was commissioned into Company D of the Eleventh Massachusetts Infantry. He was promoted to captain on September 17, 1861, and to major on August 30, 1862. He was wounded in action at Gettysburg, Pennsylvania, on July 2, 1863, and mustered out on June 24, 1864.

13. Boatner, *Civil War Dictionary,* 205. Ezra J. Warner, *Generals in Blue: Lives of the Union Commanders* (Baton Rouge: Louisiana State Univ. Press, 1964), 96–97. Robert Cowdin was commissioned colonel of the First Massachusetts Volunteers on May 25, 1861. He was recommended for promotion by Gen. Joseph Hooker for his actions at the Battle of Williamsburg and commissioned brigadier general of the U.S. Volunteers on September 26, 1862.

14. Regimental Books for the Sixth New York Independent Battery, RG 94, vols. 132–33, National Archives and Record Administration (hereafter cited as RB6). On this date, Capt. Thomas B. Bunting preferred charges against privates Thomas Ellis, Jacob H. Hatley, Charles H. Humphreys, William H. Pearse, Theodore F. Randolph, James Benward, and John H. Vennett for disobedience of an order to carry posts for a stable and for disrespect to their superior officer. According to the second charge, they stated, "We will be damned if we will be forced to carry posts for any man. No man can force us to do it. We will go in the guard house first and stay there." As of this date, the unit records still were designated Light Company K, Detached Ninth New York State Militia.

15. *Mass. Sol.*; Records of GAR Post 161, Johnson Collection, Box 74, Glennon Archives, Woburn Public Library, Woburn, MA. Albert H. Richardson, an eighteen-year-old resident of Woburn, Massachusetts, enlisted July 22, 1862, as a private and mustered into Company K, Massachusetts Thirty-ninth Infantry. He was wounded in action May 12, 1864, at Laurel Hill, Virginia, taken prisoner of war August 19, 1864, at Weldon Railroad, Virginia, and exchanged March 2, 1865 (place not stated). He mustered out on June 2, 1865. He was one of the founding members of GAR Post 161 in Woburn.

16. Capt. C. C. Marsh, USN, *Official Records of the Union and Confederate Navies in the War of the Rebellion* (Washington, DC: Government Printing Office, 1897), ser. 1, 4:593; Mary Alice Wills, *The Confederate Blockade of Washington, DC, 1861–1862* (Shippensburg, PA: Burd Street Press, 1998), 21, 106. Confederate forces captured

the *George Page* at Aquia Creek in May 1861. By December 1861 the *Page* had been armed and brought to Quantico. A report dated July 29, 1861, by Captain Rowan, of the USS *Pawnee,* stated that the Confederates had converted the *Page* to a warship while it was still lying at Aquia Creek and had mounted six guns on board. Wills states that the *Page*'s armament consisted of four thirty-two-pounder cannon and one long pivot gun. The *Official Records* contain correspondence dated December 15 and 16 from Jno. Dahlgren, commandant of the Washington Navy Yard, and Lt. R. H. Wyman, commander of the Potomac Flotilla, regarding a proposal to cut out the *Page,* then lying in Quantico Creek and Chopawamsic Creek. The proposal was rejected as being impractical.

17. Allan Nevins, *A Diary of Battle: The Personal Journals of Colonel Charles S. Wainwright, 1861–1865* (Gettysburg, PA: Stan Clark Books, 1962), 12–13, 27. In his February 5 entry, Wainwright states that a map showed a road between "Port Tobacco through Milshead to this point" (Budd's Ferry). He states that his quarters were located at Camp Hooker, about one hundred yards off the north side of the "main road" and about one and one-quarter miles on a "farm road" from the Widow Budd's abandoned house on the Maryland Potomac shore. He also states that the Sixth New York campsite was about a mile to the east of his location on a plain in the midst of a pine forest and close to the camp of the Excelsior Brigade. Wainwright confirms that the soldiers in the vicinity were slowly dismantling the Budd house for their own use. He also states that the Confederate works at Shipping Point were 2,400 yards away from the Budd House. Wainwright's March 16 diary entry states that the Chicamoxon stream ran through a ravine at the "bottom of our camp." He describes Shipping Point as "a bluff some thirty feet high, and perhaps a mile long; stretching down from the mouth of Quantico; on it are the principal rebel batteries, mounting a dozen guns or more."

18. RB6; Billings, *Hardtack and Coffee,* 146. Company Order 17 reports Pvt. Alfred T. Crane was punished in this way for using "insubordinate and insulting language to a non-commissioned officer, and also of using disrespectful and insulting language in reference to a superior officer." Billings states that some transgressors against military discipline were punished by forcing them to stand on a barrel for a half day or a full day at a time. Some officers would order both ends of the barrel to be knocked out, thus forcing the miscreant to stand on the end of the staves.

19. *Mass. Sol.* Joseph M. Phillips and Preserved B. Phillips were both from Woburn, Massachusetts. Joseph M., a twenty-one-year-old currier, enlisted June 15, 1861, as a private and mustered into the First Massachusetts Infantry on August 21, 1861. He was taken prisoner of war (date and place not listed) and paroled December 31, 1862. He mustered out May 25, 1864. Preserved B. Phillips, a nineteen-year-old currier, enlisted into the First Massachusetts Infantry on the same dates and was taken prisoner of war (date and place not listed). He was paroled October 31, 1862, and discharged for disability January 14, 1863.

20. RB6. Lt. Moses P. Clark was promoted from sergeant to second lieutenant on September 1, 1861. He was promoted to first lieutenant February 16, 1863, and to captain in March 1865. Captain Clark was the last commanding officer of the Sixth New York.

21. Stephen Sears, *To the Gates of Richmond* (New York: Tichnor and Fields, 1996), 360; Nevins, *A Diary of Battle,* 12; *NYWR.* Lt. James E. Smith was the commanding

officer of the Fourth New York Independent Light Battery. Originally mustered in at Staten Island on October 24, 1861, as Company L, Artillery Company, Serrell's Engineers, it was designated the Fourth New York Independent Battery on December 7, 1861. Along with the Sixth New York Independent Light, the First New York Light, Battery D, and the First United States, Battery H, it was assigned to the division artillery of the Second Division (Hooker's) under the command of Maj. Charles S. Wainwright. The Fourth New York was equipped with Parrott guns.

22. *Official Naval Records,* vol. 5, 12; *Official Records,* vol. 5, pp. 698, 1019, 1032–33; Boatner, *Civil War Dictionary,* 175, 315; Wills, *Confederate Blockade,* 96, 112–13. The USS *Pensacola,* a steam screw frigate, successfully passed the Confederate batteries opposite Budd's Ferry between 3:00 and 5:00 AM on January 12, 1862. Plans and preparations for her passage had been under way since at least December 28, 1861, when Gustavas Fox, assistant secretary of the navy, sent a letter to the quartermaster general of the army, requesting the loan of "two scows . . . and a quantity of hay to fill them." The plan was to lash the scows to the side of the *Pensacola* in order to protect its machinery when it passed the Confederate Potomac batteries. The navy's plans did not escape the notice of Confederate authorities. A compilation of intelligence material forwarded to the Confederate War Department by Gen. J. E. Johnston contains a report (also dated December 28, 1861) stating that "the *Pensacola* frigate, armed with the largest Dahlgren guns, is under orders to proceed down the Potomac, with other gunboats, to force the batteries on the Virginia side." The Confederate War Department received the reports on January 4, 1862. On January 12, 1862, Brigadier General Hooker, commanding Hooker's Division, reported the *Pensacola*'s successful passage to Brig. Gen. S. Williams, adjutant general, Army of the Potomac. General Hooker was dismissive of the capabilities of the Confederate artillery. Finally, Brig. Samuel Gibbs French, commanding the defenses at Evansport, Shipping Point, and Cockpit Point submitted a report to Gen. Samuel Cooper, adjutant and inspector general of the Confederate army that confirmed that the *Pensacola* had passed by his batteries between the hours of 4:00 AM and 5:00 AM on January 12. General French admitted that, despite his detailed preparations to receive the ship, the *Pensacola* had passed by his first bat-tery without a shot being fired. He blamed the failure on the tardiness of the corporal of the guard to alert the batteries to the *Pensacola*'s presence. The general claimed, however, that his gunners had hit the *Pensacola* "several times," but it appears that his claim is the product of wishful thinking.

23. Sears, *To the Gates of Richmond,* 370. Brigadier General Sickles actually commanded the First Brigade of Brigadier General Hooker's Second Division of the Third Corps of Brigadier General Heintzelman.

24. *NYWR.* Perley M. Griffin enlisted June 29, 1861, at Washington, D.C., as a private and mustered out June 29, 1864, at Washington, D.C. George Perkins's January 21, 1862, letter to the *Middlesex Journal* lists Griffin as being one of the five "Woburn boys" in the battery.

25. *NYWR.* Corporal "More" probably was Edward Saint Cloud Moore, who enlisted on June 15, 1861, in New York City as a private and mustered into the Sixth New York on June 20, 1861. He was promoted to corporal December 15, 1861. Corporal Moore was promoted to second lieutenant on June 17, 1862, and was commissioned into the Fifth New York Light Artillery.

26. *NYWR.* Henry Budelman enlisted September 27, 1861, in New York City as a private and mustered into the Sixth New York Battery. He was promoted to corporal January 1, 1863, and to sergeant July 1, 1864. He mustered out September 28, 1864, at Washington, D.C.

27. James C. Hazlett, Edwin Olmstead, and M. Hume Parks, *Field Artillery Weapons of the Civil War,* 2nd ed. (Newark: Univ. of Delaware Press, 1997), 148–50. From the information provided by Private Perkins in this letter, it is not possible to positively identify the artillery pieces mentioned. Nevertheless, it seems probable that the six-pounder rifled cannon that the Sixth New York Battery turned in were bronze model 1841 six-pounder guns that had been reamed out and rifled according to the system of Gen. Charles T. James. As modified, the guns would have fired the general's own design of shells, which were specially designed to fit the pattern of lands and grooves he invented. These would have been the James Rifles, Type 1, mentioned in Hazlett. As for the bronze "Hotchkiss field guns" that replaced them, it seems likely that they were new weapons, manufactured in 1861 according to the James system and externally very similar to the three-inch ordnance rifles that the Sixth New York would later receive before embarking for the Virginia Peninsula. These guns would have been one of the variants of the James Rifles, Type 2, described in Hazlett. In field use, it seems that the James-pattern rifles did not live up to expectations, because the rifling tended to wear relatively quickly, thus adversely affecting the accuracy of the weapon. Perkins perhaps identified them as Hotchkiss guns because the James shells they were designed to fire were not highly regarded and were replaced in service by Hotchkiss shells of about fourteen pounds.

28. RB6; *Woburn (MA) Weekly Budget,* June 21, 1861; *Middlesex Journal (Woburn, MA),* May 4, 1861. The battery books and the Woburn papers identify Furbush as being a Woburn resident. The reason for omitting him from the list of Woburn boys is unknown.

29. *NYWR.* Alexander R. Samuels enlisted August 15, 1861, at New York City as a private. He mustered out August 16, 1864, at New York City.

30. *NYWR.* Frederick A. Wall enlisted August 15, 1861, in New York City as a private and mustered into the Sixth New York Battery. He was mustered out August 16, 1864, in New York City.

31. George B. Davis, Leslie C. Perry, and Joseph W. Kirkley, *Atlas to Accompany the Official Records of the Union and Confederate Armies* (Washington, DC: Government Printing Office, 1891–95; reprint, New York: Gramercy Books, 1983), plate VIII, 1. Plate VIII shows Mrs. Mason's house about five to six miles north of Liverpool Point and about two miles south of Budd's Ferry on the Maryland bank of the Potomac River.

32. Nevins, *A Diary of Battle,* viii, 7. Major Wainwright participated as the junior member and recorder in a statutory board constituted to pass on the fitness of questionable officers to hold their commissions. The board met in Washington and was empowered to examine officers up to and including the rank of colonel. Wainwright reported that the board completed its business on Saturday, January 5, 1862. One of the officers to appear before the board was "Captain Bunting of the Sixth New York Infantry." Wainwright took special interest in Captain Bunting's case because he was awaiting orders to become chief of artillery of Hooker's Division and Bunting's battery would be part of his command. In fact, Wainwright

states that Captain Bunting had been acting chief of artillery for the past several months. According to Wainwright, in Bunting's case the board found that he "did not know the first thing; could not tell the proper intervals and distance in line; nor where the different cannoneers should sit on the boxes; indeed he at last admitted that he had never studied the tactics, so his was a very short and decided case."

33. RB6. Company Order 21 dated February 5, 1862. In this order, Lieutenant Bramhall announced his election as captain and scheduled another election at three o'clock for the post of junior second lieutenant.

34. *NYWR.* Watson Antrim enlisted September 16, 1861, at New York City as a private and mustered into the Sixth New York Battery the same day. He was promoted to corporal March 30, 1862, and reduced to private September 5, 1863. He mustered out on September 15, 1864, in Washington, D.C.

35. This word appears in various places in Homer's work. In the *Iliad,* it appears in book 1, line 35; book 2, line 207; book 6, line 344; book 9, line 182; book 13, line 795; book 23, line 57. In the *Odyssey,* it appears in book 13, line 81; book 13, line 220. In each case, it appears in the phrase "poluphloisboio thalasses," or "of the loud-roaring sea."

36. *NYWR.* Washington Augustus Roebling enlisted June 15, 1861, at New York City as a private and mustered into the Sixth New York Battery on June 20, 1861. He was promoted to sergeant September 1, 1861, and second lieutenant January 23, 1862. He was discharged for promotion May 26, 1864, and commissioned into the U.S. Army infantry the same date. He served as major and aide-de-camp. Roebling's father was John Augustus Roebling, a pioneer in the design of steel bridges and designer of the Brooklyn Bridge. Washington A. Roebling took over from his father, who was killed in a fall from the bridge on July 22, 1869, and completed its design and construction.

37. *NYWR.* Charles R. Vail enlisted June 15, 1861, at New York City as a private and mustered into the Sixth New York Battery on June 21, 1861. He was wounded in action October 14, 1863, at Bristoe Station and mustered out June 21, 1864, at New York City.

38. Boatner, *Civil War Dictionary,* 120; Nevins, *A Diary of Battle,* 19–20. Whitworth cannons were imported from Britain. Boatner says there were three varieties: two steel, breech-loading rifles (six- and twelve-pounders) and a twelve-pounder muzzle-loader. Whitworths were comparatively common in the Confederate arsenal but were rarely found in U.S. service. Major Wainwright's diary entry for Wednesday, February 26, states that the trial of the Whitworth cannon occurred on the previous day and that he assigned a detachment of "Bramhall's men" to work the guns. The guns were set up "on the plain in front of the First Massachusetts camp. Wainwright described the cannon as being "near six feet long, and not much over two inches bore." The target of the day was the Confederate works at Shipping Point, at a distance of about three miles from the gun position. Wainwright approved of the gun's range and accuracy but assessed it as not being suitable for field service, because of its excessive size and weight, small caliber, inability to fire anything but solid shot, and the great difficulty of spotting the fall of the shot.

39. Nevins, *A Diary of Battle,* vi, 11, 79. Wainwright was commissioned major of the First New York Artillery on October 17, 1861. He was ordered to report for duty

as chief of artillery of Hooker's Division on January 26, 1862, and served as such until he turned over his command on June 3, 1862, to Captain de Russy because of illness. Boatner, *Civil War Dictionary*, 883; L. Van Loan Naisawald, *Grape and Canister* (Gaithersburg, MD: Olde Soldier Books, 1960), 48–51. Wainwright was promoted to lieutenant colonel April 30, 1862, and to colonel June 1, 1862. He was brevetted brigadier general U.S. Volunteers August 1, 1864.

40. *NYWR.* James Horton enlisted August 15, 1861, at New York City as a private and mustered into the Sixth New York Battery the same day. He was promoted to corporal September 28, 1862, and to sergeant July 1, 1864. He mustered out August 16, 1864, at New York City.

41. *NYWR.* "Mr. Morgan" probably was Sylvester R. Morgan, who enlisted August 15, 1861, at New York City as a private and mustered into the Sixth New York Battery the same day. He was promoted to first sergeant September 1, 1861, and to second lieutenant October 31, 1862, when he commissioned into the Eighth New York Light Artillery Battery.

42. Sears, *To the Gates of Richmond*, 370. Brig. Gen. Daniel E. Sickles commanded the Second Brigade of the Second Division (Brig. Gen. Joseph Hooker) of the Third Corps (Brig. Gen. Samuel P. Heintzelman) of the Army of the Potomac during the Peninsula Campaign. The First, Second, and Fifth Sickles were the Seventieth, Seventy-first, and Seventy-fourth New York Infantry regiments.

43. *Dictionary of American Naval Fighting Ships*, 3:467, 6:82; 7:145. *Island Belle* was a side-wheel steamer of 123 tons. It was 100 feet long and had a beam of 20 feet 4 inches and a depth of hold of 6 feet 7 inches. It was armed with one thirty-two-pounder and one twelve-pounder rifle. *Island Belle* was assigned to the Potomac River Flotilla September 17, 1861, and served as a tug and dispatch boat. It escorted transports to Fort Monroe March 19, 1862, and March 23, 1862. It was transferred to the James River Squadron by Flag Officer Goldsborough May 24, 1862, under Comdr. William Smith, senior naval officer, and steamed up the Appomattox River on June 26, 1862, in an attempt to burn the railroad bridge at Petersburg. *Island Belle* ran aground and was burned to avoid capture on June 28, 1862. *Resolute*, a screw tug of ninety tons, was 88 feet 2 inches long. It had a beam of 17 feet and a draft of 8 feet 6 inches. It was armed with one twenty-four-pounder howitzer and one twelve-pounder howitzer. Assigned to the Potomac Flotilla, *Resolute* shelled the Confederate shore batteries at Aquia Creek on May 29, 1861. USS *Thomas Freeborn* was a side-wheel gunboat of 269 tons. It was 143 feet 4 inches long and had a beam of 25 feet 6 inches. *Thomas Freeborn* was armed with two thirty-two-pounders.

44. *Mass. Sol.* Charles H. Chittenden, a twenty-one-year-old cabinetmaker, enlisted May 28, 1861, at Boston for three years as a landsman. He served on receiving ships *Ohio* and *North Carolina* and on USS *Pensacola* and USS *Thomas Freeborn*. He deserted April 16, 1862, from *Thomas Freeborn*.

45. Naisawald, *Grape and Canister*, 591; Sears, *To the Gates of Richmond*, 370. Capt. James E. Smith commanded the Fourth New York Independent Light Battery. The Fourth and Sixth New York Independent Light batteries were part of the division artillery of Brig. Gen. Joseph Hooker's Second Division of the Third Corps of the Army of the Potomac. The other units assigned to the Second Division were Battery D of the First New York Light and Battery H of the First United States.

46. *NYWR.* Joseph Tressera enlisted September 19, 1861, in New York City as a private and mustered into the Sixth New York. He was wounded August 15, 1862,

and admitted August 17, 1862, to the Hammond U.S. General Hospital at Point Lookout, Maryland. He returned to the battery on September 8, 1862, but later deserted (date not stated).

47. *NYWR.* William Addis enlisted August 15, 1861, in New York City and mustered into the Sixth New York Battery. He was discharged for disability January 7, 1863, at Fort Monroe, Virginia.

48. Nevins, *A Diary of Battle,* 32. Major Wainwright's diary entry for Thursday, April 3 states: "Bramhall got his new three-inch guns just in time. They are infinitely better than the James guns he has had."

49. *Mass. Sol.* James W. Goodwin (residence not listed) enlisted February 27, 1862, as a private and mustered into Company D of the Eleventh Massachusetts Infantry. He was wounded in action July 2, 1863, at Gettysburg, Pennsylvania, and died of his wounds July 18, 1863, at Baltimore, Maryland.

50. Sears, *To the Gates of Richmond,* 370. The Third Sickles was the Seventy-second Regiment of New York Infantry.

51. Maj. William Gilham, *Manual of Instruction for the Volunteers and Militia of the United States* (Philadelphia: Charles DeSilver, 1861; reprint, Scotland, PA: C. J. Daley Reproductions, 1992), 491–92, 497. In light artillery tactics, the Number Two received the cartridge and shot from Number Five and loaded the ammunition into the muzzle of the piece.

52. *NYWR.* William Lowney enlisted August 15, 1861, at New York City as a private. He was discharged for disability May 11, 1864, at De Camp General Hospital, David's Island, New York.

CHAPTER 2.
SICK WITH NO CARE:
APRIL–AUGUST 1862

1. *Official Records,* vol. 11, pt. 2, p. 616; vol. 14, pt. 1, p. 98; vol. 18, pt. 1, p. 493. The weapon in question evidently was the Model 1861 Union Repeating Gun, otherwise known as the Ager, or "Coffee Mill" gun. The *Official Records* do not confirm the presence of a weapon of this type near Budd's Ferry, Maryland, in April 1862. Nevertheless, the three reports cited here prove that it was certainly employed in the Peninsula between April and December 1862. A letter dated April 14, 1862, from C. P. Kingsbury, colonel and chief of ordnance, to Brig. Gen. J. W. Ripley, chief of ordnance, requests General Ripley to forward all "Union repeating guns and ammunition on hand." In an after action report by Brig. Gen. I. R. Trimble, CSA, dated July 28, 1862, covering the June 27 Gaines' Mill battle, he reported that his brigade captured "several" of a "sort of 'repeating gun,' called a telescopic cannon, discharging 60 balls per minute." A letter dated December 25, 1862, from Maj. Gen. E. D. Keyes, Commanding Fourth Army Corps, reports that both Fort Magruder and Yorktown contained "one coffee mill (Union repeating)" gun. Since the coffee mill gun was powered by a hand crank, which fed fifty-eight caliber cartridges from a hopper into a rotating drum, it is most unlikely to have been capable of a rate of fire of 240 rounds per minute. General Trimble's report of 60 rounds per minute is probably much more accurate.

2. *NYWR,* RB6. John R. Furbush enlisted June 15, 1861, at New York City as a private and mustered out June 21, 1864, in New York City.

3. Davis et al., *Atlas,* Plates XVIII, 1, and XVIII, 2; Nevins, *A Diary of Battle,* 33, 36. Major Wainwright's diary entry for April 12 is entitled "Camp on Cheeseman's Creek." Cheeseman's Creek is a tributary of the Poquosin River, which empties into the Chesapeake Bay just south of York Point. Goose Creek is a small tributary stream on the north side of Cheeseman's Creek. Thus, the general location of the camp was about two and one-half miles south of the York River and about five or six miles to the southeast of Yorktown. Major Wainwright's April 14 diary entry states that Cheeseman's Creek would be the principal depot for the entire army.

4. *NYWR.* Augustus B. Crane enlisted on August 15, 1861, at New York City as a private. He was wounded June 9, 1863, at Brandy Station and discharged for disability July 19, 1864, at De Camp General Hospital, David's Island, New York.

5. Nevins, *A Diary of Battle,* 39. Major Wainwright's diary entry for April 18 reports that General Hooker had reviewed his batteries that morning and had pronounced himself as "well satisfied" with their condition.

6. Nevins, *A Diary of Battle,* 37; Davis et al., *Atlas,* Plate XVIII, 2. Major Wainwright's diary entry for April 16 reported that he had made a reconnaissance trip with General Hooker to select a new campsite for the division. The site was near general headquarters about four miles closer to Yorktown than the Cheeseman's Creek site and several miles to the west of the mouth of Wormley's Creek, near the Clarke house. Wainwright reported that the site was very congested and did not have space adequate for drilling his batteries.

7. *Mass. Sol.* Stephen W. Drew of Woburn, Massachusetts, enlisted on August 27, 1861, as a surgeon and mustered into the Ninth Massachusetts Infantry on the same day. He was discharged for disability on December 6, 1862.

8. Nevins, *A Diary of Battle,* 41–42; Sears, *To the Gates of Richmond,* 360; Davis et al., *Atlas,* Plate XIX, 2. Wainwright's April 26 diary entry mentions this attack, which was under the command of Brig. Gen. Cuvier Grover. General Grover commanded the First Brigade of General Hooker's Second Division of Brigadier General Heintzelman's Third Corps at Yorktown. General Grover's brigade included the Second New Hampshire, First and Eleventh Massachusetts, and the Twenty-sixth Pennsylvania regiments. Wainwright's account states that General Grover made a dawn attack on a Confederate position located to the left and front of battery number six with five companies of the First and Eleventh Massachusetts and returned with fifteen prisoners, having suffered a loss of three killed and twelve wounded.

9. Davis et al., *Atlas,* Plate XIX, 2; Nevins, *A Diary of Battle,* 43. General Heintzelman's headquarters was located at a steam sawmill about one mile south of "White House" on the main Yorktown Road. The White House was only a few hundred yards from battery position number six. Wainwright's April 29 diary entry states that he had been aroused at "two-thirty o'clock with orders to get under arms as a heavy sortie was expected." No sortie actually occurred, however, and the whole force returned to camp at daybreak.

10. Nevins, *A Diary of Battle,* 42–43. Wainwright's diary entry for April 28 relates that he had received an order for his batteries to picket the "White House" during the hours of darkness.

11. Gilham, *Manual of Instruction,* 499. Number Five's duties were to receive rounds from either Number Six or Number Seven and deliver them to Number Two, who loaded them in the muzzle of the piece.

12. *Mass. Sol.*; Boatner, *The Civil War Dictionary,* 129. Sumner Carruth of Chelsea, Massachusetts, enlisted May 22, 1861, as a captain and mustered into Company H of the First Massachusetts Infantry on May 23, 1861. He was wounded in action June 25, 1862, at Fair Oaks, Virginia. He was discharged for promotion August 19, 1862, and enlisted as a major and commissioned into the Massachusetts Thirty-fifth Infantry. He was promoted to lieutenant colonel August 27, 1862, and was wounded in action September 17, 1862, at Antietam, Maryland. He was taken prisoner of war November 14, 1862, near Fauquier White Sulphur Springs, Virginia. He was paroled, exchanged, and returned to duty February 21, 1863. He was promoted to colonel April 25, 1863, and was given a brevet promotion to brigadier general April 2, 1865.

13. Nevins, *A Diary of Battle,* 44–45. Wainwright's May 4 diary entry recounts the Confederate evacuation of their Yorktown position and the Federal pursuit. He states that General Hooker, "immediately after breakfast," rode over to head-quarters and requested permission to pursue. Permission having been granted, he was back "before nine" and issued orders to his division. Wainwright confirms that the division's wagons had gone down to the landing for provisions, thus delaying the pursuit. He also confirms the presence of torpedoes along the road, indicated by telegraph wires strung so as to act as trip wires.

14. Nevins, *A Diary of Battle,* 47–55; Naisawald, *Grape and Canister,* 48–54; Sears, *To the Gates of Richmond,* 70–75. Major Wainwright placed five of the Sixth New York's three-inch rifles in line before Fort Magruder, along with Battery H, First United States (Captain Weber), and the New York Volunteer batteries of Captains Osborn and Smith (First New York, Battery D, and Fourth New York). Confederate infantry of Longstreet's command, attacking from Fort Magruder, overran and captured twelve pieces, including those of the Sixth New York. The artillery pieces were stuck in deep mud and could not be removed before being overrun. Wainwright's diary entry for May 5, 1862, contains much detail about the action before Williamsburg. He states that Bramhall worked his guns well, firing canister against the charging rebels until the guns were overrun. In reviewing the performance of his officers, Major Wainwright stated: "Of all my officers, Bramhall and all of his lieutenants were all that I could have asked of them, cool, quiet, attending closely to their business and taking good care of their men."

15. Nevins, *A Diary of Battle,* 58–59; Naisawald, *Grape and Canister,* 60. Naisawald states that infantry recovered the Sixth New York's abandoned cannon during the night of May 5–6, the mud having prevented the Confederate forces from removing the pieces. Wainwright's diary entry for May 6, 1862, states that he rode up to his positions of the previous day and found "Bramhall's five guns and one of Webber's Parrotts still stuck in the mud; they had sunk down so deep that the rebs were not able to carry them off." He further stated that Hooker's total artillery losses for the previous day's action amounted to three Parrott guns, one howitzer, one caisson body, and one limber. The limber was from the Sixth New York Battery.

16. Boatner, *Civil War Dictionary,* 501; Sears, *To the Gates of Richmond,* 26–28, 389. Maj. Gen. John Bankhead, "Prince John," Magruder, CSA, commanded Magruder's Command and Magruder's Division at Yorktown and during the Peninsula Campaign.

17. Davis et al., *Atlas,* Plate XVIII, 2. This probably is the landing on Cheeseman's Creek, south of Yorktown.

18. Nevins, *A Diary of Battle,* 63; Davis et al., *Atlas,* Plate XVII, 1. Major Wainwright's diary entry for May 16 reports that the First Brigade of Hooker's Division, with the Sixth New York, rejoined the rest of the division, which was encamped near Slatersville on that date. Wainwright's diary places Slatersville about two miles east of New Kent Court House on the Post Road. Plate XVII confirms this location. George Perkins was with the division wagon train, some distance to the rear.

19. *NYWR.* William Colby enlisted June 15, 1861, at New York City as a private and mustered into the battery June 20, 1861. He deserted December 16, 1862, at Budd's Ferry.

20. Nevins, *A Diary of Battle,* 66–67; Davis et al., *Atlas,* Plate XVII, 1. Wainwright's diary entry for May 18 states that Cumberland was the destination of the march on that day, but the division was forced to camp two miles short of this location because of the condition of the roads and the congested traffic. Cumberland was a small collection of buildings about two miles north of New Kent Court House on the Pamunkey River. It appears that Hooker's Division camped a short distance to the west of New Kent Court House, since George Perkins mentions passing through the place on his march.

21. Sears, *To the Gates of Richmond,* 386. Through the Battle of Seven Pines, the Second Mississippi Regiment was attached to Brigadier General Whiting's Brigade (Col. Evander M. Law) of Maj. Gen. Gustavas W. Smith's Division. General Smith also commanded the left wing of Gen. Joseph E. Johnston's army. After Seven Pines, when Gen. Robert E. Lee took over command from General Johnston, the Second Mississippi Regiment was part of Law's Brigade of Whiting's Division, attached to Major General Jackson's Command.

22. Nevins, *A Diary of Battle,* 67; Davis et al., *Atlas,* Plate XVII, 1. Wainwright's diary entry for May 19 states that Baltimore Crossroads was located about twenty miles from Richmond and about six miles from Bottoms Bridge, over the Chickahominy River. Plate XVII confirms this and places Baltimore Crossroads about eight miles to the west of New Kent Court House; the location of George Perkins's stopping place on May 18.

23. Nevins, *A Diary of Battle,* 69. Wainwright's diary entry for May 23 states that the division moved about four miles on this day and camped near Bottom's Bridge. He also reports that there was a great deal of sickness in the army caused by wet ground, cold rain, an overall lack of campaigning experience in the men, and inefficient medical care. He states the most common health problems were diarrhea and southern (typhoid) fever.

24. *NYWR* and RB6. James Fulton enlisted June 15, 1861, at New York City as a private and mustered into the battery June 20, 1861. The adjutant general's report states that he mustered out June 21, 1864, at New York City; however, battery records indicate that he mustered out June 22, 1865. Joseph M. Patten, aged twenty of Rahway, New Jersey, enlisted August 15, 1861, in New York City. He was discharged from Campbell Military Hospital December 24, 1863.

25. Nevins, *A Diary of Battle,* 70. Wainwright's diary entry for May 24 states that Grover's First Brigade of Hooker's Division plus Bramhall's Sixth New York Independent Battery were sent across the Chickahominy to support Brigadier General Keyes's Fourth Corps in a fight but returned to camp in the evening without being engaged.

26. Davis et al., *Atlas,* Plates XVI and XVII, 1; Nevins, *A Diary of Battle,* 70. The "bottom bridge" of the diary is Bottoms Bridge over the Chickahominy River, about ten miles from Richmond on the Williamsburg Post Road. The Williamsburg Road passed through Baltimore Cross Roads, New Kent Court House, and Slatersville before reaching Williamsburg. It appears that the ambulances, with App and George on board, crossed Bottoms Bridge and followed the division south along White Oak Swamp Road. The ambulances must have camped along the White Oak Swamp Road, about a mile or less from the intersection of Savage's Station and White Oak Swamp Road. According to Wainwright, this was the location of division headquarters and Osborn and Bramhall's batteries.

27. Nevins, *A Diary of Battle,* 71; *Official Records,* vol. 11, pt. 3, pp. 191–92. Wainwright's diary entry for May 26 reports receiving Major General McClellan's General Order 118, which, among other things, required all wagons, except ambulances, to be left on the other bank of the Chickahominy. Wainwright's diary was in error. The order in question was General Order 128 of May 25, 1862. McClellan's order anticipated the imminent onset of a major battle and required the troops advancing beyond the Chickahominy to leave all impedimenta, except ambulance wagons, on the eastern bank of the Chickahominy. Ammunition wagons were also to be left behind, but so disposed that they could be dispatched to their parent brigades and batteries at a moment's notice.

28. Nevins, *A Diary of Battle,* 71. Wainwright's diary entry for May 28 reports a conversation with General Hooker regarding the health of the army. General Hooker, upon returning from army headquarters, stated that "a full quarter" of the army was sick, leaving only sixty-eight thousand total effectives. Wainwright stated that "not more than one in ten" of his men had been reported sick. Evidently, Major Wainwright's estimate included George and App Perkins.

29. Nevins, *A Diary of Battle,* 75. Wainwright's diary entry for May 31 states that Keyes's Fourth Corps was routed in the Battle of Seven Pines and the Fifth and Sixth New Jersey, plus Bramhall's and Osborn's batteries of Heintzelman's Third Corps were ordered to the front in order to stabilize the situation. Wainwright appears to have placed Bramhall's and Osborn's batteries in a clearing bisected by the Williamsburg Post Road about five hundred yards before Fair Oaks Station on the Rappahannock and York River Railroad. Wainwright's batteries do not seem to have actually seen action.

30. *NYWR.* "Saunders" may have been Jonathan B. Sanders, who enlisted on June 29, 1861, at Washington, D.C., as a private and mustered into the battery the same day. He was discharged for disability on June 4, 1864, from De Camp General Hospital at David's Island, New York Harbor. The adjutant general's report also lists a Herman Saunders; however, records indicate that he did not attach into the Sixth New York Independent Battery until September 10, 1862.

31. *NYWR.* Aaron S. Long enlisted August 15, 1861, at New York City as a private and mustered into the battery the same day. He deserted March 20, 1863, at Falmouth, Virginia.

32. *NYWR.* Frank V. W. Jewell enlisted December 2, 1861, at New York City as a private and mustered into the battery the same day. He was promoted to Bugler on April 20, 1862, and mustered out December 1, 1864, at New York City.

33. *RB6.* Richard W. Breese enlisted June 15, 1861, in New York City as a private.

34. *Mass. Sol.* George W. Cobbett, of Woburn, Massachusetts, enlisted August 10, 1861, as a private and mustered into Company F, Twenty-second Massachusetts Infantry the same date. He was wounded in action May 10, 1864, at Laurel Hill, Virginia. He was promoted to sergeant (date not stated) and mustered out on October 17, 1864. Cyrus L. Converse, of Woburn, Massachusetts, enlisted August 10, 1861, as a private and mustered into Company F, Twenty-second Massachusetts Infantry, the same date. He was discharged for disability on January 28, 1863, at Potomac Creek, Virginia.

35. *Mass. Sol.* James T. Newcomb enlisted August 10, 1861, as a private and mustered into Company F, Twenty-second Massachusetts Infantry. He was discharged for disability August 21, 1863, at Beverly Ford, Virginia.

36. *Mass. Sol.* Ephraim B. Penney, of Woburn, Massachusetts, enlisted on August 10, 1861, as a private and mustered into Company F, Twenty-second Massachusetts Infantry. He transferred into the Veteran Reserve Corps on February 10, 1864, and was discharged on August 11, 1864.

37. Gilham, *Manual of Instruction,* 498–99. Number Four's duties were to attach a friction primer to his lanyard and to insert the primer into the vent of the piece. At the command "fire," he jerked the lanyard, thus discharging the piece.

38. *Woburn Records of Births, Deaths, and Marriages, 1640 to 1873* (Woburn, MA: Andrews, Cutler, and Co., 1890), n.p. Zillah E. Beers was married to James Appleton Perkins. They had three children: Albert S., born April 24, 1855; Fayette Appleton, born July 12, 1856; and Cora Evelyn, born August 10, 1859.

39. *NYWR.* Ira D. Shay enlisted June 15, 1861, at New York City as a private and mustered into the battery June 20, 1861. He died of disease on July 28, 1862, in hospital at Harrison's Landing, Virginia.

40. *Register of Soldiers and Sailors of New Hampshire, 1861–65,* accessed at http://www. civilwardata.com. Henry E. Parker of Concord, New Hampshire, enlisted on June 10, 1861, as a chaplain and mustered into F&S Company, Second New Hampshire Infantry. He was discharged on August 5, 1862.

41. *NYWR.* "Frank More" probably was Franklin More, who enlisted on June 15, 1861, at New York City and mustered into the battery on June 20, 1861. He was promoted to artificer on or about December 15, 1861, but was later reduced to the ranks (date not stated). He was mustered out at New York City on June 21, 1864.

42. E. B. Long, *The Civil War Day by Day* (New York: Da Capo, 1971), 246; Gilham, *Manual of Instruction,* 499. Federal forces reoccupied Malvern Hill August 2, 1862. Number Seven was stationed in the rear of the limber, near the left wheel. He cut shell or spherical case fuses, in accordance with orders received, and delivered them to Number Five.

43. Boatner, *Civil War Dictionary,* 236; Sears, *To the Gates of Richmond,* 381; Nevins, *A Diary of Battle,* 79. Gustavus Adolphus de Russy was captain, Fourth U.S. Artillery, at the beginning of the Civil War. He was with the Artillery Reserve, Army of the Potomac, until on or about June 3, 1862, when Major Wainwright turned over his command to him and he became chief of artillery for Hooker's Division. Sears shows de Russy as commanding Third Corps Artillery Reserve during the Seven Days. The corps artillery reserve consisted of New Jersey Light, Battery B; the Sixth New York Independent Light; and the Fourth U.S., Battery K.

44. RB6. John W. Hoffman enlisted August 19, 1861, in Trenton, New Jersey, in Company D, Fifth New Jersey Volunteers. He was detailed into the Sixth New

York Battery on May 27, 1862, and was discharged on a surgeon's certificate in October 1862.

45. *NYWR.* John West enlisted April 22, 1861, at Elmira, New York, as a private and mustered into Company I, New York Nineteenth Infantry, on May 2, 1861. He transferred into the New York Sixth Battery on August 17, 1861. He was promoted to Farrier and Blacksmith on or about December 15, 1861, and was subsequently reduced to the ranks. He mustered out May 1, 1863.

46. *NYWR.* William H. Randolph enlisted June 15, 1861, in New York City and mustered into the battery June 20, 1861. He was promoted but subsequently reduced to the ranks (date not given for both events). He mustered out June 21, 1864, in New York City.

47. Battery Muster Roll (May–June 1862), Hospital Muster Roll, U.S.A. General Hospital at Master Street Philadelphia (special muster dated August 18), Record of Death and Interment (parts 1 and 2), Commonwealth of Massachusetts, Return of a Death, List of Woburn; *Woburn (MA) Budget,* Aug. 15, 1862; *Middlesex Journal,* Aug. 16, 1862. The Battery Muster Roll states that App was absent sick as of May 27, 1862, and the hospital muster roll states that he died on August 8, 1862. The record of death and interment states that he died of phthisis pulmonalis (consumption) on August 8 and that his effects were sent to Mrs. J. A. Perkins. This document also asks for "the usual military honors" to be given at interment. Both the "Return of a Death" and the "List of Woburn Soldiers" state that the cause of death was phthisis pulmonalis, while the *Woburn Budget* and the *Middlesex Journal* notices state that the cause of death was typhoid fever.

48. The *Boston True Flag* was a weekly newspaper published from November 1851 to September 1890.

49. *NYWR.* Benjamin F. Ackerman enlisted September 14, 1861, at New York City as a private and mustered into the battery the same day. He mustered out September 15, 1864, at Washington D.C.

50. *NYWR.* John McDonald enlisted August 29, 1861, at New York City as a private and mustered into the battery the same day. He mustered out on August 31, 1864, at Washington, D.C.

51. RB6. Richard Hadfield, of Derbyshire, England, enlisted as a private on August 19, 1861, in Rahway, New Jersey, into Company H of the Fifth New Jersey Volunteers and was detailed into the Sixth New York Battery May 27, 1862.

CHAPTER 3.
I DON'T LIKE THE PLAN:
SEPTEMBER–DECEMBER 1862

1. RB6. William H. Pearse was born in Dartmouth, England. He enlisted on September 28, 1861, in New York City and was discharged at expiration of his service on September 28, 1864. His occupation was listed as paper stainer.

2. Brev. Maj. Gen. J. G. Barnard, *A Report on the Defenses of Washington, to the Chief of Engineers, U.S. Army* (Washington, DC: Government Printing Office, 1871), 18, 20. General Barnard quoted the report of a commission appointed by the secretary of war in October 1862 to "examine and report on upon a plan of the present forts and sufficiency of the present system of defenses for the city." The commission consisted of senior army officers of the engineer, quartermaster, and artillery branches.

Fort Ellsworth was a component of the system of works "south of the Potomac, commencing with Fort Lyon below Alexandria and terminating with Fort DeKalb [later renamed Fort Strong] opposite Georgetown." The main purposes of Fort Ellsworth were to cover Alexandria and its railroad depot, close a gap between Forts Lyon and Worth, and prevent the rebels from establishing batteries on the heights south of Hunting Creek. Davis et al., *Atlas,* Plate VI, 1. Fort Ellsworth was located about one mile west of Alexandria, between Leesburg Pike and Little River Turnpike, and the Orange and Alexandria Railroad.

3. *The Union Army.* Since leaving its train guard duty at the end of February 1862, Jordan's regiment, the Tenth Maine Infantry, had embarked on a period of arduous active service, having been engaged most notably at Cedar Mountain and Antietam. From September 19, 1862, to September 28, 1863, the regiment was at Maryland Heights, Maryland (opposite Harpers Ferry); Berlin, Maryland (about five miles east of Sandy Hook on the Baltimore and Ohio Railroad); and Fairfax Courthouse and Stafford Courthouse, Virginia.

4. *NYWR,* RB6. One of the deserters was Pvt. John J. Anthony, a twenty-five-year-old carpenter from Richmond, Virginia, who enlisted June 15, 1861, in New York City as a private and deserted September 1, 1862, in Alexandria, Virginia.

5. *Mass. Sol.* William S. Bowen, of Woburn, Massachusetts, enlisted on August 10, 1861, as a private and mustered into Company F, Massachusetts Twenty-second Infantry, the same day. He was discharged for disability on March 26, 1863, at Potomac Creek, Virginia. "Dennett" could have been either George H. Dennett or Robert M. Dennett, both of Woburn. George enlisted on July 24, 1862, as a private and mustered into Company K, Massachusetts Thirty-ninth Infantry, and trans-ferred into the Veteran Reserve Corps on February 15, 1864. Records also indicate he mustered into Company K, Massachusetts Thirty-ninth Infantry, on August 16, 1864. He was promoted to sergeant major on February 1, 1865, wounded in action on March 31, 1865, at White Oak Road, Virginia, and promoted to second lieuten-ant on April 3, 1865, although he did not muster as such. He was mustered out on June 2, 1865. Robert enlisted August 10, 1861, as a private and mustered into Com-pany F, Massachusetts Twenty-second Infantry, the same day. He was wounded in ac-tion June 22, 1862, at Gaines' Mill, Virginia, and discharged for wounds October 3, 1862. Robert also enlisted on November 19, 1863, as a private and mustered into Company K, Thirty-ninth Infantry (the same unit that George H. Dennett served in). Robert was promoted to corporal (date not given) and was again wounded in action at White Oak Road, Virginia, on March 31, 1865 (the same date and loca-tion that George was wounded). He died of his wounds April 12, 1865, at Washing-ton, D.C. Daniel W. Moody of Woburn enlisted June 26, 1861, as a private and mustered into Company D, Massachusetts Twelfth Infantry, the same day. He transferred and mustered into Company A, Veteran Reserve Corps, on July 22, 1863. He was promoted to corporal October 11, 1864, and to sergeant January 26, 1865. He mustered out on November 14, 1865. William M. Cobbett, a twenty-five-year-old cordwainer (shoemaker) of Woburn enlisted March 3, 1862, in the First Regiment of Heavy Artillery, Massachusetts Volunteers. He was promoted to captain on June 22, 1864. He died at Andersonville Prison on September 2, 1864, and was buried in grave 7802.

6. Barnard, *The Defenses of Washington,* 22. The 1862 commission stated that Fort Runyon had lost its former importance but "should not have been permitted to

fall to decay, nor to be disarmed. As a tete de pont it should be rearmed and kept in perfect condition in every respect." Davis et al., *Atlas,* Plates VI and LXXXIX, 1. Fort Runyon was located on the Virginia bank of the Potomac River on the toll road from Alexandria to the District of Columbia and near the intersection of the toll road with Columbia Turnpike and the Chesapeake and Ohio Canal. The fort controlled the entry to the District of Columbia via Long Bridge.

7. Barnard, *The Defenses of Washington,* 22. The commission stated, "Fort Albany is a work partly bastioned, well built, and in admirable condition . . . . It is well defiladed and in a very advantageous position to cover the Long Bridge and look into the gorges of Forts Richardson and Craig. It sees the high ground in front of Fort Tillinghast and commands the valley between Forts Richardson and Scott." Davis et al., *Atlas,* Plates VI and LXXXIX, 1. Fort Albany was located on Columbia Pike, about one mile below Fort Runyon.

8. Barnard, *The Defenses of Washington,* 19–20, 35–37. The commission stated that Fort Lyon "forms the extreme left (of the Alexandria fortifications), and its function is a most important one—that of holding the heights south of Hunting Creek from which Alexandria could be shelled and our left flank exposed." Barnard states that the importance of "seeing well, and sweeping by artillery fire the deep and broad valley of Hunting Creek and the tributary valley through which the telegraph road approaches Alexandria" was recognized early in the war. Davis et al., *Atlas,* Plates VI and LXXXIX, 1. Fort Lyon was located off Telegraph Road on Mount Eagle, above Hunting Creek, just below the city of Alexandria.

9. This was the bridge carrying Telegraph Road over Hunting Creek.

10. Long, *Civil War Day by Day,* 264. At Frederick, Maryland, on September 9, Lee issued Special Order 191 for further operations north of the Potomac River. On the same day, Major General Heintzelman was put in charge of the defenses of Washington south of the Potomac River. Major General McClellan's Army of the Potomac, split into three wings, was in pursuit of Lee's army north of the Potomac.

11. Davis et al., *Atlas,* Plates VI and LXXXIX, 1. The Theological Seminary was located north of Hunting Creek, about a half mile south of Leesburg Turnpike between the turnpike and Fort Worth.

12. Long, *Civil War Day by Day,* 266. On September 14, heavy fighting occurred at Crampton's Gap, South Mountain, Fox's Gap, and Turner's Gap.

13. *Mass. Sol.* Nathaniel Ingerson, of Woburn, Massachusetts, enlisted on August 15, 1862, as a private and mustered into Company K, Massachusetts Thirty-ninth Infantry, on August 22, 1862. He was discharged for disability on November 13, 1862, at Washington, D.C.

14. The battle of Antietam Creek (Sharpsburg) occurred on September 17.

15. Barnard, *The Defenses of Washington,* 20. The 1862 commission stated "Fort Worth occupies a very commanding position. A larger work would have been desirable, but the site would not have permitted it. . . . The work is deficient in fire upon the heights directly opposite south of Hunting Creek." Davis et al., *Atlas,* Plates VI and LXXXIX, 1. Fort Worth was located about one and three-quarter miles west northwest of Fort Ellsworth, just north of Little River Turnpike and less than one-quarter mile south of the Theological Seminary.

16. *Register of Officers and Men of New Jersey in the Civil War,* accessed at http://www.civilwardata.com (hereafter cited as *New Jersey*); Sears, *To the Gates of Richmond,* 381. John E. Beam enlisted on September 3, 1861, as a captain and was

commissioned into Battery B, New Jersey First Light Artillery. Battery B, along with the Sixth New York Independent Light Battery, was assigned to the Third Corps Artillery Reserve (Capt. G. A. DeRussy) during the Seven Days of the Peninsula Campaign. Captain Beam was killed in action at Malvern Hill on July 1, 1862.

17. *NYWR.* Wardell Bunting enlisted November 23, 1861, at New York City as a private and mustered into the battery. He was promoted to sergeant on December 1, 1861. On September 15, 1862, he was discharged and promoted to second lieutenant in the West Virginia Sixteenth Infantry.

18. Boatner, *Civil War Dictionary,* 64–65; Sears, *To the Gates of Richmond,* 380. During the Peninsula Campaign, Brig. Gen. David Bell Birney commanded the Second Brigade of the Third Division (Brig. Gen. Philip Kearny) of Third Corps (Brig. Gen. Samuel P. Heintzelman). After General Kearny was killed at the Battle of Chantilly on September 1, 1862, General Birney took temporary command of General Kearny's Division.

19. *Mass. Sol.* William Coverny and James Cogan, both of Stoneham, Massachusetts, enlisted on July 14, 1862, as privates and mustered into Company D, Massachusetts Thirty-third Infantry, on August 7, 1862. Coverny was wounded in action at Gettysburg, Pennsylvania, on July 2, 1863, and was discharged for wounds on December 24, 1863. Cogan was wounded July 4, 1864 (place not stated), promoted to corporal on May 1, 1865, and mustered out on June 11, 1865.

20. *Mass. Sol.* John Howard Sullivan, of Stoneham, Massachusetts, enlisted on August 4, 1862, as a private and mustered into the Massachusetts Ninth Light Artillery Battery on August 10, 1862. He was promoted to corporal (date not stated) and mustered out on June 6, 1865.

21. Barnard, *The Defenses of Washington,* 3. The Washington Arsenal was situated "at the very angle of confluence of the Potomac and Anacostia." During the war, it was used to store "enormous quantities of guns, small arms, and ammunition." Davis et al., *Atlas,* Plates VI and LXXXIX, 1. The U.S. Arsenal was located on the site of Fort Lesley J. McNair at Greenleaf Point between the Potomac and Anacostia (Eastern Branch) rivers.

22. RB6. Captain Bramhall's letter to Maj. H. W. Brevard, assistant adjutant general of the First Division of the Third Corps, dated October 10, 1862, reported the participation of the battery in an expedition to Rappahannock Station. The force consisted of two brigades of cavalry plus the Sixth New York Independent Battery under the command of Col. L. Davies. Captain Bramhall claimed "the manner in which the Battery marched during the homewards journey attested only too well to the damaging effects of the Excessive marching it had done, and also to the wisdom of the course adopted in returning even as late as we did." He further reported that prior to the expedition, the battery "was in fine condition and excellently qualified to perform any duty which courses legitimately within the scope of a volunteer Battery, and you may well believe it to be a source of exceeding regret to me to see it reduced to such a deplorable condition."

23. *NYWR, RB6.* The battery descriptive roll lists Charles C. Morrell, a twenty-year-old clerk from New Orleans, Louisiana, who enlisted August 15, 1861, as a private in New York City and was discharged for disability August 18, 1862. The adjutant general's report states that "Morrill" was promoted to corporal on September 1, 1861.

24. *NYWR*. Edwin A. Marsh enlisted on June 15, 1861, at New York City as a private. He mustered into the battery on June 20, 1861, and was mustered out on June 21, 1864, at New York City.

25. *NYWR*. Charles S. Devoe enlisted on October 2, 1861, as a private and mustered into the battery the same day. He was promoted to corporal May 28, 1864, and reduced to private March 1, 1865. He mustered out July 8, 1865, at Hart's Island, New York Harbor.

26. *NYWR*. William Bishop enlisted June 15, 1861, at New York City as a private and mustered into the battery on June 20, 1861. He was promoted to corporal September 20, 1861, and to sergeant January 9, 1863. He was wounded in action June 9, 1863, at Brandy Station, Virginia, and was mustered out June 19, 1864, at New York City.

27. Barnard, *The Defenses of Washington,* 22, 40, 42; Davis et al., *Atlas,* Plates VI and LXXXIX, 1. Fort Craig was one of five works described as "lunettes with stockaded gorges" (the others being Forts Tillinghast, Cass, Woodbury, and DeKalb) covering the "heights of Arlington, from which the enemy would have some of the most important public buildings of the city under the fire of his rifled guns." Fort Craig was located about one-half mile from Fort Albany, north of Columbia Turnpike. Fort Tillinghast and the other small forts on Arlington Heights overlooked the present Arlington National Cemetery. The Fourteenth Massachusetts Volunteer Infantry appears to have been a six-month militia outfit and may have been assigned to Fort Albany from October 1861 to March 1862.

28. Davis et al., *Atlas,* Plate VI, 1, and *Mass. Sol.* Fort DeKalb was located on the heights above the Potomac River about a mile southwest of the aqueduct crossing between Arlington and Georgetown (site of the present Key Bridge) Edwin F. and John Henry Smith were members of Company A, First Massachusetts Heavy Artillery. Both enlisted on July 5, 1861, as privates. Edwin was promoted to corporal (date not stated) and discharged for disability on July 17, 1865. John was discharged for disability on January 21, 1864.

29. Davis et al., *Atlas,* Plates VI and LXXXIX, 1; *NYWR*. Forts Haggerty, Corcoran, and Bennett protected the approaches to the aqueduct. Fort Cass was located about a mile north of Fort Tillinghast. Charles H. Leonard enlisted at New York City on August 15, 1861, as a private and mustered into the battery the same day. He was mustered out on August 15, 1864, at New York.

30. RB6. Edward M. Rake enlisted on December 5, 1861, at Trenton, New Jersey, for three years. He transferred from Company B, Sixth Regiment New Jersey Volunteer Infantry, on May 27, 1862.

31. *NYWR*. Abram T. Cole enlisted on August 15, 1861, at New York City as a private and mustered into the battery the same day. He mustered out on August 16, 1864, at New York City.

CHAPTER 4.
THE BULLETS BEGAN TO WHIZ ABOUT OUR EARS:
DECEMBER–JUNE 1863

1. *The Parish of Saint Mary* (Piscataway, MD: Sesquicentennial Celebration Committee, 1980). Saint Mary's Catholic Church of Piscataway is located at 13401

Piscataway Road, Clinton, Maryland. The first church building on this site was begun in 1838 and completed about 1847. It was used until 1901. A new church was built on the same site and dedicated in 1904. The corner stone from the original building, bearing the date 1838, was incorporated into the new building.

2. Boatner, *Civil War Dictionary,* 418; Edward G. Longacre, *The Man behind the Guns: A Biography of General Henry J. Hunt, Commander of Artillery of the Army of the Potomac* (New York: A. S. Barnes and Co., 1977), 135; Naisawald, *Grape and Canister,* 182. Henry J. Hunt, promoted to brevet brigadier general September 15, 1862, was designated chief of artillery of the Army of the Potomac by Major General McClellan in time for the Battle of Antietam. This probably is the "Major Hunt" mentioned in George Perkins's diary.

3. Boatner, *Civil War Dictionary,* 855; Naisawald, *Grape and Canister,* 237. The chief of reserve artillery was Brig. Gen. Robert O. Tyler, who was promoted to that rank November 29, 1862. Both Boatner and Naisawald state that he was in command of the artillery of the Center Grand Division at the Battle of Fredericksburg.

4. *Mass. Sol.* John Peters Crane of Woburn, Massachusetts, enlisted on August 10, 1861, as a first lieutenant and was commissioned into Company F, Massachusetts Twenty-second Infantry on the same date. He was taken prisoner June 27, 1862, at Gaines' Mill, Virginia, promoted to captain on August 5, 1862, released from prisoner of war status on August 13, 1862, and resigned on May 18, 1863.

5. *NYWR.* Matthew Kiely enlisted on September 16, 1861, at New York City as a private. He mustered out September 16, 1864, at Washington, D.C.

6. RB6. Robert H. Fowle, a twenty-three-year-old from New York, New York, enlisted June 15, 1861, at New York City as a private. He was discharged June 20, 1864.

7. Naisawald, *Grape and Canister,* 585; *Official Records,* vol. 29, pt. 1, pp. 219, 245, 305, 677; Edwin B. Coddington, *The Gettysburg Campaign: A Study in Command* (New York: Simon and Schuster, 1968), 578. The Lieutenant French of George Perkins's diary probably was Lt. Frank S. French. Naisawald states that Lieutenant French was assigned to Battery E of the First Regiment of U.S. Artillery. The *Official Records* show that Lieutenant French commanded the First U.S., Battery I, in the Bristoe Campaign, October 9–22, 1863, when it was assigned to the Second Corps Artillery under Capt. John Hazard, and Battery E, First U.S., during the Mine Run Campaign in November 1863, when his battery was assigned to the Second Brigade, Horse Artillery, commanded by Capt. William M. Graham. Coddington states that Battery I, First U.S., was part of the Artillery Brigade of the Second Army Corps (Maj. Gen. Winfield S. Hancock) during the Gettysburg Campaign.

8. *NYWR.* Cornelius H. Miller enlisted on June 15, 1861, at New York City as a private. He mustered out on June 21, 1864, at New York City.

9. *NYWR.* Uel Freeman enlisted June 15, 1861, at New York City as a private and mustered into the battery the same day. He was discharged for disability at Falmouth, Virginia, on January 18, 1863.

10. Billings, *Hardtack and Coffee,* 102–7. Billings provides a particularly good description of this service, one of the more unpleasant aspects of army life.

11. This diary entry probably is a misspelling of Capt. James M. Robertson.

12. *Mass. Sol.* Jesse Richardson, of Winchester, Massachusetts, enlisted on July 8, 1862, as a private and mustered into Company G, Massachusetts Second Infantry, the same day. He was promoted to corporal (date not stated), first sergeant on October 1, 1863,

first lieutenant on May 24, 1864, and captain on July 3, 1865. He was wounded on July 3, 1863, at Gettysburg, Pennsylvania, and mustered out on July 14, 1865, from Company K, Massachusetts Second Infantry.

13. *Maine*; *Woburn Record of Birth, Marriages, and Deaths: 1640–1873* (Woburn, MA: Andrews, Cutler, and Co., 1890), n.p. Charles A. Green, of Portland, Maine, enlisted on August 22, 1862, as a private and mustered into Company D, Maine Tenth Infantry, the same day. He transferred into Company D, Twenty-ninth Maine Infantry, on May 31, 1864, and was wounded in action at Winchester, Virginia, on September 19, 1864. He was discharged on June 9, 1865. George Perkins's mother, Caroline Green Perkins, was a daughter of John and Elizabeth Green, of Portland, Maine. Leonard G. Jordan, an eighteen- or nineteen-year-old from Portland, Maine, enlisted on August 22, 1862, as a private and was mustered into Company D of the Tenth Maine Infantry on the same date.

14. *Official Records*, vol. 21, pp. 147, 991, 995; *Map of Field of Occupation Army of the Potomac* (corrected April 10, 1863, Brig. Gen. G. K. Warren), Fredericksburg and Spotsylvania National Military Park. Various reports by Brig. Gen. Rufus Ingalls, Maj. Gen. Franz Sigel, and others place Hope Landing on Aquia Creek, about two or three miles from the town of Stafford Court House. In a report to Maj. Gen. Ambrose Burnside dated March 19, 1864, General Ingalls stated that during General Burnside's tenure as commanding general of the Army of the Potomac "most of the Eleventh Corps and a portion of the cavalry were supplied from a depot on Acquia Creek, at Hope Landing." The map indicates Hope Landing was located about two miles from the mouth of Aquia Creek. A network of country roads or trails led from Hope Landing to Brooks Station on the Fredericksburg and Potomac Railroad.

15. Capt. James M. Robertson was commander of the First Horse Artillery Brigade of the Army of the Potomac.

16. *Official Records*, vol. 25, pt. 2, 100-101. An order dated February 25, 1863, from Col. B. F. Davis, Eighth New York Volunteer Cavalry, commanding the First Cavalry Brigade, to Major Markell, commanding the brigade pickets, identifies the location of the headquarters of the First Cavalry Brigade as being near Hope Landing.

17. *NYWR*. John Horne enlisted June 15, 1861, in New York City as a private. He was listed as being taken prisoner June 9, 1863, at the battle of Brandy Station and paroled June 13, 1863, at City Point, Virginia. He mustered out on June 21, 1864, at New York City. George Perkins's January 21, 1862, letter lists J. B. Horne as being one of five "Woburn boys" in the battery.

18. *Official Records*, vol. 25, pt. 1, 84-85, 1097; Stephen W. Sears, *Chancellorsville* (New York: Houghton Mifflin, 1996), 466. Lieutenant Woodruff was attached to Battery M, Second U.S., Lt. Robert Clarke commanding. During the Chancellorsville Campaign, Battery M was assigned to the Horse Artillery Brigade commanded by Capt. James M. Robertson.

19. RB6. Battery records in the National Archives indicate the soldier was Richard H. Paxton, of Patterson, New Jersey. The after action report of Lt. George Brown, acting commanding officer, dated March 19, 1863, states that Paxton was killed in action March 17 during the battle. Further, battery muster records confirm that Paxton was a member of the battery, enlisting at New York City on September 27, 1861, and being killed in action at Kelly's Ford on March 17, 1863.

20. Boatner, *Civil War Dictionary,* 35; and Edward G. Longacre, *The Cavalry at Gettysburg* (Lincoln: Univ. of Nebraska Press, 1986), 46. Brig. Gen. William W. Averell commanded the Second Cavalry Division at the March 17, 1863, Battle of Kelly's Ford, a ten-hour engagement in which the Federal cavalry roughly handled the Confederate cavalry of Fitzhugh Lee. Major General Hooker relieved General Averell of command on May 3, 1863, during the Battle of Chancellorsville for reporting that the country in front of the right flank of the Army of the Potomac was unsuitable ground for the employment of cavalry.

21. *NYWR.* George F. Mann enlisted on October 4, 1861, at New York City as a private and mustered into the battery the same day. He was promoted to corporal on July 6, 1864, was reduced to private (date not stated), and mustered out on October 3, 1864, at Washington, D.C.

22. Nevins, *A Diary of Battle,* 177–78. Colonel Wainwright's diary entry for April 8, 1863, mentions the presidential visit, which began with the inspection of General Pleasonton's Cavalry Corps on Monday, April 6. Wainwright has high praise for the showing of the horse batteries assigned to the cavalry and particularly singles out the Sixth New York under Captain Martin.

23. *Official Records,* vol. 25, pt. 2, 18-28, 575-586. Maj. Gen. Joseph Hooker's January 31, 1863, *Report on the Organization of the Army of the Potomac* lists Lt. R. H. Chapin as the commander of the Second United States Artillery, Battery M. General Hooker's report of May 31, 1863, lists Lt. A.C.M. Pennington as the commander of Battery M. At various times, the battery appears to have been commanded by Lt. Robert H. Chapin, Lt. Alexander C. M. Pennington, and Lt. Robert Clarke.

24. Davis et al., *Atlas,* Plate VIII; *Official Records,* vol. 51, pt. 1, 636-638; ser. 3, vol. 4, 885. In their March 1862 retreat from the Lower Potomac, Confederate forces destroyed the railroad bridge over Potomac Creek. The bridge was about four miles from Aquia Creek Landing on the Richmond, Fredericksburg and Potomac Railroad. When Federal forces occupied the area from the Potomac River south as far as Fredericksburg after the Confederate retreat, Col. Herman Haupt repaired the railroad and rebuilt the bridge over Potomac Creek. The rebuilt bridge was 414 feet long and 82 feet high.

25. Sears, *Chancellorsville,* 464; *The Union Army.* Jordan and Green's regiment, the Tenth Maine Infantry, was assigned to Major General Slocum's Twelfth Corps and served as Provost Guard at Corps Headquarters. As such, the regiment was not actively engaged at the Battle of Chancellorsville.

26. Davis et al., *Atlas,* Plate XLI, 1. This map, by Jedediah Hotchkiss, perhaps the best extant map of the Chancellorsville Campaign, shows the various positions of the two armies day-by-day.

27. Naisawald, *Grape and Canister,* 294–97; Sears, *Chancellorsville,* 289, 290, 465. The open field was Hazel Grove. The Sixth New York was assigned as artillery support for Brig. Gen. Alfred Pleasonton's First Division of the Cavalry Corps. General Pleasonton seems to have exercised some supervision of the six guns of Martin's Sixth New York and about sixteen other artillery pieces of the Twelfth Corps in the Hazel Grove position, when troops of the Fourth Georgia belonging to Rode's Division of Jackson's Second Corps attacked the position in the waning moments of Jackson's May 2 flank attack against the right wing of the Army of the Potomac.

28. Sears, *Chancellorsville,* 254–57, 459. Col. Hiram Berdan commanded a two-regiment brigade composed of the First and Second U.S. Sharpshooters. During

the Chancellorsville Campaign, Berdan's troops were designated the Third Brigade of the Third Division of Third Corps, Maj. Gen. Daniel E. Sickles. During this action, the sharpshooters captured the better part of the Twenty-third Georgia regiment in and around Catherine Furnace. The Twenty-third was acting as rear guard for Lt. Gen. Thomas J. Jackson's flank march against the right wing of the Army of the Potomac.

29. *NYWR.* Pvt. Luther Hilvesty was killed in action and Privates Edward Hart and Noah S. Laing were wounded in action. Private Hart was discharged for disability October 27, 1864, from Camp Barry, Washington, D.C. Private Laing was discharged for disability on August 24, 1864, from Grant General Hospital at Willets Point, New York.

30. *NYWR.* This was Pvt. Herman Saunders. Saunders had attached into the Sixth New York Battery on September 10, 1862, from Company G, Eighth New Jersey Infantry.

31. Sears, *Chancellorsville,* 390–91. Late in the afternoon of May 3, Maj. Robert A. Hardaway, of Maj. Gen. Richard S. Anderson's Division (Lee's First Corps) took a detachment of thirteen rifled artillery pieces on a reconnaissance toward the Federal position at U.S. Ford. Hardaway placed ten of the guns on high ground overlooking the Federal camps north of the Rapidan and opened fire at three o'clock in the morning on May 4. After firing 150 rounds, Hardaway departed.

32. Sears, *Chancellorsville,* 465. "Tydbauld's flying battery" probably was the Second U.S., Battery A, commanded by Capt. John C. Tidball. Tidball's command was assigned to Brig. William W. Averell's Second Division of the Cavalry Corps.

33. *Maine.* Leonard C. Boody, a twenty-one-year-old from Portland, Maine, enlisted on March 9, 1862, as a private and mustered into Company D, Tenth Maine Infantry, the same day. He transferred into Company D, Twenty-ninth Maine Infantry, on May 31, 1864. He mustered out and was discharged at the expiration of service on August 9, 1865.

34. Obituary of Maj. William P. Jordan, Leonard's brother, from the *(Portland, ME) Daily Eastern Argus,* January 11, 1906. The obituary states that Rev. Leonard G. Jordan resided in Oakland, California.

35. Billings, *Hardtack and Coffee,* 148. Billings asserts this was a favorite punishment in light artillery units.

36. *Veterans Graves Registry Project* (Washington, DC: Works Progress Administration, 1942), No. 165-1-14-284; G. M. Hopkins, *Atlas of the Town of Woburn, Massachusetts* (Philadelphia: G. M. Hopkins & Co., 1875). The Works Progress Administration report documents that Pvt. James A. "App" Perkins is buried in Lindenwood Cemetery, Lot 635, Grave 8, Section 3, Stoneham, Massachusetts. At the time of App's interment, Lindenwood Cemetery, on Railroad Street (or Montvale Road) was located in the town of Woburn and remained so at least until 1875, as shown by the Hopkins map of that date. That section of Woburn that enclosed Lindenwood was later transferred to Stoneham.

37. Harvard University Biographical File, n.p.; *Cambridge Chronicle,* Nov. 4, 1892; *Cambridge Tribune,* Aug. 19, 1904; *Boston Evening Transcript,* July 29, 1915. John Read was born on May 19, 1840, in Cambridge, Massachusetts, and died in Cambridge on July 29, 1915. He entered Harvard College in 1858 with the class of 1862 and graduated with his class. After his graduation, he enlisted in the U.S. Navy and served as an officer until resigning in 1865 because of ill health. He was on board

the USS *Keokuk* when that ship was disabled in action and later sank after Admiral du Pont's April 7, 1863, attack on Charleston Harbor. He later was assigned to the gunboat *Granite City* and participated in the blockade as part of the West Gulf Squadron. Mr. Read participated in land operations along the Gulf Coast under the command of General Washburn, was captured in May 1864, and spent eight months in a Confederate prison camp. After his release, he was assigned to the sloop of war *Kearsarge* but soon resigned. Postwar, John Read was active in local and state politics, veterans' organizations, and was a commissioner of the State Nautical Training School. According to the *Cambridge Tribune,* Mr. Read held the rank of captain in the U.S. Navy.

38. Strabo, *Geography,* trans. Horace L. Jones, Loeb Classical Library ed., 8 vols. (Cambridge, MA: Harvard Univ. Press, 1917–32), 13.4.11. "The surface of the plain [the Katakekaumene country in Mysia] is covered with ashes . . . and the mountainous and rocky country is black, as though from conflagration. Now some conjecture that this resulted from thunderbolts and from fiery subterranean outbursts, and they do not hesitate to lay there the scene of the mythical story of Typhon; and Xanthos adds that a certain Arimos was king of this region; but it is not reasonable to suppose that all that country was burnt all at once by reason of such disturbances, but rather by reason of an earth-born fire, the sources of which have now been exhausted."

CHAPTER 5.
I ENTERED THE SERVICE WITH VERY
LITTLE PATRIOTISM:
JULY–OCTOBER 1863

1. *Biographical Directory of the United States Congress, 1774–Present* (Washington, DC: Government Printing Office, 1989), n.p.; *Richmond Enquirer,* Mar. 4, 1862; *(Staunton, VA) Spectator,* Dec. 8, 1863. John Minor Botts was born in Dumfries, Virginia, on September 16, 1802, and died in Richmond, Virginia, on January 8, 1869. He was admitted to the bar in 1830; was a member of the State House of Delegates 1833–39; was elected as a Whig to the Twenty-sixth and Twenty-seventh Congresses (Mar. 4, 1839–Mar. 3, 1843); and was elected to the Thirtieth Congress (Mar. 4, 1839–Mar. 3, 1843), in which he was chair of the Committee on Military Affairs. He was a member of the state constitutional convention 1850–51 and a delegate to the Virginia Loyalists' Convention in 1866. The *Richmond Enquirer* of March 4, 1862, reports Mr. Botts's arrest on the previous day and his confinement in the "private jail of McDaniel's on Franklin Street, near Sixteenth." According to the *Enquirer,* Botts and others arrested the same day were suspected of engaging in "treasonable correspondence with the enemy" and "abetting the organization of a party having for its object the overthrow of the existing government." The *Spectator* article of December 8, 1863, reports on a letter that Botts wrote to the *Examiner* on October 18. In this letter, Botts admits to having met with Major General Meade, commander of the Army of the Potomac, and refers to his earlier arrest and confinement, without charges, in a "filthy negro jail," as well as a recent second arrest on unspecified charges. Botts continued to proclaim his intention to take no part in the war and to continue to adhere to his opinions and principles, which he

had held for thirty years. The letter concluded by saying that, if doing so made him a traitor, "then a traitor's life let me live, or a traitor's death let me die."

2. Warner, *Generals in Blue*, 240–41. This was Maj. Gen. Andrew Atkinson Humphreys, who became chief of staff in the aftermath of the battle of Gettysburg.

3. *Official Records*, vol. 29, pt. 1, pp. 116–18; 120–28; Davis et al., *Atlas*, Plates XLV and LXXXV, 3. The First Massachusetts Cavalry participated in the Cavalry Corps' movement from the Rappahannock to the Rapidan rivers in early September 1863. It appears that on September 14, Gen. D. McM. Gregg, commander of the Second Division of the Cavalry Corps, had directed Col. H. B. Sargent, commanding officer of the First Massachusetts, to take command of a portion of the First Brigade of the Second Division and conduct a reconnaissance toward Rapidan Station. The detachment consisted of the First Massachusetts, Sixth Ohio, and First Rhode Island cavalry regiments. Colonel Sargent reported that he was warmly engaged on September 14 and 15 by enemy forces in the vicinity of Rapidan Station and found the rebels in strength in the vicinity. This action was part of a multipronged offensive, which began on September 12. The Third Division, Brig. Gen. Judson Kilpatrick commanding, crossed the Rappahannock at Kelly's Ford on that date and drove toward Brandy Station, Culpeper Court House, linking up with Brig. Gen. John Buford's First Division at Culpeper on the thirteenth and driving Stuart's cavalry south past Pony Mountain and across the Rapidan River at Raccoon Ford.

4. Boatner, *Civil War Dictionary*, 533–44; Warner, *Generals in Blue*, 300–301. John Baillie McIntosh commanded the First Brigade, Second Division, Cavalry Corps of the Army of the Potomac, until severely injured by a fall from his horse in September 1863.

5. This Latin passage from Book 1.37 of Horace's *Odes* should read "Nunc est bibendum, nunc pede libero pulsanda tellus" (To drinking now, now all to the nimble feet that beats the earth).

CHAPTER 6.
A SHARPSHOOTER CAME VERY NEAR TO BRINGING ME DOWN: OCTOBER–DECEMBER 1863

1. *NYWR*. Rufus N. Miller enlisted on September 14, 1861, at New York City as a sergeant. He was captured on June 9, 1863, at Brandy Station, Virginia, and paroled June 13, 1863, at City Point, Virginia. He transferred to the U.S. Navy on December 24, 1863, and was promoted to master's mate.

2. Davis et al., *Atlas*, Plates XXIII, 5; XLV, 6; C, 1. The battery's line of march evidently took it about due south of Warrenton, toward Fayetteville and the Orange and Alexandria Railroad. Fayetteville was about two miles to the northwest of Bealeton (not Bealton) Station on the Orange and Alexandria Railroad.

3. *Official Records*, vol. 29, pt. 1, pp. 589, 624, 625, 627, 632. The Confederate forces engaged at Rappahannock Bridge were the regiments of Brig. Harry T. Hays's Louisiana "Tiger" Brigade (Fifth, Sixth, Eighth, and Ninth Louisiana) and three regiments of R. F. Hoke's Brigade (Sixth, Fifty-fourth, and Fifty-seventh North Carolina). Brig. Gen. D. A. Russell, who commanded the First Division of the Sixth Corps in the assault on the Confederate works on the north bank of the

Rappahannock River at Rappahannock Bridge, reported the capture of about 1,300 prisoners. Maj. Gen. J. A. Early's after action report of November 11, 1863, states that he ordered the south end of the bridge to be fired, after it became evident that Confederate resistance on the north bank had ceased and the troops assigned to the position had been captured. The four guns captured were two ten-pounder Parrott rifles and two three-inch Ordnance rifles of Green's Louisiana Guard artillery battery (commanded in this action by Lieutenant Moore). General Early reported a total loss in his division at Rappahannock Bridge of 1,630 killed, wounded, and missing, of which 1,590 were missing. If the losses (359 killed, wounded, and missing, with 309 missing) in Maj. Gen. Robert E. Rodes's division at Kelly's Ford are added to this total, it is clear that the grand total of Confederate losses on November 7 were about 2,000 experienced soldiers. Of this total, more than 1,800 were listed as missing in action.

4. Davis et al., *Atlas,* Plate C, 1. The battery seems to have retraced its steps from Rappahannock Station to Fayetteville, a distance of about nine miles to the northwest.

5. *NYWR.* James E. Tileston enlisted on June 15, 1861, in New York City as a private. He was promoted to first sergeant September 1, 1861, and to second lieutenant May 18, 1864. He mustered out on June 21, 1864, at New York City. Tileston was one of the "Woburn Boys" mentioned in Private Perkins's letter of January 22, 1862, to the *Middlesex Journal.*

6. Davis et al., *Atlas,* Plate C, 1. Sulphur Springs was about five miles northwest of Fayetteville and six miles south of Warrenton, near the Rappahannock River.

7. Davis et al., *Atlas,* Plate XLV, 6. The location of the abortive ambush may have been at the McIlhany House, shown about one mile south of Warrenton.

8. *Official Records,* vol. 29, pt. 1, pp. 552, 659. Maj. John Singleton Mosby, commanding the Forty-third Virginia Cavalry Battalion, sent a November 22, 1863, report to Maj. Gen. J. E. B. Stuart, commanding Cavalry Corps, Army of Northern Virginia. In this brief report, which covered his operations since November 5, he claimed to have captured "about 75 of the enemy's cavalry, over 100 horses and mules, 6 wagons, a considerable number of arms, equipments, &c." Major Mosby did not specifically allude to the affair of November 21 in his report; however, Brig. Gen. David McMurtrie Gregg, commanding Second Division, Cavalry Corps, Army of the Potomac, submitted an after action report on November 22 covering this incident. In his report, General Gregg stated that the guerillas had attacked a wagon train going to Fayetteville on the previous day and that he had pursued the guerillas to within a mile of Thoroughfare Gap, where they scattered into local houses. He further stated that he had captured two guerillas and recovered "seven horses and 2 mules and some United States saddles and clothing." He also reported that the guerillas had captured three men of the wagon escort during their attack but did not claim to have recovered them.

9. *Official Records,* vol. 29, pt. 2, p. 478. Brig. Gen. D. McM. Gregg, commanding Second Division Cavalry Corps, had issued orders on November 22 for all brigades to be in readiness to move at six o'clock the following morning. Brigade commanders were to have three days' rations and two days' forage.

10. Davis et al., *Atlas,* Plate LXXXVII, 2. According to this map, Morrisville would have been no more than one-half mile distant from the Sixth New York's stopping place.

11. *Official Records,* vol. 29, pt. 1, pp. 13–14; vol. 29, pt. 2, pp. 480–81. In his after action report of December 7, 1863, covering the Mine Run Campaign, Major General Meade stated that he issued orders on November 23 for his army to cross the Rapidan River "at the lower fords, in three columns, and by a prompt movement seize the plank road and turnpike, advancing rapidly toward Orange Court-House, thus turning the enemy's works, and compelling him to give battle on ground not previously selected or prepared." Third Corps, under Major General French, was ordered to cross the Rapidan at Jacobs' Mill and proceed to Robertson's Tavern. The Sixth Corps, under Major General Sedgwick, was ordered to follow the Third Corps. The Second Corps, under Major General Warren, was ordered to cross at Germanna Ford and take the turnpike to Robertson's Tavern, where the Third Corps would join it. The Fifth Corps, under Major General Sykes, was directed to cross the Rapidan at Culpeper Ford and continue via the plank road as far as Parker's Store and, "if practicable, to the crossing of the road from Robertson's Tavern." Major General Newton, commanding two divisions of the First Corps, was directed to follow the Fifth Corps. Second Cavalry Division, under Brigadier General Gregg, was ordered to cross the Rapidan "at Ely's Ford and proceed on the Catharpin road as far as Corbin's Bridge, to cover the left flank of the army."

12. Davis et al., *Atlas,* Plate LXXXVII, 2. This plate identifies the area around Ellis' Ford on the Rappahannock River as "Rappahannock City."

13. *Official Records,* vol. 29, pt. 1, p. 13. General Meade delayed the commencement of the operation until the early morning of November 26 because a storm, which occurred during the evening of November 23, made the November 24 kickoff date impracticable.

14. *Official Records,* vol. 29, pt. 2, pp. 489–90. General Meade had received a telegram announcing Grant's victory at Chattanooga and ordered it to be read to the troops before they marched on November 26.

15. *Official Records,* vol. 29, pt. 1, p. 806; Davis et al., *Atlas,* Plates XLIV, 3, and XLV, 1. The Sixth New York Independent Battery marched in company with the Second Cavalry Division along a country road between Ellis' Ford on the Rappahannock River and Ely's Ford on the Rapidan River. The force then proceeded south from Ely's Ford until it hit the Orange Plank Road leading from Chancellorsville. In his Mine Run after action report of December 4, Brigadier General Gregg stated that he halted the division for the night on or near the road leading south from Parker's Store on the Plank Road to Spotsylvania. Parker's Store was about two miles west on the plank road from the intersection that Perkins mentions in his diary. Evidently, the Sixth New York halted for the night somewhat south of the Plank Road, in the vicinity of Parker's Store. Plate XLIV, 3, does not show the ground south of the Plank Road; however, Plate XLV, 1, does show a road leading roughly south from Parker's Store on the Plank Road to a point on the Catharpin Road about two miles west of Whitehall and Shady Grove Church.

16. *Official Records,* vol. 29, pt. 1, pp. 806–8, 897–901; Davis et al., *Atlas,* Plate XLV, 1; Martin F. Graham and George F. Skoch, *Mine Run: A Campaign of Lost Opportunities* (Lynchburg, VA: H. E. Howard, 1987), 105–7, 110–11. After action reports by Brigadier General Gregg (commanding Second Division, Cavalry Corps, Army of the Potomac), Maj. Gen. Harry Heth (commanding Heth's Division of Lt. Gen. A. P. Hill's Third Army Corps, Army of Northern Virginia), and Maj. Gen. J.E.B. Stuart (commanding Cavalry Corps, Army of Northern Virginia) generally

confirm Private Perkins's account of the action of November 27. General Gregg reported that the Second Cavalry Division moved onto the Orange Plank Road in advance of the Fifth Army Corps (Major General Sykes) at Parker's Store and met the enemy skirmishers and cavalry at New Hope Meeting House. General Stuart reported that he pushed on to New Hope Church with one brigade (Gordon's) of Hampton's Division, consisting of the First, Second, Fourth, and Fifth North Carolina regiments, and engaged the Federal forces until reinforced and relieved by Heth's Division. General Heth reported that he received an order at two o'clock in the afternoon on the twenty-seventh to march east on the Plank Road and relieve Stuart's cavalry, who were engaged near New Hope Church with Federal forces. This occurred while he was located near Verdierville, on the plank road leading from Orange Court House to Fredericksburg, about two to three miles west of New Hope Church. General Gregg reported driving the Confederate skirmishers back with dismounted troopers of the First Brigade of his division, two squadrons of the Third Pennsylvania Cavalry, and one of the First Massachusetts Cavalry. He also reported successfully employing one section of Martin's Sixth New York Independent Battery to suppress a Confederate artillery piece that was firing shell and canister at the advancing Federal forces. This was the right section mentioned in Private Perkins's diary. Subsequently, Heth's Division relieved the overmatched Confederate cavalry and stabilized the front, establishing a two-brigade line of battle, with one brigade in reserve. At about the same time, General Heth's position was stiffened by the arrival of Haskell's Battalion of artillery, consisting of the Branch and Rowan North Carolina artillery and the Palmetto South Carolina Artillery. Both General Gregg and General Stuart reported that the artillery took position on the right of the Confederate line. General Gregg countered the arrival of Haskell's Battalion by employing two sections of Martin's Sixth New York Independent Battery. This was the "smart fight" mentioned in Perkins's diary. Plate XLV shows the right of the Confederate position overlapping the Plank Road about 1.5 miles to the south. Perkins states that his section, with one piece in the middle of the Plank Road and the other to the left, fired at a group of Confederate artillery that was positioned to the left of the road. Perkins reported that his battery was relieved by Battery E, First Ohio, after the Fifth Corps relieved Gregg's cavalry division. This may have been the First Ohio Light, Battery L, which was attached to the Fifth Corps Artillery under Capt. Augustus P. Martin during the Mine Run Campaign. The First Ohio's regimental history (*The Union Army,* vol. 2) reported that Battery L lost "one man and several horses killed and several men wounded."

17. Davis et al., *Atlas,* Plates XLIV, 3, and XLV, 1. The Sixth New York's November 28 bivouac evidently was located near the intersection of the Orange Plank Road with the Germanna Plank Road or Culpeper Plank Road leading northwest toward the Germanna Ford crossing of the Rapidan River.

18. *Official Records,* vol. 29, pt. 1, pp. 807, 829, 899–900; Graham and Skoch, *Mine Run,* 107, 111; Davis et al., *Atlas,* Plate XLV, 1. During the evening of November 28, Gen. R. E. Lee issued orders to Maj. Gen. J.E.B. Stuart to take Hampton's cavalry on the following day and gain the rear of the enemy forces to ascertain Federal intentions. General Stuart reported that he marched from his position near Verdierville to the Grasty and Allman houses on the Catharpin Road on the morning of the twenty-ninth. (Plate XLV shows the residences of Grasty and Almond between three to five

miles from Verdierville and about six miles from the intersection of an unnamed road leading northerly from the Catharpin Road to Parker's Store on the Orange and Fredericksburg Plank Road.) General Stuart started Rosser's Brigade of cavalry down the Catharpin Road and General Hampton followed with the two other brigades of his division (Gordon's Brigade and Young's Brigade). General Stuart directed his force to turn north from the Catharpin Road toward Parker's Store, where they encountered a brigade of Gregg's Second Cavalry Division. General Gregg rapidly reinforced his position with three regiments of Col. J. Irvin Gregg's Second Brigade plus a section (two guns) of the Fourth U.S. Artillery. Hampton brought up Gordon and Young's brigades plus Hart's South Carolina Battery, which was assigned to the Cavalry Corps. General Stuart disengaged his force and fell back toward the main line of the Confederate Mine Run positions when he learned that Major General Warren's Second Corps was marching south and imperiling the right flank of the Confederate infantry's position. General Stuart claimed to have captured one hundred prisoners and one supply wagon in this action. General Gregg admitted his loss to be four officers and forty enlisted men wounded in action (one officer subsequently died) and one officer and fifty-four enlisted men missing in action. General Gregg reported losing some rations and stated that one wagon was burned to prevent its falling into the hands of the enemy. He did not, however, admit that Hampton's attack had captured any of his wagons.

19. *Official Records,* vol. 29, pt. 1, p. 807; Graham and Skoch, *Mine Run,* 110–11. General Gregg reported that Col. Thomas C. Devin's Second Brigade of Brig. Gen. John Buford's First Cavalry Division reported to him on November 30 and was posted at Parker's Store, together with Col. John P. Taylor's First Brigade of the Second Cavalry Division. The combined outfit at Parker's Store was part of the force that covered the withdrawal of the army across the Rapidan fords on the night of December 1.

20. Davis et al., *Atlas,* Plates XLIV, 3, and XLV, 1. The Culpeper Plank Road crossed the Rapidan at Germanna (or Culpeper) Ford. The march, which began at 2:00 AM on December 1 at Parker's Store on the Fredericksburg and Orange Plank Road, turned to the left, onto the Culpeper Plank Road near Wilderness Tavern, and continued to Germanna Ford, a total of about eight miles.

CHAPTER 7.
THOUGH HE SLAY ME, YET WILL I TRUST IN HIM: DECEMBER 1863–APRIL 1864

1. Several warships of the Imperial Russian Navy visited Alexandria during the autumn of 1863.

2. This date is an obvious printer's error. George Perkins's diary entry for December 17, 1863, states, "Wrote to H.A.H., also a piece for the *Journal* on circumstance."

3. The identity of the *Hotel Egalite* protagonists appears to be the following: "Sergeant Master," 1st Sgt. James E. Tileston; "Hoplite," Pvt. George Perkins; and "Guidon," Pvt. Cornelius Miller. The identify of "Wax" is unclear, but Perkins's diary entry for December 16, 1863, states that he and Pvt. Matthew Kiely constructed their bunk from oak shingles. "Wax" therefore could be Private Kiely.

4. *Official Records,* vol. 33, pp. 119–20, 515–16. Major General Sedgwick issued orders on February 5 for a demonstration to take place on the following day, along the northern side of the fords of the Rapidan River. This action took place during the temporary absence of Major General Meade, commander of the Army of the Potomac. General Sedgwick's orders directed the Second Corps, Major General Warren commanding, to "move to the vicinity of Morton's Ford, with at least three batteries of artillery, and make demonstrations to cross the river at that point or in that vicinity, through Saturday, Sunday, and Monday, returning to its present camp Monday evening, unless otherwise ordered." The Second Corps, under the temporary command of Brigadier General Caldwell, commander of the First Division of the Second Corps (General Warren being indisposed), advanced as ordered to Morton's Ford on February 6. General Caldwell ultimately passed the entire Third Division of the Second Corps to the southern bank of Morton's Ford. General Warren resumed command of his corps about three o'clock in the afternoon of the sixth. After an engagement with the troops of Ewell's Corps during the afternoon and evening of the sixth, the Third Division recrossed to the northern bank of the Rapidan under cover of darkness. Losses were moderate on both sides.

5. *NYWR.* George's companion probably was Porter Wilson, who enlisted June 15, 1861, at New York City as a private and mustered out June 21, 1864, at New York City.

6. *The Union Army; NYWR;* Henry Woodhead, ed., *Echoes of Glory: Arms and Equipment of the Union* (Alexandria, VA: Time-Life Books, 1996), 148. The Fourteenth New York State Militia, organized in May 1861 in Brooklyn under Col. Alfred M. Wood, was also known as the Brooklyn Phalanx, Brooklyn Chasseurs, and the Chasseurs a Pied. Failing to be ordered to the front under the first call for troops, the Fourteenth Regiment, under special authority from the War Department, mustered into U.S. service and departed for Washington, D.C., on May 18, 1861. It was turned over to the State of New York in September 1861 and received its state designation as the Eighty-fourth Regiment of Volunteers on December 7, 1861. The regiment's uniform was of French Light Infantry (Chasseur) pattern: dark blue jackets with red insignia and trimmings, red trousers, and red kepis. The regiment's 1863–64 winter quarters were in the vicinity of Culpeper, Virginia. Edward B. Fowler was the regiment's colonel, having been promoted from lieutenant colonel on October 24, 1862. He served as colonel until the regiment mustered out on June 6, 1864.

7. Boatner, *Civil War Dictionary,* 188. Maj. Gen. John Newton commanded the First Corps, Army of the Potomac, from July 2, 1863, to March 24, 1864.

8. Boatner, *Civil War Dictionary,* 459–60. Brig. Gen. Hugh Judson Kilpatrick commanded the Third Division, Cavalry Corps, Army of the Potomac, from June 1863 to April 1864. General Kilpatrick led an abortive raid on Richmond February 28 to March 4, 1864.

9. Perkins mentions writing an article for the *Journal* in his diary entry for March 4. Culpeper joyrides are described in the diary entries for February 23 and March 18.

10. Boatner, *Civil War Dictionary,* 191. Maj. Gen. John "Uncle John" Sedgwick commanded the Sixth Corps, Army of the Potomac, from February 4, 1863, to May 9, 1864.

11. *Mass. Sol.;* Roster of GAR Burbank Post 33, 1867–1903, Johnson Collection, box 74, Glennon Archives, Woburn Public Library, Woburn, MA. William P. Brown,

Albert P. Barrett, and Irving Foster were all Woburn residents in the Thirty-ninth Massachusetts Infantry. Brown, a twenty-year-old clerk who was born in Pictou, Nova Scotia, enlisted on June 13, 1861, as a private, mustered into the Fifth Massachusetts Infantry on July 4, 1861, mustered out of the Fifth on July 31, 1861, and mustered into Company K, Thirty-ninth Massachusetts Infantry on August 22, 1862, and was promoted to sergeant the same day. He mustered out on June 2, 1865. Barrett, an eighteen-year-old printer, enlisted on July 19, 1862, as a private and mustered into Company K, Thirty-ninth Massachusetts Infantry, on August 22, 1862. He was wounded in action at Laurel Hill, Virginia, on May 10, 1864, and mustered out on June 2, 1865. Postwar, Barrett was a member of GAR Post 33 (Burbank) in Woburn, as was George Perkins until he left to become a founding member and first commander of GAR Post 161, also of Woburn. Foster, a twenty-one-year-old currier, enlisted on July 24, 1862, as a private and mustered into Company K, Thirty-ninth Massachusetts Infantry, on August 22, 1864. He was killed in action at Petersburg, Virginia, on June 18, 1864.

12. *NYWR.* Watson Antrim enlisted on September 16, 1861, at New York City as a private. He was promoted to corporal March 30, 1862, and reduced to private September 5, 1863. He mustered out September 15, 1864, at Washington, D.C.

13. *Official Records,* vol. 33, pp. 722–23; Nevins, *A Diary of Battle,* 335. Headquarters, Army of the Potomac General Orders No. 10, dated March 24, 1864, announced a War Department Order directing the consolidation of the Army of the Potomac into three corps from the previous five. In the reorganization, the remaining troops of the First Corps transferred to the Fifth Corps, while the First and Second divisions of the Third Corps transferred to the Second Corps. The Third Division of the Third Corps transferred to the Sixth Corps. The corps commanders were Major Generals Sedgwick (Sixth Corps), Hancock (Second Corps), and Warren (Fifth Corps). Colonel Wainwright suspected the order would cause a fair amount of ill feeling in the corps being disestablished by the order.

14. Boatner, *Civil War Dictionary,* 357. Brig. Gen. David McMurtrie Gregg commanded the Second Division, Cavalry Corps, Army of the Potomac.

15. Job 13:15.

16. *Official Records,* vol. 32, pt. 3, pp. 258–59. General Orders No. 144 of April 4, 1864, issued by the War Department Adjutant General's Office, assigned Maj. Gen. Philip Henry Sheridan to command the Cavalry Corps, Army of the Potomac.

17. Boatner, *Civil War Dictionary,* 1. "Abatis" was an obstacle formed of trees felled toward the enemy.

18. *NYWR.* Frank Bliss enlisted June 15, 1861, at New York City as a private. He was promoted to corporal September 1, 1861, and quartermaster sergeant March 1, 1862. He mustered out on June 21, 1864, at New York City.

19. *NYWR.* Smith A. Devoe enlisted September 30, 1861, at New York City as a private and mustered out on September 30, 1864, at Harpers Ferry, Virginia.

20. *Official Records,* vol. 33, p. 893. Major General Sheridan ordered Brig. Gen. Henry Eugene Davies to assume command of the First Brigade, Second Division, Cavalry Corps on April 17, 1864.

21. *NYWR.* Wade Wilson enlisted September 17, 1861, at New York City as a corporal. He was promoted to sergeant April 1, 1862, to second lieutenant June 9, 1863, and to first lieutenant March 1, 1865. He mustered out July 8, 1865, at Hart's Island, New York Harbor.

22. *NYWR.* John H. Vennett enlisted September 14, 1861, at New York City as a private and mustered out September 13, 1864, at Washington, D.C.

CHAPTER 8.
THE REGULARS WORKED THEIR PIECES BEAUTIFULLY: APRIL–JUNE 1864

1. Davis et al., *Atlas,* Plates XXII, 5; XXIII, 4; XLIV, 3; XLV, 1; LXXXVII, 2, 3. All of these maps show Brandy Station about five miles to the north of Stevensburg.

2. Ibid., Plate LV, 3; *Official Records,* vol. 36, pt. 1, p. 773; Boatner, *Civil War Diction-ary,* 840. Todd's Tavern, located at the intersection of the Brock, Piney Branch Church, Catharpin, and Spotsylvania Court House roads, was the scene of intense cavalry action during the Wilderness Campaign. Sheridan ordered Gregg's Second Cavalry Division to the aid of Wilson's Third Cavalry Division in the vicinity of Todd's Tavern on May 5. Wilson had encountered Confederate cavalry west of Todd's Tavern and had been pushed back to that vicinity. After Gregg's arrival, fighting surged back and forth between Shady Grove and Todd's Tavern along the Catharpin Road.

3. *NYWR*; RB6; *New Jersey.* Patrick Brennan enlisted October 7, 1861, at New York City as a private and was killed in action May 6, 1864, at Brock Road, Virginia. William H. Turner enlisted June 15, 1861, at New York City as a private. He was promoted to corporal September 1, 1861, and wounded in action May 6, 1864, at Brock Road, Virginia. He died May 27, 1864, at Armory Square Hospital, Washington, D.C., of complications from amputation of his leg. Daniel E. Cripps, a twenty-one-year-old farmer from Somerset County, New Jersey, mustered into Company D, New Jersey Fifth Infantry, on August 19, 1861. According to the Sixth New York Battery Record Book, Cripps was detailed to the Sixth New York Battery the same day. New Jersey records show that he reenlisted on February 28, 1864, and was killed in action at the Wilderness on May 6, 1864.

4. *Mass. Sol.*; Roster of GAR Post 161, Johnson Collection. Charles Merriam, of Woburn, Massachusetts, enlisted August 10, 1861, as a sergeant and mustered into Company K, Twenty-second Massachusetts Infantry, the same day. He was promoted to first sergeant (date not stated) and killed in action May 10, 1864, at Laurel Hill, Virginia. Cyrus Tay, of Worcester, Massachusetts, enlisted November 15, 1861, as a first lieutenant and commissioned into Company B, Thirty-second Massachusetts Infantry, the same day. He was promoted to captain on August 14, 1862, and wounded in action July 2, 1863, at Gettysburg, Pennsylvania. He was discharged on November 14, 1864. Captain Tay was a member of GAR Post 161 in Woburn.

5. Boatner, *Civil War Dictionary,* 928; Warner, *Generals in Blue,* 562–63. Brig. Gen. Seth Williams was adjutant general, Army of the Potomac, under Major Generals McClellan, Burnside, Hooker, and Meade. Shortly after Lieutenant General Grant made his headquarters with the Army of the Potomac, he selected General Williams to be inspector general. General Williams served in that capacity until February 9, 1866.

6. Boatner, *Civil War Dictionary,* 749. Maj. Gen. J.E.B Stuart pursued Sheridan with Brig. Gen. Fitzhugh Lee's Division and Brig. Gen. James B. Gordon's separate

brigade. The force engaged Sheridan's rear guard at Jarrald's Mill on May 9 and skirmished as far as Mitchell's Shop before being repulsed.

7. Boatner, *Civil War Dictionary,* 749. Major General Sheridan's force consisted of the divisions of Brig. Gen. Wesley Merritt in command of the First Cavalry Division (substituting for Brig. Gen. Alfred Thomas Archimedes Torbert, who was ill), Brig. Gen. David McMurtrie Gregg's Second Cavalry Division and Brig. Gen. James Harrison Wilson's Third Cavalry Division.

8. *Official Records,* vol. 36, pt. 1, p. 828; Gordon Rhea, *The Battles for Spotsylvania Courthouse and the Road to Yellow Tavern, May 7–12, 1864* (Baton Rouge: Louisiana State Univ. Press, 1997), 338. Col. R. A. Alger, commanding the Fifth Michigan Cavalry, submitted a report dated July 8, 1864, to brigade headquarters that substantially confirms Private Perkins's description in his diary entry for May 10. Colonel Alger stated that the brigade charged Beaver Dam Station at about four o'clock in the afternoon on May 9, recapturing 300–400 prisoners and their guard, as well as destroying the station, "three large trains, two locomotives, and a large amount of hospital, commissary, and quartermaster's stores." The Fifth Michigan, along with the First, Sixth, and Seventh Michigan, formed the First Brigade of the First Cavalry Division, commanded by Brig. Gen. George A. Custer.

9. Long, *Civil War Day by Day,* 498; Boatner, *Civil War Dictionary,* 749.

10. Boatner, *Civil War Dictionary,* 749; Rhea, *Spotsylvania Courthouse,* 199–200. On May 11, Brig. Gen. Henry E. Davies's First Brigade of Brig. Gen. David McM. Gregg's Second Division raided Ashland Station on the Richmond, Fredericksburg, and Potomac Railroad. The Second Brigade of the Second Division, under Col. J. Irvin Gregg, was engaged in an intense rearguard action with Brig. Gen. James B. Gordon's Brigade of Maj. Gen. William H. F. Lee's Division at Ground Squirrel Church or Bridge.

11. Davis et al., *Atlas,* Plate LXXIV, 1; *Official Records,* vol. 36, pt. 1, p. 857. The stream seems to have been one of the tributaries of the Chickahominy, either Grassy Creek or Allen's Branch. After destroying Ashland Station, Davies rejoined Sheridan at Allen's Station, about five miles south of Ashland Station on the Richmond, Fredericksburg, and Potomac Railroad.

12. Davis et al., *Atlas,* Plate LXXIV, 1. This was the Richmond, Fredericksburg, and Potomac Railroad at Allen's Station.

13. *Official Records,* vol. 36, pt. 1, pp. 818, 828; Long, *Civil War Day by Day,* 498. At Yellow Tavern, about six miles north of Richmond, Maj. Gen. J.E.B. Stuart was mortally wounded in an encounter with Sheridan's force. Colonel Alger's report describes the action that resulted in General Stuart's mortal wound. Custer reported, "Two pieces of cannon, two limbers, filled with ammunition, and a large number of prisoners were among the results of this charge." Other fighting took place at Ground Squirrel Church or Bridge, Glen Allen Station, and Ashland.

14. Boatner, *Civil War Dictionary,* 540. This was the railroad bridge at Meadow Bridge, on the Meadow Bridge Road from Richmond to Mechanicsville. The main bridge had been destroyed, but the Fifth Michigan Cavalry crossed by the railroad bridge and seized a bridgehead, which allowed the rest of the force to escape to the east.

15. Boatner, *Civil War Dictionary,* 749. After the fight at Yellow Tavern on May 11, Sheridan decided to move south of the Chickahominy to link up with Major General Butler's Army of the James. The night of May 11, Sheridan encountered

torpedoes (land mines) along his route. On the morning of May 12, he was faced by artillery fire from Mechanicsville and infantry forces moving out from Richmond to trap him against the Chickahominy. Nevertheless, he forced a crossing of the Chickahominy at Meadow Bridge and escaped to the east.

16. Davis et al., *Atlas,* Plate LXXIV, 1. Bottom's Bridge on the Chickahominy River was just north of White Oak Swamp and very near the 1862 battlefields of the seven days before Richmond.

17. *Woburn Records of Births, Deaths and Marriages, 1873–1890* (Woburn, MA: Andrews, Cutler, and Co., 1892), n.p.; *Middlesex Journal,* May 21, 1864; *Mass. Sol.* Woburn records indicate that Luther Flint Wyman was born on October 7, 1833, the son of Luther and Sophia Wyman. The *Journal* reported the capture and recapture of Lieutenant Wyman. Luther F. (or Luke F.) Wyman enlisted June 3, 1861, in the Fifth Massachusetts Infantry. The unit was mustered out July 31, 1861. He enlisted July 22, 1862, as a second lieutenant and was commissioned into Company K, Massachusetts Thirty-ninth Infantry. He was listed as prisoner of war May 8, 1864, at Laurel Hill, Virginia, and recaptured May 9, 1864, at the same place. He was promoted to first lieutenant February 18, 1865, and mustered out May 8, 1865.

18. Boatner, *Civil War Dictionary,* 749. Sheridan's force remained in bivouac at Haxall's Landing on the James River until May 17, when it left to rejoin the Army of the Potomac.

19. Long, *Civil War Day by Day,* 503. This was the battle of Drewry's Bluff. Gen. P. G. T. Beauregard's ten brigades attacked Butler's positions in early morning fog. Butler retreated to Bermuda Hundred.

20. *NYWR.* James Horton and Philip Roth enlisted as privates August 15, 1861, at New York City and mustered out August 16, 1864, at the same place. Horton was promoted to corporal September 28, 1862, and sergeant July 1, 1864. Roth was not promoted. George Whitney enlisted May 28, 1861, at Dunkirk as private, was mustered into Company D, New York Seventy-second Infantry, June 20, 1861, and transferred to the Sixth New York Light Battery (date not stated). Whitney mustered out June 21, 1864, at New York City.

21. In Greek mythology, Erebus was the dark region of the underworld through which the dead must pass before reaching Hades.

22. Davis et al., *Atlas,* Plates XXII and LXXIV, 1. This was the Richmond and York River Railroad.

23. *Dictionary of American Naval Fighting Ships,* 4:440; Deck Log of the USS *Morse,* National Archives and Records Administration, RG 24. USS *Morse* was a sternwheeler gunboat of 514 tons, 143 feet in length, thirty-three feet in the beam, and a draft of eight feet six inches. Her deck log for May 22, 1864, confirms that she was at White House landing for the entire day.

24. Deck Log of the USS *Morse,* National Archives and Records Administration, RG 24. The commanding officer of *Morse* was Lt. Comdr. Charles A. Babcock.

25. Deck Log of the U.S. Steamer *Mystic,* National Archives and Records Administration, RG 24. The *Mystic's* deck log for May 22, 1864, confirms that she was operating on the Pamunkey River on that date. She ran aground at 8:00 and got off again at 9:30, took on a pilot, and anchored at 11:20 PM off Indiantown in five fathoms of water. Evidently, *Mystic* went aground again at her Indiantown anchorage during the 4:00 PM and 8:00 PM watches. The deck log of *Morse* reports

receiving a boat from the *Mystic,* reporting that she had gone aground. *Morse* sent the steamer *Star* to tow her off. *Mystic* reported that the *Star* came alongside at 10:00 in the evening watch and commenced towing operations. *Mystic* was refloated at midnight.

26. *Official Records,* vol. 36, pt. 1, p. 780, 819, 829; Davis et al., *Atlas,* Plates LXXIV, 1, and LXXXI, 3. Brigadier General Custer's report dated July 4, 1864, outlines the operations of the First Brigade, First Cavalry Division, May 4–25, 1864. His report states: "May 18, crossed the Chickahominy at Jones' Bridge, and about 2 PM reached Baltimore Cross-Roads, where we encamped until the 20, when this brigade was detached from the corps for the purpose of destroying the Richmond and Fredericksburg and Virginia Central Railroads at their crossing of the North Anna. On the evening of the same day reached Hanover Court-House, where we burned two trestle bridges over Hanover Creek, and destroyed about one mile of the railroad at that place, capturing some commissary stores at the station." Col. R. A. Alger, commander of the Fifth Michigan Cavalry, submitted an after action report for May 4–25. Colonel Alger's report for May 21 stated that his regiment, supported by the First Cavalry, was ordered to determine the strength of the enemy at Hanover Court House and, if possible, destroy the railroad bridge over the South Anna River. Colonel Alger encountered a strong mixed force of infantry, cavalry, and artillery and withdrew without destroying the bridge. Major General Sheridan's report of May 22 from White House states: "I ordered General Custer's brigade by the river road near the south bank of the Pamunkey to burn the railroad bridges over the South Anna. He found them so strongly guarded by the enemy's artillery and infantry that he was unable to burn them. He, however, burned two bridges and a portion of the Central railroad south of Hanover Court-House. The bridges were respectively 30 and 100 feet in length." Plate LXXIV shows the Richmond and Fredericksburg and Virginia Central railroads crossing the South Anna River about fourteen miles north of Richmond. Hanover Court House is about twenty-two miles northwest of Baltimore Cross Roads on the south bank of the Pamunkey River, about three miles south of the Virginia Central Railroad's crossing of the South Anna River. Plate LXXXI by Jedediah Hotchkiss, shows Hanover Court House situated on the river road about two and one-half miles south of the Pamunkey River. It also shows a small tributary stream called Mechump's Creek passing through Hanover Court House before it enters the Pamunkey. This may have been the location of the trestle bridges mentioned in Custer's report.

27. Gordon C. Rhea, *To the North Anna River: Grant and Lee, May 13–25, 1864* (Baton Rouge: Louisiana State Univ. Press, 2000), 230; Boatner, *Civil War Dictionary,* 749. Sheridan had to improvise a bridge to cross the Pamunkey, since the railroad bridge had been partially destroyed.

28. Boatner, *Civil War Dictionary,* 749; Rhea, *To the North Anna,* 295; Davis et al., *Atlas,* Plate C, 1. Boatner states Sheridan was at Aylett's on May 22, where he first learned the location of the opposing armies, but the Perkins diary indicates he arrived there on May 23. Plate C shows Aylett on the west bank of the Mattaponi River, about fifteen miles north of Sheridan's earlier position at White House on the Pamunkey River and about twenty-five miles east of the leading elements of Warren's Fifth Corps as it crossed the North Anna at Jericho Mills in pursuit of Lee's army.

29. Rhea, *To the North Anna,* 304–19; Long, *Civil War Day by Day,* 507. Warren's Fifth Corps crossed the North Anna late in the afternoon. A. P. Hill's Corps hit Warren at Jericho Mills at about six o'clock and the fighting was intense until darkness set in. Wright's Sixth Corps began crossing to Warren's aid, and farther east Hancock's Second Corps was in action at Old Chesterfield on the north side of the North Anna.

30. Rhea, *To the North Anna,* 327; Long, *Civil War Day by Day,* 507–8. The Army of the Potomac continued to move across the North Anna. Hancock's Second Corps crossed at the Richmond, Fredericksburg and Potomac Railroad bridge over the North Anna at Chesterfield and Burnside's Ninth Corps dueled with Confederate defenders at Ox Ford and Quarles Mill.

31. Long, *Civil War Day by Day,* 508. The Army of the Potomac did not make a major forward movement south of the North Anna this day, because Grant realized that Lee's position was too strong to be assaulted.

32. Long, *Civil War Day by Day,* 509. Sheridan's cavalry occupied Hanovertown, south of the Pamunkey River. New Castle Ford, or New Castle Ferry, is about five miles northeast of Cold Harbor.

33. *NYWR*; RB6; *Mass. Sol.*; *Record of Service of Michigan Volunteers 1861–1865,* accessed at http://www.civilwardata.com. John R. Bunn enlisted September 9, 1861, at New York City as a private. He was wounded May 28, 1864, at Aenon's Chapel, Virginia, and died June 22, 1864, at Stanton General Hospital, Washington, D.C. William F. Johnson enlisted August 15, 1861, at New York City as a private and mustered into the battery the same day. He was captured June 9, 1863, at Brandy Station and paroled June 13, 1863, at City Point, Virginia. Johnson was promoted to Corporal July 1, 1864, and mustered out September 8, 1864, at New York City. Joshua D. Loud, a twenty-nine-year-old farmer from Boston, enlisted January 5, 1864, as a private and mustered into Company M, Massachusetts First Cavalry. Battery records show that Loud was detailed into the Sixth New York Independent Battery on April 18, 1864. He was wounded in action May 28, 1864, at Haw's Shop, Virginia, and discharged for disability on July 6, 1865, at Philadelphia. Thomas McClusky, a twenty-four-year-old laborer from Boston, enlisted July 12, 1861, as a private and mustered into Company I, Massachusetts Sixteenth Infantry. The battery descriptive roll shows McClusky was detailed into the Sixth New York from the Sixteenth Massachusetts but does not give a date for that event. In addition, information concerning the date and method of McClusky's discharge is not given. Joseph Oliver, an eighteen-year-old blacksmith from Rahway, New Jersey, enlisted on June 15, 1861, at New York City as a private and mustered into the battery on June 20, 1861. He was wounded in action at Brandy Station, Virginia, on June 9, 1863, and promoted to corporal December 23, 1863. According to the Perkins diary Corporal Oliver was also wounded May 28, 1864, at Haw's Shop. Oliver was discharged for disability on August 18, 1864, from Judiciary Square Hospital in Washington, D.C. The name "Pageatt" does not appear in the report of the adjutant general, or the battery descriptive roll. The descriptive roll, however, contains an entry for a soldier named Ezra Patch, a twenty-four-year-old blacksmith from Michigan who enlisted November 12, 1863, at Pontiac, Michigan, and was detailed from Company A, Fifth Michigan Cavalry (no date given). According to the "Record of Service of Michigan Volunteers," Patch enlisted on December 22, 1863, and mustered into the Fifth Michigan Cavalry the same date.

Patch joined the Fifth Michigan on or about February 15, 1864, at Stevensburg, Virginia, was listed as missing at Trevilian Station, Virginia, June 11, 1864, and rejoined his regiment August 5, 1864. It seems possible, therefore, that the "Pageatt" of the Perkins diary may have been Pvt. Ezra Patch.

34. *Official Records,* vol. 36, pt. 1, pp. 793, 854, 856; Boatner, *Civil War Dictionary,* 388. Major General Sheridan's report stated that, after the army crossed the Pamunkey behind the Cavalry Corps on May 28, he was ordered to "demonstrate" in the direction of Mechanicsville in order to fix the location of the enemy. Sheridan ordered Gregg's Second Division to move out from its position near Haw's Shop and proceed along the Mechanicsville Road. Gregg's division proceeded no more than three miles before it encountered a strong enemy cavalry force in its front and was closely engaged in that location for the entire day. Brigadier General Gregg's report agrees in substance with Sheridan's report and confirms the presence of the Sixth New York Independent Battery with the Second Cavalry Division until May 31. Boatner states that Gregg's cavalry made contact with Confederate forces consisting of Wickam's and Rosser's cavalry brigades, reinforced by the Fifth and half of the Fourth South Carolina, about a mile from Haw's Shop. Gregg's attacks were repulsed in a seven-hour action fought mostly on foot in dense woods. Custer's brigade reinforced Gregg's force and drove back the Confederate troops. Boatner also states Federal forces greatly overestimated the strength of their opponent, based on the volume of musketry fire that they encountered.

35. Long, *Civil War Day by Day,* 510. The army continued its forward movement south of the Pamunkey in the direction of Richmond; however, there was little contact with Lee's forces.

36. Long, *Civil War Day by Day,* 511. Fighting broke out between Grant and Lee's armies at Matadequin Creek, Old Church, Shady Grove, Armstrong's Farm, and Ashland as Grant's force moved toward the Totopotomoy Creek facing the Army of Northern Virginia north of the Chickahominy.

37. Long, *Civil War Day by Day,* 511. Grant continued to shift toward Cold Harbor, attempting to pass around Lee's right flank, but Lee adjusted his position and remained in front of the Federal army.

38. *Official Records,* vol. 36, pt. 1, p. 856. According to Brig. Gen. D. McM. Gregg, commanding Second Division, Cavalry Corps, Army of the Potomac, these were the light batteries H and I, First U.S. Artillery, Capt. A. M. Randol and Lieutenant Dennison commanding.

39. Boatner, *Civil War Dictionary,* 515. Brig. Gen. John Henry Martindale commanded Second Division, Eighteenth Corps, at Bermuda Hundred and Cold Harbor. He led the Eighteenth Corps during the Petersburg siege and resigned because of ill health on September 13, 1864.

40. Long, *Civil War Day by Day,* 512. Federal infantry continued to advance toward Cold Harbor. Confederate infantry of R. H. Anderson's Corps attacked Sheridan's cavalry near Old Cold Harbor but were repulsed.

41. *Official Records,* vol. 36, pt. 1, pp. 287, 289, 856. Brig. Gen. Henry Jackson Hunt, chief of artillery of the Army of the Potomac, submitted a report dated October 31, 1864, covering the operations of the army artillery from May 4, 1864, to October 31, 1864. This report describes the reorganization of the artillery that occurred on May 16 and May 31. General Hunt stated: "On the 16, the Reserve was by superior

orders broken up, and the batteries composing it ordered to Washington. In order to retain the organizations, men and material, in this army, the reduction of guns contemplated was, upon my recommendation, effected by reducing each mounted battery in the army to four guns, retaining the extra caissons and ordering the surplus guns . . . to Washington." Regarding the horse artillery, General Hunt reported that on May 31 Major General Meade ordered that it be reorganized by reducing it "to eight batteries of four guns each, one section consisting of Napoleons and one of 3-inch guns, and formed into a single brigade." After the reorganization, the brigade, under the command of Captain J. M. Robertson, consisted of the following batteries: "Egan's (K), First United States; Randol's (H and I), First United States; Clarke's (A), Second United States; Heaton's (B and L), Second United States; Williston's (D), Second United States; Pennington's (M), Second United States; Kelly's (C, F, and K), Third United States; Fitzhugh's (C and E), Fourth United States." General Hunt had this to say about the surplus horse artillery batteries: "The remaining batteries of Horse Artillery, viz., Porter's, (E and G), First United States; Dennison's (G), Second United States; King's (A), Fourth United States; and Martin's, Sixth New York Independent, after turning over their serviceable artillery horses and transportation for the use of this army, were ordered to Washington, to report to Brigadier-General Howe, inspector-general of artillery." Brigadier General Gregg's report of July 7, 1864, confirms that "the Independent Sixth New York Battery, Capt. J. W. Martin, and Light Battery A, Fourth U.S. Artillery, were on duty with this Division until May 31."

42. Charles Dana Gibson and E. Kay, *The Army's Navy Series, Dictionary of Transports and Combatant Vessels, Steam and Sail, Employed by the Union Army, 1861–1868* (Camden, ME: Ensign Press, 1995), n.p. SR *Spaulding* was a side-wheel steamer of about 1,090 tons. It was used as a hospital ship during the Peninsula Campaign in 1852.

CHAPTER 9.
HALF OF THE FEMALES IN WASHINGTON SEEM TO BE COURTESANS: JUNE–SEPTEMBER 1864

1. Margaret Leech, *Reveille in Washington 1860–1865* (New York: Harper and Brothers, 1941), 185–86. Leech describes the Soldiers' Rest in this way: "At the large buildings near the depot, the Soldiers' Rest and the Soldiers' Retreat, the men were well fed and lodged, efficiently policed and forwarded. As the troop trains neared the capital, the Commissary Department was notified, and gangs sent to work cutting meat, cooking, and laying the tables."

2. "Preliminary Inventory Number 17, Outline Index of Military Forts and Stations," in *Preliminary Records of the Adjutant General's Office,* comp. Elizabeth Bethel and Lucille Pendell (Washington, DC: Government Printing Office, 1949), 23; Camp Barry DC, Letters Received, 1863–1865, RG 393, pt. 4, p. 91, National Archives and Records Administration, Washington, DC; Nevins, *A Diary of Battle,* 526; Davis et al., *Atlas,* Plate LXXXIX, 1. Bethel and Pendell's compilation shows Camp Barry's location as being "near Bladensburg toll-gate." Record Group 393 contains a letter dated October 6, 1864, from Assistant Secretary of the Treasury S. Yorke complaining about the conditions of Camp Barry. Mr. Yorke, who lived

on the Bladensburg Road about two and one-half miles from the city, stated that he passed by Camp Barry, located near the tollgate, twice a day on his way to and from work. Wainwright's diary entry for May 23, 1865, noted that "the camp of artillery instruction," called Camp Barry, "occupies the ground on the right of the Bladensburg Pike just out of the gate." Plate LXXXIX, 1, a map of the defenses of Washington, dated 1865, does not show the location of Camp Barry but does indicate the existence of a tollgate at the intersection of the Bladensburg Road with Benning Road. Thus, in present-day District of Columbia, the tollgate and Camp Barry would have been located near the intersections of Florida, Maryland, and Bladensburg roads.

3. Sergeant Turner had been wounded in action in the Battle of the Wilderness.

4. RB6. On this date, Captain Martin submitted a report to Lieutenant Randolph, acting adjutant general, which listed the numbers of enlisted men who would be lost to the battery in the ensuing months because of the expiration of their terms of service. For the remainder of 1864, the numbers were as follows:

Month	Expiring Terms of Service
June	31
July	0
August	18
September	29
October	10
November	0
December	3
Six-Month Total	**91**

5. Long, *Civil War Day by Day,* 510. This engagement is known as the Battle of Haw's Shop.

6. *Mass. Sol.* Albert Wood, a thirty-year-old surgeon from Tewksbury, Massachusetts, enlisted on July 31, 1862 as an assistant surgeon. He was commissioned on August 12, 1862, into the Field and Staff Massachusetts Twenty-ninth Infantry and on August 11, 1863, into Field and Staff Massachusetts First Cavalry. He was promoted to surgeon on July 7, 1863. He resigned and was discharged for disability on November 1, 1864.

7. *NYWR*; RB6. William Conger, a twenty-two-year-old printer from Rahway, New Jersey, enlisted September 9, 1861, in New York City as a private and mustered into the battery the same day. He mustered out on September 8, 1864, in Washington, D.C.

8. *Mass. Sol.* Joseph W. Colcord, an eighteen-year-old student from Woburn, Massachusetts, enlisted July 10, 1861, as a private and mustered into Company G, Massachusetts Thirteenth Infantry. On November 11, 1863, he transferred into Company D, Veteran Reserve Corps, and mustered out on July 15, 1865.

9. Andrew Boyd, *Boyd's Washington and Georgetown Directory (Containing Also a Business Directory of Washington, Georgetown, and Alexandria)* (Washington, DC: Hudson Taylor, 1865), 116. Perkins's "Washington Market" seems to be the "Centre Market" located by Boyd's directory at "south side of Pennsylvania Avenue, between 7 and 9 West." The small "public garden" that Perkins and Colcord next visited probably was the Botanic Garden, which now resides between Maryland, Independence, and Third and First Streets near the Capitol.

10. *NYWR*; RB6. James Drake, an eighteen-year-old from Rahway, New Jersey, enlisted in New York City on September 9, 1861, as a private. The adjutant general's report states that he mustered out in Washington, D.C., on September 8, 1864; however, battery records indicate he mustered out on September 9, 1864. Frank V. W. Jewell, an eighteen-year-old clerk from Rahway, New Jersey, enlisted December 2, 1861, in New York City as a private. He was promoted to bugler April 20, 1864, and was mustered out on December 1, 1864, at New York City.

11. Boyd, *Boyd's Washington and Georgetown Directory,* 111. The Catholic Church nearest to Camp Barry was St Patrick's, which was located on F Street North, near the corner of Tenth Street. A photograph in George Washington University's Dimmock Gallery confirms that it was indeed a spacious brick edifice.

12. *NYWR*. Twenty-nine enlisted members of the original battery, who mustered in New York City on June 20, 1861, left the Sixth New York at Camp Barry on June 20, 1864. They mustered out in New York City on June 20, 1864. From June 20 to June 22, 1864, seventy members of the former Tenth New York Battery transferred into the Sixth New York.

13. Bayard Taylor (1825–78) was an American author. During the Civil War, he was minister to Russia.

14. Davis et al., *Atlas,* Plate LXXXIX, 1. This map shows a group of buildings identified as "J. A. Bartuff" about one-half mile northeast of the tollgate on Bladensburg Road.

15. Leech, *Reveille in Washington,* 11, 244. Leech gives the following description: "Other plague spots were . . . Swampoodle, an Irish colony in a marshy area near North Capitol Street." She also places it near an iron bridge on H Street.

16. Boatner, *Civil War Dictionary,* 43. A barbette is a platform that allows a gun to fire over a parapet without an embrasure.

17. Barnard, *The Defenses of Washington,* 25–27; Davis et al., *Atlas,* Plate LXXXIX, 1. Barnard reported that Fort Reno "occupies a commanding position at a point where the dividing ridge between the Potomac and Rock Creek narrows so as to expose the slopes in both direction. It commands the three roads which unite at Tenallytown. . . . A battery for eight guns has been constructed on an advanced point of the ridge, (say 300 yards northward) with magazine and enclosed gorge. This is con-nected with the work by a double line of rifle trenches, with a flanking battery, making of the ensemble a very strong position." The "Fort De Runy" of this letter is Fort De Russy. Of this work, Barnard states that it "occupies a very commanding point overlooking the valley of Rock Creek, and throwing a cross fire upon the approaches to Fort Massachusetts (Stevens) and (together with Fort Kearney) controlling the country roads between Rockville Turnpike and Rock Creek." Fort Stevens is described as follows: "Fort Massachusetts (Stevens) in conjunction with Fort Slocum, commands one of the principal avenues of approach to Washington."

18. Davis et al., *Atlas,* Plate LXXXIX, 1, shows a complex of buildings identified as "U.S. Military Asylum," to the right of Rock Creek Church Road about three-fourths of a mile to the northeast from where it branches off from Seventh Street (the present Georgia Avenue). This appears to be the site of the present U.S. Soldiers' and Airmen's Home.

19. RB6. On this day, Captain Martin sent a letter to Brig. Gen. L. Thomas, Adjutant General U.S.A., regarding the consolidation of the Tenth New York Battery with

the Sixth New York Independent Battery. This letter reported that a detachment of the Tenth New York Battery that had been serving with the Fifth New York Independent Battery had reported for duty with the Sixth New York and requested that the remaining detachments of the Tenth New York be directed to report at the earliest practicable date. This detachment may have been the group of twenty-seven men that Private Perkins reported joining on June 27. On July 20, 1864, Captain Martin sent another letter regarding the consolidation to Maj. L. H. Raymond, A.A.G. Headquarters Department of Washington, Twenty-second Army Corps. Both letters referred to Special Order 216 WDAGO, dated June 22, 1864, which had ordered the consolidation. Captain Martin was obviously concerned with the strength and integrity of his battery, given the recent and expected loss of experienced personnel due to the expiration of their terms of service. That his concern was not misplaced is confirmed by the recent conversion of the Sixth New York from a six-gun battery of three-inch ordnance rifles to a four-gun battery of twelve-pounder Napoleon guns. Private Perkins reported this change in his diary entry of July 5, 1864. The conversion implies that the battery's function was being shifted from horse artillery to infantry support.

20. No doubt the countersign actually was "Cold Harbor."

21. The identity of this place has not been verified; however, it is likely that it was Mount Olivet Catholic Cemetery, which is less than a mile from the presumed site of Camp Barry.

22. *Official Records,* vol. 37, pt. 1, 698-699, pt. 2, 543. Maj. Gen. Christopher C. Augur's report of Troops in the Department of Washington, Twenty-second Army Corps, from May 1 to June 30, 1864, included the Fourth U.S. Artillery, Battery A, commanded by Lt. Rufus King Jr. The report also states that the Sixth New York Light, Capt. Joseph W. Martin, was attached to the Artillery Camp of Instruction under the command of Brig. Gen. Albion P. Howe. In Major General Augur's report for July 1864, both the Fourth U.S. Artillery and the Sixth New York Light are shown as being assigned to the Light Artillery Depot and Camp of Instruction, under the command of Maj. James A. Hall.

23. *NYWR.* Henry Albright enlisted June 23, 1862, at New York City and mustered into the Tenth New York Light Artillery the same day. He transferred into the Sixth New York Battery on June 21, 1864, reenlisted on July 28, 1864, and mustered out on July 8, 1865, at Hart's Island, New York Harbor.

24. Gilham, *Manual of Instruction,* 493, 499. Number Six was stationed in the rear of the limber. His duties were to retrieve the rounds from the limber and to cut the fuses according to the distance or time ordered. He delivered the prepared rounds to Number Five.

25. *Mass. Sol.* The Seventh Battery, Massachusetts Volunteer Light Artillery, was organized in Lowell, Massachusetts, in April 1861 as an infantry regiment. It subsequently was reorganized as a light artillery battery and served in Norfolk, Suffolk, Portsmouth, and the approaches to Richmond. It was sent to New York City in August 1863, where it helped to suppress the draft riots. At the conclusion of this duty in September, it was sent to Washington, D.C., where it was stationed at Camp Barry until January 1864. On January 24, it was transferred to the Department of the Gulf, where it engaged in operations in Louisiana, Arkansas, Alabama, and Texas until the end of the war.

26. Boatner, *Civil War Dictionary,* 414; Warner, *Generals in Blue,* 239. Brig. Gen. Albion Parris Howe commanded the Light Artillery Camp (under Twenty-second Corps) and was inspector of artillery.

27. *NYWR.* Robert Seaman enlisted March 11, 1862, at New York City as a private and mustered into the Tenth New York Battery the same date. He transferred into the Sixth New York Independent Battery on June 21, 1864, and was killed by lighting on August 13, 1864, at Camp Barry.

28. U.S. Dept. of the Army, Quartermaster General, Internment in the Arlington National Cemetery (QMC Form 14, 1948). Pvt. Robert Seaman is interred in Section 13, Grave 8317.

29. Jeffrey D. Wert, *From Winchester to Cedar Creek: The Shenandoah Campaign of 1864* (Mechanicsburg, PA: Stackpole Books, 1997), 30–32. Sheridan's army had been pushing *up* the Valley (south) and, by August 14, was skirmishing with Early's army in the vicinity of Strasburg. Sheridan had become concerned about his exposed position, however, and, with reports coming in of reinforcements arriving for Early, was contemplating withdrawing down the valley to assume a defensible position near Halltown.

30. *Official Records,* vol. 43, pt. 1, pp. 18–19. Sheridan's August 12 report to Chief of Staff Halleck mentioned the absence of Averell's, Wilson's, and Duffie's cavalry forces and expressed concern about the reported movement of elements of Longstreet's First Corps, destined as reinforcements for Early.

31. *NYWR.* All thirteen soldiers received their discharge on August 16, 1864, in New York City.

32. *NYWR.* Privates Ellis Bunn, John McDonald, and Justus D. Trussler enlisted August 29, 1861, in New York City and were mustered out August 31, 1864, in Washington, D.C.

33. RB6; *NYWR.* Corp. William F. Johnson, Privates William Conger, Theodore Randolph, James Drake, and John W. Sym, and Artificer William M. Marsh were discharged on this date by reason of expiration of their terms of service. Johnson enlisted as a twenty-year-old farmer from New York City; Randolph, a twenty-four-year-old carriage maker from New Jersey; Sym, a thirty-five-year-old blacksmith from New Jersey; and Marsh, a twenty-four-year-old carriage maker from New Jersey. The adjutant general's report does not show William Marsh as being promoted to artificer.

34. RB6. Forty-two enlisted men were received by transfer from the Tenth New York Battery.

35. Camp Barry, DC, Letters Received, 1863–65, RG 393, National Archives and Records, Washington, DC; *Official Records,* vol. 43, pt. 2, p. 84. There are no such movement orders dated September 12 or before in the letters received file; however, two orders dated September 14 deal with the subject. One is from J. H. Taylor, assistant adjutant general, headquarters, Department of Washington Twenty-second Army Corps, addressed to Brig. Gen. A. P. Howe, inspector of artillery. This letter informs General Howe that an escort from Camp Stoneman has been provided for Martin's Battery. The second, Special Orders No. 229 from Headquarters Department of Washington Twenty-second Army Corps, relieves the Sixth New York Independent Battery Capt. J. W. Martin, from duty in the department and directs it to proceed "without delay" to Harpers Ferry to report

for duty to Major General Sheridan. This order is also signed by J. H. Taylor, records chief of staff and assistant adjutant general. Taylor also issued an order on September 14 to Col. William Gamble, commanding Camp Stoneman. The order directed the colonel to ensure that all officers and men of the Reserve Brigade and the First and Third Divisions would be prepared to move to rejoin their regiments. It also noted that Martin's battery had been ordered to march from Camp Barry to the headquarters of the Middle Military Division and ordered Colonel Gamble to send an officer to Camp Barry to ascertain when the battery would be able to move and to make the necessary arrangements.

36. RB6. The battery's daily remarks for this date report the receipt of ninety-four artillery horses, eighteen mules, the necessary harnesses, and three army wagons. The remarks also report that the battery turned in two light twelve-pounder guns and carriages to the arsenal and received in return two three-inch guns, carriages, and caissons.

37. RB6; *NYWR*. The battery's daily remarks for this date state that Privates ⌐ Benjamin F. Ackerman, John H. Vennett, Daniel S. Patton (or Patten), and Ellis F. Marsh were discharged on this date by reason of expiration of service. The adjutant general's report states that they all enlisted in New York City on September 14, 1861, as privates but does not give their residences. Ackerman was a twenty-one-year-old carriage maker from Hakensack, New Jersey; Vennett was an eighteen-year-old farmer from New Jersey; Patton was a twenty-seven-year-old tinker from Scotland; and Marsh was a twenty-four-year-old carriage maker from New Jersey.

CHAPTER 10.
BURNING BARNS IN EVERY DIRECTION
MET OUR SIGHT:
SEPTEMBER–DECEMBER 1864

1. RB6. Privates Matthew Kiely and Watson Antrim were discharged by reason of expiration of service. Kiely was a twenty-one-year-old from Ireland, and Antrim was a twenty-five year-old merchant from Pemberton, New Jersey.

2. Davis et al., *Atlas,* Plate XXVII, 1. The watering place evidently was Seneca Creek at Middlebrook, about eight miles outside of Rockville.

3. Ibid., Plates VII and XXVII, 1; RB6. The battery halted for the night at Buckeystown, on the western bank of the Monacacy River. Clarksburg, Hyatts-town, and Urbana are towns situated on the Rockville Road between the District of Columbia and Frederick City. Clarksburg, about thirteen miles north of Rock-ville, is located on the crest of Parr Ridge. Hyattstown is about halfway (three and one-half miles) between Clarksburg and Urbana. The latter town is about the same distance outside of Frederick. Sugar Loaf Mountain is a prominent terrain feature about three miles west of the Rockville Road at Urbana. This march was along the present I-270, which runs between I-495 (Capital Beltway) and Frederick. Buckeys-town was on a road that departed from the Rockville Road at Urbana and led in a more-or-less southwesterly direction to Point of Rocks on the Potomac River. From Urbana, a country road also led south, skirting the eastern flank of Sugar Loaf Mountain and passing through the towns of Barnesville and Poolesville before reaching Edwards Ferry on the Potomac River, a distance of about sixteen miles.

Edwards Ferry ran between the Chesapeake and Ohio Canal on the Maryland side of the Potomac and Goose Creek on the Virginia side. Goose Creek, about five miles outside of Leesburg, was provided with a system of dams and locks (Plate VII). Thus, Edwards Ferry may have connected the territory around Leesburg with the Chesapeake and Ohio Canal.

4. Davis et al., *Atlas,* Plate XXVII, 1. Here the march diverged from the present I-270 to the west, crossing the Monacacy and passing through Buckeystown on the Baltimore and Ohio Railroad.

5. Davis et al., *Atlas,* Plates XXVII, XXIX, XLII, 1; RB6. This portion of the march proceeded southwest toward Harpers Ferry along the present routes 180 and 340. The mountain range that Perkins describes as the Maryland continuation of the Blue Ridge is shown as South Mountain on Plates XXVII and XLII. Loudon Heights is the terminus of the Blue Ridge on the Virginia side of the Potomac River, at the confluence of the Shenandoah River with the Potomac, and commands the town of Harpers Ferry. The stopping point for this day's march apparently was between the towns of Petersville and Knoxville, near the Potomac River. The battery halted near Sandy Hook.

6. *NYWR.* Harvey Brunt enlisted on April 9, 1863, at New York City as a private. He mustered out on July 8, 1865, at Hart's Island, New York Harbor.

7. Davis et al., *Atlas,* Plate XLII, 1. Maryland Heights overlooks the confluence of the Potomac and Shenandoah rivers on the Maryland side of the Potomac. The village of Sandy Hook lies at the foot of Maryland Heights. Loudon Heights lies opposite Maryland Heights on the Virginia side of the river. The valley between South Mountain and Maryland Heights is identified as Pleasant Valley. Perkins's diary entry for September 18 places Pleasant Valley between the Catoctin Range and South Mountain on the Maryland side of the Potomac.

8. *Official Records,* vol. 43, pt. 1, 987. The abstract from the return of the Middle Military Division for the month of August 1864, Maj. Gen. Philip H. Sheridan, U.S. Army, commanding, reports that the Reserve Horse Artillery Brigade was under the command of Capt. La Rhett L. Livingston.

9. RB6. On this date, the battery received twenty-five enlisted men detailed from the Cavalry Corps.

10. Davis et al., *Atlas,* Plate XLIII, 1. Bolivar Heights is the ridge above the town of Harpers Ferry.

11. Davis et al., *Atlas,* Plates XLIII, XXVII, and XXIX, 1. Hallstown is about two miles beyond Bolivar Heights at the intersection of the Charlestown Pike with the Winchester and Potomac Railroad. Shepardstown is about ten miles north of Bolivar Heights on the Potomac River, opposite Sharpsburg, Maryland.

12. RB6. Privates W. B. Stagg, G. W. Smith, C. H. Humphreys, and W. H. Dakin were discharged on the expiration of their terms of service. Private Stagg, a twenty-one-year-old sail maker from Patterson, New Jersey, enlisted on September 24, 1861, in New York City. Private Smith, a nineteen-year-old sail maker, enlisted on the same date in New York City. Private Humphreys, an eighteen-year-old clerk, enlisted on September 23, 1861, in New York City. Private Dakin, a twenty-year-old from New York, also enlisted on August 23, 1861, in New York City.

13. Wert, *From Winchester to Cedar Creek,* 315. At the battle of Winchester on September 19, 1864, the Thirty-sixth Virginia Regiment lost 3 killed in action, 31 wounded in action, and 156 taken prisoner of war. The Thirty-sixth was part

of Smith's Brigade of Gordon's Division of Lt. Gen. Jubal A. Early's Army of the Valley.

14. Davis et al., *Atlas,* Plates XXVII and LXIX, 1; Boatner, *Civil War Dictionary,* 743–46; Wert, *From Winchester to Cedar Creek,* 22–26, 30. The village George Perkins identifies as Mill Creek probably was Bunker Hill, which was located at the intersection of Mill Creek with the Martinsburg and Winchester Pike (or Valley Pike). Bunker Hill is about three miles west of Smithfield across Opequon Creek. Lt. Gen. Jubal A. Early's Army of the Valley at various times used Bunker Hill as a base of operations, until Sheridan defeated Early's army at Winchester on September 19.

15. Long, *Civil War Day by Day,* 571. The third (and final) battle of Winchester on September 19 was a bloody affair that ended Confederate control of the northern part of the Shenandoah Valley. Long gives the following estimated losses: 4,018 total U.S. casualties (697 killed in action, 2,983 wounded in action, and 338 missing in action) and 3,921 total Confederate casualties (276 killed in action, 1,827 wounded in action, and 1,818 missing in action or captured).

16. Long, *Civil War Day by Day,* 554; Wert, *From Winchester to Cedar Creek,* 107–11; Davis et al., *Atlas,* Plate LXIX, 1. On September 20 fighting continued on the Valley Pike through Winchester, Kernstown, Newtown, and Middletown as Early withdrew his army under pressure from Sheridan and fortified Fisher's Hill, outside of Strasburg.

17. RB6. The battery's daily remarks state that the day's route was from Winchester to Strasburg to "Jackson Mountain." Mount Jackson is about thirty miles south of Strasburg on the Valley Pike (at the end of the Manassas Gap Railroad). Private Perkins's diary for this date, however, contradicts this entry. Perkins states that the battery marched from Winchester to a point just south of Strasburg, then counter-marched through Strasburg and took the road leading east toward Front Royal.

18. Davis et al., *Atlas,* Plate LXXXI, 4; Richard M. Ketchum, *The American Heritage Picture History of the Civil War* (New York: American Heritage Publishing Co., 1960), 152–53. This was Massanutten Mountain, which rises in the middle of the valley and splits the Shenandoah into the North Fork and South Fork at Front Royal. The North Fork of the Shenandoah runs close to the western flank of Massanutten Mountain. Little North Mountain (part of the Allegheny Mountains) defines the western boundary of the valley. The Manassas Gap Railroad originated in Manassas, passed through Thoroughfare Gap in the Bull Run Mountains, Manassas Gap in the Blue Ridge Mountains, and crossed the Shenandoah River at Front Royal. After skirting the northern edge of Massanutten Mountain, the railroad headed south into the valley of the North Fork of the Shenandoah at Strasburg and ended before reaching the town of New Market. Plate LXXXI is an excellent map by Jedediah Hotchkiss, chief topographical engineer of the Army of Northern Virginia. The *American Heritage Picture History of the Civil War* has a particularly good bird's-eye view of the Shenandoah Valley.

19. Davis et al., *Atlas,* Plate LXXXI, 4; *Official Records,* vol. 43, pt. 1, p. 441; vol. 43, pt. 2, p. 157. Brig. Gen. J. H. Wilson, commanding the Third Cavalry Division, sent a message to Major General Torbert at 5:15 PM on September 23, 1864, from Buckton Station reporting the arrival of Martin's battery for Merritt's division and requesting instructions as to what to do with it. Buckton Station was located on the North Fork of the Shenandoah on the northern flank of Massanutten Mountain.

Brig. Gen. Wesley Merritt's report of October 5, 1864, states that his division, with the Third Cavalry Division in company, marched on September 22 from Front Royal up the Luray Valley as far as Milford (a distance of about ten miles). Finding the Confederate position at that point too strong to be carried, the Federal Cavalry returned to Front Royal on September 23, but returned to Milford on the night of September 23, crossed Overall's Run at Milford, and bivouacked there until daylight on September 24.

20. *Official Records,* vol. 12, pt. 3, 237; vol. 29, 490–92; vol. 37, pt. 1, pp. 501, 511; Davis et al., *Atlas,* Plates C, 1, and CXXXVII, 1. Private Perkins's "Manhattan Mountains" was, of course, Massanutten Mountain. It appears that the Sixth New York's September 23 and 24 march route led south into the heart of Massanutten Mountain along Passage Creek in Powell's Big Fort Valley, before crossing into the valley of the South Fork of the Shenandoah River near the town of Luray. Gen. T. J. Jackson used Powell's Fort Valley in his May 1862 Valley Campaign to screen the approach of his forces to Front Royal and Winchester, while Gen. J. D. Imboden used it to retire to the upper valley after capturing Charlestown in October 1863. In May 1864 an intelligence report indicated that Lt. Gen. Jubal Early had four thousand troops in Powell's Fort Valley.

21. *Official Records,* vol. 43, pt. 1, pp. 429, 438, 441, 519; Wert, *From Winchester to Cedar Creek,* 316. The reports of Major General Torbert (commanding Cavalry Corps, Army of the Shenandoah), Brigadier General Merritt (commanding First Division, Cavalry Corps) and Brigadier General Wilson (commanding Third Division, Cavalry Corps) describe this action, which took place on September 24. Both the First Division and Third Division attacked Brigadier General Wickam's Brigade of Maj. Gen. Fitzhugh Lee's Cavalry Division outside of the town of Luray. Merritt reported the capture of one hundred prisoners and a battle flag of the Sixth Virginia Cavalry (attached to Col. William Payne's Brigade of Lee's Cavalry Division).

22. *Official Records,* vol. 43, pt. 1, p. 429. General Torbert and other sources make it clear that the Federal cavalry was pursuing retreating rebel forces west through Massanutten Gap, not east through Thornton's Gap, as Perkins here states. Perkins's September 25 diary entry corrects this error.

23. RB6. The battery official records claim that the march was from Jackson Mountain to "Gap W. Shenandoah River." Again, Private Perkins's diary does not agree with this entry. Although the Perkins diary is somewhat ambiguous, it appears that the battery's true route on September 23 and 24 was directly south from Buckton Station (on the North Fork of the Shenandoah), through Massanutten Mountain along Passage Creek–Powell's Fort Valley, and finally exiting Massanutten Mountain near Luray on the South Fork of the Shenandoah.

24. *NYWR.* Privates William H. Biggs, James R. Clark, Smith A. Devoe, William H. Pearse, Patrick Perryman, Bugler John W. Martin, and Sergeant John Trotter all were discharged at Harpers Ferry on September 30, 1864. Biggs, Clark, and Martin had enlisted September 27, 1861, at New York City; Pearse, Perryman, and Trotter enlisted September 28, 1861, at New York City; and Devoe had enlisted September 30, 1861, at New York City. Private Perryman had been wounded in action June 9, 1863, at Brandy Station, Virginia.

25. Davis et al., *Atlas,* Plates LXXXI, 4, and XCIV, 2. The battery passed through Massanutten Gap into the valley of the North Fork of the Shenandoah, camped

briefly at New Market, and headed southwest along the Valley Pike toward Harrisonburg (not southeast, as Perkins here states).

26. Davis et al., *Atlas,* Plate LXXIV, 1. The stream possibly was Cub Run, which flows past the southern flank of Massanutten Mountain and runs into the South Fork of the Shenandoah.

27. *Official Records,* vol. 43, pt. 1, pp. 441–42; Davis et al., *Atlas,* Plate C, 1. Brig. Gen. Wesley Merritt's report for this date states that the First Cavalry Division (less the Reserve Brigade) advanced toward Port Republic, driving the Confederate cavalry into Brown's Gap in the Blue Ridge Mountains. General Merritt's report also states that the artillery of the division was placed in position to shell the trains of Kershaw's Division, which had been discovered advancing through Swift Run Gap to join Early's Army (Swift Run Gap is about fifteen miles north of Brown's Gap). The Confederate force reacted to this threat by mounting an afternoon infantry attack on the skirmish line of the Second Brigade of the First Division. The Federal force countered this move by means of artillery fire backed up by the cavalry. This may have been the action described in Private Perkins's diary.

28. *Official Records,* vol. 43, pt. 1, p. 442; Davis et al., *Atlas,* Plates C and LXXIV, 1. General Merritt's report for September 27 states that the Second Cavalry Division (Brig. Gen. George A. Custer) was driven from its position near Weyer's Cave by an attack from a combined force of Confederate infantry, cavalry, and artillery and took up a position to the right of Port Republic. Weyer's Cave lies about five miles south of Port Republic on the South River. In response to the Confederate attack on the Second Division, the First Division fell back to Cross Keys and prepared to receive an attack. Cross Keys lies about five miles to the northwest of Port Republic on the western side of the South Fork of the Shenandoah. Instead of executing a frontal attack on the First Cavalry Division, the enemy force marched about twelve or thirteen miles southwest from Brown's Gap in the Blue Ridge to Waynesborough, where it encountered Major General Torbert on September 28.

29. *Official Records,* vol. 43, pt. 1, pp. 493–506. Major General Sheridan relieved Brevet Maj. Gen. William Woods Averell from command of the Second Cavalry Division on September 23 and appointed Col. William Powell as his temporary replacement. General Sheridan's dissatisfaction stemmed from the Second Division's alleged lack of aggressive pursuit of Early's beaten Army of the Valley. General Averell's report of October 25, 1864, includes the order relieving him from command. General Custer did not remain long as commander of the Second Division. He was appointed to command Brig. Gen. James H. Wilson's Third Cavalry Division, when the latter was detached on September 30 to assume command of Maj. Gen. William T. Sherman's cavalry.

30. Wert, *From Winchester to Cedar Creek,* 311–12. The "Michigan Brigade" was the First Brigade of the First Cavalry Division. It consisted of First, Fifth, Sixth, and Seventh Michigan Cavalry regiments plus the Twenty-fifth New York Cavalry Regiment.

31. Davis et al., *Atlas,* Plates LXXIV, 1, and LXXXI, 4. Port Republic lies on the east bank of the South Fork of the Shenandoah where the South River and North River join it.

32. *Official Records,* vol. 43, pt. 1, p. 442; Davis et al., *Atlas,* Plates C and LXXIV, 1. General Merritt's report of the operations of the First Cavalry Division for this

date states that a brigade of the First Division and of the Second Division advanced toward Port Republic after discovering that the Confederate force had withdrawn and drove his rearguard toward Waynesborough. The Sixth New York Independent Battery participated in this movement toward Port Republic.

33. Davis et al., *Atlas,* Plates LXXIV, 1; LXXXI, 4; XCIV, 2. Port Republic lies on the South Fork of the Shenandoah, not the North Fork.

34. Long, *Civil War Day by Day,* 553–54. The incident referred to may have been the vast explosion that took place at City Point on August 9, 1864. Long states that the explosion was caused by a device smuggled on board a transport vessel by two Confederate agents. It caused forty-three deaths, injured 126, and destroyed a large amount of army property.

35. *Official Records,* vol. 43, pt. 1, p. 442; Davis et al., *Atlas,* Plates LXXIV, 1; LXXXI, 4; XCIV, 2. The pike evidently was the section of the Valley Pike between Harrisonburg and Staunton. The river was the North River (not the North Fork of the Shenandoah), a tributary of the South Fork of the Shenandoah, which joins that river near Port Republic. General Merritt's report for this date states that both the First and Second Cavalry divisions (now under his command by order of Major General Sheridan) were engaged in destroying mills and forage and driving off cattle from Waynesborough and Staunton to Mount Crawford.

36. *Official Records,* vol. 43, pt. 1, p. 442. General Merritt's report states that his force remained in camp near Mount Crawford September 30 and October 1.

37. RB6; *NYWR.* James Benward, a twenty-one-year-old shoemaker, enlisted June 15, 1861, in New York City as a private. He reenlisted as Veteran Volunteer on January 4, 1864, and mustered out July 8, 1865, at Hart's Island, New York Harbor.

38. *Official Records,* vol. 43, pt. 1, p. 442. General Merritt's report states that the enemy force advanced on October 2 and skirmished with his force all day along his entire line.

39. *NYWR;* RB6. Besides Pvt. George F. Mann, Privates William B. Deyo and John Mulroy were discharged on this date. Private Deyo was from New York City and Private Mulroy from Charlestown, Massachusetts. Both enlisted in New York City on October 4, 1861.

40. Davis et al., *Atlas,* Plates C, 1, and CXXXVII, 1; *Official Records,* vol. 43, pt. 1, p. 442. Brigadier General Merritt's report of October 5 states that his command proceeded towards Cross Keys. Mount Crawford lies about twelve miles to the southwest of the southern terminus of Massanutten Mountain.

41. Davis et al., *Atlas,* Plates C, 1, and CXXXVII, 1; *Official Records,* vol. 43, pt. 1, p. 442. Brigadier General Merritt's report states that his command moved from Cross Keys on October 5 to Harrisonburg and thence to Timberville on Middle Road, destroying forage and grain and driving off cattle along the way. Timberville lies about thirteen miles north of Harrisonburg at the intersection of the present Routes 42 and 211 at the base of Little North Mountain. The town of New Market is about ten miles east of Timberville at the base of Massanutten Mountain.

42. *NYWR;* RB6. Charles S. Booth enlisted on October 7, 1861, as a private. He mustered out on October 12, 1864, at Washington, D.C.

43. Davis et al., *Atlas,* Plates C, 1, and CXXXVII, 1; *Official Records,* vol. 43, pt. 1, p. 442. This day's march took the battery northward along a country road from Timberville through Forestville and on to Edenburg, paralleling the Valley

Pike and the Manassas Gap Railroad. The unnamed town four miles north of Forestville probably was Mount Jackson, which was situated at the confluence of a tributary brook and the North Fork of the Shenandoah River at the southern terminus of the Manassas Gap Railroad. General Merritt's report confirms that his command camped on the Pike near Edenburg this day.

44. *Official Records*, vol. 43, pt. 1, pp. 446–47. Brigadier General Merritt's report of October 12 states that his division was acting as rearguard to the army. On this day, in response to an order by the commanding general, General Merritt sent his First Brigade on a reconnaissance to Woodstock (about five miles to the north of Edenburg). While the First Brigade was so engaged, General Merritt received an order from the chief of cavalry to support the Third Division, which was hotly engaged by enemy forces on the back road near Tom's Brook. General Merritt sent the Reserve Brigade and Second Brigade about four miles south on this mission.

45. *Official Records*, vol. 43, pt. 1, pp. 447–48. Brigadier General Merritt's report of October 12 covers the Tom's Brook battle on October 9. General Merritt reported that Martin's battery, which was attached to the First Brigade, inflicted severe damage on the enemy forces by enfilading their lines by fire. General Merritt reported that his command captured five pieces of artillery with limbers, four caissons, five forges, as well as numerous horses, mules, and prisoners.

46. *NYWR*. Ferdinand Drescher enlisted on December 19, 1861, at New York City as a private and mustered into the battery the same day. He transferred into the Seventeenth New York Light Artillery on June 7, 1864, and transferred back into the Sixth New York on July 3, 1864. He mustered out on December 19, 1864, at Winchester, Virginia.

47. This is an obvious typographical error for Hyattstown.

48. The battery proceeded south, which is *up* the Shenandoah Valley.

49. Long, *Civil War Day by Day*, 571. Long states the "not many" Federals killed in action totaled 697.

50. This is another obvious spelling error for Luray.

51. *Official Records*, vol. 43, pt. 2, pp. 410, 424, 436–37, 464–65. Major General Sheridan reported to Lieutenant General Grant on the results of the Cedar Creek battle in dispatches dated October 19, 10:00 PM; October 20, 11:30 AM; October 21, 4:00 PM; and October 25, 10:00 PM. It seems Sheridan's forces captured forty-eight or fifty artillery pieces with caissons and appointments (twenty-four of which were lost by Union forces on the morning of October 19 and recaptured), "at least" 1,600 prisoners, fifty-six ambulances, and numerous wagons and other equipment.

52. *NYWR*; RB6. The adjutant general's report contains a listing for Jacob D. Ancona, who enlisted on March 13, 1862, in New York City as a private and mustered into the Tenth New York Light Artillery the same day. The report also states that Private Ancona was listed as wounded at Cedar Creek, Virginia, on October 19, 1864, was transferred into the Veteran's Reserve Corps on March 10, 1865, and was discharged for disability on March 22, 1865. Private Ancona, a twenty-one-year-old tobacconist from England, was mustered into the battery by Lieutenant Church at Brandy Station on March 15, 1864, and subsequently transferred to the Veteran's Reserve Corps (date not stated).

53. *Mass. Sol.*; Wert, *From Winchester to Cedar Creek*, 193, 310. Wilbur H. Kimball, a twenty-one-year-old heeler from Lynn, Massachusetts, enlisted on August 4, 1862, as a corporal and mustered into the Massachusetts Thirty-eighth Infantry.

He mustered out on June 30, 1865, at Savannah, Georgia. Kimball's regiment was assigned to the Third Brigade, Second Division, Nineteenth Corps, of the Army of the Shenandoah during this period. Wert reports that the regiment suffered slightly more than 200 casualties at Cedar Creek, with 115 of those being captured.

54. *Mass. Sol.*; Wert, *From Winchester to Cedar Creek,* 310–11; Boatner, *Civil War Dictionary,* 191–92; *Official Records,* vol. 27, pt. 2, 71–73; vol. 36, pt. 1, 452; vol. 42, pt. 3, 94, 453; vol. 46, pt. 1, 231, 777, 785. John Damon Jr., a thirty-year-old farmer from Reading, Massachusetts, enlisted on August 5, 1864, as a private and mustered into Company E, Massachusetts First Battalion Heavy Artillery. Company E was composed of men mustered in for one year's service. Private Damon mustered out on June 28, 1865. Wert's table of organization for Brev. Maj. Gen. George Crook's Army of West Virginia does not show the Massachusetts First Heavies. Boatner states that Crook's command was sometimes referred to as Eighth Corps, since it was initially composed of the divisions of Colonel Thoburn and Colonel Duvall from that corps. The *Official Records* reports indicate that the First Massachusetts Heavy Artillery battalions and companies were present at various locations, including Maryland Heights, Cold Harbor, Petersburg, and Appomattox, from 1863 to 1865. The Perkins diary is evidence that one company served with the Eighth Corps during the 1864 Shenandoah Campaign.

55. Warner, *Generals in Blue,* 476. Brig. Gen. John Dunlap Stevenson commanded the District of Harpers Ferry from August 8, 1864, until the end of the war.

56. Boyd, *Boyd's Washington and Georgetown Directory,* 201, 434. Boyd's 1865 directory contains two entries for this establishment. The first reads "Furbush John R. restaurant. Md ave. n 11th east h do." Evidently, Furbush's home and restaurant were at the same location. The section entitled "Business Directory, Restaurants and Saloons," gives the location of the Furbush eatery at "Md ave n 14 east."

APPENDIX A. AFTER ACTION REPORTS

1. *Official Records,* vol. 11, pt. 2, pp. 105–6.

2. *NYWR.* Possibly Henry Brevord, an eighteen-year-old who enlisted as a private on May 27, 1861, and mustered into Company G, New York Eighty-third Infantry. He was discharged from promotion on September 27, 1861, and commissioned as a first lieutenant into the Missouri Fourth Cavalry. No other information on this officer is available in the *New York Official Records.*

3. Davis et al., *Atlas,* Plate VIII, 1. Bristerburg Church and store was located four to five miles southeast of Warrenton Junction and about ten miles east of Rappahannock Station on a country road between Elk Run and Town Run.

4. RB6.

5. *Official Records,* vol. 25, pt. 1, pp. 54–56; RB6; *NYWR.* The lieutenant's name is properly spelled "Brown." The ending addressed to Lt. C. F. Trowbridge does not appear in the copy of this report appearing in the battery books.

6. *Official Records,* vol. 25, pt. 1, pp. 54–56; RB6. The report in RB6 is addressed to Lt. Geo. A. Woodruff, AAAG of the First Brigade Horse Artillery.

7. Ibid., 47–53.

8. Ibid., 60–63.

9. Ibid., 785–89; RB6. The report in RB6 is written from "Camp, First Brigade, Horse Artillery."

10. *Official Records,* vol. 27, pt. 1, pp. 949–52.

11. *Official Records,* vol. 27, pt. 1, pp. 1023–26; RB6.

12. *Official Records,* vol. 27, pt. 1, pp. 1026–28.

13. Ibid., 1020–22.

APPENDIX B. WOBURN MECHANIC PHALANX

1. *Woburn Weekly Budget,* June 21, 1861, and *Middlesex Journal,* May 4, 1861.

2. *Boston Herald,* Oct. 1, 1885.

3. Charles Winslow Hall, ed., *Regiments and Armories of Massachusetts: An Historical Narration of the Massachusetts Volunteer Militia* (Boston: W. W. Potter Co., 1889–1901), 1:131–33.

4. "General and Special Statutes of Massachusetts 1840," in *Acts and Resolves Passed by the Legislature of Massachusetts in the Year 1840* (Boston: Dutton and Wentworth, 1841), 235.

5. *Boston Herald,* Oct. 1, 1885.

6. *Middlesex Journal,* May 4, 1861.

7. *Middlesex County Journal,* Feb. 18, Feb. 25, March 4, 1871.

8. Long, *Civil War Day by Day,* 59.

9. *Annual Report of the Adjutant General of the Commonwealth of Massachusetts, with Reports from the Quartermaster-General, Surgeon-General, and Master of Ordnance, for the Year Ending December 31, 1861* (Boston: William White, Printer to the State, 1861), 11.

10. *Middlesex County Journal,* Feb. 18, Feb. 25, Mar. 4, 1871.

BIBLIOGRAPHY

PRIMARY SOURCES

Manuscripts and Documents

Fredericksburg and Spotsylvania National Military Park.

Map of Field of Occupation, Army of the Potomac. Corrected April 10, 1863, Brig. Gen. G. K. Warren.

Glennon Archives, Woburn Public Library, Woburn, MA

Letters. Wyman Collection, box 27.
Records of GAR Post 161, Records of GAR Burbank Post 33, 1867–1903, Woburn Soldiers. Johnson Collection, box 74.
Woburn Assessors Lists of Polls for Ward 5, 1889 and 1890.

Harvard University Archives

Admissions Records
Biographical Files

National Archives and Records Administration, Washington, DC

Camp Barry, DC. Letters Received, 1863–65. Record Group 393, part 4.
Deck Logs of USS *Morse* and USS *Mystic*. Record Group 24.
Regimental Books for the Sixth New York Independent Battery. Record Group 24, vol. 132–33.
Report of Service and Pension Records for George Perkins.
Report of Service and Pension Records for James A. Perkins.

U.S. Bureau of the Census

Population Schedules of the Eighth Census of the United States, 1860.

Newspapers

Boston Daily Globe
Boston Daily Record
Boston Evening Transcript

Boston True Flag
Cambridge (MA) Chronicle
Cambridge (MA) Tribune
Middlesex County (Woburn, MA) Journal
Middlesex (Woburn, MA) Journal
(Portland, ME) Daily Eastern Argus
Richmond (VA) Enquirer
(Staunton, VA) Spectator
Woburn (MA) Journal
(Woburn, MA) News
Woburn (MA) Weekly Budget

Published Primary Sources

Barnard, J. G. *A Report on the Defenses of Washington, to the Chief of Engineers, U.S. Army.* Washington, DC: Government Printing Office, 1871.

Boston Directory: 1872–73, 1876, 1880–81, and *1889.* Boston, MA. Available at Boston Public Library.

Boston Manual of Public Schools, 1880. Boston, MA. Available at Boston Public Library.

Boston School Committee Report, 1872. Boston, MA.

Boyd, Andrew. *Boyd's Washington and Georgetown Directory (Containing Also a Business Directory of Washington, Georgetown, and Alexandria).* Washington, DC: Hudson Taylor, 1865.

Davis, George G., Leslie C. Perry, and Joseph W. Kirkley. *Atlas to Accompany the Official Records of the Union and Confederate Armies.* Washington, DC: Government Printing Office, 1891–95. Reprint, New York: Gramercy Books, 1983.

Gibson, Charles Dana, and E. Kay. *The Army's Navy Series: Dictionary of Transports and Combatant Vessels, Steam and Sail, Employed by the Union Army, 1861–1865.* Camden, ME: Ensign Press, 1995.

Gilham, William. *Manual of Instruction for Volunteers and Militia.* Philadelphia: Charles DeSilver, 1861. Reprint, Scotland, PA: C. J. Daley Historical Reproductions, 1992.

Hopkins, G. M. *Atlas of the Town of Woburn, Massachusetts.* Philadelphia: G. M. Hopkins & Co., 1875.

Marsh, C. C. *Official Records of the Union and Confederate Navies in the War of the Rebellion.* Ser. 1, vol. 4. Washington, DC: Government Printing Office, 1897.

Massachusetts Soldiers, Sailors, and Marines in the Civil War. Reprint, American Civil War Research Database, Historical Data Systems, Inc. http://www.civilwardata.com.

Phisterer, Frederick. *New York in the War of the Rebellion, 1861–1865.* Vols. 1–5. Albany: J. B. Lyon Co., 1912. Reprint, American Civil War Research Database, Historical Data Systems, Inc. http://www.civilwardata.com.

Record of Service of Michigan Volunteers, 1861–1865. Reprint, American Civil War Research Database, Historical Data Systems, Inc. http://www.civilwardata.com.

Register of Officers and Men of New Jersey, 1861–1865. Reprint, American Civil War Research Database, Historical Data Systems, Inc. http://www.civilwardata.com.

Register of Soldiers and Sailors of New Hampshire, 1861–1865. Reprint, American Civil War Research Database, Historical Data Systems, Inc. http://www.civilwardata.com.

Report of the Adjutant General of the State of Maine of the Union Army. Reprint, American Civil War Research Database, Historical Data Systems, Inc., http://www. civilwardata.com.

War of the Rebellion: A Compilation of the Official Records of the Union and Confederate Armies. 128 vols. Washington, DC: Government Printing Office, 1880–1901. Reprint, Carmel, IN: Guild Press, 1996. CD-ROM.

Woburn Directory: 1868, 1871, 1874, 1877, 1881, 1883, 1886–7. Woburn, MA: John L. Parker.

Woburn Record of Birth, Marriages, and Deaths: 1640–1873 and *1873–1890.* Woburn, MA: Andrews, Cutler, and Co., 1890 and 1892.

Woburn Town Report: 1865, 1870–71. Woburn, MA. Available at Glennon Archives, Woburn Public Library.

SECONDARY SOURCES

Bethel, Elizabeth, and Lucille Pendell, comps. *Preliminary Inventory of the Records of the Adjutant General's Office.* Washington, DC: Adjutant General's Office, Department of the Army, 1949.

Billings, John D. *Hardtack and Coffee: The Unwritten Story of Army Life.* Reprint, Lincoln: Univ. of Nebraska Press, 1993.

Biographical Directory of the United States Congress, 1774–Present. Washington, DC: Government Printing Office, 1989.

Boatner, Mark. *The Civil War Dictionary.* Rev. ed. New York: Vintage, 1991.

Coddington, Edwin B. *The Gettysburg Campaign: A Study in Command.* New York: Simon and Schuster, 1968.

Dictionary of American Naval Fighting Ships. Vols. 3, 4, 6, 7, 8. Washington, DC: Dept. of the Navy, 1968.

Graham, Martin F., and George F. Skoch. *Mine Run: A Campaign of Lost Opportunities.* Lynchburg, VA: H. E. Howard, 1987.

Grimsley, Mark, and Todd D. Miller. *The Union Must Stand: The Civil War Diary of John Quincy Adams Campbell, Fifth Iowa Volunteer Infantry.* Knoxville: Univ. of Tennessee Press, 2000.

Hazlett, James C., Edwin Olmstead, and M. Hume Parks. *Field Artillery Weapons of the Civil War.* 2nd ed. Newark: Univ. of Delaware Press, 1988.

Internment in the Arlington National Cemetery. Rev. ed. Washington, DC: U.S. Dept. of the Army, 1948.

Ketchum, Richard M., ed. *The American Heritage Picture History of the Civil War.* New York: American Heritage, 1960.

Leech, Margaret. *Reveille in Washington, 1860–1865.* New York: Harper and Brothers, 1941.

Linderman, Gerald F. *Embattled Courage: The Experience of Combat in the American Civil War.* New York: Free Press, 1987.

Long, E. B. *The Civil War Day by Day.* New York: Da Capo, 1971.

Longacre, Edward G. *The Cavalry at Gettysburg.* Lincoln: Univ. of Nebraska Press, 1986.

———. *The Man Behind the Guns: A Biography of General Henry T. Hunt, Commander of Artillery of the Army of the Potomac.* New York: A. S. Barnes and Co., 1977.

Naisawald, L. Van Loan. *Grape and Canister*. Gaithersburg, MD: Olde Soldier Books, 1960.

Nevins, Allan, ed. *A Diary of Battle: The Personal Journals of Colonel Charles S. Wainwright, 1861–1865*. Gettysburg, PA: Stan Clark Books, 1962.

The Parish of St. Mary. Piscataway, MD: Sesquicentennial Celebration Committee,1980.

Rhea, Gordon C. *The Battles for Spotsylvania Courthouse and the Road to Yellow Tavern, May 7–12, 1864*. Baton Rouge: Louisiana State Univ. Press, 1997.

———. *To the North Anna River: Grant and Lee, May 13–25, 1864*. Baton Rouge: Louisiana State Univ. Press, 2000.

Sears, Stephen W. *Chancellorsville*. New York: Houghton Mifflin, 1996.

———. *To the Gates of Richmond*. New York: Tichnor and Fields, 1992.

The Union Army: A History of Military Affairs in the Loyal States, 1861–65. Vol. 1. Madison, WI: Federal Publishing Co., 1908. Reprint, American Civil War Research Database, Historical Data Systems, Inc. http://www.civilwardata.com.

Veterans Graves Registry Project. Washington, DC: Works Progress Administration, 1942.

Warner, Ezra J. *Generals in Blue: The Lives of the Union Commanders*. Baton Rouge: Louisiana State Univ. Press, 1964.

Wert, Jeffrey D. *From Winchester to Cedar Creek: The Shenandoah Campaign of 1864*. Mechanicsburg, PA: Stackpole Books, 1997.

Wills, Mary Alice. *The Confederate Blockade of Washington, DC, 1861–1862*. Shippensburg, PA: Burd Street Press, 1998.

Woodhead, Henry, ed. *Echoes of Glory: Arms and Equipment of the Union*. Alexandria, VA: Time-Life Books, 1996.

INDEX